Transdisciplinary Play-Based Intervention 2 ND EDITION

TPBA Play-Based TPBI
TPBC ™

Other products available in the TPBA Play-Based TPBI TPBC™ system include:

- ***Transdisciplinary Play-Based Assessment, Second Edition (TPBA2),***
  by Toni Linder, Ed.D., with invited contributors

- ***Administration Guide for TPBA2 & TPBI2,*** by Toni Linder, Ed.D.,
  with invited contributors

- ***TPBA2 & TPBI2 Forms,*** by Toni Linder, Ed.D.
  a shrink-wrapped package of 5 complete tablets, each including key forms
  for TPBA2 and TPBI2

- ***TPBA2 & TPBI2 Forms CD-ROM,*** by Toni Linder, Ed.D.
  a CD-ROM of printable forms for TPBA2 and TPBI2

- ***Observing Kassandra: A Transdisciplinary Play-Based Assessment of a Child
  with Severe Disabilities, Revised Edition,*** produced and written
  by Toni Linder, Ed.D.
  a 50-minute DVD with workbook and forms tablet

- ***Read, Play, and Learn!®: Storybook Activities for Young Children,***
  by Toni Linder, Ed.D., with invited contributors
  a transdisciplinary play-based curriculum that includes a *Teacher's Guide* and
  individual manuals of lesson plans based on popular children's storybooks,
  packaged in modules of 8

Visit www.readplaylearn.com for excerpts, sample materials, and more information about *Read, Play, and Learn!*®

To order, contact Paul H. Brookes Publishing Co.:
  by phone: 800-638-3775
             410-337-9580 (outside the U.S.A.)
  by fax: 410-337-8539
  by web: www.brookespublishing.com
  by mail: P.O. Box 10624 Baltimore, MD 21285-0624, U.S.A.

Transdisciplinary Play-Based Intervention
2ND EDITION

TPBA · Play-Based · TPBI · TPBC ™

Toni Linder, Ed.D.

Professor
Morgridge College of Education
University of Denver
Colorado

with invited contributors

·P·A·U·L·H·
BROOKES
PUBLISHING CO ®

Baltimore • London • Sydney

Paul H. Brookes Publishing Co.
Post Office Box 10624
Baltimore, Maryland 21285-0624

www.brookespublishing.com

"Paul H. Brookes Publishing Co." is a registered trademark
of Paul H. Brookes Publishing Co., Inc.

 is a trademark of Paul H. Brookes Publishing Co., Inc.

Typeset by Integrated Publishing Solutions, Grand Rapids, Michigan.
Manufactured in the United States of America by Sheridan Books, Inc., Chelsea, Michigan.

For companion products to *Transdisciplinary Play-Based Intervention, Second Edition (TPBI2)*,
including *Transdisciplinary Play-Based Assessment, Second Edition (TPBA2); Administration Guide for
TPBA2 & TPBI2; Observing Kassandra* (DVD, workbook, and forms tablet); *TPBA2 & TPBI2 Forms*
(tablets and CD-ROM); and *Read, Play, and Learn!*® (the *Transdisciplinary Play-Based Curriculum*),
see p. ii. Visit www.brookespublishing.com and www.readplaylearn.com for more information.

This volume contains activities and suggestions that should be used in the classroom or other
environments only when children are receiving proper supervision. It is the teacher's or the
caregiver's responsibility to provide a safe, secure environment for all children and to know
each child's individual circumstances (e.g., allergies to food or other substances, medical needs).
The authors and publisher disclaim any liability arising directly or indirectly from the use
of this book.

Library of Congress Cataloging-in-Publication Data

Linder, Toni, 1946–
    Transdisciplinary play-based intervention / by Toni Linder ; with invited contributors. – 2nd ed.
        p.   cm.
    Includes index.
    ISBN-13: 978-1-55766-872-1 (spiral bound)
    ISBN-10: 1-55766-872-8
    1. Transdisciplinary Play-Based Intervention.   I. Title.
    RJ53.T7L65   2008
    618.92–dc22   2007032715

British Library Cataloguing in Publication data are available from the British Library.

2012   2011   2010   2009   2008

10   9   8   7   6   5   4   3   2   1

Contents

About the Authors

Toni Linder, Ed.D., Professor, Child, Family, and School Psychology Program, Morgridge College of Education, University of Denver, University Park, Denver, Colorado 20208

Dr. Toni Linder has been a professor in the Child, Family, and School Psychology program in the Morgridge College of Education since 1976. Dr. Linder has been a leader in the development of authentic assessment for young children and is nationally and internationally known for her work on *Transdisciplinary Play-Based Assessment* and *Transdisciplinary Play-Based Intervention*. In addition, she developed *Read, Play, and Learn!®️ Storybook Activities for Young Children: The Transdisciplinary Play-Based Curriculum* (1999), an inclusive literature- and play-based curriculum for preschool and kindergarten learning and development. Dr. Linder also is the Director of the Play and Learning Assessment for the Young (PLAY) Clinic at the University of Denver, where professional and student teams conduct transdisciplinary play-based assessments for young children and their families. Dr. Linder consults widely on assessment, intervention, early childhood education, and family involvement issues. She has conducted research on a variety of topics, including transdisciplinary influences on development, parent–child interaction, curriculum outcomes, and the use of technology for professional development in rural areas.

Tanni L. Anthony, Ph.D., Supervisor and State Consultant on Visual Impairment; Director, Colorado Services for Children with Combined Vision and Hearing Loss Project, Colorado Department of Education, 201 East Colfax Avenue, Denver, Colorado 80203

Dr. Anthony serves as a state consultant in visual impairment for the Colorado Department of Education. She also serves as the Director of the Colorado Services for Children for Children with Combined Vision and Hearing Loss Project. She is a nationally recognized trainer and author on topics specific to young children with visual impairment or deafblindness. Dr. Anthony has consulted internationally on program design of early intervention services for children with visual impairment and their families. She has worked on federal projects to design training materials for both preservice and inservice courses for personnel working with young children with sensory loss. Dr. Anthony received her Ed.S. degree from the University of Northern Colorado and her doctorate from the University of Denver in Child and Family Studies and Interdisciplinary Leadership.

Anita C. Bundy, Sc.D., OTR, FAOTA, Professor, Occupational Therapy, Faculty of Health Sciences, University of Sydney, P.O. Box 170, Sydney, New South Wales, Australia 2041

Professor Bundy's professional training is as an occupational therapist. She has taught and practiced in pediatrics for more than 30 years. Her research emphasizes children's play including the use of play to promote physical activity, mental health, and parent–child interactions. She is the author of two assessments related to play, the *Test of Playfulness,* which examines children's approach to play, and the *Test of Environmental Supportiveness,* which examines the contributions of caregivers, playmates, space, and objects to play. She also is the primary editor for *Sensory Integration: Theory and Practice* (2nd ed.), published by F.A. Davis, and is the author of several chapters in that book.

Renee Charlifue-Smith, M.A., CCC-SLP, Senior Instructor, Speech-Language Pathologist, JFK Partners, Department of Pediatrics, University of Colorado School of Medicine, 4900 East 9th Avenue, Denver, Colorado 80262

Renee Charlifue-Smith is a faculty member in the Department of Pediatrics at the University of Colorado School of Medicine. She is Director of the Speech-Language Pathology Department and is the coordinator of the ENRICH Early Intervention Team at JFK Partners. She has been a speech-language pathology consultant on a variety of federally funded demonstration, research, and training projects. Her special interests include early intervention, autism spectrum disorders, and motor speech disorders.

Susan Dwinal, OTR, Occupational Therapist, 420 High Parkway, Golden, Colorado 80403

Ms. Dwinal earned her Bachelor's degree in occupational therapy from the University of New Hampshire in 2000. She completed a fellowship in occupational therapy through JFK Partners in Denver, Colorado, which involved working as part of the Autism and Developmental Disabilities Clinic team and as a member of the ENRICH (Enrichment Using Natural Resources in the Community and Home) team. Susan has worked in a variety of pediatric settings with children and families in their homes, schools, and communities. She has worked with Dr. Toni Linder as an occupational therapist for the PLAY Clinic at the University of Denver and was also a part of Dr. Linder's rural-based Transdisciplinary Play-Based Assessment training team.

Jan Christian Hafer, Ed.D., Professor, Department of Education, Galludet University, 800 Florida Avenue NW, Washington, D.C. 20002

Jan Christian Hafer specializes in family-centered early education in the Department of Education at Gallaudet University, Washington, DC. Her scholarly interests include play, assessment of young deaf and hard-of-hearing children, and signing with hearing populations.

Natasha Hall, M.S., CCC-SLP, Speech-Language Pathologist, 181 Oneida Street, Denver, Colorado 80220

Ms. Hall earned her bachelor's degree from the University of New Mexico in speech and hearing sciences and her master's degree from the University of Nebraska–Lincoln in speech-language pathology. She is a speech-language pathologist specializing in early childhood for the Cherry Creek School District in Greenwood Village, Colorado. Natasha worked for 4 years at Presbyterian/St. Luke's Medical Center in Denver, Colorado, where she focused primarily on pediatrics. She works at the University of Denver as the primary speech-language consultant for Dr. Linder's rural-based Transdisciplinary Play-Based Assessment training team. Natasha's career expertise is in the areas of early intervention practices and developmental assessment.

Forrest Hancock, Ph.D., Early Childhood Consultant, 2305 Pebble Beach Drive, Austin, Texas 78747

Dr. Hancock is an early childhood consultant in the Central Texas area. She has been an educator in general and special education for 40 years, and her experience has spanned teaching students and practitioners from the elementary to university levels. Dr. Hancock earned her master's degree in language and learning disabilities at Texas State University and her doctorate in early childhood special education from The University of Texas at Austin where she later taught graduate courses in early language development. She develops and presents professional development trainings for preschool educators and administrators, early intervention service coordinators, and early intervention specialists, and she supports first-year special education teachers seeking certification.

Preface

Transdisciplinary Play-Based Intervention, Second Edition (TPBI2), which is greatly expanded from its original version, is designed to be used as a reference by professionals from various disciplines, educators, child care providers, and family members. Practical strategies are provided to be incorporated into functional daily routines and play activities across a variety of settings, including home, school, and community.

Each of the subcategories for each of the developmental domains has a corresponding intervention chapter in *TPBI2.* Chapters in the book include:

- A Review of the Transdisciplinary Play-Based System

- Planning Considerations for TPBI2

- Facilitating Sensorimotor Development

- Strategies for Working with Children with Visual Impairments

- Facilitating Emotional and Social Development

- Facilitating Communication Development (including Strategies for Improving Hearing and Communication)

- Facilitating Cognitive Development

- Strategies for Supporting Emerging Literacy

Within each of these sections, each subcategory of a domain has its own chapter and each subquestion within the subcategory of TPBA2 has its own area addressing what typical development looks like, how it is observed in daily routines, and how parents typically support the child's development in this area throughout the day. Individual differences are then addressed with interactional strategies and environmental modifications identified for each of the potential areas of concern. Each chapter includes a case example of how these strategies are applied.

The *TPBI2* chapters are designed to be used in combination, across domains of development, with sections of appropriate chapters providing ideas for intervention approaches with specific children. Strategies are presented in a simple, straightforward approach, so that parts of these chapters may be shared with parents, care providers, teachers, or other professionals who are interacting with the child. In addition, the system includes Functional Outcomes Rubrics (FOR) to measure progress on domains or global early childhood outcomes.

TPBA2 and TPBI2 are intended to assist individual children with special needs; however, strategies offered in TPBA2 and TPBI2 also are effective for classroom planning. The examples provided in each of the intervention chapters are taken from classrooms using the *Read, Play, and Learn!*® curriculum developed by the author. TPBA2 and TPBI2 strategies can be used with any curriculum to assist teachers in planning for individualization within the classroom.

Use of the TPBI2 strategies can be used in Response to Intervention (RTI), as well. Careful observations in the classroom using the TPBA2 Observation Guidelines and FORs will help teachers identify areas of strengths and need. Use of TPBI2 will then assist the classroom teacher in selection of interactional and environmental modifications. Because this in a transdisciplinary model, consultation with professionals from various disciplines also is needed.

The Transdisciplinary Play-Based System is a functional, holistic, integrated approach that will enable children and families to be part of a team of professionals. Findings from the TPBA2 Observation Guidelines and strategies from TPBI2 enable development of a plan to provide ongoing support to the child across a variety of environments. With frequent monitoring and ongoing modifications to the child's plan, use of the Transdisciplinary Play-Based System may help some children avoid the need for special education services later. For children who need greater support, conducting TPBA2 and then developing strategies after the child has been found eligible is another viable approach. Regardless of whether the play-based system is used for RTI or for identification of children with developmental concerns, the philosophy remains the same: Assessment and intervention should be a pleasurable and playful; should reduce family stress related to their child's development; and should result in greater independence, social interactions, and learning on the part of the child.

Acknowledgments

This revised version of the Transdisciplinary Play-Based System has been years in the making and consequently has involved the contributions of literally hundreds of children, families, students, and professionals. I know I will never be able to adequately acknowledge everyone who has been involved in this creative process, but I will endeavor to cite a few of the key people who have made significant contributions.

First, this work builds on the foundation established by the original TPBA and TPBI. For this I thank the key contributors to these volumes, Susan Hall, Kim Dickson, Paula Hudson, Anita C. Bundy, Carol Lay, and Sandy Patrick. All of these professionals helped shape the format and content of TPBA/I. When these people worked on the first TPBA and TPBI, they worked not from encouragement from the field, but purely from a belief that play was the best approach for young children and their families. Their faith in this process was critical to the completion of the first editions and the subsequent success of the TPBA system.

Those who have contributed to *Transdisciplinary Play-Based Assessment, Second Edition* (TPBA2); *Transdisciplinary Play-Based Intervention, Second Edition* (TPBI2); and the *Administration Guide for TPBA2 & TPBI2* come to the task with more of a sense of justification and validation, because there has been much research in the field of early intervention and early childhood special education to support that what we are doing is based on best practices. These people, too, are committed to providing functional, meaningful assessment and intervention for young children and their families. I again thank Anita C. Bundy who, although she has moved to Australia, has continued to offer her expertise in sensorimotor development in both TPBA2 and TPBI2. Susan Dwinal also served as a member of the PLAY Clinic team and the TPBA rural training team, and I thank her for her work on the intervention chapter for arm and hand use. Renee Charlifue-Smith has taught me much about speech and language and has been an invaluable PLAY Clinic team member. Her expertise has helped expand and build the empirical foundation for our work. Renee not only wrote significant portions of several chapters, she reviewed and contributed to all of the communication and hearing assessment and intervention chapters. Renee has been a steadfast advocate and loyal friend, and I greatly appreciate her support. Cheryl Cole Rooke and Natasha Hall came in to support Renee and gave us needed energy and input on the communication chapters. Jan Christian Hafer, from Galludet, brought her expertise in deaf education to both TPBA2 and TPBI2, adding a much-needed new hearing component to assessment and intervention. In the same way, Tanni L. Anthony contributed the vision perspective, an area that is often overlooked by those who are not vision experts. Tanni's research on the vision component of TPBA2 showed that professionals from a variety of disciplines can reliably observe vision and make determinations for the need for further vision evaluation. Ann Petersen-Smith brought her nursing background and expertise to our doctoral program, then to the PLAY Clinic, and subsequently to her research on the Child and Family History Questionnaire (CFHQ). Her work has shown the importance of this piece to both TPBA2 and TPBI2. Karen Riley has both led a PLAY Clinic team and done research on TPBA with children with fragile X syndrome. Her leadership in the clinic, her skill in report writing, her enthusiasm for research, and her undying friendship have been invaluable. Thank you, Karen! Forrest Hancock first supported TPBA and TPBI by bringing training to Texas. She subsequently contributed the assessment and intervention sections for literacy. In addition, she has a great editorial eye! Forrest's collaboration, friendship, and support have helped carry me through more than one hard night.

Numerous people have contributed to the fieldwork and research on various aspects of TPBA2 and TPBI2. I would like to thank Eisa Al-Balhan, Tanni L. Anthony, Ann Petersen-Smith, and Kelly DeBruin for their dissertation research on different components of the process. Kelly DeBruin's work on the concurrent and social validity of TPBA2 provided an important perspective on the whole process. In addition, several teams in Texas conducted evaluation research to examine the effectiveness of TPBA and were subsequently awarded a Promising Practices Award by the Texas Department of Education. Texas teams from Plano, Conroy, Round Rock, and Katy all collected data to show the effectiveness of the process and the impact of various outcomes. For example, Kellie Johnson and her team in Round Rock demonstrated that, contrary to popular belief, use of TPBA does not result in identification of more children as needing special services. In fact, Round Rock was able to eliminate two special education preschool classes due to children performing better and consequently not being found eligible for services. Children were able to demonstrate higher level skills with the TPBA approach. To all of these Promising Practices teams, thank you for your dedication to implementing and sharing child- and family-friendly practices. In addition, I'm grateful to Forrest Hancock, Elaine Earls, Jan Andreas, Margie Larsen, Lynn Sullivan, Stacey Shackelford, and the other Independent School Districts and Texas Regional Service Centers. Thank you for your leadership, field testing, and feedback! AnneMarie deKort-Young, Corrine Garland, and Stella Fair have been supportive colleagues throughout.

Many people also reviewed manuscript segments. I'd like to thank Carrie Davenport, from the Ohio School for the Deaf, who gave important feedback on the hearing chapter. I also would like to thank John Neisworth, Phillippa Campbell, Sarah Landy, Marci Hanson, Angela Notari-Syverson, Kathleen Stremel, and Juliann Woods, in addition to Anita C. Bundy, Karen Riley, Renee Charlifue-Smith, and Tanni L. Anthony, for their participation in the cross-domain influences study that demonstrated the validity of the transdisciplinary construct. I believe this work will lead to interesting future research on intervention planning.

One incredibly gratifying aspect of the work on TPBA2 has been the opportunity to share TPBA and TPBI with people from various cultures around the world. Because of the flexible nature of both the assessment and intervention models, they are easily adapted to different situations. I would like to thank the people who have begun to use TPBA and TPBI (both the first and second edition materials) for their support and ongoing research and feedback, in particular, Jenny Hsing and Anne-Merete Kleppenes in Norway; Margaret Galvin, Kevin McGrattin, and Ruth Connolly in Ireland, Manuela Sanches Ferreira and Susana Martins in Portugal; and Chen Xuefeng in China. You all have been an inspiration to me for how you advocate for and create change for children and families. Thank you!

Of course, as every professor does, I have worked with my students in many ways. Although I cannot thank each one individually, I would like to extend global thanks for all their hard work throughout the years. I have learned from each one of you! In particular, I'd like to thank Keri Linas, Kim Stokka, and Jeanine Coleman for their collaborative efforts throughout their doctoral programs. Each of you has embraced play as an important part of your studies and each of you will contribute much to our field. Thank you for your positive, can-do attitude! Go for it!

To all of the people at Paul H. Brookes Publishing Co. (past and present), including Paul Brookes, Melissa Behm, Heather Shrestha, Tara Gebhardt, Jan Krejci, and Susannah Ray, I am grateful for your continued support, tolerance, patience, and hard work.

And finally, to my family and friends, who have been virtually abandoned during this seemingly overwhelming and endless task, I thank you for your unwavering love and support (even when *I* was wavering, you kept me going!). Your love sustains me and provides my emotional refueling! Thank you!

*To all the children and families with whom I have worked over the years,
I am grateful for all you have taught me about development,
learning, patience, flexibility, determination, and love.*

1

A Review of Transdisciplinary Play-Based Intervention

In *Transdisciplinary Play-Based Assessment, Second Edition* (TPBA2), a vignette was presented that illustrated the traditional and TPBA approaches from the child's point of view. In the following vignette, the difference between traditional intervention and transdisciplinary play-based intervention (TPBI2) is presented from the child's point of view. Because intervention at home and at school or child care may look very different, both situations are exemplified. Note that the role of the child, the therapist, and parent or teacher is similar in both settings, but very different depending on the approach.

TRADITIONAL INTERVENTION AT HOME

Imagine yourself as a 2½-year-old boy with cerebral palsy and overall developmental delays. You are sitting on your Mommy's lap looking at pictures in a book when the doorbell rings. Mommy puts you down on the floor and goes to answer the door. She smiles and tells Rosa to come in. Rosa brings in her bag of toys and you smile at her too. You know what is in that bag. Rosa has fun toys! You crawl over to the bag and try to get into it. Rosa and Mommy are talking about you and what you have been doing all week. You start pulling out Rosa's toys, looking for the one that has lights and makes noises. Oh, here it is! You start banging on it, trying to make it go. Rosa pushes the button for you. Mommy sits in her chair and watches you play with Rosa. Rosa takes out another toy, the one with rings you put on a stick. This is not your favorite toy. It is hard. So you go back to the first toy and bang on it some more. Rosa gets the "doughnuts" again and helps you put them on the stick. Rosa then gets out markers and paper and puts them on the coffee table. She tries to get you to stand up and come play with the markers. She helps you stand and hands you the marker. You bang the marker on the paper a couple of times and then sit down. Standing up is hard and writing is not fun. You crawl over to Mommy so she will pick you up, but instead, Mommy says, "I'll let you two play for a while. I need to clean up the kitchen while you guys are busy." Mommy leaves the room. You try to follow her, but Rosa pulls you back and hands you another toy. Okay. Playing is fun. You stay in the living room and play on the floor until Rosa packs up her toys to leave. Mommy comes back and tells her, "See you in a couple of weeks." Rosa says, "Maya will be out next week to work on some of his motor issues." I'm not nuts about Maya. She makes me do hard things.

TRANSDISCIPLINARY PLAY-BASED INTERVENTION

You are sitting on your Mommy's lap looking at pictures in a book when the doorbell rings. Mommy puts you down on the floor and goes to answer the door. She smiles and tells Rachel to come in. Rachel talks to me and plays with me with my favorite pop-up toy, while she asks Mommy about our week and what was fun and what was hard. Mommy says she is having trouble getting her work done at home, because I need attention and lots of help. It's true. I like my Mommy to spend time with me! Rachel asks what Mommy would like to be doing right now, and she says, "I really need to be cleaning up the kitchen from breakfast *and* lunch. It's one o'clock, and I can't seem to get time to do what I need to do. It's better on the days that he goes to child care. I get a little time to myself." Rachel says, "Then let's go into the kitchen and look at how Sam can help out and learn some new skills!" We all go into the kitchen, which (Mommy is right) is a mess! Rachel says, "Let's see. We want him to be motivated to stand independently, to be able to use two hands together, to learn some useful new words, and to entertain himself independently. Right?" "Especially, that last one!" my Mommy laughs. "Okay. Let's think about this for a minute," Rachel says. "What in this room does Sam like?" Mommy laughs, "Aside from food? He loves water." (She's right about that!) "He likes getting into my cupboards and pulling things out!" (She's also right about that!) Rachel says, "Let's let him help with washing dishes." Rachel looks around then goes into the living room, comes back with my little plastic table and cube chair, and puts the table up against the wall. "This way," she says, "the table is stabilized and Sam can pull up on it without pushing it away. Do you have a plastic tub or pot we can put some water in?" I crawl over to see what Mommy is doing in the cupboard, and I see lots of fun pots and pans. "Let's let him pick one," Rachel says. "That lets him make choices and be independent." "Sam, get a pan *out*." No problem there. I pull out a big one in front. Rachel says, "How about some spoons and stuff like that?" Mommy opens a drawer and I pull up to stand and look inside. "Great!" Rachel says, "He wants to see in the drawer. That's a great way to motivate him to pull to stand!" Mommy lets me pull out a few things and throw them on the floor, then she shuts the drawer. Rachel puts water in the pan, shows me, and takes it to my little table. "Wa-wa!" I shout and crawl to the table. "Yes, Sam. It's *water*. Come help Mommy clean the dishes." I pull up and reach for the water. Rachel moves the chair so I can sit down by myself. Mommy brings over the stuff I threw on the floor and puts them in the pot of water. I reach in and get a spoon and start playing. Rachel asks Mommy for a sponge and then shows me how to squeeze the sponge. It's hard, but I like watching the water come out. She shows me how to wipe the spoon. Hey, this cleaning is fun!

Rachel says, "Okay. Now that he's cleaning, we can start." Mommy and Rachel go to the sink and Mom puts water in the sink and starts to wash her dishes. Rachel tells her about how to "model" for me, says, "Sam, spoon," when we are washing spoons, and tells Mommy to give me something new to wash when I get bored. I'm not bored, though. I love playing in the water. Mommy keeps showing me what she is washing, then tells me it's my turn to wash. I show her how to squeeze the sponge. Mommy says, "Great, Sam. You are such a big helper." I really am! Mommy and Rachel and I are talking while Mommy and I are washing dishes. When we are all done, Mommy lets me use my sponge to clean up my "mess." Mommy laughs and tells Rachel that maybe she'll have me help put the clothes in the washer and dryer too. Rachel says that that is a terrific idea, because if the laundry basket is on the floor, I will need to get up and down to take out each piece and then put it in the dryer, and I'll need to use two hands on the bigger pieces. I like taking things out and putting them in. I think we should do that now. I say, "out" and Mommy and Rachel look at each other, smile, and nod. Mommy says, "I never thought about how a 'chore' for me is play for him. But, this gives me all kinds of ideas about how we can do things together that will help both of us!"

TRADITIONAL INTERVENTION IN CHILD CARE AND EARLY EDUCATION

I am sitting with my friend, listening to my teacher read a book, when Miss Mary comes in to get me. She tells my teacher she'll bring me back in time for snack. Good. I like snack, but I'd like to have heard the end of the story before we left. She carries me to her office where she has a little table and chairs. She has a doll and some cars on the table, so that looks like fun. I sit in the chair and Miss Mary asks me to show her the baby's mouth, eyes, and nose. I point to them. "What is this?" she asks and points to the baby's head. I tell her it's "har." I don't know why we are pointing to these things. Can't we just play with them? I start pushing the cars around and making noises like my daddy's car. She hold up a car and says, "C-A-R. Say 'car,' Sam." I try to imitate her. Then I go back to pushing the car and making car noises. Miss Mary gets out a book and starts to show me pictures in the book. She asks me what the pictures are. Doesn't she know? After the book, Miss Mary takes me back to my class and tells me she'll see me next week. Good. I'm back in time for snack!

TRANSDISCIPLINARY PLAY-BASED INTERVENTION IN CHILD CARE AND EARLY EDUCATION

Mr. Bob comes in before story time and talks to my teacher. I am sitting in my cube chair, 'cause Mr. Bob told me and my teacher that I will be able to sit better, talk better, and pay better attention in my cube chair. I think he is right. We used to all sit on carpet squares, and I had to work so hard to sit up I couldn't pay attention to the story or talk to the teacher! Other kids have cube chairs too, and some sit on the floor or on a special cushion. Mr. Bob brought my book for me to look at while we are listening. Mr. Bob made my book for me. It has just has three pages and they are thick pages, so I can turn them myself. This book helps me see what the teacher is talking about. We all take turns helping the teacher tell the story. Sometimes, when it is my turn to tell the story, I get to use Mr. Bob's talking book. My teacher holds up her book, and I push the buttons on my talking book, and the book tells the story. I try to talk as much as I can. I tell my friends what I want them to shout out, like what the cow says. I like being the teacher. We do the same story every day for many days and pretty soon I know a lot of the words in the story and can tell other people what I know.

Mr. Bob stays after story time. That's when we all have choices about what we want to do. Mr. Bob helps us tell the teacher what we want to do, and then he goes around and helps some of us. He likes to help us talk to our friends and say what we're doing. Sometimes he uses sign language or pictures. My friend Alison has a machine that Mr. Bob helps her use. When she pushes on part of it, the machine talks for her! It is really cool. Mr. Bob is teaching my teacher (how neat is that!) how to make it talk. Sometimes Mr. Bob brings in his friends. He calls them part of his "team" to teach *him* what to do. There is a lot of teaching going on in this classroom!

Now it is snack time, and Mr. Bob is eating with us today. He says he is going to eat his cracker and cheese in his ear! I shout, "Mouth!" Mr. Bob says, "Stop, Bob!" He laughs, tells me 'thank you,' and eats it with his mouth. Good thing I told him what to do. Then he said he is going to listen to me with his nose. I laugh. Mr. Bob is so funny.

Marisa tells him, "Stop, Bob!" He stops and looks at her. She points to her ear. "Ear, Bob." I say it too. "Ear, Bob!" My teacher asks me if I want to smell the cheese and holds the cheese to my eye. Everybody laughs, and says, "Stop, Ana!" My teacher says, "Where should I hold the cheese?" Everyone shouts, "His nose!" "Nose!" I yell too. She holds it up to my nose and I smell it. It's fun to tell the teacher what to do!

2
Planning Considerations for TPBI2

The purpose of *Transdisciplinary Play-Based Intervention, Second Edition* (TPBI2) is to present a process for planning, implementing, and evaluating intervention for children from birth to 6 years of age who need supports to enhance their development. Within TPBI, the intent is to provide a structure for that process, a framework for conceptualizing intervention strategies, and a means for monitoring and evaluating the effectiveness of the strategies selected.

TEAM MEMBERS

Team members in TPBI, whether the same or different from the TPBA team, work together to support the family members, care providers, and early educators who interact with the child daily. During the postassessment planning phase, the team members listen to family members and, along with them, provide input as to what the child's needs are, what services would best meet those needs, and what form intervention should take. Either during the postassessment planning time or during a preintervention planning phase, the team moves from talk of services to a plan for implementing actual strategies. During the preintervention planning phase, the whole team, or possibly a couple of representatives of the team if TPBA was done in the home, meet with primary caregivers and teachers to talk about the specifics of what outcomes are desired, what functional objectives will guide intervention, and what strategies can be used across the day to support development and learning. For children in school, separate planning meetings may be held with parents and teachers, although this is not recommended because all caregivers need to be on the same page, even if issues at home and school are different. The team members help the primary caregivers think about possible outcomes and help them identify times of the day, activities, or events for which they either need intervention ideas or identify times when their positive interactions with their child are ripe for interventions to be introduced. This is a brainstorming time, and parents and teachers may agree or disagree with ideas presented, talk about what has already been tried, reveal personal struggles, and/or share their own perceptions about what strategies might work. The team's role is to listen, support, help weigh the options, and then facilitate the development of the actual intervention plan. During the intervention phase, the role of team members varies depending on the age of the child, location of services, and level and type of strategies identified. Both for the child and the parents or teachers, the goal is to provide intervention based on the system of least support, meaning that, as much as possible, the team members play a consultation role, stepping in to provide more guidance or structure as needed. The goals for the child, parents, caregivers, and educators are independence and the ability to think for oneself and solve problems creatively and independently. Team members' roles vary with each individual person, in accordance with their need and desire for varying levels of support. During the evaluation phase, team members provide observations, elicit parent perceptions, and try to pull together an objective view of progress and next steps.

TPBI is not like traditional therapy, in which specialists meet with a child and do hands-on, direct intervention for their areas of expertise. TPBI is a team approach, with a concerted effort made to provide holistic intervention. In an earlier analogy, the relationship between the child, family, and team was described as a wheel, with the child as the hub, the team as the spokes, and the family as the rim, holding all together and making it roll. An alternative way of perceiving the relationship might be that the child is the hub, the family members, teachers, and other significant people in the child's life are the spokes, and the team is the rim that provides the support to the inner pieces. The rim cannot function effectively if part of it is missing or ineffective. The team must be in constant communication, support each other in many ways, and function as a unit. In short, the child, family, teachers, and team must function in a collaborative whole for intervention to be maximally effective. Most of us do not get to choose our teams, our families, or our children, but we do our best to make it all work. When intervention "works," it does so because each member of the team contributes information, suggestions and advice, training, coaching, supervision, and emotional support. Intervention works when team members are caring, nonjudgmental, open, willing, honest, tolerant, and patient. Intervention works when parents are caring, nonjudgmental, open, willing, honest, tolerant, and patient. And intervention works when all parties listen to each other, integrate ideas, and collaborate in making them work. Although this doesn't always happen, just think what could happen if the wheel rolled in a straight line without wobbling.

Everyone on the team implements intervention in a different way, playing different roles as called for. One model for thinking about implementing TPBI is that each team that provides early intervention (EI) and/or early childhood special education (ECSE) support consists of members from a variety of different disciplines, depending on the needs of the population served. The team conducts the TPBA together, as described in Chapter 1 of TPBA2. The team holds the postassessment meeting. Things then can become unclear, because different states and agencies function in different ways. At some point in the process, an intervention team is assigned to work with the child and family, and hopefully the same team also works with the caregivers and teachers (although this is not a given). For each child, a *family facilitator* should be assigned. Ideally, the family facilitator is a person who already has connected well with the family or has expertise in the area of the child's primary disability or needs. The family facilitator should remain the family contact and develop a trusting relationship with the family in order to provide continuity. The rest of the team should support this facilitator.

The team, including the intervention facilitator, should meet on a weekly basis to discuss the children and families in order to garner ideas and support. Intermittently, a short video clip of the child involved in various daily activities should be presented for the team to watch and provide input. Discussion should revolve around key issues and questions the intervention facilitator brings to the team. Whenever possible, home visits or classroom visits should be made by pairs of team members. This is important for several reasons. Two team members can offer fresh perspectives on the child and family, provide coaching in their own areas of expertise, provide feedback to the primary intervention facilitator on how they think the child or family is responding, and/or provide peer mentoring. Taking different team members at varying times expands the opportunities for rethinking intervention strategies. In addition, when team meetings are held and the child and family are discussed, the team members have more "real life" perspective to bring to the table.

A key factor to remember in TPBI is that all team members are merely supporters for the true primary interventionists—the parents, caregivers, and teachers who spend many hours with the child each day. The role of the intervention facilitator is to help those people gain knowledge, skills, and confidence in their interactions with the child, while at the same time helping them to "keep it real," to make learning and developing more fun and motivating than ever before.

TYPES OF INTERVENTIONS

Within TPBI2, ideas for intervention are presented in several ways. General principles that promote development are offered along with strategies to help adults create supportive learning environments. Suggestions also are presented for fostering development and learning across cognitive, emotional and social, communication, and sensorimotor areas through modification of interpersonal interactions. Examples are shared of applying strategies in various activities and routines across the child's day at home and child care or school. Developmentally appropriate suggestions also are illustrated. The team, therefore, has a repertoire of ideas from which to draw. The type of strategies that are identified to try in intervention will vary depending on the child's age, type of disability, and degree of severity of disability; the setting in which intervention is taking place; the adult's relationship with the child; and the adult's confidence in using the strategies. The professional's role with the child and adults in the child's life will also vary, depending on the type and level of support needed and desired.

MATERIALS

No specific materials are required to conduct intervention in the TPBI approach. TPBI is a process, using whatever is in the natural environment. In addition, therapists may recommend modifications of the environment or materials or the use of therapeutic materials or equipment that may enhance the child's functioning. Whenever possible, the team (including family members and teachers) should use the same materials in the home and classroom as the peers or siblings without disabilities. Adaptations or special toys, materials, and equipment are included when doing so will increase the child's motivation and increase skills or independence. The most important "materials" are the forms used in the planning process for TPBI.

Forms are merely an aid to the TPBI2 process. They give structure to the process and provide a guide for thinking about, planning, implementing, and evaluating intervention. Modifications of the included forms or substitutions with specific program forms may be needed to meet state or agency requirements. A summary of the forms used in TPBI and their descriptions follow (note that all forms are included on the TPBA2 & TPBI2 Forms CD-ROM):

- Postassessment/before intervention:

  Child Assessment and Recommendations Checklist (see Appendix in *Administration Guide for TPBA2 & TPBI2*)

  Family Service Coordination Checklist (Forms CD-ROM only)

  Team Intervention Plan (see Appendix in *Administration Guide*)

- Beginning intervention and ongoing

  Collaborative Problem-Solving Worksheet (see Appendix in *Administration Guide*)

  TIP Strategies Checklist: Home and Community (see Appendix in *Administration Guide*)

  TIP Strategies Checklist: Child Care and Early Education (see Appendix in *Administration Guide*)

- Ongoing and postintervention (optional, as other monitoring tools may be used)

  Functional Outcomes Rubrics (FORs) by TPBA2 Domain (4) (sensorimotor, emotional and social, communication, and cognitive; see Appendix in *Administration Guide*)

  Functional Outcomes Rubrics by OSEP Child Outcome (3) (CD-ROM only)

  Team Assessment of Progress (TAP) Form (see Appendix in *Administration Guide*)

  OSEP Child Outcomes Reporting Form and Worksheets (CD-ROM only)

Description of Forms

Child Assessment and Recommendations Checklist

This optional form can be completed after TPBA2 and after services and interventions are determined. It summarizes what the child and family's needs are, what type of interventions and services will be provided and by whom. It also notes the time for a review of progress.

Family Service Coordination Checklist

This optional form can be used for IDEA Part C service coordination. It identifies areas of potential need and family strengths, as well as who will be responsible for helping to access services in these areas.

Team Intervention Plan

This form is meant to be used after the TPBA and any other assessments are completed. It identifies selected global outcomes and priority intervention subcategories, as well as specific functional targets for intervention.

Collaborative Problem-Solving Worksheet

The Collaborative Problem-Solving Worksheet (CPSW) is used to record the subcategories selected and functional intervention targets determined. Other developmental areas that also can be addressed along with intervention targets can be indicated as well. Specific interactional and environmental strategies and resources for intervention are noted on this worksheet.

TIP Strategies Checklist: Home and Community

This TIP checklist identifies, in brief format, ideas for types of activities or routines at home and in the community where intervention can be embedded, along with suggestions for types of interactional and environmental strategies that may be considered. This checklist is meant to stimulate ideas and can be used when completing the CPSW.

TIP Strategies Checklist: School and Child Care

This TIP Strategies Checklist identifies, in brief format, ideas for types of activities or routines at eduaction and child care settings where intervention can be embedded, along with suggestions for types of interactional and environmental strategies that may be considered. This checklist is meant to stimulate ideas and can be used when completing the CPSW.

Functional Outcomes Rubrics by TPBA2 Domain

These charts provide a matrix of Goal Attainment Scales for each of the domains of development, by subcategory. The Goal Attainment Scales show the progression from minimal to functional skills for the subcategory. The scale is used to indicate baseline of performance (behavior on implementation of intervention) and level of performance at two subsequent measurement intervals.

If desired, priority subcategories can be chosen by domain from these charts. Once the priority subcategories are determined by the team, functional intervention targets are written.

Functional Outcomes Rubrics by OSEP Child Outcome

These charts provide a matrix of Goal Attainment Scales for each of the OSEP Child Outcomes. These include the same Goal Attainment Scales as on the FOR by TPBA2 Domain but organized by OSEP Child outcome. Once the priority subcategories are determined by the team, functional intervention targets are written (for more information, see OSEP Child Outcomes Reporting with TPBA2 on the optional TPBA2 & TPBI2 Forms CD-ROM.

Team Assessment of Progress (TAP) Form

The TAP Form is meant to be used to evaluate the child's progress on the Goal Attainment Scales for the subcategories selected as priorities for intervention. These are completed at least twice a year, but preferably more frequently. (A more comprehensive review of all subcategories by the team can also be done using the FORs; refer to the instructions on the optional CD-ROM for translating this information into outcomes reporting categories.) The Team Intervention Plan is then revised by reexamining desired global outcomes, identifying new subcategory priorities, and writing new intervention targets.

OSEP Child Outcomes Reporting Form and Worksheets

States, and therefore programs within states, are required to report the percentage of children receiving IDEA services who improve, maintain, or do not improve functioning on three federally designated child outcomes. (For additional information, see OSEP Child Outcomes Reporting with TPBA2 on the optional TPBA2 & TPBI2 Forms CD-ROM.) This form and its worksheets enable programs to track a child's progress using the Goal Attainment Scales and the FORs by OSEP Child Outcome.

TPBI PROCESS

TPBI is meant to be a flexible process. It is meant to be used in conjunction with TPBA2, because TPBA serves as an initial experiment in intervention and thus provides a foundation for planning approaches that may be beneficial. The TPBI process can be used following any assessment that results in obtaining sufficient functional information to be used for intervention planning. Once the team has information on the child's skills, behaviors, learning style, interactional preferences, and functional needs, intervention planning can proceed. The TPBI process involves several steps before actually beginning intervention. These steps establish the direction for intervention efforts, narrow down the focus of efforts to functional targets the family and other providers can address, and then lay out a plan for intervention. Specific forms are provided to facilitate thinking through each step of the TPBI process. Teams may choose to use their own forms, may use the TPBI2 forms in addition to agency forms, or may use only the TPBI2 forms. The core of TPBI2 is not in the paperwork, it is in the use of recommended strategies with children, families, and professionals. The forms are meant to support this work, not detract from it. Therefore, use the pieces that are needed and helpful.

The Twelve Steps (in the following section) outline how the TPBI process is completed and illustrate the means by which the state-of-the-art theories, research, and methodologies outlined in Chapter 9 of the *Administration Guide* (Fundamentals of TPBI2) have been incorporated into the process. As with TPBA2, professionals are given various tools and options for how to use them to meet individual program or team needs and preferences. The various means provided to plan intervention are described in the following sections, along with descriptions and examples of how the TPBI2 planning process can be used with a diverse population of children.

THE TWELVE STEPS

Step One: Identify Strengths, Needs, and Desired Outcomes

It is useful to have a goal and to know if progress is being made toward that goal. For this reason, the first step in the intervention process is to identify the overall outcome or outcomes that are desired as a result of intervention. As described previously, the field has moved away from global goals such as "Improve fine motor skills" to working toward long-term functional outcomes that relate to successful functioning and quality of life. Depending on your home state, your agency requirements, and/or your professional preferences, outcomes can be determined in many ways. TPBI2 uses several different sources to identify the direction and focus intervention should take: 1) preliminary information from families obtained on the Child and Family History Questionnaire (CFHQ) and Family Assessment of Child Functioning (FACF) Tools 2) TPBA2 Observation Guidelines and Observation Summary Forms from each domain, 3) TPBA2 Age Tables from each domain, 4) Goal Attainment Scales for each subcategory of TPBA2, and/or 5) the Functional Outcomes Rubric (FOR) for each TPBA2 domain (see Appendix in the *Administration Guide*), or 6) the Functional Outcomes Rubric (FOR) by OSEP Child Outcome. Because multiple measures should be used to identify outcomes and specific targets, a combination of these tools is recommended (Sandall, McLean, & Smith, 2000).

Preliminary Information from Families

First, information from the Child and Family History Questionnaire (CFHQ) and Family Assessment of Child Functioning (FACF) Tools, is used in determining desired outcomes for the child and family. In particular, several questions at the end of the All About Me Questionnaire (the second part of the FACF) ask the parents what they would like to see for their child in terms of independence, control, skills, and so forth. Even if the child is of preschool age and an individualized education program (IEP) is being developed, it is still recommended that the program include outcomes both for the child in the school context and within the family and community contexts. Risk and protective factors are important to note in building the support elements of the intervention plan, because they are helpful in identifying priorities, strengths, resources, and concerns.

TPBA2 Observation Guidelines and Observation Summary Forms

The TPBA2 Observation Summary Forms for each domain identify overall patterns of strengths and needs (see TPBA2 Observation Summary Forms and Observation Guidelines for each domain in *TPBA2*) and contain a 9-point Goal Attainment Scale (seen in each section of TPBI2) for rating the child's level of functioning. A quick review of these forms will help distinguish broad areas of strength and focus of intervention for the child. For areas of concern, a review of the TPBA2 Observation Guidelines for those specific subcategories will enable the team to identify qualitative processes that need further development or attention in intervention.

TPBA2 Age Tables

The TPBA2 Age Tables also can be used to identify strengths and needed skills and monitor progress in specific subcategories of concern (see Age Tables relating to each domain of TPBA2 in Appendix in the *Administration Guide for TPBA2 & TPBI2*). Higher level skills are strengths that can serve as a foundation for further development. Skills that are noted as "gaps" or skills the child has not yet accomplished but that provide a foundation for further learning ("ready for") should be identified. The TPBA2 Age Tables enable the team to identify specific areas or skills to target.

Using this information, the team can build on their discussion of strengths and needs to determine outcomes. Three different options are provided for determining which potential long-term global outcomes are appropriate for the child: identifying TPBA2 developmental domains needing a higher level of performance, OSEP Child (ECO Center) Outcomes, and personal outcomes.

Identify TPBA2 developmental domains needing a higher level of performance. In this method, the team has the option of selecting one or more of these outcomes as a global outcome:

1. *Sensorimotor:* Moves independently and effectively and regulates and uses sensory input for learning.

2. *Emotional and social:* Effectively relates to others and controls emotions and behaviors.

3. *Communication:* Understands and actively and effectively uses verbal and nonverbal communication.

4. *Cognitive:* Understands ideas, effectively solves problems, and actively participates in learning.

Identify OSEP Child Outcomes. The outcomes described by the ECO Center (2005) are another set of global outcomes for children that programs may wish to target. These outcomes are not labeled by domain but require skills from each domain to accomplish. They have the advantage of already being transdisciplinary, and TPBA2 Goal Attainment Scale information can be recorded on each FOR by OSEP Child Outcome (see CD-ROM for more information). Because states must report on children's progress toward these outcomes, the TPBA2 subcategories for each of the domains of development were analyzed for their contribution to these global outcomes. Programs receiving IDEA funds and using the OSEP Child Outcomes for accountability purposes may want to use these outcomes to plan intervention.

At the time of publication, the three outcomes identified by OSEP include the following (ECO Center web site: http://www.fpg.unc.edu/~eco/pdfs/ECO_COSF_Training2-1-07.pdf):

1. Has positive social relationships.

2. Acquires knowledge and skills.

3. Takes appropriate actions to meet own needs.

Please note that OSEP requirements for accountability may change or be refined over time. If you choose to use these outcomes, it will be important to double-check with the ECO Center to make sure the outcomes you are using are still accurate.

Identify personal outcomes. The third option is the approach that traditionally has been used in programs for professionals and families to write their own outcome(s) that are meaningful for their child and family. In this option, the family is asked what goals they have for their child, and their answers become the "long-term" goals. Although there is nothing wrong with this approach, it precludes agencies from looking across children and programs at progress toward uniform global outcomes (i.e., outcomes that are the same for all children). If every child has a different desired outcome, comparative measurement of the progress of all children is more difficult. Narrowing global outcomes down to three or four enables comparison of all children on their progress toward these outcomes. The intent is to enable program administrators and legislators to examine the overall effectiveness of programs. Programs that are not bound by federal, state, or agency requirements, however, may still prefer to use this more open-ended approach.

All of the methods discussed here can be used separately or in combination. The approaches are meant to address both qualitative (developmental processes) and quantitative (age-level skills) types of outcomes. Depending on the child and family, the most useful means can be chosen. Once the outcomes are determined, they are written on the Team Intervention Plan (see Appendix in the *Administration Guide for TPBA2 & TPBI2*). The information included on this form helps determine services needed and becomes the first document in the intervention plan. Figure 2.1 illustrates the global outcomes selected by Ben's parents and teacher.

Step Two: Identify Priority Subcategories Contributing to the Outcome

Once the outcome has been selected, the next step is to break down that "big" outcome in areas that will contribute to reaching the ultimate goal. This is easily done by looking at the subcomponents of the outcomes chosen and identifying which subcomponents are priorities for the child and family. For two of the methods of identifying outcomes (FORs by TPBA2 Domain and by OSEP Child Outcome), a corresponding approach to determining contributing skills is provided. For the personal outcomes approach, the team must use professional judgment to determine subcomponents of the outcomes selected. If either the FORs by TPBA2 Domain or FORs by OSEP Child Outcomes are used, these can be easily be referenced. The team should look at the subcategories listed on the FOR and prioritize among the subcategories those that are the most important for the child. The team already rated subcategories as part of TPBA2, so unless parents view the rating differently (which should be discussed), a look at each profile of ratings will provide a picture of areas that may need intervention. After discussing which areas take precedence, a selection is made for intervention. These are

TPBI2 Team Intervention Plan

TPBA **Play-Based** TPBI
TPBC ™

Child's name: _Ben B._   Birth date: _____   Age: _3 years_

Person determining intervention plan: _____   Date: _2-07-06_

Relationship or role: _____

Projected month of reevaluation follow-up: _____

Contact person: _____   Phone: _____

Directions: Select the TPBA2 Domain Outcomes column *OR* the OSEP Global Outcomes column. Prioritize as a team (1, 2, 3, 4) one or more outcomes below based on their importance for the child in home and community (H/C) and school and/or child care (S/CC) settings. The priorities may be the same or different, depending on the child's needs in each environment.

TPBA2 Domain Global Outcomes			OSEP Child Outcomes		
H/C	S/CC		H/C	S/CC	
		Ability to move independently and effectively and to regulate and use sensory input for learning (Sensorimotor Development)			Positive social-emotional skills
1		Ability to effectively relate to others and control emotions and behavior (Emotional and Social Development)			Acquisition and use of knowledge and skills
2	1	Ability to understand and use verbal and nonverbal communication (Communication Development)			Appropriate behaviors to meet needs
	2	Ability to understand ideas, solve problems, and learn (Cognitive Development)			

Figure 2.1. Ben's priority outcomes.

then recorded on the Team Intervention Plan under the priority subcategories selected for intervention along with the agreed-on ratings. In addition to ratings, age levels can be noted if the parents desire. Age levels will note the age range at which the child was primarily functioning. In some cases, no age levels are available because the subcategory is qualitative rather than age-based. (See Figure 2.2 for an example of this section of the form.)

Step Three: Determine Baseline

A unique approach to identification of intervention targets and progress monitoring was developed for TPBI. This approach has combined a Goal Attainment Scale and an evaluation rubric (either). Both the TPBA FOR and the FOR by TPBA2 Domain or FOR by OSEP Child Outcomes contain a Goal Attainment Scale for each subcategory of each outcome. The TPBA2 subcategories from each of the domains that directly relate to the global outcome are listed in the column on the left side of each FOR. Once the team identifies desired outcomes, the FOR can be used to identify where the child is on the scale for a particular subcategory or across all subcategories. By identifying where the child is on the FOR, the team can help families determine what targets of intervention will assist the child in reaching the selected outcomes.

Looking at the Goal Attainment Scales often helps parents narrow down their child's functional level without feeling the stress and sadness that looking at TPBA2 Age Tables may elicit. On the Goal Attainment Scales, parents circle where they see their child (e.g., "I think he's between a 3 and a 5 on Regulation of Emotions and Arousal States. He still has bad emotional outbursts, but he's beginning to start to go off by himself to calm down after I hold him and talk to him. So I think I'd call that a 4"). After reviewing the Goal Attainment Scales for the areas selected, the team is ready to identify targets for intervention. Only those Goal Attainment Scales with comparatively lower ratings for a given child need to be targets of intervention. For children with relatively flat patterns, with almost all ratings falling at the same level, a target may be chosen based on additional assessment data and the parent's priorities. Although many items could be selected, it is wise initially to select two or three priority subcategories. Each subsection within a given chapter of TPBI2 has a Goal Attainment Scale for its subcategory. If desired, the team can copy each Goal Attainment Scale for the subcategories selected as priorities and combine them to make the child's own mini-rubric as part of his or her file.

By identifying where the child is on the FOR, the team can help families determine what targets for intervention will assist the child in reaching the selected outcomes. (See Figure 2.3 for an example of a completed FOR by TPBA2 Domain and Figure 2.4 for examples of a rubric developed for Ben from the priorities and ratings selected.) By making the child's own FOR, the priorities are identified more easily and seem less overwhelming. As Ben begins to use more words to communicate, and listens and understands more, he will be better able to control his emotions, communicate his needs, follow others' instructions, and learn new words. This, in turn, will help him progress in other areas of development, such as play, social interaction, and problem solving. Because of the transdisciplinary nature of development, is not necessary to specify intervention priorities in every domain and subcategory.

The three components of outcomes assessment combined—global outcomes (GO), the FOR, and the functional intervention targets (FITs)—provide the basis for evaluat-

---

After prioritizing outcomes for the child, look at the Functional Outcomes Rubrics (FORs) that correspond to the outcomes with the highest priorities. Examine the Goal Attainment Scales that were completed during the TPBA that are listed on the FOR selected. Discuss the assessment/intervention areas that have the lowest ratings with the family. Determine what subcategories across the domains identified are the most important to helping the child's learning and development. Indicate the subcategories selected for intervention and the rating given on the line next to the subcategory. Place the age level for that subcategory (if available) on the following line.

The priority subcategories selected for intervention:	Rating	Age level
Regulation of emotions and arousal states	1	12–15 months
Behavioral regulation	3	12–15 months
Expressive language	4	12–15 months
Conceptual knowledge	3	12–15 months

Figure 2.2. Ben's priorities at home and school (from his Team Intervention Plan).

ing developmental progress and planning the next steps. These components can be remembered by the acronym "GO FOR IT." The following section describes developing appropriate intervention targets for the priorities that are identified.

Step Four: Write a FIT or Objective

Professionals in the field of EI and ECSE are long used to writing goals and objectives. These goals and objectives, however, often are not functional. Goals such as "Will increase vocabulary" could be written for anyone. Objectives taken off of a checklist, or a missed test item such as "Will put six blocks in cup," do not lend themselves to developing functional skills. Why do you want the child to put blocks in a cup? What skills are you trying to develop? And who needs blocks served in a cup, anyway? The field of EI has wisely moved toward trying to support the development of functional skills as they are used in a child's everyday life.

The same, unfortunately, is not always true of preschool, where the push for testing academic skills to meet the requirements of the No Child Left Behind Act of 2001 (PL 107-110) tends to compel teachers toward purely academic targets and away from functional skills. TPBI2 attempts to address both. The TPBA2 Observation Guidelines, Goal Attainment Scales, and FORs address developmental processes and functioning and qualitative aspects of learning. The TPBA2 Age Tables provide developmental sequences and skills specific to various developmental age ranges, including academic skills.

As with TPBA2, TPBI2 is meant to address both skills and processes to maximize a child's functioning. The FITs that are written can, and should, relate to both. The team should try to ensure that families and teachers address a range of developmental priorities, not just academic skills. Team members may need to provide information about foundational learning and social processes, the importance of language basics to literacy, the importance of sensory and motor development to learning, and so forth. Use the information gained from TPBA2 so that family members and professionals understand how these foundations contribute to academic, social, and athletic skills.

Once the team has determined priorities jointly, the more difficult step is turning those priorities into functional, measurable objectives. Once a priority is established, the parent is asked about next steps.

BEN

After his mom, Marcy, rated her child, Ben, on her priority of Emotional Regulation, a team member asked, "What would you like to see him do for next steps in controlling his emotions?" Marcy said, "Well, I'd like Ben not to blow up at all, but I know that's not going to happen any time soon! I guess I'd like for him to not need me to have to help him so much. I spend a lot of time holding him! Maybe if Ben could find another way to calm down that didn't need me. That would be a good step."

The team member then said, "You said Ben 'loses it' at least once an hour right now. How about if we also reduce the number of tantrums he has?"

"I'd nominate you for sainthood," Marcy said. After further discussion, the team constructed the following FIT:

For 1 month, Ben will have three or fewer tantrums per day at home, that last less than 10 minutes each, and he will be able to calm himself using a calming object or a "safe spot."

Functional Outcomes Rubric (FOR) by TPBA2 Domain: Emotional and Social Development

Child's name: Ben B.   Age: _____   Birth date: _____   Date of initial rating: _____

Person(s) completing the form: _____

Outcome: Ability to effectively relate to others and control emotions and behavior

Directions: The following transdisciplinary Goal Attainment Scales address the skills necessary for effective emotional and social development. Family members, other caregivers, professionals who provide education or therapy services, or the team as a whole can complete the rubric. For each subcategory, circle the corresponding number that most characterizes the child's behavior or skill. Subsequent assessment findings are noted in the columns marked 2nd and 3rd rating. Please note that the Goal Attainment Scales on the TPBA2 Observation Summary Forms are the same as these. The ratings assigned on the Observation Summary Forms are supposed to be the initial rating here, and the "Date of initial rating" is the same as the "Evaluation date" on the Summary Forms. More than three can be given if the team desires.

	Date of 2nd rating:	Date of 3rd rating:

TPBA2 subcategory	Level of the child's ability as observed in functional activities									Date of 2nd rating:	Date of 3rd rating:
	1	**2**	**③**	**4**	**5**	**6**	**7**	**8**	**9**		
Emotional expression	Expresses emotions related to comfort and discomfort using sounds and physical movements.		Experiments with different types, levels, and forms of emotional expression to communicate needs.		Often expresses extremes of emotions to get needs met and to elicit a response from others.		Expresses full range of emotions, with the predominant emotions being positive.		Easily communicates full range of emotions in appropriate contexts, with an acceptable level of intensity.		
Emotional style/ adaptability	① Does not adapt to new people, objects, events, or changes in routines without extreme, long-lasting emotional reactions.		Adapts to changes in people, objects, events, or routines with much verbal preparation and environmental support.		Adapts to changes in people, objects, events, or routines using motivating, logical connections to the transition situation.		Adapts to changes in people, objects, events, or routines with verbal preparation.		Adapts to new people, objects, events, or changes in routines independently, with an appropriate amount of caution and emotional reaction.		
Regulation of emotions and arousal states	① Has a difficult time controlling arousal states and emotions; needs extensive environmental support and physical and verbal support from a caregiver. Regulation takes more than 1 hour.		Is able to control arousal states and emotions in a soothing environment when receiving physical and verbal support from a caregiver. Regulation takes 30–60 minutes.		Is able to control arousal states and emotions in a quiet environment or when physical or emotional support is received from an adult. Regulation takes 15–30 minutes.		Is able to control arousal states and emotions with self-regulatory strategies (e.g., a blanket or special toy) or verbal suggestions from an adult. Regulation takes just a few minutes.		Is able to independently control arousal states and emotions in a way appropriate for the situation.		

Transdisciplinary Play-Based System (TPBA2/TPBI2)
by Toni Linder.

Figure 2.3. Ben's TPBA FOR in the emotional and social domain.

(continued from previous page)

FOR by TPBA2 Domain: Emotional and Social Development **TPBI 2**

TPBA2 subcategory	Level of the child's ability as observed in functional activities									Date of 2nd rating:	Date of 3rd rating:
	1	2	3	4	5	6	7	8	9		
Behavioral regulation	Does not understand or respond to adults' requests to stop actions.		(3) Beginning to understand what not to do, but does it anyway. Resists adults' input and control.		Understands right and wrong with adult input, so sometimes chooses appropriate behavior. Is beginning to look to adults for input on what to do.		Independently understands right and wrong and chooses appropriate behavior most of the time, but needs adult assistance to choose and manage behavior.		Chooses appropriate behavior and responds to adults' requests most of the time; tolerates a balance of control.		
Sense of self	Is dependent on others to meet needs.		(3) Tries to access toys and people, shows adults objects, and smiles when others respond to his or her actions. Does not request assistance when needed.		Focuses on specific goals related to movement, objects, or interactions with people. Often requests help or needs reinforcement to maintain effort.		Is motivated to independently reach multiple types of goals; is persistent, confident, and pleased with successful efforts. Knows when help is needed.		Is goal-oriented, persists in the face of challenges, feels confident of success and proud of accomplishments. Aware of own strengths and weaknesses.		
Emotional themes in play	Demonstrates limited range of emotions in play and/or lacks awareness of or concern for emotions of others in the play situation.	(2)	Demonstrates a range of emotions in play through verbal and nonverbal means, but emotions reflect reaction to play itself rather than the meaning of the play.		Recognizes and labels own and others' basic emotions in play situations. Has repetitive unresolved emotional themes in play.		Is able to attribute emotions to inanimate characters in dramatic play, and uses play themes to experiment with resolving emotional conflicts.		Is able to appropriately represent own and others' emotions and can resolve emotional conflicts in interactions and themes within symbolic and sociodramatic play.		

(continued)

Transdisciplinary Play-Based System (TPBA2/TPBI2)
by Toni Linder.

Figure 2.3. *(continued)*

FOR by TPBA2 Domain: Emotional and Social Development **TPBI**[2]

TPBA2 subcategory	Level of the child's ability as observed in functional activities									Date of 2nd rating:	Date of 3rd rating:
	1	2	③	4	5	6	7	8	9		
Social interactions	Watches caregivers and reacts to their initiations with vocal or physical responses.		Is responsive to affection and initiates positive interactions with others. May have difficulty with separation from key caregivers.		Takes turns in prolonged interaction with family members and familiar people. May be shy or anxious with unfamiliar people. Plays alongside peers but may have frequent social conflicts.		Primarily has positive reciprocal relationships with family members and peers in daily activities. Is able to initiate interaction and engage a peer for several minutes. Uses adults for conflict resolution.		Discriminates among familiar people and strangers, has close relationships with family, and maintains several friendships. Is able to initiate and maintain interactions in reciprocal, goal-oriented play and can negotiate conflict situations independently.		

TPBA2 Subcategory	Level of the child's ability as observed in functional activities									Date of 2nd rating:	Date of 3rd rating:
	1	2	3	4	5	6	7	8	9		
Regulation of emotions and arousal states	① Has a difficult time controlling arousal states and emotions; needs extensive environmental support and physical and verbal support from a caregiver. Regulation takes more than 1 hour.		Is able to control arousal states and emotions in a soothing environment, when receiving physical and verbal support from a caregiver. Regulation takes 30–60 minutes.		Is able to control arousal states and emotions in a quiet environment or when physical or emotional support is received from an adult. Regulation takes 15–30 minutes.		Is able to control arousal states and emotions with self-regulatory strategies (e.g., a blanket or special toy) or verbal suggestions from an adult. Regulation takes just a few minutes.		Is able to independently control arousal states and emotions in a way appropriate for the situation.		
Behavioral regulation	1 Does not understand or respond to adults' requests to stop actions.		③ Beginning to understand what not to do, but does it anyway. Resists adults' input and control.		Understands right and wrong with adult input, so sometimes chooses appropriate behavior. Is beginning to look to adults for input on what to do.		Independently understands right and wrong and chooses appropriate behavior most of the time, but needs adult assistance to choose and manage behavior.		Chooses appropriate behavior and responds to adults' requests most of the time; tolerates a balance of control.		
Language production	1 Expresses needs reflexively (e.g., crying, grimacing, body movement).		3 Uses eye gaze, facial expressions, body movement, gestures, and vocalizations to communicate.	④	Uses gestures, vocalizations, verbalizations, signs (words, word combinations, or phrases), and/or AAC to communicate.		Uses gestures, words, phrases, signs, and/or AAC to produce sentences (not grammatically correct) and to ask and answer questions.		Consistently uses well-formed sentences and asks and answers a variety of questions.		
Conceptual knowledge	1 Recognizes familiar sounds, smells, tastes, people, actions, and objects.		③ Notices salient properties, sees similarities and differences, and has simple labels for some animals, people, objects, actions, and events.		Recognizes, discusses, or uses concrete similarities and differences to categorize or group animals, people, objects, actions, and events into constructs, such as type, location, use, relationship, and/or causality.		Recognizes, describes, and organizes thoughts and actions by both concrete and abstract concrete and abstract concepts, and categories. Is forming a classification system into which new concepts and rules are structured and related.		Describes, compares, differentiates, and understands both featural and dynamic (e.g., who, where, when, why and how) aspects of concepts. Has an understanding of logical relations among mathematical, physical, biological, psychological, and literacy concepts, and can share ideas through symbolic representations.		

Figure 2.4. Ben's rubric for home and school

In order to know if a child has done a skill "well enough" to consider it accomplished, it is important to know what the child needs to do functionally in the environment and what constitutes "success." What quality of skill is needed? How many times must a skill be seen at this level of quality? Under what circumstances? As the number of intervention targets being addressed at one time is limited to 3 or 4, it is worth the time to think out what exactly the child needs to do to function better in his or her life, and what level of skill or behavior will demonstrate successful functioning. This way, everyone is on the same page.

Step Five: Select Activities, Settings, and Routines

Step Five is the beginning of what is carried out in Step Seven, identifying and creating strategies. Before determining where and how intervention supports will be provided, an understanding is needed of what daily life is like for the child. Once the targets for intervention are identified, the team needs to address how the intervention will take place. The TPBI process is one that should occur in natural environments, within natural interactions, and with targets embedded in daily experiences, activities, and routines. The planning tools provided are meant to be used in consultation with families, caregivers, teachers, or therapists to guide implementation of intervention in a way that is consistent with these philosophical tenets.

Several steps are needed to complete the Team Intervention Plan (see Appendix in *Administration Guide*). These are listed on the Team Intervention Plan for team members and the family, but the steps also will be iterated here.

It is important to embed whatever interventions are planned into the child's actual life, rather than provide only treatment, therapy, or education that does not carry over into functional activities. Therefore, another critical aspect of planning intervention is talking about actual situations, routines, events, and activities in which intervention could 1) help the child function better, 2) help the family members or adults function better, 3) capitalize on the child's strengths, and/or 4) capitalize on the family members' or adults' strengths. In addition, the team should consider including difficult interventions in ways that could be more fun or pleasurable; fun activities that provide an opportunity for including more learning; or activities that occur frequently over the course of the day or week, and thus offer opportunities for practice. The initial conversation begins with the team but needs to be extended into a more protracted discussion in a more personal and private level before the actual start of intervention.

Step Six: Complete the Team Intervention Plan

The previous steps contribute to completing the Team Intervention Plan. Once the functional intervention targets (FITs) are specified, the team can then determine how intervention will take place to address them. Designation of who will be the primary intervention facilitator and the roles of various team members is important to ensure that everyone knows what will happen and in what ways support will be provided. See Figure 2.5 to see how Ben's Team Intervention Plan was completed.

Step Seven: Identify or Create Strategies

Because preliminary discussions with families, caregivers, and teachers can be quite lengthy, it is best to plan discussion time outside of a formal meeting to talk about strategies to use in intervention. Have an in-depth conversation with key adults about their day, the fun times, the stressful times, the moments of joy, and the moments of desperation. In short, talk about the good, the bad, and the ugly. It is important to discuss not just the negative aspects of the day, because some of the most joyous times are the best for incorporating language, movement, social interaction, and conceptual thinking. Humor is a wonderful way to motivate children. Discussion of these times leads easily to a discussion of strategies that can be incorporated into each type of situation.

The fun part of working in early childhood/EI and ECSE is that professionals are able to be creative. They have a storehouse of knowledge and ideas, but every child, every family, and every situation is different, and what works for one may very well not work for another. The more ideas the intervention facilitators have, the better. Once the team has determined several FITs on which to focus, and they know the fabric of the child's daily life, they are ready to think about what strategies will help the child and family or teacher be successful.

TPBI2 is meant to be a source for ideas—a jumping off place for professionals to problem solve with key adults in the child's life. There is no one way to use TPBI2. It is a resource, not a cookbook. It is especially helpful for people in transdisciplinary roles, because every discipline is not represented during each visit. This is a team process, so conversation about the child and family with the whole team is critical. During team discussions, have each professional review various strategies in his or her domain of TPBI2 and talk about how certain strategies might be useful to the child or family. Using collaborative problem solving, the team ideas will help all interested parties to generate a plan of action or, more likely, numerous plans for how the day can be full of special moments for teaching and learning. TPBI2 serves as a resource for ideas across all domains and is a reminder for all team members of how to incorporate holistic strategies. It is important to stress that families are not being asked to become therapists. They are being supported with strategies that can make their own lives and those of their children fuller, more meaningful, and more successful just by doing what they already do in slightly different ways.

In the same way that the number of targets for intervention should be limited, the number of strategies selected to be tried also should be limited so as to not overwhelm the family and to clarify what strategies are having a positive effect. Use the TIP Strategies Checklists as a basis for beginning discussion, spending more time on one or two ideas with which the adults involved in the intervention are confident.

Step Eight: Individualize Environmental and Interpersonal Strategies

As discussion proceeds, what started out as general strategies, suggestions, observations, or ideas need to be developed into an individualized approach for the child and family or the teacher. The intervention facilitator and other team members will want to observe what is happening, talk about the parents' perceptions, and perhaps try new strategies through experimenting or demonstrating for the parents. All of these efforts build insights into how the child and adults in the child's life respond and learn. Individualization for adults may involve providing reading material, visual guides, and examples; using video for feedback; or going out into new environments to try novel experiences. The team should take time to get to know the family as people, not just as "clients," so that interventions devised will have an increased likelihood of success. At the same time, professional boundaries will need to be maintained.

Step Nine: Write Concrete Examples

Writing down ideas gives everyone a concrete reference. Much is discussed in a short time, and just as much is forgotten. After a couple of initial discussion and brainstorming sessions with key adults, it is useful to put a more specific plan down on paper. Write down one or two of the FITs that were developed for the Team Intervention Plan, then begin talking about the day and how the strategies discussed previously may be implemented. Use the Collaborative Problem-Solving Worksheet (CPSW) (see Appen-

---

Functional Intervention Targets

1. For 1 month, Ben will have three or fewer tantrums per day at home that last less than 10 minutes each, and he will be able to calm himself using a calming object or a "safe spot."

2. Once Ben is giving the person who is speaking eye contact, he will respond to a simple one-step request by doing what is asked, within two repetitions of the request, 75% of the time for 1 month.

3. Ben will be able to request what he wants using gestures and simple labels for two new common objects in his environment each week for 1 month.

4. Ben will be able to use appropriate actions on specific objects or toys five consecutive times once the actions are demonstrated and he has had practice with using the object or toy in a functional way.

A.   How the above Home and Community Services will be provided:

By whom: The speech-language pathologist, Judy P., will serve as the primary intervention facilitator.

Frequency/intensity/duration: Judy P. will make home visits every other week to consult and coordinate intervention strategies. Visits will become less frequent as the family and teacher feel things are progressing well.

Role of intervention facilitator(s):   Judy P. will observe the situations in the home and school that are most difficult for Ben. She will provide feedback, suggestions, demonstration, and consultation as new strategies are tried. Other team members will make visits to provide additional ideas as needed. Judy will occasionally videotape situations to take to team problem solving meetings.

Role of family members: Mr. and Mrs. B. are the key people in Ben's life and, as such spend many hours interacting with him. They will lead the intervention by trying various strategies related to the identified goals for Ben. They will monitor what works and what does not so that they can share progress and problems with the intervention support team. They will maintain ongoing communication with Ben's teacher to ensure consistency of approaches.

B. How the above Child Care/Early Education Services will be provided:

The intervention team will observe classroom routines and provide consultation to the teacher to coordinate intervention and help ensure consistency between home and school.

By whom: Judy P., SLP, is the primary intervention facilitator.

Frequency/intensity/duration: Classroom visits will be made every other week, alternating with home visits.

Role of intervention facilitator(s):   The intervention facilitator will assist by demonstrating, providing needed support materials or readings, doing joint problem solving, and involving other team members as needed.

Role of educators/caregivers: The teacher is the primary provider in the classroom. Intervention services will be provided in the classroom, with the intervention facilitator as a support to the teacher.

Projected month of reevaluation follow-up: 5/08
Contact person: Judy P.
Phone: 666-7777

Figure 2.5.   Ben's functional intervention targets and team roles.

dix in *Administration Guide*) format. *TPBI2* is, once again, a helpful reference. When completed, the CPSW serves as a visual reminder of ideas, or tips, for all to keep in mind when interacting with the child. Dunst found that visual reminders serve to increase the use of the ideas presented (Dunst, 2001). See Figure 2.6 for an example of a section of Ben's CPSW.

The team should then consult with the family and other service providers as intervention takes place and provide further explanations, models, or feedback as needed. The worksheet can be modified continually, with more intervention targets added as progress is made or new strategies added if progress is slower than desired. The CPSW also serves as a way to talk about what happened since the last discussion with regard to other areas of development, environmental changes, and whether specific ideas that were written down were successful.

Step Ten: Share Information

Whether or not the child participates in child care or school, there are usually other important adults in the child's life. Even if these other people have not been included formally in the intervention process, the child will benefit from having congruent strategies across people and contexts. Families should be encouraged to inform and coach others who spend a lot of time with the child in the strategies the families themselves are learning. With the family's permission, the intervention facilitator also may play an important role by including others in the child's life in informal discussions, information through written materials, or inclusion in support or information groups.

Step Eleven: Implement Intervention

Every part of the TPBA2/TPBI2 process is part of intervention. Beginning with TPBA, when the strategies that seem to promote higher levels of thinking and action are explored; through the assessment discussion and intervention planning process, when the family's and team's experiences are shared; to when actual day-to-day strategies are implemented, evaluated, and modified, TPBA2 & TPBI2 guide the evolving process. The ongoing relationship with the child, family, and teachers provides the basis for being part of a highly rewarding, if at times frustrating, process. The role of the professional as intervention facilitator takes many forms, and on any given day this person will listen, talk, demonstrate, practice, or coach. Intervention is full of surprises. Some days, no one will be there when the professional shows up. Some days, nothing will go well. Other days, a first word will be said or a step will be taken. The professional needs to be ready to assume all roles as needed and, in addition, help the key adults build outside networks; serve as an advocate with other agencies; provide access to needed resources; stay informed on legal issues and within ethical boundaries; and on top of all that, keep excellent records on visits, with detailed progress notes (Klass, 2003).

Step Twelve: Evaluate Progress

Evaluation also is an ongoing process. As with the rest of the intervention process, documentation of progress should be a joint effort. In Chapter 9 of the *Administration Guide*, several approaches are presented to help in collaboration. In addition to informal checks and discussions with family members, caregivers, and teachers, more formal measures are needed. Depending on the age of the child and agency requirements, official evaluation may take place two to three times per year. Progress monitoring can be done using the individual child's rubric (see Figure 2.4). Both home and school or child care can monitor progress on the selected priorities. Even though only a few priorities were selected, all areas are interconnected, and progress on these areas will un-

TPBI2 Collaborative Problem-Solving Worksheet (CPSW)

Child's name: _Ben_

Date: _02-07-06_   For home/community ☒   For child care ☐   For school ☐

Person(s) completing the form: _____

1. In the first column, write the functional intervention targets (FIT) that were selected and recorded on the Team Intervention Plan after the assessment.

2. In the second column, write related areas that also need to be addressed as part of accomplishing this target.

3. In the third column (T), list priority times of the day, routines, or activities when the FITs can be addressed. In the fourth column (I), brainstorm possible interactions supports. (Refer to TPBI2 under the domain and intervention subcategory related to that target for suggestions.) In the fifth column (P), brainstorm potential environmental modifications that could be tried. For each column, refer to the TIP Strategies Checklists for suggestions.

4. At the bottom of the worksheet, indicate any resources that might be helpful for implementing intervention, including reading material, Internet sites, videos, equipment, toys, assistive devices, and connections with community agencies.

5. Indicate any assistance needed to implement the intervention and/or access resources.

Functional intervention targets and subcategory	Related areas	T Times for natural intervention	I Interactions that support development	P Potential environmental adaptations
Ben will be able to request what he wants using gestures and simple labels for two new common objects in his environment each week for 1 month.	Cognitive: understanding concepts Language: using nouns to label Social: communicating to a person Motor: using gestures to support communication	Meals: labeling food, utensils Bath: labeling toys, body parts Dressing: labeling clothing, body parts Play: labeling toys, people Books: labeling pictures, real objects, animals	Use simple 1- to 2-word phrases. Obtain eye contact before talking. Touch shoulder, wait. Hold object near mouth when labeling. Use exaggerated, rhythmical speech. Use gestures or signs to support speech.	Use real objects as cues to what happens next (e.g., key to car for going out). Use pictures of real objects to support labels (e.g., cereal box of Cheerios next to the bowl to help him see relationships between objects and pictures).

Figure 2.6.   Segment of Ben's Collaborative Problem-Solving Worksheet for home.

doubtedly contribute to progress in other areas. If desired by families or teachers, progress on other Goal Attainment Scales can also be checked.

WHERE INTERVENTION TAKES PLACE

Not limited to home and school, intervention should take place as many places as possible, as often as possible, and be implemented by as many people as possible. Repetition of new skills across a variety of functional contexts is the key to learning, particularly for children with special needs. In specific cases, additional private or pull-out therapy may be warranted, but even specialized therapies should be integrated into the total picture of the intervention process, so continuity is maintained.

RESULTS OF SUCCESSFUL INTERVENTION

The desired results of intervention are many. We want children with special needs to become more functional and independent in their daily lives. We want them to become motivated to learn and use new ideas and skills. We want children to be able to give and receive love; to have meaningful friendships; and to share life's activities with joy, sensitivity, and reciprocity. We want children to express themselves in as many ways as they can, with their eyes, their gestures, their body, and their words, through art, music, and movement. We want them to love and participate fully in as many aspects of life as they can. We want the same for their families.

In TPBI2, options are provided for addressing the progress toward outcomes: 1) use of the TPBA2 Age Tables to measure skills accomplished and changes in level of performance, and 2) use of the FORs to measure progress toward global outcomes. Use of both together is recommended.

The FORs by TPBA2 Domain are completed initially by the professionals as part of TPBA2. A 9-point Goal Attainment Scale is included as part of the summary information with each of the subcategories of TPBA2. This is completed by individual professionals on the team during the first assessment of the child. Because most assessments are traditionally done by developmental domain, the scales are arranged by domain (completion by the family, caregivers, and/or educators can be done as well). As noted previously, examining these rubrics and discussing them with parents helps identify target areas for intervention. During intervention planning, either the FOR by TPBA2 Domain or FOR by OSEP Child Outcomes is used to identify global outcomes and priority subcategory outcomes. Whichever Goal Attainment Scales are selected for planning intervention targets and strategies (they are the same in both, just organized differently) should be used for measurement of progress. (See Appendix in *Administration Guide* for both sets of FORs.)

The FORs are designed to help programs measure the child's progress toward attaining global outcomes and identifying new targets after intervention has occurred. To measure progress, the team can re-rate the child on identified target subcategories (as in the child's individual rubric in Figure 2.3) or across all subcategories in a specific rubric for a more comprehensive reevaluation. By doing this, the team can identify what outcomes and targets have been obtained and which outcomes and targets a child needs to work on attaining.

As described previously, the child's FORs should be reviewed on a regular schedule (usually two to three times per year, determined by the intervention team). If progress has been made and the child has moved up on the scale, the team needs to evaluate whether or not new outcomes or targets need to be identified. If the child has not made progress, the team needs to discuss whether new intervention targets, different strategies, or both are needed. When a new plan is made, the Team Intervention Plan and the CPSW should be revised and updated. In the case of federal outcomes monitoring, measurement of progress on global outcomes is done at entry into the program and on exit or transition from EI, to ECSE or a kindergarten or first-grade program. (See the TPBA2 & TPBI2 Forms CD-ROM for additional information.)

The TPBA2 Age Table(s) for identified targets also should be reviewed to determine performance-level changes and examine what specific skills may have been accomplished or are still needed. It is recommended that the professionals and teachers on the team use the TPBA2 Age Tables. Depending on the child's level of functioning, it may be difficult for families to look at the child's functioning age level or skills he or she is missing. For this reason, it is recommended that families use the Goal Attainment Scales and the professionals use the TPBA2 Age Tables. In combination, the two give a good quantitative and qualitative view of the child's level of functioning. There is a paradox in the EI/ECSE field that both functional outcomes and measurement of specific skills is desired, but typically age levels are emphasized.

Progress over time can be noted on the Team Assessment of Progress (TAP) Form (see Appendix in *Administration Guide* and Figure 2.7 for Ben's TAP Form). Both the Goal Attainment Scale rating and the child's age level are indicated on the TAP Form. The parent, teacher, or team (individually or together) can indicate where they see the child functioning on this continuum at each reevaluation. This can be done as frequently as is desired. Goal attainment scaling has the advantage of ease of involvement for all participants in the child's ongoing evaluation, because the scales are easy to understand and rate. Examination of this information in combination with information from the TPBA2 Age Tables should provide formative evaluation data as well as summative data at the end of each year, and at transition times. Both formative and summative data should be used to revise and update the Team Intervention Plan for the child.

STATE AND FEDERAL OUTCOMES MEASUREMENT

Federal requirements for accountability reporting include measuring functional progress (qualitative) for the child as well as progress in closing the gap between the child and same-age peers (quantitative). Both can be measured with TPBA2/TPBI2.

TPBI2 can be used to measure functional, qualitative progress across TPBA2 domain outcomes (see FORs by TPBA2 Domain in the Appendix in *Administration Guide*) or across the OSEP child outcomes that have been adopted by the U.S. Department of Education, Office of Special Education Programs (see the FORs by OSEP Child Outcome in the Forms CD-ROM). During the entry and exit assessments, the team should complete the set of three Functional Outcomes Rubrics (FORs) by OSEP Child Outcome. Each FOR is composed of a series of Goal Attainment Scales for the TPBA2 subcategories that represent skills needed for the child outcome. The team can use the Goal Attainment Scale ratings that have been collected on the TPBA2 Observation Summary Forms. For further information about using TPBA2 and TPBI2 for OSEP Child Outcomes reporting, please refer to the TPBA2 & TPBI2 Forms CD-ROM.

In addition, the TPBA2 Age Tables from each domain indicate quantitative growth against same-age peers. The Age Tables for each priority subcategory, as well as other areas, also can be used to look at progress over time. Reevaluation across the subcategories that have age tables is only needed when the child transitions from one program to another.

The OSEP Child Outcomes Reporting Form and its worksheets, allow the intervention team to document whether the child is making progress toward the global outcomes across five ratings, from no improvement in functioning to functioning at the level of same-age peers. Cumulative data across children enables providers to examine group progress and can contribute to program evaluation.

CONCLUSION

Transdisciplinary Play-Based Intervention (TPBI2) is a functional approach to intervention that views family members, caregivers, and teachers as key players in the child's intervention program. They are involved in the assessment, in assessment review, in intervention planning, and in implementation and evaluation. Such involvement may lead to more "ownership" and involvement on the part of these important people in the child's life. The movement of intervention out of the therapy room and into the settings where the child needs to use his or her skills is an important shift in the field of early intervention and early childhood special education. This transfer of focus requires a transition in the role of therapists and other related services personnel to one of consultation and support. It requires acquisition of new skills in communicating with

TPBI2 Team Assessment of Progress (TAP) Form

Child's name: _Ben_ Birth date: _1-15-03_ Date: _____

Person(s) providing information to complete the form: _____

The TAP Form helps the team monitor progress. Using the initial team intervention planning form as a starting point, the key team facilitator completes the TAP form with the significant adults in the child's life. This process should be done for both home and community and school or child care settings, as appropriate.

1. List the *priority subcategories* that were identified on the TPBI2 Team Intervention Plan.

2. Indicate the date the evaluation update was done in the appropriate column (with the first date being the date of the initial assessment). Three dates are indicated below for measurement (more can be added if desired).

3. Help the parents, caregivers, or teachers complete the Goal Attainment Scale (GAS) for each corresponding priority subcategory.

4. Indicate the rating on the Goal Attainment Scale for each measurement time.

5. Using the TPBA2 Age Tables, determine the child's age level for each subcategory at the time of the evaluation update. After completing and updating either the TPBA2 domain FOR or the OSEP FOR (the scales are the same on both FORs but are organized differently), discuss with the family and all providers the areas of progress. The Team Intervention Plan can then be revised by reexamining desired global outcomes, identifying new subcategory priorities, and writing new intervention targets.

6. To translate this information into federal child outcomes reporting categories, refer to the optional CD-ROM, OSEP Child Outcomes Reporting Worksheet and Form instructions.

Home and Community Evaluation

| Priority intervention subcategory | Date 1: _2-07-06_ | | Date 2: _5-28-06_ | | Date 3: _____ | |
	Rating on Goal Attainment Scale	Age range	Rating on Goal Attainment Scale	Age range	Rating on Goal Attainment Scale	Age range
Expressive language	1	12–15 mo.	4	18–21 mo.		
Conceptual knowledge	3	12–15 mo.	5	15–18 mo.		

School and Child Care Evaluation

| Priority intervention subcategory | Date 1: _2-07-06_ | | Date 2: _5-28-06_ | | Date 3: _____ | |
	Rating on Goal Attainment Scale	Age range	Rating on Goal Attainment Scale	Age range	Rating on Goal Attainment Scale	Age range
Expressive language	4	12–15 mo.	5	18–21 mo.		
Conceptual knowledge	3	12–15 mo.	4	18–21 mo.		

Figure 2.7. Team assessment of progress for Ben.

adults, as partners in intervention, rather than recipients of information. It also entails learning how to shift knowledge about the child and share skills in how to intervene to address particular issues influencing the child's development to others—other team members, family members, and educators. TPBI provides a framework for working through this process and also summarizes key interactional and environmental strategies that may be useful across all domains of development. When implemented with a transdisciplinary team in play and in motivating, meaningful daily activities and routines, intervention can assist children to become more independent, more physically and communicatively skilled, more knowledgeable, and more emotionally secure and socially successful.

REFERENCES

Bailey, D., & Bruder, M.B. (2005, January). *Child and family outcomes for early intervention and early childhood special education: Issues and considerations.* Menlo Park, CA: Early Childhood Outcomes Center. Retrieved March 15, 2008, from http://www.fpg.unc.edu/~eco/pdfs/COSFTraining_11-7-06_module2.pdf

Dunst, C.J. (2001). Participation of young children with disabilities in community learning activities. In M.J. Guralnick (Ed.), *Early childhood inclusion: Focus on change* (pp. 307–333). Baltimore: Paul H. Brookes Publishing Co.

Klass, C.S. (2008). *The home visitor's guidebook: Promoting optimal parent and child development* (2nd ed.). Baltimore: Paul H. Brookes Publishing Co.

No Child Left Behind Act of 2001, PL 107-110, 115 Stat. 1425, 20 U.S.C. §§ 6301 *et seq.*

Sandall, S., McLean, M.E., & Smith, B.J. (Eds.). (2000). *DEC recommended practices in early intervention/early childhood special education.* Longmont, CO: Sopris West.

3

Facilitating Sensorimotor Development

I. Strategies for Improving Functions Underlying Movement

with Anita C. Bundy

Goal Attainment Scale

1	2	3	4	5	6	7	8	9
Needs to have total body support in all positions.		Holds head steady and can sit with support.		Moves between variety of sitting and prone postures. May stand alone briefly.		Shows anticipatory postural adjustments. Stands independently and sits on chair.		Is able to assume and maintain functional positions and move smoothly and independently between them.

The development of gross and fine motor skills requires integrity of the sensory-neurological and musculoskeletal systems. If these systems are damaged, foundations for skillful movement such as postural control and muscle tone can be negatively affected.

Postural control, which is composed of *postural orientation* and *postural stability,* provides a means of stabilizing the body, enabling controlled but free movement of various body parts. Postural orientation allows the child to move the body into desired positions in order to complete desired activities. Sensory information from the muscles, joints, skin, ears (including both hearing and the sense of movement), and eyes help the child know the location of various body parts in relation to the environment. Vision and hearing give the child spatial information about where he or she is in relation to other aspects of the environment, whereas touch to the skin, vestibular input (i.e., sense of movement), and pressure to the muscles and joints inform the child about what various body parts are experiencing in relation to each other.

Postural stability is required to maintain balance. Children maintain balance by moving various body parts to establish a base of support that allows them to comfortably engage in activities. For example, a toddler walks with feet far apart, so as to be more stable; when reaching for something, a child may lean on the opposite hand for support; or when falling backward, a preschooler will extend his hands backward to support his body.

Muscle tone, or the degree of tension in muscles when they are at rest, is important for postural orientation and control. A certain amount of muscle tone is necessary for both maintaining stationary positions, such as sitting and for movements, such as reaching, walking, running, and kicking. The amount of muscle tone present influences the child's ability to prepare for an action, respond to stimuli, and maintain postures and movements. Too much or too little muscle tone can have an impact on the child's postural stability and ability to perform functional movements easily and efficiently.

APPROPRIATE FUNCTIONS UNDERLYING MOVEMENT

Children who have good postural control and muscle tone typically accomplish normal developmental movement patterns and milestones within expected age ranges. They look comfortable both in stationary positions and when moving. They are able to maintain an upright posture with head and trunk well aligned. They can easily change positions and maintain balance as they move. Children with good postural control also are able to anticipate what the body needs to do and prepare for movements or changes in position so that they can accomplish a goal. For example, when someone tosses the child a large ball, the child will prepare his or her feet, arms, and hands so that when the ball comes, he or she will not be thrown off balance. Children with good postural control are also able to both extend (straighten) and flex (bend) their muscles as needed in order to maintain balance. In ball-catching, for example, the child needs to be able flex (bend) the arms and legs to counter the pressure of the incoming ball. Children with strong foundations for movement can perform actions easily, efficiently, and fluidly.

Appropriate Functions Underlying Movement in Practice

▊▊▊▊ **I. A. Posture supporting action**

Daily Routines (Home and Classroom)

- *Infant/toddler:* The infant is lying on her tummy in the crib and when her father enters the room, she lifts her head, arms, and legs in excitement. The toddler squats down to pick up cereal that has dropped on the floor, and then reaches up and puts it on the table.

- *Young child:* The young child at snack time is sitting in a chair at a table. He leans sideways to pick up his fallen napkin and catches himself when he starts to fall by placing a hand on the table for support.

Play Routines (Home and Classroom)

- *Infant/toddler:* The infant sits upright on the floor without support, reaches forward to pick up a toy, and sits back up to examine it. The toddler plays a chase game with her father, running with feet spread apart and hands raised at her sides.

- *Young child:* The young child positions himself in front of the ball, raises both hands, stands on one foot, pulls the other foot back, and then lofts the ball high into the air with a kick.

Classroom Routines

During circle time, the children sit on carpet squares with their legs crossed in front of them. They are passing around a conch shell. As the shell comes around, each child, in turn, rotates toward his friend on the left, reaches for the shell, explores and listens to it, and then turns and passes it to the next child on his right.

I. B. Muscle tone supporting posture

Daily Routines (Home and Classroom)

- *Infant/toddler:* The infant is standing in her crib, holding on to the side rail, bouncing up and down. Her legs bend and straighten with ease. The toddler sits on the potty chair looking at a book. His back is straight and he holds the book up with both hands in front of his face.

- *Young child:* The young child is helping his father clean the house. He is pushing and pulling the vacuum cleaner back and forth across the carpet independently.

Play Routines (Home and Classroom)

- *Infant/toddler:* The infant crawls toward her puppy. Her head is up and she moves her head from side-to-side following the puppy's movements as it runs back and forth. The toddler has a bucketful of ping-pong balls. He holds the bucket with his left hand, takes the balls out one and a time, and throws them at a clown face on the wall.

- *Young child:* The young children are doing wheel barrow walking. A friend holds up a child's feet, so the child can walk on his hands. They then walk down the mat.

Classroom Routines

In the literacy area, the children are making books. They are stapling papers together or using a hole punch and then fastening a ring through the hole. Both methods require squeezing and pushing with the hands.

GENERAL PRINCIPLES FOR SUPPORTING FUNCTIONS UNDERLYING MOVEMENT

Adults perform a variety of activities, both consciously and unconsciously, that support the child's use of postural orientation, postural control, and muscle tone. Adults typically encourage the development of motor skills and independence, but at the same time, these strategies support the use of functions underlying movement.

Encourage the Next Developmental Step

Parents and other caregivers are particularly aware of next developmental steps with infants and toddlers. They look for and encourage first holding the head up, rolling, then sitting independently, crawling/creeping, pulling to stand, standing independently, walking with support, then walking and running. In doing this, they often place the child in the desired "next-step position" (e.g., sitting, standing) and then remove some of the external support.

Provide Practice

Repetition is important for accomplishing new skills. Adults provide a variety of opportunities for practice by placing children in situations that will enable them to practice actions needed for new motor skills. For instance, they may place desired objects to the side of the child's head and just out of reach to encourage the child to roll over. They may move toys up onto the couch, a chair, or a table to get a child to pull to stand. Setting up situations that require the child to move to a new position is a common parenting strategy.

Encourage Independent Action

Another strategy adults use is to encourage children to accomplish a task without adult support. They will provide a high level of social support by cheering and clapping for the child's independent efforts. For example, one parent may support the child in standing, while the other parent stands 2 feet away and encourages the child to walk to him or her. The child's efforts are celebrated whether the child is successful or not. Such encouragement motivates the child to continue to work toward the accomplishment of the skill.

THE PRINCIPLES IN PRACTICE

Adults use a variety of approaches throughout the day to support the child's motor development. Here, examples are provided of how caregivers use the above strategies during the day at both home and school. These examples are approaches that most caregivers use naturally in their daily interactions with children. They also are appropriate for most children with disabilities as well.

Daily Routines (Home and Classroom)

Feeding/Eating

While feeding the infant in the high chair, the adult will often place food so that the child needs to reach for it. This requires the child to shift position and adjust balance. As the child moves out of the high chair, sitting on stools, benches, or other types of "adult" chairs require the child to be able to support the trunk using postural muscles without support on the back or sides of the body.

Diapering/Toileting

As the child moves to independent toileting, the child has to give up the support of lying down for diapering. Potty chairs provide side and back support but require the child to sit erect and keep his or her feet on the floor. Potty seats that fit onto toilets give no back or side support or support for the child's feet and thus require the child to have more trunk stability and balance. Parents typically move the child from the more supportive device to the less supportive as the child gains stability and, therefore, confidence. Encouragement of independence is important.

Dressing

Independent dressing requires movement of individual body parts, the ability to coordinate both sides of the body as they perform different actions, balance, and coordination. Caregivers typically support the child by isolating the child's body part and corresponding piece of clothing and helping the child to maneuver, push, and/or pull as needed. As the child becomes more skilled, the adult encourages increased self-sufficiency and helps the child less often. Activities such as putting on pants add the need for increased balance. Adults may provide physical support until the child can manage to stand on one foot for a few seconds with minimal support. The adult also may have the child sit to put on the top part of the pants and then stand to have the adult pull them up. Both methods enable the child to have success while he or she is working at developing balance, strength, and coordination.

Play Routines (Home and Classroom)

Face-to-Face Play

Face-to-face games, such as Peekaboo, songs and finger plays, and playing ball usually are done while the child is sitting down first, so the child has better balance. Later, adults may play such games while the child is standing or walking. Such activities require the child to move arms and hands and maintain balance and control of individual arms, hands, and fingers. Typically, until they have good orientation and stability, children will stop and sit down to engage in this type of play.

Physical Play

Physical play with adults challenges a child's motor skills. Adults may chase the child as he or she crawls or runs; let the child "tackle" and crawl over them; or play bouncing, jumping, or throwing games. All of these require the child to shift weight from side to side, use balance, isolate body parts, and exert and resist pressure. These are activities that support the development of the foundations of movement.

Manipulative Play

Adults encourage the development of postural stability through use of toys that require the child to move in a variety of ways. Adults encourage children to play while sitting, standing, and moving. They provide toys such as trucks to push across the floor while crawling, balls to stand and throw, bats to swing, and tricycles to ride. They encourage building, drawing, and manipulative play. All of these require the child to have stability, balance, and coordination of individual body parts. Proximal stability provides a stable base for a child to use his or her hands to manipulate toys successfully and with good dexterity.

Sensory Play

Activities involving messy play include playing in the mud or splashing in puddles, playing with crayons or finger paints, making things with playdough or clay, or painting with a brush. Again, adults who encourage their children to engage in such activities are supporting the use of balance; use of pressure; and isolation of fingers, hands, and feet.

Reading and Learning Routines

Circle Time

Teachers use circle time primarily for cognitive, social, and communication purposes. Stability and balance, however, are required when children sit on the floor, when they sing and dance, when they raise their hand to answer a question, when they turn to respond to a friend, and so forth.

One-on-One Book Reading

When an adult reads to a young child, the parent often sits the child on his or her lap in a supported position. As the child gets older, the child may sit next to the adult. Although these routines are not meant to promote motor development, they still require the child to use balance to crawl up and down, to rotate to look at the adult and the book, and to use hands together and independently.

Science and Math

Many math and science activities involve movement. Children measure and count small and large things, compare by lifting and weighing, and push and pull to maneuver objects around. Again, motor development is not the end goal, but actions involved in science and math often encourage use of foundations underlying motor development.

PLANNING INDIVIDUALIZED INTERVENTIONS FOR IMPROVING FUNCTIONS UNDERLYING MOVEMENT

▨▨▨▨ I. A. How well does posture support action?

Conditions that affect movement can be caused by neurological trauma or brain deficits that result in disorders, such as cerebral palsy; by musculoskeletal system disorders, such as muscular dystrophy; or by biological, developmental, or environmental problems that result in physical impairment. Because the causes and effects of difficulties with the foundations underlying movement can be complex, medical and therapeutic monitoring is recommended. In general, children who have conditions that result in difficulty with postural orientation and postural stability require help to improve 1) righting reactions (i.e., head and trunk movements which enable a child to remain upright and assume new body positions); 2) protective extension (i.e., extension of a limb to prevent falling); 3) balance (i.e., compensatory reactions of the head and trunk that keep the center of gravity over the base of support); 4) alignment of head, trunk, and limbs to enable movement in and out of positions; 5) sensory awareness of where the body is in space; 6) intention for purposeful movement; and 7) voluntary control of actions.

In addition to the strategies indicated above that adults use with children without disabilities, children with motor disabilities may need extra assistance. The following are general principles for adapting interactions and making environmental modifications to support the development of better postural orientation and control.

Interaction Strategies

1. *Motivate the child to move.* Motivation on the child's part is critical. Passive movement by an adult provides some input to the brain for building neurological pathways, but movements controlled by the child involve more brain centers and will have a greater effect. For this reason, adults need to motivate the child to move independently. For infants and developmentally younger children, social interaction with people is motivating. For older children, interaction with people and/or objects may be more motivating.

The adult should position his or her face or the object in front of the child in such a way that the child needs to pull the head up to orient toward the desired interaction target. Slowly moving the interaction target can encourage changing the position while allowing the child to adjust body position to stay in alignment. For example, if the parent is playing Peekaboo in front of a child who is sitting in a slanted infant seat, the child does not have to try to orient or move. The parent is doing all of the work. If the parent has the child on the floor on hands and knees, however, and then pops up from behind a chair or couch, the child needs to lift his or her head to orient to the adult.

2. *Incorporate interaction.* Positive interaction with others can shift the child's attention from a difficult movement to the social interaction taking place. This can help the child move less consciously. Turn-taking games prompt the child to imitate the actions of the adult, sibling, or peer. Children are more likely to try to pull to stand at the coffee table, for example, if another child models this next to him, particularly if the child

obtains a toy or food. Adults also can act as the playful role model. For example, the parent who blows bubbles and then models stomping on them is encouraging the child to use balance skills.

3. *Provide slight challenge.* If the challenge to orient or maintain balance is too great, the child will collapse, fall, or give up. The adult needs to be able to modify activities to provide only a slight challenge. In the previous example of blowing bubbles, if the child does not yet have sufficient standing balance skills, the adult can change the activity to incorporate less difficult balance requirements. For instance, the child might be able to sit on a small chair or stool and then lean forward and to the side to poke the bubbles. This still requires the child to shift body weight to maintain balance but provides lower body support so the child can be successful.

4. *Make practice fun.* Toys and games can integrate opportunities to use balance and stability, but so can daily activities. Making those daily activities into fun is one way to motivate children to practice and build skills so they can move independently and fluidly. For example, bath time can involve a game of throwing toys into the tub from a basket on the floor (requires shifting up and down, extending one arm forward, and balancing as the body moves); in the tub the child can play games racing boats (encourages rotation to the side, extending back and forward); and after the bath, helping to dry off can be a movement game done to the "Hokey Pokey" (shifting individual body parts out to be dried requires stability and balance).

5. *Provide positive verbal prompts.* Verbal supports can include encouragement to do something independently (e.g., "You can get it!"). Adults can also provide verbal directions (e.g., "Lift your foot") or suggestions (e.g., "See how I do it"). The adult's level of positive affect is also important for motivating the child to continue to move.

6. *Provide minimal physical supports.* Children with motor disabilities may take longer to move, may display negative affect when trying to move, or may resist doing motor activities. As a result, adults often just pick the child up and carry him or her or do the necessary task for the child. Although this may save time, it teaches the child that being dependent is acceptable, and "learned helplessness" may be the consequence. Adults need to determine what is the *least amount* of support they can give to enable the child to accomplish his or her goal. The amount of support given should be continually reduced until the child can do the task independently.

Environmental Modifications

In addition to interpersonal strategies that may support the child, environmental modifications often are useful. Depending on the findings from TPBA2, the team may want to consider some of the environmental modifications outlined here.

1. *Use adaptive seating.* Children who lack balance and stability will expend much energy trying to stabilize themselves. Adaptive seating can provide support where the child needs it (e.g., back, sides, front) so that attention can be focused on something other than balance. Such support can free a child's hands so that he or she is able to play and manipulate objects. Seating the child so that feet are on the floor or supported on a bench helps stabilize the child. A chair with an appropriate back also is important for children with balance and stability issues. For most children, a back that allows the child to sit at a 90-degree angle encourages upright posture. For children who have difficulty supporting their heads, however, a seat that slants backward may be helpful. If this is the case, then adjustments need to be made to how toys and materials are presented to the child so that he or she can see and manipulate them. For example, a slant board may be needed for a book, so the angle is such that the child can look at it independently. The seat of the chair also may need modification depending on what motor

concerns are present. Placing supports in between, under, or at the side of the child's legs may help the child maintain a more appropriate orientation to activities and make manipulation of objects easier. Assistance and consultation from therapists should be sought to plan seating supports appropriately.

2. *Incorporate practice into routines.* Using supports such as those described in the previous section removes the need for the child to "work" at maintaining orientation and stability. This is desired when the child needs to be thinking about cognitive or social engagements. However, such modifications do not encourage the further development of stability and balance. It is important to introduce opportunities throughout the day for the child to practice using righting reactions, equilibrium responses, and body adjustments for orientation to people, objects, and events. Even if the child needs a great deal of support, the caregivers should engage the child in small increments of participation for each daily activity. For instance, the child can make efforts to move toward, get up, get in, get off, reach for, and so forth with each daily routine (e.g., eating with the family, going to the bathroom, playing with siblings, taking a bath, going to bed).

3. *Position toys and materials.* The placement of toys and materials that are motivating to the child is important. If everything the child wants is placed right in front of him or her at eye level, the child needs only minimal effort to be steady. As with the description of seating given previously, this is appropriate when the goal is for the child to accomplish quickly what is needed. However, for the encouragement of further development of balance skills, placement of objects in more challenging positions is needed. The adult can place objects the child desires up higher, so the child needs to reach up with one hand and stretch one side of the body or balance on toes; to the side so the child needs to lean to one side and retain balance; just out of reach in front of the child, so the child needs to lean forward and extend, and so forth. The placement should not be frustrating, but just enough of a challenge that the child is successfully working against gravity.

4. *Adjust level of sensory input.* Some children have sensory issues that preclude them from obtaining sufficient sensory information to know exactly where their body is in space. Children who are hard of hearing or have vision impairments, who need extra tactile or proprioceptive input to feel environmental input, or who need intense input to register movement may have difficulty orienting to or responding to activities that do not provide enough input. Adults may need to make adjustments to lighting, sound, or intensity of input so the child is capable of responding with the movements necessary. For example, if the child cannot see the ball in the bright light, he will not move toward it. If the child does not hear the parent's voice, she will not orient toward the adult to see what is happening. If the child does not register the fact that she is moving quickly, appropriate body adjustments will not be made so she can stop.

5. *Use assistive devices.* Children who have difficulty with stability may benefit from various types of assistive devices to help them balance and function more easily. Orthotic devices such as splints or casts can provide support for ankles, hips, knees, wrists, and so forth. Walkers and crutches also can provide additional stability. By stabilizing various body parts, the child may increase ability to orient to tasks and function against gravity. Again, medical and therapeutic consultation should be sought to determine whether these are appropriate.

▓▓▓▓ I. B. How well does muscle tone support posture?

Children with neurologically based disabilities (e.g., cerebral palsy, Down syndrome, dyspraxia) often have muscle tone that is too high, too low, or apparently "fluctuating" in one or more quadrants of the body. When muscle tone is too high, movements look "rigid" and forced, and task difficulty increases tone in all involved limbs.

Children with increased muscle tone have difficulty controlling their actions. It requires concentration to start to move, to sustain, and to stop movement, particularly in affected limbs. Children with high tone in the upper body often maintain flexed arms and fisted or clawed fingers, while children with high tone in the legs extend rather than flex them.

Children with abnormally low muscle tone look "floppy" and have an increased range of movement and unusually flexible postures. They may sit, stand, and walk with legs spread wide for more support. As with children with high tone, children with low tone may have difficulty starting and stopping movements. Consequently, they have poor gradation of movements, or no gradual transitions between actions. For example, they may "plop" to sit down. Because sustaining a position requires effort, the child may compensate by leaning against supports or "stacking" one body part on another (e.g., by pulling the shoulders up around the neck). Children may also stiffen body parts by "locking" joints as a means of compensating for lack of stability. Children with low tone in the limbs generally also have decreased tone in the trunk.

Two other types of motor dysfunction, *ataxia* (characterized by tremors and unbalanced walk) and *athetoid cerebral palsy* (characterized by constant, writhing, involuntary movements) show unusual muscle tone patterns. Muscle tone also can be high in one part of the body, such as the limbs, and low in another (typically the trunk). Careful developmental monitoring also is important, because what appears as low tone in an infant can develop into athetosis later.

Muscle tone is dependent on signals from the brain telling the muscles to contract or extend, and, therefore, neurological conditions affecting muscle tone are not "cured." Environmental activities, however, can have a temporary impact on tone and, consequently, can improve motor functioning if used repeatedly and at pivotal times. The following strategies are recommended for improving muscle tone related to performing specific actions. Consultation with medical and therapeutic professionals is needed for specific children.

Interaction Strategies

1. *Do preparatory activities to normalize low tone.* Before engaging in an activity requiring use of fingers, hands, arms, trunk, legs, or feet, adults can do preparatory activities to temporarily increase the muscles' response to input. Activities that involve pushing or pulling activate muscles. Sensory activities that involve quick compression movements, cold temperatures, or staccato pulsing input also may have the effect of "waking up" the nerves and muscles. For example, bouncing on the legs before walking, playing with playdough before writing, washing the hands in cold water before fine motor play, and so forth may help the child with low tone have increased motor control.

2. *Do preparatory activities to normalize high tone.* Children with high tone need ways to relax muscles before they try to use them. Preparatory activities that help to decrease muscle tension include slow stretching and massage, warmth, slow rhythmic movement, and deep pressure. For example, before playing outdoors in gross motor activities, a warm bath, deep hugs with a soft towel, a massage with warm lotion, and stretching games may help the child have more control and thus practice more normal movement patterns.

3. *Modify affect.* The affect of the adult can have a calming or excitatory effect on the child. For children with low tone, excitement, louder voice, and more rapid speech may increase attention and enthusiasm and thus increase muscle tone. For children with

high tone, the opposite is true: a soft, slow, modulated voice is preferred. Excitement can cause the tension in the muscles to increase, so a calming affect is preferred.

4. *Modify interaction during activities.* In the same way that affect influences muscle tone, actions during an activity can have the same effect. The way an activity is done influences how the child's muscles react. The same principles as stated previously apply. For low tone, rapid, bouncing, staccato actions are helpful. For example, the child may be sitting in a rocking boat with another child. To increase the child's ability to rock the boat, encouraging rapid movement back and forth with frequent starting and stopping will provide more opportunity to give input to the muscles. Sing a fast song and have the children stop rocking when you stop singing. For the child with high tone, such an approach would increase muscle tone. Instead, the adult will want to sing a slow, rhythmic song with steady movement.

5. *Teach the child deep breathing and relaxation techniques.* Children with cerebral palsy or neurospinal defects may also have compromised respiratory functioning. Monitoring of breathing patterns and respiratory functioning is important for these children.

6. *Pay attention to eating.* Children with high tone burn extra calories, because their muscles are contracting more. Frequent snacks and high protein foods are needed to maintain body weight and energy. Children with cerebral palsy may have eating disorders as well and may need medical intervention. Children with low tone tend to burn fewer calories and gain weight more easily. Watching the amount of food and caloric intake is important for these children. Added weight makes it more difficult to move.

Environmental Modifications

In addition to interpersonal strategies that may help normalize tone, environmental modifications often are useful. Depending on the findings from TPBA2, the team may want to consider some of the environmental modifications outlined here.

1. *Modify the environment.* The amount and type of stimulation in the room can have either a calming or excitatory effect on children. Loud noises, bright lights, and raucous activity arouse a child and may lead to increased tension in the muscles. Soft lights and colors and reduced activity may lead to relaxation of tension. This may help parents plan the home environment for the child. Many teachers have children with both high tone and low tone in one classroom; thus, it is important to have different areas of the room that can promote diverse responses.

2. *Alternate the level of activities.* A child's day is full of a range of activities, from vigorous to calm. How activities are sequenced and how they are performed can influence how the child responds. Activities that are more intense, such as running around outside, should be interspersed with calm activities, such as reading. This enables the child to use his muscles and then recover for the next round of activity. Children with high tone and those with low tone can benefit from this pattern.

3. *Modify activities for individual needs.* Any activity can be modified to involve different toys or materials to respond to a child's needs. Heavier toys or materials can be introduced to require pushing, pulling, or more exertion. Toys with an element of surprise, such as pop-up toys, or toys that "explode," can increase excitement. Toys that rock, swing, or move up and down can be adjusted for speed and tempo. In the dramatic play area, heavier dolls and real materials can be substituted for light, plastic ones. Textures can be modified to provide more (or less) stimulation. Adults need to

analyze the characteristics of each play situation and routine to determine what can be modified so the child can respond more easily or effectively.

4. *Use adaptive devices.* Devices such as massagers, heating pads, electric toothbrushes, and electronic swings or rockers can be used with children as needed.

5. *Involve children in the use of appliances around the home.* Household appliances such as the vacuum cleaner, kitchen blender, and other appliances with buttons and noises can be stimulating and motivating for children with low tone. Children with high tone, alternatively, may be calmed by the sound of the dryer or the low sound of music on the radio. Adults should consider which activities can involve children in ways that are not contraindicated for their condition. For example, trying to help water the lawn with a long, stiff hose that is shooting cold water may increase the tone of a child with spastic cerebral palsy, but it may provide resistance and cold stimulation to increase the motor abilities of the child with Down syndrome.

ROUTINES FOR THE CHILD WHO NEEDS SUPPORT TO IMPROVE THE FUNCTIONS UNDERLYING MOVEMENT

The following are examples of how the previous strategies can be incorporated into the child's daily routines at home and school. In addition to the strategies noted at the beginning of the chapter, used by caregivers of children who do not have special needs, these may support the development of increased proficiency with functions underlying movement.

Daily Routines (Home and Classroom)

Feeding/Eating

To help the child gain independence in eating, pay attention to the child's position. If the child cannot sit in a stable position when unsupported, supports should be provided in any place the child is collapsing, sliding, or stiffening. For example, if the child has no head control, a chair with a slight backward incline and side head supports may be needed. If the child in a high chair is sliding forward onto the tail bone, provide support under the knees to push the bottom back. If the chair is too big and the child is falling to the sides, a baby's bath foam support may be inserted into the chair to add support all around. Placing the child's feet in a flexed position on a step, in addition to using bolsters, foam, or towel rolls under the knees to break up high tone, can help the child maintain a flexed, rather than extended, position. Once the child is in a stable position, his or her hands will be free to explore or help with self-feeding.

Diapering/Toileting

Lying on the back for diapering provides a stable position unless the child arches back and goes into extension. In this case, a small roll under the neck and under the knees may help break up the tone and allow the child to have greater freedom of movement. Placing toys to the sides for play before and/or after diapering also can allow the child to practice maintaining stability in side-lying; placing the child on the tummy with toys at the head will encourage pushing up and develop shoulder stability.

As independent toileting emerges, children with high tone in the legs may benefit from a potty chair that is fully supported around the body and is slightly higher in the front than the back. This pulls the legs into increased flexion, inhibiting the tendency to extend the legs. As the child moves to a potty seat on the regular toilet, additional adaptations may be added to the back, sides, or front as needed to provide support. It is important for children to have their feet supported, either on the floor or on a step, as this will also increase stability. Children are more likely to tend to their toileting when they are not worried about falling over or off the potty.

Dressing

Dressing requires ability to isolate body parts, strength, coordination, and balance. Adults can help children by using clothing that is easy to put on and take off. Velcro fasteners; large head, arm, and leg holes; and loose-fitting clothing are easier to manage. Positioning the child for dressing also is important. Doing preparatory relaxation with the child with high tone may be helpful, as is helping the child to maintain flexion in the limb being dressed. For children with low tone, playing games to get them to extend limbs through the appropriate hole may be helpful. For example, "Here's your baby looking at you up your sleeve. Can you get her?" As the child is developing balance skills, the adult can encourage the child to stand and use the dresser or the adult's arm for support. Applaud the child's efforts at independence!

Going Out

Children who lack stability and have high or low tone often are trapped in a car seat in the back of the car, unable to explore or play with toys. Adapting seating so the child can see out of the window can open up a new world to explore. Placing a tray with a Velcro strip on the car seat with toys with corresponding Velcro attached may allow the child to play. Attach a string to the toys and tray as well, so if dropped they can be retrieved.

Involve the child in shopping. Provide appropriate supports (see Feeding/Eating, above) in the shopping cart child seat, so the child is stable. Once secure, reaching for items to the front and sides is a good way to practice balance. Shopping centers also provide opportunities for the child to practice walking and running. Some shopping malls have child play areas that encourage crawling in and out, climbing over, and going through play equipment. These often are cleaner and safer than outdoor playground equipment.

Play Routines (Home and Classroom)

Face-to-Face Play

Begin face-to-face games, such as Pat-a-cake while the child is sitting comfortably right in front of you. As the child gets more involved, encourage her to play while sitting without support or while standing. With attention on the adult right in front of her, balance will not be as challenged. As balance increases, the parent can move to the side or behind the child to get her to turn to find the parent. This will challenge new balance skills.

Physical Play

By its very nature, physical play provides many opportunities to support the foundations underlying movement. As children crawl, walk, run, climb, jump, hop, wiggle, and dance, they are providing input to muscles and joints and challenging balance. Adults need to encourage children with balance and muscle tone issues to engage in physical activities that promote higher levels of ability. Roughhousing on the floor, jumping on the bed, walking on or throwing pillows, and playing chase and Hide-and-

Seek in various rooms of the house require many different types of movements. Children are highly motivated to participate in these exciting games. (For children with spasticity, the pace can be slowed, with physical interaction of a less intense nature.) Children should also be allowed to play in playgrounds where grass and sand surfaces offer a different balance challenge, and in restaurants or shopping mall play areas where they can play safely with other children. As the child gets older, opportunities for peer play should be made available as often as possible. Music and dance activities with peers also provide opportunities for inspiring movement.

Manipulative Play

Manipulative play often is difficult for children with stability or muscle tone issues. Although for many children, once they are seated securely and feel stable, they can use their hands and fingers more freely. Positioning is thus critical for manipulative play done at a table, such as play with puzzles or drawing. For most children, sitting in a chair so feet are flat and ankles, knees, and hips are bent at a 90-degree angle is important. (For children with increased extension, however, a greater angle may be recommended.) The position of the trunk also is important, because the back needs to be straight and the body oriented to the manipulatives with which the child is playing.

Because many children prefer to play on the floor rather than at a table, adults also need to address the best position for the child on the floor. If children have low tone, they may play while lying on the floor or by propping on their arms. These are typically not the best positions for using two hands together to manipulate objects. Other children may sit with their legs in a W position or another position in which the legs give a wide base of support. Although functional, such positions often put strain on the ligaments around the joints, leading to even greater range of motion or even susceptibility to hip dislocation. Alternatives include providing pillow supports, such as a C-shaped pillow or Boppy-type pillow that curves around the child to provide support. Changing the child's base of support, so that he or she is sitting on knees and heels or side-sitting, with both legs bent to one side, may help the child practice another position. Using low tables or benches also can allow children to extend their legs in front under the bench and also have the toys more at eye level. This can help the child with low tone raise the head and straighten the back. Consultation from therapists can help generate ideas appropriate for individual children.

Sensory Play

Sensory play with paints, clay, glue and so forth is typically done while sitting at a table (see Manipulative Play, above). Many sensory activities in preschool, however, are done at a "sensory table" that is filled with water, sand, mud, shredded paper, mashed potatoes, or any number of sensory items. Children with stability and tone issues may have difficulty standing in a stationary position to play. The child with low tone may lean on the table, curve his back in and lean his tummy on the table, lock his knees, rock on his ankles, or leave the activity after just a few minutes. Children with high tone also may lean on the table or use an arm to support themselves. They also may lock joints to stabilize. For children who lack balance in standing, alternatives may include providing seating at the sensory table or using a standing slant board or other adaptive device. Because slant boards are confining and feel restrictive, an alternative that provides some degree of support but also has flexibility may be preferred. For instance, some walkers have seats that can come down, allowing the child to stand for a while and then sit. The goal here is to maximize the child's opportunity to explore and manipulate.

Dramatic Play

Dramatic play is difficult for the child who is unstable, because often it involves other children moving around without concern for another's ability to move quickly. Provide stable furniture in the dramatic play area for the child who needs extra support to hang onto or lean against. Handles can be added to the side of a table or to a sturdy shelf to allow the child to move around the space with occasional support. Provide extra room for children who need space for walkers or other mobility devices. The goal in dramatic play is not to practice balance, but rather to think, communicate, and interact; thus, teachers should provide whatever supports are necessary to enable the child to move freely in this area. For example, the child may use a chair in some centers, a walker in others, sit on the floor in a supported pillow in another, and use an electric wheelchair in the dramatic play area. The teacher needs to match to goals of the center with the needs of the child, so that motor issues do not prohibit learning and interaction.

Reading and Learning Routines

Circle Time

Circle time is a group activity, and although sharing is part of the goal, it is a larger social event. For this reason, positioning so that the child can see the teacher and the other children is important. If the child has difficulty turning, a swivel chair can help her see everyone. A cube chair may provide the support that sitting on a carpet square does not, enabling the child to attend rather than collapse, fidget, or lean on others. Participation in the group also is a goal, so the child should be able to use his or her hands freely. For some children, preparatory activities can help the child sit and attend better. For the child with low tone, active play before circle time may be helpful. For the child with high tone, relaxation to music may be calming.

One-on-One Book Reading

As discussed for dramatic play, the goals of one-on-one reading also are related to communication and interaction. Adults should make this time one of nurturance and closeness. Although the child could sit with more support in a separate chair or adaptive seat next to the adult, this would deny the child one of the main benefits of one-on-one reading—feeling close to the adult and sharing touch and interactions. For this reason, whenever possible, it is recommended that until the child is too large to comfortably sit on the adult's lap, the lap is the "chair" of choice. The adult may need to use pillows, bolsters, or body parts to break up extension or provide adequate support, but the one-to-one body contact is important. This is a time for sharing funny sounds, words, laughter, comments, and stories. The security provided in these moments far exceeds that of any chair.

Science and Math

Science and math activities often are done at a table while sitting, or at a table or easel while standing. The suggestions provided for preparatory activities and positioning are applicable here as well. Because attention, manipulation, and comprehension are keys for learning in this center, the focus should be on the child being stable so that mind and hands can function freely.

DOMINICK

Dominick is a 9-month-old African American boy with cerebral palsy. He demonstrates low tone in his trunk and high tone in his extremities. He smiles easily at all adults and shows interest in pictures and toys that create a sound or action. He is able to sit with support, but not independently. He is able to roll from front to back and is able to turn toward the right side from his back, but not roll completely over from back to front. He sits in his high chair to eat but falls to one side or the other, depending on where he is leaning. He likes to look at books on his mother's lap and will look at them on his stomach for a several seconds before collapsing. He cries when in his car seat all the way home from child care, which is frustrating for his mother, who picks him up.

Environmental Supports

1. *Place supports around Dominick when he is in the high chair. A foam bath support placed under and around him will help keep him from falling over and help him to sit directly facing his food. The high chair also can be used for play, because this supported position will enable Dominick to use his hands freely with toys.*

2. *Place Dominick on his tummy frequently and place him on his forearms to look at his favorite book. This will help him build stability in his shoulders and arms.*

3. *Place a band of bells on different limbs for a few minutes while he is being diapered. This will encourage Dominick to move individual limbs to see what they can do and to try to reach them. Encourage him by shaking the limb to have it make noise, then wait to see if he tries it himself.*

Interactional Supports

1. *Although he cannot yet sit unsupported, hold Dominick on your knee with another person in front and slightly above him. Have this person make faces and noises with Dominick to encourage him to hold up his head and play face games.*

2. *After bath time, give Dominick a slow massage with warm lotion. This will help decrease the tone in his limbs.*

3. *Play games with Dominick when he is relaxed. Help him to retrieve toys to each side, to look at pictures in supported sitting, and to bear weight on his feet. Make these games fun with lots of slow movements, soft singing, and smiling. Encourage his independent efforts.*

KEYS TO INTERVENTION BY DEVELOPMENTAL AGE

The following ideas are directed toward children who are functioning at approximately the following levels. The suggestions are not meant to be all-inclusive, but rather indicative of potential areas for exploration.

Developmental age	Postural foundations	Keys to intervention
Birth to 3 months	Muscle tone (by 3 months) Muscle tone: Unsupported head flops forward or backward.	Place child on tummy frequently and entice to look up at face and sounds.
	Posture and Gross Motor—Supine: Head in midposition and posture symmetrical. Brings hands to midline; kicks with both feet. Moves limbs reciprocally or arms together, legs together.	Hold face and objects of interest directly over child. Talk to child and shake objects. Attach bells to wrist or ankle to encourage child to notice action–sound relationship.

(continues on next page)

Developmental age	Postural foundations	Keys to intervention
Birth to 3 months (*continued*)	**Posture and gross motor (by 3 months)** Prone: Symmetrical head lifting 45–90 degrees. Shoulders slightly abducted. Sitting: When supported, helps maintain position; minimum head bobbing. Unsupported, maintains head in midline, supports weight on arms briefly in front. Standing: Held in standing, presses feet against surface and takes some weight briefly (0–3 months). May bend and straighten knees. When picked up, brings body up compactly; keeps head in line with body.	Hold child up on shoulder to look around, on lap with minimal head support to look at people and objects of interest. Place child on forearms on stomach with an object of interest to explore. This will encourage the development of shoulder stability and head control. Hold child under arms and let the child feel the weight of his or her body on the feet. This will encourage bouncing on the feet and experimenting with feeling pressure on the legs.
3–6 months	**Posture and gross motor (by 6 months)** Supine: Contacts feet with hands (5–6 months). May bring feet to mouth and suck on toes. May roll from back to belly. Prone: Landau reaction complete when held in prone position. Head held vertically. Increased head, hip, and trunk control allows free movement; turns, twists in all directions. Bears weight on extended arms; may push backward. Movement of trunk, head, and limbs counteracts tipping. Sitting: Sits unsupported momentarily (5–6 months) with head in extension, arms lifted off surface and shoulder blades retracted; cannot maintain indefinitely or move in and out. May extend arms forward to catch self and prop. Can move head freely. Cannot move in and out of sitting. Standing: When supported can take full weight on legs (5–6 months). Movement: Propels self on tummy with legs, steers with arms, goes backward or forward.	Place interesting socks or bells on the child's feet to encourage exploration of the feet. Place interesting objects to the side of the child's head and encourage the child to turn toward the object. Give hip a little help in roll over. When on the tummy, move a desired object to various positions so the child tracks the movement and tries to reach it. After the child retrieves it and plays with it, move it to a new position. Play singing games in the air or on the knee with swaying movements. Sit the child in a seated position with arms propping up body. Have a book for the child to look at to encourage him or her to maintain the position for a minute or two. Encourage child to work into and out of positions with support from the adult. Practice standing on legs, while supporting under the arms, for continued experience with the feel for the upright position. Place child on stomach and get in front of him or her on the floor, face-to-face. Move backward and entice the child to come after you.
6–9 months	**Posture and gross motor (by 9 months):** Most babies are combining gross and fine motor activity. Prone: Rolls tummy to back with rotation. Can assume quadruped and rock. Lies propped on one side and reaches; rotation in trunk. Sitting: Uses arms behind body and head and trunk to counteract backward falls. Standing: Stands briefly with one hand held. Pulls to stand, shifts weight; may rotate; may remove one hand from support. Movement: Crawls on belly. May propel self forward by falling. May pull self from hands and knees to standing and cruise along furniture.	Place desired objects in a variety of places around the child when the child is lying on his or her back or side, on the stomach, in sitting, or on all fours. Challenge the child in these positions with a slight movement, so the child tries to recover position. Place object on chairs or low tables where the desired object is visible. Encourage the child to pull up to stand to get the object. Move the object to one side a bit to encourage movement. Use social interaction and objects to entice the child to crawl.
9–12 months	**Posture and gross motor (by 12 months)** Sitting: Uses rotation to attain a sitting posture. Reaches for distant objects, with one arm to lean on while the other reaches. Reaches above the head with both arms, alternately, and without losing trunk stability. Reaches behind the back with exaggerated twisting. Standing: May stand alone briefly (9–12 months). Actions: Rolls ball to adult. Movement: Active and independent. Walks with hand held or may take several steps independently; some children use walking as primary locomotion.	Use toys and food to encourage the child to sit by holding the desired item slightly above the child's head. Provide opportunities to reach in all directions, with some efforts requiring the child to support his weight on a hand and arm. Provide opportunities for the child to cruise around furniture picking up pieces of cracker or chasing a moving car. Hold the child under the arms while the child is standing examining an object of interest. Reduce support when the child is not aware.

Developmental age	Postural foundations	Keys to intervention
9–12 months (continued)		When walking, provide support as the child wants or needs. Increase the amount of time the child walks with support, and gradually reduce support (first holding the hand, then onto the parent's pants).
		Use preferred adults as "targets" for walking, especially when they are holding a desired item.

12–18 months	Posture and gross motor (by 15 months)
	  Standing: Stands, squats and stoops.
	  Movement: Slower walking speed. Creeps upstairs.
	Posture and gross motor (by 18 months)
	  Sitting: Sits in small chair. Climbs into adult chair.
	  Actions: Picks up toy from floor. Flings ball (9–18 months).
	  Movement: Walks well, pulling toys. Begins to run. Walks upstairs with one hand held.
		Place objects at different heights so the child needs to squat and stand.
		Having the child pick up objects from the floor and hand them to the adult encourages movement up and down.
		Allow the child opportunities to climb onto and under furniture and play equipment.
		Attach strings to cars and other toys so the child can pull them. This encourages the child to turn and walk backward to watch the toy.
		Provide opportunities for the child to maneuver up and down small stairs.

18–24 months	Movement (by 21 months)
	  Movement: Moves ride-on toy with no pedals. Climbs down from adult chair.
	Posture and gross motor (by 24 months)
	  Standing: Balances when stationary. Can stand briefly on one foot.
	  Actions: Flings ball forward at large target. Kicks ball forward (20–24 months).
	  Movement: Walks with arm swing at elbow, heel toe progression and balanced gait. Jumps off floor (17–24 months). Walks upstairs holding on (12–23 months). Walks downstairs holding on (13–23 months).
		Provide opportunities to climb up and down on low playground equipment and ride-on toys that the child can propel with both feet.
		Sing songs and dance to stimulate balancing, jumping, and body rotation.
		Play ball games of throwing and catching to encourage anticipation, weight shifting, and body adjustment.
		Practice climbing on equipment at parks, walking up steps of different sizes, and maneuvering through obstacle courses.

24–36 months	Movement (by 30 months)
	  Movement: Walks up stairs with no support (18–30 months). Walks downstairs with no support (19–30 months). Jumps from bottom step (19–30 months). Begins to pedal tricycle. Climbs up and down furniture independently (24–30 months).
	Movement (by 36 months)
	  Actions: Catches 10-inch ball against chest (30–35 months).
	  Movement: Walks with rotating trunk and reciprocal arm swing. Walks up and downstairs alternating feet (23–36 months). Climbs nursery apparatus (30–36 months).
		Play games requiring the child to isolate different body parts and use them in different ways, for example, Simon Says and the Hokey Pokey.
		Provide games and begin doing activities that use reciprocal movements, such as riding a tricycle, swimming, and racing.
		Begin games of throwing and hitting that require the child to coordinate eye, hand, and foot.
		Participate in play dates at the park.

36–48 months	Movement (by 48 months)
	  Actions: Catches ball with elbows bent in front of body (3–4 years).
	  Movement: Walks like an adult. Exhibits true running with trunk rotation and arm swing. Can steer tricycle around obstacles.
		Demonstrate how to anticipate movements, modify body position, and respond to different actions, such as throwing and hitting.
		Begin to involve in preschool gymnastics and sports.
		Pretend to be different animals.

48–60 months	Movement (by 54 months)
	  Actions: Uses forward weight shift to throw ball further. Throws with some directional accuracy.
	  Movement: 33% of 4-year-olds able to hop on one foot and 43% can gallop, but only 14% can skip (Clark & Whitall, 1989).
		Practice motor skills the child likes to improve accuracy, speed, and fluidity.
		Introduce group games requiring turn-taking, with running, throwing, hitting, and jumping.
		Practice balance by dancing, walking, and tumbling.

(continues on next page)

Developmental age	Postural foundations	Keys to intervention
48–60 months (*continued*)	Movement (by 60 months) Actions: Throws smoothly, releases on time and in line with target (3–5 years). When catching, adjusts body position in line with ball and has elbows at sides (54–59 months). When striking with a bat, the body is a good distance from object, contact is made with extended arms. Movement: Skips with coordination (alternate step-hop pattern, body suspended momentarily, reciprocal arm swing). Hops on one foot (3–5 years). Can stand on one foot for several seconds and walk along curb without falling. Jumps down from high step; jumps forward. Climbs ladder (4–5 years).	Provide gross motor toys, such as hula-hoops, shovels, rakes, and balls.
60–72 months	Movement (by 66 months) Movement: Mature running pattern develops (5–5½ years); tests skills by racing. Movement (by 72 months) Actions: Kicks to a target. Movement: Skips effortlessly with elbows flexed, landing on balls of feet. Gallops with full coordination (5–6 years). Hops in straight line.	Involve the child in team sports or club activities involving movement. Have group play dates at the park so children have room to race and climb. Introduce a bicycle.

3

Facilitating Sensorimotor Development

II. Strategies for Improving Gross Motor Activity

Goal Attainment Scale

1	2	3	4	5	6	7	8	9
Remains wherever placed; no active movement out of a position.		Moves by rolling and commando crawl.		Moves around the environment on all fours, cruises, and takes a few steps.		Walks and runs easily.		Is able to do complex gross motor actions (e.g., hopping, skipping).

Although it is possible to learn, have social interactions, and communicate without movement, all of these can occur more easily through physical engagement and discovery. It can be difficult to differentiate fine from gross motor skills, and activities often require both. In TPBA2, we have distinguished between activities primarily involving the large muscles of the trunk and lower body and arm and hand use. This in no way implies that lower body movements constitute gross motor activity and upper limb movements are fine motor. In fact, throwing, which has an important upper limb component, is a gross (or large) motor task. Gross motor skills are needed for the child to roll over, sit, pull up to stand, stand independently, and run. They contribute to participation in physical games and sports, and performing any number of functional activities such as bathing, dressing, and so forth. Clearly, these latter activities also involve cognitive and fine motor skills. This section deals with only the gross motor component.

APPROPRIATE GROSS MOTOR ACTIVITY

Gross motor skills should be fluid, not halting or awkward. Gross motor actions also should be easy to perform. The child should be able to make developmentally appropriate functional movements automatically. Gross motor actions should be effective, meaning the child should be able to move various body parts in concert in such a way as to accomplish the intended action. Even if the preschool child is not accurate, for instance, in kicking the soccer ball into the net, the child's movements should reflect the necessary sequence of skills to connect with and move the ball. Appropriate gross motor skills also should enable the child to enjoy a variety of types of activities requiring a range of slow to fast actions.

Gross motor skills are refined through practice before the child achieves ease, efficiency, and effectiveness. Adults need to be aware of where the child is in the developmental process to understand the level of proficiency that can be expected. Gross motor skill tends to appear from the head down to the feet, and from the trunk out toward the extremities. By preschool, children walk and run efficiently; they can climb, jump, and maneuver their bodies in and out of spaces. As they get older, their skills become more precise, and children's movements increase in efficiency and effectiveness.

Appropriate Gross Motor Activity in Practice

████████ II. A. Quality of gross motor movements and interference with function

Daily Routines (Home and Classroom)

- *Infant/toddler:* The infant kicks his feet, then reaches down and puts his foot in his mouth after his bath. The toddler runs, with feet apart, to the kitchen when his mother calls him.

- *Young child:* The young child climbs out of the tub and dries off with little assistance.

Play Routines (Home and Classroom)

- *Infant/toddler:* The infant crawls to the couch, pulls to stand, and waits for her father to pick her up. The toddler runs into the ball in an attempt to kick it.

- *Young child:* The young child throws the ball to her father, then holds out her hands to catch it when he throws it back.

Classroom Routines

During outdoor time, the young child independently climbs the jungle gym, crawls through the tunnel, then goes down the slide.

████████ II. B. Play positions

Daily Routines (Home and Classroom)

- *Infant/toddler:* The infant lies in her crib on her back, legs and arms out wide, and slightly bent. The toddler sits on the floor with legs outstretched, eating a cracker.

- *Young child:* The young child sits on the toilet, feet dangling, hands on the toilet, body leaning forward to call her mother.

Play Routines (Home and Classroom)

- *Infant/toddler:* The infant sits on the floor, legs bent into a circle in front of her body, propped on her arms. The toddler sits in a small chair with feet on the floor at a child-sized table, coloring.

- *Young child:* The young child sits on the floor in a tailor sit with legs crossed in front of him, playing a game.

Classroom Routines

The young child sits in her cube chair at circle time listening to the teacher read a story.

▮▮▮▮ II. C. Independence when moving between positions

Daily Routines (Home and Classroom)

- *Infant/toddler:* The infant sits unsupported in the crib; he turns to look as his father enters the room, then pulls to stand on the crib rail. The toddler climbs up onto the couch and sits next to his mother to read a book.

- *Young child:* The young child takes off her pants, walks to the washing machine, climbs a step ladder, and throws her pants in the machine.

Play Routines (Home and Classroom)

- *Infant/toddler:* The infant rolls over on his stomach to get the toy lying up by his head. The toddler squats down to watch an ant crawling on the sidewalk.

- *Young child:* The young child dances and twirls around to the music on the tape recorder.

Classroom Routines

During recess, the young child gets on a tricycle, rides around the bike path, and then gets off to let another child have the tricycle.

▮▮▮▮ II. D. Environmental movement, independence, and quality

Daily Routines (Home and Classroom)

- *Infant/toddler:* The infant turns her head to the side, reaches over with arm and leg to reach her bottle, and flips onto her stomach. The toddler stands independently but needs assistance to support his body when he lifts his leg to put his pants on.

- *Young child:* The young child climbs up into the car independently and gets into the car seat without assistance.

Play Routines (Home and Classroom)

- *Infant/toddler:* The sitting infant leans forward to get a toy, falls forward, then brings her legs behind her and pushes forward to get it. The toddler climbs up on a chair and reaches for the dinosaur toys.

- *Young child:* The young child kicks the ball, chases it, leans over, picks it up, and throws it to his friend.

Classroom Routines

The young child gets a puzzle out of the cupboard, carries it to the table, sits, and plays.

▮▮▮▮ II. E. Bilateral coordination

Daily Routines (Home and Classroom)

- *Infant/toddler:* The infant lies in the crib flailing both arms and legs in unison. The toddler walks with reciprocal movement of the legs as he "helps" push the laundry basket.

- *Young child:* The young child climbs into bed by putting his arms and one leg on the bed, then pushing off with his other leg.

Play Routines (Home and Classroom)

- *Infant/toddler:* The infant crawls to the spinning top with alternating movements of his arms and legs. The toddler climbs the ladder on the slide by sliding her hands up the rails and then bringing one foot at a time to the next step.

- *Young child:* The young child climbs stairs to the play loft by sliding his hands up the rail at the same time that he raises one foot and then the other to a higher step.

Classroom Routines

The young child walks sideways around the table, holding paper plates and placing one at each seat.

GENERAL PRINCIPLES FOR SUPPORTING APPROPRIATE GROSS MOTOR SKILLS

Provide Gradually Decreasing Support

Parents and other adults naturally support young infants at the head, back, and bottom. As children gain head control, their parents gradually reduce support until the child holds the head in a stable, upright position independently. As children develop stronger trunks, parents provide less bracing with their own body and start to lean their child against pillows, high chair backs, and infant seats. As children gain stability, props and other supports gradually are diminished until the child is able to sit without any external support. The same is true for other gross motor skills the child acquires. As children acquire skill, parents allow them to climb on to furniture or come down steps with less assistance. As the child gains gross motor abilities, the parent continually monitors how much assistance the child needs.

Encourage Effort

Young infants hear adults cheering and clapping for each of their accomplishments. As the child becomes more independent, adults need to provide less assistance, so parents and caregivers are particularly motivated to see these changes occur. Adults encourage skill development not only by reducing support, as mentioned previously, but also by providing verbal and emotional encouragement. For example, as the infant begins to take first steps, the adult will be just inches away, gently encouraging, "You can do it. Come on. That's it. One more step. Yay!" Most parents are cheerleaders during children's first three years. Such encouragement helps motivate children to continue their hard work.

Provide Models

Adults both intentionally and unintentionally provide a model for motor actions. Probably more powerful than the adult model, however, is the peer or sibling model. To most children, the standing adult must look like a pair of legs with a head! A small person provides a more accurate representation of what they themselves can do and gives the child something to imitate. When the infant sees another infant cruising around a table, for example, the infant is likely to want to follow, literally, in that child's footsteps. Older children serve as untiring models—another plus.

Provide Varied Opportunities for Practice

As children are learning new gross motor skills, parents and other caregivers try to provide opportunities for practice. When infants are learning to sit, adults prop them against all types of soft surfaces. When infants are learning to crawl, adults entice them with desirable objects to crawl toward. When they are pulling to stand, adults place objects of interest on chairs, coffee tables, laps, and other available objects of child height. These enticements give children needed practice so they can refine their motor skills, doing them more quickly, easily, and efficiently.

THE PRINCIPLES IN PRACTICE

Daily Routines (Home and Classroom)

Feeding/Eating

Although eating is largely a fine motor activity, the way in which the child is positioned for feeding or eating influences his or her success. Other than when they are nursing, parents place their children in increasingly upright positions (usually sitting) for meals, making sure that they have the support they need to use their arms and hands effectively. As the child becomes more stable, seating with less support to the trunk is provided.

Diapering/Toileting

For independent toileting to occur, independent sitting or a stable squatting position is necessary. Parents and caregivers support the transition to the toilet by first providing physical support to the child's back and sides by holding or providing a potty chair. Attention to the size of the potty chair is important to ensure a secure feeling on the part of the child.

Dressing

Dressing involves a variety of gross motor actions, including moving arms and legs independently and with precision, changing body position, balancing the body as weight shifts from one side to another, and coordinating both sides of the body. Adults first control these actions and require nothing on the part of the child but flexibility. As the child gains more control, the adult need only direct actions, providing cues for what comes next and rewarding efforts and success. For example, the adult might say, "Now lift your foot and put it in the pant leg. Oops! Wrong leg. Let's try the other leg. That's it!"

Play Routines (Home and Classroom)

Face-to-Face Play

With infants, games involving making faces and noises may be played while the child is lying down or in a supported sitting position in an infant seat or on the lap. Toddlers may play face-to-face games, such as singing rhymes, while sitting or standing in front of the adult. Young children are independent and can move in and out of increasingly varying positions. Preschool teachers often do group activities involving following a leader or moving on command. Children learn by watching adults and each other.

Physical Play

Physical play is the primary means by which gross motor skills are practiced. As they roll, crawl, squat, run, jump, and twirl, children increase their strength and refine their balance and coordination. Parents encourage this through provision of opportunities for outdoor play, play on playground equipment, play with peers in large spaces, and through organized recreational activities such as gymnastics.

Manipulative Play

Toy play involves use of the hands and arms, but also often involves gross motor movements. Floor play, such as building with blocks, involves moving from one position to another as the structure grows. Table play involves movement in and out of the sitting position. Dramatic play can involve a variety of movements as characters run, chase, drive vehicles, and so forth. Adults support children playing in various ways by providing toys that encourage movement. Active play with toys is important for development.

Sensory Play

Parents like to take messy play outdoors. Squirt guns, sand play, and similar play activities tend to encourage gross movements, running, getting up and down, leaning, reaching, and so forth. Art activities at easels or on murals on the wall also encourage movement of the body in different planes.

Reading and Learning Routines

Circle Time

Although circle time typically involves sitting, teachers also use this time for movement activities such as dancing, dramatizing a story, or demonstrating actions. Allowing children to move in between sitting activities often enables them to attend better when they are sitting.

One-on-One Book Reading

Book reading is also a sitting activity, but trips to the book shelf, the library, and the book store encourage both reading and movement.

Science and Math

Science and math for young children should involve discovery through exploration. Finding bugs on the ground, in plants, and in trees, for example, involves gross motor movement and thinking. The combination of action and thinking is motivating to children, and the gross motor actions keep children stimulated.

PLANNING INDIVIDUALIZED
INTERVENTIONS FOR IMPROVING GROSS MOTOR ACTIVITY

■■■■■■ **II. A. In general, how do you describe the child's gross motor movements? How much do gross motor problems interfere with function?**

Gross motor movements are necessary for the performance of a great number of daily functional activities. Children who have difficulty moving easily may avoid movement, struggle to accomplish tasks effectively, expend more effort, and tire more easily. Challenges with movement can result from delays in development, concerns related to posture or muscle (see TPBI2, Chapter 3, Section I. Strategies for Improving Functions Underlying Movement), problems with basic coordination, or motor planning issues. For children with special needs, identifying what is contributing to gross motor challenges is important. When delays are involved, experience and increasing challenge may be needed to move the child into more competent movements. For children with issues related to muscle tone, balance, and other components of movement, targeted strategies may be helpful (see TPBI2, Chapter 3, Section I. Strategies for Improving Functions Underlying Movement). Coordination and the ability to plan motor movements (see TPBI2, Chapter 3, Section IV. Strategies for Improving Motor Planning and Coordination) require practice and effort. It is important for adults to observe and understand normal patterns of movement, so they can identify when children need assistance.

In general, helping children move more efficiently involves all of the subcategories under sensorimotor development. Effective movement relies, in part, on integrity of the sensory and motor systems. When these systems are compromised, adults may need to help children

1.   Gain a better intuitive understanding of their body and where it is in space.

2.   Organize and execute movements.

3.   Control and adapt movements (increase or decrease speed and force; change direction (see TPBI2, Chapter 3, Section IV. Strategies for Improving Motor Planning and Coordination).

Children with motor delays or disabilities may lack certain basic skills (e.g., walking), or they may have the basic motor milestones but the quality is poor. Speed, agility, or coordination may be a problem. This section is concerned with helping children acquire and refine gross motor abilities. The following strategies are suggested in addition to those identified at the beginning of the chapter for use with typically developing children.

Interaction Strategies

1. *Capitalize on the child's motivations to move.* Self-initiation is critical to movement. The child needs to *want* to do something (see TPBI2, Chapter 5, Section V. Strategies for Improving Sense of Self). Adults can provide incentives for movement by enticing the child with desired objects or events. If the child is hungry, food can be a motivator. If the child wants to be with her father, she is motivated to crawl several feet away to be next to him. Children need a reason to move, and the adult can help to provide that reason.

2. *Provide slight challenge.* As children initiate new movements, adults can modify the level of challenge (see TPBI2, Chapter 7, Section III. Strategies for Improving Problem Solving). If the parent is two steps away, the child who is beginning to take steps may see this challenge as "doable." On the other hand, if the parent is across the room, the child will probably choose the type of movement that is safe and comfortable—crawling.

3. *Encourage effort.* The adult's level of affect and words of encouragement can help motivate children to try novel or challenging movements. However, if adults get too excited, the effect can be the opposite: The child may refuse. Monitor the level of affect that is optimal for encouraging the particular child. Encourage continuing effort, not just results. "You tried so hard! Let's play again."

4. *Monitor the child's energy level.* Children who find movement difficult will expend inordinate amounts of energy to move. It is important for adults to monitor the degree of fatigue the child is experiencing, because motivation will flag as energy drains. If the adult continues to urge the child to move, the child may resist future efforts. For the child, as long as it is fun, it is worth doing. Once it is boring or stressful, it is not worth the effort.

5. *Do daily chores in tandem.* Adults can provide a physical model as well as a motivational model for young children. While children are young, they want to emulate everything their parents do! Sweeping the floor, carrying the laundry basket together, and pushing the grocery cart are all exciting when done with Mom or Dad. Instead of carrying the child around, leaving the child to play alone, or setting the child in front of the television, think of ways to involve the child in meaningful ways in everyday chores. Again, make the activity so exciting that the child will *want* to do it. For example, "Are you strong enough to help Mommy take the pans out of the dishwasher and put them away?"

6. *Involve the child in choosing activities and methods for movement.* Because motivation and purpose are so critical to practicing gross motor movements, adults need to think of ways to give children options that will spark their initiative to challenge themselves. For example, "I'm going to hop to the car. Are you going to walk, run, or hop?"

7. *Talk about what the child did.* Children get feedback from their actions. They either accomplish what they intended (e.g., walked to the parent) or they didn't (e.g., fell on their bottom). The child who fell knows he did not succeed; he may feel bad or he many not understand why he fell. The adult can help by offering feedback. "That was just a little too far. I'll move closer."

8. *Help children anticipate what they need to do.* Some actions take forethought for success. The child needs to anticipate what movements are needed. When kicking a ball, for example, the child has to think about positioning the ball in relation to the toes. Thinking about the options improves accuracy. Some children can make self-corrections based on environmental feedback from their actions (e.g., after the child misses the ball, he repositions the ball and kicks it again), whereas others don't understand why their efforts failed. Adults can comment on what the child did and provide suggestions. For example, "First touch the ball gently with your toes. Then pull your foot back and kick."

9. *Prioritize efforts to encourage motivation.* Adults have all sorts of goals for children. Adults want children to move without assistance, to do self-help skills (e.g., dressing) independently, and to entertain themselves. For children with gross motor delays, it is important to prioritize what is important to the *child.* "Therapy" to "work on" specific goals that are important only to an adult is asking a child to expend a lot of energy for something that means little to her. Once children accomplish *their* most important goals, they have new skills and new confidence that they can apply in new situations—likely to activities their parents particularly value.

10. *Use humor and competition.* Laughter is highly motivating. Children often repeat actions simply to get adults to laugh and to experience their own pleasure again. Adding physical roughhousing or competition can make movements into a highly charged game. For instance, having a "race to the bathroom" can be fun (if the child wins) or funny (if the parent goes to the kitchen instead!). The repetition incited by humor and competition also results in practice of skills (see TPBI2, Chapter 7, Section V. Strategies for Improving Complexity of Play, and Chapter 5, Section VII. Strategies for Improving Social Interactions).

11. *Help the child achieve an optimal level of arousal.* Motivation and purposeful actions are supported by an optimal level of arousal. Some children may need to be calmed so they can attend and focus on their actions and the consequences of their actions, whereas others may need to be stimulated to activate their bodies. Different types of sensory stimulation (e.g., sights, sounds, movement, touch) may serve to awaken or dampen arousal levels (see TPBI2, Chapter 3, Section V. Strategies for

Improving Modulation of Sensation and Its Relationship to Emotion, Activity Level, and Attention).

12. *Encourage typical patterns of movement, but accept alternatives if they are functional for the child.* Children with special needs may find it necessary to adapt the ways in which they move. As long as the adaptation does not exacerbate the child's condition (e.g., hyperextend already lax joints), the adaptation solves a problem and creates no additional concerns. For example, children with muscular dystrophy often stand up by locking their knees and walking their hands up their legs. This adaptation is functional for children with this disability and allows them to be independent in rising to standing. In contrast, a child with cerebral palsy may choose to W-sit because it gives her a stable position for playing on the floor with her friends. Although it solves one immediate problem, in the long run W-sitting is likely to cause other problems with joints and pain. It is easy to say that children should not be allowed to W-sit, but it is difficult to enforce this rule. Furthermore, playing with friends may be worth the possibility of later problems, and there may be other ways of offsetting those. Consultation with physicians and therapists may be necessary to address adaptations for specific children.

Environmental Modifications

In addition to interpersonal strategies that may support the improvement of gross motor skills, environmental modifications often are useful. Depending on the findings from TPBA2, the team may want to consider some of the following environmental modifications.

1. *Create a safe environment for movement.* Children with motor delays may have bumps and falls as a result of their lack of coordination. Creating an environment that reduces the possibility for injury without unduly limiting the child's independence is important. Eliminate sharp corners; provide large spaces where the child will walk; and provide safe, soft places for jumping and falling.

2. *Present props that encourage movement in play.* Certain toys entice children to use gross motor skills. Push toys, balls, tricycles, sit-on toys that require two feet to propel, and climbing equipment are good examples. Use parks and structured recreational activities geared to getting children to play together. Peers can be highly motivating.

3. *Provide opportunities to build stability.* Children build stability—a foundation for movement—through having to support their bodies in challenging positions (see TPBI2, Chapter 3, Section I. Strategies for Improving Functions Underlying Movement). For infants, this may be propping up on the arms to look around; for toddlers, it may mean standing to catch a ball; and for young children, this may be walking on their arms in a "wheel-barrow walk." Thoughtful consideration of play activities that can promote both stability and coordination can be very important.

4. *Provide opportunities to practice balance.* Balance underlies many coordinated acts and, like stability, also can be improved in the context of gross motor activity. Walking on uneven surfaces causes the child to make trunk and limb adjustments. Activities such as play in a sand box, walking on "stones" made of pillows or boxes of different sizes, or climbing up or running down a hill also challenge balance.

5. *Provide obstacles to movement.* Small obstacles build persistence and coping skills. When the child wants to move toward a goal but something interferes, adaptation is needed. If the child wants to get to his mother but she is upstairs, the child needs to climb the stairs. If the ball rolls behind the couch, the child needs to crawl to get it. Such obstacles require the child to use movement patterns that may be a challenge in order to accomplish his or her goals.

6. *Alternate active and passive activities.* Alternating active and quiet activities can help the child "recharge" in the case of the underresponsive child, or calm down in the case of the overresponsive child. Conscious thought about the sequence of activities also can prevent physical fatigue or emotional burnout on specific types of activities. For instance, the child may love dancing to his favorite song, but if this is followed by another action-packed activity the child may not have the will or stamina to do it. However, if book reading follows the dancing, the child may be more than ready for the next action event.

7. *Pair peers in motor play.* Peers provide wonderful role models and encouragers. If peers with proficient motor skills lead the activity, the child with lesser abilities will imitate the more competent child. It is important to have the role model be sensitive to the child's limitation so as not to intimidate the child with delayed skills.

8. *Provide a variety of activities in different situations.* Generalization is best promoted by the child using his or her developing gross motor skills in a variety of different situations. Each situation provides slightly different characteristics and environmental conditions and, therefore, enhances the utility of the skill. Each also offers a different type or level of support. The more opportunities the child has to practice skills in varying situations, the more likely it will be that the child will internalize the movements and be able to move from a conscious to subconscious level of performance. For instance, walking on the wood floor at home, carpet at Grandpa's, sand at the park, grass in the front yard, and in the river on vacation all provide slightly different walking experiences. All lead to increased confidence and proficiency.

9. *Use adaptive equipment to aid mobility.* Adaptive equipment such as walkers, canes, and crutches enable children to become mobile. Some children use these devices while they are developing the ability to walk and then discard them when they progress into independent mobility. Others will adopt devices as they grow older and the effort of walking uses energy they prefer to use in other ways. Consultation with a physical therapist and mobility specialist is recommended to select appropriate alternatives.

II. B. What positions does the child play in?

Helping children to maintain a stable position is important for attention and the ability to have hands free for activity. Likewise, being able to assume positions without fear ensures that children have the same opportunities available to their peers. Children with postural issues, children with delayed motor development, and children with disorders that make them fearful of movement may have difficulty assuming or maintaining appropriate positions for daily activities or play. A child may have serious delays in acquiring motor milestones, may "collapse" or lock into a position due to lack of stability, or may find that sitting on a small stool is inordinately scary. As noted previously, some children require adapted or supportive furniture to sit or stand independently. Adapted furniture can be awkward or uncomfortable to use or it may not be available at the precise place and time when a child needs it. Thus, some children compensate by leaning—on an arm, another person, or an object (e.g., a table). Other children use positions that allow them a wider base of support, such as the "W" sit, or the "long" sit with legs extended straight and wide. Still others may avoid tasks that are too demanding. Whereas some of these compensatory behaviors are adaptive, others cause later difficulty. Some children may be helped by "warm-up activities" to counteract difficulties arising from muscle tone or level of arousal. (See TPBI2, Chapter 3, Section I. Strategies for Improving Functions Underlying Movement, and Chapter 3, Section V. Strategies for Improving Modulation of Sensation and Its Relationship to Emotion, Activity Level, and Attention.)

Interaction Strategies

1. *Provide verbal guidance.* Although it is important not to verbally bombard and thus overwhelm a child with words, verbal guidance can help a child find an appropriate position. For example, if the child is sprawled across a chair and leaning on the table to support himself while trying to color, the adult might suggest, "Let's turn you around so you are facing the table and put a block under your feet so that you can sit more comfortably." This helps the child know what to do and how it will help him.

2. *Provide verbal feedback.* Sometimes, children are unaware of the position they are using. A verbal prompt may help them. For example, saying, "You only have half of your bottom on the chair," may be enough to cause the child to reorient. Let the child know what works for him or her, as well. For instance, "You color much easier when you sit with your feet on the stool."

3. *Provide visual cues and modeling.* A visual model or demonstration may be needed for the child to understand what is meant. The adult or another child can demonstrate. In other cases, a visual cue or a representational gesture can provide a prompt. For instance, the teacher could hold up crossed fingers to remind the child to cross his legs in front of himself rather than use a W-sit. After this gesture is used and paired with words and a demonstration a couple of times, the gesture alone may be a sufficient cue.

4. *Assist the child to move into a more stable position.* Some children may need physical assistance to get into a more stable position. If this is the case, move the child in a pattern that recreates the movements the child would use to change position. This provides input to the muscles about that pattern and offers a form of practice for moving in that pattern.

5. *Encourage trying new positions.* Although all children have favorite positions for play and other routines, it is a good idea to watch to make sure that the patterns used are not potentially problematic (such as a W-sit that strains the muscles and tendons around the hip, knee, and ankle joints).

6. *Allow the child with postural difficulties to focus on one thing at a time.* Because the child needs to work on posture, it can be tempting to provide less support when she is working at the table, thus providing another chance for practice. However, if the table-top activity is at all demanding, the child may have difficulty concentrating on both at the same time, causing her to fatigue very rapidly. This is similar to asking an adult to sit on a one-legged stool while using chopsticks for the first time!

Environmental Modifications

In addition to interpersonal strategies that may support the child assuming and maintaining appropriate play positions, environmental modifications often are useful. Depending on the findings from TPBA2, the team may want to consider some of the following environmental modifications.

1. *Provide adaptive supports.* Children with motor disabilities may require adaptive equipment, such as a wheelchair, special chair, slant board, and so forth, to provide adequate support for interactions within the environment. For some children just the addition of couch pillows or reading pillows or rolled towels behind or around them can provide sufficient support. Infant Boppy (C-shaped) pillows are curved and can encircle an infant, toddler, or young child who needs extra stability to sit on the floor and play. Swimming "noodles" cut to the appropriate size can be placed around the child for support or under knees in sitting to give the child a better position to encourage flexion and upright posture (see TPBI2, Chapter 3, Section I. Strategies for Improving

Functions Underlying Movement). Adaptations of table size—for example, using a small bench instead of a table—can allow the child to sit supported on the floor rather than at an inappropriate table.

2. *Play games and provide activities that build strength and stability.* Games that require pushing and pulling, jumping, or hopping give input to ankles, knees, and hips. For example, children can pretend to be various animals with songs and in their dramatic play. This will help children develop the needed underlying skills to support their bodies in different positions.

3. *Play games and provide activities that challenge balance and require protective reactions.* Sitting on a "T"-shaped stool or a large ball requires the child to make body adjustments to maintain balance. Games that challenge sitting and standing balance, such as Musical Chairs, also will encourage children to make needed body adjustments to maintain a stable position.

4. *Remove supports as the child becomes more comfortable.* As the child becomes more stable and secure, provide less support. If the child spreads out all over the floor, gradually move the legs to a narrower base of support. For example, if the child needs a chair with back and sides, move him to a chair with just a back, and then to a stool with no back or sides.

5. *Ensure proper alignment with appropriately sized chairs, tables, and so forth.* Have a variety of options for sitting. For stable sitting, provide sitting that keeps the child's ankles, knees, and hips at 90-degree angles. This encourages an upright posture.

6. *Change the location of activities to require different positions.* Children with motor disabilities may not change positions as frequently as their typically developing peers. By moving the activities to different locations, adults can encourage children to assume and maintain different positions. For example, a bingo game can be played at a table, requiring the child to use a traditional chair position; it can be played on a coffee table, encouraging the "tall kneeling" position, or on the floor, encouraging a cross-legged or side-sit position. Other games or activities can be planned that are done in standing, such as painting a mural.

II. C. How independent is the child when moving between positions?

Moving requires use of muscles different from the assumption of stationary positions. To move in a planned way, children generate the specific patterns of muscle contraction and relaxation that enable the legs to move in a certain way, the body to lower, the body to turn or raise—whatever is necessary. Movement also requires stability. Thus, children with postural or muscle tone concerns may have difficulty transitioning from one position to another. Many of the previous suggestions may be helpful here as well. (Also see TPBI2, Chapter 3, Section I. Strategies for Improving Functions Underlying Movement.)

Interaction Strategies

1. *Help the child practice a more typical pattern of movement with physical guidance and verbal support.* Children with special needs may have unusual patterns of movement. For example, they may move into a sitting position by "plopping" from standing. Adults can help children learn a more typical pattern by physically guiding the child through a different pattern. After physical prompts have been offered a sufficient number of times, the child may begin to initiate these movements independently or with just a verbal prompt.

2. *Provide verbal feedback and reassurance.* Some children may experience fear or anxiety when changing positions. Provide reassurance, remain close to the child to give a sense of security, and offer whatever assistance is needed.

3. *Reduce need for "thinking" about movement through practice.* The more frequently the child moves in a particular way, the more likely those movement patterns will become a habit. In addition, the child will gain confidence.

4. *Reduce the amount of time the child is carried—especially while leaning full body weight against the adult.* Rather, when necessary, carry the child with his back toward you. In addition to the postural benefits, the child will be able to see more of the world around him. Even a little effort on the child's part can encourage future self-initiation.

Environmental Modifications

In addition to interpersonal strategies that may support the improvement of gross motor transitions, environmental modifications often are useful. Depending on the findings from TPBA2, the team may want to consider some of the following environmental modifications.

1. *Provide reasons to transition.* Many children who have difficulty moving prefer to stay in a comfortable stationary position. To encourage them to move to a new position, the environment can be arranged so that the child needs to move to obtain desired objects. For example, when the child is sitting on the floor, toys can be placed on a low shelf so the child needs to move into a stand-and-reach position. Conversely, when the child is standing, placement of toys on the floor, under a table or behind a chair, can encourage changing positions.

2. *Play movement games.* Dramatic play often involves movement. Pretending to "go camping," for example, can involve sitting at the "camp fire," hiking in the "woods," crawling into a "sleeping bag," stepping over "rocks and logs," or jumping over the "stream." The sequence of these activities can encourage transitions from one position to another.

3. *Provide objects to support transitions.* Furniture and other stable objects can be used to help the child, particularly when pulling to stand. Low tables, ottomans, or heavy footstools may be particularly useful.

▮▮▮▮▮ **II. D. How does the child move through the environment? How independent is the child? How good is the quality?**

Moving independently fosters development in other areas as well. Thus, children who have a reduced ability to move are at risk for secondary disabilities in other areas. For example, children who cannot move are dependent on others to approach them for social interaction or conversation. They have difficulty exploring the environment fully and making discoveries about it. Reduced social and environmental engagement means lack of practice, which can further impede development. In addition, dependence on another person for movement can have a negative impact on self-confidence. Thus, enhancing autonomous mobility is an important goal.

Interaction Strategies

1. *Decrease physical support as the child becomes more able.* Provide support at key points—that is, places that help the child to be the most active with the least support.

Depending on the skill the child is attempting and the parts of her body where tone is abnormal, support is offered at the needed control point (e.g., shoulders or hips when the child is trying to crawl or walk). As the child gains confidence and control, even minimal support with a finger may be sufficient to enable her to move.

2. *Provide maximal encouragement.* Facial expressions with smiles and a look of expectation tell children they are doing well. Vocalizations and verbal support also encourage the child to increase independence. Reinforce the child's efforts as well as her accomplishments.

3. *Provide verbal suggestions for movement of body parts.* As the child understands the names of body parts, talk about the body parts that need to move. For example, the adult can suggest, "Lift your foot."

4. *Model actions.* Children may need a visual model for a required action. The child may be more motivated to jump, for example, if the adult shows him or her how and demonstrates pleasure with the action.

5. *Accept unusual patterns of movement.* Some children with high muscle tone, physical abnormalities, or other motor impairments may acquire unusual patterns, such as a "crab crawl," "scissor walk," or other atypical ways of moving. The child should not be discouraged from moving because of these abnormal patterns. Rather, adults can encourage movement and then enhance preferred patterns through other activities. For example, if the unusual crawling pattern is due to tactile sensitivity when the knees are on the floor, activities to desensitize the child to various textures may be helpful. If the movement patterns are due to increased tone in one or more parts of the body, stretching or reduction of tone prior to movement may be helpful. Children also may benefit from careful adult guidance of correct movement patterns to enable the child to "feel" and experience more typical coordination of the legs. Consultation with a therapist may be necessary to develop specific ideas for a particular child.

Environmental Modifications

In addition to interpersonal strategies that may support independent movement, environmental modifications often are useful. Depending on the findings from TPBA2, the team may want to consider some of the following environmental modifications.

1. *Provide adaptive equipment.* We are all familiar with braces, crutches, walkers, and wheelchairs. More recently, mobile scooters have begun to appear in the market. Of course, tricycles, Big Wheels, and other riding toys can be used or adapted for particular children.

2. *Use environmental supports.* A child may be able to push a small chair, large weighted box, child-sized shopping cart, or other moveable object across the floor as he or she learns to walk.

3. *Plan the environment to enable independent movement.* Children may need more space between furniture to maneuver adaptive equipment. Conversely, the child who can walk with a little support may be able to cruise through the environment, moving from one piece of furniture to another. In this case, placement of furniture in such a way that something stable is always within reach is important. Bars on the walls of bathrooms or in the hall also can help children be independent.

4. *Place "movement motivators" in the environment.* Place objects the child likes within a realistic distance. This will motivate the child to move independently. Placing objects

too far away will discourage movement, whereas placing them too close provides too little challenge.

▨▨▨▨ II. E. How well does the child use two body sides together? (Bilateral coordination)

Sometimes, the two sides of the body need to move in unison, as when jumping with both feet together. At other times, body parts need to move reciprocally, as with walking. Still other times, body parts to do completely different things, as when standing on one foot and kicking a ball with the other. The legs and arms need to coordinate, whether moving together or separately, to accomplish gross motor tasks. Movements performed symmetrically (with both sides of the body moving together at the same time) are easier than alternating movements. When a bilateral action is difficult, a child may not be able to inhibit "associated" movements of other body parts. Learning to control both wanted and unwanted movements is important for coordination.

The body can be thought of as divided into planes, split down the center from right side to left side, split down the center from front to back, and split in half from top to bottom. Children need to be able to move their limbs from side to side, from front to back, up and down, and across the middle of all of these planes. Children who have gross motor disabilities may have difficulty coordinating actions across or within these planes to make these desired movements. They may only be able to move one body part at a time; they may have "mirror" movements, in which one side does the same thing as the other side; they may not be able to cross one or more of the three midlines; or they may not be able to move both sides of the body with the same degree of accuracy in all directions. In all of these instances, the goals of movement may be compromised.

For children to maintain interest in games, activities, and daily routines involving coordination of both sides of the body, increased ease, control, and accuracy of movement is needed. The following suggestions are provided to improve bilateral coordination in the lower body. (See TPBI2, Chapter 3, Section III. Strategies for Improving Arm and Hand Use, for bilateral coordination in the upper body.)

Interaction Strategies

1. *Encourage movement.* Children who have difficulty coordinating both sides of their bodies may avoid situations that challenge them. Adults need to encourage movement by providing interesting reasons to move. Climbing the stairs may not seem interesting, but climbing the stairs to get a piggyback ride down may be motivating.

2. *Provide guidance.* Physical guidance may help the child learn motor patterns. For example, supporting one foot while helping the other to kick will give the child the feel of the movement. Success will lead to increased motivation and desire to practice. Give as little support as possible, because self-initiated movements are important.

3. *Provide verbal and visual prompts.* Some children may process information with verbal guidance, whereas others may need to see a model demonstrate the action. Once the child is engaged in trying to accomplish an activity, a combination of both visual and verbal support can be used, unless the child becomes overloaded with too much input.

4. *Encourage movement toward nonmoving objects before moving objects.* Kicking a stationary ball is easier than kicking a moving ball. When encouraging movement, make it easy for the child to succeed and increase the challenge as the child's skill increases.

Environmental Modifications

In addition to interpersonal strategies that may support the improvement of coordination of both sides of the body, environmental modifications often are useful. Depending on the findings from TPBA2, the team may want to consider some of the following environmental modifications.

1. *Take the child to the playground.* Playground equipment offers many opportunities for using both sides of the body independently. Climbing the ladder of the slide, crawling through a tunnel, and climbing onto a sit-on toy are all activities that require movement of body parts in a sequence of independent movement. Pumping the feet together on a swing requires movement of the legs in unison. Park activities are generally highly motivating to children.

2. *Use the stairs.* Skip the elevator and escalator and use the stairs. Encourage children to climb stairs by alternating feet, lifting one foot up onto the step and the other foot up and past that foot to the next step.

3. *Incorporate climbing into play.* Provide cardboard boxes, wagons, or other objects that entice children to climb in by standing on one leg and lifting the other. A sturdy object, such as a climbing structure, can encourage such movements and at the same time provide a prop for support as the child moves.

4. *Provide a safe environment.* Children are more likely to experiment and practice movement when they feel safe. Carpeting, mats, close supervision, and adult assistance may promote practice.

5. *Use community recreation programs.* Children's gym classes, such as Gymboree, or a group gymnastics class offer a supportive, fun environment for practicing movements and getting adult assistance for movement.

ROUTINES FOR THE CHILD WHO NEEDS SUPPORT TO IMPROVE GROSS MOTOR ACTIVITY

The following are examples of how the preceding strategies can be incorporated into the child's daily routines at home and school. In addition to the strategies noted at the beginning of the chapter, used by caregivers of children who do not have special needs, these may support the development of increased proficiency with large muscle movement.

Daily Routines (Home and Classroom)

Feeding/Eating

Eating typically involves sitting, without much gross motor movement, but adults can encourage children to participate in getting to and into the chair or highchair for meals. If the child has difficulty eating, distraction with physical games may help. For a highchair baby, let the child kick a swinging toy in between bites of food. The fun of kicking may be a good reinforcement for eating.

Diapering/Toileting

For the infant, play kicking games on the changing table. Hold a bell or sound-producing object slightly above her foot and talk to her. When she gets excited, she will kick her feet. Once she kicks the bell, she may kick again. Once she gets the idea that she can produce the sound with a kick, hold the toy so she can see it above her foot, and wait. She may then try to kick the toy to make the sound. Alternate this game with both feet. Even better, depending on the infant's age, try to get her to kick with both feet together. This requires considerable postural control also. For the toddler and young child, a step-stool to the toilet and sink encourages alternating the feet to climb.

Dressing

Putting clothing on requires using both sides of the body. At first, the parent may put both of the child's feet in the pants and have the child pull up the pants. Putting pants on one leg at a time and encouraging the child to push the foot through is a functional way to practice bilateral use of legs. If the child can stand independently, encourage him to stand on one foot to put the other foot in his pants leg. Provide a support with your arm or shoulder for him to lean against. Children typically put on shoes while sitting down. Encourage the child to try stepping into shoes while standing briefly on one foot and lifting the other to place it in the shoe. This will encourage balance and alternate weight shifting.

Going Out

Going out of the house provides opportunities for the adult to encourage the child to walk, go down steps or the curb, climb into the car, climb into the grocery cart child seat or up on a restaurant bench, and so forth. The adult can encourage independence by letting the child perform these actions with as little support as possible (remembering, of course, what the primary purpose of the activity is). Older children can push the grocery cart or their sister's stroller, practice hopping and jumping to and from the car, or walk on the curb or low wall.

Play Routines (Home and Classroom)

Face-to-Face Play

Games that involved turn-taking are great for babies. For example, as babies use their feet and push against the mother's tummy, the mother can respond by moving backward. When she moves forward again, she can wait for the child to push again. This can become a game accompanied by sounds, words, or a song.

Physical Play

An endless variety of physical games can incorporate bilateral coordination. Riding tricycles and bicycles, ball games, running, and jumping, climbing, wrestling, and so forth all require the child to use his limbs in different ways, both together and alternately. Children who are not good at coordinating their bodies may avoid such play or find it difficult to learn. Adults can encourage play by introducing games that require practice using balance or shifting weight in a gradual way. Jumping on a trampoline (or a bed), climbing a jungle gym, and pumping higher in a swing are independent activities that can be done with other children but do not require the child to compete. The adult can offer "just enough" support to allow the child to be successful with each activity. The adult also can make the play into a game by having the child try to kick an object with both feet as she swings, jump on a bean bag or the trampoline, or kick a flag as she comes down the slide. As competence increases, the child will usually seek out greater challenges and more competitive play. Floor games can include kicking a ball back and forth while sitting or doing exercises (such as leg lifts) to music along with Mom or Dad.

Manipulative Play

Playing with manipulatives typically involves playing on the floor or sitting on a chair at a table. Hands are more involved than legs (see TPBI2, Chapter 3, Section III. Strategies for Improving Arm and Hand Use). However, seating for manipulative play can encourage gross motor movements in different ways. Side-sitting on the floor, a half-kneel (one knee up and one knee on the floor) at a short table, or sitting with one leg bent and one leg straight in front all encourage children to shift weight and move legs differently as they move to pick up toys or rise from the floor.

Sensory Play

Sensory play can involve stomping, jumping, or hopping in various textures such as grass, hay, sand, or water. Pretending to "skate" on shaving cream or sliding across a smooth floor in socks are fun activities. Learning to swim involves learning to kick in different ways and can help children who don't navigate as well on land build confidence.

Dramatic Play

Depending on the story or event being dramatized, a variety of motor activities may be required. Pretending to be a cowboy can involve climbing on a rocking horse or tricycle, chasing cows, and climbing fences. Pretending to be an astronaut can include making a space craft from cardboard boxes, crawling inside, and walking in space (on pillows). Even toddler-play with dolls involves much bending over to put the baby doll to bed, standing and leaning over to put the food in the oven, pushing strollers, and rocking the baby.

Reading and Learning Routines

Circle Time

Circle time can involve a variety of ways to sit and move. Teachers can use circle time for games such as Simon Says, which can encourage movement in unusual ways; dancing; pretending; or dramatizing actions in stories.

One-on-One Book Reading

Reading typically is a quiet activity involving little action. However, many books lend themselves to dancing or acting out various actions in the book. Adults can interject these opportunities while the book is being read or after it is finished.

Science and Math

Science and math can encourage children to explore time, speed, force, exertion, and cause and effect related to various actions. Moving like animals to see how they live, walking on stilts made of coffee cans to explore height, trying to balance on various widths of boards to test balance, and so forth all encourage children to learn concepts through motoric exploration. Teachers who consciously think about integrating movement into science and math support both cognitive and motor development.

GRIER

Grier is a 3-year-old boy with hemiplegia. Although his cognitive and language skills are good, he struggles with gross motor skills. He has good use of his left side but impairment of functioning on his right side. He avoids using his right arm and drags his left leg when he walks. He has difficulty with balance, body rotation, weight shifting, and coordinating both sides of his body. Although his right side will not become "normal," he can learn to function well in his various environments. When developing recommendations for his family and his teacher, the following suggestions were made for environmental modifications and interpersonal interactions.

Interaction Strategies

1. Grier has increased tone on his right side. Consultation from a therapist on how to reduce tone and do stretching with Grier to prevent contractures is recommended. Do these activities in a fun, interactive way, with Grier choosing the music as background for the games. Make these activities into turn-taking games, with Grier "preparing" your feet, legs, and arms, and you preparing his. Follow this activity with an interaction or activity of Grier's choice.

2. Support all self-initiated efforts that Grier makes to use his right arm as a reason for celebration.

3. Play games involving Grier alternating his feet or arms. For instance, let him lie on his back and try to kick or hit bubbles that you blow or a tennis ball suspended from a string. Encourage him to use one leg at a time.

4. Pick Grier up by the left arm and leg and swing him with his head slightly downward. This is a fun position for using his right arm to hit a ball back to Dad.

5. Grier loves roughhousing. Play wrestling games on the bed, where he needs to "pin you" by straddling your legs to hold you down. This will encourage him to climb up and over you and separate his legs. Playing on the bed will challenge his balance, especially when he stands up.

6. Encourage Grier to use a variety of sitting positions. Demonstrate how to sit with legs crossed in front of you. Give him a lap board to balance across his crossed legs to provide a surface for drawing. This will require him to keep his legs in this position to support the board.

Environmental Modifications

1. Because Grier has balance concerns, make sure the environment is safe. Place protectors on table corners.

2. Grier often reverts to crawling, especially down the stairs. Add hand rails on the right side of the stairs and encourage him to use both hands on that railing as he goes down the stairs. Rotating his body to the right will place more weight on his right leg and may help him use it better.

3. Place toys in various spaces around him, particularly on his right side, so that he needs to turn in all directions and use his right side.

4. Have "play dates" with other 3-year-olds at the park. This will motivate Grier to do what his friends are doing. Offer support only when requested or when Grier is frustrated and will not try. Then offer only minimal support to enable him to do the activity.

KEYS TO INTERVENTION BY DEVELOPMENTAL AGE

The following ideas are directed toward children who are functioning at approximately the following levels. The suggestions are not meant to be comprehensive, but rather indicate potential areas for exploration.

Developmental age	Developmental issues	Keys to intervention
Birth to 3 months	Control of head and upper trunk beginning through development of muscle tone to resist gravity. At 3 months, child lying on the back can hold head in midline and bring hands to midline on chest. "Kicks" arms and legs reciprocally. When held in sitting or standing, can keep head in midline. Beginning to keep head in line with body when picked up. May briefly take some weight when held in standing.	Intervention is focused on building neck and upper trunk control. Use visual or auditory stimulation during "tummy time" (time spent on the stomach) to motivate the child to lift the head. When the child is lying on the back, use visual or auditory prompts to encourage following with the head and eyes. Give the child opportunities to play while lying on the back with visual stimulation such as a mobile. This will encourage the child to focus the eyes and may promote swiping and kicking. Encourage movement of the legs and arms by attaching sound-making devices to the ankles or wrists.
4–6 months	Developing greater control against gravity in all positions. Control extending into lower trunk and legs. On back, grabs feet with hands and brings them to belly. Moves by kicking against flat surface. On belly, rests on elbows or hands, legs wide apart and back nicely extended. Learning to reach with one arm. May begin pulling legs up into crawling position. Propels self on tummy with legs, steers with arms, goes backward or forward (5–6 months). Rolling begins, at first by accident, from stomach to back. By 6 months can roll either way using trunk rotation and lifting head. Gradually increases amount of time in supported sitting until it is up to 30 minutes by 6 months. Beginning to sit unsupported first by propping on arms. While supported, stands and moves body up and down, stamps feet. Gradually takes more weight on legs and with support from adult can move from under arms to hips.	Intervention is focused on improving control against gravity in an increasing variety of positions and beginning movement in those positions. Placement of objects is very important because it helps to motivate the child to assume new positions and to move. Toys placed to the side encourage rotation, rolling, and reaching. Placement in front while the child is on tummy motivates head lifting and moving forward. Placing the child on a hard surface gives something to push against and makes it easier to move independently. Help the child roll from back to front by gently rolling one hip forward to help that leg lead. Physical play, holding the child up into the air in the "airplane" position makes the child push his trunk, arms and legs up against gravity. Games that involve this position can support the child using large muscles to hold the body up. Be sure the child has plenty of times to practice standing with weight on feet and legs. Support somewhere between the chest (under the arms) and the hips. The lower your hands, the more the child is controlling.
7–9 months	Increasing movement and stability, building on the control acquired in earlier months. Huge variety in sitting positions. Rolling, pivoting, assuming quadruped and bear-standing, trying to crawl, coming to sitting, and pulling to stand are hallmarks of this time. Likely to resist being in supine except to sleep. Acquires ability to sit independently and play with toys. Can resist falling if bumped gently. By 9 months can be left alone in sitting. Pushes up to sit independently.	Play games where the child sits in a supported position on the lap or in supported seating. Place toys to the front and both sides of the child's body so the child needs to shift body weight to get the object. Lean with your own body to help the child get the idea. When the child can sit unsupported, place toys slightly out of reach in front and to both sides. Place desired objects at various points on the "clock" around the child to challenge balance reactions, encourage rotation, promote use of muscles in the trunk, and encourage coordination of both sides of the body.

Developmental age	Developmental issues	Keys to intervention
7–9 months (*continued*)	Sits in both W and side-sitting positions. Most babies are playing with toys while sitting. On tummy, rocks with head and chest high off surface, limbs extended and back arched. Uses arms and legs to pivot. Can assume quadruped and rock. Moves forward on belly. Stands briefly with one hand held. Pulls to stand, may remove one hand from support. May pull self from hands and knees to standing and cruise along furniture.	Trucks, balls, and other moving objects can be used in turn-taking and back-and-forth games. Place the child next to a low table or couch to help with pulling to stand. Present motivating objects to persuade the child to try to pull up. For children who need help, position the knees and hips so that they can rise more easily. Hold on to the child's hands and pull upward, letting the child push against the floor to come up to stand. Play music and bounce to the music. While holding the child's hands, encourage him or her to step into a shallow box containing interesting materials (this can vary in depth from the lid of a box to an actual low box as the child can adjust the height the foot is lifted). While holding the child at the hips let the child reach down for toys and help him or her squat, get the toy, and stand.
10–12 months	The hallmarks of this time period are crawling and standing. Children are very active (static sitting is rare) and always exploring. Crawls on hands and knees. Moves from hands and knees to sitting or half sitting and back again. Reaches while on hands and knees Stands with little support. Sits down from standing without falling. May assume stand by going through half-kneel. May stand alone momentarily. May walk (usually leaning on furniture or holding someone's hand).	Play physical games and roughhouse with the child. Tickling can stimulate the child to "escape." Let the child get away, then watch for the cue that the child wants to repeat the game. Place small objects, such as pieces of cereal, as a trail for the child to follow, first when crawling then when cruising sideways around a low table. Use toys that move to motivate the child to chase the toy. Place obstacles in the child's path so the child has to maneuver up, over, or around the obstacle. For example, when on the floor, place a desired object on the opposite side of your body so the child needs to pull up on you and crawl over. Pillows, chairs, and other large objects can also become a simple obstacle course. Watch patterns of movement to ensure that both sides are used equally. Encourage movement and use of limbs that are underused by presenting preferred objects or activities to the less used side. Provide incentives to crawl or climb into boxes or under objects. This requires the child to adjust the height of movements of various body parts. Play movement games such as kicking the feet in the tub or a wading pool. Try to "get" the moving light from a flashlight. Reduce the amount of support in standing as much as possible. Having the parent as a "target" for movement is motivating. Food or a special toy can also prompt that first independent step. As the child begins to take steps without support, be there to offer assurance and prompt continued effort.
13–18 months	The hallmarks of this period are walking and moving around while upright, squatting, stooping, varying the speed of walking, picking up toys from floor, pulling toys. Begins to run. Walks upstairs with one hand held. Seats self in small chair. Climbs into adult chair. Creeps up stairs.	Study tiny objects. Bugs, small pieces of paper, and crumbs of food are all fascinating and encourage children to squat in order to study or pick up what they see. Place desired objects on different surfaces, chairs, tables, or steps to encourage climbing.

(continued on next page)

Developmental age	Developmental issues	Keys to intervention
19–24 months	The hallmark of this stage is the appearance of the fundamental motor skills. Can stand briefly on one foot. Moves ride-on toy with no pedals. Climbs down from adult chair. Flings ball forward at large target. Kicks ball forward. Jumps off floor. Walks up and down stairs first holding on and later with no support. Jumps from bottom step.	Try to step on bubbles, leaves, pieces of grass, or other small objects to encourage standing on one foot for a second. Play games requiring movement at different speeds (e.g., chasing a puppy, following an ant). Walk on paths of different widths, angles, and substances (e.g., the wide sidewalk, narrow curb, thin ribbons, slopes and hills, steps, bumpy stepping stones, mounded dirt). Begin dramatic play with props requiring movement (e.g., getting in and out of a toy car, on and off a "horse," lying down to sleep).
24–36 months	In this stage, more of the fundamental motor skills appear. Begins to pedal tricycle. Climbs up and down furniture independently. Catches 10-inch ball against chest. Walks up and downstairs alternating feet. Climbs nursery apparatus.	Tricycles are good for encouraging reciprocal movement of the legs and use of alternating force from first one side of the body and then the other. Water play in a swimming pool also encourages kicking against the resistance of the water. Play movement imitation games, acting out actions in songs, such as ducks swimming, frogs jumping, and so forth.
36–48 months	More fundamental motor skills appear and others are refined. Catches ball with elbows bent in front of body. Exhibits true running with trunk rotation and arm swing. Can steer tricycle around obstacles.	Develop increased control of movement through games where targets are involved, such as jumping on specific numbers or colors or playing games requiring change of speed (e.g., Red Light/Green Light). Introduce dramatic play involving more complex movement. Dramatization of stories involving movement can include everything from going on a safari to being a firefighter and saving a child in a burning house. Adults can facilitate movement in dramatic play by providing props (a big box for a safari Jeep or a fire truck, a hose, and a ladder for the fireman)
48–60 months	More refinement and development of fundamental motor skills. Learns to skip, hop on one foot, and gallop. Can stand on one foot for several seconds and walk along curb without falling. Jumps down from high step; jumps forward. Uses forward weight shift to throw further. Throws smoothly and with some directional accuracy. Releases on time and in line with target. When catching, adjusts body position in line with ball and has elbows at sides. When striking with a bat, the body is a good distance from object, contact is made with extended arms.	Children become more involved in group physical activities in this period. Parents arrange play dates and teachers plan group physical activities. Provide physical play materials such as jump ropes, balls and bats, and mini trampolines. Adults can also demonstrate more complex action sequences and, if children have verbal comprehension, begin to "coach" them about how to hone their skills. Repetition of movement patterns leads to more fluid actions. Incorporating novel movements into every aspect of the day is important.
60–72 months	Fundamental motor skills continue to refine. Strength and coordination improve. Kicks to a target. Skips effortlessly. Gallops with full coordination. Hops in straight line.	Children are able to understand the rules of group sports and may now choose to be involved in them.

3

Facilitating
Sensorimotor Development

III. Strategies for Improving Arm and Hand Use

with Susan Dwinal and Anita C. Bundy

Goal Attainment Scale

1	2	3	4	5	6	7	8	9
Tracks objects. No voluntary control of arms, hands, and fingers.		Reaches for objects and people; bats at objects without grasping.		Uses gross grasp to obtain objects; little active release.		Grasp matches size and shape of objects; gross release.		Can use arms, hands, and fingers efficiently and effectively to reach, grasp, manipulate in hand, and precisely release and place objects.

Arm and hand use in TPBA2 includes reaching for and batting objects as well as grasping and releasing, isolating finger movements, in-hand manipulation, construction, and tool use. Use of arms and hands is complex and depends on a number of functions. These include cognition to generate ideas (see TPBA2, Chapter 7, Subcategory III. Problem Solving; and TPBI2, Chapter 7, Section III. Strategies for Improving Problem Solving), cortical control of actions, integrity of the muscles and joints of the limb, and control of the trunk. The trunk provides a stable base for moving the arms (see TPBA2, Chapter 2, Subcategory I. Functions Underlying Movement). Arm and hand movements are needed for most functional activities including eating, dressing, grooming, bathing, and playing. Children learn through their hands. Infants and children grasp and manipulate objects, thus learning the characteristics of the objects (e.g., texture, size weight). Playing with toys and manipulating objects, in turn, contributes to the development of cognitive skills (i.e., attention, problem solving, memory, written expression, creativity, and imagination). Arm and hand skill is imperative to some language and communication (e.g., gestures and sign language) and provides a means for social exchanges, greetings, and expression of love and affection.

APPROPRIATE ARM AND HAND USE

Arm and hand use should be automatic, intentional, and fluid. Children should be able to use their arms and hands both symmetrically (i.e., both do the same thing) and asymmetrically (i.e., one hand stabilizes and the other acts). The infant's ability to grasp and release begin as gross, automatic movements and gradually become more precise (i.e., better matched to the task) and under increasingly voluntary control.

Children practice arm and hand skills through play. Resistance to movement is an important contributor to the development of arm and hand skill. Thus, infants are working on arm and hand use whenever they are weight bearing on open hands— while lying on the stomach and later while crawling on hands and knees. The pressure that comes through weight bearing on the hands helps to build the muscles of the shoulder girdle and develop arches in the hands. Later, these arches will allow the child to shape the hand in the way needed to manipulate objects. Similarly, older children hanging from the rungs of a climber or propelling a swing are working on the development of arm and hand skills.

Toddlers and older children also are developing arm and hand skill through play with construction toys and tactile media (e.g., playdough) and through beginning tool use including eating utensils and writing tools. These involve isolated finger use, bilateral control, grasp tailored to the object, and the ability to reposition objects in the hand in preparation for use (in-hand manipulation).

The ability to use the hands in a lead/assist fashion, with one hand stabilizing a toy while the other manipulates it, is an important aspect of arm and hand skill. The toddler is able to turn pages of a book and complete simple puzzles. Preschoolers are able to manipulate objects with dexterity and use tools for a number of different purposes. They use two hands together effectively to construct towers with blocks, make necklaces with beads, cut with scissors, and color pictures with crayons.

Appropriate Arm and Hand Use in Practice

■■■■　**III. A. Arm and hand use**

Daily Routines (Home and Classroom)

- *Infant/toddler:* The infant is soothed by putting a rattle in his mouth after waking up from a nap. The toddler takes off her shoes after they are untied when she gets home from the park.

- *Young child:* The young child undoes the zipper on his jacket and the snap on his snow pants when he comes in from playing.

Play Routines (Home and Classroom)

- *Infant/toddler:* The infant grasps a rattle and shakes it to make a sound. She brings the rattle to her mouth to explore it and gain an understanding of how the object feels. The toddler uses one hand to hold the drum while he uses a stick to hit the drum with the other hand.

- *Young child:* The young child plays dress up and independently puts on a dress with buttons in the front and high heeled shoes. She opens her purse and gets her lipstick.

Classroom Routines

During center time, a child chooses to write a letter to her mother, including drawing a picture, writing her name, folding the paper, and putting it in an envelope.

▮▮▮▮ III. B. Reach; III. C. Grasp; III. D. Release

Although these are each separate motor skills, they are most often used in combination and so are considered together in this section.

Daily Routines (Home and Classroom)

- *Infant/toddler:* The infant transfers toys from one hand to the other while he is getting his diaper changed. The toddler grasps a spoon using all of his fingers and the palm to feed himself applesauce during snack time.
- *Young child:* The preschooler holds a crayon with thumb and first two fingers and colors by moving her whole arm.

Play Routines (Home and Classroom)

- *Infant/toddler:* The infant bangs the toy on the highchair tray and then, each time the adult replaces the toy, throws it on the floor again. The toddler successfully puts the shapes of a shape sorter into the correct holes.
- *Young child:* The young child throws beanbags into the target while playing in the backyard.

Classroom Routines

The child uses scissors to cut out heart shapes from construction paper for Valentine's Day.

▮▮▮▮ III. E. Isolating finger movements

Daily Routines (Home and Classroom)

- *Infant/toddler:* While at the zoo, the infant points to the monkeys with excitement to show her mom. The toddler dips his finger in the brownie batter to taste it while baking with his mother.
- *Young child:* The young child pushes the buttons on the elevator as he goes to visit the doctor.

Play Routines (Home and Classroom)

- *Infant/toddler:* The infant activates cause-and-effect music toys with her index finger. The toddler points to pictures in her favorite book.
- *Young child:* The young child counts the number of kids in the class on the fingers.

Classroom Routines

During circle time, the young child is able to isolate finger movements to participate in songs with finger plays.

▨▨▨ **III. F. In-hand manipulation**

Daily Routines (Home and Classroom)

- *Infant/toddler:* The infant rakes two Cheerios from the tray on the highchair into his palm. He cannot deftly transfer them to his fingers and so he eats them by opening his fingers and taking them with his mouth. The toddler turns pegs over to place them in the pegboard by using whole arm movements rather than by rotating them deftly in her fingers.

- *Young child:* The child gets coins out of her pocket, holds them in her fist, and then puts them into the machine one at a time to buy candy.

Play Routines (Home and Classroom)

- *Infant/toddler:* The infant moves a toy from one hand to the other and then puts it in the bucket. The toddler strings large beads on a string to make a necklace.

- *Young child:* The child shows his friends the different rocks in his rock collection by holding the rocks in his hand and shifting them to his fingers.

Classroom Routines

The child shifts the marker into position for writing with ease when she wants to color a picture.

▨▨▨ **III. G. Constructional abilities**

Daily Routines (Home and Classroom)

- *Infant/toddler:* The infant sees relationships when she bangs one object on another. The toddler stacks the paper plates on the table and puts them into the trash after dinner, showing understanding of functions of objects.

- *Young child:* The child helps his father build a cage for the pet turtle by helping to hold the wood and hit with the hammer.

Play Routines (Home and Classroom)

- *Infant/toddler:* The infant combines objects, placing one object on or in another. The toddler stacks three blocks to make a tower and enjoys knocking it over again and again.

- *Young child:* The young child completes a 10-piece interlocking puzzle.

Classroom Routines

During recess, the child makes a fort by stacking rocks and sticks with her friends.

▨▨▨ **III. H. Tool use**

Daily Routines (Home and Classroom)

- *Infant/toddler:* The infant imitates combing her hair when she watches her mother combing her sister's hair. The toddler helps his mom make a cake by stirring the batter with a big spoon.

- *Young child:* The child uses cookie cutters to cut out dinosaur-shaped cookies to bring to school for a birthday.

Play Routines (Home and Classroom)

- *Infant/toddler:* The infant bangs a xylophone with a mallet to make music. The toddler plays with the tool set, pretending to hammer nails and screw in screws.

- *Young child:* The child draws a picture of his mother with markers and asks her to put it up on the refrigerator.

Classroom Routines

The child digs dirt with a small shovel to plant seeds for the school's garden.

GENERAL PRINCIPLES FOR SUPPORTING APPROPRIATE ARM AND HAND USE

In day-to-day life, parents, caregivers, teachers, and other professionals naturally provide opportunities for a children to practice and develop arm and hand skills. The following are strategies that can be used with all children, consciously or unconsciously, to support the development of arm and hand use.

Encourage Effort and Praise the Child for Attempting Tasks

Children have an inner drive to succeed and be independent. Encourage and allow the child to do things for him- or herself. Self-help skills provide many opportunities for encouraging independence and practicing arm and hand skills. From dressing to grooming to eating, the child has opportunities to practice and refine arm and hand use. Praising a child for attempting a new skill, ("Oh, what a big boy you are! Nice job putting on your shoes!"), provides positive reinforcement and increases the likelihood that the child will attempt that task again and eventually be independent.

Include Children in Activities You Are Doing and Make Them Fun

Many daily activities involve arm and hand use. Chores around the house—putting laundry into the basket, carrying grocery bags, cleaning (spray bottle to dust or clean windows, vacuuming, sweeping), and cooking—involve a lot of use of arms and hands. Most of these activities provide considerable resistance to movement as well as require coordinated use of two arms.

Provide Extra Time

When children are first learning new tasks that require them to use their arms and hands in a skilled way, they need extra time to complete the task. The best time to work on putting on your coat is not when you are running late! Parents and other caregivers must allow extra time for the child to practice and learn new tasks.

Model Skills and Encourage Imitation

Children love to imitate adults. During toy play, adults model new actions and encourage the child to participate in play with his or her hands. Building different structures with blocks, making animals with playdough, or playing dress up will foster imitation.

Do Things *with* Children, Not *for* Them

When a child encounters a new toy, he may need help. When the child asks for help (verbally or nonverbally), parents may help the child by doing the task hand over hand. Once the child learns how to do the task, parents gradually reduce their assistance to help the child be independent.

Backward Chaining Methods

Some skills that require arm and hand movements (e.g., self-help skills) are best taught using *backward chaining.* Most parents, caregivers, teachers, and other professionals naturally use chaining procedures when teaching new skills, either consciously or subconsciously. In backward chaining, the skill is broken down into steps and the child is helped through all of the steps except the last step. The child performs the last step independently. Once the child is doing the last step independently the adult may work backward, having the child do more steps until he is independent. For example, if a child is just learning to tie the shoes, the adult may help him with all of the steps leading up to the last step of pulling the two loops. The child is then encouraged to finish tying the shoes which gives him a sense of accomplishment for having finished the task.

PLANNING INDIVIDUALIZED
INTERVENTIONS FOR IMPROVING ARM AND HAND USE

III. A. In general, how do you describe the child's arm and hand use? How much do problems with arm and hand use interfere with function?

Children who have difficulty with arm and hand use may avoid activities that involve manipulation or refuse to perform basic activities of daily living because they are just too hard. This can lead to delays in development in other areas including cognition, communication, and social emotional. When difficulties with arm and hand use are identified, it is important to find out what is contributing to the child's decreased abilities. The ability to use arms and hands may be affected by poor postural control or abnormal muscle tone (see TPBA2, Chapter 2, Subcategory I. Functions Underlying Movement). If a child is not able to maintain an upright supported posture, use of the arms and hands will be compromised. Postural and muscle tone issues need to be addressed through intervention or compensation techniques including providing appropriate support for the body before—or simultaneous with—addressing use of the hands (see TPBA2, Chapter 2, Subcategory I. Functions Underlying Movement). Difficulties with sensory processing including sensitivity to touch, decreased awareness of body in space, or difficulties with motor planning also can affect the way children use their arms and hands (see TPBA2, Chapter 2, Subcategory IV. Motor Planning; and TPBA2 Chapter 2, Subcategory VI. Sensorimotor Contributions to Daily Life).

When a child's arm and hand skill seems delayed or compromised, adults may need to help children develop these skills or compensate for them. Development of skills may occur through practice or adaptation (e.g., pencil grip, adapted scissors). When determining underlying difficulties with arm and hand use (e.g., poor posture, abnormal muscle tone), an occupational therapist should be consulted.

The following questions should be asked:

1. Is the child able to maintain the body in an upright position? If not, is there a way to help support the child through use of positioning equipment to maintain upright position with hips, knees, and feet at a 90-degree angle?

2. Is the child sitting in a chair that allows the feet to touch the ground for added support and stability?

3. Does the child need support to keep the body upright and prevent leaning to one side or the other?

4. Is increased or decreased muscle tone interfering with use of the arms and hands? Do techniques need to be used to either increase or decrease muscle tone before activities that require hand use? (see TPBA2, Chapter 2, Subcategory I. Functions Underlying Movement).

5. What are the sensory processing abilities of the child? Is the child sensitive to touch and could this be affecting the willingness to use the hands to manipulate toys? Does the child have difficulty regulating the use of force (too much or too little force) due to difficulties processing input to muscles and joints? Is the child able to use the vision to guide arm and hand movements effectively? (see TPBA2, Chapter 4, Strategies for Working with Children with Visual Impairments).

6. Does the child have difficulty with motor planning that is affecting the use of the arms and hands for functional tasks? (see TPBA2, Chapter 2, Subcategory IV. Motor Planning).

7. Does the child have a hard time using two hands together to complete tasks?

After determining the underlying causes for arm and hand use difficulties, often with the help of an experienced professional, intervention can begin. General principles for adapting interactions and making environmental modifications to support the development of arm and hand use are outlined here.

Interaction Strategies

1. *Identify the child's motivation to use arms and hands.* Motivation is key to the development of arm and hand use. While passive movement provides some input to the brain for building neurological pathways, movements controlled by the child have a greater effect. That is why capitalizing on the child's motivation to use the arms and hands is so important. For infants and young children, objects that make noise, have lights, spin, shake, or vibrate often are motivating and draw the child's attention. Holding highly desired objects just beyond the child's reach will encourage him to exert more effort to get them. (But don't do this repeatedly, because children learn quickly that you have no intent to let them play with the desired object and thus will stop reaching for it.) For older children, a new game that requires problem solving or construction may appeal to their motivations.

2. *Encourage independence and effort.* Be a cheerleader and encourage children to do things for themselves. Provide the least amount of assistance to help children be successful, and praise their efforts.

3. *Give honest praise.* Children know when they have done a good job and they know when adult praise is genuine. "Good try!" or "Almost!" may be genuine when "Good job!" or "Well done!" is not.

4. *Provide just right challenge.* Create the "just right challenge." Children must be challenged but not frustrated. Taking into account the child's abilities and the demands of the activity will give the adult an idea of the appropriateness of the task. The just right challenge is characterized by use of one's best skills to meet a significant challenge. There must be some chance for failure. We neither want the activity to be so hard that it provokes anxiety or frustration nor so easy that it is boring.

5. *Do daily chores and play activities in tandem.* Most children love to help an adult. Children love to be involved in "adult" activities and young children love to be involved in "big kid" activities. Start the chore or play activity and ask the child to help you finish it or wait for the child to initiate the activity or movement and then provide a little bit of assistance. Giving "high fives" and talking about doing the activity together provides motivation.

6. *Model how to do things and then encourage the child to practice.* Children often learn new skills by watching and then attempting the task on their own. Model actions slowly and describe what you are doing so the verbal explanation supports the actions. Some children can process auditory information better than visual, and they can then "talk themselves through" an action.

7. *Break multistep tasks down into small steps to increase success.* Help children be successful by breaking tasks down into small steps. This is especially important during daily routines. When the child is learning how to get dressed, for example, "walk" the child through the steps of putting on the pants (i.e., hold pants, step one foot in, step the other foot in, pull up, and straighten) through physical and verbal guidance, requiring the child to complete only the last step of the process. Gradually add more steps as the child is successful.

Environmental Modifications

In addition to interpersonal strategies that may support improvement of arm and hand use, environmental modifications are often useful. Depending on the findings from TPBA2, the team may want to consider some of the environmental modifications outlined below.

1. *Provide opportunities for the child to use her hands.* Give the child numerous natural opportunities throughout the day to explore, manipulate, build, create, feel, and perform daily living tasks. More practice using the hands in different ways increases the child's strength and coordination needed for successful arm and hand use.

2. *Choose toys that draw the child's attention and that require use of the hands.* Choose toys with bright colors or lights, or toys that vibrate or make noise when activated. This will increase the young child's motivation to use his hands to activate the toy to get the desired response

3. *Provide optimal positioning for a child and adaptive seating if needed.* For the child who has difficulties with postural stability (see TPBA2, Chapter 2, Subcategory I. Functions Underlying Movement), make sure that the child is in a supported position to be able to use the arms and hands effectively. Children need a stable base of support for using the hands without losing balance. Children should be supported in an upright position with knees and hips at a 90-degree angle and feet supported on the floor or other surface (i.e., stepstool, box, phone book). Adapted seating may be needed for children with increased or decreased muscle tone that affects trunk muscles (see TPBA2, Chapter 2, Subcategory I. Functions Underlying Movement).

4. *Adjust level of sensation.* Some children dislike certain sensations that, in turn, preclude them from using their hands to explore different materials or textures. These children may avoid messy play or avoid using their hands to explore materials (see TPBA2, Chapter 2, Subcategory V. Modulation of Sensation and Its Relationship to Emotion, Activity Level, and Attention). For a child who shows sensory sensitivities to tactile input to the hands, activities such as finger painting, sand box play, or play with shaving cream or playdough may need to be modified. A child with these sensitivities should be encouraged gently to participate in this type of play. The adult can offer the child the option of doing finger painting or shaving cream play with the hands or with a paintbrush or other tool. The child also can have the option of having a towel near him to be able to wipe the hands whenever he wants to.

▨▨▨▨　**III. B. How well is the child able to reach?; III. C. How effective is the child's grasp?; III. D. How well does the child release objects?**

The development of reach, grasp, and release is an intricate process that involves the use of vision and motor control. Control for reaching comes from proximal muscles (i.e., shoulder, trunk). Manipulation needed for grasping and releasing comes from the wrist, hand, and forearm. Reaching develops from visual regard of objects, to swiping at objects, to visually directing reach, to reaching toward an object with the hand in the appropriate orientation to grasp. Grasping develops from gross (full fisted grasping), to grasping with the little finger side of the hand, to more refined use of the thumb in opposition to the other fingers when grasping an object. Release develops from the presence of a strong grasp reflex with hand closed, to involuntary releasing, to transferring objects between hands, to pressing down on a surface to release, and finally to controlled release with wrist extended (bent up). When a child has difficulty with reaching, grasping, and releasing, the nature of the difficulty needs to be defined and then the challenge can be addressed. Activities to help develop these skills involve working on improving proximal stability (see TPBI2, Chapter 3, Section I. Strategies for Improving Functions Underlying Movement), adapting activities based on the visual needs of the child (see TPBI2, Chapter 4, Strategies for Working with Children with Visual Impairments), and directly addressing the child's decreased hand function.

Children with high, low, or fluctuating muscle tone (see TPBA2, Chapter 2, Subcategory I. Functions Underlying Movement) often have difficulty with arm and hand use. Children with high muscle tone and stiff muscles may have decreased ability to use their arms to reach or may have persistently fisted hands. Children with low or fluctuating tone may show decreased strength or precision needed to successfully reach against gravity, grasp an object with precision, and release with coordination. The following sections provide interaction strategies and environmental modifications to help develop a child's ability to reach, grasp, and release.

Interaction Strategies

1. *Encourage independence and effort.* Children who have difficulty with reaching, grasping, and releasing need encouragement to contact, manipulate, and transfer toys while playing. Adults should encourage these activities and praise the child's efforts. One means of encouraging children to use their hands may be to leave them alone with a highly desired toy.

2. *Use people as targets to get the child to reach.* Familiar people are often good targets for a child to reach for while playing. Set up situations in which the child has the opportunity to use both hands to reach for a loved one. The adult also can motivate the younger child to reach by holding an object slightly out of the child's immediate grasp.

3. *Provide the least amount of physical prompting needed for success.* Using most to least physical prompting for a child who has difficulties with reaching, grasping, and releasing is recommended. When the child is reaching for a favorite toy, start by prompting near the shoulder and gradually move down closer to the hand as the child gains more control. When prompting a more mature grasp (with the thumb side of the hand), start off by helping the child fold the little finger and ring finger into the palm when picking up small objects. Once the child gets the idea, have him hold a small object in the little finger and ring finger to decrease the need for adult prompting. For a child who needs help with releasing, helping the child by stabilizing the forearm and wrist on the table or helping him to flex (bend down) the wrist will naturally force the fingers to open. Similarly, extending (bending up) will cause the fingers to close around objects, helping with grasp.

4. *Provide frequent breaks based on the child's nonverbal signs.* Working on these skills can be frustrating and exhausting for a child with motor or visual challenges. Reading a child's nonverbal cues to determine level of frustration or fatigue is imperative. Intersperse pleasurable activities that do not require use of fine motor skills.

5. *Incorporate work on reaching, grasping, and releasing during highly motivating times within the child's routines.* For a child who enjoys mealtimes, provide numerous opportu-

nities for the child to reach for the cup, spoon, and plate. Provide food cut up in different orientations and varied sizes to force the child to use her fingers to grasp in different ways. During bath time, have the child reach for sponge letters or animals that are stuck on the sides of the bathtub, grasp the letters, and then release the letters into a bucket.

6. *Remember, the child just wants to play.* Do not try to get children to reach repeatedly for an object without giving them time to play with it. Similarly, when children grasp objects in unusual ways, do not be too quick to correct them. Children are more interested in acquiring the object than in grasping in the most developmentally appropriate manner. Although performing arm and hand skills in the most efficient and effective way possible is important, constant correction of their attempts may cause them to avoid activities that call for those skills and may set up negative interactions with caregivers.

Environmental Modifications

In addition to activity-based strategies that support children's reach, grasp, and release, environmental modifications often are useful. Depending on the findings from TPBA2, the team may want to consider some of the following environmental modifications.

1. *Provide optimal positioning for a child, and adaptive seating if needed.* For infants and young children, early reaching skills are most easily developed while lying on the back or in a semireclined position because the arms are free and the head and trunk are supported. For an older child, a supported sitting position provides a stable base from which to reach and use the hands effectively.

2. *Provide attractive toys nearby.* Toys that make noise, light up, vibrate, or have characteristics that are motivating to the child should be presented just within reach so that the child is enticed to reach and grasp. Toys that are suspended provide a good target for reaching (e.g., balloons, beads, bubbles). Toys that are switch-activated (e.g., push, turn, poke, slide) work on grasp. Wind-up toys, Lite-Brite, piggy banks, Jack-in-the-Box, peg boards, and vibrating pens all work on improving grasp. Games such as Connect Four, Hi Ho! Cherry-O, Don't Break the Ice, and Don't Spill the Beans all involve working on grasp and release.

3. *Vary the placement and spatial orientation of objects.* This will allow the child to develop the coordination of the shoulder, trunk, arm, and hand needed to reach forward, to the side, up, down, diagonally, and behind the body. It also will force the child to learn how to grasp objects with the hand in different positions; that is, wrist in neutral (palm to side, thumb up), in supination (palm up), and in pronation (palm down) or any variation between these positions.

4. *Use sensory-based materials to help motivate reaching and grasping.* Children often are motivated by toys that make noise or provide stimulation when activated. Playing games with balloons during which the adult blows up the balloon and holds it in front of the child often will result in the child reaching for the balloon, contacting it, and letting the air out. Playing with shaving cream on a mirror will often entice the child to reach forward to contact the shaving cream with her hands. Hiding toys in a water or sand table may motivate a child to reach and grasp toys. Water toys that involve squeezing a toy to make water shoot out also are motivating for children. Sticker activities are a great way to have the child work on grasping and releasing. Toys that make noise, including the Dropper Popper (looks like a half of ball, use fingers to turn it inside out, put it on the table and it pops in the air), help with improving grasp strength.

5. *Vary the size and shape of objects to be grasped.* Developmentally younger children will find it easier to pick up bigger objects and often use more of a whole-hand gross grasp or a raking grasp with the little finger side of the hand. When thinking about how to modify activities, take into consideration the developmental level of the child and choose appropriate materials for the next step.

6. *Use of adaptive equipment or switch-operated toys.* Some children who have difficulty with reach, grasp, and release need to have toys adapted to help them be successful. Cause–effect toys can be adapted to include single-switch devices that can be activated by pushing, pulling, or tilting.

7. *Play games that have targets.* Throwing balls into a bucket or hoop or at a target on the wall or on the floor is a great way to work on grasp and release.

8. *Cleaning up toys together.* Having the child pick up toys as part of the daily routine provides opportunities for reaching, grasping, and releasing, in a naturalistic way.

9. *Provide adaptive equipment for the child with difficulty grasping and releasing.* Products such as a universal cuff (a Velcro strap that goes around the child's hand to make grasping and holding easier, used for eating utensils, toothbrushes, and to help the child play musical instruments); specialized hand or wrist splints fabricated by an experienced occupational therapist based on need; art tools (Sammons Preston; special holders for art materials for the child with decreased ability to grasp); and the crayon holder (Southpaw Enterprises; more than doubles the diameter of regular-sized crayons making it easier for a child with decreased grasping ability) or other pencil grips can help a child be more independent with grasping and holding objects.

■■■■■ III. E. How well does the child isolate finger movements for pointing, poking, and tapping?

Finger isolation is needed to perform a variety of functions within the sensorimotor, communication, self-care, emotional and social, and cognitive domains. Children use finger isolation to point in order to request items and indicate wants and needs, to show items to adults and peers and initiate joint attention (the ability to use eye contact and pointing for the social purposes of sharing experiences with others), to activate cause–effect toys or to turn things on, to express themselves through nonverbal communication or sign language, and to perform a variety of self-care tasks (e.g., opening and closing containers, using a telephone, participating in cooking activities). When a child has difficulty with finger isolation, he may have difficulty specifying wants and needs, communicating effectively, independently activating toys, or participating in or becoming independent in self-care tasks. The following sections provide interaction strategies and environmental modifications to help develop a child's ability to isolate the fingers.

Interaction Strategies

1. *Set up situations that elicit joint attention and help the child isolate the index finger to point.* Help the child point out and share interesting things throughout the day. While reading a book, model pointing out the child's favorite characters and/or pictures. Help the child point proximally to the pictures and share them with you by helping him gently close the other fingers against the palm. Giving him something to hold in the other fingers (e.g., small ball, cotton balls) will help keep the other fingers closed against the palm and allow the index finger to point. Children also can be taught to point with an isolated index finger to make choices or express wants and needs by using a colored sticker in the shape of a circle. Place the circle sticker on desired objects

and help the child learn that he needs to isolate the index finger and touch the circle to request the toy. When outside encourage the child to point with an isolated index finger to things he sees in the environment, an airplane flying by, a bird in the trees, and/or a train going by.

2. *Sing songs and finger plays that require isolated finger movements.* Children often are motivated by music and singing familiar songs. Many songs have arm and hand movements that go along with the words. There are many songs that require finger isolation. Some examples include, "Where Is Thumbkin?" "Five Little Monkeys Jumping on the Bed," "Five Little Ducks," "Ten in the Bed," "Open, Shut Them," and "Twinkle, Twinkle, Little Star."

3. *Children love to imitate the actions of adults.* Model actions that require the child to isolate the fingers and encourage the child to imitate the action or perform it by herself. Some daily examples include turning things on and off or activating things (e.g., lights, appliances, tape or video player, elevator); letting the child push buttons on the pretend phone or use an old turn dial phone as the adult talks on the real phone; providing the child with an old keyboard or electric typewriter so he can pretend to type as the adult works on the computer; playing musical instruments with the child (e.g., keyboard, piano); or including the child in cooking activities that involve opening and closing containers, poking, pouring, stirring, tearing, and so forth.

Environmental Modifications

In addition to interaction-based strategies to support the child to isolate the fingers, environmental modifications often are useful. Depending on the findings from TPBA2, the team may want to consider some of the following environmental modifications.

1. *Choose toys that help elicit finger isolation.* There are a variety of toys that help the child isolate the fingers. Finger puppets are available in different colors and characters and often are motivating for the child. The child can make certain puppets talk or do actions while other fingers are held against the palm, working on isolating particular fingers. Cause–effect toys often are motivating; the child can push buttons to make sounds, play songs, or have the toy perform an action. Games for older children that provide opportunities for finger isolation are Jenga (a wooden block tower building game) and Tricky Fingers (a game that requires use of isolated fingers to move colored balls within a self-contained box to make patterns). Individual finger weights also are available to help provide more feedback for a child's fingers as he plays.

2. *Set up arts and craft activities and cooking activities that elicit finger isolation.* There are a number of arts and crafts activities that help a child work on finger isolation: finger painting, playdough, finger paint brushes (little brushes that fit over a child's individual fingers), stamp pad people and animals (use fingertips to make people's heads or animal's bodies), Modeling Dough Fingertip Stampers (fit on a child's fingers and act as stamps). Cooking activities are great for using fingers to isolate and poke cookie or bread dough; pushing buttons on a mixer or microwave also is a good way to elicit finger isolation.

3. *Play with musical instruments or musical toys.* Playing musical instruments naturally promotes finger isolation. Playing a piano, keyboard, accordion, or guitar helps the child use the fingers in an isolated way. Play with musical toys often requires the child to isolate the fingers to push buttons that play specific songs. Some books have buttons that children can push to hear songs as they read. Turning on a CD or tape player also requires finger isolation.

III. F. How effective is the child's in-hand manipulation?

In-hand manipulation involves repositioning objects in the hand once they have been grasped so that they are ready for use. Thus, its function is to make hand use more skillful and efficient. When children have difficulty with in-hand manipulation, accomplishment of fine motor skills may look awkward and require more time for completion. In-hand manipulation is one of the last of the fine motor skills to develop. The earliest of the skills appears at approximately 18 months. Even 7-year-olds, who are capable of performing even the most sophisticated in-hand manipulation, may choose not to do so, reverting to more simplistic hand patterns. Children who have well-developed grasp patterns but who show difficulty with in-hand manipulation probably simply need opportunities to practice these more complex skills.

Interaction Strategies

1. *"It's Magic!"* Some children may view manipulating an object within the hand without stabilizing it against the body or another surface as a magic trick. Adults can provide a model that children try to copy. For example, the adult can hold a coin or small pebble in the fist, palm down, so the child cannot see it, then manipulate the object up between the thumb and forefinger. The child can then try to do the trick to show another family member.

2. *Encourage manipulation in daily tasks.* When checking out at a store, for instance, give the child a couple of pennies and ask them to give the clerk one penny. Hold the child's other hand to encourage her to use in-hand manipulation, or pick the child up and hold her on your hip, so that one arm is behind your back.

3. *Incorporate manipulation into play interactions.* When pretending to play house, for example, use poker chips as "cookies" and hand the child a stack of cookies. Then hand the child a pretend glass of milk. Once the child has both hands full, she will need to manipulate the pile of cookies to get one or hand the adult one.

Environmental Modifications

In addition to interpersonal strategies that may support the child to perform in-hand manipulations, activity-based modifications often are useful. Depending on the findings from TPBA2, the team may want to consider some of the following modifications.

1. *Have the child help with daily tasks.* Activities like putting coins in a piggy bank or vending machine, twisting caps, and repositioning a writing implement in the hand encourage children to perform in-hand manipulations.

2. *Color with crayons and markers.* Coloring with crayons and markers inherently requires in-hand manipulation from taking off the cap with the same hand holding the pen to flipping it over to color.

3. *Use playing cards.* Fanning the cards with one hand is a good "trick" that involves in-hand manipulation. Playing card games that require the child to hold several cards at one time encourages repositioning the cards as each card is removed from the hand.

4. *Use materials that require manipulation to accomplish a goal.* Threading a string through beads or macaroni involves in-hand manipulation. Filling a jar with a narrow opening with small items, such as counting beads or beans, necessitates in-hand manipulation if the child has more than one item in both hands.

▩▩▩ **III. G. How good are the child's constructional abilities?**

Construction refers to the creation of something new in two or three dimensions—drawing, writing, building with blocks. Children may have difficulty with construction for many reasons: motor, perceptual, or cognitive. Thus, understanding the underlying problem can be crucial to improving construction.

Interaction Strategies

1. *Build something together and then have fun knocking it down.* Building and knocking down and building again can provide endless fun. The level of difficulty can be modified based on the child's ability, from a simple tower to a complex bridge that then gets rammed by a truck.

2. *Color and draw together.* Take turns drawing on request—dogs, horses, dinosaurs. You are limited only by your imagination. Drawing pictures together on one sheet of paper encourages imitation, problem solving, and conversation. Taking turns making suggestions about what is needed in the picture not only promotes dialogue, but also gives the adult the opportunity to suggest drawing items that require different types of movements (e.g., a circle for the sun, a line for a road).

3. *Create props for play or make crafts for presents.* Make creating playthings fun by planning what is needed and making them together. For example, if the child wants to be a princess, you can plan what the princess needs (e.g., a crown, a wand, a bead necklace) and make these items together. The adults help think of what is needed and provide the materials, while letting the child lead the way in planning and making the props. The adult suggests, models, and supports only as needed.

4. *Construct cards for friends.* Cut out or tear pictures from magazines, newspapers, or old greeting cards to glue onto paper. Fold the paper to make a card and then write or draw on the inside. Doing this together can be a fun activity using a variety of fine motor skills.

5. *Choose activities that involve building something and then playing with it.* Put together train set and then play with it. Build with dominoes, K'NEX, Bead Buddies, or tiles. Build a structure with Legos or Tinkertoys from a model. Turn-taking is important to make this a social interaction and to model different construction actions.

Environmental Modifications

In addition to interpersonal strategies that may support the child's developing skills in construction, environmental modifications can be useful. Depending on the findings from TPBA2, the team may want to consider some of the following environmental modifications.

1. *Use medium or large objects.* In general, big or medium-sized objects are easier than small ones for construction. Modify the size and shape of objects to fit the child's level, but still provide a slight challenge.

2. *Use objects with a purpose.* Construction play using objects without a defined purpose (e.g., sand, water) is much less stressful for young children. Using objects purposefully, however, provides a goal for children to guide their actions. For example, playing in the sand with a stick may encourage some fine motor use, but the addition of a dump truck, action figures, small rocks, and a shovel or a spoon provides an incentive for the child to combine these items in a meaningful way. Support from another child or adult adds further motivation.

3. *Computer use.* The computer provides an excellent medium for doing virtual construction. Software is available for creating art, puzzles, and whole virtual towns. Varying types of modifications of keyboards, control pads, and other control devices can be used to modify the computer so that children with more severe motor disabilities or children who are developmentally more immature can use the computer successfully.

III. H. How effectively does the child use tools?

Tool use is critical to many functional activities. If children cannot use tools effectively and efficiently, their actions will not be successful. To be efficient and effective, children must be able to use tools as an extension of their bodies. This is as true whether the tool is a bat or a pencil. The most effective method for improving tool use is practice.

Interaction Strategies

1. *Make practice fun.* Young children are more interested in the activity than in holding the tool perfectly. It's okay to help the child hold an implement correctly, but unless the grasp is interfering with doing the task, don't worry too much about correcting it. The adult needs to encourage repetition in a fun activity that the child wants to continue.

2. *Encourage the child to color or draw pictures.* Outlining pictures before coloring them provides young school-age children with a very pleasing outcome as well as practice following lines. Give the child a reason to draw that is motivating; for example, drawing pictures of what to get at the grocery store, so the child can take his own "grocery list." Make pictures of favorite pets, people, or activities to share with other family members or to take to school to share with teachers and friends. The adult's role during this interaction is to comment on what is seen, problem solve with the child about what else could be added or how something could be represented (e.g., rub a crayon over a texture placed under the paper to show grass), and help the child add written labels to the picture.

3. *Use prewriting activities before ever placing a pencil in a child's hand.* Children who have difficulty with fine motor activities often can benefit from additional proprioceptive (pressure) input to the muscles and joints of the fingers, hands, and arms. Resistive activities give children a clear sense of where these body parts are and what they are doing. Play activities that involve pushing or pulling materials with the fingers, hands, and arms provide such resistive input. For example, picking up and moving a heavy item, such as pouring from a pitcher into a cup or container, provides input to the whole arm. Children can form shapes or letters with clay or in sand, lentils, or rice to provide additional input as well.

4. *Do not force young children to write or copy letters before they are ready.* Children write when they have a reason, when they are motivated to convey a message, and when they feel they can. The adult can play a role in helping children to be interested and motivated to write but should not demand that writing be practiced for the sake of writing.

Environmental Modifications

In addition to interpersonal strategies that may support the child using tools, environmental modifications often are useful. Depending on the findings from TPBA2, the team may want to consider some of the following environmental modifications.

1. *Modify the tools a child is using.* Practice with markers or paint brushes first, because these are easier to control. Modify materials so that the child can grasp and manipulate the tool more easily. Pencil grips; pencils that are smaller, heavier, lighter, or bigger (easier); or those that have a modified shape may be helpful.

2. *Use different scissors.* Many types of adapted scissors are available commercially: self-opening scissors, loop scissors, Short Cuts scissors adapter (the bumper between the handles prevents the scissor blades from closing, allowing only short, successful cutting strokes on the line). Modification of the activity (snipping paper to make a fringe instead of cutting a long strip) can give the child needed practice and enable him to be successful.

3. *Use utensils.* Many children enjoy using utensils such as tongs, strawberry pickers, or tweezers. These encourage grasp patterns similar to those used on writing implements. By creating fun activities with a useful purpose (e.g., picking up ice cubes with tongs to put in the child's drink, picking up beads with tweezers to make a necklace), the child is encouraged to do a task that might otherwise be uninteresting or avoided.

4. *Use a slanted surface.* Drawing or writing on a slanted surface encourages good posture and also facilitates copying from a vertical surface.

ROUTINES FOR THE CHILD WHO NEEDS SUPPORT TO USE ARMS AND HANDS

The following are examples of how the above strategies can be incorporated into the child's daily routines at home and at school. In addition to the strategies noted at the beginning of the chapter, used by caregivers of children who do not have special needs, these may support the development of increased proficiency with arm and hand use.

Daily Routines (Home and Classroom)

Feeding/Eating

Eating provides a good opportunity to encourage hand use and development. Finger feeding encourages grasp and hand-to-mouth patterns for infants. The child's position for eating greatly affects the ability to use the hands (see TPBA2, Chapter 2, Subcategory I. Functions Underlying Movement). Once the child is positioned in a supportive upright position, using the hands to feed himself is easier. Finger foods help the child refine reach, grasp, pinch, in-hand manipulation, and release. Using age-appropriate sized utensils helps the child with early tool use. Older infants and toddlers learn to use a spoon and drink from a cup. Preschoolers master a fork and older children learn to cut with a knife and fork. Mealtime is a great time to promote using the hands in a lead/assist fashion. One hand holds the bowl while the other hand scoops with the spoon. Mealtime also provides opportunities for independence in opening containers promoting increased wrist movements and pinch. Adults can model, encourage, provide slight assistance, and provide modified tools as needed. Playful activities involving proprioceptive input (pushing and pulling) before mealtime also may be helpful.

Diapering/Toileting

For the infant, diapering may provide opportunities for playing with toys with two hands together at the midline of the body. It also may be a time for the child to reach and swipe at mobile toys. Adults can provide both the opportunity for such play, but also the motivation. Encourage the child to look and reach, comment, and show enthusiasm when the child is successful. Modify the placement of the toys of mobiles to require increasing effort.

Diapering and toileting provide the opportunity for the child to undo and do fasteners and to use two hands to pull down and pull up pants. For children with disabilities, modified fasteners such as Velcro closures may be helpful (see TPBI2, Chapter 3, Section VI. Strategies for Improving Sensorimotor Contributions to Daily Life). Use of reverse chaining, or having the child complete the final step and then going backward to add each additional step, helps children feel successful. Providing opportunities to use fasteners on dolls during play, on the adult when dressing to go outside, or on siblings or peers encourages practice, which facilitates efficiency of movements. Use of toilet paper to clean oneself, a task not mastered for several years, allows children to practice using hands without the advantage of vision. Although young children should not be expected to successfully complete the wiping task, they should be given the opportunity to try, because this motivates the child to achieve independence. Washing hands after toileting is important and gives the child a chance to practice grasping and rotating, and screwing/unscrewing of faucets. Children should have step stools or be positioned in such a way that they can reach the faucets. Grips or handle modifications can be used for children with more involved motor difficulties.

Dressing

Dressing is reliant on coordinated arm and hand use and on bilateral coordination. During dressing activities, the child will use two hands in different ways at times (one hand stabilizes the zipper, the other one pulls it up), and then at other times he will use two hands together for the same purpose (both thumbs hook the sock and pinch it, then put it on the foot). In addition, doing fasteners demands independent and skilled use of fingers and the ability to use two hands to align and manipulate the fasteners. Working on fasteners helps improve and refine grasp skills and wrist movements. Adults may support dressing skills with the use of successful approximations (e.g., adding small steps the child can do successfully) and encouragement for effort and independence. Adaptive fasteners or clothing may be needed (see TPBI2, Chapter 3, Section VI. Strategies for Improving Sensorimotor Contributions to Daily Life). Putting on and pulling off garments requires movement against resistance, accurate movement of body parts, and strength. Children who have low tone, high tone, or reduced strength may find dressing challenging and need additional assistance. Activities that assist children with increased or decreased tone, such as positioning techniques or relaxation or arousal strategies, may be needed before and during dressing (see TPBI2, Chapter 3, Section I. Strategies for Improving Functions Underlying Movement). In addition, buttons or sashes fastened in back require the coordinated use of hands in the absence of vision. Consequently, activities that help children know where their body parts are and help them understand how to plan motor movements also may be required (see TPBI2, Chapter 3, Section IV. Strategies for Improving Motor Planning and Coordination).

Going Out

Going out on errands provides numerous opportunities for skilled arm and hand use: opening and closing doors, handling coins, reaching for objects on a shelf. Going out also may include a stop at the park or a restaurant, both of which provide opportunities for arm and hand use (see the following sections). Adults can make these outings into opportunities for functional practice of fine motor skills. Instead of having the child passively sitting in the car seat, stroller, or grocery cart, the adult needs to involve the child in the actions for each outing. The child can help manipulate and push in the seat belt fastener (arm, hand, and finger coordination and manipulation); pick up items (grasp);

examine them (two-handed manipulation); and place them in the basket (release). While paying for items, the child can find and pick out coins (pincer grasp and in-hand manipulation) and give them to the clerk (reach and release). Conscious thought on the part of the adult as to how the child can participate in each activity of the day will enable the child to have numerous opportunities for practice of fine motor skills, thus facilitating the development of fluidity and efficiency of movement.

Play Routines (Home and Classroom)

Face-to-Face Play

Young children enjoy songs and games with actions. Such play provides opportunities for repetition of arm, hand, and finger movements. For instance, Peekaboo provides the opportunity for the infant to grasp, move the arms up and down, and release a blanket. Tickle games encourage the infant or child to reach to initiate and/or continue the social routine. Songs and fingerplays, such as "Itsy Bitsy Spider," motivate the child to imitate finger movements, remember sequences of actions, and provide opportunities to practice coordinated bilateral finger movements.

This play is almost always interactive in nature, and thus the adult can facilitate more precise movements by slowing down the actions modeled, exaggerating the movements, and providing wait time. When needed, the adult can give physical cues or assistance for shaping the hands or fingers or moving the arms. Children with cognitive delays may need additional wait time, modeling, or assistance, whereas children with motoric challenges may need supportive positioning or strategies to facilitate changes in muscle tone (see TPBI2, Chapter 3, Section I. Strategies for Improving Functions Underlying Movement) or motor planning (see TPBI2, Chapter 3, Section IV. Strategies for Improving Motor Planning and Coordination).

Physical Play

Physical play provides opportunities for children to build arm and hand strength through climbing, pushing, pulling, and carrying heavy items. Play on the monkey bars, climbing structures, and rock-climbing walls builds upper arm and hand strength needed for functional play. Ball games help build coordination and use of two hands together. Resistive movements are inherent to physical play (e.g., swings, climbers, rough-and-tumble). These promote development of strength and bilateral coordination and give children a clear sense of where their limbs are in space. Adults support the development of arm, hand, and finger use by providing opportunities for the child to play on equipment that encourages such activity. The adult can encourage the child to pull a peer or sibling in a wagon or stroller, and can help support the child as they try to maintain balance while holding on to the sides of a moving wagon or stroller.

Manipulative Play

Manipulative play is one of the most important ways to develop hand skill, and a variety of different toys, games, and daily activities promote development of a child's arm and hand use. Rattles provide opportunities for the infant to grasp, carry, and release and work on exploring toys with the mouth. Later, children love putting things on top of and in various containers, and they begin to combine small objects in various ways. Puzzles and construction-type toys strengthen eye–hand coordination and fine motor grasp and release. Children are highly motivated to build with Duplos or Legos, make necklaces of tiny beads, do crafts, dress dolls, create with playdough, and engage in other similar activity. Car and train sets allow opportunities for pushing cars on the floor to build up arm and hand strength. Tool sets allow for banging, pushing, pulling, and twisting promoting development of the wrist. Toys that require more refined pinching, such as Lite-Brite or the Operation game, help strengthen pinch. All of these activities build fine motor skill. Many involve resistive movements to the fingers, which promote strength and give children a clear sense of where their fingers are in relation to their bodies and the environment.

Adults not only should provide materials that are developmentally appropriate for children with special needs, but also they must find ways to encourage the use of fine motor skills in manipulative play. Adults who interact with children with delayed fine motor skills or challenges due to motor disabilities also can provide needed supports for successful manipulative play. They need to ensure that the child's body is adequately supported so that the child's hands are free to play; provide toys that motivate the individual child's interests so the child *wants* to manipulate the object; modify toys so that the hands and fingers can accommodate the toy or tool needed; have social interactions that encourage and reward the child's efforts; and use assistive devices as needed to ensure that the child experiences success in meeting his or her goals.

Sensory Play

Manipulative experiences require tactile sensory input. It is, therefore, important that the child have an interest in and tolerance for some form of tactile play. Playing with playdough using cookie cutters and play tools (knife, fork, pizza cutter, playdough press, scissors) provides sensory play opportunities and also requires use of the hands in a skilled manner. The child gets the opportunity to open the container, take out the playdough, and put it away, while using two hands together. Fingerpaint and shaving cream provide the chance for exploring textures with the hands and isolating fingers while making pictures. Playing in water, sand, lentils, rice, beans, finger paint, and other media provides lots of tactile input to the hands and arms. They also generally involve resistance to movement of the fingers, hands, and arms, thus providing a clear sense of where these body parts are located. Children who have difficulty tolerating tactile input of various kinds may need additional support to benefit from these experiences (see TPBI2, Chapter 3, Section V. Strategies for Improving Modulation of Sensation). The adult initially may need to provide textures that are more appealing to the child to decrease sensitivity, provide increased weight (through heavier objects) to give more input to the child, or give the child tools to use that decrease the child's direct contact with the aversive textures. Tool use in sensory play is recommended, because it enables the child to try various means for manipulating materials while giving the child an opportunity to practice manipulating the hand and fingers. Sensory play can take place throughout daily routines as well, when the child takes a bath (e.g., with bubbles, sponges, wash cloths); plays on the carpet or in the bed (picking up lint and other small items); and plays outdoors in the grass, rocks, sand, and/or leaves.

Dramatic Play

Dramatic play provides innumerable opportunities for use of arms, hands, and fingers. Children need to manipulate dress-up costumes, props, and dolls or action figures during dramatic play. Almost every play sequence involves the need to use fine motor skills to represent the actions of the child's story. Thus, it provides the same opportunities for hand and arm use described previously in dressing, manipulative play, sensory play, and so on. Dramatic play is a combination of all forms of play. For children with special needs dramatic play may be challenging for a variety of reasons (e.g., cognitively limited ideas, difficulty carrying out the actions needed, lack of social skills needed for interaction, or lack of communication skills needed to express dramatic play ideas). As dramatic play provides a stimulating, purposeful means for practicing fine motor skills, the adult needs to intervene in any of the areas of need to ensure that the child can carry out dramatic play. Particularly for children with motor challenges, the adult may need to provide assistive devices or interactional supports to enable the child to successfully play with peers within dramatic play. As a play partner within the dramatic play, the adult can observe and assist as needed when the child is frustrated or avoiding tasks requiring arm and hand use.

Reading and Learning Routines

Circle Time

Circle time provides an ideal opportunity for songs and games with actions. During circle time, the child has the chance to explore props from the book with the hands and then pass them to her friends. She uses the arms and hands to do motions to her favorite songs and also to raise her hand when the teacher asks a question, all working on the development of arm use. Adults need to ensure that all children in the circle participate in these type of activities. It is easy to overlook the quiet child who sits passively and does not get involved in movements. The teacher may need to have that child sit or stand near him, so that the child can "help" the teacher show the other children what to do. Even if some assistance is needed, the child will most likely like to be the "leader." Another alternative is to have a classroom aide assist the child by modeling or prompting needed actions. It is important, however, to address fine motor skills at other times throughout the day. It is very difficult for a child with motor concerns to keep up with a group. Preparatory activities involving proprioceptive input may be helpful, as described previously.

One-on-One Reading

For the infant and young child, book reading involves primarily visual-motor, cognitive, communication, and social skills. In the fine motor area, book reading allows opportunities for the child to hold the book with one hand and turn the pages with the other. It also provides chances for the child to isolate the finger to point to interesting pictures, letters, or words in the book. For children with fine motor difficulties, adaptations can be made to make participation in book reading easier. Board books with heavier pages can be easier for developmentally younger children to handle. Adaptations such as "page fluffers" (e.g., a thick substance placed on the corners of pages to place a space for fingers to go between the pages); tabs for the child to manipulate to turn the page (e.g., the end of a Popsicle stick); or pop-up, moveable parts, or tactile books that encourage manipulation also are motivating to children. Adults also can choose books that entice the child to explore and examine. Books with simple large, colorful pictures; pictures of real objects and people; simplified stories; and intriguing characters provoke the child to examine details and turn the pages to see what happens next. Adults can track the words of the story with their finger, ask questions that require the child to point to pictures, and request that the child help by turning the pages. For children with severe motor impairment, a control pad on the computer can enable the child to turn the pages of books on-line or scanned in to the computer. Positioning also is important, so that the child can see optimally and manipulate the book freely.

Science and Math

Science and math projects require the use of the child's hands to dig in the dirt, feel bugs or other animals, or explore rocks. This helps promote the child's sense of touch and pressure and discrimination of these senses through the hands. Science and math are not primarily about hand use, although both often involve use of manipulatives. Thus, a secondary gain from math and science may be the opportunity to practice hand skills. Teachers may need to encourage exploration, because some children may avoid tasks that are difficult. Give the child the adaptive tools if needed (e.g., larger handles, Velcro strap attached to hand, a rubber grip, visual cues for finger placement). Materials also may need to be modified so the child can be successful. For example, holes may need to be made larger to enable the child to get objects inside. Exploratory tools may need to be bigger or have adaptive handles or grips. The environment may need to be modified so the child can more easily reach and use the materials. Seating may need to be adapted so the child can be in a position that facilitates use of both hands. The adult needs to watch, comment, suggest, model, and modify as needed.

▓▓▓▓▓   KEN

Ken is 4 years old. He attends all-day child care while his mother, a single parent, works. Ken is charming and enthusiastic. However, when compared with classmates, his fine motor and construction skills are quite poor. Consequently, Ken avoids most activities that demand these skills. Ken holds crayons in a primitive fashion, grasping them with a cylindrical grasp, much like one would typically hold a small glass. He colors by moving his whole arm. His in-hand manipulation also is poor and once he has grasped an object, he finds it very difficult to move the object around in his hand without stabilizing it against his body or the table. When attempting to cut with scissors, he places his thumb and first finger (rather than the middle finger) through the loops. He does not enjoy crafts or building with blocks. When developing recommendations for use at home and in the classroom, the team made these suggestions for interactional supports and environmental modifications.

Interaction Strategies

1. *Consultation from a therapist on the development of fine motor skills is recommended. Do activities suggested by the therapist in a fun, interactive way. Perhaps you and the therapist can take turns or she can instruct you as to how they should be done.*

2. *Support all self-initiated efforts that Ken makes to engage in fine motor or construction activity as a reason for celebration.*

3. *Do not require Ken to engage in fine motor or construction activities for too long, because these activities take a lot of energy and concentration.*

4. *Ken loves knocking things over. Build towers together from blocks or boxes. When the tower is at its highest, knock it over with great ceremony.*

5. *Do crafts or bake cookies and decorate them together. Ken loves the company of adults and is more likely to engage in difficult activities if he gains your company while doing it.*

Environmental Modifications

1. *Make sure Ken has lots of opportunities to dig in sand, play in water, and engage in other activity that provides resistance to the movements of arms and hands. This will help him understand how the arms and hands move.*

2. *Large-diameter crayons or markers may be easier for Ken to use than pencils or pens.*

3. *Adapted scissors with four loops (two for an adult; two for Ken) may provide a mechanism for teaching him to use scissors effectively.*

4. *Provide Ken with lots of fun opportunities for engaging in fine motor activity (e.g., crafts, dress-up, clay). These might be centers in preschool because many children will enjoy them. Do not insist that Ken do those activities, but invite him to join in the fun.*

KEYS TO INTERVENTION BY DEVELOPMENTAL AGE

The following ideas are directed toward children who are functioning at approximately the following levels. The suggestions are not meant to be comprehensive, but rather indicate potential areas for exploration.

Developmental age	Arm and Hand Skills	Keys to intervention
Birth to 3 months	Grasp develops such that the child can hold object placed in hand. Tries to swipe at objects.	Provide high-contrast, visually stimulating objects (e.g., mobiles) placed within child's reach so he can swipe. Attach rattles or other objects to the wrist to draw child's attention.
3–6 months	Grasp is getting stronger. Can hold a small toy or rattle while shaking or banging. Transfers objects hand to hand. Can move object to mouth. Rotates wrist, turns, and manipulates objects crudely. Is developing use of two hands together for reaching and holding. Can brace large objects against the body with two hands.	Place rattle, spoon, or cracker in the child's hand. Applaud child's efforts at banging, shaking, bringing object to mouth.
6–9 months	Is developing control of objects between thumb and fingers. Increased finger and thumb dexterity allows baby to pick up and manipulate small objects. Begins to point and poke with index finger. Purposeful release of objects. Inspects toys. Plays with two toys, one in each hand, banging together. Can combine hand skills with standing, sitting, and so forth.	Place objects on the tray, coffee table, or floor for child to grasp and manipulate, poke (e.g., soft books, small blocks). Encourage child to hand objects to you or to place them in large containers. Blow bubbles and encourage child to pop them.
9–12 months	Is developing the ability to use an increasing number of grasps: 3-jaw chuck, spherical grasp, neat pincer. Can move small objects from finger to palm. Begins to make appropriate wrist and hand adjustments to accommodate for different weights. One hand stabilizes and the other manipulates. Develops control of release from flinging to putting 1-inch tiny objects into small holes. Objects still do not always land where intended. Can stack up to six 1-inch cubes. Reaches across midline. Begins to prefer one hand.	Offer objects of all shapes, sizes, and weights for child to grasp, manipulate, push, and pull with one or both hands. Offer containers of varying sizes for child to place objects in. Stack blocks together and knock them down.
12–18 months	Increasing strength and control of fingers enables child to use tools and manipulate objects. Much better use of two hands together. Can perform sequences of alternating two-hand movements.	Continue to offer objects of varying sizes, shapes, weights. Encourage child to use a spoon independently. Provide toys that can be pulled apart.

Developmental age	Arm and Hand Skills	Keys to intervention
12–18 months (*continued*)	Beginning of two-hand tool use. Release continues to become more precise.	Introduce crayons or markers in supervised sessions. Sing simple songs and clap along. Stack boxes.
18–24 months	May begin to string beads. Uses hands consistently in a lead-assist fashion. Grasps crayon in palm and turns hand thumb up or grasps crayon with fingers. Can move one or two small objects from palm to fingers. Can unscrew bottle cap (simple rotation). Can turn pages of book. Construction: Builds tower of 4 blocks. Completes 4–5-piece puzzle. Tool use: Begins to use simple tools (e.g., toy hammer).	Provide small objects for the child to combine, put inside. Use objects that require two hands: jars with lids, beads, wind-up toys. Place small objects such as poker chips or cookies in the palm to encourage the child to manipulate them to the fingertips. Provide opportunities to construct with large blocks, simple puzzles, plastic tools. Provide exposure to a variety of picture books.
24–36 months	More ability to manipulate grasped objects (e.g., can unscrew bottle cap). Greater precision and control of release. Increasing competence in two-hand tool use. Stronger hand preference.	Offer increasingly sophisticated objects for opening, closing, operating. Do simple puzzles. Roll and toss balls.
36–48 months	Uses precision (tripod) grasp on pencil or crayon; uses effective power grasp on tools. Improving ability to manipulate grasped objects in one hand: can move coin from palm to fingers, separate pages, and/or roll a small piece of clay into a ball. Can throw small ball at least 3 feet. Can stack 9–10 small blocks. Stabilizes paper when coloring, drawing.	Increased use of construction toys. Encourage child to draw simple shapes and scribble. Use pegboards and puzzles. Play simple dress-up. Play catch with a large ball.
48–60 months	When drawing, movement comes from fingers rather than arm and hands. Can reposition crayon in one hand following grasp.	Introduce scissors in supervised situations. Encourage snipping, simple cutting. Drawing, puzzles, card games.
60–72 months	Manipulates tiny objects in fingertips without dropping. Can "walk" fingers down marker or pencil to get it into position for drawing. Uses two hands together well.	Offer increasingly small objects and encourage child to reposition them for use; for example, placing coins held in one hand in a piggy bank one at a time. String beads or macaroni. Cut out shapes. Do simple crafts.

3

Facilitating Sensorimotor Development

IV. Strategies for Improving
Motor Planning and Coordination

with Anita C. Bundy

Goal Attainment Scale

1	2	3	4	5	6	7	8	9
Has volitional movements for simple, routine actions or events. Does not attempt novel or multistep actions independently.		Has difficulty understanding what to do with objects or things in the environment. Uses repetitive actions without a functional goal and has difficulty executing even simple, nonroutine action sequences.		Can conceive of a goal, but needs prompting, demonstration, conscious effort, and multiple opportunities for practice to organize and execute a multistep task. Actions may appear awkward and slow and results may be inaccurate.		Can conceive of a goal, but needs prompting or demonstration and conscious effort to sequence and execute the necessary actions to achieve a multistep, complex task. With effort and practice, can achieve accuracy.		Can conceive of a goal, and with little conscious effort, can organize and sequence a complex sequence of actions effectively and efficiently to achieve the intended objective.

Motor planning is part of larger umbrella term, *praxis.* Praxis is the ability of the brain to organize—to conceive of a goal, to structure, and carry out a sequence of events to achieve the plan. Motor planning is the ability to organize and carry out motor activities to accomplish unique tasks. This often is broken into three processes: *ideation,* or knowing what one wants to do; *organization,* or creating a nonconscious physical plan for actions; and *execution,* or the actual physical completion of the actions needed to accomplish the task. Simply stated, motor planning is the ability to carry out multisequence tasks quickly and efficiently. Motor planning involves all types of movements, including gross motor, involving organizing the actions of the trunk and all extremities; fine motor skills, involving the ability to control arms, hands, and fingers; and oral motor skills, involving the coordination of tongue, teeth, lips, and jaw.

Motor planning is important because it is involved in learning all purposeful physical acts. Motor planning skills are necessary for social interaction, academic skills, language and communication, and all tasks requiring movement.

Once action sequences are practiced and learned, they become automatic and do not require conscious thought. This happens with the movements required to walk, talk, eat, and read and write. Adequate motor planning skills are essential for independent functioning and learning new skills.

APPROPRIATE MOTOR PLANNING AND COORDINATION

Children with good motor planning skills are able to look at a situation and determine what actions need to be taken to accomplish what they want to do. They can initiate an action and sequence the necessary steps to complete the task. They understand where their body parts are in space and can move them in the required direction, for the required amount of space, with the appropriate amount of speed and the necessary force to achieve their goal. When done, they can then turn their attention to other tasks. Children with good motor planning skills are able to coordinate their actions effectively to organize themselves and their environment. When asked to perform a routine skill, they can do so quickly and efficiently. When asked to perform a novel set of actions, they can perform them—even if not totally accurately—relatively smoothly after observation of the skills and verbal instruction. Children with good motor planning skills have an awareness of where their body parts are in space and how to coordinate movements and integrate actions with objects in the environment.

Appropriate Motor Planning and Coordination in Practice

IV. A. Does the child have good ideas for using toys?

Daily Routines (Home and Classroom)

- *Infant/toddler:* The infant reaches for the bottle, grasps it, and puts it to her mouth. The toddler pokes her spoon in the jar of applesauce, scoops, then pulls the spoon out, and eats the applesauce.

- *Young child:* The young child sets the table for snack, placing a plate, napkin, and plastic fork at each place.

Play Routines (Home and Classroom)

- *Infant/toddler:* The infant picks up a block in each hand and bangs them together, smiling. The toddler picks up a small baby bottle and puts it to the doll's mouth. Then she puts the doll in the doll crib.

- *Young child:* The young child puts on a fire hat, grabs a stick to use as a hose to put out a make-believe fire, and climbs into a cardboard box as a fire truck.

Classroom Routines

During music time, the children do the Chicken Dance, making their arms into wing shapes and stomping their feet. Then the teacher plays music and the children make up dances to go with other animals.

IV. B. How well does the child initiate, terminate, and sequence actions?

Daily Routines (Home and Classroom)

- *Infant/toddler:* The infant is laid on the diaper table by his mother. He lifts his legs, anticipating the diaper, and then puts them down while his mother finishes diapering him. The toddler pulls off his pants and then steps out of his diaper. He runs to the tub and calls his mother to put him in the tub.

- *Young child:* Mom tells the young child to get his jacket and shoes on and get his lunch bag. He complies.

Play Routines (Home and Classroom)

- *Infant/toddler:* The infant dumps the balls out of the container, puts the lid on, and starts putting them one by one in the hole in the lid until all the balls are in the container. The toddler gets a piece of paper and pencil and makes scribbles on it. She then takes it to the adult and says it is a movie ticket.

- *Young child:* The young child rides the tricycle around the sidewalk loop, stops at the stop sign, rides around little orange cones, then comes back to the "finish" line. "I made it!" he shouts.

Classroom Routines

During the time for centers, the young child picks up his picture tag, places it on a piece of Velcro on the chart by the center he chose, completes his activity, and then takes his picture to another center.

IV. C. How good are the child's spatial and temporal abilities?

Daily Routines (Home and Classroom)

- *Infant/toddler:* Mother holds out her hands and says, "Come see Mommy." The baby stands at the coffee table and doesn't move. Mom moves to within a foot of her and holds out her hands again. This time, the infant takes a step forward. The toddler climbs up onto the step stool in front of the toilet, turns, and waits for her father to lift her up.

- *Young child:* Mom has the laundry basket at the foot of the stairs. The young child is throwing dirty clothes down, trying to hit the basket.

Play Routines (Home and Classroom)

- *Infant/toddler:* The infant drops a ball down the ramp toy and watches as it swirls down the ramp. She waits for the ball to come out of the bottom. The toddler runs away, turns, looks, waits for the adult, then runs off again until he gets to the wall, where he stops and waits for the adult to scoop him up.

- *Young child:* Hula hoops are set out all over the playground. The young child takes big and little steps to be able to step in and not on the hoops. When the teacher says, "Go faster!" he goes faster on the ones closer together, but slower on the ones farther apart.

Classroom Routines

In the block area, a young child constructs an airplane runway with a long string of blocks and then builds a control tower. After this, he stacks two blocks and places a long block horizontally across the top. He places this structure on the "runway" and pushes it for take-off.

▰▰▰▰ **IV. D. Does the child seem to have a good sense of the body? Of objects as an extension of the body?**

Daily Routines (Home and Classroom)

- *Infant/toddler:* The infant crawls across the crib, pulls up on the crib bars, and reaches over toward the pet cat. The toddler hangs on to the railings of the banister as she climbs the steps. At the top, she turns around and scoots down on her stomach.

- *Young child:* The young child's mom wakes him up and tells him to get dressed. He puts on his underwear, pants, and shirt independently.

Play Routines (Home and Classroom)

- *Infant/toddler:* Dad is holding the infant and tips her backward so she is looking up-side-down. The infant laughs, and when Dad pulls her up, she throws herself back again. The toddler climbs up on the couch and jumps on his father. Dad lifts him into the air above his head. The toddler raises his arms and legs and says, "Fly me, Daddy."

- *Young child:* The young child climbs up on the chair and spreads his arms, saying, "Superman!" He jumps down and runs around the room pretending to fly. He leaps onto a pillow and says, "Got you, bad guy!"

Classroom Routines

When feeding the hamster in its cage, the young child uses a stick to slip under the top of the cage and prop it open. She then takes a scoop with a long handle, scoops pellets out of the food jar, puts her arm into the top of the cage, and empties the scoop into the food cup. She fills another long-handled scoop with water at the sink and returns to fill the water cup.

▰▰▰▰ **IV. E. How well does the child organize clothing and personal space?**

Daily Routines (Home and Classroom)

- *Infant/toddler:* The infant crawls to the open drawer, pulls out a shirt, and puts in on top of his head. Mother tells the toddler to pick up her toys. She puts the doll in the doll bed, the book on the shelf, and the toys in the toy box.

- *Young child:* Arriving at school, the young child puts his backpack in his cubby, takes of his boots and puts them on the boot shelf, takes off his coat and hangs it up, and goes into the classroom to play.

Play Routines (Home and Classroom)

- *Infant/toddler:* The infant stands up in the crib and one by one starts to throw out the stuffed animals, the blankets, and all the items in the crib, laughing as each one hits the floor. The toddler picks out an animal puzzle, dumps out the pieces, and one by one fits the animals in their appropriate spots.

- *Young child:* In the dramatic play area, the young child is dressing her friend as the princess. She carefully places the crown on her friend's head, wraps a feather boa around her neck, and puts plastic high heels on her feet.

Classroom Routines

The bell rings and the young child starts to pick up his blocks. He places each one on the shelf in the space marked for that shape block.

IV. F. Does the child generate appropriate force?

Daily Routines (Home and Classroom)

- *Infant/toddler:* The infant is requesting more cereal by slapping the tray on the high chair, nodding his head, and bouncing on his bottom. The toddler gently pats and then kisses her new baby brother.

- *Young child:* Mom says, "Be quiet, now. The baby is sleeping." The young child walks on tip toes and gently closes the bedroom door.

Play Routines (Home and Classroom)

- *Infant/toddler:* The infant carefully stacks one big foam block on top of another. The toddler is pushing a baby stroller around the room. She pushes slowly, then faster, saying, "Hurry, Baby."

- *Young child:* The young child and his friend are building a spaceship with Tinker-Toys. He looks for the pieces he wants and pushes them together. Then he looks and finds another piece; when it doesn't go in, he pushes harder until it fits.

Classroom Routines

As the class lines up to go out for recess, the young child assigned to be "Door Person of the Day" pulls open the heavy door and then holds it open for her classmates to go through.

IV. G. Does the child perform actions in response to verbal request or demonstration?

Daily Routines (Home and Classroom)

- *Infant/toddler:* Mother is dressing the infant, she raises her hands and says, "Lift your arms!" The infant lifts her arms and waits while her Mother puts on her shirt. Mom is pouring syrup on the pancakes. "Me do it," the toddler insists. Mom gives him the plastic bottle and says, "Slowly. Pour slowly, so you don't get too much." He holds the bottle and tips it gently at first, then a little more until the syrup starts to come out.

- *Young child:* The young child watches as his Dad shows him how to open the adhesive bandage wrapper, take the plastic shields off of the ends, and put it on his knee. His Dad hands him another bandage and says, "Now you do one." The young child carefully does each step, checking in with his Dad for help when needed.

Play Routines (Home and Classroom)

- *Infant/toddler:* Dad makes a "raspberries" sound with his lips. The infant laughs and does the same. The caregiver is singing songs and fingerplays. The toddler watches and imitates the actions of the adult's fingers and body.

- *Young child:* On the playground, the young child is walking across the tilting teeter-totter. When his friend instructs him to "Don't hold on!" he takes his hands off the support bars and says, "Look! No hands!"

Classroom Routines

During story time, the teacher acts out the actions in the story and the young children watch and imitate her.

GENERAL PRINCIPLES FOR SUPPORTING
APPROPRIATE MOTOR PLANNING AND COORDINATION

Parents and caregivers, teachers, and other professionals do not think of their typical interactions with children as intervention to promote motor planning. Much of what they naturally do in their interactions, however, does promote the development of organized movements. The following are strategies that adults use with children, consciously or unconsciously, to support the development of coordinated movements.

Motivate

As children learn new movements, adults offer encouragement through words and gestures. They help set initial goals for the child to achieve (e.g., walking to Daddy), they encourage effort (e.g., "You're almost there!"), and they reinforce accomplishment (e.g., "You did it all by yourself!"). Motivation is critical for learning anything, and adults help move the child from wanting to do things to please the adult to the child learning new skills in order to please him- or herself.

Demonstrate

Showing the child how to do something is a commonly used strategy. From the first infant game of Peekaboo to more complicated activities such as learning how to bat a ball, parents and other significant adults model for children the actions they want them to perform. Usually, the total action is demonstrated and the child watches and then tries to imitate. If that is unsuccessful, the adult demonstrates the individual steps involved in a complex sequence of actions. For instance, the adult may have the child throw him a ball and model how to catch it. The adult will then throw the ball back to the child and say, "Catch." If the child stands there and gets hit by the ball, the adult may then say, "Put your arms out like this."

Give Physical Assistance

Physical assistance usually is given when a child is learning a skill initially or when the child is struggling with an action in a skill sequence. For example, the teacher who is helping a child learn to write may first demonstrate drawing a particular letter. If the child has difficulty with an aspect of the writing, the adult may then assist the child to physically feel the correct movement. For instance, when the child is learning to write a "C," the adult may help the child move the pencil in the correct direction.

Set a Goal

Adults help children select new skills they can accomplish. They constantly place new challenges in front of them. From crawling to the top of the stairs, to dressing oneself, to being able to being able to throw a ball into a basketball hoop, children respond to the challenges presented to them. Adults often select the challenges for young children. They decide when it is time for the child to do various activities independently (e.g., brushing teeth); buy specific toys to promote valued skills (e.g., a bat and ball); interact with the child in selected activities (e.g., putting together a puzzles vs. playing chase); choose to involve them in various community activities (e.g., swimming lessons or soccer); and they select the type of leisure and educational programs in which the child will participate (e.g., a play-based focus versus a structured academic focus).

All of these decisions influence the type of skills the child will experience, practice, accomplish, and perhaps those in which the child will learn to excel.

Give Directions

One strategy all parents use in teaching new skills, particularly motor skills, is to give directions on what the child needs to do. Instructions include what body part to move, how to move it, where to put it, how fast to move, what to change, and when to start and stop. For example, when the parent is trying to help a child make "cookies" from playdough, one might hear directions such as, "Use two hands. Roll it around like this. Put it down here, and push it flat. Push harder. That cookie is too big. Let's start over. Take some of the dough off. Now roll it real fast. That's it. Now, press it flat."

Comment or Ask Questions

Adults ask questions to get children to think about what they want to do or what they are doing. This helps children think about a goal or plan and helps children monitor their actions. For example, the parent might say, "What are you going to build with those blocks?" If the child does not have a plan, the parent may make a suggestion. If the child says something like, "I'm building a castle," the parent watches and comments or asks questions to stimulate ideas. For example, the adult may say, "Does this castle need a door?" or "The knights need a tower to watch for the dragon."

Break Down Actions

Adults help children learn complex motor skills or activities by breaking down the task into smaller motor challenges. For instance, when the child is learning to ride a tricycle, the adult may first push the child and help him or her learn to steer without pushing the foot pedals. Once the child is comfortable sitting on the tricycle and understands how to turn the handle bars, the adult then puts the child's feet on the pedals and helps him or her push first one and then the other pedal. After the child can pedal, the adult lets the child learn to pedal and steer at the same time.

Experiment

In addition to trying to get children to do skills the "correct" way, adults encourage children to try new actions and approaches. After a child learns to throw and catch, for example, the adult may start to throw the ball under his legs, over his head in a "hook shot," or backward. Experimenting allows children to have fun feeling different types of input and using their body parts in unusual ways.

THE PRINCIPLES IN PRACTICE

Adults employ a variety of strategies to support the child's motor planning skills. The following are examples of how caregivers use the previously mentioned strategies during the day at both home and school. These examples are approaches that most caregivers use naturally in their daily interactions with children. They are appropriate for most children with disabilities as well.

Daily Routines (Home and Classroom)

Feeding/Eating

Adults help children learn to scoop, to stab food with a fork, and to apply the correct pressure and direction to be able to cut pieces by directing their hand or providing some physical support. Children learn to balance a cup, pour without spilling, and carry their own utensils and dishes to the sink without spilling or falling when adults give the child encouragement and many opportunities to practice.

Diapering/Toileting

Although diapering is performed by the adult, infants learn to anticipate the movements needed and participate when adults encourage them to help. Toileting involves many complex action sequences, and parents help children learn these sequences by providing smaller versions of adult equipment (potty chairs) and prompting them for each step of the process.

Dressing

Learning independent dressing is supported by adults when they break down each task and let the child participate in each step in whatever way he or she can. For infants, this may mean raising their hands above their head to accept a t-shirt. The adult gives the toddler support and directions for how to participate, such as "Lift your foot." The older child is typically able to accomplish most of the gross motor tasks involved in dressing but may need prompting or physical assistance to handle small buttons or zippers.

Play Routines (Home and Classroom)

Face-to-Face Play

Most face-to-face games are played with infants and involve the parent demonstrating actions and waiting for an imitative response from the child. Toddlers often initiate the songs and fingerplays they are learning and adults help them shape their fingers, demonstrate new movements, and move with the rhythm of the songs. By preschool, children are able to learn to manipulate the pieces of board games and to take turns with adult support.

Physical Play

Physical activities often are a way to practice the skills that children are learning, such as crawling, rolling, and then running. With older children, physical play often involves equipment such as balls, kites, tricycles, or playground equipment. Adults help children take on the new challenges these pieces of equipment present by giving them the opportunities to experience different kinds of movement, encouraging practice and perseverance, and demonstrating or assisting as needed.

Manipulative Play

Toys can involve both fine and gross motor skills, but each new type of toy introduced requires children to either generalize patterns of skills they used before the new toy or to learn a new sequence of skills. Adults support learning by suggesting uses for the materials, asking questions, and demonstrating approaches.

Sensory Play

Different types of materials require varied approaches to manipulations. Fingerpaints and glue require a light touch with individual fingers. Cookie dough and playdough require more pressure and more whole-hand movements for much of the shaping. As the child develops the ability to draw, more fine motor precision is needed. Parents set limits and/or model how to play with messy materials and make suggestions for how to use paint brushes, markers, and pencils.

Reading and Learning Routines

Circle Time

Circle time requires being able to sit and participate in a group activity and then do actions as the teacher requests, either when called on or in unison. Children often are expected to be able to comply without much assistance from the teacher other than verbal directions.

One-on-One Book Reading

Parents assist young infants in turning pages by getting the task started and letting the child complete it. Toddlers are encouraged to get books by themselves, share them jointly with the adult, and return the book to the shelf. Young children often are taught by teachers how to make a book, first through modeling and dictation, and then through encouraging the child's drawing and writing. Adults can write additional words on the pages if necessary to convey the story.

Science and Math

For many science and math activities, children are required to separate, compare, and group materials in specific ways. Teachers model, suggest, question, direct, and encourage children's manipulation of objects to help them organize and develop patterns with the materials.

PLANNING INDIVIDUALIZED INTERVENTIONS FOR IMPROVING MOTOR PLANNING AND COORDINATION

Motor planning concerns are commonly seen in children with sensory integration issues and other developmental challenges. In infancy, motor planning issues may not be as evident because adults assist the child in most activities. However, as the child transitions from sensory exploration of the environment to movement with intent to achieve mastery, control of actions becomes increasingly necessary. Action sequences become longer and more complex. Children who have difficulty with functional use of objects, imitation of others, and conceptualizing and carrying out a play may have difficulty with learning new skills and have strained social interactions. Skills such as writing may be difficult and, consequently, negatively influence academic success. Motor planning difficulties can affect communication as well, if the child cannot produce and organize sounds, or sequence sounds into words and words into sentences. In addition, inability to accomplish desired goals can lead to frustration and lack of self-confidence.

For this reason, it is important for parents and professionals to be knowledgeable about a variety of strategies to help increase children's ability to move effectively through their environment and to know what they want to do and how to do it. In addition to the common strategies typically used by caregivers and teachers outlined earlier, the following techniques may be used to individualize programs for children with concerns relating to various aspects of motor planning.

▬▬▬ IV. A. Does the child have good ideas for using toys?

Children with motor planning concerns may not automatically know what to do with a novel toy. This is a problem with *ideation* that may limit the child's use of toys to a familiar pattern. For instance, children with autism spectrum disorders, fragile X syndrome, or limited cognitive abilities may repeat the same action with a toy innumerable times. Typically these children are using the toys because they enjoy the sensory input, rather than using the toy for a functional purpose. The child does not see the toy as having a variety of useful purposes, but rather performs the same actions that he or she has done before. These children may get "stuck" in a motor pattern, either because that is the only known action with a specific object or because that specific pattern provides satisfactory sensorimotor input (see TPBA2, Chapter 2, Subcategory V. Modulation of Sensation and Its Relationship to Emotion, Activity Level, and Attention). Children also may be limited in their ability to think of an action sequence (see TPBA2, Chapter 7, Subcategory V. Complexity of Play, and Subcategory III. Problem Solving). It should be noted that children who get into repetitive patterns often are resistant to physical assistance or direction. It is, therefore, necessary to use less directive and controlling methods. The following recommendations may support the child in conceptualizing more complex actions.

Interaction Strategies

1. *Create a relationship of trust.* For children to learn from adults, they need to feel safe, nurtured, and supported. Developing such a relationship can occur through playful interactions. Follow the child's lead, which means seeing what the child is interested in and directing your attention to that. Use any toy or object that is of interest. Watch what the child does with the toy spontaneously and then imitate the child or play next to the child with another similar toy. The child should not feel pressured to pay attention to the adult's agenda; rather, the child needs to know that what he or she is doing is fine. Once trust is established, mutual play can begin.

2. *Demonstrate a related action.* Build on the child's interests and familiar actions by taking the toy the child is using (a duplicate or similar toy) and modeling a different interesting action. For example, many children repetitively run a car or truck around or just crash them together. The adult can put another idea into the child's head by showing him or her an interesting "next" action. The adult can introduce a bridge, a tunnel, or a thin paper road into the play. This requires the child to modify his or her actions slightly.

3. *Demonstrate an unusual action.* Capture the child's attention by introducing an intriguing action that motivates the child to try something novel. For example, for the child who is moving toy cars repetitively, introducing a drive-through "car wash" may be captivating, especially if real water is involved. With a cookie sheet as a flat surface to catch the water, a makeshift tunnel, a bowl of soapy water, a dish "mop" with a handle, and a towel, the car wash is ready. While the child is playing with a car, the adult takes another car and models running it through the car wash, washing it, and drying it. This is a multistep task; when the child starts to imitate the adult's actions, the child will probably need verbal and physical prompts to move from one step to another. Repetition of this game with other cars (usually every car and truck available is tried!) leads to the child being able to complete the sequence without adult assistance.

4. *Create a need for a new action.* When the child encounters a problem, he or she needs to find a way to resolve the issue. This is sometimes done by obtaining an adult's assistance and sometimes by demonstrating behaviors (such as screaming) that bring in adult support. By creating a slight challenge, where the child can see a means for solving the problem independently, the child is encouraged to try a new action. For example, if the child has a favorite toy, the toy can be placed in a spot where the child has to use new movements, for example, climbing up on a chair to get his car off a shelf, or driving the car under the bed, so the child needs to commando crawl to get it.

5. *Suggest another idea.* A verbal suggestion may be sufficient to prompt a new idea. Depending on the child's hearing and attention to others, a verbal suggestion may pro-

vide a sufficient stimulus for modifying actions. For example, the child who is repetitively lining up blocks in a row may respond to the verbal suggestion, "Those blocks look like a train! Here comes the train, *toot-toot*! Push the train!"

6. *Prompt child-initiated ideas.* Raise questions such as, "What else could we do with . . . " or "How many ways could we . . . ?" Encourage the child to look at different aspects of the toys, equipment, or situation and think about the implications of each. For example, "What do you think this button does?" or "I wonder what would happen if. . . ." Encourage thinking of more than one answer: "That's one way to get up the hill. What is another way?"

7. *Motivate the child by making a new game.* Take the repetitive actions of the child and show the child how this can be a fun new game. For example, if the child is continuously throwing objects instead of using them functionally, the adult might make this into a game by showing the child how to throw balls into a basket instead, giving cheers for each successful attempt. This changes a purely sensory activity into a game with a goal and parameters. The child may respond positively to this slight modification of his actions, whereas if given a direction to do something else, he would resist.

8. *Use physical support as needed.* Some children may need a physical prompt or physical assistance to carry out a new task. Support should be the least amount necessary to enable the child to complete the action independently. Physical support should be reduced as soon as possible, so the child is actively performing self-initiated actions.

Environmental Modifications

In addition to interpersonal strategies that may support the child's understanding of how to use toys, environmental modifications often are useful. Depending on the findings from TPBA2, the team may want to consider some of the following environmental modifications.

1. *Provide related toys.* Arrange the environment so that the materials available are somehow potentially related. Instead of a random selection of toys, present toys that can help the child connect ideas. For example, instead of having a toy box or shelf full of varied play items, such as cars, dolls, books, and so forth, set out related toys. A doll, a baby bottle, and a tooth brush may provide a stimulus for higher level, functional play.

Teachers like to organize the storage of toys and materials by category (e.g., cars go here, blocks go there). For the child who has limited ideation, the arrangement by category may encourage limited play. Adults can use the arrangement of like materials to teach categorization, but then prompt higher level ideation by selecting a few related toys to place out on the floor or table to help children see relationships and combine toys for play.

2. *Use previous knowledge and experience.* Present toys and materials that are related to the child's experiences, so the memories of actual experiences may prompt ideas for action sequences. If the child has recently been to a zoo, plastic zoo animals and pretend food may prompt feeding the animals or making a zoo.

3. *Arrange the environment.* The location of objects or toys and materials in the environment is important. If all toys are visible, the child may be overwhelmed and retreat to the familiar. Have room dividers, doors on shelves, or a cover over the open shelves to limit the visual stimulation and temptation to just pull things off of the shelves.

4. *Use picture cues.* Action picture sequences, in combination with verbal suggestions, help children who are visual learners to see options. Some children may not re-

spond to adult verbal suggestions but will be interested in recreating actions seen in pictures.

5. *Eliminate toys on which the child perseverates.* Many children get "stuck" repeating actions with favorite toys. Eliminating these as an option for play can encourage the child to try new actions. Use the favorite toys as reinforcement for playing with other toys first.

6. *Start with familiar objects and materials in familiar environments, and add new actions.* Later, add unfamiliar objects and materials to the familiar environments and increase the actions with these new materials; then perform familiar actions in unfamiliar environments and, finally, unfamiliar actions in unfamiliar environments.

▪▪▪▪ IV. B. How well does the child initiate, terminate, and sequence actions?

Every action sequence requires initiation of a preliminary movement, transitions to subsequent actions in the sequence, and the ability to stop the actions in order to move on to something else. Children who have difficulty with organization of thoughts and/or actions, or who have trouble executing what they want to do, may struggle with part of or all of the steps in an action sequence. Assuming the child has an ability to think of what he or she wants to do, issues relating to difficulty carrying out the actions may stem from sensory processing concerns (e.g., avoidance of certain types of sensory input), ability to coordinate bilateral movements or movement of individual body parts simultaneously or in sequence, or ability to control the speed and precision of the desired movements.

Children with concerns related to action sequences have a difficult time planning how they should respond to actions as they are occurring (e.g., kicking the ball as it is approaching) and/or anticipating how they should respond to something that has not yet happened (e.g., positioning the glass so the adult can pour liquid into it). The following strategies may help the child learn all steps in an action sequence.

Interaction Strategies

1. *Start with simple movement sequences.* Some actions (e.g., waving an arm) are easier to perform than others (e.g., finger isolation). When trying to get children to initiate one action and follow it with another, start with actions that are easier to perform. For instance, playing Peekaboo with a baby requires only two simple actions, covering the face while holding the object to obscure the child's view, and then lowering the object. Playing Pease Porridge Hot is a more difficult sequence, requiring slapping the knees, then clapping, then slapping another person's hands. Gradually increase the complexity of the actions and games the child needs to do. The child will help determine the desired level, because most children resist or avoid activities they know are above their capability or will be frustrating. Make all actions fun and motivating for the child.

2. *Begin with whole-body movements.* Activities that require body parts moving together are easier than activities requiring the movement of specific body parts and inhibition of other body parts. For example, a game in which the child lies on the floor and kicks a ball with both feet and then bats the ball with both hands is easier to do in sequence than kicking with one foot and then batting with one hand.

3. *Start with activities that give self-corrective feedback.* Figuring out how to sequence a series of nesting dolls is difficult, but the child gets immediate feedback if one does not fit inside of another, or if a top does not fit on the base. The child can then try another size doll, using trial and error to succeed. Actions that require the child to think ahead and anticipate what will happen, such as riding a tricycle around a plastic cone, call for

the child to make adjustments in advance. This is more challenging, and often more frustrating, because the child is not sure what needs to be adjusted. Break this down into fun sequences. For example, the child does not have to get on a tricycle, pedal, and steer all at once. Make learning each step motivating. Just pushing the pedal forward and down so it knocks over an object can motivate the child to push that one foot. Moving the object to the other side or having another one set up slightly ahead of the first one will motivate pushing the second foot.

4. *Modify a familiar sequence.* After the child has performed a sequence numerous times, the actions of the sequence become routine. Once a routine becomes familiar, the messages to the brain and consequent physical responses become automatic, thus requiring less thinking. It is therefore less demanding for a child to add on to or modify one element of a sequence than it is to change the whole activity. For example, switching from diapers to underpants requires changing the starting position of the body, moving from lifting both legs at once to lifting one leg at a time and adding a step of pulling the pants up the body. For many children, this may seem like a totally new challenge rather than a modification of a routine. A slight modification, such as having the child lie down, having him lift both legs while the underpants are put on, and then standing him up and having him pull the pants up may offer just enough of a change of sequence for the first step in the new motor planning sequence. The other steps can then be added after this new sequence becomes familiar.

5. *Provide support for novel sequences.* The adult is not always able to break down or modify every situation a child encounters. Under these circumstances, it may be necessary to provide physical guidance and verbal directions or support. For example, the child care teacher may have a group of toddlers on the playground trying to climb up the ladder on the plastic sliding board. For the child who is struggling to figure out how to lift a foot and pull up at the same time, the teacher may both instruct and provide a physical prompt, lifting the child's foot.

6. *Add steps to familiar sequences.* As the child develops familiar routines or play sequences, the adult can prompt the addition of another step in the sequence. For example, as the child learns the first steps in the sequence to wash his or her hands (e.g., climbing the steps and turning on the water), the adult can model holding a bar of soap in both hands, rolling it over, placing it back on the dish, rubbing the hands back and forth, and rinsing. Even these steps may need to be broken down and practiced one at a time before moving on to the next step in the sequence.

7. *Use known objects to demonstrate a new sequence.* If the child has a favorite doll, it can be incorporated into teaching many new sequences, washing the baby's hair, brushing the baby's teeth, dressing the baby, and so forth. Even though the actions are different when performed on a doll, acting them out helps build a mental image of the action sequence. Having a mental image of the actions enhances memory.

8. *Involve favorite people as role models.* Children like to do the things they see their favorite people do. Children often will attempt a sequence that a peer does, even though it is difficult, whereas encouragement by an adult might result in resistance. Use their favorite people as role models whenever possible. Again, this helps to build a mental image of actions.

9. *Tell the child what action will finish the activity.* Tell the child the steps involved, what is first, next, and last. Knowing what is last helps the child to have a goal and also know when they are finished with a task.

10. *Develop a signal for termination of an activity.* Children with motor planning problems may have difficulty knowing when to stop. In addition to telling them what is the

final action, the adult can develop a signal (e.g., the sign for "all done") that is a cue for the child that it is time to do something else.

11. *Use backward chaining.* Teach the last step first, then add the next-to-last step, and so forth. This allows the child to be successful as he or she learns the sequence. This can be done for learning to brush teeth, get dressed, or almost any routine.

Environmental Modifications

In addition to interpersonal strategies that may support the child's ability to initiate, sequence, and terminate actions, environmental modifications often are useful. Depending on the findings from TPBA2, the team may want to consider some of the following environmental modifications.

1. *Use favorite books, movies, and television shows as stimuli.* The characters in favorite books, movies, and television shows perform numerous action sequences. Adults can take advantage of these characters by pointing out what they are doing and how they are doing it. They also can have the child point out what the child did first, next, last, and so forth. Both the visual and verbal input provide a mental rehearsal for the child.

2. *Use picture action sequence cues.* Some children can use specific action pictures as cues for what they should do next. For example, pictures of the child putting on her coat could be hung next to her coat. She can then look at these for a reminder when she gets stuck.

3. *Arrange objects in action sequence cues.* Some children need concrete reminders of what is involved in an action sequence. For example, when a class was dramatizing a book with a sequence of actions at Halloween, the teacher hung up a sequence of objects on a clothes line to remind the children of the next action in the sequence. The boots went "stomp, stomp," the shirt went "shake, shake," the hat went "nod, nod," and so forth. The visual cues reminded the child of the word sequence and the actions that accompanied the words.

4. *Apply learned sequences in new situations.* Once a child has learned a sequence of actions in a familiar situation, such as home or school, take the need to use the actions into a different environment. For example, once the child has learned how to play catch with Daddy in the backyard, go to the park where the grass is different, there is different terrain, and there are new distractions. The ability to apply new skills and modify them for new situations is important.

5. *Reduce distractions in the environment.* Auditory, visual, tactile, or other sensory distractions can reduce ability to focus attention on the task at hand.

6. *Reduce the number of battery-operated toys.* Battery-operated toys require only a push of a button. Children need toys that they actually need to wind up, push, and pull themselves and maneuver without benefit of a remote. Although battery-operated toys are undoubtedly easier for the child to use, they do nothing to increase the child's ability to carry out a sequenced plan of action.

IV. C. How good are the child's spatial and temporal abilities?

Children with motor planning difficulties may have difficulty taking space and time into account. For example, they may not realize that if a person is farther away, they need to throw the ball harder to get it to go farther. If someone kicks them a ball, they may not realize that they need to adjust for how fast the ball is coming. They may not be able to adjust their movements based on visual and auditory information about where things in the environment are located in space and time. In order to learn how to control for space and time, a child needs to be able to be stable while moving, plan a path and control the speed of movement of body parts, coordinate the sequence of the movement of different limbs to stop where and when they need to stop, adjust the force the various parts of the body exert during an action, and move the body in relation to both stationary and moving objects in the environment. These skills require automatic responses and quick adjustments for accuracy. Children with motor planning problems may have difficulty with these skills and, consequently, have difficulty maneuvering their bodies through a group, be unable to avoid a moving object, or lose their balance when they try to start or stop movements quickly.

Interaction Strategies

1. *Discuss space and time.* Help children understand the concepts of *near* and *far, moving* and *still, fast* and *slow.* Use these terms to help them evaluate what is happening as they watch others responding to space and matching timing with movement. For instance, as the child watches other children throwing bowling balls at pins down the hall, the teacher might say, "Look, Justin pulled his arm way back and threw the ball hard to get it to go fast and far."

2. *Try actions at fast and slow speeds.* The adult can experiment with doing familiar actions quickly and slowly in fun games. Describe the action and then let the child tell what happened and how it felt. Imitate the child's actions and describe how you feel. Model moving fast and slow; talk about the consequences of both.

3. *Do the same activity with different people.* Everyone interacts differently with children, so when the same activity is done by various people, the interactions with the child will naturally alter. This requires the child to adjust to the requests and interpersonal communication style of various people.

4. *Change the requirements of a task.* Once a child has learned a routine, change the spatial or temporal requirements. For example, instead of eating in the high chair or at the table, have a picnic on the grass. This will require different postural orientation, varying movements to access the food, and adjustments to coordinate movements.

5. *Do songs and fingerplays.* The adult can first lead and help the child to learn the sequence and then have the child lead the adult or other children. The combination of rhythm and words help guide the actions. Adults can put almost any activity to words and rhythm.

6. *Provide opportunities for changing direction in space.* Play chase games and other games that require starting and stopping. If the adults engage in an exercise routine, have the child join in. Doing exercises together (e.g., touch your toes, stretch your arms) to music helps the child with temporal understanding. Change the tempo of the music to alter the speed of the movements.

Environmental Modifications

In addition to interpersonal strategies that may support the child learning spatial and temporal skills, environmental modifications often are useful. Depending on the findings from TPBA2, the team may want to consider some of the following environmental modifications.

1. *Change the spatial orientation of objects or people.* Placing and using objects in familiar ways is important for the child learning an action or action sequence. However, the

child also needs to be able to modify actions, because the demands for performance will seldom be strictly routine. Therefore, intentional modification of positions and demands of a task is important. Move objects from expected locations to new locations. Try the same actions from different distances or directions (e.g., near/far, high/low, side/side). This will require the child to make slight adjustments to his or her orientation and movements. Let the child direct your actions to increase motivation to play the game. For example, when playing a Break the Bubbles game, ask the child, "Should I blow them close to you or far away?" When getting dressed, "Do you want to stand up or sit down?"

2. *Change the expectations and outcomes.* Once a child has learned a routine, or has a set way of playing with toys, change the expectations. For example, if the child has learned to stack blocks and then knock them down, create a need for the child to change the outcome. For example, "drive" a small car into the blocks to knock them down and say, "Oh, no! I wrecked my car. Let's build a garage for it." Building a garage requires the child to think of a different spatial configuration.

3. *Repeat action sequences numerous times and in different situations.* Children learn about spatial and temporal modifications based on experience. It is important for children to have as many contrasting experiences as possible in order to be able to make comparisons and draw conclusions about the consequences of their varied actions. For example, the child will learn to maneuver around people when exposed to people at parks, in the grocery store, in the mall, at a party, at a festival, and so forth. Each of these experiences requires the same skills, with different spatial and temporal requirements. Under varying circumstances, the number of people in the crowd, the degree and speed of their movement, and their expectations of others all require the child to move in response to the varying demands of the situation.

4. *Do the same activity with different objects.* Changing an aspect of a game can require temporal adjustments. For example, if a child is batting a softball and the adult switches to a large rubber ball, the child will need to adjust the speed and force of hitting. If a balloon is then substituted for the rubber ball, another adjustment will be required. The same can be done with objects used in daily routines. A sponge can be substituted for a wash cloth or child chopsticks (like tongs) for a fork. The adjustments help the child practice new strategies.

5. *Create a need for problem solving around spatial and temporal actions.* Have the child help think of ways do things. For instance, place objects the child wants in places that he or she cannot reach, then have the child think of ways to get to them.

6. *Match actions to music and rhythm.* Play clapping, bouncing, stomping, and marching games to the rhythm of a beat. The sound rhythms help the child develop underlying rhythmic patterns for movement, making movements smoother and less reliant on visual cues (i.e., watching the body parts move).

7. *Provide small comfort spaces.* Children with motor planning difficulties often feel overwhelmed and disorganized in large spaces. They like to find small, tight spaces in which to curl up and feel secure. Some children find these spots for themselves, but adults can recognize the need and make a spot that is special for the child. The space can be a bean bag chair in a quiet corner, a space with a big pillow behind a couch or chair, or a big cardboard box filled with soft pillows or blankets. Children can use these spaces to "pull themselves back together" whenever they feel the need, or adults can suggest the child relax for a while in his or her special spot if they see that the child is becoming overwhelmed or frustrated with the demands of various activities.

8. *Develop a daily schedule.* The child with organizational issues does better with a predictable routine. Have a picture chart of activities for the day. If the activities are different on a specific day, the daily activity picture chart can change from day to day. Put Velcro on the chart so pictures can be changed to correspond to activities of the day. Talk about the chart and use it to help the child organize his thoughts about the activities of the day (e.g., the child can talk about what is going to happen that day, what the next activity is going to be, what needs to happen before a desired activity) (see TPBI2, Chapter 5, Section III. Strategies for Improving State and Emotional Regulation).

9. *Provide auditory and/or visual cues to prepare the child for transitions.* Stopping and starting activities can be helped by giving the child a sound cue or signal that the routine is going to change. This enables the child to have time to prepare both mentally and physically for adapting movements.

██████ IV. D. Does the child seem to have a good sense of the body? Of objects as an extension of the body?

Children with motor planning concerns often have difficulty perceiving where their various body parts are in relation to other body parts, to objects in the environment, and in space in general. Body awareness derives from the brain's ability to interpret tactile information from what the body is touching and proprioceptive information from the amount and type of input the muscles, joints, tendons, and connective tissue are receiving. Children with poor body awareness may not realize they are sitting on the edge, rather than in the center, of the seat. They may frequently break objects, crash into furniture, trip, or bump into others. They may have to look at their feet or hands to do tasks. They may seek extra sensory input by chewing on their clothing or doing other actions to gain extra feedback from various body parts.

Body awareness helps children move efficiently and effectively through space. It also helps children know where their body is in relation to objects that support them in some way, such as tables and chairs, swings, the toilet, and so forth. Use of tools also requires an understanding of how objects can be used as an extension of the body. Poor body awareness may contribute to social conflict, difficulty learning new tasks, reduced mastery motivation, and a lack of self-confidence.

Interaction Strategies

1. *Provide "just enough" support.* If the child feels secure, movements will be more readily attempted. Offer a finger or a hand first, and more support only if needed. Build the child's self-confidence.

2. *Model different actions.* As the child learns new movements or skills, the adult can model using objects in new ways. For example, if the child can kick a ball, the adult can model hitting the ball with a stick, or play a racing game, pushing the ball with the head, while on hands-and-knees. Simple routines also can be modified. If the child typically uses a wash cloth in the bath, the adult can introduce a bath brush with a handle. These modifications require the child to reorient the body parts and use them in new ways.

3. *Help the child learn movement words.* In order to be able to follow instructions related to movement, children need to know the names of body parts, action words, and prepositions. They also need to be able to interpret gestures. For example, when the child is learning to put on shoes, the adult says, "Put your foot in *the shoe and push.*" The child needs to understand what all of these words mean. Gestures may help give clues to meaning, but the child needs to learn the meaning without gestures as well, so that

later he or she can follow instructions given by the teacher in a group. To teach these words, 1) use the words for the body part needed while showing the body part, 2) gesture to illustrate the preposition while saying the word for the preposition, and 3) demonstrate the actions paired with the word for the action.

4. *Practice all the things body parts can do.* Play games like Simon Says, Hokey-Pokey, or other songs and fingerplays that require the child to watch and imitate someone doing various actions. Involve the child in making up new actions to go with the songs. Try fun things, like coloring with a marker between the toes, or finger painting with your elbow. These "silly" actions are highly motivating to children and help them try unusual patterns.

5. *Start with simple one-step actions.* Adults need to figure out what the child *can* do in simple actions, and then add more complex movements. For example, if the child can step over the side of the wading pool, the adult can suggest optional ways to get in the pool. The child could crawl in with arms first, and then legs; or he could crawl in sideways or backward. The child might try sitting and putting both feet in, and then pushing back and then forward with his arms to lift his bottom and project it over the side of the pool. All of these variations require a change in movement pattern from what the child typically experiences.

6. *Create problem situations.* Children can learn to try new approaches when they are motivated to solve a problem. For example, if the glue is not coming out of the bottle, they need to shake it, push harder, or make the hole bigger with a tool. If the playdough is not coming out of the container, they need to use a finger, dump it over and pound on the bottom, or use a tool to get it out. The adult not only can create the problem situation, but also suggest alternative movements to try.

7. *Motivate the child to repeat action sequences numerous times.* Repetition is important because each time the action sequence is done, the neurological pathways for that sequence are strengthened. Children often repeat actions numerous times because they like to feel competent and experience mastery. For children with motor planning problems, however, practice may not be motivating in its own right. Adults may need to provide the motivation through encouragement, reinforcement with a hug, or a reinforcing consequence (e.g., when the child jumps on the pillow, the squeak toy underneath makes a sound).

Environmental Modifications

In addition to interpersonal strategies that may support the child developing a sense of body and an ability to use objects as an extension of the body, environmental modifications often are useful. Depending on the findings from TPBA2, the team may want to consider some of the following environmental modifications.

1. *Ensure a safe, motivating environment.* Children with motor planning problems may not realize where their body is in relation to objects around them. They may, therefore, trip over or bump into things. Make sure all sharp edges are covered and loose objects, such as rugs or scattered toys, are secured or removed. Reduce the number of unnecessary objects that could become obstacles, such as toys lying around on the floor. Provide interesting objects and situations that will motivate the child to want to explore and try new movements. For example, kicking a ball may not be as motivating as trying to kick a pillow up onto the bed.

2. *Provide opportunities for forceful, jarring input.* Jumping on a bed, a trampoline, or couch cushions or the floor sends a message to the brain from many parts of the body,

from the feet up through the legs and the spine. Increased information to the brain contributes to improved understanding of what is happening to the various body parts.

3. *Provide opportunities for unfamiliar movements in relation to objects.* With practice, children with motor planning problems learn to navigate in familiar situations; for example, climbing stairs, crawling up on the couch, and so forth. Novel situations, however, provide a challenge. Set up games that require the child to use her arms and legs in new ways. For example, the kitchen table and chairs can become a "tunnel" and a "cave" for the child to pretend to be a bear or other animals. A cardboard box can become a space ship, a puppet stage, or a space for Hide-and-Seek.

4. *Provide opportunities for pushing and pulling.* Children like to push and pull heavy objects. This is particularly good for children with motor planning concerns, because it provides more input to the muscles and joints. After the child has been given a ride in a wagon, let the child push or pull someone or something in the wagon. Provide real food cans and other heavy household items in a dramatic play situation. A laundry basket or cardboard box can be used for a shopping cart to push around. Have the child help with household or classroom chores requiring pushing and pulling (e.g., vacuuming, moving the chairs in the classroom, pushing the box that was just delivered).

5. *Provide the need for a tool.* Tools are an extension of the body that assist the user in accomplishing tasks that body parts alone cannot complete. Children with motor planning difficulties often have difficulty figuring out how to coordinate the actions of the body parts with the actions of the tool. Provide lots of opportunities for using tools by making activities interesting and motivating. For example, hot things can be picked up with a hot pad, or ice cubes with tongs. Cookie cutters are needed to make the cookies, a spatula to get the biscuits off of the tray, a fork to stab the pickle in the jar, a toothpick to pick up the marshmallows, and so forth.

6. *Incorporate objects that can be used as tools.* Even if a tool is not needed for an activity, one can be added to enable the child to practice. For example, for fingerpainting, a popsicle stick or plastic fork may be used instead of fingers. Use tweezers, tongs, or chopsticks to pick up beans or small objects.

7. *Let the child wear a backpack or vest with heavy objects in the pockets.* The additional weight on the body helps give the child more sensory information about body location.

IV. E. How well does the child organize clothing and personal space?

Learning to organize belongings in the environment typically does not occur without adult support. Some children, however, have more difficulty than others in seeing how objects relate to the surrounding environment. They do not know where to look for things they want or where to return them when they are finished. Retrieving and putting things away requires having a mental image of where something is located and a plan for how to move it to where it is needed or belongs. Children with motor planning problems may struggle with this process. Organizing thought and actions is a challenge that becomes evident in everything that has not become routine. For this reason, establishing routines and cues to help the child remember or learn a new routine is important. Organizational structure in addition to routines also can be helpful.

Interaction Strategies

1. *Comment on the positive.* Acknowledge the child's efforts to help, even if he is not totally accurate or successful in his attempts. Comment on what he did do. For example, "You put all of the cars in a box. Good for you!" or "You are helping Mommy put your shirt on!" These comments encourage the child to continue his efforts.

2. *Reinforce effort.* Don't wait for the child to finish the task to provide reinforcement. Look for effort and reinforce that (e.g., "You are trying so HARD!" or "You are getting it. Keep trying!").

3. *Prompt thinking through questioning and guidance.* "Where should we put the . . . " "We need to find a shelf for the books." "I see the baby's bed over by the door."

4. *Break down the organization task.* A mess is overwhelming for everyone. Help children learn to structure their environment and their tasks by breaking them down into small steps. "What do you want to pick up first, the dishes or the baby's clothes?"

5. *Model and take turns.* Show the child and expect the child to take a turn. Do not do it for him or her. Make it into a game (e.g., "I'm going to put away the ball. I get a high five! What are you going to put away? Great! Now you get a high five!").

Environmental Modifications

In addition to interpersonal strategies that may support the child learning to organize clothing and personal space, environmental modifications often are useful. Depending on the findings from TPBA2, the team may want to consider some of the following environmental modifications.

1. *Provide visual, tactile, and auditory cues.* Pictures or objects can provide clues for children about where to put things. For instance, adults know that books go on a shelf and they know which shelf by seeing other books already in place. Children with motor planning issues may not understand where objects belong. Having categorized spaces for objects is important. Children also may need a visual gesture, a verbal suggestion, and a picture or object cue to help them. The picture of a car on a plastic box for the toy cars, for example, will provide guidance. For lower functioning children or children with vision impairments, actual objects attached to a container or space on a shelf may be helpful. Children's clothing also can be organized to encourage independent dressing. Place pictures of shirts on the drawer that holds the shirts, pants on the pants drawer, and so forth. Cardboard or wooden dividers also may help the child see where to put different articles of clothing. For example, socks go in this side, underwear on that side. All children (and adults, for that matter) can benefit from organizational structure.

2. *Develop dressing routines.* Dressing routines can help the child organize a series of actions. For example, determine a sequence for dressing and use that same sequence every day. As each step of dressing is completed, have the child initiate the next step. Soon, the child will be able to help with all steps.

3. *Use mirrors to look at specific aspects of appearance.* Develop a visual guide to check off while the child looks in the mirror. Is the shirt straight, the zipper up, the buttons closed, the shoes tied, the hair combed, and so forth? Again, learning this "checklist" will give the child a guide for when he is older and no one is there to "straighten him up."

4. *Develop scheduled routines for putting things away.* The child who has motor planning problems is at greater risk for tripping over or breaking things. Develop a system associated with each daily routine for putting things away. Even though the same toys or objects may come out many times a day, teaching the child to organize and put away materials several times during the day will serve several purposes: It will help the child learn the organization of the materials; it will help the child learn the sequence for the actions involved in putting them away, and it will make the environment safer for the child. A picture chart of a sequence of actions may help (e.g., first pick up the books, then the cars, then the dolls).

5. *Simplify the task.* When putting toys away, instead of making a separate trip for each toy, use a basket, big container, or wagon to gather them up. Then sort them at each stop (e.g., stuffed animals go in the hanging net; balls go in the barrel). This also helps children learn to categorize and organize their thoughts. Reducing the number of steps the child needs to perform is important as well.

IV. F. Does the child generate appropriate force?

Using the appropriate amount of force to accomplish a task requires the ability to interpret tactile information relating to pressure and visual information relating to changes in the environment. For example, if you have ever misjudged the number of steps when going up or down the stairs, you know that you can get quite a jolt if you think there is another step and there isn't one! You are anticipating needing to move in a certain way and your movements do not match the requirements of the situation. Vision and tactile sensations together guide our movements and adjustments to movements. Children with motor planning issues often cannot anticipate the amount of movement or degree of force necessary to be successful in an activity. They use too much or too little force initially and then cannot make adjustments to correct their movements. Activities to help children coordinate what they feel with what they see can help children develop this ability.

Interaction Strategies

1. *Use vocal intonation and affect to cue the child.* Loud noises and fast movements tend to stimulate more activity and, consequently, often more force. The opposite is true with soft sounds and slow movements. For instance, when adults want a child to walk on tiptoes, they often whisper. This strategy can be used in an activity where different types of force are needed. For example, when pushing on playdough to make a "pancake," the adult might grunt loudly and make an intense facial expression to indicate effort.

2. *Teach verbal labels by modeling use of appropriate force.* It is important to teach the child labels for words that indicate doing things with different amounts of force while at the same time demonstrating what the words mean. For instance, the adult might pet the kitty slowly and gently while saying, "soft," "gentle," or "slow."

3. *Experiment with what happens with different types of force.* Make a game out of giving each other instructions for whether to be "hard" or "soft." For example, try bouncing a ball hard and soft in a game of catch. Then take turns telling each other how you want the ball thrown. This gives the child an opportunity to experience both throwing hard and anticipating how to adjust position for catching the ball he has told someone else to throw hard. This can be done with other activities as well, such as turning on the faucet, spinning the spinner on a game board, washing the car, and so forth.

4. *Explain the consequences of too much force.* Children with motor planning concerns often do not realize how hard they are hitting, jumping, and so forth. They may unintentionally hurt other children, break toys, or damage things in the environment. When the child hits and hurts another child, help him to understand the consequence by explaining and having the other child express his or her feelings. When a toy is broken, the child can help fix it, so he understands what happened as a consequence of too much force.

5. *Involve peers in supporting the child's actions.* Help peers to understand that the child's hurtful actions are unintentional. Peers can be taught to help their friends moderate their actions by using the words, "gentle," "careful," "slowly," and so forth. Peers also can be taught to model actions for other children.

Environmental Modifications

In addition to interpersonal strategies that may support the child learning how to generate appropriate force for specific activities, environmental modifications often are useful. Depending on the findings from TPBA2, the team may want to consider some of the following environmental modifications.

1. *Provide target games.* Target games help children adjust motions and force. Whether throwing a bean bag through the holes in a target board, a tissue into the trash, clothes into the laundry basket, or a ball through a hoop, target games encourage children to think about what they need to do to make the shot. Changing the distance also will change the amount of force needed.

2. *Provide self-correcting activities.* Some activities provide immediate feedback about whether appropriate force is being exerted. For example, a stapler and a hole punch will not work unless sufficient pressure is exerted. One needs to pull gently on tissues on a roll of toilet paper or the whole roll unravels. Such instant feedback gives information about what needs to be done. However, the adult also may need to give verbal explanation or demonstration to help the child understand what needs to be done.

3. *Use toys and materials of varying weights.* Most children's toys are lightweight so that they can be manipulated easily. It is important to vary the weights of materials children use, so they learn to judge how much force is needed. Adults can have the child help carry the phone book, groceries, and tools. They can involve the child in shoveling in the garden or sandbox. Shoveling materials of different weights, such as water, sand, dirt, packing peanuts, and so forth, helps children learn to control movements based on the feedback they get from the weight of the material.

4. *Use strong toys and materials.* Children who use excessive force may break toys easily. Make sure materials the child uses are strong (e.g., wooden toys are better than flimsy plastic, construction or heavy weight paper is better than tablet paper, markers are better than easily broken crayons).

5. *Vary activities and routines to include the need for different types of input.* Provide activities that alternate between requiring heavy and light force. In a classroom, this might include an art activity requiring carefully gluing small pieces to paper and then stapling the paper to another piece of paper or using a hole punch to put a trim around the paper. The first set of actions necessitates more precise, delicate work, whereas the stapler and the hole punch require increased pressure.

▮▮▮▮▮ IV. G. Does the child perform actions in response to verbal request or demonstration?

Some children have difficulty responding to a request for action or imitating others' actions. Their motor planning processes may be such that they cannot listen to an instruction and translate that into an action sequence, or see an action and figure out how to make their bodies do the same thing. They need to *feel* the action performed. For these children, structure and physical assistance are needed in order to create neurological pathways related to the motor actions.

Interaction Strategies

1. *Provide physical support.* Physical guidance in the form of hand-over-hand assistance or movement of specific body parts may be needed at the initial stages of a child learning a new task involving movement. For instance, the child who is learning to open a jar lid may need the adult to stabilize the jar, put his hand on top of the child's

hand, help the child apply pressure to the lid, and turn it slowly. Depending on the child's ability to process auditory information, this movement can be accompanied by labeling of the actions. After numerous repetitions, the child then may be able to respond to the words or the demonstration as a cue for what to do.

2. *Some activities may need practice on each step.* Many children can practice a multi-step sequence as a whole and learn the task. Other children may have difficulty learning more than one action at a time. For these children, practice each action in the sequence, in order, numerous times before combining it with the next action. For example, when learning to step in to or over something (e.g., in to a wading pool, over an object), the child may need to practice the first step of lifting the foot over something many times with physical support to be able to perform that action accurately. The next action, that of putting the weight down on the foot that stepped over and then lifting and bringing the other foot over, requires a whole different set of movements. These may need to be practiced after the first step is understood and internalized.

3. *Reduce the amount of support provided.* As indicated in a previous section, it is important for the adult to provide the *least* amount of support possible for the child to succeed. As the child improves in the ability to make movements without physical assistance, the adult should reduce the prompts from physical manipulation of the child's body parts to guidance, then to a touch prompt, then to a gesture or demonstration paired with words, and finally to just words.

4. *Make the actions motivating.* Do not "practice" for the sake of learning. Incorporate whatever actions the child is learning into a meaningful activity that is of interest to the child and will result in an outcome the child will enjoy. For example, if the child hates water, do not practice "stepping over" the side of a wading pool. Instead, step over a toy to get to reach for another desired toy on a shelf.

5. *Show enthusiasm.* Model an excited affect to increase the child's desire to do what the adult is asking; the child should feel that it is worth the effort. If the adult makes the activity into "work," "practice," or "therapy," the child will not be as motivated to participate.

6. *Keep in mind the child's perspective.* Children with motor planning concerns may have difficulty translating what they see in front of them to their own perspective. When the adult is in front of and facing the child and is moving a right foot and right arm, the child may move her left arm and left leg because that is what the child sees the adult doing (as if in a mirror). If the adult is in front of the child, facing away; behind the child, prompting movement of appropriate body parts; or beside the child, demonstrating movement, the child may be able to imitate more easily.

Environmental Modifications

In addition to interpersonal strategies that may support the child performing actions in response to demonstration or request, environmental modifications often are useful. Depending on the findings from TPBA2, the team may want to consider some of the following environmental modifications.

1. *Reduce the difficulty of the task.* If a task is too challenging (for any of us), the inclination is to give up or revert to a behavior that is easy to do. Rather than frustrate the child with an activity that will result in discouragement, modify the task. For example, if the child is learning to climb stairs, don't choose stairs that are high and steep. The child will either resist the task or revert to crawling. Take the child to a place where there is a low rise to the stairs and there are few steps to conquer. After the child feels confident with those stairs, increase the difficulty level slightly.

2. *Use picture cues.* For children who have difficulty comprehending verbal requests, a combination of demonstration and picture cues may be helpful.

3. *Provide physical supports.* Some tasks are challenging because the child lacks the underlying abilities to do the task independently. For instance, if the child has high muscle tone or low muscle tone, the movements required to accomplish the task may be too difficult. A hand support, brace, appropriate positioning, or other modification may be helpful.

4. *Use a mirror so the child can see actions performed.* Stand behind the child so the child can see him or herself and the adult. The adult can then do interesting actions that the child can see and imitate.

ROUTINES FOR THE CHILD WHO NEEDS SUPPORT TO ENHANCE MOTOR PLANNING AND COORDINATION

Daily Routines (Home and Classroom)

Feeding/Eating

Eating involves wanting the food, accessing the food, and getting the food into the mouth, chewing, and swallowing. Children can have a problem with any of these steps. The adult can determine which of these steps is hindering the process by observing the child's attempts to eat. If motor planning (i.e., getting the food to the mouth, manipulating the food around the mouth) is the problem, then helping the child requires supporting his or her arm and hand movements and oral motor movements (see TPBI2, Chapter 3, Section VI. Strategies for Improving Sensorimotor Contributions to Daily Life). Modification of the tool (e.g., so the eating utensil is angled to get to the mouth more easily) can make motor planning easier. The adult also can verbally direct the child's actions or model actions that the child can imitate. Repeated physical support of the child's movements also can help the child plan motor sequences for eating.

Diapering/Toileting

In diapering, motor planning is not required because the adult typically performs the necessary actions. Toileting, however, requires the child to perform a sequence of actions independently. Climbing onto the toilet or positioning the body in such a way as to discharge bodily fluids requires balance, coordination, and control. Helping the child feel secure is the first step. This can be done by determining how much support the child needs to get into "position." The child then needs to have adequate support to maintain stability, so he or she feels secure enough to allow the release of sphincters. Steps, railings, or other supports may be needed.

Dressing

Dressing is a complex process requiring balance and stability in order to implement the movements needed to carry out the actions required to dress. Arms and legs need to be lifted, directed, and controlled in order to place them accurately in a piece of clothing. Adults first direct physically but should, as soon as possible, allow the child to assume increasing control. Physical direction allows the child to practice necessary patterns, and reduced control allows the child to practice independence in these patterns. A visual picture sequence may be helpful.

Dressing also requires that the child reorient clothing so that the limbs go into the correct openings. Placement of the clothing in such a way that children do not have to figure out how to reorient them to get them on is suggested. Clothing may need to have larger openings, modified closures to aid manipulation, or elastic waistbands so the child can be independent in dressing.

Going Out

Each new environment provides a new set of challenges for motor movements. Children may resist going into new environments because they know it may be difficult. Adults can help children with special needs by making sure the child learns the routines of each part of "going out," such as getting into and out of the stroller or car seat, getting into the grocery cart or walking through a parking lot full of cars, and so forth, so they become familiar. Practicing these routines as a pretend game may help the child see them as motivating actions rather than challenges. Prepare the child verbally for what is to be the next event and what he or she will need to do (e.g., crawl into the booth in the restaurant and look at the pictures on the menu). Provide the physical support necessary, but encourage independence.

Play Routines (Home and Classroom)

Face-to-Face Play

Games played face-to-face often involve movements of hands and fingers or other body parts. Learning fingerplays, for example, may be very difficult for the child with motor planning issues. She needs to coordinate action sequences and words, often mirroring the adult. It may be helpful for the adult to hold the child on his or her lap, so that the child can see the adult's hands moving in the same perspective as she sees her own. The adult can then model slowly and provide support as needed to help the child form the needed actions. Make it high energy and fun, so the child will want to repeat the game again. Repetition will promote learning the sequence of actions.

Physical Play

Even more than in face-to-face play, physical play involving action sequences requires the child to see what someone is doing and "turn it around" in his mind to be able to use the same arms, hands, and legs as the adult. If the child is unable to imitate the adult when the adult is in front of him, another person (peer, sibling, or other adult) can demonstrate while the first adult stands behind the child and provides verbal and physical prompts. This can be done in group games as well, until the child learns the sequence of actions and use of tools (e.g., a bat and ball). Physical games that require the child to use specific actions can be incorporated into play as well. For example, relay games in which children transport objects in different ways, swinging games involving kicking a target, or obstacle courses can be fun, especially if done with a friend (who also serves as a model and assistant).

Manipulative Play

For the child who struggles with motor planning involving manipulation of hands and fingers, play requiring complicated sequences can be very difficult. Even picking up a glue bottle, opening the top, turning it over, squeezing it gently, stopping when a small amount has come out, turning it back over, and closing the lid may be a huge challenge. Demonstrating the sequence may be helpful, but backward chaining may allow the child to be more successful. This means that the adult or another child does all of the steps of the sequence up until the last one, putting the lid back on. The child then performs that step. When he can do that successfully, the preceding step is added, and so forth. This approach can be used with activities like puzzles, building with blocks, making puzzles, and other fine motor play.

Sensory Play

Children with motor planning problems may seek out proprioceptive input, meaning that they like play involving pushing, pulling, jumping, and so forth. They crave this type of input to provide more information to their muscles and joints about where their body is in space. Adults can incorporate proprioceptive input into other activities, either as preparation for an activity requiring awareness of body parts or as an integral part of an activity. For example, before drawing or art, the teacher might have an activity making things out of playdough. This provides increased awareness of muscles and joints before engaging in an activity requiring more precise control. Alternatively, an activity such as making an art project with different stamps requires pressure as part of the activity. The child has to push down on the ink pad and then push down again on the paper.

Dramatic Play

Children with motor planning problems may choose to do the same dramatic play sequence repeatedly (usually a familiar daily routine), rather than try to develop new action sequences. New costumes and new props require modification of movements. The child may need verbal prompts or a physical assist to start a new sequence. Incorporate other children as motivators and models for actions. Having costumes that are modified so they are easy to put on is important. Incorporate some props and actions that are familiar to encourage joining the play. Add new actions as these are learned.

Reading and Learning Routines

Circle Time

Movement often is a part of circle time, especially for songs, dance, and group games. Children with motor planning problems often like to stick to the same routine that is familiar, so new activities should be included along with familiar ones. Give the child an opportunity to select a favorite song or game and give him or her the chance to lead the group. This will help build self-confidence so that when a new movement game is introduced, the child will be motivated to participate. Teach new movements slowly, and make sure one action sequence is learned (or at least approximated) before adding more.

One-on-One Book Reading

Reading involves motor planning by requiring moving the eyes across the page and then back to the beginning of the line of print right under it, and then across again. It requires turning just one page at a time, and the ability to scan pictures for important information. The adult can help the child practice these movements by helping the child to scan the picture, following the adult's point as various aspects are talked about. The child can then take her turn telling the adult about the next picture. As the child begins to understand that the print on the page is associated with the words being spoken, the adult can start to track the line of print with his or her finger. This encourages the child to use that movement pattern with her eyes. It is important to not just focus on the print, however, because the meaning is coming from the pictures as well as the words being spoken.

Science and Math

Math and science should be taught to young children through manipulation and discovery and through discrimination and comparison. Activities often involve novel actions (e.g., crawling under the bushes to capture a bug, chasing a butterfly with a net, moving heavy rocks to see what is underneath). Such activities can be great motivators for movement and problem solving. The adult may need to provide suggestions about what might be tried or to use adapted materials to assist the child. For example, the child with motor planning problems may need a larger, heavier butterfly net. The added weight gives more sensory input, and the larger net reduces the need for precision.

▬▬▬   ### MANUELA

Manuela is a 3-year-old from Portugal. She received TPBA at a university in Porto. She was receiving private occupational and speech and language therapy, along with consultation from a special educator in her school program. Her parents had her assessed in order to determine if she should be in a different program and what they could do with her at home.

Manuela was a happy, excited little girl. She raced from toy to toy, pulling her mother with her. She was able to do simple, familiar actions but used few words throughout the session. In addition to cognitive and language delays, Manuela demonstrated concerns in motor planning abilities. Manuela was very active and demonstrated a short attention span in her play. She tripped over toys on the floor, stumbled into her mother when she was sitting on the floor, and fell off of her chair when sitting at the little table. She played forcefully with toys, banging the baby's bottle into the doll's mouth while pretending to feed her, brushing the adult's hair roughly with a toy brush, and banging loudly on musical toys. She frequently acted impulsively, throwing objects or hitting things when frustrated because she couldn't figure out how to operate them.

Her parents indicated that her behaviors were causing her social problems at school. Other children avoided playing with her, because she often unintentionally hurt them. After the assessment, the team discussed how Manuela's language delays compounded her learning and interaction challenges. In addition, motor planning difficulties were having an impact on her development, influencing both her cognitive learning and her social interactions. The team and family developed an intervention plan that included the following suggestions to address motor planning concerns.

Interaction Strategies

1. *Let Manuela help dress you and do other household tasks. This will give her practice in matching clothing to body parts and will help her learn to orient the clothing appropriately. You can guide her gently.*

2. *Let Manuela help with tasks that require gentle movements, such as combing your and her hair, drying plastic dishes, and putting clothing away. Use language that supports her movements, such as "gently," "lightly," "carefully." Comment on how she is doing things, so that she associated the words with the actions; for example, "You did that so gently!" said in a soft voice.*

3. *Play "Stop and Go" games. You can help Manuela learn to start and stop by making activities into a game and giving her cues (e.g., while stirring dough for cookies say, "Stop! Stir the other direction. Go! . . . Stop! Now stir fast! Go! . . . Stop! Now stir slowly! Go." [said slowly]). This also will help her learn to modify her direction and speed of movement.*

4. *Provide only as much support as is needed when Manuela is performing actions. Try verbal suggestion first, then model and give gestural cues, then give a little assistance. You want her to feel proud that she can do things independently. Give her lots of verbal reinforcement.*

Environmental Modifications

1. *Organize Manuela's environment so it is safe. Reduce the number of unnecessary obstacles in each room, and cover sharp corners. She has difficulty maneuvering around things, so she just walks on them or trips over them. Keep her environment simple.*

2. *Dressing is hard for Manuela, so break down each dressing activity into parts. Tell her the names for the body parts, clothing, and movements she is making. Lay the items out so she can see what part goes on first. Go slowly, and let her figure out as much as she can before you guide her. This way, she will feel successful and want to do it herself.*

3. *Let Manuela do activities throughout the day that enable her to push and pull, run and jump, and roughhouse. Give her lots of heavy input, such as rubbing her with a towel after her bath, letting her take heavy toys with her in a backpack, and having her help stir dough. Buy her sturdy, heavier toys rather than light, plastic toys that are harder for her to notice and are easily broken.*

4. *Alternate activities with heavy input and activities that make Manuela change her speed and force of movement. For example, after playing a rough game, tip-toe into the other room to surprise Mommy.*

KEYS TO INTERVENTION BY DEVELOPMENTAL AGE

Developmental ages and related strategies are not provided for this subguideline, because much of motor planning is qualitative processing, rather than age related.

3

Facilitating Sensorimotor Development

V. Strategies for Improving Modulation of Sensation and Its Relationship to Emotion, Activity Level, and Attention

with Anita C. Bundy

Goal Attainment Scale

1	2	3	4	5	6	7	8	9
Despite modification attempts, over- or under-reactivity to sensory input has a markedly negative impact on engagement with objects, people, or events in the environment.		Requires major and/or frequent modifications of environment or interpersonal interactions to demonstrate appropriate responses to sensory input.		Demonstrates appropriate responses to sensory input with moderate modification of environment or interactions.		Demonstrates appropriate responses to sensory input with minimal modification of environment or interactions.		Is nearly always able to appropriately respond to all types of sensory input without environmental modifications.

Children take in sensation in a variety of ways, through vision, hearing, touch, taste, smell, movement, and pressure on muscles and joints. Sensory modulation refers to the ability to filter, process, and respond to these sensations in such a way that a child can function appropriately in his or her environment. Processing sensory information involves the neurological processes of detecting, receiving, modulating, integrating, and organizing sensory information such that the resulting behaviors match the demands and expectations of the environment. The way the child processes various sensations is thought to influence emotion, arousal, and activity level. Children who can modulate sensory input can easily and accurately interpret incoming sensation, adjust or regulate their level of arousal, and respond appropriately. They respond as expected to activities and events, with typical emotional responses, level of activity, and focus of attention. Thus, sensory modulation is critical to adaptive interactions with objects and people and, thus, to children's optimal engagement in play and other daily life activities.

APPROPRIATE MODULATION OF SENSATION AND ITS RELATIONSHIP TO EMOTION, ACTIVITY LEVEL, AND ATTENTION

Children who have appropriate sensory modulation demonstrate an appropriate level of attention and an acceptable range of emotional and physical response to objects, people, activities, and events that occur within their daily life. Children who have appropriate sensory modulation also enjoy a wide range of activities and a wide range of types of sensory input. They have preferences for various types of stimuli, such as preferred foods, smells, materials, and actions, but they do not limit their experiences to only certain types of sensory input or activities. They can attend appropriately to a range of types of experiences in order to achieve their desired goals. Children who have appropriate sensory modulation demonstrate a range of emotional responses to things they like and do not like, but they do not overreact or lack responses to typical functional activities of the day.

Appropriate Modulation of Sensation and Its Relationship to Emotion, Activity Level, and Attention in Practice

▆▆▆ **V. A. Regulation of responses to sensory experiences and the effect sensory experiences have on the child's emotional responses**

Daily Routines (Home and Classroom)

- *Infant/toddler:* The infant fusses initially when placed in the warm tub of water, but calms and begins to smile when Dad dribbles water on his tummy. The toddler lunch consists of a variety of tastes, including bland chicken, salty chips, and sweet fruit. All of these are eaten with gusto.

- *Young child:* The young child is playing in a mud puddle in the backyard. He squeals with delight as he splashes his hands in the muddy water.

Play Routines (Home and Classroom)

- *Infant/toddler:* The infant is playing "horsie" by bouncing on his father's knee. Every few bounces, his father will bounce him higher and the infant squeals with delight. The toddler is hiding behind the chair. Mother leans over the top of the chair and shouts, "Boo!" He screams in surprise.

- *Young child:* The young child is riding her tricycle. She turns a corner too sharply and the bike falls over. Her knee is scraped and she starts to cry.

Classroom Routines

The young child is mad because another little girl took his hat and ran away. The girl returns the hat and gives the child a hug, saying, "I'm sorry." He hugs her back and says, "That's okay."

▆▆▆ **V. B. Effect of sensory experiences on the child's activity level**

Daily Routines (Home and Classroom)

- *Infant/toddler:* The infant is tossed in the air by her father when he takes her out of the crib. She kicks her feet and waves her arms to get him to do it again. The toddler has been playing actively and is excited. His mother holds him on her lap and begins reading him a book, while rocking slowly. He calms, puts his thumb in his mouth, and attends to the book.

- *Young child:* At the grocery store, the young child sees all the options available and excitedly runs up the aisle, looking at all of the different cereal boxes. "I want this one and this one and this one!" he shouts to his father.

Play Routines (Home and Classroom)

- *Infant/toddler:* The infant is lying in the crib watching the mobile above him. His mother turns it on and as it begins to move and play music, the infant's legs and arms begins to move. The toddler is running around in circles; then she sees the doll stroller, puts several dolls in the stroller, and slowly pushes the stroller around the room.

- *Young child:* The young child is out on the playground. She looks around at what the other children are doing and then climbs the jungle gym, crawls through the tunnel, goes down the slide, and then runs back around to do it again.

Classroom Routines

Before nap time, the teacher has all the young children lie on their cots and breathe deeply. He then plays slow, soft music.

▬▬▬ V. C. Effect of sensory experiences on a child's attention

Daily Routines (Home and Classroom)

- *Infant/toddler:* The infant smells the chocolate chip cookies her mother is baking and hears her mother opening cupboards. She crawls into the kitchen to find her. The toddler hears a dog barking outdoors and goes over to window, looking for the dog. She points and says, "Daddy, doggie woof, woof!"

- *Young child:* The young child is playing in the leaves his mother is raking. He waits for her to make a pile then jumps in and rolls around, while giggling and laughing.

Play Routines (Home and Classroom)

- *Infant/toddler:* The infant pushes the button on his pop-up toy. The lamb pops up. The infant pushes the lid down on the lamb and pushes the button again. He repeats this action sequence for all of the optional lids on the toy. The toddler is putting lotion on her doll. She rubs each part with the white lotion, while saying, "On your face, and hands, and feet, and tummy."

- *Young child:* The young child is listening to music and dancing. When the music stops, she stops dancing and looks her mother. "Play another one, Mommy."

Classroom Routines

During circle time, the teacher does a fingerplay and song about five little ducks. All of the young children watch and try to imitate her.

GENERAL PRINCIPLES FOR SUPPORTING APPROPRIATE MODULATION OF SENSATION AND ITS RELATIONSHIP TO EMOTION, ACTIVITY LEVEL, AND ATTENTION

Parents and other adults often tell children what is going to happen in advance. This preparation lets the child anticipate events and adjust responses. For example, the adult may say, "After breakfast, we'll go outside and play." This tells the child what type of activities and, therefore, sensory input to expect. The child starts thinking about what is coming and starts planning in his or her mind what possibilities exist for play outdoors. The mind and the body "get ready" for the next experiences.

Regulation

Adults help children regulate sensory input that may be too much or too little. They watch the child's response to various activities and determine whether modifications need to be made. For example, when the adult is giving the child a bath, the adult will test the temperature of the water and then watch the child's response when he or she gets in the tub. If the child lifts a foot, makes a face, or starts to cry the adult will say, "Is that too hot?" or "Is that too cold?" Adults watch and interpret children's reactions to various environmental events and then make judgments about what will make the child more comfortable, happier, more interested, or more involved. For instance, the parent may see the child getting scared when the swing starts going higher. The adult will then slow the swing and reassure the child that everything is okay. Adults also learn what activities the child likes and will arrange opportunities for the child to experience these types of situations. If the child loves movement, for example, the parent may take the child to local outdoor recreation areas or amusement parks. If the child dislikes noises, they will avoid going to events with fireworks or loud music.

Discussion

Adults help children understand what they are experiencing. They describe the sources of sounds, label tastes, textures, and smells, talk about movements, describe forces they are experiencing (e.g., pushing or pulling), and talk about the characteristics of things they are seeing (e.g., shiny or bright). Discussion helps children understand what they are experiencing, which reduces anxiety or uncertainty that can occur with introduction of novel experiences.

Build Tolerance

Adults naturally introduce new experiences to children as gradually as they can. They will say, "Just take a tiny bite" or "Just touch it with your finger." As the child demonstrates increased tolerance for novel experiences, the parent or caregiver will introduce more of the experience. Although the child initially may have demonstrated fear at seeing Big Bird, after reading books and seeing him on television the child may then request activities relating to this character.

THE PRINCIPLES IN PRACTICE

Adults employ a variety of strategies to support the child's ability to moderate sensory input. Following are examples of how caregivers use the previous strategies during the day both at home and at school. These examples are approaches that most caregivers use naturally in their daily interactions with children. They also are appropriate for most children with disabilities.

Daily Routines (Home and Classroom)

Feeding/Eating

All children have food preferences, but most children can be enticed to try a variety of different tastes. Parents often use tricks to entice children to expand their options. They may mix a preferred food with a nonpreferred food. For example, the child might like a certain topping or dressing that can be put on top of the food, or the child can "dip" the food in the topping. Small tastes of a new food also may be introduced after the parent tastes it and shows the child that it is "yummy."

Diapering/Toileting

Moving from the diaper to the toilet involves tolerating new actions and sensations. Children are encouraged to feel pride in their new abilities. Parents also involve the child in washing their hands so that they can smell and feel the slippery soap, feel the water, and dry with a towel. As parents applaud the child's new independence, they also encourage expanded sensory experiences.

Dressing

Children often have favorite clothes they like to wear. They may prefer certain colors, textures, or styles that fit in a certain way. Adults help children expand their tolerance for these different sensory characteristics by varying the clothing the child wears each day and by talking about the favorable aspects and how nice the child will look and feel in the clothing.

Play Routines (Home and Classroom)

Face-to-Face Games

Face-to-face games involve primarily visual, auditory, tactile, and movement experiences. The turn-taking involved in these games encourages the child to imitate the adult and, thus, to try new sensory experiences.

Physical Play

Physical play involves visual and auditory experiences, but more importantly, vestibular, tactile, and proprioceptive play. The adult helps the child by modeling and showing positive emotions related to the actions. Turn-taking enables the child to tickle the adult, chase the adult, jump on the adult, and see the adult's responses as well as to experience these sensations.

Manipulative Play

Play involves all types of sensory input. Most parents try to expose their children to a wide range of play opportunities, including toys that make sounds, have numerous visual aspects, require movement with various parts of the body, and so forth. They talk about what the toys do, demonstrate use and response, and encourage exploration of all of the possible uses within the environment.

Sensory Play

Art and messy play provide opportunities for adults to encourage exploration of numerous types of materials. Although some parents are concerned about messes, most parents allow their children to discover characteristics of materials as long as they are safe. Children touch, smell, taste, and manipulate whatever they find when they are young. Parents monitor what their child is doing and provide suggestions, comments, and admonitions when appropriate.

Reading and Learning Routines

Circle Time

Teachers use circle time primarily for visual and auditory input, but children can be encouraged to use all of their senses in group activities. Teachers who use circle time in this way enable peers to observe and imitate each other in a variety of sensory experiences. Such group activities encourage active participation by all children.

One-on-One Book Reading

Book reading is primarily visual and auditory, but many books for young children include tactile components such as furry material on a cow picture or rough-textured material on a picture of a beach. Parents also use the content of books as stimulation to reenact the actions in books, thus exposing children to other sensory experiences.

Science and Math

Discovery of math and science concepts requires use of multiple senses. Good teachers use experimentation and physical exploration and manipulation using smell, taste, touch, hearing, vision, movement, and physical effort to help children internalize concepts related to the sensations experienced.

PLANNING INDIVIDUALIZED INTERVENTIONS FOR IMPROVING MODULATION OF SENSATION AND ITS RELATIONSHIP TO EMOTION, ACTIVITY LEVEL, AND ATTENTION

▬▬▬ **V. A. How well can the child regulate responses to sensory experiences? What effect do sensory experiences have on the child's emotional responses?**

Although research is just beginning to document issues related to sensory regulation, there is increasing evidence that across all sensory systems, how the nervous system handles sensory input has an impact on behavior. Children who have difficulty with sensory modulation seem to require either more or less sensory input than typical children in order to function effectively. Their thresholds of tolerance for one or more types of sensory input are thus either higher or lower than those of most children. Children who have a *high* threshold for sensation need a great deal of input before they will respond, whereas those with a low threshold need very little. Children with high sensory thresholds may not react to what typical children do; therefore, they seek additional input in order to respond adequately. Children with *low* sensory thresholds, alternatively, find what other children consider a "typical" level of input to be too much input.

The result of poor sensory modulation may be seen in the child's emotional responses to various situations. Sensory modulation issues may affect any of the sensory systems, and children can have low reactivity to one type of sensory input and high reactivity to another. For example, the child may need more intense input to the proprioceptive system to register where his or her body is in space but at the same time be hypersensitive to sounds and react with crying to loud noises.

When children need more intense stimulation to register input, they may respond in one of two ways. Because they are not registering input in a particular sensory area, they may appear to have dampened affect. However, children with high sensory thresholds also may act with intensity and more emotionality. They need more input and, thus, they run and jump more, push harder, and seek out intense experiences. Often their emotions match that intensity. However, intense input also can have a calming effect for these children. Increased proprioceptive input—for example, through hugging or pushing on something—can have a calming effect.

Children with low thresholds of responsivity also can demonstrate emotionality in one of two ways. Because they react to a small amount of stimulation, they may avoid a certain type of sensation and appear withdrawn and resistant to certain types of activities. When exposed to situations with stimuli they experience as aversive, however, they may have an intense emotional response; they may run away or get angry and frustrated. They may show *flight* (e.g., moving away, withdrawal, distraction), *fight* (e.g., anger, aggression), or *fright* (e.g., reluctance, whining, clinging).

To make matters more complicated, some children seem to demonstrate alternate responses at different times and in varied environments. Children with fragile X syndrome seem to move between underresponsiveness and defensiveness.

Adults need to determine the child's sensory needs across all sensory areas and situations to effectively plan intervention strategies. Children may need adaptations to the environment, activities, or routines, and interaction patterns with adults or peers to help them function optimally throughout the day.

The following are characteristics that may be seen in children who have sensory modulation issues that may interfere with the child's ability to function adequately in his or her environment. These issues can have an impact on the child's level of arousal, emotionality, attention, and activity level.

Tactile defensiveness. Children who are overly responsive to touch may demonstrate tactile defensiveness, or clusters of behaviors that indicate consistent avoidance of various types of tactile input that would be considered nonirritating to most people. They may avoid touch contact with others, avoid touch to certain parts of the body, or pull away from anticipated touch. They may appear to need a large amount of personal space. Children with tactile defensiveness also may have an aversion to certain textures, such as rough materials. They may avoid daily routines involving tactile input such as washing, brushing hair or teeth, or cutting hair or fingernails. They also may avoid messy play or any play involving unusual textures.

Tactile seeking. Children who constantly seek out things to touch may be underresponsive to touch. They may constantly holding things, touch everything they see, or seek out unusual textures such as feathers and fur.

Vestibular and proprioceptive avoidance. The vestibular system is important for organizing sensory input to coordinate movement of the body and eyes and for awareness of the body's position in space. Children who are overresponsive to vestibular and proprioceptive input may demonstrate discomfort or nausea with certain types of movement. Children with hypersensitivity to vestibular and proprioceptive input also may demonstrate gravitational insecurity, or fear of having the body in an unstable position or out of contact with direct support. They may fear even slight movements, particularly of the head.

Movement seeking. Some children seek out movement experiences. They cannot seem to get enough vestibular and proprioceptive input.

Pressure seeking. Some children appear to seek intense input to muscles and joints by hitting, pushing and pulling, falling, and performing actions with great force.

Oversensitivity to visual stimuli. Some children demonstrate averse reactions to certain types of visual stimuli, such as bright lights, flashing lights, and so forth. They also may appear to not be able to isolate the visual stimuli on which they need to focus.

Oversensitivity to auditory stimuli. In a similar fashion, children may have an averse reaction to sounds they register as "too loud" or irritating, or they may not be able to screen out sounds that should not be a focus of attention.

The following are suggested strategies to deal with emotionality concerns associated with these characteristics.

Interaction Strategies

1. *Stimulate internal motivation.* Children may be motivated to try an anxiety-provoking activity if they believe the physical, emotional, or social reward will be worth the anxiety caused. For instance, if the child sees other children engaging in the activity and having fun, the child may be motivated to try it. If the child has anxiety in large groups, the adult can point out the fun the children are having and suggest an action the child might enjoy too. If the adult encourages the child's attempts, the child may want to try the activity in order to feel success or to please the adult. The adult should not put the child down for lack of effort or compare the child with other more successful children.

For children who become angry, the adult wants to motivate the child to remain in control and find positive aspects of the experience. Pointing out factors that are nonaggravating may help. For instance, if the child gets aroused easily in a line where other children are too close, the adult can point out that the other children want to be near him because they like him, and that way he will have a friend in front and a friend behind him.

Children may withdraw from sensory experiences that seem overwhelming or that do not provide enough input. To motivate children to participate, the adult may add elements that supply motivation. Helping children determine a goal they want to accomplish can motivate them to participate. For instance, a child may withdraw from art activities involving tactile input. The adult may be able to help the child determine an outcome he or she wants to achieve, even if it is just watching and supporting a friend by giving advice or "fingerpainting" with a stick instead of a finger.

Children who get overexcited or stimulated easily may escalate into volatility. The adult may want to motivate the child to maintain a calmer demeanor; for example, "Let's count ten breaths before you do it again. Great! You did it!"

2. *Provide reassurance and physical comfort and verbal support.* Children may demonstrate anxiety or fear for several reasons: 1) they may remember previous negative experiences associated with the particular sensory input, 2) they may anticipate a negative feeling on seeing the activity, or 3) they may experience the feelings during the activity. Adults can help children by preparing them for an activity. Acknowledge that the activity sometimes feels "scary" to the child, but that is okay. Talk about what is going to happen (e.g., "You are going to climb the steps"), what the child can do (e.g., "You can hold on to the railing"), what the adult will do to help (e.g., I will stand right behind you"), and how the child can approach the activity (e.g., "You can go as slowly as you want," "Tell me when you are ready," "Ask me for help if you need to").

Acknowledge the child's discomfort in certain situations. Provide verbal prompts to help the child monitor the situation. For example, if the child gets angry when other children intrude into his or her space, the adult may help the child analyze and modify actions and reactions: "That's a good idea, Chloe; sit on the end where you have more space." "I like how you asked your friend to move over." "Can you tell your friend how you feel?"

If the child exhibits withdrawal and lack of emotion, acknowledge the child's lack of interest ("Does that look boring?") or anxiety ("Does that look too messy for you?"). Then support the child in thinking of a way to make the activity more fun (e.g., "What if you jump over to get your coat instead of walk?") or tolerable (e.g., "I'll bet it would be fun to cover it with plastic wrap and then touch it! That way you won't get messy!"). Reassure the child that he or she is able to do a particular action.

Help the child monitor his or her affect by commenting on what the child is doing and asking questions. For example, "You look like you are getting silly. Can you slow down a little so you don't get too excited?"

3. *Help the child pair emotionally charged activities with activities that stimulate contradictory emotions.* If the child has a calming toy or object to hold, he or she may attempt the activity (e.g., "Let's have a picnic in the grass with your teddy bear. I brought juice!"). Distraction from what is bothering the child to another more interesting activity or event may help deflate the emotional intensity (e.g., "Look, Sam, the people behind you are waiting for you to lead them outside").

Withdrawal from an overstimulating activity can be reframed for the child by pairing the activity with calming words and actions (e.g., "Let's you and I dance slowly over here"). For activities that lack stimulation, the adult can add excitement with his or her voice and enthusiasm and include a preferred sensory component. For example, when the child resists sitting at a table to play, the adult might suggest blowing bubbles before sitting down and after the child is finished with his puzzle.

Children whose actions and emotions escalate during an activity may be able to be calmed by introducing a calming action. For example, after the child races around the playground on the tricycle several times, the teacher may introduce a stop sign or give the child a "speeding ticket" to encourage her to slow down.

4. *Structure verbal parameters for the child; preparation, monitoring, and closure are important.* Help the child understand the parameters of each situation. For example, "We are going into the store to buy milk. We won't stay. I need for you to hold my hand and help me pick out the milk. You also can give the clerk the money." Later, "You did a great job helping me at the store." This will help the child who has difficulty with new places and overstimulation to understand how long the anxiety-provoking situation will last. It also gives the child a role to engage her and focus her attention.

Children need verbal parameters for behavior. Adults can tell children what is appropriate in certain situations. "We are going to church. In church, people are quiet and listen." Later, "We are in church now. You need to be quiet. You can sit between Daddy and me, and I will give you a book to read." Later, "I know it was hard to sit a long time, and you tried very hard." Parameters also can help the child calm when an emotional "explosion" occurs. "Okay. I know you are mad that you have to sit in the car seat. I will count to ten and then it is time to stop crying."

Adults can help children by introducing step-by-step boundaries. This way, they can gradually introduce situations. For example, "Let's move a little closer. I can't see." "Now I want to catch the ball. Tell me when." "Now I'll throw the ball to you and you can throw it to Tony."

5. *Modify the speaker's affect.* By modifying their own affect, adults can influence the affect of the child.

- A quiet, firm voice and serious demeanor transmits security, calmness, and gravity.

- A quiet, rhythmic voice with a smiling face conveys nurturance.

- An animated voice with a joyful expression relates excitement.

Children tend to respond to the emotions conveyed by others, so modeling affect appropriate to the situation can have a significant impact on the child.

6. *Help the child develop self-regulation.* Talk to the child about what he or she is feeling and when these feelings occur. Help the child notice when he is experiencing these emotions and what he can do about it. For example, "It looks like you are getting upset (mad, bored, worried). What would make you feel better?" or "Do you need to go to a quiet space (ask for help, change activities)?" After many repetitions of the pattern, the child may begin to recognize the onset of emotions and act to readjust his or her actions. Reinforce the child's efforts at self-regulation.

Environmental Modifications

In addition to interpersonal strategies that may support the child, environmental modifications often are useful. Depending on the findings from TPBA2, the team may want to consider some of the following environmental modifications.

1. *Modify the environment.* Increase or decrease the stimulation in the environment, including, as needed, lighting, noise, amount of visual distraction, materials, or toys. Decrease the space available for play or movement to lower affect. Depending on the child's sensory issues, playing in a small space indoors is usually calmer than playing in the wide-open outdoors (unless the child is stressed by lack of parameters). Small, closed spaces may be comforting. Children need a place to go when they need to be alone. Provide soft, soothing transition objects or a calming "cuddly" for the child. This can be a blanket, a cuddly toy to hold, or an object to suck.

2. *Modify the activity.* Raise or lower arousal level. How the activity is presented— calmly or with excitement—models emotions for the child. The structure of the activity itself also influences emotions. Activities with no boundaries, such as bubble blowing, playing in the sand, or running around, tend to excite emotions; whereas activities that have structured parameters, such as filling up a bucket with sand or water, tend to be more calming. Adults can provide structure to activities by giving the activity a goal (e.g., cutting fringe all around a paper), by adding a sequence requiring changing actions (e.g., playing doctor), or by providing step-by-step instructions. For some children, predictability in play sequences provides security. The adult needs to modify play gradually.

3. *Make activity purposeful.* Activities that are done because the child wants to accomplish something tend to help the child maintain moderated emotions. If the child is kicking to get a ball in the net, he is more determined than if he is just kicking the ball anywhere. The focus and goal orientation can help the underresponsive child become more responsive, whereas the overresponsive child can become more observant, which requires a calmer demeanor.

4. *Provide physical parameters.* Physical parameters, such as a table, a tray, or a marked-off space on the floor, help the child to control actions and also keep emotions in check. A chair with arms, a cushion, or a ball to sit on also provides a means of containing the child who tends to get "out of bounds." Alternatively, standing and moving to do an activity can be arousing for children who need extra input.

5. *Modify toys and materials.* The level of difficulty a child encounters in play and routine activities influences the child's emotional level and responsiveness. If an activity is too easy, the child will become bored, distracted, or seek more exciting actions. If the activity is too challenging, the child can become frustrated, angry, or just give up. Adults need to adjust activities so that there is a slight challenge, but not too much.

Toys, materials, and activities can be modified to help achieve this level of difficulty: Add a handle to a cup that is difficult to hold, modify clothing on dolls to make them easier to take off and put on, substitute different types of blocks (e.g., magnetic, bristle blocks) that offer interest and motivation to manipulate, introduce balls that are easier to catch and throw (e.g., softer and larger), and so forth.

6. *Modify sensory characteristics.* Children may seek out or be aversive to different kinds of sensory input. Toys can be modified to add the types of sensory input that arouses pleasurable emotions. Visual interest (e.g., adding fingernail polish to the doll's fingers and toes); auditory supplements (e.g., adding bells to a bracelet), tactile embellishments (e.g., books with textural features), olfactory (e.g., using lotion after a bath), and taste (e.g., using real food in dramatic play) all add interest and elements that can help modify emotions.

7. *Provide adaptive equipment.* Adaptive equipment can reduce frustration. Adaptive seating, communication devices, auditory enhancements or amplification, glasses, and so forth are all important to maximize the positive aspects of interacting with the environment and reduce stress and frustration.

8. *Modify the child's position.* Make sure the child is comfortable and stable. Children who feel insecure, off balance, unstable, or too constrained will feel discomfort, anxiety, or fear. Whether the child is lying down, sitting, standing, or moving, adults need to attend to the child's feeling of security. Sometimes all that is needed is a supportive hand; other times, moving the child into a more stable position is needed.

9. *Modify schedule or routine.* Predictable routines reduce stress and anxiety for children. Particularly for children who have difficulty regulating their state of arousal, predictable patterns for getting up going through daily routines, and going to bed are important.

■■■■■■ **V. B. What effect do sensory experiences have on the child's activity level?**
V. C. What effect do sensory experiences have on the child's attention?

The child's level of arousal, which is influenced by sensory regulation abilities, not only has an impact on emotions, but also on attention and activity level. Children with poor sensory modulation may be distractible, impulsive, and disorganized and may have increased anxiety and inappropriate levels of attention. For example, when the child cannot filter sensory information appropriately, his or her attention may be scattered among all sensory changes going on in the environment or, alternatively, be diverted to only specific stimuli. In either case, attention is not optimal.

Activity level, emotions, and attention all interact and are influenced by the child's ability to modulate sensory input. Children who are overly reactive to various types of sensory input may react by becoming overaroused, and therefore they become overly active and inattentive. Conversely, some children who are overresponsive "shut down" in an attempt to control the input. Children who are underresponsive need more input to maintain activity level and attention.

All of the sensory areas influence the child's level of arousal, activity level, and attention. Underresponsiveness or overresponsiveness in one sensory area can have a profound effect on the child's behavior. However, the child's response to all of the sensory areas needs to be taken into consideration, because how the child responds to one sensory area can be used to offset the child's reaction to another sensory area. For example, the child who is hyperreactive to tactile input may become less active and more attentive when deep touch-pressure is applied to her arms or proprioceptive input is applied to her shoulders. Thus, observation of the child's patterns of response is critical to intervention.

The following are general principles for intervention with children for whom over- or underresponsive sensory systems are having a negative impact on activity level and/or attention. Consultation with professionals trained in sensory modulation techniques is recommended.

Interaction Strategies

1. *Modify frequency, intensity, duration, and/or rhythmicity.* Adults need to watch the child's initiations, repetitions, and avoidance of behaviors. Children typically seek out what they like, repeat what is pleasurable, and avoid what is unpleasant.

For children who are overly responsive to sensory input, adults may need to modify the frequency, intensity, duration, and/or rhythmicity of input in order to increase attention and decrease activity level of children. Needs vary by child and may alter as environmental demands change.

Alternatively, for children who are underresponsive to sensory input (including touch, noise, visual stimuli, or certain smells or tastes), in general an increase in the frequency, intensity, duration, and/or rhythm of input is needed. Monitor reactions of the child to determine when stimulation is "just the right amount." Light touch and colder temperatures are stimulating and thus, when appropriate to the situation, may be used to arouse the underresponsive child. Children who are underresponsive may increase activity level and attention when encouraged to perform quick, staccato movements (e.g., dancing or jumping) or in response to unpredictable intonation (e.g., talking in an unusual or exaggerated speech pattern or singing instead of talking) or other intense input from adults (e.g., bouncing or tickling). However, some children who appear underresponsive are actually withdrawing because they are *overly* responsive. In other words, they become overstimulated easily and they withdraw from engagement with the environment and/or people. Because it can be difficult to determine what is happening with some children, professional consultation is recommended to determine what is needed.

2. *Reduce anxiety and/or activity level through calming activities.* Increased anxiety resulting from sensory defensiveness (including touch, noise, visual stimuli or certain smells or tastes) may be reduced through activities that are calming. Deep touch pressure and warmth is calming, so putting warm lotion or powder on the child's back, arms, and legs with deep, slow rhythmic massaging movements may reduce activity level. Talking slowly and calmly also increases attention and reduces activity level. (If signs of distress are seen in the child, stop.)

3. *Let the child control actions on his or her own body when possible.* Children who are defensive often get upset because they feel no control over the input they receive. Allowing them to put lotion on themselves, adjust the loudness of the radio, or control the rheostat on the lights gives them a sense of control. The adult also can ask for the child's input if the child is unable to participate in controlling input. For example, the adult can add input in increments (e.g., touch, sound, light) and ask the child "Are you ready for more?" Preparing the child verbally for the sensory input that is coming also is important, so the child is not surprised or startled.

4. *Hold the child close.* Children normally move through a progression of being held close to the body, interacting a few inches away, and then being comfortable exploring independently. Some children benefit from remaining in one of these first levels of "se-

cure base" longer. In other words, holding the child on the lap or between the legs may provide comforting input, decrease activity level, and increase attention.

5. *Be aware of sensitivity to movement.* Parents who frequently carry children and move them through space for various purposes (e.g., getting in the car seat or into the tub) need to be aware of hypersensitivity to movement and of how they are holding the child as they move him or her. Some children have difficulty when the head position is moved from upright or they have difficulty with nonlinear movements, so this should be monitored.

6. *Reduce stress.* Stress affects attention negatively and can result in either an increase in activity level or in immobilization. Stress reduction strategies include helping the child to breathe rhythmically, to slow down, and to concentrate on something he or she enjoys (see TPBI2, Chapter 5, Section III. Strategies for Improving State and Emotional Regulation). Adults can help children by suggesting, modeling, and helping them to regulate their actions.

7. *Model affect, actions, and responses.* Adults can provide a role model for children as they regulate their own attention and activity level. Tell the child what you are doing and why it is helping.

8. *Play turn-taking games.* Involve the child in turn-taking games involving sensory experiences (as appropriate to the child's needs). For example, giving each other a massage, using a back massager on each other, drying each others' hands with a towel, or putting lotion on each other (some children may prefer to do these things in turn, rather than on each other) will have different effects on children, depending on their sensory needs. Games such as blowing and jumping on bubbles, playing catch, or batting a ball may increase attention and activity level, whereas other interaction games, such as lotto, fingerplays, or reading may lower activity levels while at the same time increasing attention.

Environmental Modifications

In addition to interpersonal strategies that may support the child learning to control attention and activity level, environmental modifications often are useful. Depending on the findings from TPBA2, the team may want to consider some of the following environmental modifications. Consultation with professionals with expertise in sensory modulation is recommended.

1. *Create a safe environment.* Children with sensory modulation issues may not pay attention to location of objects in the environment or be able to modify actions to avoid risks. They need an environment that is free of clutter, has furniture secured, and presents no dangerous options.

2. *Provide toys that match the child's sensory needs.* Be aware of how much sensory stimulation the child's toys provide and how the child reacts to each element. Some children need extra sensory input, and some children get sensory overload if too much stimulation is provided. Many of today's toys are loaded with sensory stimulation of all types. They have lots of "bells and whistles." The toys have multiple tactile elements; lights and sounds are produced; music is played; words, letters, or numbers are elicited; or the toys have parts that vibrate or begin to move. For children who need extra sensory input to attain an optimal level of arousal, these type of toys serve to awaken the various sensory systems and, thus, the child's attention and interest. It should be noted, however, that overuse of this type of toy can lessen its therapeutic value because the child can become immune to its effects. It is better to vary the type of toy and the type of sensory input.

Children who are underreactive also may benefit from toys that involve both movement and proprioceptive input. Sometimes called *heavy work*, activities such as pulling a wagon that is lightly loaded or pushing another child on a sled can "wake up" the system. Moderation here is important, because too much heavy work for a child who tires easily can result in withdrawal.

For children who are overly responsive to sensory input, "less is more." Provide less complexity of stimuli. Blocks may be less excitatory than a toy cash register. A puzzle may cause less activity and anxiety than a whistle.

3. *Provide musical toys, such as drums and bells, and equipment to play tapes and CDs for dancing and singing.* Much in the same way that multisensory toys arouse children, musical toys, particularly when used with loud, staccato rhythms, can arouse the child. For children who are underresponsive to sensory input, musical instruments and equipment can motivate children to move, dance, sing, and interact.

4. *Provide calming music as a background.* For children who are overly responsive to sensory input, classical music, lullabies, or music with slow rhythms can be calming when played in the background while the child is engaged in the activities. Calming music, for example, may help children who are over stimulated by the events of the day to relax for sleep.

5. *Provide materials that can be used rhythmically or hugged to provide deep pressure.* Objects that the child can hold and rub or manipulate in a repetitive fashion (fidget toys) can help the child calm. A squeeze toy can serve the same purpose for a child as an adult's stress ball. For children who are overly responsive to sensory input something to hug can be comforting. A stuffed animal or a cuddly doll can serve as both a transition object and an object that can provide proprioceptive input through hugging. The child needs to be given these when over stimulated and then talked to softly as he or she calms down. The child will soon associate the objects with the calming effect.

6. *Provide familiar toys and materials, because familiarity may be less overstimulating.* For children who are overly responsive to sensory input, new toys, materials, and situations may be overly arousing. Children who get easily overstimulated by novelty can benefit from sameness and routine. Introduce novel events gradually and with preparation. Taking along a familiar toy and using familiar routines and words can have a stabilizing effect. It makes the situation more predictable for the child and enables the child to relate to known calming strategies.

7. *Provide a variety of foods with more spicy flavors and varied textures.* Spicy foods and crunchy textures have an arousing influence. For children who are underresponsive to sensory input, mealtimes with flavorful foods can serve to increase the child's attention and arousal level.

8. *Incorporate oral sensory activities.* Movements involving the mouth can have an impact on attention and activity level, because they provide proprioceptive input to this area and require rhythmic activities of breathing and swallowing. Use of thick drinks and straws encourages sucking, a proprioceptive activity. Chewing food that is rubbery, stringy, or crunchy also requires extra effort and proprioceptive input. These oral activities can replace nonfunctional actions such as chewing on clothing or toys.

9. *Introduce aromas into the environment.* The part of the brain that processes aromas is closely connected to the limbic system, which is concerned with emotion and memory; consequently, smell can have an effect on affect. Aromatic essential oils that are arousing, such as cinnamon or vanilla, and those that are calming, such as rosemary, orange, lavender, and rosewood, can be used in bathwater, compresses, or on scent rings during various times of the day to awaken or calm the child's senses.

ROUTINES FOR THE CHILD WHO
NEEDS SUPPORT FOR EFFECTIVE MODULATION OF SENSATION

Daily Routines (Home and Classroom)

Feeding/Eating

Make sure the child feels stable and secure. Support efforts at experimenting with new tastes and smells. Reduce distractions and involve the child in the discovery process. Support efforts at independence and experimentation with food. Sucking thick liquids through a straw also provides extra input and proprioceptive input to the lips, tongue, and cheeks. Sucking may thus help the child attend to the eating process.

Diapering/Toileting

For infants, diapering can include play with sights and sounds, and comments on smells. Because children want to move they may "fight" being constrained for diapering. Give them a reason to lie still by involving them in a preferred activity requiring their concentration. As the child gets older, involve her in sensory activities such as washing hands with soap and water, drying with a towel, putting on lotion and powder, massaging arms and legs, and so forth. Provide supported potty chairs and later secure potty seats, so the child feels safe.

Dressing

Some children prefer the feel of being naked, whereas others find it to be "too cold." Sensitivity to the child's preferences is important. Be aware of texture preferences and types of clothing the child finds comfortable. (Children who like being naked may not like confining, tight clothing; however, some children may prefer heavy, snug clothing because it feels comforting.) Dressing involves balance and can prompt insecurity. Encouraging the child's efforts and providing reassurance and, whenever needed, physical support is important.

Going Out

Because going out involves a major transition from one environment to another, it may be difficult for children with sensory modulation difficulties. Preparation for the outing (verbal and physical), provision of a motivating task (meaningful to the child), and attention to the child's sensory concerns (reducing irritations, increasing preferred sensations) is important to make outings successful.

Play Routines (Home and Classroom)

Face-to-Face Play

Face-to-face play may seem overwhelming to some children with defensiveness to close proximity or touch. Sensitive interactions, in which the adult reads the child's cues and stops when the child turns away or averts his or her gaze can help the child become more responsive. Wait for the child to turn back to the adult to reinstigate contact. Face-to-face games also should respect the child's need for more distance. For some children, focus on fingerplays or object play may allow turn-taking interactions without the intensity of face-to-face contact.

Physical Play

Physical play can provide opportunities for children to do "heavy work" or get more intense proprioceptive and/or vestibular input. With attention to the child's individual differences, physical play can provide either arousal or dampening of sensory systems. Rapid movements (e.g., riding a tricycle) and light touch (e.g., poking at bubbles) tend to arouse, whereas deep pressure and slow, rhythmic movements with pushing and pulling (e.g., pushing another child on a swing) tend to calm. For children with underresponsive systems, provide arousal activities before an activity on which the child needs to concentrate. For children with hyperresponsive systems, provide dampening or calming activities to increase focus and attention.

Manipulative Play

Manipulative play often requires focus and attention, so preparatory activities such as those described previously under Physical Play may be helpful. Manipulative play itself also can provide different kinds of input. Activities such as squeezing playdough, art activities using hole punches or staplers, or construction with TinkerToys or small Legos requires pushing and pulling, or proprioceptive input. Coloring with force to make darker shades also encourages the child to use pressure.

Sensory Play

Sensory play involving such materials as water, sand, and other textures may be particularly aversive to children with tactile defensiveness. Start with larger, less "sticky" substances, such as torn paper, wood chips, and other exploratory materials, and gradually modify the textures the child explores to include those that are smaller or more glutinous or gooey. Meaningful activities, such as making bread or cookie dough, are more involving than simple exploration and thus may be more motivating to the child. Art activities using materials such as fingerpaints, glue, feathers, glitter, and so forth provide tactile input. Some children with tactile defensiveness first may be able to participate using a tool, then gradually be able to use a fingertip, then have increasingly more contact with more fingers and the hand. Proprioceptive activities with the hands, such as cutting a hard material that requires force, in preparation for more aversive tactile experiences may reduce avoidance.

Dramatic Play

Dramatic play can enable the meaningful use of many different sensory systems. During role play, the child can push and pull a baby carriage or wagon (proprioceptive input), pretend to "drive" a tricycle (vestibular input), give the baby a bath and dress it (tactile input), and so forth. Awareness of sensory needs enables the adult to provide props that provide the needed sensory input. As a play partner, the adult can then model, suggest, or assist the child to use these materials in the play. The child is more motivated to use the materials in the dramatic play context. For example, when playing fireman, the child is motivated to drive the "fire truck," carry the heavy hose, climb a ladder, play in water or some material representing water, "carry" the injured people, and so forth.

Reading and Learning Routines

Circle Time

Spacing and seating of children can address sensory issues. Some children may need parameters, such as with a chair, carpet square, or hula hoop, to delineate "their" space. Other children may benefit from preparatory activities involving arousal (for children with underresponsive sensory systems) or proprioceptive (pushing the chairs into a circle) input to help increase focus and attention. Some children benefit from having a "fiddle" or squeeze toy to play with during circle time, to help them focus. For other children, chewing gum or other chewy food is helpful.

One-on-One Reading

Lap reading is a great way to provide parameters for children who need boundaries and to give proprioceptive input through holding and hugging. For children who do not like being touched, allowing them to hug a favorite stuffed animal or doll during reading gives them some extra sensory input but allows them to retain control of that input.

Science and Math

Centers such as math and science typically involve manipulation of materials, thinking, and problem solving. Use of manipulatives that provide extra effort to construct, such as three-dimensional models that need pressure to connect, can provide proprioceptive input to calm the sensory system and increase attention. Adults can select manipulatives that provide different types of sensory input depending on the child's needs. One child may be able to count and sort colored feathers, whereas another may do the same with heavier colored blocks.

■■■■ SOLEDAD

Soledad is a 4-year old Hispanic child in a Head Start program in a rural area. Her teacher is concerned because Soledad has a short attention span, is easily distracted, is aggressive with other children, and is constantly chewing on the neck of her shirt or some other object. Soledad's mother reports that Soledad will only wear certain clothing (soft) and that she needs to "microwave Soledad's clothing in the morning to warm them up," or she won't get dressed. She also stated that she has found Soledad in her room, under (rather than on) the mattress on her bed. A play-based assessment and a developmental and sensory history revealed that Soledad has tactile defensiveness. She does not like being too close to people or wearing clothing that does not feel comfortable because of texture or temperature. She also is sensory seeking in relation to oral stimuli and deep pressure. Many of Soledad's aggressive behaviors seem to be in response to being too close to peers. Her reaction, striking out, appears to be a defensive reaction rather than an aggressive response. She also seeks oral stimulation that gives her proprioceptive input, such as biting and chewing. The patterns of her behavior indicate a sensory regulation disorder. The following recommendations were made for environmental and interactional adaptations to support Soledad's functioning at home and at school.

Interaction Strategies

1. *Acknowledge Soledad's feelings and things that make her uncomfortable. Help her to think of ways to calm herself. For example, "It makes you upset when someone gets too close to you. What could you do so that Sara will not touch you?" or "I see that you are getting angry—try taking deep breaths. That's good. Now, what can you do with your hands instead of hitting?"*

2. *Prepare Soledad for upcoming changes to the routine or new events. Give her choices of what she wants to take with her to make her feel comfortable. Let her know what behavior is expected of her and reward her with big hugs when she responds.*

3. *Use a calm voice with Soledad, because she may get more excited or angry if you model the same affect she does. Help her hear what a quiet voice sounds like and see a calm demeanor.*

4. *Give Soledad backrubs and massages on the arms and legs to calm her or as a preparation before an active movement experience.*

Environmental Modifications

1. *Maintain a predictable routine.*

2. *Provide alternatives for Soledad to get appropriate proprioceptive input. This is calming for her and meets her need for extra input to muscles and joints. Give her opportunities to push and pull things in her environment, such as wagons. Let her carry heavy objects.*

3. *Give her objects to squeeze or an action to do when she is upset. Perhaps she could hit one fist into the other palm, or squeeze her hands together.*

4. *Give her a quiet place to go when she needs space and time to calm down.*

5. *Make an animal sock friend for Soledad that is stuffed with heavy beans or rice and covered with soft material or fur. During circle time or at work time, her "friend" can be placed on Soledad's lap for her to stroke. This will be calming for her and will help her to attend.*

6. *Let Soledad use a straw for drinking and give her thicker liquids, such as yogurt, to provide oral stimulation and proprioceptive input to the mouth.*

7. *When Soledad is upset or needs to attend, chewing gum may be helpful.*

8. *Use a bean bag, sleeping bag, or box stuffed with foam rubber or soft materials for Soledad to relax or rest in and on. This will give her input and can be used for comfort and calming.*

KEYS TO INTERVENTION BY DEVELOPMENTAL AGE

The following ideas are directed toward children who are functioning at approximately the following levels. Age milestones are not included, because sensory processing does not evolve in developmental progression. Suggestions are provided, however, related to children's sensory activities at different ages. These are not meant to be all-inclusive, but rather indicative of potential areas for exploration.

Developmental age	Key to intervention
Birth to 3 months	Notice what calms or arouses the child: different kinds of movement (e.g., up/down, side-to-side, rocking), cuddling, certain textures, and so forth.
	Notice response to faces, voices, noises of different pitches and intensities, and so forth.
	Provide opportunities to suck, both for calming and during focused attention on people and objects.
	Face-to-face talking, smiling, and singing are important.
3–6 months	Notice preferences for toys and the different types of sensory input they provide.
	Encourage interactive face-to-face play with noises, facial expressions, and vocalizations.
	Watch for signs of displeasure and the associated sensory input to determine the child's avoidance patterns.
	Child will begin to reach for preferred toys and materials, so the adult can provide options of different types of sensory play materials and see what the child chooses.
	Introduce a variety of different sensory toys.
	Be careful not to overstimulate with toys with too many sensory aspects. Encourage rolling over to get toys.

Developmental age	Key to intervention
6–9 months	Provide opportunities to lie on and explore different textures, rugs, blankets, tile, and so forth.
	The adult can use preferred toys as a motivation for the child to reach, scoot, and explore.
9–12 months	Exploration of tastes, smells, and different textures can be introduced.
	Watch for the child's sensory self-calming techniques (e.g., rocking, sucking thumb, rubbing blanket).
	Move toys into different positions in relation to the child to encourage movement through rotating, crawling, and pulling to stand.
	Play turn-taking face-to-face games and games involving tickling and throwing the child into the air.
12–18 months	Expand food textures and tastes. Play chase games and turn-taking games with faces and objects.
	Observe reactions to self-initiated movement and movement by others.
	Make bath time a playtime and let the child use the wash cloth independently to maintain control of input.
18–24 months	Observe child's awareness of sensations related to toileting.
	Let the child choose clothing to wear.
	Provide a variety of different types of play: manipulative, movement, dramatic play.
	Introduce sensory play with safe materials (dough, sand and water).
	Roughhouse play and chase play provide opportunities for turn-taking with sensory input.
24–36 months	Experiment with different sensory means for self-calming (e.g., quiet spot, hugging).
	Encourage tub play with kitchen utensils for exploration.
	Provide opportunities for expansive motor play at the park and on playgrounds.
	Provide materials for manipulation and construction that require pushing and pulling efforts.
	Introduce art materials for exploration.
	Introduce new dramatic play themes from the child's books, daily observations, and movies.
	Change sensory materials in the sensory table on a regular basis to encourage exploration of new textures.
36–48 months	Role play situations involving anxiety (e.g., doctor, dentist, going to bed) or movement themes (e.g., fireman, fisherman, circus).
	Play games with peer partner involving movement, such as dancing.
	Build large structures with various materials, including boxes, large blocks, paper, and so forth, and use art materials to decorate them.
	Use textures, movement experiments, and discovery of characteristics of real objects and situations in science and math.
48–60 months	Do "performances" to showcase talents.
	Play group movement games (Tag, Duck-Duck-Goose, Farmer in the Dell).
	Involve child in cooking new recipes for the family to expand tastes.
	Encourage dramatic play with props and themes that incorporate movement and sensory exploration (e.g., camping, going to the beach).
	Play in a variety of places (e.g., table, floor, outdoors).
	Do science and math activities that involve classification through discovery of characteristics.
60–72 months	Play movement games with rules (e.g., Mother May I; Statues; Musical Chairs).
	Encourage making up own dramatic play stories, creating floor games and movement games, songs, dances, and musical creations with instruments.

3

Facilitating Sensorimotor Development

VI. Strategies for Improving
     Sensorimotor Contributions to Daily Life and Self-Care

with Anita C. Bundy

Goal Attainment Scale

1	2	3	4	5	6	7	8	9
Is dependent on adults for all aspects of self-care because of difficulty with motor skills.		Is able to minimally help adult with motor aspects of self-care activities.		Can participate in all forms of self-care with moderate assistance from adults for motor aspects.		Needs minimal help with self-care activities and routines.		Is able to use motor skills to independently conduct everyday self-care activities and routines, including fasteners and use of cutlery.

Most activities of daily life have sensorimotor components. Two that are routinely a part of TPBA2 are addressed here: eating and dressing. These are particularly important for autonomy. As children take over, their sense of self-confidence soars and their parents are freed to do other things.

APPROPRIATE SENSORIMOTOR CONTRIBUTIONS TO DAILY LIFE AND SELF-CARE

Feeding/Eating

The oral mechanisms for eating are the same ones involved in speech (see TPBA2, Chapter 5, Subcategory VI. Oral Mechanism). They include the physical structures of the mouth and jaw, including the teeth and the musculature of the lips, tongue, and cheeks. Children who have the sensorimotor foundations for eating are able to take in food and manipulate it within the mouth, swallow, and breathe without aspirating or choking. They can use fingers and/or utensils to get food to the mouth. They know when they are hungry and can tolerate a range of textures, tastes, and smells in a variety of foods. They readily regulate the quantity of food that they take in.

141

The skills necessary for eating develop through typical stages. These include a suckling-swallow pattern for taking in liquids present at birth; to coordinated sucking, swallowing, and breathing for taking in semisolid foods in later infancy; to biting and chewing with up-and-down jaw movements as toddlers; to eating solids with utensils and chewing with rotary movements—patterns that begin to develop in young children and persist through adulthood.

From birth to about age 2, children rely on adults to provide both nourishment and the support for eating, but children regulate their own intake. They increasingly take on more responsibility, touching the breast, holding the bottle, then a cup, eating from a spoon, then controlling the spoon, and finally skillfully using a fork and knife. By age 2, children have acquired preferences for foods. They also have the necessary control over the large muscles of the arms and small muscles of the fingers to feed themselves. They begin to take greater control over self-feeding and take pride in using utensils. By age 5, children can participate in pouring, cutting, and spreading with a dinner knife.

Dressing

As with other daily life skills, the young infant is dependent on the adult for dressing and undressing for purposes of maintaining warmth and comfort. Older infants begin to help by removing simple garments (e.g., socks) and by holding limbs out for dressing by the adult. Toddlers are better at undressing than dressing. Young children gradually acquire the skills needed to put on clothing and can manage most garments except for fasteners. By the time they start school, most children are mastering fasteners and learning to tie their shoes.

Appropriate Sensorimotor Contributions in Practice

VI. A. Eating a simple snack

Daily Routines (Home and Classroom)

- *Infant/toddler:* The infant opens his mouth in anticipation of the spoonful of baby food. The toddler picks up a piece of ground meat with his fingers, puts it in his mouth, and chews with his mouth closed.

- *Young child:* The young child puts butter on her knife and presses it down on the bread, tearing a hole.

Play Routines (Home and Classroom)

- *Infant/toddler:* The infant places her fist in her mouth. The toddler takes a plastic spoon and pretends to feed the baby doll.

- *Young child:* In dramatic play, the young child brings a tray of plastic food to the table.

Classroom Routines

During snack time, the young child sets the table with bowls and spoons, carefully pours cereal and milk in a bowl, and eats from a spoon with little spilling.

VI. B. Performance of simple dressing tasks

Daily Routines (Home and Classroom)

- *Infant/toddler:* Mother puts the baby's arm in the sleeve of his shirt and pulls it through. The toddler holds out her arm. Her mother places the sleeve of the shirt over her hand and she pushes it through by herself.

- *Young child:* The young child dresses herself and then asks her mother to help with the buttons on her shirt.

Play Routines (Home and Classroom)

- *Infant/toddler:* The infant pulls up her shirt and shows her tummy so Daddy will blow on it. The toddler picks up her mother's hat, puts it on her head, and runs away laughing.

- *Young child:* The young child takes off her shoes, puts on plastic high heels from the dress-up box, and wraps a boa around her neck.

Classroom Routines

Before going outdoors, the young child puts on his jacket and boots but needs help with the zipper and ties.

GENERAL PRINCIPLES FOR SUPPORTING APPROPRIATE SENSORIMOTOR CONTRIBUTIONS TO DAILY LIFE AND SELF-CARE

Adults use a variety of strategies to promote daily life skills, particularly eating and dressing. The following are strategies often used by adults to help children develop independent skills. These strategies also are useful for children who have difficulty with accomplishing these skills.

Follow the Child's Signals

Adults respond to children's cues. When infants cry, they feed them or respond to dressing needs when they think the child is wet, hot, or cold. As the child gets older, adults read physical cues (e.g., pointing at the refrigerator, or tugging at pants) or respond to vocal or verbal requests. They also respond to cues the child provides about what he or she does not like and when he or she does not want assistance, respecting the child's need for some control. Children also give cues when they are ready to move to the next phase of self-feeding. They reach for the bottle, hold it, lean forward to pick up food, and so forth.

Respond to Cues About Tempo

Adults respond to children's needs for activities to happen at a faster or slower pace. For instance, when feeding the child the pace of feeding may be fast initially, as the child is hungry and wants more. The pace slows as the child gets full. The same is true for dressing. The child's restlessness may cue the parent to hurry the pace of dressing, or the child's efforts to dress himself may slow the pace.

Develop a Routine

Routines help children anticipate and learn action sequences. Each family develops a routine that reflects the culture and needs of the family. Each teacher also develops a routine that supports the needs of the children and curriculum. The setting, time, utensils, food, and clothing may differ, but the routines help the child learn what is expected for each environment. Adults develop routines for bathing, toileting, dressing, eating, and other daily life skills.

Set Limits and Standards

Adults also help children learn acceptable practices for carrying out daily life skills. Adults teach children what to eat and what to wear. They teach them how to use uten-

sils appropriately, whether the eating tools are a spoon and fork or chop sticks. They in-
still good manners and knowledge of how to dress appropriately for the situation.

Make Eating and Dressing Fun

Adults make eating a social event and getting dressed an enjoyable learning experience. Meals are times for interactive sounds, games around eating, and talking about
food and how the child is doing in gaining new eating skills. Dressing is a time to learn
the names of body parts and to praise the child for acquiring new skills.

Encourage Participation and Independence

Adults encourage participation in daily life skills in numerous ways. They allow children to make choices about what, how much, and when to eat. They support the child
in taking greater control of the eating process; model and aid in the use of utensils, and
gradually provide greater challenges for independence. In the same way, children are
encouraged to select the clothing they will wear and assist the adult in putting them on
until they can do this task independently.

Reward Accomplishments

Children want to please adults. They will do almost anything to get a smile, a hug, or
applause. As they gain skills, children want to do things for themselves because of the
sense of accomplishment they feel. Adults support children's growing skills by acknowledging them and encouraging them to learn the next step, so they will be "a big
girl" or "a big boy."

THE PRINCIPLES IN PRACTICE

Adults employ a variety of strategies to support the child's development of self-help
skills. Following are examples of how caregivers use the previous strategies during the
day at home and in school. These examples are approaches that most caregivers use
naturally in their daily interactions with children. They also are appropriate for most
children with disabilities.

Daily Routines (Home and Classroom)

Feeding/Eating

As the child is learning the new skills, the adult provides verbal and physical prompts.
For example, Mother hands the spoon to the child and gently guides it to her mouth.
"Here it comes. . . . You did it! Good for you!"

Diapering/Toileting

Diapering and toileting involve partially undressing and re-dressing. This provides an
opportunity for adults to help children learn the steps involved in each process. Typically, with the infant, the adult comments on what he or she is doing ("Let's pull the
pants off"). With toddlers, more independence is desired and the adult asks for assistance ("Lift your legs"). Adults encourage young children to do much on their own
("Are you done? Pull your pants up").

Dressing

Similar to diapering and toileting, adults give the child increasing responsibility. First
they label the body parts and pieces of clothing as they are dressing the child, then ask

for participation and help in getting various clothing pieces on the body, and then watch and assist the child only as is needed.

Play Routines (Home and Classroom)

Face-to-Face Play

Eating often involves face-to-face play. The adult opens his or her mouth in imitation of the child, makes noises ("Yum yum!"), and makes faces in imitation of the child. The adult also entices the child to eat with games of "Zoom! Here comes the airplane," with the food zooming to the child's mouth on the spoon. Although these may not be thought of as games by some adults, the interaction process is a turn-taking game involving food, faces, and sounds.

Physical Play

When children are young, parents and caregivers often incorporate physical play into dressing. They blow raspberries on the tummy, bounce and cuddle the child while pulling up pants, tickle and kiss feet as they pull on socks.

Manipulative Play

Dressing and eating often are incorporated into doll play. Adults often use doll activities to practice dressing skills and using fasteners such as snaps, buttons, and zippers. Pretend play with plastic utensils also occurs through playing "tea party" with Mom, Dad, siblings, and peers.

Sensory Play

Adults often encourage children to practice new skills such as dumping, pouring, and stirring in the tub or the sand box. Plastic cups, shovels, and spoons are provided for the messy play, giving the child practice in an environment that does not involve food.

Reading and Learning Routines

Circle Time

Teachers use circle time to read books about the seasons and the clothing worn in various seasons, and about planting, harvesting, cooking, and eating. They read about children helping their younger brothers and sisters learn new skills. Group songs and fingerplays also enable children to pretend, "This is the way we comb our hair . . . ," and so forth.

One-on-One Book Reading

Books about independence, "getting bigger," and doing things "all by myself" often are read by adults as a way of encouraging the child's efforts and acknowledging his or her growing abilities. Children love to talk about what they can do.

Science and Math

Teachers incorporate information about eating and nutrition into science and math centers, games such as food lotto, and cooking experiments such as making gelatin or pudding.

PLANNING INDIVIDUALIZED INTERVENTIONS FOR IMPROVING SENSORIMOTOR CONTRIBUTIONS TO DAILY LIFE

Many children with special needs have difficulty with being fed or eating independently and/or carrying out daily life skills such as bathing, dressing, and caring for personal hygiene. Causes for the difficulties may relate to physiological problems, physical restrictions, cognitive or language comprehension limitations, poor sensory processing, behavioral concerns, or motivational issues. Daily life skills involve attending, comprehending social and communicative intentions, understanding what needs to be done, planning actions, processing sensory information, having the physical abilities to carry out sequences of actions, ability to monitor accuracy of movements, and sense of pride in accomplishment. Thus, all areas of development are involved, with gross and fine motor movements being only the most visible requirements.

This section does not attempt to address all of the potential problems that children with special needs may encounter. The following are offered primarily as considerations for children with mild to moderate special needs. Children with severe or profound multiple disabilities may lack self-sufficiency for all daily life skills and need full caretaking. For children who are extremely compromised in daily life skills, a team including medical, therapeutic, and educational professionals will be needed to adequately address all of the potential adaptations and approaches needed. Most children will be able to assist adults, at least partially, with their daily life skills, whereas the majority will be able to learn to become independent either with or without environmental adaptations and supports.

In this section, only eating and dressing are addressed because these are observable in TPBA. Many of the recommended strategies, however, apply to other daily life skills as well.

▭▭▭ VI. A. How well does the child eat a simple snack?

Many children with specific types of disabilities, such as cerebral palsy, vision impairment, mental retardation, or other disabilities, may have difficulty eating because of 1) abnormal muscle tone that affects postural support and movements for eating, 2) abnormal movement patterns in the mouth or in limbs that make eating difficult, 3) problems associated with abnormalities of the oral structures, 4) learning problems, or 5) medical issues. In addition, conditions such as Prader-Willi syndrome, phenylketonuria, or disorders affecting metabolism or the breakdown of specific amino acids or proteins may result in specific dietary concerns that have an affect on eating. Physiological disorders affecting the esophagus, stomach, or intestines (e.g., gastric reflux) or cardiac or respiratory issues also can negatively influence eating patterns. In addition, medications should be monitored because they can have an impact on eating and digestion. Eating is a life-and-death matter, and problems with eating should be taken seriously.

Eating and drinking involve the skeletal system, the muscular system, the nervous system, and cognitive and emotional functioning. Difficulties may relate to any of these areas, and comprehensive medical and therapeutic evaluations by a speech or occupational therapist may be needed to identify causes of problems. Depending on the findings of such evaluations, various supports may be recommended. The following are basic strategies and environmental considerations that are applicable to many different types of eating problems.

Interaction Strategies

1. *Modify the presentation of food.* Take time and make eating enjoyable. Meals should be a social time for talk and turn-taking. Present new foods numerous times. Use the "rule of 15" (present new foods at least 15 times over a period of time). Do not force

foods the child does not like. Sit in front of the child and present food from below the child's eye level to encourage a flexion pattern (to ease swallowing) and sitting symmetrically. Presentation from above (while standing) may encourage extension patterns. Where the food is presented in the mouth elicits various oral motor responses in the lips, cheeks, jaw, and tongue, so consultation with an expert is recommended. Present only three foods at one time, and then only one tablespoon of each per year of the child's age.

2. *Monitor the presentation of food and drink.* Some children with disabilities have a difficult time coordinating breathing and swallowing when eating or drinking and consequently are at risk for aspiration. To reduce the risk of aspiration, adults should 1) present small amounts of food or liquid at a time; 2) pace the feeding by waiting until the child has swallowed successfully before presenting more, 3) avoid rushed or forced feeding, 4) alternate offering food and drink, 5) determine the viscosity that is best tolerated (thinner liquids may be more easily aspirated), and 6) obtain medical evaluation and consultation for positioning if problems are persistent.

3. *Use language to support learning.* Tell the child what is happening (particularly for children with sensory, visual, motor, or auditory impairments). Use consistent tactile, gestural, and word cues. Tell children what they are eating (e.g., label foods, actions). Label the food at least three times while the child has the food in his or her mouth to help make the association between the food and the label. Offer choices. Combine words with nonverbal gestures or movements. Use praise for efforts at self-feeding, for trying new tastes, and for successes in eating. Eating should be a time for nurturing. For children with visual impairments and hearing loss, use multisensory ways to provide encouragement because the children may not be able to see facial cues and/or hear comments. Use touch signals, signs, or Body Signs. Use signs and gestures to support language. Tell the child how to move the food in his or her mouth or if more pressure is needed (e.g., for hard food such as carrots). Have conversations at mealtime about the day's events. For children with both hearing and vision impairments, tactile Body Signing may be used up against the child's body to cue them to what is happening and to provide directions (e.g., "Open wide"), ask questions ("More?"), or comment ("Banana").

4. *Provide physical support as needed.* Control of jaw, lips, and tongue may require manual assistance for children with motor control difficulties. Use of the thumb and finger of the nondominant hand on the chin or cheek can assist the child to control the jaw and other oral structures. *Do not use these techniques unless instructed by a professional, however, because doing them improperly can inhibit eating.* Placement of the hand on top of the head can help keep the child from extension of the neck, which may inhibit eating. *Keep your hands away from the back of the head because that may encourage pushing and too much extension.*

5. *Model routines and skills.* Involve the child in food preparation—washing, peeling, stirring, pouring, cutting—as the child is able. This encourages ownership of dishes that are to be served.

Let the child watch you eat and feel you chewing and swallowing (feeling is especially important for children with vision impairments). Label what you are doing: "chew" or "swallow." Overemphasize the actions so the child can see and/or feel what you are doing.

6. *Tell the child what to do instead of what not to do.* Provide positive supports to encourage continued effort.

7. *Encourage independence.* From the first days, encourage exploration and participation (e.g., touching the breast, holding the bottle, feeling the food, taking food to the mouth, playing with the spoon). Do not prop bottles in the child's mouth (it increases risk of ear infections and dental problems) or leave the child unattended, both for safety reasons and because meals are a time to build attachment and social interaction. Involve the child in all aspects of the meal: preparation, serving, eating, removing food, and clean-up. All of these activities provide opportunities to practice necessary self-help and other skills.

8. *Use a coactive approach.* Sit beside and slightly behind the child. Place hand-over-hand and guide the child's hand gently. Do this just a few times for each meal at first, so the child does not avoid the assistance. Phase out support as the child takes more control. Use a cue, such as a touch to the wrist or arm, to remind the child to keep eating.

9. *Teach needed skills.* Break down the task into smaller steps and determine whether the skills can be shaped through approximation; with subskills chained (forward or backward); prompted with touch, gesture, or words; or modeled and imitated. The following suggestions include both interactions and environmental considerations grouped by the skill being addressed.

10. *Increase sucking.* Extra long nipples, nipples with an enlarged hole, or specialized nipples may stimulate sucking. (A feeding team, speech-language pathologist, or occupational therapist can recommend an appropriate nipple. *Do not try to prescribe a nipple without assistance.*) Use the lightest bottle and little liquid to encourage holding the bottle for self-feeding.

11. *Increase chewing.* Begin with purees. Then make the purees slightly lumpy. Use hard biscuits that soften when sucked. Small, moist chunks will break off for chewing. *Food that does not soften (e.g., carrots) can be dangerous to children with poor oral motor skills. Feed hard foods only on the advice of a professional, and supervise carefully.* Provide hard rubber toys to chew (e.g., teething rings). Use a spoon that has been coated with rubber for children who have a bite reflex, or atypically strong closure of the jaw, stimulated when teeth or gums are contacted. This will prevent damage to the teeth and reduce the chances of breaking a spoon, which could be dangerous.

12. *Assist swallowing.* Make sure the first bite is swallowed before another is presented; do not allow "stuffing" or storing food in the cheeks. Press the finger under the jaw at the back of the tongue if needed to stimulate a swallow. *(Check with a professional first.)* Thicker liquids are easier to manage than thin liquids. Use naturally thickened liquids, such as nectar juices or yogurt mixed with milk. Placement of the food to prevent aspiration is important. *A professional should be consulted for assistance.*

13. *Assist finger feeding.* Encourage visual or tactile scanning of the tray or table to search and find food (tactile search will be needed for children who are blind). Start finger feeding with a favorite food at the beginning of the meal (when the child is most hungry). Start with food that is soft, easy to pick up, and no bigger than a fingernail. Encourage dexterity with fingers (see TPBI2, Chapter 3, Section III. Strategies for Improving Arm and Hand Use). Stand behind the child to direct his or her hands, because this helps the child create the appropriate movements.

14. *Assist drinking.* Teach the child to pick up a cup before putting it down. Cutting a notch out of one side of a cup (the side opposite where the child's mouth will be) can allow adults to see what is happening as the child takes liquid. This also minimizes the

need for the child to tip the head backward while drinking because the nose does not hit the rim of the cup. For this reason, cut-out cups are sometimes called "nosy cups." Use a two-handled cup, little liquid, and preferred flavors in the cup. For open-mouth cup drinking, start with a small amount of water. Present the cup on the bottom lip, encouraging a lip seal and avoiding a bite reflex. To aid control, present just a few drops of liquid at a time at first. Thickened liquid may be easier initially than very thin liquid. Provide assistance until the child can control the cup independently.

15. *Increase the use of a spoon.* Use a child-size spoon so the child does not become frustrated. Demonstrate bringing the spoon to the mouth. To assist in holding and using a spoon, present spoons for play during mealtime before the child uses a spoon to feed. (He or she will then associate spoons with meal time.) Letting the child have a second spoon decreases negotiation over who has the spoon and encourages imitation of what the adult is doing in between the adult feeding bites. Place just a little food at the front of the spoon, touch the food to the child's lips to encourage opening the mouth, then just partially into the mouth to prevent gagging and to preserve the ability to tip the spoon up. Demonstrate putting food in the spoon with fingers first, before scooping. Later, demonstrate getting food on the spoon in a bowl. Use food that clings to the spoon easily. Consider if an adaptive spoon is needed for gripping or getting spoon to mouth. (Consult with professionals.) The adult may need to prevent finger feeding to encourage spoon use.

16. *Teach fork use.* Forks actually are easier than spoons for many children, because the food does not fall off when the utensil is rotated. Use a child-size fork so it fits easily into the child's mouth and is easier to control. To reduce frustration, practice using a fork when it is not needed for eating. For example, let the child help with cooking, pressing cookie dough with a fork or mashing soft foods. Try using a "spork," a combination of a fork and a spoon. Use toothpicks to poke marshmallows, raisins, and other soft items. This will help the child get the idea of spearing things.

17. *Teach knife use.* Involvement in food preparation is a nice way to model, take turns, and support the child. Cut cookie dough, soft cheese, hard-boiled eggs, pieces of ripe fruit, pieces of stale bread to feed the birds, and so forth. Spread soft materials on hard foods first, so the child does not break or poke holes in the underlying food item. For instance, spread peanut butter on celery, spread soft butter on an English muffin, or spread oil on a cooking tray. The child can help make sandwiches (and if a piece of bread is ruined, it is no big loss), spreading soft butter or softened cheese spread. Children love playdough. Use a plastic knife with homemade playdough, which is softer than commercial brands.

18. *Teaching serving (e.g., pouring, passing).* Cooking is useful for taking turns in a supportive way, without the demands of a meal. Children can pour ingredients into a bowl using containers with a small amount of liquid or solid, such as milk, flour, or sugar. Keep the amount small, so that it is lighter and easier to manipulate, to increase chances for success and reduce mess. Let the child carry items to the preparation area. You can use the child's pretend cups and pitchers if they are easier for the child to manipulate. Let the child carry a small cookie tray to the oven for you to insert. Have the child carry items to the table on a basket or tray to set the table (e.g., napkins or spoons).

19. *Play pretend games involving family members, peers, and dolls.* Plastic utensils are easier to handle and do not require accuracy for the pretend situation. Occasionally include real snacks and utensils.

Environmental Modifications

In addition to interpersonal strategies that may support the child to improve eating skills, environmental modifications often are useful. Depending on the findings from TPBA2, the team may want to consider some of the following environmental modifications.

1. *Modify the environment.* Eliminate interpersonal stress. Feeding a child with disabilities may be challenging. Try to relax and take your time. Make the environment quiet, calm, and pleasant. Soft music may help. Make sure the child can see your face (avoid back lighting for children who are deaf). Protect environment and clothing so that mess is not a worry.

2. *Modify the foods presented.* Match the consistency of the food to the abilities of the child. Increase the thickness of liquids (e.g., potato flakes, commercial thickeners, gelatin products) and move toward solids to encourage the development of chewing; reduce constipation, cavities, or vitamin deficiencies; or lessen the impact of deformed oral structures. Avoid very hot or cold foods for children with high tone or sensory dysfunction; they may have a negative response to temperature extremes. Monitor the amount, type, and consistency of food. Introduction of solids should be directed by the child's overall development. Try to approximate the typical sequence for digestive and dental development. Introduce frequent variety and try new foods at beginning of meal, followed by a favorite. Modify color (place different colors of food on the plate to help the children identify them) and taste (children need to learn to tolerate different flavors, so introduce new tastes each week). Spicy, tart, or sour foods may increase oral movement in hypotonic children, whereas cold food may increase hypertonicity.

3. *Encourage smell.* Let the child smell foods as well as taste them.

4. *Vary texture.* Some children have difficulty with different textures. Start with textures that form into a bolus, such as mashed bananas. The most difficult textures to handle are those that separate in the mouth, such as rice or vegetables.

5. *Promote self-feeding.* Use dips (e.g., ranch dressing, mild salsa, ketchup) and dippers (e.g., carrots, pretzel sticks) to encourage eating new foods and to promote self-feeding.

6. *Rule out food allergies.* For children with allergies, present the same food 3 days in a row to rule out allergic reactions.

7. *Modifying the feeding schedule.* Teaching feeding skills may be accomplished best in small, frequent meals. The child can learn new skills in short practice sessions and enjoy the meal with the rest of the family in a less stressful situation. New tastes and textures also may be tolerated more easily in a new situation. Establish a routine for time, sequence of events, and position of the food and drink.

8. *Modify the utensils.* Although using typical utensils is better for the child to function in a "normalized" environment, modifying utensils can assist the child in tolerating feeding better, reducing negative reactions, and/or becoming more independent. Utensil size, configuration, and material can make a difference in feeding. Use adaptive dishes or utensils if needed. Colors on handles of utensils, cups, and edges of dishes help children with attentional issues or vision impairment find the utensils. A cutaway (nosy) cup has part of the top of the cup cut out so the top of the cup does not hit the nose. Clear plastic cups allow the adult to see the child's lips and tongue, so adaptations can be made if needed. Use modified spoons: a spatula spoon to minimize stimulation to the inner mouth, or nylon, plastic, or rubber-coated spoons for children who are hypersensitive or who have a bite reflex. Use nonslip bowls, plates, cups, and mats to stabilize dishes.

9. *Modify the position of the child.* Modifying the position of the child can increase stability so the child can use oral motor skills and fine motor movements more adaptively. No one, not even infants, should ever be fed while lying flat on the back. Sitting is the most desirable position for eating. Head and trunk control or support are important prerequisites for feeding in sitting. For children with disabilities, consultation with professionals is needed to ensure that the child is positioned for good trunk, head, and arm and hand control. The following may be helpful for various types of motor issues:

Hypertonicity: Children with too much tone may have neck and head thrust backward, making swallowing difficult and aspiration easier. Open jaw, jaw thrusting, and lip and tongue retraction also may be seen and are good cues that too much extension is present.

- Use upright posture, if possible, and head flexed slightly (not more than 15 degrees) to break up extension. *Professional assistance is vital in this area.*

- Placing a wedge under the legs to increase the angle of the hips to greater than 90 degrees may reduce leg extension or thrusting.

- Based on the amount of head control the child has, modify support to the child's head (e.g., headrest extension, neck support, head support).

- Use rolled towels behind the shoulders to bring them forward.

- If upright posture is not possible, consult with professionals on the best position for feeding.

Athetosis: Uncontrolled movements of the legs, arms, and/or head can interfere with feeding and eating.

- Restricting the movements of the limbs (e.g., padded straps, wheelchair tray) may assist with feeding the child.

- Restrict head movement. This is done most effectively with your hand on the top of the child's head. *Seek assistance from a professional.*

- Present food at midline or slightly to the other side (opposite the side toward which the child typically turns). This may help the child maintain a midline orientation.

Hypotonicity: Trunk and head control is key for children with low muscle tone.

- Head control may require a head positioner to support the head on a stable base.

- Supports to the side of the chest can aid trunk control. Avoid placing straps across the child's chest because this may interfere with breathing.

- Raise the tray or table to bring body up straighter.

- Low facial tone may require monitoring for pooling of liquid or pocketing of food. *A trained professional can provide techniques for helping to increase muscle tone.*

10. *Modify sensory input.* Modifying the amount and type of sensory input can reduce oral-facial hypersensitivity. Procedures administered directly to the tongue, gums, and face help reduce or increase reactivity. *(However, before attempting any of these procedures, request input from the team.)* Increase flavor, spices, and intensity of food to heighten awareness (see No. 2 under Environmental Modifications). If oral hyposensitivity is present, placement of food, texture of food, and smell and taste should be considered. *Seek assistance from the team.* Provide oral input through toys and oral games for

the child who is tube fed to reduce oral hypersensitivity or increase lack of sensitivity to help transition the child to oral feeding. *Be guided by the team.*

11. *Inhibit primitive reflexes that may inhibit eating.* Asymmetrical tonic neck reflex (ATNR), or the "fencer's" position, may interfere with getting the hand to the mouth. Placing the child's hand on a dowel at midline can help the head stay in midline and enable the child to control the other hand. Present food slightly off midline from the side away from which the child generally turns the head. Symmetrical tonic neck reflex (STNR) inhibits sitting and hand-to-mouth movements, because the movement of the head affects the head and arms (i.e., neck extension = arms extend, legs flex; neck flexion = arms flex, legs extend). Generally, placing a hand on the child's head to bring it into an optimal position is enough to offset this tendency. A tray can support the elbows in a flexed position, and raising the tray or table to mid-chest can assist with trunk stability. Oral motor reflexes including rooting, gagging, sucking-swallowing, and biting can all interfere with eating. Stable body position, positioning of head and neck, placement of hands and fingers with regard to the mouth, control of utensils, and placement of food in the mouth all may need to be considered. *Consult with professionals.*

VI. B. How well does the child perform simple dressing tasks?

Both gross and fine motor skills of almost every body part are required for dressing. Children need to use postural supports, balance, fine and gross motor planning, sensory regulation, bilateral coordination, fine motor manipulation, as well as cognitive, communication, and social skills. Children with motor concerns, such as cerebral palsy or motor planning disorders, may have problems with both dressing and undressing. Cognitive impairments may affect attending, imitating, and learning skill sequences, and communication concerns may inhibit understanding directions or requesting assistance. Social and emotional skills also are needed, particularly when initially learning skills through turn-taking and participation, because children need to have adequate motivation, emotional regulation, and compliance. Even typically developing children are 12 months old before they participate in dressing and at least 6 years of age before they are independent in dressing. Ability to achieve independence in dressing can, thus, present a challenge for many children with special needs.

The following suggestions may provide support to adults attempting to help children acquire skills in dressing.

Interaction Strategies

1. *Have calm interactions.* Watch and react to the child's cue to slow down, stop, or assist. Patience is needed to allow independence to emerge. Have conversations about what the child is wearing and why, what is going to happen after dressing, and so forth.

2. *Make dressing into a game.* Take turns with each step, so the child can imitate your actions. Make silly faces and exaggerate efforts. Break down skills into small steps. Backward chaining may allow the child to be successful. This means letting the child do the last step in the sequence of actions needed, and then, when this is done successfully, adding the step before that, and so forth.

3. *Sing songs to add interest.* "This is the way we take off our shoes, take off our shoes . . . ," and so forth.

4. *Teach what is important.* Teach skills with a mind to complexity and sequence, according to family preference, need, and usefulness. For example, think about what dressing actions are needed most frequently. For example, do not worry about teaching the child to put on gloves if these are rarely worn. On the other hand, if the child is

learning independent toileting, the ability to pull the pants up and down is very important. Family preference also should be taken into consideration. In one family, learning to tie shoes may be important, whereas in another, learning to wrap a scarf over the head may be necessary.

5. *Reduce tone in the limbs before dressing.* Using massage or relaxation techniques, reduce tone in the limbs before dressing (see TPBI2, Chapter 3, Section I. Strategies for Improving Functions Underlying Movement).

6. *Be careful of unintended consequences.* Particularly when dressing a child, adults have a tendency to pull on body parts to get them into the clothing. Be conscious of the fact that these actions may have the unintended result of increasing tone in children with hypertonicity. For example, pulling on the child's fingers or extremities can increase tone, making dressing even more challenging. Guide the extremities slowly through the clothing to avoid increasing tension. Push rather than pull whenever possible.

7. *Dress the most affected limb first (and undress the most affected limb first).* This allows the most flexibility for positioning the clothing.

8. *Encourage participation and independence.* The adult needs to convey positive expectations and confidence in the child's ability to gain independence. Reward effort (not just success) with praise, hugs, and kisses.

Environmental Modifications

In addition to interpersonal strategies that may support the child in improving dressing skills, environmental modifications often are useful. Depending on the findings from TPBA2, the team may want to consider some of the following environmental modifications.

1. *Use positioning techniques.* Avoid having the child lie down to dress, to prevent extension and to allow the child to see the process. Use the sitting position as soon as developmentally possible. Lean the child against a support if needed (an adult's body or a hard surface). Side-lying may relax the child who has too much tone. Infants who go into extension can be dressed while lying on their stomachs across the adult's lap.

2. *Consider clothing construction.* Double stitching at seams and crotch and well-attached buttons and well-made button holes are desirable. Front-opening shirts typically are easier to put on. Use tube socks.

3. *Consider the fabric.* For children in wheelchairs, breathable cotton or cotton blends are helpful for relieving the tendency toward moisture buildup. For children with sensory regulation issues, choose fabrics that are preferred by the child. Avoid stiff or scratchy fabrics. For children with spasticity, stretchy material will allow more "give" for children with a restricted range of movement. Choose material with flame-retardant finishes. Avoid fabric with a loop pile that can catch on rough surfaces. Choose washable permanent press for easy care. Use easily cleaned materials as a cover. A smock or vest of vinyl-like fabric can be wiped clean and worn over other clothing. Use lightweight, but warm, material. Thinsulate and fleece are lightweight and warm for winter.

4. *Consider the size.* Larger clothes may allow more ease of movement. However, too much material in sleeves catches on crutches. Larger pant legs are optimal for children with contractures or braces. Larger head openings are better for ease of putting on pull-on shirts.

5. *Modify clothing closures.* Use shoes with Velcro closures. Use Velcro closures of different sizes and stress for clothing fasteners. Add a ring or interesting pull tab onto

large-toothed zippers (a key ring with fun objects attached, old jewelry, fabric flowers, leather strips, and so forth can be used as zipper pulls). Use buttons with shanks (they have more movement). Sew buttons on with elastic thread to allow sleeves to stretch open when the arm is put through.

6. *Adapt.* Have everything ready for diapering or toileting, dressing, and undressing so the child does not have to wait and become uncomfortable. Capes can be worn instead of outer coats, especially for girls. Boys may like Batman or Superman capes. Elastic waistbands on skirts and pants are desirable. Add fabric patches to reinforce areas prone to extra pressure or wear. Change buttons or hooks to Velcro (hook side of Velcro on button position, loop side to behind buttonhole). Add fabric loops on pants, skirts, and socks to assist in pulling them up. The following are specific adaptations for children with special needs:

- Sensory regulation disorder: Remove tags from clothing if the tag is irritating to the child.

- Nonambulatory: Consider pants for children who crawl. Dresses and skirts inhibit crawling.

- Wheelchair

    Short jackets and shirts to prevent bunching

    Full skirts to provide more comfort

    Wraparound tops with side or back closures

    Capes rather than coats

- Limited arm movement

    Use few or no buttons on clothing.

    Make pullover shirts into front-opening shirts with Velcro or zippers.

- Vision impairment

    Sew knots into the inside of the garment with a color code (e.g., one knot is red; two knots, green).

    Add brightly colored trim to openings in clothing to help the child with low vision see the contrast and identify the opening.

- Language impairment or delay: Use communicative devices to enable the child to make choices, comment, request assistance, and so forth. Communication boards, picture sequence cues, voice-output devices, and sign language all can be used.

ROUTINES FOR THE CHILD WHO NEEDS SUPPORT TO IMPROVE SENSORIMOTOR CONTRIBUTIONS TO DAILY LIFE

Daily Routines (Home and Classroom)

Feeding/Eating

Positioning is the first and most important step. The child's feet should be supported, the trunk should be stable and in midline, and extension or flexion of body parts should be inhibited. Use adaptive devices if needed. When feeding the child, the adult should sit in a chair in front of the child and present the food or drink from below eye level. Use adaptive utensils if needed, such as a cutaway or nosy cup. Watch the intake and moderate the amount of food and liquid that the child takes in. For the child learning to feed him- or herself, coactive movements with the adult positioned at the side or behind the child may be used initially, then phased out as the child gains control of movements. Have a routine that includes time, seating, placement of utensils, and participation style.

Diapering/Toileting

For the infant with too much tone, diapering while the child is lying on the stomach, over the adult's knee, may prevent forceful movements of the legs together. For older children, provide supports to enable the child to stand and squat to push down pants. For example, the adult can stand behind the child and move the child's hips, tipping them down and inward, so the child can squat to push the pants down. Use adaptive clothing, such as pants with an elastic waist or Velcro closures to aid undressing. Loops on the sides of pants near the top can aid in pulling pants up.

Dressing

Position the clothing so it is aligned with the child in the way it will be put on. Provide supports for the child to enable independence, first sitting down, then standing using the adult's shoulder or arm for support. Begin with participation in undressing because this is easier. When dressing, let the child choose the clothing to motivate participation. Use adaptive closures, flexible material, and oversized arms and legs when needed. For children with too much tone, dress and undress the most affected limbs first.

Going Out

Encourage the child to get the jackets or hats needed and participate in dressing. Bulky coats are hardest to put on, so have the child experience success with other outerwear first. Hats are easiest to put on and take off; mittens are easy to take off, but hard to put on. For children with more involved motor difficulties, adapt buttons or change to Velcro fasteners, and add zipper pulls to make zippers easier to operate. Use capes for children in wheelchairs or children with extremely restricted movements. When children participate and feel pride in dressing accomplishments, they will be more motivated to go out.

Going to restaurants can be a challenge. The child may feel more comfortable if his or her own utensils are brought along, especially if adaptive utensils are used at home. To increase interest in eating, offer the child choices about what is ordered. Make available items that are easier for the child to manage with less adult support.

Play Routines (Home and Classroom)

Face-to-Face Play

Play games that will increase the child's oral motor and fine motor control. For instance, playing imitation games in the mirror can be fun and may encourage the child to move lips, tongue, and jaw in specific ways. For example, make kissing movements, open-mouthed yawns, grimaces, and so forth. Play tongue games where you take turns sticking out the tongue faster and faster. Play Simon Says with facial expressions and tongue movements with older children. Check with your speech-language pathologist to learn the best movements for your child. Fingerplays can increase fine motor skills and imitation abilities. Many songs and fingerplays involve food or dressing.

Physical Play

- *Make food.* Let the child help you make "shakes" by shaking the ingredients in a small jar (e.g., bananas the child mashes plus milk, orange juice and milk the child pours, powdered flavoring and milk the child measures). Add music, and the child can dance and shake at the same time.

- *Pretend to "be" food.* Be popcorn, boiling water, or dough being rolled out.

Manipulative Play

- *Food play.* Use foil and plastic wrap to wrap pretend food (or real food when helping in the kitchen). Children can play while dinner is being fixed. Give them a large plastic bowl and let them help tear lettuce, snap beans, break carrot strips, or crack eggs. This also is sensory play because they will experience different textures and smells as well. Include cooking tools in dramatic play that require manipulative skills (e.g., hand egg beater, masher, strainer, tongs).

- *Dressing play.* Use doll clothing with fasteners the child can manipulate. Use dress-up clothes the child will want to wear, including hats, coats, dresses, shoes, and various costumes.

- *Puzzles.* Use varying levels of puzzles for different children relating to fruits, vegetables, clothing, body parts, and so forth. Higher level, multipiece puzzles may relate a story (e.g., growing food, going to the grocery store or restaurant).

- *Games.* Board games and lotto games related to dressing and eating involve children in sharing their ideas and experiences.

Sensory Play

- *Water play.* The child can scrub plastic food with brushes or sponges, and wash dishes (especially plastic ones in dramatic play). Give the child cups, pitchers, measuring cups, and spoons in the tub, wading pool, or dish-washing container. Take dolls into the tub and shampoo their hair, wash, dry, and dress them.

- *Food play.* Dip foods into different textures (e.g., salad dressing, peanut butter, cheese dip). Do finger painting with pudding, applesauce, or yogurt. Let the child help shuck corn and peel hard-boiled eggs or oranges. Smell spices and foods when cooking. Play games at mealtimes in which family members close their eyes, smell the food, and guess what it is.

- *Incorporate textures.* Incorporate textures into dramatic play (e.g., feather boas, playdough for "cooking").

- *Art activities.* Use utensils in art activities (e.g., squeeze bottles for glue, a plastic fork or knife or rolling pin for shaping playdough, a shaker for sparkles, pitchers for mixing paints). Use food materials, plants, seeds, pasta shells, and so forth. Make dyes for art from berries, grapes, beets, or purple cabbage. Make prints with potatoes or fruit halves, or other interesting leftover food parts from nature.

Dramatic Play

Dramatic play should offer an opportunity to practice skills in a safe environment without criticism.

- *Food play.* Help the child prepare and serve a pretend tea party, birthday party, or picnic. Include plastic containers and utensils along with real ones. Pretend play can be motivating and offers an opportunity for practice. Include real snacks in the play to make the practice authentic. This play can include preparation, serving, and washing up. Include foods of different cultures (e.g., restaurants or travel play).

- *Dressing play.* Costumes and props enable children to practice dressing. Involve the child in discovery of costumes or dress of different cultures and discovery of dress for different activities or settings. Make prop boxes with cultural dress and make-believe food to use with stories of different cultures and lifestyles.

Reading and Learning Routines

Circle Time

Circle time is an opportunity to talk about and develop narratives about the day's activities, create story boards, sing, and dance. All of these activities can involve the sequences of actions relating to dressing or eating. Children can share their own preferences and family experiences. Circle time also can involve reading books about learning to do things by one's self, helping others with daily activities, and discovering how things are made.

One-on-One Reading

Reading books about how children learn new skills gives adults an opportunity to talk about children's experiences and feelings about what they are learning to do. Children with disabilities may enjoy books about how animals or children struggle to overcome challenges to be independent. Talk about the foods and articles of clothing pictured in the books. Discuss what you like and do not like.

Science and Math

- *Concepts.* Name and identify body parts, foods, and clothing. Sort and classify what, when, where, and how to dress and eat. Order, sequence, and comprehend using the following activities:

  - *Activities for eating.* Cooking and eating involve measuring amounts; counting utensils and foods; and studying plant and animal growth, nutrition, shapes, smells, portions, and how food changes form.

  - *Experimenting.* Depending on the child's level, each of the above-mentioned topics can be introduced and explored using real foods. They can be explored by examining, manipulating, comparing, and cutting apart.

  - *Reading.* Read books and play games relating to food and dressing.

  - *Activities for dressing.* Compare clothing of seasons, cultures, and ages. Experiment with textures, weights, and sizes. Plan outfits for travel.

▰▰▰ **SOHNI**

Sohni is a 2-year old Pakistani child with an unidentified genetic syndrome. She has extremely low muscle tone in both her trunk and oral musculature. Her mouth is open most of the time; she drools and has a tongue thrust. She can sit alone but has a curved back and sits on her tailbone with shoulders rolled forward and chin thrust forward. Sohni also has cognitive and visual impairments, with extremely low vision. She currently is ready to finger feed herself but is primarily fed by spoon. She is dressed by her parents and caregiver in child care. The goal is to increase Sohni's participation in feeding and dressing and move her toward more independence in daily living skills. The following are a few of the suggestions offered to her caregivers.

Interaction Strategies

1. *When encouraging finger feeding, stand behind Sohni to guide her. Let her know what you are doing. "It's time to eat." Touch her arm to let her know where you are. "Let's find the banana." Move your hand down her arm to her hand and gently guide her hand in a searching motion around the tray. Feel for a reaction in her fingers when she touches the food. "You found a banana! Get it!" When she picks it up, release your hand from hers and see if she takes it to her mouth independently. Provide assistance if needed. Tell her what she is eating. "Banana. You found a banana. Bananas are good." Repetition of the word when she is eating it will help her learn what a banana is. Gradually fade out physical support as she learns to search, but keep talking to her so she is motivated to continue.*

2. *Use the above-mentioned search strategies in play and in dressing and bathing routines. Let Sohni feel and hear the toy, if it makes sound. Tell her, "Let's play. Here's your top!" labeling the toy so she learns its name. Then remove the toy and when she reaches for it, put it down and help her begin to search. Do the same for finding her bath toys, wash cloth, and soap (as described above).*

3. *When dressing Sohni, let her feel the clothing and smell it (use a fabric softener with a scent she likes). Tell her it is time to dress, and label the piece of clothing you gave her. Lay the piece of clothing open across her body, and help her feel it. For example, lay the t-shirt across her chest and arms and say, "Here's your shirt. Let's put it on." This will prepare her for what is coming. Get her arm or leg positioned in the opening of the clothing and then tell her to "Push." The goal is for Sohni to learn to participate and learn the actions involved in dressing.*

Environmental Modifications

1. *At mealtimes, provide support for Sohni's trunk and neck to allow her to take in food and swallow more easily. Provide seating with a straight back and raise her feeding tray to mid-chest height to help her keep her head up while eating. Use a wedge or rolled towel under her knees to help keep her hips back and at a 90-degree angle. Make sure the foot rest is under her feet, so her feet also are at a 90-degree angle.*

2. *On Sohni's tray, provide a plastic sheet of a contrasting color to her food (e.g., black plastic for bananas and noodles) or a plate with a bright trim so she can find the food more easily. Start with her favorite foods. Begin with many pieces of food on the tray so she will be successful when she begins to search. Gradually reduce the number of pieces of food on the tray.*

3. *Use a cutaway cup to see where Sohni's tongue is and how much liquid she is getting. Slight pressure under the jaw at the back of the tongue may help her pull in her tongue. Manual support of her jaw and lip (as demonstrated by the speech-language pathologist) will help Sohni get lip closure and lose less liquid.*

4. *Currently, Sohni is being dressed while she is lying down. This gives her a lot of support for her head and trunk. Once she is participating in lifting her feet, offering her arms, and so forth (see the table at the end of this section), move her into a supported sitting position, which will enable her to participate more fully.*

KEYS TO INTERVENTION BY DEVELOPMENTAL AGE

The following ideas are directed toward children who are functioning at approximately the following levels. The suggestions are not meant to be all-inclusive, but rather are indicative of potential areas for exploration.

Developmental age	Eating and dressing skills	Keys to intervention
Birth to 3 months	Eating: Sucking increases to approximately 20 seconds before pausing. If offered pureed foods, uses a suckling pattern. Dressing: Body parts are easily manipulated by the adult for dressing.	Eating: Watch and respond to the baby's need to stop sucking and rest. Dressing: Talk to child about what is happening. Use warm wipes if child is reactive to cold, and leave clothing or cover on upper body while diapering.
4–6 months	Eating: Opens mouth adaptively. Closes lips. Gums soft cookie, although may revert to sucking it. Ejects food with tongue. May begin to eat pureed solids regularly. Helps bring bottle to mouth. Takes one or two swallows from a cup. Rarely drools in supine, prone, or sitting unless babbling or attention is engaged elsewhere. Dressing: Becomes more active and excited when dressed by adult.	Eating: Stimulate mouth opening by touching food on spoon to lips, and press lightly on tongue with spoon to encourage lip closure. Present bottle; let child help with bringing it to his or her mouth. Touch cup to child's bottom lip to stimulate lip closure. Dressing: Encourage participation; hold up shirt or pants for child to reach for. Let child hold clothing before dressing. Name body parts and clothing pieces. If spasticity is involved, dress and undress the more involved limbs first.
6–9 months	Eating: Mouth open in anticipation of spoon; beginning cup drinking; beginning to be able to move food from tongue to side of mouth. Feeds self soft biscuit with one hand (7 months). Takes ground or junior foods and mashed table foods. Can use upper lip to assist in removing food from spoon (8 months). Sitting in chair, no external support is needed; seat belt used for security, not support. No longer loses liquid during sucking initiation or when breast/bottle is removed (9 months). Uses an up-down sucking pattern for semisolids. Dressing: Child anticipates adult's actions and starts to offer leg or foot.	Eating: Introduce cup with or without spout, depending on child's ability and need. Provide soft foods that will encourage the development of chewing. Make sure child has postural support needed to sit in a highchair. Play imitation games with mouth and face. Dressing: Diaper or dress with child on stomach and over the knee for children with extension patterns. Encourage child to help push arms or legs through clothing openings. Use sitting position for dressing if child has extension patterns.
10–12 months	Eating: Chewing is more refined; independent finger feeding Helps hold cup and spoon. Feeds self whole bottle (10 months). Helps hold cup and spoon (11 months). Drooling is under control. Can take coarsely chopped table foods, including some easily chewed meats. Takes liquid primarily from a cup. Often insists on self-feeding (12 months). Dressing: Holds out foot for shoe or arm for a sleeve. Pushes off pants if soiled (12 months).	Eating: Let child have spoon to hold. Use adaptive spoon if needed. Let child practice finger feeding with soft items, such as pudding, placed on the tray to encourage hand-to-mouth action. Place 1–2 small pieces of food on tray; encourage child to pick up. Use coactive movements, if needed, at first. Consider positioning as child begins self-feeding. Make sure child is stable, food is of manageable and safely sized bites. Pace presentation and provide moderate amount. Play games with lip smacking and tongue movement. Label body parts as they are used. Label foods several times while in child's mouth. Dressing: Use elastic waist pants for ease in undressing. Encourage child to finish the last step in pulling off each item of clothing.

(continued on next page)

Developmental age	Eating and dressing skills	Keys to intervention
13–18 months	Eating: Eats ground and chopped foods. Has controlled bite. Starting to chew with lips closed (15–18 months). Good lip seal for drinking. Sucking-swallowing from a cup well-coordinated, with choking rarely occurring. Dips spoon in food and brings to mouth. Holds cup by handle but likely to tip. Fills spoon, turns in mouth, spilling. Lifts cup to mouth, may drop food (18 months). Dressing: Tries to put shoes on, usually getting half way. Pulls off hat. Begins to remove hat, socks, mittens and helps with other clothing.	Eating: Fork may be easier to control than a spoon. Stabilize cups, plates, and so forth to allow child more control with spoon. Use bowl with lip curved in and suction cup on bottom. Use dips for food to encourage trying new things. Label foods and actions of eating. Dressing: Involve child in taking off clothing. Let child make choices in clothing. Partially put on clothing pieces and let child finish the task. Give child dolls to wrap with blankets and hats to put on. Add padding on knees of pants if child is using crawling as primary movement method due to motor concerns.
19–24 months	Eating: Easy lip closure; no loss of food or liquid; eats variety of textures. Handles cup well. Unwraps food. Can suck and use straw. Opens jars. Point of spoon enters mouth. Dressing: Can take off shoe if lace is untied. Helps to push down/pull up trousers (18–24 months). Is able to find large sleeve hole (21–24 months).	Eating: Introduce various textures and new foods each week. Involve child in food preparation to encourage eating new foods. Consult with specialist on appropriate type of cup for child, if child has oral motor difficulties. Use plastic food, dishes, and utensils in dramatic play. Dressing: Use Velcro shoe closures and easy, pull-on clothing. Front closures are easier for children than pullover styles.
25–36 months	Eating: Eats the same food as the rest of the family; can grade jaw opening to size of food. Holds fork in fist (28+ months). Can pour from small pitcher (24–30 months). Holds cup by handle with one hand. Dressing: Can remove pull-down lower body garments with elastic waist (24–30 months). Buttons one large front button. Can untie lace and take off shoe (2–3 years). Can put on shoe, but it may be on the wrong foot. Is independent with pull-down garments. Opens front and side buttons. Closes front snaps. Removes all clothing. Can put on socks, shirt, coat.	Eating: Make mealtime a conversational time. Involve child in preparation and setting the table. Give child small pitcher and small amount of liquid to pour (e.g., own milk on cereal). With three different foods on plate, have child help choose which utensil to use. Talk about food's smells, colors, textures, tastes. Do "tea party" dramatic play and pretend to cook. Dressing: Adapt closures on clothing if needed. Give child time to do all of the tasks for undressing for bath or bed and dressing after toileting. Do dramatic play with dolls, involving undressing, bathing, diapering, dressing. Involve child in folding and putting away clothes. Child sorts sizes and colors, turns clothing right-side out before folding.
36–48 months	Eating: Chewing quite refined; can handle most types of food. Obtains drink from tap (36–42 months). Dressing: Opens front zipper on pants or jacket (39+ months). Buttons series of three buttons. Undresses rapidly and well. Dresses self.	Eating: Involve in food preparation (e.g., scrubbing, mashing, cutting with plastic knife), passing food at mealtimes, washing and drying plastic dishes. Practice spreading soft foods with a knife. Eat in different situations, requiring different seating, utensils, foods, manners, and so forth. Provide a variety of real utensils in dramatic play for practice (e.g., tongs, spatula, food brush). Dressing: Provide child with physical support but as little assistance as possible in dressing. Provide dress-up clothes for dramatic play with different types of closures, openings, and wraps. Have different types of shoes for dramatic play (e.g., boots, high heels, sandals, slippers). Have child help dress a sibling or friend in dress-up play.

Developmental age	Eating and dressing skills	Keys to intervention
48–60 months	Eating: Eats with fork held in fingers rather than fist (51+ months). Chooses fork over spoon where appropriate. Dressing: Unbuckles belt or shoe (45+ months). Needs little assistance with removing t-shirt or sweater, or with putting on underpants, shorts, trousers, or socks and shoes (except laces). Distinguishes front and back of garment and turns clothing right-side out. Can insert belt in loops. Buttons/unbuttons most buttons (4–4½ years). Closes front zipper and locks tab (4–4½ years).	Eating: Provide meals with a variety of textures. Keep introducing new foods. Describe and talk about the foods, where they come from, how they are made, and so forth. Involve child in all aspects of the meal, including grocery shopping. This will increase child's interest in preparing and eating what he or she bought. Have child help serve others in the family or the class. Make and cut sandwiches to practice knife use. Use knife and fork together. Dressing: Dramatic play can now involve costumes with more complex clothing such as a fireman's or policeman's uniform, cowboy outfit, space gear, an action hero suit, and so forth. The more unusual and complex, the better.
60–72 months	Eating: Child is efficient at all aspects of eating. Use of knife and fork is being refined. Dressing: Is able to dress with care. Can open back zipper (57+ months). Puts shoes on correct feet (4½–5 years). Unties back sash on dress.	Eating: Eat a variety of ethnic foods for variety in tastes, textures, and so forth. Try chopsticks. Dressing: Involve child in shopping for own clothing. Involve child in helping to dress younger siblings.

Resources: www.enablemart.com; www.mayerjohnson.com

4

Strategies for Working with Children with Visual Impairments

Tanni L. Anthony

TPBA2 does not include an assessment of a child's vision but offers a screening opportunity to determine whether a child's general visual performance appears to be within normal ranges or if there appears to be a concern that should be evaluated further. This chapter addresses general strategies for children who have been found, through other diagnostic means, to have visual problems such as needing prescriptive glasses or having a visual impairment.

The visual system involves three primary mechanisms working together: the eye which collects the visual information of light, color, and form; the optic nerve, which serves as the transmitter of visual information to the brain; and the brain, where visual information is interpreted. If there is damage to any one or more of these components, the visual image will be distorted, misinterpreted, or even absent. If there is a problem, it may be readily correctable with glasses or another type of medical intervention. Some visual problems, however, are not fully correctable and the child may have a permanent visual impairment.

VISUAL DEVELOPMENT

Visual development is usually quantified by measures of acuity, field, eye teaming, color, and interpretation. Each will be reviewed briefly.

Visual Acuity

The most recognized form of vision-related measurement is visual acuity or the clarity of our vision. The measurement of 20/20 is the norm for optimal visual clarity. Infants are not born with adultlike acuity and it takes several years for a young child to achieve 20/20 vision. Visual acuity is tied to the optical abilities of the eye. The cornea—the clear cover of the eye—is responsible for about 70% of our visual acuity.

The ability to see a very small object such as a thread on a coat or that last bit of cereal in the bowl involves near visual acuity. Distance acuity is used to watch a movie on the television screen across the room or to look for oncoming cars before crossing the street. Near acuity is used for reading a book and distance acuity is used for reading what is written on the classroom board or the PowerPoint presentation projected on the screen at the front of the classroom.

Visual Field

A normal visual field extends about 180 degrees from one side of the head to the other side when a person is looking straight ahead. To find the boundaries of your visual field, *look straight ahead and without moving your eyes* try the following: Bend your elbows so your hands are at ear level, slowly bring your hands forward until you detect their presence. Now place one hand over your head and slowly move it forward until you detect its presence. Finally, place a hand under your chin at chest level and slowly move it forward until you see its presence. In doing this exercise, you have found the general parameters of your visual field.

We use our visual field to gather information in front, to the side, above, and below us. When we notice a person coming up to us from the side, we are using our peripheral vision. As we walk, our lower visual field provides information about something on the ground that may be in our way. Our central field provides access to the face of the person we are looking at or the dial of a watch when we tell the time. Reading print involves one's central vision.

Eye teaming

Eye movements are controlled by six eye muscles and three cranial nerves (Langley, 1998). The eyes are designed to move together; when we look in any direction, both eyes should move in unison. This eye teaming is called *binocularity*. By moving our eyes, we are able to shift our central vision (our best detail vision) to whatever we want to see. As the tennis ball goes from one side of the court to the other, spectators can keep their eyes on the fast moving ball to keep up with the game. Tracking or following a moving object is important in most recreational activities involving a moving target object (e.g., ball, puck) and/or moving people. Another form of eye teaming movement is called *saccades*, which involves moving both eyes across a series of stationary items. Coordinated saccadic eye movements are important for reading print; the eyes should move efficiently back and forth across the printed page from one line to another.

Eye movement skills typically are present at birth and continue to refine quickly over the course of the next several months. Eye movements should be well synchronized by 6 months of age (Bishop, 1988); the eyes should move in unison and have full range of side-to-side and up-down movement capabilities. There should be no evidence of an eye turning in, out, up, or down. Any noted misalignment of the eyes should be reported to an eye care specialist.

Color Vision

The cones in the retina allow us to perceive the colors and their many shades. Colors offer both aesthetic pleasure, such as appreciating the color changes of the autumn leaves and the look and visual feel of artwork, and support the mood of a room. Colors serve to get our attention and provide information. The red stop sign alerts the driver to prepare to stop and the neon yellow-green of a fire truck catches our eye as the vehicle pulls out of the station two blocks ahead of us before the siren is activated. Maps use different colors to define subway paths or roads. In the early grades, colors are used as attributes for matching and classifying. Our language is embedded with color references when we describe people and events and offer directions to others.

Interpretation

The interpretation of a visual image is tied to visual recognition, the ability to assign meaning to what is seen. The brain seeks to understand what it sees. When we look at cloud formations, we often "see" something familiar such as a face, animal, or other object in our visual imagery repertoire. Very young infants learn quickly to visually identify their caregivers. With experience, they recognize familiar objects such as bottles and pacifiers. With language, the visual items assume labels. As the child matures symbolically, visual images such as pictures and symbols have representational meaning.

Vision is one of two distance senses, with hearing being the other sense that provides information away from one's body. The sense of sight has ties to every developmental domain. Much of what is learned in the early years and throughout life is through incidental learning or being able to observe one's environment and the activities occurring away from one's body. Incidental learning undergirds much of a young child's understanding about objects, people, and events. To help illustrate this idea, envision a young child in a highchair watching his mother prepare a snack for him. He observes her walking to the counter, where she takes the yellow banana from the bunch in a bowl by the sink, opens a drawer to take out a silver knife, peels the banana, and cuts the banana with the knife so the slices fall onto his highchair. He watches his mom pick up a slice of banana and bring it to her mouth. Within these few minutes of observation, the child has information about where items are kept within the kitchen, what a banana looks like before and after it is peeled and sliced, that a knife is used for cutting, and that his mother eats food just like he does. For a child who does not have the visual advantage of such incidental learning, a banana may seem to just appear on the highchair tray and may exist only in its sliced format.

In addition to incidental learning, vision guides movement. Early hand watching behavior occurs typically by 3 months of age when the infant brings her hands up to her eyes for observation and watches as they move away from her body. With experience, the baby learns to move her hands toward an object of intention. Over time and repeated practice, the child learns to use her eyes and hands for laserlike reaching accuracy and precision grasping of even the smallest objects. Vision will also be the impetus for whole-body propulsion toward desired people and objects. As gross motor development skills increase, the child will ambulate with specific intent toward something she sees across the room and wants to investigate.

Vision invites imitation of other's movements. The toddler playing next to other children will mimic his peers' actions with toys. As daddy claps his hands, so will the baby. The child observing his mother putting her clothes on in the morning has a model for performing the same actions with his shirt and pants. Sibling actions are definite motivators for a child's personal repetition. Imitation has significant ties to literacy as the child copies lines, shapes, and ultimately letters and words from others.

Another visual link to literacy is the ability to discern the detail and gestalt of pictures. A young child's first books are usually picture books of familiar objects, animals, and people. Pictures invite the handling and review of books, as well as provide key information about the context of a story.

APPROPRIATE VISION

Although vision is present at birth, babies are not born with complete visual abilities. The very young infant is visually drawn to faces and images with high contrast and patterns and can follow a slowly moving object. Visual development occurs typically very quickly and automatically over the course of the first 18 months of a child's life.

Babies will not have adultlike visual acuity but typically are able to demonstrate eye contact from an 8–10-inch focal distance. By 6–7 months of age, infants can visually detect a very small object from 10 inches away. This might be first observed when a child notices food crumbs or a small cake decoration. By 6 months, the infant expands her focal distance to up to 5 feet away, and by 18 months the child can visually locate a small ball from 20 feet away. Children at 3–4 years of age should have visual acuity of 20/40 or better.

Visual acuity can be screened through a school-based or community-based vision screening program to determine whether it is within normal ranges. If a child fails a vision screening, he or she should be referred to an appropriate pediatric eye care specialist. Only an eye care specialist can provide an eye examination to determine whether the child has a refractive error. A refractive error occurs when a person is nearsighted, farsighted, and/or has astigmatism. These problems are usually fully correctable with prescriptive lenses such as glasses or contact lenses prescribed by an eye doctor.

Appropriate Visual Abilities in Practice

■■■■■■ Quality of visual acuity

Daily Routines (Home and Classroom)

- *Infant/toddler:* The infant looks into his mother's eyes as she holds him close and talks to him. The toddler looks across the room, from 10 feet, to check in visually with his mom, and he smiles when she smiles at him.

- *Young child:* The preschooler sees his Dad's white car coming down the block and shouts, "Mom, Dad's home!"

Play Routines (Home and Classroom)

- *Infant/toddler*: The infant reaches up and swats at the overhead mobile, delighting in its movement. The toddler grasps the winder on a toy and makes an attempt to wind it up.

- *Young child:* The young child notices that the Mr. Potato Head 3 feet away is missing an eye.

Classroom Routines

The children are gathered around the teacher during story time. As she reads from the books, she holds it up so the children can see the pictures. She points out small details and the children nod as they see them too.

■■■■■■ Ability to track moving objects

Daily Routines (Home and Classroom)

- *Infant/toddler:* The infant follows an object moving slowly from midline to each side. The toddler watches his cat cross the room to his food dish.

- *Young child:* The young child follows the movements of his mother as she works to prepare his afternoon snack in the kitchen.

Play Routines (Home and Classroom)

- *Infant/toddler:* As the swatted mobile begins to swing, the infant watches it move to and fro. The toddler watches the blown soap bubbles fall from her teacher's mouth above to the floor.

- *Young child:* The young child keeps his eyes on his friend who is running from the slide to the swing set.

Classroom Routines

The teacher has a flashlight in the dark and moves its light across the room; the children follow the beam of light and guess where it might land.

▨▨▨▨▨ Ability to distinguish figure–ground relationship

Daily Routines (Home and Classroom)

- *Infant/toddler:* The infant locates her pacifier on the busy-blanket next to her. A toddler points to the small ladybug sitting in the multicolored flowers in the garden.

- *Young child:* The young child finds the matching missing button to her shirt in the pile of different colored and sized buttons.

Play Routines (Home and Classroom)

- *Infant/toddler:* The infant reaches for her rattle that is partially covered by other toys. The toddler finds his new favorite toy in the pile of toys left by the Christmas tree.

- *Young child:* The young child locates the wig she is looking for in the "dress up" box.

Classroom Routines

The teacher asks the children to find Waldo in the book, *Where's Waldo,* and they shout with glee when he is located on page after busy page.

▨▨▨▨▨ Quality of visual discrimination

Daily Routines (Home and Classroom)

- *Infant/toddler:* The infant visually distinguishes her mother from another person. The toddler points to her dog when she sees a picture of a dog in a storybook.

- *Young child:* The young child picks up the red crayon and announces, "This is red!"

Play Routines (Home and Classroom)

- *Infant/toddler:* The infant smiles when she sees her yellow fuzzy duck in her mom's hand. When given a choice of three shoes, the toddler picks out the matching shoe to put on her doll's foot.

- *Young child:* The young child finds the spoon that is the biggest in the silverware drawer.

Classroom Routines

The teacher makes a bulletin board with everyone's baby picture. The children can identify which picture is of them.

GENERAL PRINCIPLES FOR SUPPORTING CHILDREN'S AGE-APPROPRIATE VISUAL ABILITIES

Most of the typical activities presented to young children involve vision. Parents and other caregivers automatically encourage eye contact as they interact with children, fixation as objects are held up for a child to see or as they look at books together, tracking by moving objects across the child's line of vision, watching people and objects moving in the environment, and so forth. Although such activities do not "develop" vision, they encourage the use of a child's vision.

The most important way to support a young child's visual skills is to work with the family to obtain appropriate eye care for the child. The American Academy of Ophthalmology (1996) recommends that all children have an eye examination by their third birthday. An earlier examination should occur if there is a family history of serious eye problems and/or if there are any concerns about the child's visual performance. Only an eye care specialist, such as an optometrist or ophthalmologist can examine the internal health of the eyes and prescribe needed glasses or medical treatments for optimal visual performance. School personnel involved in vision screening can screen for eye problems but cannot do a clinical visual evaluation, diagnose a visual problem, and/or offer possible needed treatment.

GENERAL PRINCIPLES FOR ENHANCING VISUAL ABILITIES

If a child has reduced vision due to eye and/or brain damage, perception and/or interpretation of the visual image may be affected for different reasons. If the child cannot decipher the image due to visual acuity challenges, the lack of or reduced interpretation is tied to poor visual input to the brain. For example, when the cornea or the lens of the eye is cloudy, the visual image will be distorted. When any structure of the eye, including the optic nerve, is damaged or incomplete, there will not be a complete visual message to the brain. If there is neurological damage to the visual pathways or visual cortex, which is called cortical or cerebral visual impairment (CVI), the brain may not be able to interpret the visual image.

In the event that a child has a potentially correctable vision problem such as a refractive error or poor eye alignment or a permanent and uncorrectable visual impairment, the early intervention and educational teams should follow the eye care specialist's recommendations and take care to individualize the child's program needs.

Comply with Medical Recommendations

If glasses have been prescribed, they should be worn as recommended. Usually, prescriptive lenses are worn throughout a child's day, but there are times when the recommended wearing time may be restricted to certain types of visual activities. For example, there are times when glasses are needed only for close viewing or for distance viewing. Care should be taken daily to keep the glasses clean and in good shape. There are types of frames and lenses that have been designed just for young children to minimize weight on tiny noses and ears and to decrease the likelihood of breakage.

Children with permanent visual impairment may benefit from glasses to correct their refractive error. For example, a child with *retinopathy of prematurity*, an eye condition affecting the premature infant's retina, also may have a high level of nearsightedness. Although glasses cannot correct the vision problems due to the retinal condition, they can assist the child with seeing better by correcting the refractive error. Children who are light sensitive, such as the child with albinism, will benefit from light absorption lenses. This is an important reason why all children should be followed by an eye doctor: to ensure that vision is corrected at an optimal level.

If another medical treatment has been prescribed, such as patching an eye because of a lazy eye or amblyopic condition, caregivers, early interventionists, or educators should talk to the family to determine how to support the patching schedule. It is always important to follow carefully the exact medical instructions of how long an eye should be patched. Often it is a good idea for the child to be exposed to visual tasks while an eye is patched. It may be helpful to find tasks that are especially motivating for the child to maintain his efforts to use the unpatched eye. This allows the unpatched eye the opportunity to work. The child, under these conditions, may demonstrate early visual fatigue that should be respected by taking breaks or discontinuing the visual tasks.

Team with a Teacher Certified in Visual Impairment

In the event that a child has been diagnosed as having a visual impairment, the educational team should include a certified teacher of students with visual impairments (TVI). This individual is a university-trained special educator with specific expertise in the instructional needs of children who have a visual impairment. A TVI is trained to address the effects of vision loss on development and a child's academic school experience, to assess for and procure needed specialized equipment, and to provide specialized instruction unique to children with visual impairment, such as braille and low vision device training. A TVI will conduct a *functional vision assessment* (FVA) to determine the status of the child's vision in everyday settings and what low- and high-tech strategies will help to improve visual efficiency. A FVA will address the following components of a child's visual performance: appearance of the eyes, eye movement abilities, focal distance abilities, eye dominance, color awareness, visual motivators, lighting needs, sensory compensation needs, and an overall individual sensory/learning style (Anthony, 2000).

A FVA can be completed by a trained TVI within the context of TPBA, although this is not a routine component of TPBA2. The vision guidelines of TPBA2 are not for functional vision assessment, but for general vision screening purposes only. These vision guidelines will help a team determine whether a child should be evaluated by an eye care specialist. When a TPBA team knows that they will be conducting a play-based assessment with a child who is visually impaired, they will benefit from the expertise of a TVI to discuss possible assessment adaptation needs for all the developmental domains.

In addition to a FVA, the TVI will complete a separate assessment called a *Learning Media Assessment* (Koenig & Holbrook, 1995) to determine the learning and literacy media needs of the child with visual impairment. For example, the assessment findings may indicate that the child is primarily a tactile learner and should be taught braille. For a young child, this will involve following a tactile sequence of development with real objects, tangible or tactile symbols, and, ultimately, braille instruction. Another child may also benefit from both braille and visually enhanced materials such as large print or the use of a magnification device, as another means of literacy media. A TVI will work with the child's family and educational providers to ensure that all sensory information is presented in an optimal learning manner for the child.

The next six areas of consideration are important for all children, but especially children with visual impairment.

Promote Postural Security

All children benefit from good postural security during visually related tasks. A child who is competing with gravity during visual tasks will be distracted by working to stay upright. For example, the baby who does not have great head control will not be able to sustain eye contact with his mother as long as his head is lagging to one side. If the child's head is stabilized, the eye contact will become the primary task of his attention. The child in a wheelchair who does not have good upright support will be less able to concentrate on seeking and finding a wanted visual symbol on her communication board. When children are sitting in chairs, their feet should be able to be flat on the ground. For best viewing results, children should be in well-supported positions when they are expected to visually attend to a person, object, symbol, or eye–hand coordination task.

Ensure Adequate Wait Time

Children with neurological impairments and/or medical fragility may benefit especially from inflated wait time to respond to presented visual material. As a child receives the sensory input, it may take considerable time for him or her to organize a motor response such as fixating on the object, following the object, reaching toward the object, and so forth. The child's specific need for wait time will be an important aspect of his or her educational programming, and it is necessary for all the team members to understand so that there is consistency across team members who interact with the child.

Eliminate Competing Auditory Distraction

A quiet environment will assist children in their visual concentration. During home visits, it may be prudent to talk to the family about turning off the television or moving to a quieter room if there is a lot of background noise of other children. If a preschool setting has a high level of noise, it may be helpful to find a quiet corner to work with the child or even to move to another room. The more medically complex or neurologically involved the child, the more attention should be paid to a quiet environment where the sole demand on the child is to attend to the presented visual information.

Creating a quiet learning environment also will involve paying attention to adult voices that may distract the child from the visual task. Well-intended adults may want to provide language input during learning tasks and, although modeling vocabulary is important, there must be a balance of providing information to the child and respecting her need to have a quiet learning environment for visual learning. Once the child has engaged visually, the adult(s) can determine how best to provide verbal input to support the visual experience. For example, after one child leaned into a picture book and intently studied the illustration, the early interventionist offered, "Yes, Sara, that is a bunny. We have a pet bunny at school." With the picture in mind, more information could be offered about the picture and the real-life rabbit in the classroom.

Pay Attention to Focal Distance and Angle of Viewing

Children, if physically able, will self-regulate their need to see an object better. An object might be brought closer to the child's eyes or the child might lean forward to bring his eyes closer to the object. Some learners will turn their head and/or their eyes a certain way when looking at something. If a child has not been evaluated by an eye doctor and is demonstrating these behaviors, such behavior would be a good reason to schedule an eye examination. In the event that the child has a visual impairment that cannot be improved with glasses or other medical procedures, these behaviors should not be discouraged because the child is doing what he needs to do to see at an optimal level.

For a child with low vision (the term *low vision* describes corrected and useable vision in the better eye starting at 20/70 distance visual acuity [Corn & Koenig, 1996]), it might be helpful to experiment with the positioning of objects that free his or her hands from needing to bring the object closer or from neck strain of bending continually to see something. For example, a reading stand is often used with school-age students to keep the reading materials upright and within closer visual access of the learner. For a younger child, a play board to which objects are attached safely will provide easier visual and physical access to the objects the child wants to investigate.

Another aspect of visual presentation involves the child's visual field. There are many types of field loss associated with damage to the eyes and/or brain. Children with cerebral palsy or certain types of retinal disorders have a high incidence of visual field loss. Visual field loss may be minimal or extensive and may be static or progressive. Some field losses involve compromise to half the child's visual field in each eye, such as when a child has hemianopsia. Others conditions may result in lower field loss, peripheral or side vision loss, and or central vision loss. Field loss may also be random within a person's visual field such as the case of a scotoma, or blind spot.

If the child has a visual field loss, the certified TVI can offer guidance as to where best to present visual materials. A child with a lower visual field loss, for example, will need materials elevated and angled for better visual access. If a child has a right field loss, materials will be positioned to the midline and left side. In all cases of field loss, however, one aspect of visual efficiency training will be to ensure that the child has the appropriate scanning techniques, as much as possible, to visually check the field area that may be neglected due to a field loss.

Pay Attention to the Visual Display

Imagine if your world was the equivalent to a *Where's Waldo* book. For some children, especially those with neurological damage resulting in cortical/cerebral visual impairment, the amount of information in a visual display can be overwhelming. To assist with looking and interpreting the visual information, less visual information often is better. It is advisable to literally assume the position of the child and look around at the visual environment. Even if an object is presented directly in front of the child, it may be that it is competing with a very busy background. The background may actually be the teacher's visually busy shirt or it may be the competing presence of a variety of different objects within the child's visual field. For some children, it will be important to present objects against a solid backdrop that shields the child from other extraneous visual information. For the child who cannot suppress unnecessary visual information, it might be helpful for education personnel to wear a solid-colored smock when working with him or her.

Pay attention to the following characteristics of the visual display in front of the child who has a visual impairment:

Contrast. Is there good contrast between the object of interest and its background? It is easier to discern a light-colored object when it is presented against a dark background, and vice versa.

Color. Bright colors may be helpful to attract a child's visual attention. A child may identify personal belongings because of their particular color (my red backpack, my mom's white car). Colored borders may also be used to frame a picture. Children with cortical visual impairment or CVI may demonstrate strong color preferences that can be tied into objects used throughout their day. A child with CVI, for example, may attend visually to a red cup over a soft blue cup.

Visual array. The "congestion" of a visual display may interfere with a child's visual attention or discrimination. For some children, it will be important to minimize the number of visual targets on one display and to pay attention to the busyness of the visual background of a display. White space is necessary around pictures and/or letters in order to highlight what should be looked at on a page. Visual crowding of information may result in the inability of a child to distinguish one item from another. This is especially true when a child has poor visual acuity and/or visual interpretation abilities.

Visual complexity. Pictures or visual displays that have competing backgrounds or have a lot of internal "busyness" will be difficult for some children. It is important to pay attention to the clarity of pictures when working with children who have reduced visual acuity and/or neurological conditions that affect visual performance.

Choose Optimal Lighting

The amount of lighting needed for visual tasks is dependent on both the task at hand and the individual needs of a child. Some visual impairment conditions result in light sensitivity, such as albinism or aniridia. For these children, bright light may be uncomfortable and they may benefit from light-absorption lenses and/or caps with brims or bills. Other children may do better with increased illumination. Often, task lighting or lighting that falls directly on the visual display is helpful. For example, most people do not need a bright room to read a book but are content with a lamp that directs light onto the book. The rule of thumb is that lighting should come from behind the child and fall over his or her shoulder for optimal lighting conditions.

PLANNING INDIVIDUALIZED
INTERVENTIONS FOR IMPROVING VISUAL ABILITIES

▮▮▮▮ What if the child is blind/visually impaired?

There are many eye conditions that can result in an early-onset visual impairment. Children with disabilities, in general, have an increased risk for visual complications. This is especially true for children who have a history of neurological compromise due to prenatal and postnatal infections, complications at birth, accidents, or trauma. Visual impairments or blindness can be an isolated disability or comorbid with other disabilities. Although differing approaches often are indicated for specific eye conditions or for a diagnosis of cortical/cerebral visual impairment, this chapter does not attempt to address strategies for each individual child with visual impairment. A certified TVI should assist in planning individual programs.

In the sections that follow, more generic strategies are presented for consideration. The intent is not to present ways to correct the child's vision, but rather a means to help the child compensate for vision difficulties so that development and learning are affected to the least extent possible.

Interaction Strategies

1. *Repeat presentations or opportunities to interact with materials.* As with all children, repetition is important for learning. A child with limited or absent vision will benefit from opportunities to repeatedly see, touch, and/or hear objects, pictures, and symbols. Play boards with attached objects and/or trays with raised edges will help contain the items for repeated access.

2. *Include and/or inform the child of environment and/or routine changes.* If there are changes made, care should be taken to talk about the changes and, as far as possible, show the child what has been changed. This allows the child to anticipate what is occurring and to make an adjustment based on other sensory input. If the child has an

object or symbol system of communication, it is helpful to include an object that means "Something is different" to help highlight the routine change for the child.

3. Watch for fatigue. Watch for cues that might indicate visual fatigue, such as looking away, closing or rubbing the eyes, or irritated-looking eyes. Respect the child's need for breaks, and give him or her free time.

4. Use a hand-under-hand approach. Establishing trust before physically guiding a child is paramount (Miles, 1993). It is critical that the team be trained not to grab or physically direct the child's hands. A hand-under-hand approach involves letting the child know what you are doing ("I want to show you the eggs in the bird's nest"), then placing your hand under the child's as an invitation for the child to move his or her hands with yours.

5. Use real-life objects and activities that are motivating to the child to teach new concepts. If it is fun to do, it is worth learning. Real-life objects and hands-on activities are the crux of addressing the impact of a visual impairment. Activities should be active and involve participation and discovery on the part of the child.

6. Determine what sensory system gives the child the most accurate information (visual, tactile, auditory). Talk with the TVI about the results of the LMA. The LMA will guide the types of sensory materials and activities that are most appropriate for the child. All team members should be familiar with the individual sensory learning style of the child.

7. Introduce new objects with more than one sense. Let the child feel, smell, experiment with, and listen to the object. Some children may need to use just one sense at a time. Again, talk to the TVI about how to best "package" the child's sensory learning. Some children benefit from an immediate multisensory approach, whereas others will need to have one sense activated at a time in order to allow time for true sensory integration.

8. Present objects or pictures in isolation or contrasting pairs if the child is being given a choice. The more the child can focus on relevant objects, the easier it is for him or her to determine what is being presented. If the child is given a choice of two objects, it might be helpful initially to present objects that are dissimilar in appearance and feel.

9. Use consistent language for common visual referents, and provide opportunities for generalization with objects. This ensures that the child knows that the cup he is looking at or touching is the one he knows as *his* cup. For example, "Here's your 'Dora' cup." To assist with generalization, the child should have opportunities to experience different objects in the same categories, such as a variety of cups, so that the Dora cup is distinguishable for its unique characteristics and the child understands that there are many different types of cups.

10. Use descriptive language that matches the child's developmental language level. Description is important for the child with visual impairment, so adults communicating with the child must be aware of not only the child's productive language level, but also the child's ability to comprehend abstract concepts. Furthermore, it is important to determine what type of description is meaningful and relevant. Too much information may serve to just tune the child out or pull the child away from his or her activities and self-discoveries. Use concrete terms that help the child locate what you want him to see (e.g., "Find the baby doll with the red shirt," rather than, "Give me the baby" or "It is the doll with the fuzzy ribbons in her hair"). Avoid terms such as "over here" or "over there." Be specific: "The puzzles are on the top shelf by the door."

11. *Give the child needed wait time.* Processing and interpreting input from various senses can take time. Let the child explore objects before requesting a response. Be patient!

12. *Avoid clutter.* Remove unnecessary items from the table or play area.

13. *Avoid standing in front of a window when talking.* The glare and backlight may make the adult's face difficult to see. Instead, position yourself at an appropriate distance and height from the child's face.

14. *Encourage the child to build self-advocacy skills.* Model the language that a child might use to self-advocate for his or her needs for breaks and accommodations: "You need more lighting for this task; let's turn on this lamp" or "What could help you see the picture better? Good you brought it closer to your eyes."

15. *Prepare the student for contact or interaction.* Provide verbal or auditory cues to prepare the child. Before touching, feeding, or helping a child, address the child by name and tell him what you are doing. For example, "Anthony, here comes a bite of banana." If you walk away from the child, be sure to let him know that you are leaving.

16. *Play listening games and highlight auditory cues.* Because listening is particularly important for children with visual impairments, reinforce the need to listen carefully and interpret what is heard. Point out sounds, ask children what they hear, and interpret the meaning of sounds. For example, "Violet, do you hear the sound outside? What do you think it is? That's right. It is raining. Do you think we should go outdoors today?" Be aware that the child may be tuned into environmental sounds that others do not pay attention to because of their focus on visual information. These sounds should be highlighted as learning opportunities. For example, a child may be tapping his cane back and forth on the grass and sidewalk instead of making his way to the school bus. The teacher may comment, "Your cane makes a different noise when it's on the grass and not the sidewalk."

17. *Play "I Spy" Games.* This type of game is a fun way to encourage the child to use vision and discriminate familiar objects, and to learn more about the child's distance and/or figure–ground visual abilities.

18. *Model and help the child develop organizational skills.* Organization is critical for children who have visual impairment. The preschool classroom should have defined spaces and containers for play and learning materials. Help the child organize his or her own space, create a mental map of the environment, and be able to maneuver through that environment independently. Many programs have found success with a "finished" bucket or basket; the objects used in a specific activity are placed in this container after they have been used in the activity. There is a defined place for them to go after they have been used and there is a clear way to announce, "We are finished," which helps with the transition to another activity.

19. *Teach other children to give the child with visual impairment clues* about what is happening, to give assistance, but not to do things for the child. Adults are in a great place to provide social mediation to increase peer interaction.

Environmental Adaptations

In addition to interpersonal strategies that may support the child who has a visual impairment, environmental adaptations often are useful. Depending on the findings from the FVA and discussion with the TVI, the team will want to consider the following types of environmental adaptations outlined below.

1. *Use meaningful objects and simple pictures.* Objects that are used to represent an activity and/or are used as a communication tool must be meaningful to the child. Too often, a well-intended service provider might want to use a miniature to represent a concept or activity. Simple pictures without internal busyness or complicated backgrounds will assist in the child's ability to interpret the picture.

2. *Provide color contrast to help with visual discrimination tasks.* Use contrasting background color to help the child see the key focus of attention from the background. Light-colored objects or symbols can be presented on a dark background, and vice versa.

3. *Use personalized color as tools for visual attention and visually based learning.* Use a child's favorite or preferred color to highlight personal objects such as backpacks, books, and so forth. Children with cortical visual impairment or CVI often demonstrate a strong preference for certain colors. These colors can be used to increase visual attention and visually based learning.

4. *Attend to lighting.* Reduce glare in the classroom and on any instructional materials by covering reflective surfaces and closing curtains or blinds (as needed). Adjust lighting type and strength. Placement of lighting usually is best behind or to the side of the child so the light beam falls on the task materials and not directly in the child's eyes. Incandescent lighting may be preferred over fluorescent lights, which emit a distracting noise. Some children may need reduced lighting if bright lights are bothersome. Glare can also be a problem. For example, white boards or pictures that have been laminated may be hard to see.

5. *Reduce distractions.* Auditory distractions, such as outside and inside noises or competing conversations, can make visual concentration more difficult. Pay attention to a child's ability to habituate to background noise; some children will not be bothered and others will be pulled from the visual task. Remove extraneous toys and materials from the visual environment when wanting the child to focus on a particular visual target.

6. *Determine size preference for pictures, symbols, and print.* Set out the same picture in different sizes and see which one the child chooses. A TVI will conduct specific assessments to determine visual efficiency with various print font sizes.

7. *Space objects on a page far apart.* As children begin to look at pictures or words, reduce the clutter on a page with only a few, large items. As appropriate, help the child learn to use a finger to guide the eyes from one element to another. Cut complicated pictures in books apart and place them on more than one page, so the child can differentiate characters and actions. If the child has a field loss, it is important to monitor whether spreading objects out is or is not beneficial to the child.

8. *Use tactile information to enhance and/or substitute for pictures and/or provide access to braille.* Tactile adaptations need to be made with care. Sometimes they "look" good, but they are not meaningful to the child whose dominant learning style is touch. The goal of tactile items in books should be to invite a child's exploration and to reinforce, as far as possible, a concept. For example, a feather would be a better tactile referent for a bird character in a book rather than a dried glue outline of the bird. A TVI will be responsible for a child's braille instruction and will assist with where to procure braille books or provide braille to the existing classroom books.

9. *Cover unnecessary material on a page.* Depending on the complexity of a picture or the content on a page and the child's need to minimize the amount of visual information, covering part of the picture or page can help a child focus on what is important.

10. *Use bright tape or glue on tactile cues for key parts of toys or materials.* Brightly colored tape or a tactile marker made with glue might be used to indicate, for example, the play button of a CD player or tape recorder. Many children will not need such an accommodation because they will tactilely map the locations of these buttons.

11. *Use a light box.* Light boxes, which illuminate transparent pages and objects, may help children focus, see contrast, and delineate specific shapes and figures. A TVI can assist with the procurement of this equipment and provide guidance on how best to use these materials.

12. *Place opaque markers on glass windows and doors.* This is an important safety precaution for all children, but especially those with vision impairments.

13. *Use adaptive equipment.* A slant board may be helpful to elevate and support print materials. Audio materials may be a wonderful way for the child to listen to stories. The TVI and motor specialists can assist with low- and high-technology needs for visual enhancement and postural support. Low-vision devices, such as magnifiers and telescopes (for distance viewing), should be prescribed by a specialist in low vision.

14. *Work with the TVI to determine the need for large-print books and computer screen adaptations.* Many states have a system for ordering large-print books; a TVI will be knowledgeable about how to procure these materials. Computer monitors can be adapted for font size and color/contrast needs.

15. *Pay attention to seating.* In groups, make sure the child is seated so he or she can see the teacher and instructional materials.

■■■■ What if the child has a limited visual field?

Interaction Strategies

1. *Talk to the certified TVI.* Discuss the nature of the field loss to learn about where to present visual information and/or where to position yourself when signing to the child who also is Deaf/hard of hearing.

2. *Present only a small amount of clear, uncluttered material.* Take advantage of where the child can see, and focus on what is important. Be aware that by enlarging material, the visual presentation may be more difficult for the child with a field loss.

3. *Recognize that searching for what can be seen is tiring.* Let the child help control the pace of the engagement and the break between looking and acting. Be aware of signs of visual fatigue (e.g., eye rubbing, looking away, irritated eyes).

4. *Help the child decode visual images.* Children who cannot see all of a situation may need verbal clues or descriptions to help them make sense of what is seen or what is happening outside of their visual field. If possible, encourage the child to take the time he needs to explore each part in order to build an understanding of the whole display. The adult also can help interpret the whole so the parts make sense.

5. *Follow the child's lead.* Let the child tell or show what he or she sees or does best.

Environmental Adaptations

In addition to interpersonal strategies that may support the child with a limited visual field, environmental adaptations often are useful. Depending on the findings from functional vision assessment completed by the TVI, the team may want to consider some of the environmental modifications outlined below.

1. *Place objects in the child's preferred visual field.* The TVI will help with determining the child's functional visual field, where there might be visual neglect, and useable areas of visual field.

2. *Match the size of objects presented to the child's visual field.* If the child has a small visual field and a large picture or object is presented at close range, the child will only be able to make out a fraction of the whole thing, making recognition and use difficult or impossible.

3. *Pay attention to the visual array of communication boards.* If a child has a visual field loss, care should be taken to arrange object, picture, or symbol systems to accommodate the field loss *and* the ability of the child to move her head for scanning purposes. Both are important considerations, because many children will accommodate for the field loss by moving their heads to take in the full visual array. If a child has cerebral palsy and cannot move to accommodate the field loss, the array will need to be minimized to accommodate the child's visual field.

▆▆▆▆▆ What if the child has poor depth perception?

Depth perception involves good visual acuity and the ability of both eyes to work together to perceive changes in depth.

Interaction Strategies

1. *Verbally help the child anticipate changes in depth.* Comment on what the child needs to do (e.g., reach up, step down).

2. *Encourage the child to use vision and touch in combination.* If vision alone does not provide accurate information, the child may need to explore through sound, movement, touch, and pressure. All are useful and should be encouraged. If a very young child pauses before a perceived or real surface change, encourage the child to feel with his feet or hands for the possible surface change. If this is a common occurrence, the child may need to be referred for an orientation and mobility (O&M) assessment consultation.

3. *Work with an O&M specialist to determine the need for an adapted mobility device or a long cane.* One of the purposes of these devices is to clear "the next step." Only an O&M specialist can prescribe a cane for a child who has visual impairment.

Environmental Adaptations

In addition to interpersonal strategies that may support the child with poor depth perception, environmental modifications often are useful. Depending on the findings from TPBA2, the team may want to consider some of the environmental modifications outlined here.

1. *Highlight edges.* Fluorescent colors are good for delineating edges of steps, tables, doors, and so forth. Colored tape can highlight the beginning of steps, as can a deliberately placed rug.

2. *Highlight dangerous areas on the playground.* Paint poles on the playground in bright colors. Highlight the edges around hazards and the edges of the playground area and the sidewalk. Remove low hanging branches.

▬▬▬ **What if the child has limited visual motor/visual cognitive skills?**

Children with vision problems or visual impairments may also have motor problems, because the two can go hand-in-hand, with vision typically guiding and encouraging motor exploration and development. At times, motor difficulties may appear to be vision problems and vice versa. It is, therefore, important to look at both concurrently and provide intervention that is addressed to the coordination of vision and motor development. The following are strategies that may be useful for children who have difficulty coordinating vision and motor skills within activities.

Interaction Strategies

1. *Provide verbal support.* Use words to guide the child's actions and tell the child what is happening. For example, "Oh, you are drawing such a straight road! Keep going, keep going, you are almost at the garage."

2. *Allow the child to place his or her hands in yours to feel how the actions are done.* Physical hand-over-hand may be forced and not allow the child to gain the same perception of movement.

3. *Accept alternative approaches.* For some children with visual impairment, particularly CVI, "head-reaching," or leaning toward an object with the head, may precede hand reaching. This is a compensation that should not be discouraged, because the child is actively exploring, and the shift to hand reaching can occur later.

Environmental Adaptations

In addition to interpersonal strategies that may support the child using visual-motor skills, environmental adaptations often are useful. Depending on the findings from the FVA and the fine motor section of TPBA2, the team may want to consider some of the environmental adaptations outlined here.

1. *If glasses have been prescribed for near-viewing tasks, be sure they are worn.* Be sure the glasses are clean and comfortable for the child.

2. *Pay attention to the positioning of the materials.* It might be easier for the child if the materials are elevated on a table where the objects in use are at eye level, as opposed to on the floor where the child has to lean over the materials.

3. *Use shiny balls or balls with stripes of bright tape or Mylar glued on.* When the balls move, they will be easier to see and catch, hit, or kick. A similar strategy can be used with other objects that require eye–hand coordination.

ROUTINES TO SUPPORT THE CHILD WITH VISION IMPAIRMENT

Daily Routines (Home and Classroom)

Feeding/Eating

When feeding her 12-month-old, the mother puts cereal bits out on the tray in a line across the tray. She then taps the tray on the left side beside the first piece and says, "Sara, start here where my finger is, the first piece is on your tray. (Avoid "over here" as it does not provide full description.) Sara searches to the left where she heard the sound, finds the first piece of cereal by her mom's finger and then systematically moves across the tray, finding each other piece.

Diapering/Toileting

During diapering, an infant stares at the shiny Mylar mobile his father made him. His dad occasionally hits it to make it move, and the baby reaches up to try to touch it.

Dressing

Mom says, "Can you get your socks out, Ben?" Ben moves across his bedroom to his dresser. Each drawer has a white knob that contrasts with the dark wood of the dresser. Ben reaches for the middle drawer handle, pulls it open, finds the sock bin on the right, and takes out a pair of rolled up socks.

Play Routines (Home and Classroom)

Face-to-Face Play

Mom and Andrew are singing "Old MacDonald." Andrew is sitting on her lap on a chair in front of the window, watching her face in the light. When she makes an animal sound, she makes exaggerated mouth movements and Andrew feels her mouth and laughs. Then he sings it and Mom feels his mouth and laughs.

Physical Play

Dad and Wayne are playing ball after dinner. Dad has a brightly colored beach ball. Dad asks Wayne if he wants to catch it or kick it. Wayne says, "Kick it!" Dad says, "Okay. Here it comes. Watch—it's coming at you!"

Manipulative Play

Wanda is putting an animal puzzle together. She brings a piece up close to her eyes and says, "Duck," then looks at the spaces on the puzzle that have the same outline as the puzzle piece. When she finds what she thinks is the right one, she rotates the piece. When it goes in, the puzzle piece "quacks." "Duck," says a beaming Wanda.

Sensory Play

Gene is "reading" a tactile book. He finds the main character, a corduroy swatch for a dog named Boo, on each page, which talks about all the mischief the dog gets into. Gene tells his mom, "Boo is funny."

Dramatic Play

Mark is playing with his army men. One set of army men has tiny felt hats glued on. Mark says these are the "good guys." The ones without the hats are the "bad guys." His mother has set up a desk lamp on the floor so that it shines on the "battlefield." When they fight, he holds them under the light and says, "Got ya!" and one falls to the floor.

Reading and Learning Routines

Circle Time

Lee sits up front by the teacher at circle time so he can see the big book the teacher is holding. She has a basket of corresponding objects that are in the book. As she reads the story, she stops to pull out the object being discussed, so that Ben and the other kids can touch it.

One-on-One Book Reading

Mom holds Meribeth on her lap. They are reading her favorite book. Each page has simple pictures. Meribeth holds the book so it is positioned up close to her face. She is turning the pages and telling her mom the story. "And then what happens?" asks her Mom. Meribeth says, "And then she gives her mommy a hug." She turns the page, looks closely at it and touches the picture and says, "Yup. I'm right. See?"

Science and Math

During the science activity, Alexa looks at the large pictures of the sequence for mixing colors. She looks hard, and then goes to the tape machine and pushes the green button. The tape says, "First, find the yellow paint and put a little in the empty jar under the light. Stop the tape until you are ready for the next step." Alexa did that and then pushed the green button again. "Next, find the red paint and put some red paint in the jar under the light. Stop the tape until you are ready for the next step." Alexa complied and then pushed the green button again. "Now take a stick and stir the colors together. What color did you get?" "Orange!" cried Alexa. "Now pour a little of your new color on a piece of paper to dry. Your teacher will help you write the name of the color you made and your name on the paper."

▮▮▮▮ JOSEPH

Joseph is a 13-month-old with optic nerve hypoplasia and cerebral palsy. His optic nerves were underdeveloped at birth and he has a significant visual impairment. He has learned to search for the toys he wants by crawling and feeling around him. He is making noises to call his mother and dad for help and beginning to use a few labels for his favorite things. He calls Cheerios, "O's"; his bottle, "ba-ba"; and his dad, "da-da." Although a little delayed in motor and language skills, he is very interactive with his parents and older brother. He loves roughhouse play with his father and singing with his mother. He loves to look toward the window and the light.

Interaction Strategies

1. *Talk to Joseph before you touch him or pick him up. Your voice will make him aware of your presence. Tell him what will happen to him before moving him, "Joseph, it is time to change your diaper. Up, you go!"*

2. *Play interactive games in which you get him to look toward you to get you to repeat an action. Imitate any sounds he makes as communication, and repeat the game when he moves or makes a noise. Use vibrating toys and action toys as part of the game. This will give him increased awareness of body parts.*

Environmental Adaptations

1. *Use toys with sounds and lights, where one or the other or both can be activated. This will draw Joseph's attention to the toy. Change what is activated to keep him motivated to explore the toy. Help him find the activator by placing his hand on top of yours.*

2. *Use tactile books and books with buttons to push to create sounds. This will help Joseph become interested in books, learn new words, and associate tactile input with a label. The TVI can assist with adding braille to his favorite storybooks. A tactile label can be placed on his books to help him identify them.*

3. *Use brightly colored or reflective toys to engage him and structure his environment (e.g., around his food tray, the edge of his floor mat, the color of his toy box).*

KEYS TO INTERVENTION BY DEVELOPMENTAL AGE

Because visual impairment is not connected with age, no intervention key is given. Please refer to the chart titled "Visual Development Indicators," in TPBA2, Chapter 3.

REFERENCES

American Academy of Ophthalmology. (1996). *Policy statement: Vision screening for infants and children.* San Francisco: Author.

Anthony, T.L. (2000). Performing a functional low vision assessment. In F.M. D'Andrea & C. Farrenkopf (Eds.), *Looking to learning: Promoting literacy for students with low vision* (pp. 32–83). New York: American Foundation for the Blind Press.

Bishop, V.E. (1988). Making choices in functional vision evaluations: "Noodles, needles, and haystacks." *Journal of Visual Impairment & Blindness, 82*(3), 94–99.

Corn, A.L., & Koenig, A.J. (1996). Perspectives on low vision. In A.J. Corn & A.J. Koenig (Eds.), *Foundations of low vision: Clinical and functional perspectives* (pp. 3–25). New York: American Foundation for the Blind Press.

Koenig, A.J., & Holbrook, M.C. (1995). *Learning media assessment of students with visual impairments: A resource guide.* Austin, TX: Texas School for the Blind and Visually Impaired.

Langley, M.B. (1998). Alignment and ocular mobility. In M.B. Langley (Ed.), *Individualized systematic assessment of visual efficiency for the developmentally young and individuals with multihandicapping conditions* (Vol. 1, pp. 1–33). Louisville, KY: American Printing House for the Blind.

Miles, B. (1993, 2003). *Talking the language of the hands to the hands: The importance of hands for the person who is deafblind* (Fact sheet). Monmouth, OR: DB-Link: The National Consortium on Deaf-Blindness. (ERIC Document Reproduction Service No. ED419331) Retrieved June 14, 2007, from http://www.dblink.org/lib/hands.htm

5

Facilitating Emotional and Social Development

I. Strategies for Improving Emotional Expression

Goal Attainment Scale

1	2	3	4	5	6	7	8	9
Expresses emotions related to comfort and discomfort using sounds and physical movements.		Experiments with different types, levels, and forms of emotional expression to communicate needs.		Often expresses extremes of emotions to get needs met and to elicit a response from others.		Expresses full range of emotions, with the predominant emotions being positive.		Easily communicates full range of emotions in appropriate contexts, with an acceptable level of intensity.

The means by which we demonstrate how we are feeling is considered *emotional expression*. The range, clarity, intensity, duration, and frequency of expression of various emotions influence many aspects of development and learning. Emotions have an impact on motivation, attention and cognitive processing, social relations, communication, and even physical health.

Children demonstrate emotions in numerous ways: through facial expression, body language, vocalizations, and words. The basic feeling states of *happiness, surprise, fear, anger, sadness,* and *disgust* can be inferred from universal facial muscle movements and expressions. Facial expressions for *interest, contempt,* and *shame* are less universal but are identifiable within specific cultures.

Signs of many emotions are present at birth, with more subtle emotions and those requiring cognitive understanding appearing later. In early infancy, children demonstrate clearly when they are unhappy by fussing or crying. They show interest and contentment by staring intently and within a few weeks by smiling. By 18 months of age, children demonstrate the full range of emotions, including self-conscious emotions such as shame and pride. As language develops, children begin to use words, in addition to body language, to express feelings.

Emotional expression is a fundamental aspect of communication. Clarity of emotional expression is important to help others know how they should respond to the child, both behaviorally and emotionally. It enables adults and other children to gauge whether activities are motivating and should be continued, modified, or terminated. Intensity of emotional expression determines how easily the emotional cues are read and also somewhat determines the emotional response of others. For example, if a child falls and shows no negative emotional response, the adult reads this behavior as indicating that the child is not hurt and does not need attention. However, if the child screams loudly and cries, the adult will immediately race to aid the child and offer consolation. If children do not register readable emotional cues, it is more difficult for adults to respond appropriately.

Emotions help us see how children perceive themselves or others, how they interpret events in their environment, and how well they self-regulate when confronted with challenging situations. Intensity, duration, and frequency of various types of emotions also influence how children are perceived by others. If children respond consistently with intense emotions that are seemingly out of line with the demands of the situation, adults may begin to ignore or view these emotions negatively, rather than responsively. Moderation of emotional expression is, therefore, important to convey accurate communicative intentions and for the development of synchronous, reciprocal social interactions. Without emotional expression, adults do not understand how a child feels; with too much emotional expression, adults may misinterpret feelings.

APPROPRIATE EMOTIONAL EXPRESSION

Emotional cues need to be readable. Adults can respond quickly to children whose cues are easily interpreted. Children with clear facial cues and body language can get adults to respond to their needs.

Positive emotions need to be accessible. Positive expressions of emotion are extremely important because they reinforce adults' efforts at interaction with children. If a child is happy, yet expresses no emotions, adults may keep increasing the intensity or variety of experiences in an effort to gain a positive response. If positive responses are not obtained, they may cease their efforts. It is devastating for parents or caregivers not to be able to elicit positive emotions in a child.

Emotional expression needs to be accurate, in that it should express what the child actually feels. If a child is hurt and laughs, for example, adults will have a different response than if he cries. For infants, toddlers, and young children, what is felt is what is expressed. This is important for the adult to respond appropriately.

As children get older and they begin to understand and gain control over emotions, however, they may be able to display emotions contrary to what they are actually feeling. Older children may do this kind of behavior intentionally in order not to convey what they are actually feeling—pain and embarrassment, for example. This type of intentional suppression of feelings or conscious choice of which emotion to display is a normal part of the development of emotional regulation (see TPBA2, Chapter 4, Subcategory III. Regulation of Emotions and Arousal States). As children understand what others may be thinking or feeling, they begin to respond based on what others may be thinking or feeling (see TPBA2, Chapter 7, Subcategory IV. Social Cognition). Emotions also need to reflect accuracy in terms of level of intensity of emotion experienced.

Appropriate Emotional Expression in Practice

▓▓▓▓▓ I. A. Expression of emotions

Daily Routines (Home and Classroom)

- *Infant/toddler:* During lunch, the infant makes a face of disgust and spits out the new baby food. The toddler opens her mouth and eyes wide with surprise when the Jack-in-the-Box pops out.

- *Young child:* The young child drops his head and looks down when admonished for taking a toy.

Play Routines (Home and Classroom)

- *Infant/toddler:* The child smiles, giggles, then squeals as her Dad tosses her in the air and swings her around.

- *Young child:* The young child watches her friend dancing in circles, she smiles, starts to dance, and then laughs and says, "I'm twirling."

Classroom Routines

During outdoor play, the child makes a face, sticks out his tongue at another child and says, "I don't like you. Stay away."

▮▮▮ I. B. Emotional range, including positive emotions, emotions of discomfort, and self-conscious emotions

Daily Routines (Home and Classroom)

- *Infant/toddler:* Throughout the day, the child demonstrates happiness with getting bananas for breakfast, fear when the dog jumps on her, shame when she drops her cup of milk on the floor, disgust at the smell of her diaper, and unhappiness at having to take a nap.

- *Young child:* When Dad says it is time for bed, the young child shakes her head, frowns, and says, "I'm not ready to go to bed!" He replies, "You can have 5 more minutes, then we will put you and your doll to bed." She smiles and goes back to her doll.

Play Routines (Home and Classroom)

- *Infant/toddler:* The toddler hides shyly behind his mother's legs when his brother chases him; he then laughs and runs away; when his brother tackles him, he cries; and when he tickles him, he laughs.

- *Young child:* The young child is pretending to be a doctor. She frowns and says, "You need surgery." The other child says, "I already had surgery." The "doctor" looks surprised, smiles, then says, "You need more surgery. You are still sick."

Classroom Routines

During story time, the child watches the teacher with interest, smiles at the characters in the story, laughs at the teacher's joke, and frowns when the teacher says story time is over.

▮▮▮ I. C. Experiences that make the child happy, unhappy, or self-conscious

Daily Routines (Home and Classroom)

- *Infant/toddler:* The infant enjoys interesting sensory experiences, such as bath time and mealtime. He does not like his mother leaving him alone for his nap.

- *Young child:* The young child enjoys the daily activities that are structured and predictable. He is unhappy when routines are changed or something unexpected occurs.

Play Routines (Home and Classroom)

- *Infant/toddler:* The toddler enjoys running and moving her body and investigating toys that make something happen.

- *Young child:* The young child is playing outside riding his tricycle, and gets upset when his father wants him to stop playing for dinner.

Classroom Routines

During bathroom time, the child plays in the water at the sink, laughing and splashing the water. He cries when the teacher says he needs to turn off the water and dry his hands.

GENERAL PRINCIPLES FOR SUPPORTING APPROPRIATE EMOTIONAL EXPRESSION

Most adults look for and notice the various cues a child gives that demonstrate how he or she is feeling. The adult's response is typically dependent on what he or she thinks the child is feeling. Adults support the appropriate expression of emotions by helping children in several ways: 1) by identifying what the child's expressions and behavior tell the adult about how the child is feeling, 2) by explaining how others react to the child's behavioral expressions, 3) by modeling and explaining the adult's own behaviors and emotions, and 4) by helping the child moderate the intensity of his or her emotions.

Identify What the Child Is Feeling

When the adult understands how the child is feeling, either as a result of stated words or because body language was interpreted, the adult can help the child understand those emotions. If the child is crying because he is not getting the candy he wanted, the adult may say, "I know you are mad that I said, 'No' to candy, but it is almost time for dinner." This tells the child that he or she is understood and gives an explanation for the adult's response. Putting words to children's feelings helps them to label the emotions that they feel and will lead to them using these words to express their feelings.

Explain What Others Are Feeling

Explaining to the child how emotional responses affect adults helps children develop social cognition (i.e., understanding the thoughts and feelings of others). For example, the parent may say, "When you scream like that it makes me mad. I feel like I want to help you when you are *not* screaming. Just ask me for help."

Explain Reasons for Feelings

Adults help children understand emotions by expressing their own feelings in clear ways and explaining their reactions. For example, the adult may say, "Mommy is sad because Grandma is sick. Sometimes when people are sad they cry. It is okay to be sad. I will feel better in a few minutes."

Help Children Moderate Feelings

Adults help children monitor their emotions and judge when they are ready to modify their emotions. The parent may say, for example, "Okay. That's enough. Bobby said he was sorry he took your doll. You have it back. You don't need to cry."

THE PRINCIPLES IN PRACTICE

Daily Routines (Home and Classroom)

Feeding/Eating

During mealtime, the caregiver watches the infant's face and says, "Mmmm. You like applesauce." When the toddler pushes the peas away, the parent says, "I know you don't like peas, but take two bites."

Diapering/Toileting

When the toddler points to the poop in the potty and smiles, his mother says, "Look at what you did! You should be so proud!"

Dressing

The young child dresses herself in mismatched clothing but appears in the kitchen with a big smile on her face. "Look, Mommy. I dressed all by myself!" Her mother smiles and says, "You certainly did! I'm so proud of you!"

Play Routines (Home and Classroom)

Face-to-Face Play

Dad hides behind the blanket, then drops it, saying, "Peekaboo!" The infant giggles and grabs the blanket, pulling it over her face.

Physical Play

Mom pretends to be the "tickle monster" and chases after the toddler. He screams and runs away. Mom talks in a deep voice, with a stern look on her face, saying, "You better run. I'm going to get you!" When she catches him, she starts to laugh and tickle him.

Manipulative Play

The young child holds the dinosaur and his Dad holds the male action figure. Jimmy says, "You should be afraid, because I am going to eat you!" Dad speaks for the male doll, saying, "I'm not afraid of you. I am brave."

Sensory Play

While making a finger painting, the toddler makes a face and looks at the red paint on his hand. His mother says, "Don't you like the paint on your hands? It's okay. It will wash off. Let's see if you can make a circle with your finger."

Reading and Learning Routines

Circle Time

While reading the book, *A Porcupine Named Fluffy,* the teacher models being embarrassed like Fluffy when the rhinoceros laughs at him. She has all of the children lower their heads and look down like they are embarrassed.

One-on-One Book Reading

While reading to her infant, the mother points to the picture of the crying baby and says, "Look. The baby has tears coming out of his eyes. He is sad."

Science and Math

At the sensory table, the children are feeling the different textures of cotton batting, pine cones and pine needles, and other materials. The teacher asks which ones they like to feel and which ones they don't like to touch. She then describes the textures as "soft," "prickly," "sticky," "sharp," and so forth.

PLANNING INDIVIDUALIZED INTERVENTIONS FOR IMPROVING EMOTIONAL EXPRESSION

I. A. How does the child express emotions?

Some children demonstrate little affect or unusual expressions due to a disability. For example, motor disabilities may influence expression of emotions. Children with low tone have more flaccid muscles, and consequently, facial expressions, gestures, and movements that demonstrate emotions may be more subtle. In the same way, increased tone also may limit emotional expression. Children with spastic cerebral palsy may create a smile that looks like a grimace due to lack of motor control.

A variety of environmental and/or neurological dysfunctions can result in lack of emotion, depressed affect, or emotional extremes. For children who demonstrate a lack of affect, adults may need to demonstrate and explain affect and learn how to read idiosyncratic or subtle emotional cues.

In addition, some children express emotions in excess of what they are actually feeling, feel more emotion than the situation demands, or have difficulty bringing their emotions back to a moderate level (see TPBI2, Chapter 5, Section III. Strategies for Improving Regulation of Emotions and Arousal States). In these situations, the adult helps children assess the situation and respond appropriately. For instance, when the child falls and is screaming intensely, the adult may say, "It's just a little scrape. Let me kiss it, so it will feel better." When the child is overly sensitive, the adult might say, "I know you hate getting water in your face. Let me wipe it off." For the child who can't calm down, the adult might say, "I am going over here to sit until you are calm and ready to play again" (see TPBI2, Chapter 5, Section III. Strategies for Improving State and Emotional Regulation). Children with drastic emotional shifts or extremes of emotions also may need professional support.

Helping children accurately express what they are feeling is important for the development of social skills. If people cannot understand what the child is feeling, it is more difficult to respond appropriately in interactions. The following strategies may help children express their emotions more clearly.

Interaction Strategies

1. *Read every action or movement as having an emotional context.* Label what you believe the child is feeling and watch for a positive or negative reaction on the part of the child. A look, a movement, or a sound all can indicate emotional responses. Adults need to observe the child carefully and let the child know how his or her actions are being interpreted. For instance, if the child turns away from an attempted kiss on the cheek, the adult might say, "You don't like me kissing you on the face. Okay. I'll squeeze your hand instead." Watch for and attempt to elicit the full range of emotions in order to better understand the child's reactions.

2. *Position face and body so the child can read emotional cues.* Although children can determine many feelings from tone of voice, many children need multiple cues to read emotions in others. Others provide an emotional mirror for young children, so it is important that they be able to see (or in the case of children who are blind, to feel) the expressions of others.

3. *Demonstrate affect with exaggerated expression or movements.* Many children with disabilities have difficulty reading emotions in others. This may be a result of lack of attention to others, reduced understanding, or sensory limitations that restrict the amount of information the child receives about emotions (e.g., the child who is deaf can see facial expressions but cannot hear tone of voice). For this reason, adults need to help children who have difficulty understanding emotions by using exaggerated affect and movements. Combine tone of voice, facial expression, and gestures to get the message across. This will not only encourage children to attend to emotions, but also to imitate the adult's expressions

4. *Use words to label feelings that are being expressed.* Just because the child is attending to or imitating the adult, does not mean he or she understands the emotion expressed. Teach the child words for feelings and then use those words to label feelings. Ask the child to determine what expressions mean. For example, "Look at Mommy's eyes and mouth. How do you think I feel?"

5. *Talk about how the child is feeling.* In the same way that adults should talk about their own feelings, they need to talk about what the child is feeling. The adult should label the child's emotions or ask about how he or she is feeling if the adult is unsure. *Happy, sad,* and *mad* are the most frequently discussed emotions for children. Discuss other emotions as well, such as *embarrassment, shame, guilt, pride, fear, surprise, disappointment,* and *frustration.*

6. *Point out emotions in a variety of situations.* Children have the opportunity to see emotions being expressed hundreds of times a day—in interaction with others, when observing others in real-life situations, on television, in movies, and in play situations. For example, within one day the child may play an exciting chase game with his brother, watch a cartoon in which a character is afraid, see an angry mother scold a child in the shopping mall, see his dad spill something on the carpet and feel guilty, and so forth. These are all opportunities to illustrate what different emotions look like and why the people feel the way they do.

Environmental Modifications

In addition to interpersonal strategies that may support the child's expression of emotions, environmental modifications often are useful. Depending on the findings from TPBA2, the team may want to consider some of the following environmental modifications.

1. *Involve the child in high affect situations.* Toys, materials, and events that involve surprise, movement, and high sensory input are likely to evoke emotions. If the child does not make facial expressions or gestures, the adult can model them. The child may then try to imitate these expressions. Repetition of the events may lead to the child spontaneously expressing emotions.

2. *Use pictures in the environment and books to point out emotions.* Pictures of emotional expression are seen in ads, on billboards, in magazines, and in books. Take advantage of these pictures as an opportunity to discuss expressions and what caused them. Books are particularly good to stimulate discussion of actions and their relation to emo-

tions. Select books that have topics that are of interest to the child, with clear depictions of facial expressions.

3. *Use a mirror to reflect expressions.* Children do not know what their faces look like when they are feeling various emotions. Use of a hand mirror can help show them what they look like. As described earlier, role play is good for "pretending" emotions and a mirror can help them see what they look like to others.

4. *Pay attention to lighting.* Backlighting from a window can make faces difficult to see. This is particularly relevant for children with vision impairments. Adults should be aware of the location of lighting in relation to their faces to optimize the child's chances of seeing subtle emotional cues. How children read and interpret cues influences their own emotional responses.

▨▨▨ I. B. Does the child demonstrate a full range of emotions, including positive emotions, emotions of discomfort, and self-conscious emotions?
I. C. What types of experiences make the child happy, unhappy, or self-conscious?

Some children clearly express a limited range of emotions. Their cues are clear for the emotions they reveal; they just don't demonstrate a full range of emotions. Happiness or excitement and anger or frustration are most commonly recognized by adults. However, children also need to demonstrate a sense of pride when they know they have done something well. This sense of mastery motivation is critical for the continuing desire to learn new skills (see TPBA2, Chapter 4, Subcategory V. Sense of Self). Children with delays or disabilities may have a reduced sense of pride, especially as they begin to compare their skills to those of others. Without a sense of pride, children with disabilities may give up easily. Instead of persisting when frustrated with a difficult task, they may choose to ignore the activity, try once and then quit, or get angry. A moderate level of tension and frustration can be positive, because these emotions often motivate effort.

In addition to pride, children need to recognize when they have done something harmful or hurtful and feel a sense of regret. This emotion may not be exhibited in children who lack understanding of cause and effect (i.e., the effect of their actions on others); who have limited social cognition (i.e., awareness of others' emotions); or who act impulsively, without thinking of the effect of their actions. These children may need adult support to be able to understand and express regret.

Children who are hypersensitive to sensory input may be easily overwhelmed by almost any stimuli and may demonstrate predominantly negative emotions such as whining or crying. Helping children to adapt to sensory input, in addition to communicating when they are feeling uncomfortable, is important.

For children with a predominantly depressed affect, investigation of what makes the child happy is important, along with exploration of the causes of the depression. Children who are diagnosed with depression or other emotional disorders need further psychological evaluation and support from other professionals.

For children with identified disabilities or syndromes, it is important for parents and professionals to become familiar with the emotional and behavioral characteristics associated with the specific conditions. For example, children with Angelman syndrome may exhibit predominantly happy expressions. They often exhibit inappropriate laughter or bouts of laughter that are inconsistent with occurring events. These children also have difficulty with motor planning necessary for imitation of adults' facial expressions and retardation that also may limit their understanding of emotions. Concrete demonstration of the relationship of events to subsequent emotions is necessary, along with embellished facial expressions and gestures. Children with Williams syndrome may show emotions related to excessive fears, anxieties, and phobias but also show friendliness, caring, and empathy for others. Their unusual linguistic strengths enable them to talk about and describe what they and others may be feeling.

Knowing what elicits various types of emotions is important so that adults can prepare a child for different situations and respond in a supportive way. Understanding what makes children happy or unhappy is especially important for planning intervention. Children repeat activities they enjoy or at which they are successful. They avoid activities that are not pleasurable or at which they are unsuccessful. By selecting toys, materials, and activities that elicit positive emotions, adults can motivate children to practice new skills and also integrate activities that are not as pleasant.

Activities the child likes can also be used to motivate children to do tasks that are less interesting. For example, if the child wants to play with the dog and doesn't want to get dressed, the parent can say, "You can play with the dog as soon as you get dressed."

Interaction Strategies

1. *Use what makes the child smile.* Positive emotions encourage children to explore, practice, and accomplish their goals. Adults can make almost any activity into a pleasurable one by building on the characteristics that children prefer. For example, for children who love movement, the adult can incorporate actions before or during an activity. For children who enjoy social interaction, turn-taking in a gamelike manner can make a nonpreferred activity fun.

2. *Help children know when they should feel proud.* It is important for adults to help children see their strengths, not only in relation to others but also in relationship to their own growth. For instance, "Last week you couldn't pull up your own pants, and now you can! Soon you will be able to dress all by yourself!"

3. *Help children understand regret.* Adults can help children recognize when they should feel bad about their actions, not by shaming children by calling them names but by helping the child analyze what happened, how it was harmful, and how to prevent it from happening again. For example, "When you bumped into Alison, she fell and it hurt her. What might make her feel better? Let's help her wash off her knee and see if that makes her feel better."

4. *Reinforce all effort on the part of the child.* Particularly for children with delays or disabilities, who may not be immediately successful in accomplishing a desired goal, the adult needs to encourage the child to keep trying. Acknowledge and praise the child's attempts and persistence in doing something independently. For example, "You are trying so hard! You've almost got it. Yea!"

5. *Read the child's facial cues and actions and acknowledge the emotions that are demonstrated by the child.* As noted previously, some children do not give clear visual signs of their emotions. The adult can help the child recognize the importance of a range of emotions by modeling when various emotions are appropriate, labeling the feelings, and talking about what the child might be feeling.

6. *Talk about emotions of discomfort.* Acknowledge that everyone feels sad or mad at times, and talk about when that happens and what people do to feel better. Emotions of discomfort are natural and adults should not disparage children for expressing "negative" emotions, but rather help them to moderate these emotions and express them at appropriate times (see TPBI2, Chapter 5, Section III. Strategies for Improving Regulation of Emotions and Arousal States).

7. *Emphasize the emotions that are lacking or restricted in the child's repertoire.* For children who predominantly exhibit one type of emotion, it is important for adults to attempt to broaden the range of experiences so that variations of emotion are elicited. For example, various games can elicit surprise and gradual challenge can be introduced to generate interest, then accomplishment, and then pride.

8. *As children begin to engage in dramatic play, use role play to reenact emotional situations.* Dramatic play allows children to "try on" different emotions, such as fear or anger, in a safe way. Adults can encourage this type of discovery but at the same time be available for problem solving if emotions escalate or become overwhelming to the child. Role play of specific situations that involve strong emotions can help children gain some distance from the emotions and think about their responses more objectively. For example, role play about how to handle angry emotions when someone hurts you can be done without the immediacy of the actual situation. The adult can then remind the child when the actual situation occurs to think about what he did when they role-played a similar situation. Social skills groups for older children often use practice activities such as this, but they also are effective with younger children. When situations are repeated or practiced frequently, responses become more automatic.

9. *Pay particular attention to what motivates a happy response.* As noted previously, both positive and negative emotions can guide intervention. Activities that elicit positive responses should provide the foundation for planning intervention, with activities that bring forth more negative emotional responses woven in so that the unfavorable aspect is reduced or eliminated. For example, if the child does not like fine motor activities but likes dramatic play, fine motor tasks can be incorporated into pretend play. While playing house, for instance, a pencil and paper can be used to make a grocery list. A can opener can be used to pretend to open a can. Coins can be put in a piggy bank. Knobs and levers can be manipulated to activate the stove, the phone, and so forth.

Environmental Modifications

1. *Modify the environment to respond to the individual child's needs.* Adults need to recognize patterns of behavior and determine what environmental or interpersonal interactions trigger positive or negative emotions. The adult can then alter the environment to increase or decrease the desired emotions.

2. *Read books reflecting different emotions.* The full range of emotions are expressed through the actions and responses of characters in books. Selection of books related to emotions that are not expressed by the child or need to be explored more by the adult (e.g., anger or sadness) can help children think and talk about emotions. Books also can help children relate to someone else's situation. The adult's role is to help the child explore how the characters' actions and feelings relate to the child's own actions and feelings or those of his or her family and friends.

3. *Incorporate props into dramatic play to stimulate emotional thoughts.* Dramatic play typically elicits emotions of some kind because children represent what they have seen others do in real life. For children who express limited or minimal emotions, props in dramatic play can encourage more intense emotional expression or facilitate expression of certain types of emotions. For example, props that elicit emotions include a doctor's kit (e.g., elicits pretend discomfort, nurturance), dinosaurs (e.g., anger, aggression), or magic wands. Use of puppets can facilitate a range of emotions (see Table 3.1 in *Administration Guide for TPBA2 & TPBI2*, Chapter 3).

4. *Find community resources.* Some children and families may need additional supports to help them explore their feelings. Awareness of what resources exist in the community for children's mental health is important.

ROUTINES FOR THE CHILD WHO
NEEDS SUPPORT TO EXPRESS EMOTIONS

Daily Routines (Home and Classroom)

Feeding/Eating

Acknowledge the child's likes and dislikes related to various types and textures of foods. Label the emotions you see. "You're spitting it out. Does it taste disgusting?" When trying to get a child to taste a new food, model taking a bite and demonstrate a high level of positive affect.

Diapering/Toileting

For infants, diapering is more of an emotional experience for the adult! However, interactive games and turn-taking can make diapering an opportunity for fun. As the infant gets older and the desire to move increases, diapering may become more frustrating for the child. This presents an opportunity to use labels such as "fidgety," "frustrated," "patient," and "anxious." The move to independent toileting provides opportunities for discussion of these same terms, but also "satisfaction" and "pride." Exaggerated affect and gestures may be helpful.

Dressing

Dressing often is a challenging event because body parts are bent and shoved, clothes are tugged and pulled, and movements must be coordinated. Adults can emphasize the importance of effort and persistence and teach words and phrases such as "frustrated," "stick with it," and "keep trying." Comments such as, "You did it! You should be proud of yourself!" will help children identify feelings associated with accomplishment.

Going Out

Going out enables children to see the expressions of other people besides their close family members. Watching other children is important because children often imitate each other. Adults can point out the emotions of other children and talk about why they are expressing various emotions. Watching others enables discussion of emotions, especially emotions of discomfort, that may be difficult to talk about when the child is in the throes of a temper tantrum.

Play Routines (Home and Classroom)

Face-to-Face Play

Face-to-face play presents a perfect opportunity for games with emotional expression. Children have the chance to see others' facial expressions, interpret them, and respond. For children who have difficulty creating identifiable emotional expressions, adults can make up imitation games. "I'm going to make a face like a mad lion!" "What animal do you want to be? Are you going to be a happy cow or a mad cow?"

Physical Play

Physical play tends to arouse intense emotions. This type of play is great for children who need to learn to express emotions more clearly. Hide-and-Seek can elicit surprise, Tag engenders excitement, playground play can prompt motor effort and pride, and so forth. Incorporate emotion words in the play: "Ah-ha! I surprised you!" "You are so excited!"

Manipulative Play

Many types of manipulative play involve construction or combining objects in some way. For children with disabilities, these types of tasks may present fine motor challenges that are frustrating. Acknowledge the frustration and help the child come up with a solution to the problem. "This is hard, isn't it? Let's see if we can do just this part first, so it won't be so frustrating." As described previously, incorporating elements that are motivating can help the child to persist. For instance, if the child does not like puzzles and avoids such tasks or becomes upset, the adult can change the focus of the task to make it a social game: "I need a blue piece. Can you help me find a blue piece? You found one!"

Sensory Play

Sensory play of various forms (e.g., music, movement, tactile play) also may produce intense feelings. As with physical play, sensory play provides many occasions for expression and discussion of feelings.

Dramatic Play

Dramatic play can encourage expression of many different emotions. Dramatization of favorite stories and movies is a great way to encourage children to experiment with expression of different emotions in a safe way. It also is a means for children who have experienced trauma or loss to express emotions that they may feel uncomfortable expressing in other ways. Inclusion of props, such as those described in the Environmental Modifications section, also can provide a stimulus for acting out and talking about emotions.

Reading and Learning Routines

Circle Time

Reading to a group is not as intimate as one-on-one reading, but it presents the advantage of allowing children to hear others' thoughts and feelings. They may also have the option of listening or sharing. Teachers should take advantage of stories about characters who are afraid, embarrassed, brave, proud, jealous, and so forth, to discuss emotions, dramatize, or reenact scenes from the book.

One-on-One Book Reading

Lap reading with young children is a wonderful time to share discussion of what characters in books are feeling, why they are feeling that way, and what they should do about their feelings. It also enables adults to talk to children about when they might have felt the same way as the characters in the book. Such discussions can help children to see that others may feel the same way they do. The intimacy of the one-on-one reading also can provide a secure base for discussion of issues that are troubling a child.

Science and Math

Emotions are a part of psychology—one of the sciences that children can investigate in preschool. The science involves social cognition or understanding what others are thinking and feeling. Presenting this as an important area for investigation can lead children to acquire meaningful insights. For example, a young child can do a survey of what makes others feel certain emotions and how they act when they feel that way (e.g., What makes you happy? Sad? Mad? Frustrated?). The child can then make a chart comparing boys and girls, young people and old people, and teachers and parents. Such investigation helps children learn about similarities and differences in feelings.

▓▓▓▓ *RAJEEV*

Rajeev is a 12-month-old foster child who was removed from his home due to abuse and neglect. Rajeev shows little facial expression and rarely reaches toward his foster mother. He rarely cries and will just lie in his crib until someone comes into the room to see if he is awake. His foster mother reported that he often was left unattended with no one responding to his cries. She is concerned that Rajeev does not demonstrate emotions and that will impair his ability to form relationships, which could have a negative impact on potential adoption. The TPBA team who assessed Rajeev observed this "flat" affect throughout the play session. The following recommendations were made to address this issue.

Interaction Strategies

1. *Play hugging, kissing, tickling games, while modeling lots of smiling and laughing. Carefully watch for movements or facial expressions that may indicate he wants more or less input. Rajeev needs to learn that positive emotions are associated with play and interaction and that his cues will be responded to.*
2. *Listen for any sounds and watch for movements. Read these as communication and respond immediately. Use words to tell Rajeev what you think he is feeling. "You like that? You want more?"*
3. *Experiment with different types of play—sensory, face-to-face, toys, and motor activities—to see what Rajeev prefers. Play more of the preferred activities and escalate activities (intensity or duration) to elicit more emotions. Stop when emotions begin to change.*

Environmental Adaptations

1. *Provide toys that surprise or have a large auditory or visual effect, so that Rajeev is motivated to attend closely. High effect toys are more likely to arouse emotions.*
2. *Make exaggerated faces in the mirror next to Rajeev. Try to get him to imitate you. Place a mirror in front of Rajeev so he can see his face. This may interest him in watching himself in the mirror and smiling.*

KEYS TO INTERVENTION BY DEVELOPMENTAL AGE

The following ideas are directed toward children who are functioning at approximately the following levels. The suggestions are not meant to be all-inclusive, but rather are indicative of potential areas for exploration.

Developmental age	Emotional expression	Key to intervention
Birth to 3 months	Recognizes and demonstrates distress, rage, happiness, joy, and surprise.	Acknowledge and respond to emotions immediately, so child learns making faces and sounds is communication to which adults will respond.
3–6 months	Shows excitement; pleasure at social interactions. Demonstrates fear of loud noises.	Take advantage of face-to-face games to make faces for the child to imitate. Demonstrate sources of sounds.

(continued on next page)

Developmental age	Emotional expression	Key to intervention
6–9 months	Distinguishes angry voices. Demonstrates fear of heights. Expresses anger, distrust, disgust. Shows elation at social games.	Respond to child's nonverbal cues. Label child's emotions, and comment on what is causing them. Provide a predictable routine and reassure child when changes are disruptive. Let child investigate heights with adult support and comfort. Children read adults' facial cues to see how child should be responding, so adult should model appropriate emotions for child.
9–12 months	Shows fear of strangers. Shows surprise and shyness.	Respond to fear with soothing; gradually introduce new people by letting child look, touch, and get close as he or she feels comfortable. Use toys that have elements of surprise to motivate exploration.
12–18 months	Shows beginning guilt, pride, shame. Demonstrates fear of more things. Expresses depression at loss. Demonstrates jealousy; anger tantrums.	Learning what is right and wrong should be supported with explanations of why something is the right or wrong thing to do. Reinforce child's effort of working toward independence. Talk about how to deal with the uncomfortable emotions of sadness, jealousy, and so forth. Child may need support to think of options for ways to handle feelings.
18–24 months	Reacts to others' sadness. Shows embarrassment and clear shame and guilt.	Encourage child to watch others' facial expressions and actions to see how they are feeling. Comment on and reinforce child's growing awareness of and response to others' feelings. As child becomes more self-conscious about how others feel about him or her, support individual differences (e.g., "I know you don't like to meet new people, so I'll hold your hand and you can just watch everybody for a while. Let me know when you want to play too"). Acknowledge that everyone makes mistakes, and talk about how the situation could be handled differently "next time."
24–36 months	Shows empathy; extremes of emotion. Demonstrates fear of change. Shows complex emotional expression.	When child demonstrates empathy, remark on how that makes the other person feel better. Acknowledge fears and concerns and provide supports to help child handle them independently (e.g., transition objects). Note that mixed emotions are okay (e.g., "I know you are excited to see Santa, but I can tell that you are also a little worried. Do you want me to go up to see him with you, or do you want to do it all by yourself?").
36–48 months	Demonstrates fear of visual appearances. Expresses loving. Displays physical anger.	Before going to the circus, a parade, or out for Halloween, use a mirror to put on makeup or paint child's, doll's, and adult's faces. Talk about who is under the makeup. Guess what others may look like when made up. Provide opportunities for child to nurture stuffed animals, dolls, pets, or siblings. When child is angry, acknowledge that it is okay to be angry, everyone gets mad sometimes. Then help child find appropriate ways to express anger (e.g., with words, stomping feet, squeezing a ball).

Developmental age	Emotional expression	Key to intervention
48–60 months	Shows extreme jealousy. Displays silliness. Expresses fear of parent loss, sleeping alone, being lost, and extreme differences. Gets "hurt" feelings.	*Bibliotherapy,* which involves using books related to emotions that are troubling, can be helpful. Talk about what characters in stories feel and do, and how the child feels and acts. Discuss options for actions to manage feelings. Give child concrete means for dealing with fears.
60–72 months	Displays resentment of correction. Expresses fear of ghosts, witches, insects, thunder, fire, wind, storms, blood, injury, death.	Help child with problem-solving strategies (see TPBI2, Chapter 7, Section III. Problem Solving) and assure him or her that mistakes are a way to learn. Help child learn about the concepts he or she fears. Explain that knowledge is a way to have control over uncertainties.

5

Facilitating Emotional and Social Development

II. Strategies for Improving Emotional Style/Adaptability

Goal Attainment Scale

1	2	3	4	5	6	7	8	9
Does not adapt to new people, objects, events, or changes in routines without extreme, long-lasting emotional reactions.		Adapts to changes in people, objects, events, or routines with much verbal preparation and environmental support.		Adapts to changes in people, objects, events, or routines using motivating, logical connections to the transition situation.		Adapts to changes in people, objects, events, or routines with verbal preparation.		Adapts to new people, objects, events, or changes in routine independently, with an appropriate amount of caution and emotional reaction.

Emotional style (adaptability) refers to how the child typically approaches and responds to various stimuli, including new or modified experiences. Emotional style includes 1) reaction to novelty, or how easily the child accepts and engages *new* things, including people, objects, or events; 2) flexibility, or how easily the child handles *changes* or modifications of activities, routines, settings, or interaction patterns; and 3) emotional reactivity, or the child's *typical* level of positive or negative response to various types of stimuli.

These factors are important for several reasons. Interest in and openness to novel objects and events are important for learning. Learning requires integrating new information into what one already understands. Children need to investigate unique things to discover their characteristics, relationships, and potential uses. Conceptual development is based on being able to compare aspects of the environment and group them in various ways; thus, tolerance of new experiences is a critical part of gaining knowledge. Children who have fear, anxiety, or excessive caution are more likely to "stick to what they know" than to explore new things. Children who are interested in novelty are eager to discover.

Response to new people also is a significant issue for children, because the development of social relationships beyond the immediate family depends on the child being able to meet, become friendly with, and eventually form friendships with others. Although caution around new people is necessary, the ability to know whom to trust and how to socially engage someone new is an important skill. Children who are overly cautious or fearful, or who are indiscriminately friendly, may have difficulty forming meaningful social relationships.

Being able to handle changes in activities and routines is an important aspect of emotional style. Activities and routines are constantly changing throughout the day, sometimes based on what the child needs and sometimes based on what adults and others in the child's life need to have happen. Flexibility therefore is needed so the child can function well throughout the day. Children who have rigid expectations and negative emotional responses to change or who need to be in control of what and when changes occur may have stressful relations with others during these transition times. Resistance to change also may result in less involvement, as described previously.

A third element, emotional intensity, is a significant factor in children's learning and social interactions. Children should show a range of emotions and the ability to express varying levels of intensity of emotions appropriate to the situation. As discussed in TPBA2, Chapter 4, Subcategory III. Regulation of Emotions and Arousal States, they also should be able to adjust their emotional intensity as needed. In relation to emotional style and adaptability, the intensity of emotions expressed when new situations are introduced or transitions are necessary can affect how the child learns or interacts as well. Children who have intense negative responses to change or to certain people, types of materials, or specific experiences often need support from adults to determine the cause of the aversive reaction and to potentially modify the input, process, or situation to enable the child to benefit from the experience.

APPROPRIATE EMOTIONAL STYLE/ADAPTABILITY

Children who can adapt easily and show interest in new aspects of the environment experience less stress than children who have difficulty adapting. Children should be cautious but demonstrate enough interest to determine the characteristics of each situation and evaluate its value. They also should be able to demonstrate a moderate level of emotional intensity that enables them to focus on the object, person, or situation at hand. Too much or too little emotional intensity may negatively affect learning and engagement.

Appropriate Emotional Style/Adaptability in Practice

▨▨▨▨ **II. A. How does the child approach new people, activities, or situations?**

Daily Routines (Home and Classroom)

- *Infant/toddler:* The infant sees a stranger approaching and buries his face in his father's shoulder. When Mommy's friend comes to the door, the toddler studies the person, recognizes her, and approaches slowly.

- *Young child:* The young child looks at the new art materials on the table, picks them up and examines them, and starts experimenting with gluing them on paper.

Play Routines (Home and Classroom)

- *Infant/toddler:* The infant is rolling a ball back and forth with his father. The father puts the ball behind his back and introduces a toy truck that he rolls to the infant. The infant looks surprised but rolls the truck back to Dad. The toddler stands at the edge of the sand area in the playground and watches the other children. His caregiver encourages, "Come on, let's dig in the sand." Slowly he steps into the sand and moves toward his caregiver.

- *Young child:* The young child is playing with the blocks when the new child in class comes up to watch. The young child looks up and says, "Do you want to play with me?"

Classroom Routines

During circle time, the teacher says, "We have a new book today. Who wants to help me?" The young child raises her hand.

▓▓▓▓▓▓ **II. B. How easily does the child adapt to transition in activities and/or changes in routines?**

Daily Routines (Home and Classroom)

- *Infant/toddler:* The infant is playing on the floor. Her mother says, "Time for lunch. Let's go eat." The infant raises her arms to be lifted up. The toddler is waking up from his nap. His mother says, "You need to wake up so we can go to the store." He fusses briefly, then snuggles into his mother's shoulder.

- *Young child:* The teacher says, "Today we are not going outside for recess. We are going on a field trip to the park!" The young child shouts, "Yeah!"

Play Routines (Home and Classroom)

- *Infant/toddler:* The infant has been mouthing a rubber ball. His mother takes the ball and says, "Let's go play with the ball outdoors so you can throw it." The infant reaches toward the ball, fusses, and then quiets as they enter the backyard. The toddler has been going up and down the slide repeatedly. His mother says, "That's enough sliding. Let's go back to the car and go home." The toddler happily runs toward the car.

- *Young child:* The young child is playing a game on the computer when her mother says, "Time to stop. Let's go downstairs now and find some other things to play with." The young child says, "But I'm not done!" and starts to whine. Her mother says, "I bought new markers at the store. Let's go find them." Pouting, the young child reluctantly follows her mother downstairs.

Classroom Routines

During center time, the young child plays alone with the action figures, then moves to the dramatic play area where he puts on a costume and begins to play with his friends.

▓▓▓▓▓▓ **II. C. How intensely does the child react to various stimuli?**

Daily Routines (Home and Classroom)

- *Infant/toddler:* Although initially fussy when put onto the changing table, the infant quickly calms when her mother talks to her and points to the mobile over her head. The toddler happily splashes in the bath. When Dad announces that the bath is over and it is time for bed, the toddler screams and kicks. "No, I don't want to go to bed!" Dad takes him out of the tub, kicking and screaming, but he calms when Dad wraps the towel around him, hugs him, and says, "Let's go read a story."

- *Young child:* The young child screams and physically twists her body to try to get away as her mother tries to gently comb her hair. The screaming and crying continue as her mother gently reassures her and tells her it will only take a minute to comb her hair.

Play Routines (Home and Classroom)

- *Infant/toddler:* Dad winds up the toy monkey and it begins clapping tiny cymbals. The infant laughs and claps her hands. The toddler is feeding the baby doll a bottle, and the caregiver says; "Now the baby is tired." The toddler takes the doll to the toy crib and quietly says, "Nite-nite, baby."

- *Young child:* The teacher places shaving cream on the table and adds drops of food coloring for the young child to rub into the shaving cream. The young child slowly puts her hand in and starts to rub the cream around. "Oooh. It's cold and gooey!"

Classroom Routines

The young child gets up groggily from his nap and wanders around the room, holding his stuffed bear.

GENERAL PRINCIPLES FOR SUPPORTING APPROPRIATE EMOTIONAL STYLE/ADAPTABILITY

All children need to be able to adjust to changes in activities and routines throughout the day. Although expected, emotional reactions to new situations and modifications in daily routines need to be moderate and controllable in order for the child to be able to function, learn, and interact. Children become better able to adjust as they learn to predict the consequences of change. Adults help children predict results, learn how to approach new situations, make transitions across activities, and control the intensity of their emotional responses to change. The following are strategies that often are used by parents and other caregivers.

Let the Child Know What Is Coming

Children are less likely to have difficulty with new situations or changes in routines if they know what is going to happen. Parents typically let children know in advance when someone is coming over, where they are planning to go, and so forth. This advance warning enables the child to think about the upcoming change and thus be more prepared for it. For example, the adult might say, "As soon as we're through with lunch, we'll go for a walk around the block."

Talk About Upcoming Events

Talking about the positive aspects of what is going to happen next helps the child focus on less anxiety-producing elements of a situation. The adult attempts to get the child to look forward to, rather than fear, the change. For the situation described in the preceding paragraph, the adult might say, "When we're on our walk, we'll look for birds and flowers. Maybe we'll see that little doggie you like." The adult also may frame upcoming events by talking about the beginning and the end; for instance, "We will start at our house and walk around the block and end up back home again."

Give Warnings

Another strategy frequently used by adults is to "count down" to the change. Abruptly announcing, "We have to go *now*" can result in stress and rebellion on the part of the child. By giving frequent warnings of an upcoming change, adults often can lessen the negative response. Because young children have a limited concept of time, using concrete referents is helpful. For example, "You finished all your lunch. Mommy is going to put your dishes in the dishwasher and then we'll get ready for our walk." Later, "Okay, we have your coat on. We're ready to go. Let's go get the stroller."

Use Transition Objects

Transition objects provide a connection to the familiar for the child. Many children have special objects that provide a secure base for them. A blanket, a stuffed animal, or a pacifier is the most common. These objects help the child to self-calm in situations in which he or she may feel anxious. For example, the child who is upset at having to stop playing to take a nap may calm immediately when given the "blankie" to take with her to the crib.

Pair the New Experience with Something Pleasurable

By combining a new experience with a familiar experience, the adult can reduce the amount of stress for the child. For example, if the child likes running and jumping, the parent might make a game of running and jumping on the path through the zoo. In this way, the child is doing something fun and not concentrating on the new experience.

Reflect Feelings and Remain Calm

Trying to get a child who is happily playing to leave the house or change activities can be challenging. Yelling and excitability on the part of the adult, however, may cause escalation of the child's emotions. The calm tone of the adult can lower anxiety related to changes or transitions. Reflection of the child's feelings also can help keep the intensity of emotions the child feels within acceptable boundaries. For example, the parent says, "You are being shy, aren't you? You don't need to be afraid. This is a new friend of Mommy's."

Give the Child an Element of Control

Children are more likely to be able to make a transition if they have control over some element of the change. Parents and other caregivers often give children choices as a means of helping them to participate in decision making. When the child hears, "Do you want to ___ or ___?" the focus changes from change or no change to *how* the change will occur. For example, instead of saying "Do you want to go to bed?" the parent may say, "It is time for bed. Do you want to sleep with your bear or your kitty?" Choices reduce oppositional behavior and extreme emotional responses in the face of loss of control.

THE PRINCIPLES IN PRACTICE

Such strategies can help children make adaptations throughout their day. The following are specific examples of how these techniques are implemented on a daily basis.

Daily Routines (Home and Classroom)

Feeding/Eating

Children often are hesitant to eat new foods. Parents may encourage experimentation by comparing the new food with something the child likes. For example, the parent says to the toddler, "Here is a mango. It is orange like your doll's hair. It is sweet like bananas and strawberries."

Diapering/Toileting

Sitting on a toilet is a new experience for the child being toilet trained. Sitting is usually not a motivating experience. The adult can encourage patience by giving the child some way to occupy him- or herself on the potty chair. For example, the parent might give the child a plastic bowl as a "potty chair" for her doll. The child can then sit the doll on the potty and show her how to use it by modeling.

Dressing

Dressing can be a transition issue, particularly if the child is comfortable in his warm "jammies." It also can be a problem if children are asked to wear new or unfamiliar clothes. Adults may help the child make the transition by talking about what the child can do when dressed. For example, "Let's get your pants and shirt on so you can go play with your friends next door. They are waiting for you to play in their sand box!"

Play Routines (Home and Classroom)

Face-to-Face Play

Sudden changes may feel intrusive. The parent who knows the child is easily upset may talk the child through the game as they play. For instance, when playing Peekaboo, the father may talk to the child while he is behind the blanket: "Where is Daddy?" Can you find me? I'm hiding!"

Physical Play

Physical games may release intense emotions for the child. The adult may need to help the child calm by gradually slowing down the vigor of the activity or by physically holding the child. For example, after an active chase game, the young child was screaming and jumping up and down. Mother approached him and gave him a big hug while giving him slow, gentle kisses.

Manipulative Play

The child has been playing Superman with his action figures. It is time to stop and go to bed. The child starts screaming. Mother says, "Let's put Superman to bed too. Does he want to sleep here in the living room or in the hall outside your bedroom?" In this case, the parent is giving the child some aspect of control over the transition. By letting the child participate in the change, he is more motivated to make the transition.

Sensory Play

Messy play or art play involving touching various materials can be highly motivating or highly aversive. Parents often skip these types of activities if the child does not like them, because they are not viewed as imperative and "messy" often means a mess is made! Parents frequently introduce messy activities into bath time and outdoor play, where it is easy to control. When adults are not stressed by a messy activity, children feel more relaxed as well.

Reading and Learning Routines

Circle Time

Getting children into circle time from active play often is demanding. Teachers frequently use signals, such as flashing the lights or playing a specific song, to warn children and let them know that it is time to make a transition (e.g., they have only 5 minutes more to play).

One-on-One Book Reading

For most children without disabilities, making the transition out of one-on-one book reading is difficult because children often do not want to end this special time. Adults frequently use the limit or parameter of "one more book." This helps the child anticipate the end time for reading together.

Science and Math

Making the science and math area an interactive center, with many options and concrete manipulatives, draws children in. Transitions out of the center may be made by having an equally motivating option or by using a transition object such as the child's picture, which is then moved to the new center.

PLANNING INDIVIDUALIZED INTERVENTIONS FOR IMPROVING EMOTIONAL STYLE/ADAPTABILITY

Children with disabilities may resist new activities or situations. The unfamiliar may seem threatening or complicated. New people may seem intimidating or frightening. They may resist new toys and materials because they lack the strategies to figure out how to use them. Novel situations may feel uncomfortable because the child lacks the skills necessary to analyze what is happening and make appropriate adjustments to behavior.

Transitioning to a new activity or routine also may be difficult for children with special needs, because they are being asked to leave something familiar for something unknown. Even if the activity to which the child is moving is a known activity, stopping one thing and starting another may feel daunting. The child would prefer to stay with a habitual pattern rather than have to create new behaviors.

Because learning takes place when children add new information or skills to their existing repertoire, it is important to help children with disabilities increase their flexibility and adaptability to change. In addition to the strategies discussed previously, the following sections provide suggestions for supporting the development of an emotional style that tolerates and adapts more easily to modifications in routines and activities.

▨▨▨▨ **II. A. How does the child approach new people, activities, or situations? (Consider age)**

The child who is shy, avoidant, inhibited, or fearful may move away from unfamiliar people or objects, resist eye contact, protest or cry, or seek proximity to more secure people (e.g., a parent) or objects (e.g., known toys or transition objects available during TPBA). Children who resist or avoid new situations need emotional support to help them feel comfortable so they can begin to explore their environment.

Interaction Strategies

1. *Anticipate problems and provide support rather than pressure.* Some of the child's resistance to the novel may be due to neurological differences that influence adaptability. It is best not to force the child into a new situation, but rather find ways to entice the child. Pushing or demanding may result in more resistance and increased negative emotional response, making the situation even more untenable. It is important for the adult to anticipate the new situations that will be challenging for the child, so that techniques can be planned.

2. *Draw relationships between the familiar and the new.* Adults can help children see the relationships between new and familiar situations. Pointing out similarities can help the child recognize common factors and help reduce anxiety. For example, "Look, she is wearing tennis shoes just like yours!" or "You have a ball like that at home. Yours is yellow." or "When we get to the library we'll see if we can find your favorite book."

3. *Avoid surprise.* Some children with special needs may easily become alarmed or overwhelmed when new activities are introduced unexpectedly. Children who are deaf or hard of hearing may not hear approaching people or noise-making objects. When objects or people suddenly appear or come up from behind, they may become startled and cry. Use a visual warning in combination with a gentle, gradual touch to let the child know something new is approaching. In the same way, children who have visual impairments may become upset when an unexpected touch or loud sound is imposed. When playing with a child with visual impairment, a soft verbal warning before touching them is important. For instance, "Mommy is going to pick you up now, so we can go eat." Children who are hypersensitive to touch also need a gentle verbal warning before being picked up or introduced to tactile material.

4. *Know the child's sensitivities.* Be aware of aspects of new activities that may be overwhelming to the child, and enable the child to adjust gradually. For example, the child who does not want to try new things may let his Barney doll touch the toy, look at the book, or "throw" a ball. The doll, in effect, does the exploration while the child watches. Using the stuffed animal as an intermediary may allow the child to see that the activity is fun, and he then may be able to try these activities himself. This same approach may be used with the adult or peers modeling an activity for the hesitant child.

5. *Give the child words to say he or she is uncomfortable.* Children often cry, scream, or resist activities when they do not have the words to express their feelings. The adult can teach the child to say a phrase such as, "I'm not ready," "I don't like it," or "Not yet." If adults respond to these words, children will begin to use them to express concern with less physical expression. Adults also can express confidence that the child will adjust to a change by saying, "Tell me when you are ready" or "Let me know when you want to play."

Environmental Modifications

In addition to interpersonal strategies that may support the child's adaptation to new objects, people, or events, environmental modifications often are useful. Depending on the findings from TPBA2, the team may want to consider some of the following environmental modifications.

1. *Bring a transition object.* Just as children without disabilities often like to have a transition object, children with special needs also may gain comfort from a familiar object. The object selected may be unusual; for example, a ball, truck, or even just the last

object held when leaving the house. For children who are having difficulty with new people due to separation issues, a picture of the parent or an article of clothing the parent has worn, such as a scarf, may be helpful.

2. *Provide a familiar element.* Keeping one thing recognizable—the setting, the people, or the toys and materials—can provide a sense of familiarity for the child. Seeing new toys or new people in the home is less stressful than encountering them in a new environment. In the same way, bringing a favorite book or toy to a new environment also can help the child become comfortable. Playing with something familiar can enable the child to "settle in" and then become interested in the new surroundings. New people can then gradually relate to the child through the child's familiar books or toys. Having familiar adults introduce novel items or take the child to new settings also is advisable.

3. *Anticipate overwhelming aspects.* For example, if the child is easily upset by loud noises and you are going to an amusement park or other loud venue, letting the child wear ear muffs or ear phones may help lessen the sound. If the child does not like situations with many new people, bring a favorite toy to distract the child. Stay with the child to provide a secure base until the child is comfortable with the new situation.

II. B. How easily does the child adapt to transitions in activities and/or changes in routines?

Beginning new activities or ending a familiar activity is difficult for many children with special needs. Children with autism spectrum disorders, for example, may fixate or perseverate on one activity (e.g., pushing a car) or aspect of play (e.g., lining things up) to the exclusion of others (see TPBA2, Chapter 7, Subcategory V. Complexity of Play). Narrow interests or restricted focus of attention may contribute to the child's difficulty with transitions. Lack of comprehension of event sequences also can cause children with cognitive delays to resist change. If the child does not understand what is coming next, anxiety about change may be evident.

Children with emotional and social concerns also may demonstrate problems with making transitions from one activity or routine to another. Some children may have issues with control and reject any efforts on the part of adults to redirect their attention (see TPBA2, Chapter 4, Subcategory IV. Behavioral Regulation). Fear of the unknown (e.g., "What will happen next?") also may contribute to difficulty making transitions across activities or routines.

Children with motor planning problems (see TPBA2, Chapter 2, Subcategory IV. Motor Planning) also may stick with familiar, practiced activities. Making a transition to new activities requires organizing new motor sequences, which may be difficult for the child. Many children tend to avoid activities they know will be difficult, and they prefer to stay with an activity they have mastered.

All children need predictable routines, but some children with special needs become very rigid about how routines are to be done. They may insist on the same order of actions in a routine, such as how they get dressed; the same foods for each meal; or the same sequence of routines each day. For some children, the smallest changes can cause huge disruption. This lack of flexibility can cause adults great stress in their interactions with the child. The tendency may be always to let the child have his or her way in order to avoid conflict, or to engage in numerous battles. Neither approach is beneficial. The following suggestions may help children who have difficulty with change or transitions.

Interaction Strategies

1. *Give choices so the child retains control.* Let the child have control over some aspect of the situation. Choosing what they will take, how they will make the transition, what they will do in the new activity or routine, and so forth, gives the child a reason to want to enter into a new situation. For example, if the child is going out in the car, the parent might ask, "What would you like to play with in the car: your ABC book or your Spiderman?" or "When we get to school, do you want to stop and say 'Hi' to Mary or go hug Big Bear?" Involving the child in making decisions takes away some of the worry that may result from introduction to new situations or having to stop one thing and start another.

2. *Concentrate on the means rather than the ends.* Help the child focus on the immediate actions. This helps the child focus on the present, rather than what comes next. For example, the adult might say, "Do you want to walk, run, or hop to the door?" Make the process of transition fun.

3. *Reinforce flexibility.* When the child does tolerate change or makes a nice transition, praise the child's effort and point out what the child gained. For example, if the child agrees to eat a new food, the parent might say, "Look at you! You are being so brave to try new things! Yea!"

4. *Introduce change gradually.* When possible, introduce changes in routine gradually. For instance, if the child is going to start preschool or a new child care center, the child needs to be prepared in advance. The parent needs to talk about the change in a positive way (e.g., "You will have so much fun!"); introduce elements with which the child can become familiar (e.g., drive by and look at the new site and watch the children going in); talk about choices the child may have in the new setting (e.g., "You will be able to play with cars or blocks"); introduce another element (e.g., take a trip to look at the classroom and watch the children play); and involve the child in planning the transition (e.g., what to wear, what to take along on an outing).

5. *Downplay the change.* Do not talk about what the child will be missing (e.g., "Mommy will miss you when you are at school"; "I know you would rather have French fries, but you need to eat something different!"). Talk positively about the current situation.

Environmental Modifications

In addition to interpersonal strategies that may support the child in making transitions more easily, environmental modifications often are useful. Depending on the findings from TPBA2, the team may want to consider some of the following environmental modifications.

1. *Remove the object of perseveration.* When the child persists in playing with the same object all the time, remove the object from the child's sight when the child's attention is diverted. Play physical games that do not involve objects to get the child engaged, then gradually introduce a new object into the play. The child may require adult support as a play partner until new play patterns can be developed.

2. *Combine toys and materials from the preferred activity with toys or materials from the next activity in unique ways to entice the child to transition.* The material that is transferred then functions like a transition object for the child and helps the child connect the ideas, rather than seeing the various actions as termination of one activity and commencement of another. For example, if the child is playing with a farm set and is fixated on putting the cow in the barn to make the "Moo" sound, the adult might take the cow to another area and show the child how the cow can play somewhere else. For example,

the cow might be put on top of one of the lids of a pop-up toy, so that when the activating device is pushed, pulled, or turned, the toy will make a noise and the cow will fly through the air. This may be intriguing to the child and entice him or her to begin experimenting with the different actions of the knobs and sounds of the different lids.

3. *Use picture cues for routines.* Many children with special needs can benefit from visual cues to guide them. Picture cards that can guide the child's actions can be made from actual pictures of the child, from pictures created by the family, from web sites, or from professional materials (see, e.g., Do2Learn [http://www.dotolearn.com]; The Internet Picture Dictionary [http://www.pdictionary.com]; Beyond Autism [http://trainland.tripod.com/pecs.htm]). Once the child learns how to use picture schedules and action picture sequences, the visual cues can serve as a reminder of activities, reduce perseveration, and also lessen stress related to lack of understanding of event sequences.

4. *Use object cues.* Object cues are real or simulated objects that are used by adults to remind children of routines or upcoming events (e.g., a wash cloth for the bath, a key for a car trip, a toy shovel for the park, a spoon for time to eat). Such object cues can be useful for children with developmental delays, visual impairments, and other disorders affecting attention, memory, and behavior.

▮▮▮▮▮ II. C. How intensely does the child react to various types of stimuli?

The intensity of a child's reaction to transitions and change also is important to intervention. Children who have extreme responses can be extremely challenging for parents, caregivers, and teachers. In order to avoid the tantrums, parents may avoid outings in the community, caregivers may let children "have their way," and teachers may let the child repeat familiar activities rather than introducing new experiences to the child that may then disrupt the entire class. Dealing with an emotional style characterized by extremes of behavior requires thought and sensitivity.

Alternatively, the child who has the opposite response—that of quiet withdrawal—often is ignored because he or she is not a "problem." These children, however, also may suffer the loss of important engagement experiences for their learning as a result of lack of attention or anxiety. These children also need adult support. All of the previous strategies provide a foundation for intervention with children on the extreme ends of the spectrum of emotions. In addition, see TPBI2, Chapter 5, Section III. Strategies for Improving Regulation of Emotions and Arousal States, and Chapter 5, Section IV. Strategies for Improving Behavioral Regulation.

Interaction Strategies

1. *Maintain a calm demeanor.* The adult's own temperament is important to the outcome of a transition experience. It is easy for the adult to become frustrated and also demonstrate intense emotions. Although this is always important when dealing with children's emotions and behavior, it is especially important when the child's emotions are intense. The adult needs to model the desired behavior and intensity.

2. *Avoid too much talking.* For many children, simultaneously trying to deal with emotions, think about what is happening, and listen to an adult increases the intensity of response. It is just too much to handle. Reduce the amount of input and gently touch or guide the child as he or she is ready. As noted previously, giving the child some control through options of how he or she wants to be involved often is helpful.

3. *For some children, holding or a tight hug can be calming.* The use of holding should be done when the child is out of control and is hurting himself or others or is being de-

structive to materials in the environment. The holding should be nonpunitive, and as gentle as possible, while the adult says nothing or softly explains what can happen when the child calms down (depending on the child's level of comprehension and attention).

4. *Analyze the consequences for the child.* If the child is benefiting from the attention the adult gives the child, the behavior may escalate or be maintained. For a child who does not want to make changes or transitions, however, ignoring the child is reinforcing. He gets to continue doing what he wanted to do in the first place. For children who have difficulty changing because of the stress of the process rather than the need for attention, the adult needs to focus on making the process less anxiety producing. See the previous suggestions.

Environmental Modifications

1. *Calm the environment.* Reducing anxiety is important for children with intense transitional issues. The environment should be made less attractive to the child so that change is a preferred option. Bright lights or loud noises may encourage the child to change environments.

2. *Provide transition objects.* If leaving an object of interest is the cause for anxiety, removing the object the child does not want to leave, while at the same time providing a transitional substitute the child likes and can take along, will reduce anxiety. For example, if the child is playing with a favorite toy and it is time to go outdoors to play, perhaps the child could bring the toy with her. If the child's anxiety is related to uncertainty, it may be helpful to provide reassurance and information in the form of pictures of what is to come.

ROUTINES FOR THE CHILD WHO NEEDS
SUPPORT WITH EMOTIONAL STYLE/ADAPTABILITY

Daily Routines (Home and Classroom)

Feeding/Eating

For children who are "picky" eaters and do not exhibit flexible eating patterns, adults can look for special ways to introduce new foods. Try to find a dip or sauce the child likes (e.g., salad dressing, cheese sauce, honey). Any food can then be dunked in this dip. Find a pattern the child likes for the food. Food can be placed in the shape of a face, by color, or on a specific part of the plate. Choices will give the child control. For example, "Should I put the potatoes on the clown's face or on the lion?" "Do you want 5 beans or 6 beans?"

Diapering/Toileting

Transitions from diapers to underpants may be a difficult transition for some children. They have to move from an interaction with the parent to independence, have to recognize internal feelings of pressure and gain control of bodily functions, and then organize a sequence of actions to maneuver through the toileting experience. Children may be challenged by, and therefore resist, shifting to this new approach. It is only when the child's discomfort or pride in accomplishment exceeds the comfort of the familiar routine that the child transitions to the more independent routine. Parents can take advantage of this fact by not using "pull up" style toilet training pants that mask the child's sensation of wetness. They also can gradually replace the old diapering routine with a set toileting routine. Clarify each step for the child, use picture or object cues if needed, and keep the toileting routine consistent so that the child learns the sequence. Help the child recognize and take pride in learning each step of the process, not just the final outcome.

Dressing

For children who have difficulty with transitions, the hardest part of dressing is that more than one routine is involved. First, there is a routine to take off what is already on (e.g., pajamas), which involves a series of complex actions. Then the child must adjust to being naked. For some children, this is problematic because they may be sensitive to temperature changes. Putting on clothing involves another shift, another temperature change, and another balance of control between the parent and child. Again, a routine for these separate aspects is helpful, with the child leading as much as possible and anticipating the next step. Allowing the child a reasonable amount of control over clothing choices, speed of dressing and undressing, and order of the routine is preferable. For children with sensitivity to temperature change, warming the towels after a bath or the clothing before putting it on may make dressing more pleasant.

Going Out

Leaving the comfortable environment of the home often is difficult for children with transition issues. Several of the ideas mentioned previously may help: using transition objects, discussing the next event with anticipation, planning what the child will do on the way and once there, making the leaving process a game, and letting the child participate at his or her comfort level once at the destination. Once the adult has informed the child of the planned outing, prepared the child, and set out, it is important to stick with the plan. Adding additional activities (e.g., a stop at another store) can undermine the coping strategies the child is using. It also is important to end the outing while the child is happy, rather than extending the time because the child is behaving well. Pushing the limits may lead to the child not trusting the adult's comments about what will happen on future outings.

Play Routines (Home and Classroom)

Face-to-Face Play

Face-to-face play with unfamiliar people is difficult for many children, particularly children with autism spectrum disorders or fragile X syndrome. Sudden movements, certain types of touch, or play that feels too intrusive also may cause the child to react negatively in face-to-face play. Adults should develop a comfortable, trusting relationship with the child before engaging in this type of play. Read the child's cues carefully so you can respond when the child seems to be overstimulated or resisting the game. Slow, rhythmic movements tend to be calming, and fast, jerky movements are arousing. Adults can moderate their pace of interaction depending on the child's cues. Children with fragile X syndrome, in particular, may find face-to-face play threatening. For them, other types of play may be more rewarding.

Physical Play

Physical play often involves movement and touch, especially when roughhousing is involved. Because of the intense nature of physical play, children tend to either enjoy this type of play or resist it. For children who enjoy the sensations, physical play can provide a means for transitioning to a less desired activity. For infants, being tossed, swung, or tickled on the way to a new activity can act as a pleasurable distracter. For toddlers and young children who love to move, moving in different ways, such as crawling, jumping, or hopping to another area, can help them transition. For children who do not enjoy physical activity, the challenge becomes how to transition them *into* play where active movement is involved. Children who have tone that is excessively high or low, children with motor planning problems, or children with hypersensitivity to vestibular or proprioceptive input may avoid active physical play. Because this type of play is important for sensorimotor and social development, figuring out how to get children involved in physical games is important. Adults can address this by integrating the types of play the child does enjoy into physical games. For instance, if the child likes puzzles, adults can make putting together the puzzle into a fun physical game. Using turn-taking, the adult and the child or the child and peers can create games to put together a floor puzzle. With a pile of puzzle pieces on one side of the room and the puzzle on the other side, they could take turns running or jumping with a puzzle piece across the room to place the piece. They could wrestle to see who gets the last puzzle piece. If the child likes pretend play, they could pretend to be puppies sitting up, rolling over, crawling, and so forth. The adult needs to consider what motivates the child, then integrate that with physical play.

Manipulative Play

Children who avoid manipulative play often have fine motor or visual concerns that inhibit their success. They can be transitioned to such play by capitalizing on aspects of the play that will entice them or enable them to feel success. These two approaches often can be combined. Begin with larger objects that are easier for the child to manipulate. Make sure the toys or materials selected have characteristics that appeal to the specific child. For instance, some children like toys that have mechanisms that cause the toy to have a visual, auditory, or movement effect when activated. Other children like toys that are bright and shiny or make music. Some children like toys that can be combined to create interesting patterns or structures, such as puzzles, paper and markers, or blocks. A second consideration is to select toys and materials that will not be too challenging for the child's developmental abilities. If pieces are too small to see or manipulate, the child either will avoid the play or will not experience success and will not want to try again. Start with larger versions of the manipulatives, so the child can experience success. It also is helpful to have a model for the child at the beginning of the process, so they can see what their efforts can produce. The adult's excitement or pleasure in the activity also can be a motivator for the child to choose to try this kind of play.

Sensory Play

Sensory play is any play that involves the various sensory systems. It is important that children be able to experience a range of different types of sensory input to promote neurological and physical development. In addition, sensory experience helps children understand various sensory concepts so they can fit these concepts into classification systems (see TPBA2, Chapter 7, Subcategory VI. Conceptual Knowledge). Although some children like all types of sensory play, children often have preferences for the type of sensory play in which they want to engage. As described earlier, some children will make the transition easily to physical play involving vestibular and proprioceptive input. Other children will avoid this kind of play. In the same way, children who are "tactually defensive" may seek out or avoid tactile input of various kinds; for example, play with messy or gooey materials or play with certain smooth or rough textures. Some children may react negatively to play with loud, noisy toys. Children may avoid play with certain kinds of textures. Desensitizing children who have an extreme aversion to different types of sensory input may be necessary before they can fully enjoy such play. By gradually introducing mild forms of the avoided sensory input paired with pleasurable play, the child may be able to develop a tolerance for the sensation. For example, if a child is averse to any soft or mushy texture, the adult may introduce these gradually into play. Playdough, bath foam, and fingerpaints all can be enjoyed first with a tool such as a stick or roller, then with a finger, and finally, as the child's desire to explore increases, with the full hand. Allowing the child to eat mushy foods with the fingers also is helpful and can be incorporated into dramatic play by "feeding the baby." The adult needs to think of creative and fun ways of "softly" introducing the type of sensory stimuli the child avoids.

Dramatic Play

Dramatic play, or play that involves representing events by acting them out either alone or with others, often is difficult for children with cognitive, language, social, or motor limitations. Children with cognitive delays may not be able to remember, conceptualize, or sequence a series of real-life events. Children with language delays or disorders may have difficulty with sequencing thoughts and actions or communicating within sociodramatic play. Children with emotional or social concerns may not be able to understand the thoughts and feelings of others within the dramatic play scenario and may not be able to relate to integrate and coordinate their play with others. Children with sensorimotor concerns may be able to conceptualize what they want to act out but not be able to perform the actions necessary. Any of these concerns may lead children to resist dramatic play. In each of these situations, the adult can draw the child into dramatic play by building on the child's skills and strengths. For children with cognitive delays, beginning with simple manipulative and combinatorial play, such as pushing a car and then moving into the child himself pretending to drive a car, makes an important connection for the child. For the child with language delays, using signs, gestures, or picture cues in combination with concrete language and actions may motivate the child to want to play. For the child with autism or other kinds of social skills issues, giving the child a "script" for what to say and do may be helpful. The adult can help the child with motor problems by using assistive devices, letting the child guide the adult's actions (where the adult acts "for" the child), and involving the child in a meaningful way so that the child understands how his or her thoughts can be included.

Reading and Learning Routines

Circle Time

Transition into and out of circle time often is a challenge. Children are usually into their various activities before circle time. Use of transition songs or transition activities often is helpful. First, give children a warning (e.g., flicker of the lights, sound of a bell) that they have 2 minutes left before cleanup. This gives them time to think about winding up their activity. Then use another signal (e.g., song or specific routine words) to indicate that it is time to clean up. Some children may need a model or assistance with this aspect. Give children choices about where and how they want to sit, because some children may feel overwhelmed sitting close to others in a group, some may need a more supportive chair, and some may need to sit next to an adult. It is desirable to have a routine to start circle time so that children know what to expect, but it also is important to have an exciting start to circle time so children will anticipate coming to something fun. Some days might involve props, costumes, real materials, and so forth that entice children to participate.

One-on-One Book Reading

Children may avoid one-on-one reading because of lack of interest in or understanding of books, a short attention span, or avoidance of social intimacy. To motivate children to want to transition from a more active play to the quiet of one-on-one reading, the adult at first may need to make one-on-one reading more like the child's preferred form of interaction. For example, if the child enjoys physical play, dramatic play, or manipulative play, the adult can lead into book reading by acting out the actions on the page; adding fingerplays; or using miniatures, real objects, or stuffed animals to portray characters in the books. Actual objects may be of more interest to children with disabilities, and the comparison of the object with the picture may draw the child in. The adult and child then can use these objects to depict the actions in the book while reading the story.

Science and Math

As with circle time, centers such as the science and math area need to contain materials that are exciting and fun for children to manipulate. Having the same puzzles, counting bears, and boring worksheets every day will not encourage children to want to transition to this area (unless they are children who dislike change, and that should not be encouraged anyway!). Before moving to centers, let the children know what to expect and tell them why the center will be fun, and also show them a prop or action that will motivate them and help them remember what they have been told about the center. Use picture cues at the center to guide action sequences. Use peer pairing because this will enable children who have limited memory or attention to have a social model. (It will be necessary to train the peers about how to support their friend's play.)

JAMAL

Jamal is a 4-year-old boy who has been diagnosed as having fragile X syndrome. For boys, this syndrome is characterized by perseveration; hyperactivity and attention issues; hypersensitivity to tactile and auditory stimuli; social anxiety with new people; language delays; difficulties with short-term memory; and problems with organizing, planning, and sequencing information. They do best in familiar contexts or situations that build on long-term memory, use simultaneous processing, and have a visual or hands-on component. Predictable activities and events are handled best.

Jamal has a difficult time meeting new people and transitioning to new activities. He is enrolled in a preschool that uses Read, Play, and Learn!, *an inclusive curriculum based on integration of activities related to the concepts and actions within a story book over a period of time. Jamal's teacher reads the story every day, using props from the story, asks the children questions, and has the children involved in dramatizations of the actions of the story. After circle time, where the story is shared, the children go to centers for art, dramatic play, sensory play, physical play, science and math, table play and other areas. All of the centers involve concepts that relate to the story, use visual cues to remind children of the concepts, and Jamal typically chooses the puzzles or blocks in floor play or table play. He seldom chooses dramatic play or activities involving social interaction. Jamal's use of vocabulary and comfort with the concepts and activities increases over the course of each module, and he is able to use the phrases and concepts learned appropriately and become involved in re-enacting the story.*

The following are suggestions that were incorporated into Jamal's intervention plan.

Interaction Strategies

1. *Do not require eye contact, because this will raise Jamal's anxiety and reduce his desire to interact. Let him look away and then look back to the interaction when he is comfortable.*

2. *Because boys with fragile X syndrome often do relatively well with daily living skills, let Jamal be a leader for these aspects of the day. This will help others in the class see him as competent.*

3. *Use patterned phrases and responses to teach social skills, and practice these in role play situations related to familiar stories.*

4. *Jamal can be a peer partner in the physical games he loves to play. Help him to play the leader in Follow the Leader physical play in the gym and on the playground. Train the peer to imitate Jamal's actions. Then trade roles and show Jamal how to be the follower.*

5. *Use one-to-one reading of the focus book with Jamal to help him understand concepts and be ready to participate in circle time. Pick aspects he knows and understands when discussion takes place in circle so that he can participate.*

Environmental Modifications

1. *Reduce auditory and visual distractions by separating the room into separate zones with just a few children in each at one time.*

2. *Use a visual schedule and a predictable routine during each aspect of the day. Also use visual picture sequences for aiding memory for sequential tasks.*

3. *Begin with stories related to events that are familiar to Jamal, so he can relate the new concepts to familiar contexts. This will help him learn how each of the centers relate to the story and will help him apply the visual schedules with less familiar material.*

4. *Use music, quiet area, and relaxation techniques when Jamal is upset. Consult with the occupational therapist about setting up a "sensory diet" to assist in modulation of sensory input.*

5. *Let Jamal use tools to explore sensory materials that are distressing to him. Gradually encourage him to explore materials with body parts, such as fingers or toes.*

6. *Use Jamal's interests in horses to involve him in a variety of activities. His toy horse can help him draw, watch him in the dramatic play area, gallop through the sand in the sensory table, and so forth.*

7. *Use real props, costumes, and materials in each of the centers to increase the relevance to Jamal.*

8. *During circle time, let Jamal hold a "fidget" toy such as a squeeze ball. This will help him maintain attention. Keep circle time short and give him functional reasons to get up (e.g., "Jamal, could you get our book?").*

KEYS TO INTERVENTION BY DEVELOPMENTAL AGE

The following ideas are directed toward children who are functioning at approximately the following levels. Emotional style and adaptability are not so much influenced by developmental age as by neurological and temperamental differences that influence how the child reacts to various types of experiences. For this reason, age levels for this area indicate the type of interests the child typically has for this age rather than how emotional style changes. Intervention suggestions then address how to increase the child's adaptability to these types of interests. The suggestions are not meant to be all-inclusive, but rather are indicative of potential areas for exploration.

Developmental age	Typical interests	Key to intervention
Birth to 3 months	Faces Black and white contrast Movement of objects Sensory input such as sounds, music, and movement	Begin face-to-face play. Gently introduce sensory input of all types. In one-on-one reading, look at books with pictures of babies and people.
3–6 months	Own face, body, hands, and fingers Familiar routines and objects	Use mirror play, more face-to-face play. Keep schedule and routine, but modify routines slightly to develop tolerance for change. Engage in one-on-one reading.
6–9 months	Preferred toys, new objects Parts of objects Smells, sounds, and new movements Familiar words Pictures	Rotate toys so child has change each day. Introduce new smells, tastes, music, and so forth. Increase one-on-one reading, looking at pictures of objects, people, and animals and matching with real objects, sounds.
9–12 months	Shows interest in objects and adult responses to objects and actions Has preferred toys Shows increased interest in action toys and speech sounds made by adult	Increase manipulative play; cause-and-effect play with turn-taking. Vary type of sensory result of cause-and-effect toys (e.g., sound, lights, movement). Play face-to-face sound games.
12–18 months	Specific physical aspects of objects and what they do Naming or identifying pictures in books	Increase functional play with object manipulation, sensory play with variety of materials. Dramatize life events and actions in books. Increase one-on-one reading of simple rhyming and story books.
18–24 months	Focuses on others' actions Looks at books Intense interest in own play	Increase social play situations. Read stories. Vary types of play, including dramatic play with familiar routines and simple actions. Increase exploration of sensory aspects of objects. Experiment with varying types of movement.
24–36 months	Attends to stories in books Likes problem solving with small objects and figuring out how things work Pretends in social interactions Combines objects in unusual ways and experiments	Increase reading of stories and dramatizing situations and actions in stories. Increase use of manipulative problem-solving toys. Increase sensory exploration and discovery of sensory aspects of toys and materials. Allow time for exploration of physical play alone and with adults and peers.
36–48 months	Attends to amount, likeness and difference, symmetry, balance, directionality, classification Engages in visual-motor problem solving Performs dramatic play sequences	Promote "scientific" investigation of characteristics in play through manipulation, trial-and-error with different types of sensory materials. Encourage sociodramatic play with social situations and event sequences. Hold brief circle time with high-interest involvement. Encourage physical play individually and in pairs. Maintain one-on-one reading time and circle time.

Developmental age	Typical interests	Key to intervention
48–60 months	Attends to multiple sensory characteristics of objects and events Analyzes behaviors and situations	Encourage investigation of all sensory aspects of situations and events. Support individual strengths as a means to develop flexibility. Play in pairs and groups to promote social interaction in dramatic and physical play. Maintain one-on-one reading time and circle time.
60–72 months	Focuses on multiple attributes of objects Orientation and identification of letters and numbers Complex sociodramatic play with storyline Attends to difficult tasks Attends to long stories, complex tasks Can plan, implement, and evaluate own efforts	Routines and activities should involve all types of play and sensory exploration. Integrate art, literature, science, and math so it is meaningful and motivating to the child and encourages self-discovery and functional use of information. Encourage use of symbolic props in play. Encourage creation of own stories and dramatizations. Maintain one-to-one reading time and circle time. Encourage peer sharing of "reading."

5

Facilitating Emotional and Social Development

III. Strategies for Improving
Regulation of Emotions and Arousal States

Goal Attainment Scale

1	2	3	4	5	6	7	8	9
Has a difficult time controlling arousal states and emotions; needs extensive environmental support and physical and verbal support from a caregiver. Regulation takes more than 1 hour.		Is able to control arousal states and emotions in a soothing environment, when receiving physical and verbal support from a caregiver. Regulation takes 30–60 minutes.		Is able to control arousal states and emotions in a quiet environment *or* when physical or emotional support is received from an adult. Regulation takes 15–30 minutes.		Is able to control arousal states and emotions with self-regulatory strategies (e.g., a blanket or special toy) or verbal suggestions from an adult. Regulation takes just a few minutes.		Is able to independently control arousal states and emotions in a way appropriate for the situation.

REGULATION OF EMOTIONS AND AROUSAL STATES

Regulation of Arousal States

Regulation of arousal states involves strategies we use to adjust the flow of incoming stimulation in order to maintain a comfortable (or satisfying) state of arousal. It is the ability to move through various states of arousal, from asleep through groggy, to awake, to alert and attentive in a manner consistent with individual bodily needs and environmental demands.

At times during the day we may become irritable, fussy, or even cry in certain situations. Our awareness fluctuates depending on the situation and our ability to regulate our state of arousal. All of these states serve various purposes. Sleep allows us to take a break from external stimulation and rejuvenate. The drowsy or groggy state helps us gradually move in and out of sleep. Fussiness or crying enables us to communicate what we are feeling and "release" internal emotions. The quiet, alert state is the most important for learning, moving, interacting, and communicating. If we spend too much time in one state it can interfere with the balance needed by the mind and body. We need enough sleep, but not too much. We need to be awake and alert, but not to the extent that the body cannot rest. We need the state "in between" asleep and alert to help us transition, but getting stuck in that state hinders functioning. We need to express irritation and frustration, but not in excess. Being able to move smoothly between states and being able to control the amount of time we spend in each is an important process, as the ability to utilize these various states appropriately is important for healthy functioning.

State regulation is closely related to other types of self-regulation, but for most people state regulation cycles are resolved within the first year of life. After that, we learn to adjust according to environmental demands and internal needs. Infants need an average of 16 hours total sleep at 1 month of age. This gradually diminishes to an average of about 10.5–11 hours by the age of 6. As sleep states are regulated, so are other states of arousal; for example, the quiet, alert state increases as sleep needs decrease, allowing more time for interaction and learning. State regulation issues that persist, such as inability to sleep, brief alert states, or prolonged fussy states, may have a negative impact on learning, development of relationships, and general functioning. As state regulation is concerned with level of arousal, it also is closely associated with emotional regulation. Issues with one often are associated with concerns about the other.

Regulation of Emotions and Arousal States

Emotional regulation involves the modulation of the full range of emotions and overlaps with state regulation. The basic emotions of happiness, interest, surprise, fear, anger, sadness, and disgust are discernable early in infancy and become expressed more clearly as the infant matures. "The goal of emotional development is to gain the ability to fully experience a wide range of feelings but to do so in a regulated manner" (Gowen & Nebrig, 2002, p. 29). Emotional regulation is related to state regulation and is defined as the ability to appropriately control and adjust the level of emotional expression across the range of emotions. Temperamental factors contribute to emotional regulation. How the child reacts to environmental events, general mood, and activity level also are related to emotional regulation.

Children need to be able to tolerate intense feelings without losing control, modulate the intensity and duration of emotions, transition smoothly from one emotional state to another, and regain equilibrium. Children need the capacity to identify their own emotions, develop empathy, and manage their feelings constructively. Difficulty with emotional regulation can be seen in young children who exhibit a "flat" affect or predominantly a sad, depressed affect, pervasive anxiety and fear, or angry behavior problems.

APPROPRIATE REGULATION OF EMOTIONS AND AROUSAL STATES

A desired characteristic of state regulation is the ability of a child to move from sleep to a quiet, alert state of attention that enables the child to focus and interact for learning. A child also should be able to effectively regulate the degree of sensory input, so that fussiness and irritability is minimized and the child can easily recover and return to the quiet, alert state. In addition, a child also should be able to shut down input, so that drowsiness and sleep is possible.

A desired characteristic of emotional regulation is the ability of a child to respond to situations that elicit various emotions and be able to adjust his or her emotional state and level of intensity of emotional response in order to be able to maintain appropriate functioning. Emotional regulation also requires that the child be able to focus attention, shift attention, and inhibit thoughts and behaviors as necessary to be able to reduce negative emotions. As the infant's brain develops, the infant becomes better able to tolerate stimulation that arouses emotion. The infant moves from using the caregiver to help soothe and control distress (e.g., through rocking, soothing) to being able to shift attention from unpleasant events and being able to sooth him- or herself in a variety of developmentally appropriate ways (e.g., sucking a thumb, rubbing a soft object). The young child will learn to avoid or move away from unpleasant stimuli, use language to understand and express his or her feelings, request assistance when needed, and find other strategies for self-calming. As the child develops, he or she also will be able to substitute new goals for ones that have been frustrated and will be able to use increasingly sophisticated strategies for managing emotions with different people and in different environments. The following examples illustrate how typically developing children regulate their states and emotions.

III. A. How easily is the child able to regulate physiological states of awareness?

Daily Routines (Home and Classroom)

- *Infant/toddler:* When waking up, the infant may cry or vocalize for attention from the adult. When the adult responds, the infant quickly quiets and begins social interaction. The toddler fusses and whines when overtired, holds her blanket to her face, and falls asleep.

- *Young child:* The young child wakes up, plays quietly in bed, and then gets up to go find her parents, demonstrating a gradual transition from asleep to alert.

Play Routines (Home and Classroom)

- *Infant/toddler:* When startled by the noise of the toy, the infant starts to cry but quiets and becomes alert as the adult holds the toy up for him to see. The toddler is playing quietly with a doll. When another child takes the doll, the toddler screams and starts to cry.

- *Young child:* The young child may need parental support and a model in order to move from active play to quiet, focused play.

Classroom Routines

After running around at recess, the children come in and select books. One child fusses because he doesn't want to come in. Slowly he calms, looks at a book, and comments quietly to a friend.

III. B. How easily is the child able to regulate (control and move in and out of) emotional states?

Daily Routines (Home and Classroom)

- *Infant/toddler:* When being bathed, the young infant may find the initial exposure to the water surprising, causing the child to cry. He soothes as the parent pours warm water over him and sings to him. The child who is developing emotional self-regulation will be calmed by the gentle touch and reassuring voice of the caregiver during stressful daily routines.

- *Young child:* The young child has already learned to anticipate the environmental changes and will be able to prepare him- or herself for the different sensations presented by anticipated events.

Play Routines (Home and Classroom)

- *Infant/toddler:* The young infant who is playing with a caregiver initially may find the interactions pleasurable and demonstrate happiness through smiling and laughing. If the caregiver persists in play beyond the point of enjoyment for the child, the child may look or move away and direct attention to something else in order to reduce distress. When the child is frustrated because a toy won't work, the child may fuss or cry briefly but recover and try again after seeking assistance or verbal support.

- *Young child:* During outdoor play, the children are playing by jumping in the snow. One child slips, falls, and starts to cry. When he sees other children laughing and falling on purpose, he laughs too. He gets up and falls again, this time on purpose.

Classroom Routines

The child displays distress when looking at "scary" pictures in a book. She points to and verbalizes fear and seeks a hug from the caregiver in order to remain emotionally calm.

▓▓▓ III. C. Are there identifiable patterns or "triggers" when the child has difficulty modulating emotions?

Daily Routines (Home and Classroom)

- *Infant/toddler:* The infant cries when the parent wipes his bottom with a cold cloth. The toddler wants macaroni and cheese for lunch and screams when his mother places tiny raviolis on his plate.

- *Young child:* At bedtime, the young child cries and fights his mother when told it is time to put away his toys and go to bed.

Play Routines (Home and Classroom)

- *Infant/toddler:* When the Jack-in-the-Box pops up loudly and unexpectedly, the infant cries. When playing with the train set, the toddler screams and cries when another child invades his space, sits down, and picks up the train engine.

- *Young child:* When shooting off the rocket in the backyard, the child screams, laughs, and jumps up and down each time it goes off.

Classroom Routines

During song and dance activities, the children swing their arms, jump around to the beat of the music, and laugh with excitement.

▓▓▓ III. D. How easily is the child able to self-calm when emotions become intense?

Daily Routines (Home and Classroom)

- *Infant/toddler:* The infant calms within 5 minutes when his father holds him and walks him around the house. When getting her hair washed, the toddler screams but then calms quickly when she realizes the hair washing is done.

- *Young child:* The young child gets mad and shouts when told he has to eat "three string beans." When the family makes a game out of taking their turn and making a face relating to how much they like beans, the child makes a mad face, eats a bean, then laughs when everyone imitates his face.

Play Routines (Home and Classroom)

- *Infant/toddler:* The infant squeals when her father blows on her stomach. She then stops, watches, and waits until she sees her father moving to blow again on her tummy before she starts to laugh again. The toddler is running away from her father and laughing as he chases her. She hides behind the couch, quiets, then pops up and laughs as he pretends to search for her.

- *Young child:* The young child is angrily chasing his friend who is riding his bike. When the friend stops the bike and says, "Here. I just wanted to try it," the young child calms down and says, "Well ASK! Okay?"

Classroom Routines

The young child is frightened when the scuba diver enters the classroom dressed in full underwater diving gear. He starts to cry, but calms when the man takes off his mask and says, "It's okay. I'm Damon's daddy and this is what I wear when I swim in the ocean."

■■■■ **III. E. How well is the child able to inhibit impulsive actions and emotions (e.g., physical, vocal or verbal outbursts) in order to attend to tasks?**

Daily Routines (Home and Classroom)

- *Infant/toddler:* The infant reaches for the pretty glass bowl on the coffee table, stops, looks up at her mother, and when her mother shakes her head "no," she picks it up anyway. The toddler grabs for a cracker, and her mother stops her and says, "What do you say?" The toddler says, "Please" and then takes the cracker.

- *Young child:* In the car, the young child asks, "If I am really, really good at Grandma's house, can we stop at Burger King on the way home?"

Play Routines (Home and Classroom)

- *Infant/toddler:* At the park, the infant crawls over to the sandbox, reaches down, and puts a handful of sand in his mouth, demonstrating the infant's typical lack of impulse control. When a peer takes the toddler's doll, the toddler grabs his arm and bites it. She then begins to cry along with the bitten peer.

- *Young child:* There is only one mini-trampoline in the gym and the young child and his friend both race for it. When they get there at the same time, one says, "You can go first, but then I get to jump longer."

Classroom Routines

At the writing center, the young child is bored and starts squirming and making silly noises. He quiets when asked by the adult to calm down and find something else to do.

■■■■ **III. F. What is the child's predominant mood and how long do feeling states or moods last?**

Daily Routines (Home and Classroom)

- *Infant/toddler:* The infant's moods change quickly depending on whether he is hungry, wet, sleepy, or interested in engaging people or the environment. The toddler is driven not just by inner needs, but also by desires. She cries longer when she doesn't get what she wants to eat or can't do what she wants to do, but she can be calmed within 10–15 minutes, even if she does not get what she wants.

- *Young child:* Depending on overall temperament and how effective tantrums have been in the past, the young child may persist in demonstrating negative moods for long periods of time. On the other hand, for young children who have learned compromise and have self-calming techniques, negative moods may be brief, and focused attention and contented engagement may last for long periods of time.

Play Routines (Home and Classroom)

- *Infant/toddler:* During play, the infant is interested and content until tired of the activity. The toddler's moods during play primarily are contented but may shift quickly when a challenge is encountered. They can shift back to contentment just as quickly, however, once a novel or interesting event occurs.

- *Young child:* Playtime typically is a time for interested or excited moods. Shifts occur quickly, but negative moods typically do not persist beyond 15 minutes.

Classroom Routines

The young child typically adopts the mood of the classroom, adjusting to the mood corresponding to those of his peers during various activities.

GENERAL PRINCIPLES FOR SUPPORTING APPROPRIATE REGULATION OF EMOTIONS AND AROUSAL STATES

For the child who demonstrates typical patterns of state and emotional regulation, the following suggestions are designed to provide ways caregivers can continue to assist children in developing strong regulatory and coping mechanisms. These strategies also are helpful for children who have difficulty regulating emotions, but exploration of modifications for these children will be discussed in more depth later.

Provide Regular Routines

A regular routine helps children anticipate sequences and outcomes. Adults need consistent approaches to dealing with the child's needs and emotions. For example, adults provide a consistent sequence for going to bed, getting up, eating meals, and so forth. These consistent patterns are important to enable children to understand what is going to happen next. The predictable routine offers a sense of comfort. Consistency in response to emotions also is important.

Accept Emotions Expressed by the Child

It is important for children to understand that it is okay to have strong feelings, that expression of emotions is normal and expected, and that the child has the ability to control how he or she expresses emotion. The caregiver can verbalize what the child appears to be feeling. ("You don't like it when I move your food.") This helps the child to identify words to go with the feelings he or she is experiencing. As language develops, the child will be better able to express feelings verbally rather than having to act them out physically. Caregivers also can let the child know that "It is okay to be mad." Adults can reassure the child that expressing feelings is all right; we all have feelings, but it also is important to let children know that there are limits to how emotions are expressed. Caregivers can set parameters to help the child understand, for instance, that "it is okay to be frustrated when your block tower falls down, but it is not okay to throw the blocks at your brother." Adults can identify appropriate ways for the child to show anger, frustration, jealousy, fear, or sadness and help the child substitute appropriate means of expression of feelings for inappropriate means. Caregivers need to realize that as the child develops, he or she is experiencing an increasingly more sophisticated range of emotions with a concurrent range of emotional intensity. The adults in the child's life need to support the child's efforts to deal with these emerging feelings by helping the child develop coping skills.

Help Children Identify the Strategies That Are Effective for Them in Moderating Emotions

The caregiver can play an important role in helping children identify what works to get their emotions under control. Adults need to be good observers of what types of activities stimulate or calm a child. These activities, or elements of these activities, can then be introduced to the child at emotional times. ("Why don't you go rock in your rocker while you are calming down. That always seems to make you feel better.") Such verbalization will enable the child to think about "what works," and at some later time when he or she is upset, the child may be able to remember this strategy and begin to employ it independently.

Model Appropriate Coping Strategies

It is important for parents to model emotional regulation strategies for the child. Taking a time out, a deep breath, or redirecting actions can be helpful in reducing intense emotions. Letting children see how adults effectively manage emotions is helpful. Even the best caregivers, however, may occasionally lose control of their emotions and say or do inappropriate things. If this happens, discuss the emotions experienced and express regret to the child if the resulting behavior was inappropriate. Caregivers also can discuss alternatives to their actions. Try to ensure that the negative interaction ends on a positive emotional note, with a kiss, a hug, or a laugh.

Provide a Variety of Experiences for the Child that Elicit a Range of Emotions

It is not necessary to shelter children from experiences that may elicit strong emotions. Children will learn to handle their emotions when they are confronted with situations that bring out their feelings. Experiences at amusement parks, natural history museums (with dinosaur bones or animal scenes), movies, books, and new and different environments not only provide opportunities for the child to learn new concepts, but also provide opportunities to face new feelings and come up with coping strategies, either independently or with the support of an adult.

THE PRINCIPLES IN PRACTICE

Although the following examples do not address every aspect of the day or every possible situation, they are typical of successful strategies often employed during daily routines, play, and reading routines. Reading routines, at home, in school or child care, and in the community, are included because they are of critical importance to children's learning. Other learning routines also are essential, and the following strategies generalize to those situations as well.

Daily Routines (Home and Classroom)

Feeding/Eating

Eating a meal typically is a social event and a time that is full of pleasant emotions for the child. Talking to the child about the food, the tastes, the events of the day, and what will happen later typically are all calming and pleasurable for both caregiver and child. For young infants, feeding games such as "Here comes the airplane" are fun. Children, although not parents, often enjoy the game of "throwing food on the floor." Young children often express intense emotions about *what* they will or will not eat. Caregivers support the child in moderating emotions during mealtime by setting limits on what can be done, by not letting the child get too excited, and by giving the child opportunities to make choices and have as much independence as possible.

Diapering/Toileting

During the diapering routine, the child has many sensory opportunities, including experiencing the body clothed and naked; feeling wet and dry sensations, perhaps the texture of powder, the temperature of cold lotion, the pressure of adult hands and a diaper; listening to the caregiver talk; and looking at the sights around the changing table. The child with good emotional regulation will handle all of these changes with aplomb. The caregiver can support the child by following the same routine each time so the child is not surprised by changes. The caregiver also can let the child know what is going to happen next, or introduce new sensations a little at a time.

For older children, learning control of bodily functions can be an emotionally challenging experience. Adults can support children by acknowledging their emotions and providing tools to help them internalize strategies. For example, parents are typically good at reading facial and body language and stating, "You are wiggling and making a face. Does that mean you need to go to the bathroom? I'll go with you to help you get settled." Developing a routine, such as sitting, looking at a book, wiping, flushing, and washing also is good, particularly when the adult assists the child toward feeling independence and confidence.

Dressing

Dressing is an activity that often can involve conflict for children once they begin to gain skills enabling them to dress independently. The child may want to dress more slowly than the working parent needs or he may want to wear different clothing than the parent would select. The child may become angry or frustrated if the parent takes over the job of dressing. The parent may handle this by 1) acknowledging that the child is angry (providing a label for the child's emotions), 2) telling the child how he or she feels (providing a model of verbal expression of emotions), 3) giving the child options as to what he can put on or wear (demonstrating a method for negotiation), 4) praising the child for taking a deep breath and calming down (noting what worked) and making a decision (encouraging self-confidence).

Going to Sleep

Children with good emotional regulation typically have good state regulation as well. Going to sleep is not a problem if the routine is regular and consistent. Activities that result in intense emotions, such as hysterical laughing or crying, should be avoided just before sleep times. However, if the child becomes intensely aroused before sleep, the parent can help regulate the emotions. Parents need to note what activities calm the child and are likely to help return the child to equilibrium in order to prepare the child for sleep.

Going Out

Children with good emotional regulation may look forward to outings. They are able to handle new sights, sounds, and experiences without undue emotional response. Caregivers should prepare the child by discussing what is going to happen, what the child will see, and so forth. Even young infants who do not understand this conversation will benefit from the calm voice of the caregiver as the child is moved into the car seat. Car seats position the child in such a way that the child can only see the seat in front of them (and the back of the parent's head). Placing items for the child to look at in his or her line of vision can keep the child from experiencing negative feelings when the parent is not able to hold the child. In addition, talking to the child, playing music, or singing may hold the child's interest and help him or her self-calm.

Play Routines (Home and Classroom)

Face-to-Face Play

Face-to-face games with children can generate intense emotions. Children with good emotional regulation typically enjoy face-to-face games and use coping skills such as gaze aversion, turning away, or thumb-sucking when they become overstimulated. Caregivers can assist a child by carefully observing and reading his or her cues, so that they can back off when the child registers signs of having had enough. Gradually increasing the stimulation or intensity of turns is another strategy to ensure that the child can "keep up" with the game. Older children often can verbalize when they have had enough.

Physical Play

As with face-to-face games, physical games also need to be monitored by the parent. Physical games have the potential of escalating quickly, with commensurate emotional acceleration. For this reason, particularly with tickling and wrestling games, it is important for the caregivers to watch the child's nonverbal signals and listen to verbal requests. Activities that are pleasurable can quickly become overwhelming and distressing. Children with good emotional regulation are able to monitor their emotions and attempt to control the situation. The caregiver's role is to respond to those cues.

Manipulative Play

Children are less likely to lose control of their emotions in toy play than in either face-to-face or physical games. Play with toys is usually less personally intense and, because toys are controlled by the child, the child can move or divert attention from the stimulating events, if necessary. Play with toys that evoke violent actions or encourage smashing, beating up, fighting, and so forth can involve extreme emotions. Children with good emotional regulation, however, are able to monitor their emotions and divert their actions, change their language, or use other strategies if they become too angry or frightened. Caregivers also can help moderate play by monitoring the intensification of the play and by modeling deescalation of interactions.

Sensory Play

Sensory play often stimulates intense emotions. Input from movement, touch, sounds, and pressure may be particularly arousing. The type of stimuli children like or dislike will vary. Children seek out pleasurable stimuli and avoid unpleasant stimuli. Adults who are in tune with the type of sensory input the child prefers become adept at using sensory stimuli to help the child increase motivation or decrease intense negative responses. For example, adults know the favorite blanket, toy, or song the child likes that helps him or her calm. They also know the toys and actions that arouse the child and get him or her excited.

Reading and Learning Routines

Circle Time

Depending on the curriculum, circle time is used for various purposes, including welcoming individual children, book reading, singing and dancing, and doing other group activities. Adults can use group circle time activities for increasing arousal (through song and dance) or calming children (through quiet book reading). Adults help moderate the children's emotions by varying their voice level, intonation, and activity level and their means of encouraging children's participation.

One-on-One Book Reading

Book reading usually is a calm activity between caregivers and children. Books, however, can have themes that can be scary or sad for young children. Caregivers need to anticipate the themes of the books and the emotions attached to those themes and be able to discuss those emotions with the child. For very young toddlers, the caregiver may just identify emotions, such as "sad," "mad," or "happy," represented on the faces of characters in the books. For the older child, talking about more subtle emotions such as embarrassment, discussing what child does in similar situations, or deciding what the character should do is important to help the child discuss coping strategies.

Everyday Literacy

Children may get very excited or upset if they see symbols or pictures associated with things they want or things they find upsetting. Before a child can communicate with words, nonverbal communications and actions are used. Caregivers can use *joint referencing* (looking at what the child is looking at) and watch the child's emotional response. Label what is being looked at and talk about what you think the child likes or does not like. For example, if the child sees a picture of a peach on a can and starts to grunt and reach for the can, the caregiver can comment, "Peaches. You love peaches. You can play with the can now, and I'll give you some for lunch." If the child begins to lose control, the parent can divert the child's attention to another picture or activity.

For older children, using pictures and symbols may help them address their emotions more consciously. For example, looking at family pictures or class pictures in which everyone is having fun may help a child to calm.

Community Literacy

Emotional response to community literacy is based on children's previous experience with the signs and symbols in their community travels. Symbols such as the McDonald's arches may evoke crying for the caregiver to stop at the restaurant. The sight of words and pictures on a candy wrapper may cause a temper tantrum. Children with good emotional regulation usually can be diverted or calmed when attention is diverted or they are given another choice.

Science and Math

Many activities for science and math involve manipulation of various materials, measuring, concocting, discovering similarities and differences, and so forth. For some activities calm, focused attention may be required, whereas for other activities children may be encouraged to use sensory exploration and more active engagement. At first, adults may need to facilitate the child's modulation of attention and emotions. For example, an activity involving children measuring each other's height using different types of objects could easily become a physical game leading to emotional escalation. The teacher helps children focus on the goal of the activity and the steps involved, which also serves to help children moderate their emotions.

PLANNING INDIVIDUALIZED INTERVENTIONS FOR IMPROVING REGULATION OF EMOTIONS AND AROUSAL STATES

The previous section addressed how adults naturally interact with children in a way to help them learn to moderate their state and emotions; this section discusses how to assist children who have difficulty with state and emotional regulation, those who appear overly emotional, and those who have difficulty elevating or moderating emotional responses when desired. Examples will be provided of how routines or interactions can be modified to help children gain better awareness and internal control over states of awareness and emotions.

III. A. How easily is the child able to regulate physiological states of awareness (e.g., sleeping to waking)?

Many children with disabilities have issues with regulation of states of arousal. Children may have difficulty falling asleep or staying asleep. Sleep issues may be due to a variety of factors, including central nervous system (CNS) immaturity (e.g., night terrors), physical problems (e.g., obstructive sleep apnea, illness), or behavioral concerns (e.g., night awakenings and bedtime resistance), and may be temporary, intermittent, or chronic.

In addition to children who have difficulty falling asleep or staying asleep, some children may take a prolonged time to move from sleep into an alert state. Other children, once agitated into a fussy state, have difficulty quieting. Many times these issues are related to temperament, but they are also more common in children with learning difficulties or developmental delays. Children with concerns related to states of arousal have not settled into expected patterns for moving through their day and night. This may be extremely stressful for parents and siblings, because the resulting behavior is disruptive to their own regulatory patterns. The child may not be able to go to sleep at a reasonable hour, giving parents no break for themselves, or he or she may be up in the middle of the night or sleep for only a few hours. Caregivers, consequently, become exhausted and exasperated and often resort to less than optimal strategies, such as locking the child in his or her room, in order to get some peace. Children who require extended time to become alert, and who are fussy for long periods as they struggle to gain equilibrium, also are challenging for caregivers. State regulation issues can be seen in children without disabilities, but because these concerns often are neurologically based, they are more commonly seen in children with disabilities. Children with autism spectrum disorders and emotional regulation dysfunction, discussed in the following section, are particularly vulnerable to problems with state regulation.

Interaction Strategies

Moving from one state to another—particularly from awake to asleep, or asleep to awake—is problematic for many children. Difficulty with falling asleep and staying asleep can be tremendously disruptive to a family. The following ideas may be helpful for some children. For persistent problems, a medical review is recommended.

1. *Make the hour before bedtime a special, nurturing time, with quiet play and loving interaction.* This makes children feel more secure, and reduces sleep problems due to attachment issues and insecurity. A transition object such as a blanket or an unwashed t-shirt that retains the parent's scent may comfort the child.

2. *Let the child self-calm.* Avoid patterns in which the child falls asleep while the adult is rocking, rubbing the child's back, or lying down with the child. This encourages reliance on the adult to move the child into the sleep state, rather than helping the child self-calm and fall asleep alone. *Sleep-onset association disorders* are the most common cause of children not being able to go back to sleep when they wake, because they need the pattern they associate with sleep to be able to settle back to sleep.

3. *Be positive and confident.* Demonstrate confidence that the child will be able to go to bed and to sleep on his or her own. Do not check on the child constantly, because this will only show the child that the adult is anxious and will reawaken the drowsy child.

4. *Have rules about bedtime and be firm.* Children will quickly learn ways to get additional attention (e.g., needing a drink or snack, one more book). Make rules about what happens at bedtime (e.g., stay in bed, no snack) and stick to them. If the child needs reassurance, give it quickly and settle the child back down.

5. *If both parents are in the home, take turns putting the child to bed.* This can avoid problems if the parent who typically puts the child through the bedtime routine is unavailable.

6. *Make bedtime a positive time, not a punishment.* Use of bedtime as a punishment may lead to negative associations and resistance.

7. *If the child wakes, be comforting but unexciting.* Children may wake wanting to play. Avoid any stimulating interaction or games. Reassure the child with a soft voice, but do not pick him up (unless the child is ill or in pain). If waking and crying is a pattern, wait 5–10 minutes at each episode before going in to calm the child. Hopefully, the time between waking and crying bouts will lengthen and the child will begin to self-calm.

8. *Rule out medical concerns if waking persists.* A variety of health issues may contribute to sleep issues. Consultation with a doctor may be needed to rule out allergies or food sensitivities, gastroesophageal reflux, colic, urinary tract or other infection, pain from ear infection, gas, teething, or skin conditions causing itching or discomfort.

9. *Give the child choices.* As children seek independence and control, give them limited choices such as what stuffed animal to take to bed or in what order to do bedtime activities. This can help the child feel in control of the process and reduce conflict.

10. *Monitor and comfort when needed.* Parasomnias are events that disrupt sleep, such as nightmares or night terrors. When the child has a nightmare, or bad dream, the child is scared and upset. The adult can reassure the child and soothe the child back to sleep. During a night terror, a neurological occurrence during sleep, the child is unaware of the presence of the adult and calming does not work because the child is still asleep. Just stay close to monitor the child's safety until the child goes back to sleep.

Environmental Modifications

1. *Reduce personal and environmental discomfort.* Make sure the child is dry, warm, and wearing comfortable pajamas that keep the child warm but not hot. Moderate the temperature in the room to take into account the child's clothing and bed covers, because children have individual temperature needs, with some preferring warmth and others liking it cooler for sleep.

2. *Keep a consistent bedtime routine.* Bedtime should be at the same time every night (even on weekends), with the same simple sequence of comforting events (e.g., warm

bath, pajamas, book, cuddling). Make the sequence one that can occur anywhere, so it is replicable in situations outside of the home. Habits form quickly, so establish a routine early (between 3 and 5 months of age). If the child does not have a set routine, old habits must be broken while establishing a routine. Consistent routines for the rest of the day (e.g., waking up, eating, napping, playtime) also are important.

3. *Start bedtime before the child is overtired.* Establish when the child starts to slow down and make this the time to start the bedtime routine. If adults wait until the child is overly tired, the child may become fussy and have more difficulty falling asleep. Children also may "get a second wind" after a slow down time, so take advantage of the down time to get the child ready for bed.

4. *Set bedtime to ensure that the child gets enough sleep.* Insufficient sleep can make it difficult for the child to wake up, may result in a cranky or irritable child during the day, and may lead to falling asleep in the car or taking long naps that then can interfere with nighttime sleep. From 1 month to 1 year of age, the infant moves from sleeping an average of 16 hours a day to 13.5 hours a day, then to about 12 hours at the age of 3 years, and 10.5 to 11 hours at the age of 6. Children need a lot of sleep, and after the age of 4 most children do not take a nap, so night time sleep is even more important. Lack of sufficient sleep affects both learning and behavior.

5. *A soothing "white" noise may block out noises for children who are sensitive to sounds.* A fan, humidifier, or white noise machine may help.

6. *Change the lighting to trigger the sleep/wake cycle of the brain.* Dim lights as bedtime or naptime approaches and use bright lights in the morning (e.g., open shade, turn on the lights).

7. *Pay attention to what the child drinks and eats before bedtime.* Avoid using anything other than water in a bottle to soothe the child at bedtime. Milk or juice can cause baby bottle tooth decay. Avoid caffeine in drinks or food, such as soda or chocolate, because these can disrupt the sleep cycle. In addition, feeding solids to the infant before 6 months of age can cause digestive problems and discomfort leading to loss of sleep.

8. *Keep the bed a place to sleep.* Minimize the number of toys in the bed to one or two cuddly toys. Too many toys can encourage play rather than sleep. Televisions, computers, and other visual electronics should *not* be kept in the bedroom or be used to put the child to sleep!

9. *Give the child a one-time pass.* Some children may respond positively to a "permit" or a card that allows them to get up once for a specific purpose. The permit is then surrendered to the parent and the child is expected to remain in bed for the rest of the night (except for bathroom needs).

▨▨▨▨ **III. B. How easily is the child able to regulate
(control and move in and out of) emotional states?**
**III. C. Are there identifiable patterns or triggers
when the child has difficulty modulating emotions?**
III. D. How easily is the child able to self-calm when emotions become intense?

These three questions related to emotional regulation are addressed together because the interventions related to them overlap. Depending on the child, numerous strategies discussed here may be combined effectively.

Regulation

Many children have difficulty regulating their emotions, or adjusting their emotions to appropriately match the requirements of a given situation. Emotional regulation is important for the development of social skills, empathy and caring behaviors, problem solving, and coping skills. Lack of ability to regulate affect has been shown to be closely associated with the development of behavioral and emotional problems.

As indicated previously, emotional self-regulation is related to state regulation and children who have difficulty with state regulation also may demonstrate problems with emotional regulation. They may become emotional quite easily and then not be able to deescalate or moderate their emotions. For example, once the infant begins to get mad, fearful, or sad, he or she quickly escalates to crying, the crying intensifies, and the infant is unable to be soothed. Even tickling games that begin with giggles may become overwhelming and result in crying. Often other behaviors, such as hitting or kicking, may accompany the outburst.

Children who have cautious temperaments and are slow to warm up also may get overwhelmed easily by their emotions and demonstrate excessive anxiety and distress. As they become overwhelmed by emotions, they may withdraw into themselves and "hide" their emotions. These children may display fearfulness and reticence to interact with peers. For example, they may cling to their parent and cry easily when encouraged to explore new environments or engage with other children.

Lack of appropriate emotionality also is a reason for concern. Children who are oblivious of their own and others' emotions, who display emotions in inappropriate contexts, or who display emotions out of proportion to the demands of the situation also may have emotional regulation difficulties. Children with autism spectrum disorders, for instance, may not recognize or respond to their parents' or peers' emotions; may become excited, sad, or fearful in inappropriate situations; or may display screaming, tantrum behaviors when a simple change is made in their routine or environment (see TPBI2, Chapter 7, Section IV. Strategies for Improving Social Cognition).

Patterns or "Triggers"

Adults need to observe the types of activities and experiences that cause the child to experience extremes of emotions, such as anger, fear, sadness, or even uncontrolled excitement. Understanding what sets off emotional outbursts can help adults respond appropriately with both interactional supports and environmental modifications. The type and range of activities that arouse extreme emotions will vary from child to child. Some may become easily upset in social situations in which they do not have total control. Just being told "no" may "send them off the deep end." Others may become overly excited by specific types of experiences, materials, or toys (e.g., things that spin). Transitions to new people or situations may set off other children. Although varying approaches may be needed for each of the situations described previously, some general strategies are recommended in the following sections. Planning intervention approaches begins with understanding what triggers the child's loss of emotional control.

Self-Calming

Some children escalate to great states of excitement, anger, sadness, anxiety, or frustration and then quickly, and independently, transition back to a state of stability. Other children, however, have a very difficult time bringing themselves back to equilibrium. Children whose emotions get out of control often exhibit negative behaviors such as crying, screaming, hitting, kicking, and biting. Children can get overly excited with positive emotions as well. When this happens, children may become loud and boisterous, laugh hysterically, and demonstrate out-of-bounds motor activity. For these children, adults can play a mediating role to help them calm down. Children who are emotionally labile also need to learn strategies to help monitor their emotions so they can modulate their emotions independently and not rely on adult support. Such strategies can start when the child is very young but will need to be developed as the child gains cognitive understanding and a more sophisticated understanding of cause and effect.

Extremes of emotionality, whether excessive anger, sadness, or fearfulness, in addition to lack of emotional expression, all cause concern for caregivers and require special interaction techniques to assist the child in developing emotional self-regulation strategies. Often, external supports are needed to help the child regain emotional equilibrium. The intent, however, is that the child be able to develop personal strategies or techniques that lead successfully to self-calming. The structure and support provided, as well as the communication and interaction patterns caregivers use, can help children develop the ability to regulate their emotions.

Keep in mind that the environment itself can influence emotional regulation. The amount of sensory stimulation may need to be addressed. Children who are hypersensitive to noise, light, too much visual stimulation, touch, or movement may need environmental modifications to reduce one or more aspects of the stimulation (see TPBI2, Chapter 3, Section V. Strategies for Improving Modulation of Sensation and Its Relationship to Emotion, Activity Level, and Attention).

Interaction Strategies

1. *Give the child words for feelings and words to use to let the adults know when support is needed.* Label feelings of discomfort so the child learns to associate labels with his or her feelings. "That scared you." "You don't like loud noises." Also provide suggestions for ways the child can request assistance with emotions, such as "Can you hold me?" "I need my blankee."

2. *Use verbal preparation.* Tell the child ahead of time when a situation that may be distressing or overwhelming to the child is going to happen. Point out the aspects of the situation that will be positive, and give the child assurance that a caregiver will be there for support.

3. *Avoid using negative statements about the child or the child's emotions.* Negative statements may result in further escalation of emotions. Do not make fun of the child or dismiss the child's feelings; rather, talk about how the child is feeling and ways in which the child can handle the emotions.

4. *Encourage self-talk.* Encourage the child to use self-talk to calm and reassure him- or herself or to change strategies for self-calming. For example, give him or her words such as, "Say 'deep breath'" or "You used to be afraid of clowns, but not now."

5. *Encourage verbalization of feelings.* Once the child has calmed (after the crying, screaming, kicking tantrum), hold the child and gently talk about the situation. Help the child to verbalize his feelings. Talk about what happened to his body inside and out when he got upset. This will help the child recognize changes in his body (e.g., tightening muscles, faster breathing) and internal sensations (e.g., "tummy feels excited") that may signal that something is making feelings escalate. If the child can learn to recognize these signs and verbalize them to an adult, the adult can then provide reminders of what helps the child feel calmer. Eventually, the child may be able to use these strategies without support from an adult. Adults can also keep alert for physical changes that denote an escalation of feelings, talk about what they are seeing, and help the child do something to "stop the runaway train!"

6. *Discuss consequences of behaviors.* Help the child understand the consequences of his or her behaviors for others. Separate the feelings from the behaviors. All feelings are okay. All behaviors are not. Provide reinforcement for the child's efforts at self-regulation.

7. *Model calm behaviors.* Help the child notice facial cues and body language. This will help the child understand how others handle the situation. For example, model putting your finger to your lips for quiet, hugging yourself to calm down, or closing your eyes and breathing deeply.

8. *Encourage role play.* Young children may be able to use dramatic play to act out situations ahead of time, thus giving them strategies they can use in the actual situation. Go through the actions and words that may occur and then the corresponding actions and words the child can use.

9. *Demonstrate a substitute behavior.* Demonstrate a substitute behavior (language or action) for the unacceptable behavior. For example, model speaking quietly and moving gently instead of yelling, screaming, and hitting.

10. *Distract the child to other interesting objects or events.* When the child *begins* to escalate, try to redirect attention to another activity that is less excitatory (e.g., watching the doggie out the window or playing with another toy with interesting effects).

11. *Set limits for what is acceptable behavior and what is not.* Talk about acceptable ways to express emotions and the reasons some behaviors are not acceptable ways of expressing emotions. Reinforce efforts at deescalating emotions. Help the child to learn the consequences of his or her behavior. Be consistent with enforcing limits.

12. *Do not give in to tantrums.* Do not give in and give the child what he or she is having a tantrum over. This will only increase the recurrence of tantrums. Offer a choice between two acceptable options. This allows the child to retain a sense of control. For example, when the child is crying for candy, the adult can say, "Do you want crackers and cheese or Cheerios?"

13. *Provide challenges.* Provide slight challenges for the child to practice emotional regulation of feelings such as frustration, but provide support and encouragement. For example, if the child has difficulty with going into busy grocery stores, practice by going to the small convenience store. Give the child a small task, such as holding a written list, to help him focus on something other than the environment.

14. *If changes are a trigger, introduce routine.* If the situation occurs frequently (e.g., going to bed, going in the car) develop a routine of pleasurable steps that lead up to the activity. This will help the child develop an internalized set of expectations for dealing with the situation.

15. *Prepare the child for overarousing or triggering situations.* Help the child to understand situations he may want to avoid or ignore because they are overarousing, and give him words to help him seek adult assistance in difficult situations. Let the child know that all of us have different things that bother us, and help him recognize what is bothering him and how to handle the situation.

Environmental Modifications

Caregivers can use materials within the environment to help children calm or prepare for an upcoming uncomfortable situation. It also may be possible to modify aspects of the overwhelming situation. Knowing what is overwhelming to the child helps caregivers modify the environment to help prevent situations that cause stress. It is better to modify the environment before a negative situation arises, but that is not always possible; modification "on the spot" may be needed.

1. *Use cues to mark the time approaching an event.* Use a signal, such as flashing lights or the sound of a timer, to let the child know that a change is coming and he or she must stop playing and go to dinner in 5 minutes. Then use a different signal to tell the child that time is up. Use the same sequence of signals consistently. The first signal allows the child to mentally and emotionally prepare for a change, whereas the second signal lets him or her know it is time to change.

2. *Introduce pictures or objects associated with the event or person.* For example, if the child hates going to the grocery store, give the child pictures of fruits and cereals that she likes to look for at the store or coupons they can "spend" when she gets there. A picture schedule of the day also may be useful if changing activities is a trigger for loss of self-control. The pictures help the child anticipate that what is coming is familiar.

3. *Let the child see or hold an object that is calming.* The child can use transition objects such as a blanket or objects associated with a loved person (e.g., such as the mother's t-shirt at naptime or bedtime). A transition object also can be something associated with the next activity; for example, a favorite cup that is used for snack.

4. *Use prevention strategies.* Structure the environment so that the child does not have too much stimulation, either through toys and materials that tend to "hype him up" or through interactions that are intrusive to the child. Pay attention to the level of sensory stimulation that seems optimal for the child. Use the "Three Bears" test to determine what type and amount of visual, auditory, tactile, taste, smell, movement, or pressure are "just right" for the child. Try to keep environmental stimulation within the child's acceptable range (see TPBI2, Chapter 3, Section V. Strategies for Improving Modulation of Sensation and Its Relationship to Emotion, Activity Level, and Attention). For example, if the child is overwhelmed by too many people, it may be possible to take him or her to a separate, less busy, part of the room to watch the others from a distance.

5. *Give the child a special quiet space for self-calming.* This space is not punishment, but a special spot for time away from the activities that are exciting or distressing the child. Let the child know this special place is for "quiet time" to help calm him or her down. Give the child a book, stuffed animal, or other "quiet" toy that can help refocus attention.

6. *Eliminate negative triggers.* If you know the characteristics of the situation that will bother the child, try to make modifications ahead of time. Let grandma know to put the dog outside, not have too many toys out, or not to have soap operas on the television.

▓▓▓▓▓ III. E. How well is the child able to inhibit impulsive actions and emotions (e.g., physical, vocal or verbal outbursts) in order to attend to tasks?

Children who have difficulty regulating emotions often have concurrent problems with impulse control. They "want what they want, and they want it NOW!" Emotions interfere with their ability to think, plan, and wait. Children with poor impulse control act without thinking about the potential negative consequences of their words or actions. They have rapid, unplanned reactions to stimuli before they process information inherent in the situation. Although most young children at times are demanding and speak and act without thinking, some children seem to be unable to act otherwise. Various types of sensorimotor, cognitive, and emotional disabilities are associated with poor impulse control in young children, including attention deficit disorder and attention-deficit/hyperactivity disorder, autism spectrum disorders, fragile X, sensory integration dysfunction, and bipolar disorder. Children with an inability to regulate emotions and control corresponding physical impulses also are at risk for being more aggressive and for having interaction difficulties with authority figures and social problems with peers. Their impulsivity is a pattern of responding, rather than an occasional thoughtless act. Therefore, it is important to find strategies to help children inhibit behaviors perceived as negative within their culture and to think about consequences before acting.

Interaction Strategies

1. *Teach "mindfulness."* For children who lack impulse control, adults need to help children learn to focus on the task at hand, think about what is happening in their environment, and plan ahead (see TPBI2, Chapter 7, Section I. Strategies for Improving Attention; Chapter 7, Section II. Strategies for Improving Memory; and Chapter 7, Section III. Strategies for Improving Problem Solving). Several of the following strategies may help the development of mindfulness.

2. *Keep expectations within the child's ability.* Children with minimal impulse control need to take things in smaller steps, because they become distracted easily. Break down what needs to be done, so that each step can be reinforced. This will help the child stay on task and reduce the likelihood of the child suddenly switching to a more preferred activity. For example, if the parent tells the impulsive child to "clean up the toys and bring me a book to read," the child may not comply—not out of willful noncompliance, but because there are too many interesting things that will draw her interest, and the goal will be forgotten. Instead, the adult may need to give one small task (e.g., "See if you can put away 10 blocks") and then immediately reward success.

3. *Involve the child in thinking about what to do and how to do it.* More active involvement in planning helps the child build a "mind set" for a task. For instance, in the previous example of cleaning up the toys, the adult could say, "It's time to clean up. Look around. What do you want to put away first?" This question stimulates the child to think and plan a sequence and gives the child ownership or control of the thoughts and actions involved.

4. *Talk about consequences.* Help the child think about both positive and negative consequences. Help the child learn that all words and actions have consequences.

- Tell the child how it feels when she does something (both right and wrong).

- Tell the child the consequences of her actions in terms of results or outcomes.

- Ask the child, "What do you think will happen if . . . ?" Then discuss what actually happened after the behavior, action, or event.

- Ask the child, "How do you think you will feel when you . . . ?" Then discuss how the child actually feels after the behavior, action, or event.

- Remind the child about previous similar situations, and see if she can recall consequences.

5. *Provide consequences immediately.* Logical, reasonable, and fair consequences should be clear to the child. Frequent restatement and clarification may be needed. Ask the child what consequences are appropriate for specific situations, to encourage him to think about and relate his actions and the consequences. If the child is unable to communicate this verbally, give him options to choose from; for example, "The rule is

to play together. You took Maddie's doll. Do you want to give Maddie the doll and choose something else?" or "Do you want to play with the doll *and* Maddie?"

6. *Reinforce desirable behaviors.* Reward the child for following rules, staying on task, accomplishing a goal or steps toward a goal, planning ahead, and talking about consequences. In the previous example, if the child chose to play with Maddie and the doll, the adult should say, "Good for you. Now both you and Maddie can have a good time with the baby!"

7. *Maintain a calm atmosphere and a consistent approach.* Children who have difficulty with inhibition of impulses present challenges that are frustrating to adults. The child may interrupt, scream for attention, hit others when he does not get his way, and display other noncompliant behaviors. Adults need to try to maintain a calm disposition and, when needed, be able to disengage and separate from the stressful interaction with the child. This may mean having the child go to a calm, secure place while the adult does the same. Both children and adults are able to think and communicate more clearly when they are calm. Consistency is important. Keep the rules the same, the consequences noncontradictory, and communication clear.

Environmental Modifications

1. *Have a few simple positive rules.* State what the child *should* do, rather that what the child should not do. Children need to know what actions are expected. Having only a few important rules to remember makes it easier for the child to adhere to the rules.

2. *Use visual and auditory reminders.* Visual reminders, such as a picture schedule of events or a series of activity sequence cards, may help keep children from wandering away or being distracted by another activity. Teachers have long been flashing the lights or using a schedule of activities chart to help notify children of shifts in activities. An auditory cue such as a bell, timer, or verbal prompt, when combined with a visual cue such as a gesture or sign, gives the child two types of input to help maintain focus and resist digressions.

3. *Structure reinforcement.* It is important to use reinforcement in a systematic way. Increasing levels of reinforcement can keep the child motivated to stay on track with behaviors. Always provide the promised reinforcement, even if numerous requests are made and success takes a long time.

4. *Change reinforcement frequently.* Changing the type of reinforcement can keep children interested. After all, how long can stickers be rewarding?

5. *Avoid making temptations accessible.* Children respond to the stimuli in their environment. Children who lack impulse control have a difficult time ignoring the enticing elements within the environment and have an overwhelming urge to act on them. By reducing distractions, the child is better able to stay on the intended course. As often as possible, have the television off, toys put away, and any other temptations out of sight and hearing.

6. *Practice risk management.* As described previously, temptations increase the risk of impulsive behaviors. The presence of a group of children does the same. Keep parties or play interactions to two children to avoid challenging the child's behaviors in group situations. Certain toys and materials also challenge risk taking. Climbing toys, bats and balls, and fast-paced activities often encourage more intense actions and more impulsive actions. Structure and adult supervision are important when the child is engaging in these activities.

7. *Have a special sanctuary for the child.* We all need a place to "get it together." This is especially true for children who have intense emotional responses or act without thinking. Have a special place for the child to think quietly. It is important that being in this place not be seen as a punishment by the child, but rather a place to breathe and calm down, think about what has occurred previously, and plan next steps. The adult can help the child by offering suggestions for ways to think about these things in a nonpunitive manner. The quiet place should also be nonstimulating visually and lack materials that will encourage activity.

III. F. What is the child's predominant mood and how long do feeling states or moods last?

Psychological Concerns

Contrary to some beliefs, mood swings or depressed behavior can be seen in young children. Such pervasive affect influences attachment, communication behaviors, and social interactions. Identification of lasting feeling states should lead to intervention addressing adult–child interaction patterns, environmental modifications, and potential psychological treatment. Children who frequently exhibit long-lasting moods (of longer than an hour at a time) during which they are angry, sad, or have intense mood swings need to be referred for individual and/or family therapy.

"Flat" Mood

Some children may not be clinically depressed but still do not experience and express a full range of emotions in appropriate situations. They may exhibit a lack of positive affect, engage in self-stimulating behaviors rather than social behaviors, and/or avoid social exchanges. For example, children raised in an orphanage, who have spent many hours unattended in a bed, may exhibit a sad appearance, rock back and forth, and appear unaware of others. Children also may experience a flat affect as a result of lack of responsiveness to the environment. These varying causes of a lasting mood need to be addressed, both through interaction and environmental techniques, and may require additional therapy.

Some children demonstrate a low intensity of expression of emotion. These children often are described as having a "flat affect." They demonstrate low levels of excitement, smiling, and enjoyment of activities. Although behavior may not be difficult, adults, siblings, and peers may find interaction with these children to be unrewarding. As a consequence, attachment with parents and other caregivers, friendship with peers, and social interactions in general may be negatively affected. Others also may find it difficult to "read" what the child enjoys or dislikes. For this reason, it is important to assist children with low intensity of emotional expression to increase their affective responsiveness and expression of emotion to a higher lever.

Differentiation of emotions across people and situations also is difficult for some children. During the first year of life, children learn to differentiate family members from non-family members and children from adults. They learn to read the emotional cues of others and respond accordingly. Beginning in the first 6 months, children develop a growing sense of humor, enjoying first physical play and then more subtle incongruities of things that are funny—they are not in the "right" place, used in the "right" way, or used by the "right" person. The same is true of fearful situations, because children use social referencing to determine what situations are worthy of distress. Some children need assistance to learn to differentiate emotions and when and how emotions should be expressed. Children need to learn to "read" other people's emotions, to identify emotions related to various situations, and to express emotions appropriate to their actual feelings. The following strategies are recommended to help children understand and respond to emotions of others (see also TPBI2, Chapter 7, Section IV. Strategies for Improving Social Cognition).

Interaction Strategies

1. *Identify and label emotions.* Help children understand what expressions are associated with different emotions. When the child demonstrates an emotion, even with unusual or mild cues, the caregiver should take the opportunity to label what he or she thinks the child is feeling. This will help the child attach meaning to his or her feelings. Demonstrate an exaggerated expression of what you think the child feels.

2. *Model appropriate affect and describe feelings.* Whenever possible, the caregiver can point out how he or she is feeling. Label the emotions and relate them to actions (e.g., "Mommy is mad. I am shaking my head 'no.'").

3. *Label emotions in pictures, books, or as people are expressing them.* Point out the expressions on the faces of people and characters in books. Talk about emotions as part of discussions about what the child or others are doing.

4. *Look in the mirror and practice making faces.* Let the child see his or her face and expressions next to others'. Play games of making faces. Try to get the child to imitate expressions of emotions. Label each emotion.

5. *Discuss emotions that are appropriate for specific situations.* Let the child know that expressing and talking about emotions is good.

6. *Encourage expression of more intense emotions.* For children who exhibit little expression of affect, encourage expression of more intense emotions. Exaggerate affective expressions of "surprise," "happiness," "disgust," "sadness," and so forth, and label the emotions.

7. *Engage in highly stimulating social games.* Engage in highly stimulating social games involving bouncing, tickling, hiding, and so forth. Model exaggerated affect in turn-taking games to elicit imitation.

Environmental Modifications

1. *Provide a stimulating environment.* Depending on the child, different types of sensory input will arouse the child's emotions. For some children, rapid music, bright lights, or movement toys will awaken the flat affect (see TPBI2, Chapter 3, Section V. Strategies for Improving Modulation of Sensation and Its Relationship to Emotion, Activity Level, and Attention).

2. *Modify the too-stimulating environment.* Children who have rapidly shifting moods may respond to a calmer environment with softer lights, sounds, and predictable changes.

ROUTINES FOR THE CHILD WHO NEEDS SUPPORT TO REGULATE EMOTIONS AND AROUSAL STATES

The following are examples of the previous strategies as they might be implemented for various children during the day across different environments and contexts. These strategies have not been broken down by infant, toddler, and young child because children with special needs may demonstrate a wide range of developmental abilities and behaviors. In the appropriate instances, examples are given for children functioning at younger or older developmental levels. Strategies that may be indicated for children functioning at specific developmental levels for this subcategory are included later in the chapter.

Daily Routines (Home and Classroom)

Feeding/Eating

Some children are very "picky" eaters as a result of hypersensitivity to specific tastes or textures of foods or restricted preferences. They may refuse to eat many foods. A gradual introduction of new flavors (in repeated trials) is important. Children who have had feeding difficulties as infants or who have been tube fed may need professional assistance to move into being able to eat real food with the family. Issues with oral motor sensitivities, lack of sensory stimulation to the mouth and esophagus, and previous eating habits all may contribute to the child having a hard time with making the transition to regular eating patterns. These children may react with intense negativity to introduction of food, making mealtimes stressful for the whole family. Such problems require extreme understanding and patience on the part of caregivers and professional support to help with sensory, physiological, and behavioral issues. The parent can support the child's feelings by identifying the child's fears, anger, and frustrations. It is important to try to make mealtimes a positive, fun experience, because hormones for digestion are released with pleasurable feelings. Make eating fun by taking turns, making noises, modeling enjoying eating, and talking as a family. Eating should not be forced. Set up a routine that includes positive incremental steps toward eating. Let the child have control of as much of the situation as possible, including getting bowls and spoons out and playing with them. It is important to not let bad habits become established, because children who react negatively to meals or certain foods can become very manipulative of the situation. It is easy for parents to "give in" in order to try to avoid a tantrum; however, this only establishes a negative pattern.

Landy (2002) recommends the following tips:

- Have meals and snacks at regular times.

- Do not use food to comfort the child, or between scheduled snack and meals.

- Keep mealtime and snack times short.

- Let the child self-feed as much as possible. This gives the child a sense of control and independence.

- Do not watch TV or allow the child to play with toys at mealtime.

- Cut down on milk and juice to keep the child from filling up on liquids.

- Combine new or disliked foods with foods the child likes, such as on pizza.

- Let the child help prepare the meal so he or she is interested in the result.

- Let the child decide when to stop eating. Do not force the child to "finish" everything.

For children who exhibit a flat or inappropriate affect, exaggeration of appropriate affect is helpful. For the child who just swipes the baby food jar off the tray onto the floor, the caregiver needs to do more than indicate that the behavior is not appropriate. It is important that the child learn how to indicate dislike or unhappiness. Give the child a gesture or sign, combined with words and a facial expression, to indicate "all done," "no," or "don't like." Help the child to practice these gestures and expressions in appropriate situations. In addition, give the child gestures, signs, words, and facial expressions for other emotions that may be related to mealtime, such as pleasure and surprise.

Diapering/Toileting

Diapering is a stressful experience for children who are sensitive to changes in temperature or varying textures. Exposure to the cool air or cold lotion after having been warmly dressed, or having the legs pulled up and manipulated, may result in some children screaming throughout the diapering process. This, in turn, is stressful to the parent who then hurries through the process without interacting positively with the infant. A negative situation can be modified into a more positive experience for the child. Again, a routine is important so that the infant can begin to anticipate the sequence of events to follow. Although diapering cannot always be done in the same place, try to use the same type and texture of baby pad, wipes, and so forth, each time. Talk softly to the infant and let her know what is coming. "Let's take off that stinky diaper." "Here's the wipe for your bottom. Feel it. It's wet." When applying lotion, warm it by rubbing it between warm hands for a few seconds before applying it to the infant's body. Let the child play with a toy or watch an interesting mobile. This may distract the child from the actions she finds distressing. Giving the child a special toy that is comforting to her to hold also may be calming. Talk about the child's body parts while firmly holding the "hands," "feet, "tummy," and so forth. Light touch often is too stimulating. Labeling body parts helps the child to develop body awareness. As the child begins to anticipate the sequence of events by lifting her legs, getting the diaper, and so forth, encourage the child's independence and assistance.

Moving to independent toileting introduces a whole new set of experiences to the child. The requirement for control of physical processes often is emotionally stressful for the child. Reduce the child's anxiety by remaining calm, demonstrating patience and tolerance for accidents, and praising even the slightest efforts at independence.

As with mealtime, diapering provides an opportunity to demonstrate the expression of emotions related to disgust, pleasure, surprise, and so forth. In addition, the caregiver can play physical games, such as blowing on the tummy, tickling, and so forth, to encourage laughing and smiling. Watch the child's facial expressions and body language carefully to ascertain what the child may be feeling. Give words to those emotions and demonstrate corresponding exaggerated facial expressions. Wait to see if the child imitates the expressions and reinforce these by imitating his expressions.

Dressing

Dressing is another activity that can be frustrating for a child. Getting the head through a small neck hole and bending arms and legs into sleeves and pants can be stressful for young children. Children may become angry when the parent tries to manipulate the body parts or when clothing is tight or the textures uncomfortable.

As the child becomes more independent, efforts at self-dressing may cause frustration and crying. Describe the feelings the child is experiencing, so that as language develops he or she will be able to use words rather than actions to express frustration. Give the child gestures, words, or signs to help him or her indicate the need for assistance. Allow the child as much independence and control as possible in dressing. Let the child choose desired clothing (matching clothes are less important than independence), and the parent can retain some control by limiting the options.

Dressing frequently can be done in front of a mirror. This gives the child an opportunity to see her own facial expressions. The caregiver can then model sounds, words, and expressions in the mirror as the child is dressed or attempts to dress herself. Expressions of effort, frustration, pride, and happiness can be practiced at this time. The mirror encourages the child to imitate the adult's expression and provides visible reinforcement for her efforts. The modeling also can be done without a mirror if one is not available.

Going to Sleep

Young infants spend much time sleeping. As they spend more time awake, parents frequently rock their infant to sleep after feeding. As the infant grows and develops, a sleep routine is needed. Children who need help with emotional regulation may exhibit anger or crying when told it is time for bed. They also may wake in the night and not be able to soothe themselves back to sleep. For such children, parents need to begin early to establish good patterns and prevent sleep problems. Landy (2002) suggests the following:

- Be firm about a set time for bed and have a bedtime routine. Children need to know what to expect.

- Have a quiet time before bedtime. This is a good time to read books together.

- Children like to have a special blanket or "cuddly" to take to bed. This object often serves as a comforting "companion" to the child.

- Let the child cry for a brief time when he goes to bed or awakens. This will allow time to try to calm himself.

- Do not lie down with the child until she falls asleep. This encourages the child to depend on the adult for soothing and relaxation.

- Help the child develop strategies for dealing with fears. For example, provide a night light for the child and let her turn it on. This will give the child a sense of control over the dark. Look for "monsters" and reassure the child.

- Use naps to help the child keep from becoming overtired and cranky.

- If sleep problems have become chronic, a systematic approach is recommended. (See the resources listed on p. 123 of Landy, 2002.)

Bedtime raises a variety of emotions for children, including anger, frustration, fear, and happiness. Do not exaggerate negative emotions at this time, but rather work toward helping the child find bedtime a calming, satisfying routine worthy of a smile. With each step of the bedtime routine (e.g., undressing, washing, brushing, reading, putting stuffed animals to bed), pride of accomplishment can be modeled and practiced.

Going Out

For the child who has difficulty regulating emotions, leaving the house may be threatening. New sights, sounds, and events may arouse intense emotions, such as anxiety, or be overstimulating. Consequently, the prospect and process of leaving the house may become traumatic. Give the child sufficient notice that you are going somewhere, with the time frame adjusted to the end of some activity; for example, a television show, the end of a meal, or after a nap. This will allow the child time to adjust to the plan. As with other daily routines, having a ritual or set of procedures around leaving the house will help the child develop self-regulation strategies. For instance, the child may get items they like to look at or listen to in the car. Make a game out of going out. For instance, the caregiver and child can each choose something to take and can count the steps or sing a song on the way to the car. Let the child help to get ready to go by getting the clothing and traveling items that are needed. Give the child positive reinforcement for helping to get ready. If going to a familiar place, the caregiver may want to help the child anticipate positive or fun activities that will happen on the trip and at the destination.

Help children anticipate and look forward to forays into the world. Show excitement about new sights, sounds, and events. Make sure the child can see your responses. Also make sure the child can see you express caution (at street crossings), surprise at the unexpected (falling leaves), fear when appropriate (an approaching siren), happiness (going down the slide), and differentiated emotions to friends and strangers. Children will learn about how to respond to new events by reading the adult's emotional cues (social referencing). As the young child often is in a car seat, stroller, or baby pack on outings, it is hard for the child to see the adult's emotional reactions. It is, therefore, important for the adult to take time to talk to the child about what is happening and vocalize emotions. Take the time to stop on outings, particularly stroller outings, to bend down next to the child, point out events, and show facial and verbal expression. Let the child experience, touch, or watch events with you and make a game of responding to these events.

Play Routines (Home and Classroom)

Face-to-Face Play

Face-to-face games can be intense. Young infants will adjust to overstimulation by gaze avoidance, turning away, or crying. As infants get older, those who have difficulty with emotional regulation may react in different ways. They may continue to "turn off" when unable to regulate input, they may react with crying, or they may have a positive reaction that is overly intense. It is important for the caregiver to read the child's cues and back off as the child begins to either escalate or break down. Let the child lead the play turns, with the adult providing wait time in between turns. As the infant's emotions calm down, the parent should wait until the child looks back to reinstitute the game. Giving the child wait time also is important because it allows the child an opportunity to "regroup," a self-regulating skill. It is important for caregivers to realize that a fun game can turn overstimulating and unpleasant quickly, that giggles and laughter can turn to crying and screaming almost instantly, and that it may take time for the child to recover and be ready to reengage.

For the withdrawn child, face-to-face games with peers can be highly stressful. It is important to allow the child time to "warm up" to the peers. Use physical and verbal support and gradually encourage the child to join the play. Focus on the nonthreatening aspects of the play, such as the toys and materials the child is interested in, rather than the play with the peer. Discuss the emotions of the peer, pointing out the smiles, interest, and nonthreatening aspects of the peer's body language (e.g., "See, she is smiling at you. She wants to share the toy with you").

Face-to-face games provide a possibility to take turns reacting to events and making faces. Songs and finger plays provide opportunities for the child to use gestures, words, and facial expressions relating to emotions. Songs like "If you're happy and you know it" and "There's a spider on the floor" give the parent and child venues for practicing emotional expressions.

Physical Play

Physical games can be even more intense than face-to-face games. Depending on the sensitivity of the child's tactile and proprioceptive systems, the child may be able to tolerate varying amounts of physical play. Tickling, roughhousing, chasing, and bouncing may arouse the child to high levels of emotion. This does not mean that caregivers should avoid such play. Unless this type of play results in an intense negative reaction, the caregivers can engage in physical games, again with the child taking the lead in turn-taking. Physical games are a good medium for working on self-regulation. The adult can instigate the game, monitor the child's reaction, and then give the child methods for self-calming. For example, the caregiver may have the child take deep breaths or move more slowly, or just hold the child gently until the child calms. It is important to let the child know what is happening, because these strategies may be ones the child may be able to use for self-regulation as he or she develops. In some cases, the child may escalate into aggression in physical games by hitting, kicking, biting, or pushing. If this occurs, it is important to set limits on inappropriate behavior. Let the child know that this type of behavior is not acceptable. Have the child discuss the reasons for biting. For example, if the child wants to stop playing, he or she can say, "Stop." When the child becomes aggressive, stop the physical games and divert the child's attention to other activities.

Physical games with peers can be threatening to the shy and withdrawn child or to the child who is not interested in peers. Encourage the child to watch the play between the other children before encouraging his involvement. As the child sees the positive affect of the peers, he may want to enter the play. Give the child plenty of wait time. Support the child by being a co-player with the other children until he is comfortable. Let the child lead the physical play whenever possible. Don't force interaction, because this will increase anxiety, fear, and resistance.

Physical games can help to rouse the positive affect of children who have low affect. The intense level of play can take children with high thresholds of reactivity into the range of pleasurable play. For children who need this type of intensity to rouse emotions, physical games can be worked into many daily routines, including bathing, diapering, waking up, and just playing.

Manipulative Play

Toy play also can stimulate intense emotions. The caregiver can note the types of toys that raise intense emotions in the child. Some children may become overexcited with various types of toys and need adult support to assist them in dealing with these emotions. Children with autism may become repetitive in their play, with excitement mounting as they play. The adults need to introduce new materials and toys to expand the child's focus. As children become older, toy play involves dolls and can include acting out emotions. Dramatic play can assist children in dealing with emotions. Caregivers can use doll play to help children talk about their emotions, act out situations that involve emotions, and practice using self-regulation skills. As children play, caregivers can observe their reactions to different types of toys and materials and note which toys cause them to lose emotional control.

For some children, independent play does not cause the child to lose control; rather, peer play is where issues arise. Children begin to play with peers in the second year. Aggression and anger become more evident when siblings and peers encroach on toys perceived as "mine." The adult needs to analyze the situation to determine whether supportive strategies are needed. Caregivers can help the child see alternative behaviors, problem solve, and use words instead of actions. If necessary, calming strategies, separation, or diversion may be needed.

As with physical games, toys that give a big response for a little action on the child's part can produce a positive emotional reaction. Toys that spin, have lights, make noises, sing songs, and so forth, may result in emotional excitement. Watch the child's response to various toys and materials to determine which result in emotional responses. Make sure that the toys selected do not result in perseverative (nonmeaningful repetition) play that excludes adult or peer interaction. It is important for the child to learn to share emotions in play and not "get stuck" in repetitive, noninteractive sensory stimulation.

Reading and Learning Routines

One-on-One Book Reading

Books provide a wonderful medium for discussion of emotions. Infant board books with pictures of babies conveying various emotions are perfect for putting verbal labels on facial expressions. As children get older, books can be used to discuss the range of emotions, what causes emotions, how we deal with our own emotions and those of others, and how we can solve problems. Books also can be used to help children deescalate when they are upset, to calm down before a nap or bedtime, and as a self-calming strategy to introduce to children.

Again, books provide a means of illustrating emotions and demonstrating when and how they are exhibited. Young children who have limited emotional expression need to be exposed to board books and simple story books that display children's emotions and how various situations are handled. Books are available that illustrate the full range of emotions, from excitement to fear. Such books give adults the opportunity to discuss situations, demonstrate emotions, problem-solve reactions, model solutions, and discuss children's reactions and feelings.

Household Literacy

Point out the faces of people on cereal boxes, in the newspaper or magazines, and on television. Talk about the emotions displayed through the expressions on the faces in the pictures. Discuss what the people are doing or should do to feel better, calm down, and so on.

Community Literacy

Look for happy, sad, and angry faces on billboards, signs in store windows, and boxes for toys. Go to the library for story time and talk about the feelings and actions of the characters in the books the librarian reads.

▆▆▆▆   *JUSTIN*

Justin is a 3-year-old diagnosed with autism. His parents and caregivers report frustration with his lack of sleeping through the night, his tantrums, and his behavior, which escalates into squealing and screaming when he is excited. Justin sleeps only 2–3 hours a night and is up the rest of the time roaming the house, playing, or watching television. They also are concerned that Justin has difficulty controlling his emotions. He is quick to have a tantrum when things are "not going his way," and also gets overly keyed up when something is of interest to him. He jumps up and down, flaps his hands, and squeals. This continues until someone helps him to regain control. Justin's difficulty with state and emotional regulation is causing stress in his family and also is interfering with Justin's ability to attend to relevant activities in his environment and to learn through meaningful engagement with people, objects, and within emotionally charged events. The team first recommended that the family have a complete neurological workup and a sleep study done for Justin. The team wanted to rule out any neurological or medical concerns that might be influencing Justin's sleep pattern. Results indicated no identifiable condition, other than the autism, that was contributing to the sleep issues. Medication was prescribed to help him sleep.

The following are a few of the ideas the team and family generated to address the family's priorities.

Interaction Strategies

1. *Prepare for change. Give him a warning with a timer or a watch alarm a few minutes before he needs to stop what he is doing, and tell him what is coming next.*
2. *Offer choices. Make sure you get Justin's visual attention, and then tell him what needs to happen and give him a choice; for example, "We need to go to the car. Do you want to walk or run?"*
3. *Use music to transition. Because Justin loves music, make up songs about what is going to happen next. Use a tune he knows and sing about what is going to be fun. For example, to the tune of "Frère Jacques" sing, "Justin loves to take his bath, take his bath. Justin loves to take his bath, and play with BUBBLES!"*
4. *Change the routine slightly. Justin likes to repeat the same familiar sequence. At every opportunity, introduce a new action, new words, and a slightly different way of doing things. You want to try to increase his flexibility and tolerance for new things, so model one more step to Justin's meal routine, a different action to his block-stacking routine, or a new word to his sentence. Try to get him to imitate you and take turns with the new behavior. Make it fun by showing exaggerated facial expression, voice inflection, and laughter.*

Environmental Modifications

1. *Provide a calming routine for going to bed. Justin needs to learn to expect a routine series of events that lead to sleep. He currently goes to bed at varied times. Establish a set routine with him for going to bed, and stick with it so that he anticipates that he is going to sleep. Experiment with various calming strategies before bed. These might include*
   - *A warm bath, followed by a back and body rub with warm lotion*
   - *Soft music played while he goes to sleep*
   - *Eliminating toys and other distracters from his room when he is going to sleep*
   - *Using picture sequence cards to remind Justin of the bedtime sequence and help him become more independent in going to bed*

2. *Provide a bed that "cocoons." Try different ways of giving Justin calming input while he is lying down in bed; for example*
   - *A water bed may provide calming movement.*
   - *Heavy blankets or a weighted blanket may provide calming input.*
   - *A sleeping bag may help Justin resist kicking off the covers. The activity of quick movements and the resulting change in body temperature may contribute to his waking up.*

3. *Help Justin find calming activities during the night. Justin seems to be able to function on far less sleep than the rest of the family. Although increasing the amount of sleep he gets is desired, other adjustments may be needed. Helping Justin be calm and quiet throughout the night, so his activity does not interfere with the sleep of the rest of the family, is important.*
   - *Use picture sequence cards next to his bed to show him what to do if he wakes up during the night. Place these cards right next to the object he can use; for exam-*

ple, pictures of putting on earphones, followed by the sequence to operate the tape player. This may help Justin resist waking a family member, because he will have a visual guide for what to do. You may want to try taping yourself reading a book to him, and leave the book for him to look at while he listens. Soft music also may be calming.

- *Place a large stop sign on the back of the inside of his bedroom door, and teach Justin what this means. (Practice by placing the sign on different doors during the day, and then stopping and saying, "Here is the stop sign. It means 'stop.' Don't open the door now."*
- *Avoid having a television in his room, because this active visual stimulation may keep him awake.*
- *Give Justin activities that will engage him quietly if he does wake up; for example, a set of foam blocks, a peg board that has numerous holes to fill with small pegs, or a picture card game that he can play by himself. Remove most toys from his room, leaving just the few that he can use along with their sequence picture cards to show him what to do.*
- *If he comes to your room, walk him silently back to his room, show him his picture sequence cards, sign to him that he needs to be quiet, show him the stop sign, and leave.*

4. *Use transition objects. Use transition objects in combination with sequence picture cards to help Justin understand what is coming next.*

REFERENCES

Gowen, J.W., & Nebrig, J.B. (2002). *Enhancing early emotional development: Guiding parents of young children.* Baltimore: Paul H. Brookes Publishing Co.

Landy, S. (2002). *Pathways to competence: Encouraging healthy social and emotional development in young children.* Baltimore: Paul H. Brookes Publishing Co.

KEYS TO INTERVENTION BY DEVELOPMENTAL LEVEL

The following ideas are directed toward children who are functioning at approximately the following levels. The suggestions are not meant to be all-inclusive, but rather are indicative of potential areas for exploration.

Developmental age	Regulatory issues	Keys to intervention
Birth to 3 months	Can be comforted and calmed by touching and rocking.	Experiment with calming strategies, which may vary from child to child (e.g., some children may like rapid rather than slow movements).
	Uses gaze aversion when overstimulated.	
	Sleeps regularly (3 months).	Read the child's cues and stop interaction when the child turns away.
	Is able to be calmed down or to self-calm.	
	Quiets for brief periods.	Provide visual and tactile distractions.
	Uses sucking, looking, or other sensory modalities to calm.	
	Cycles through various states with less crying and more alert times.	
3–6 months	Has ways to soothe self.	Provide favorite toy or blanket to hold.
	Stops crying when people talk to him or her (5 months).	Talk quietly to the child, while not holding him or her, to encourage self-calming.
	Can recover from distress with caregiver support within 15 minutes.	Bring the child's attention to a mobile or other interesting object or event.
	Sleeping and waking bouts begin to lengthen and consolidate.	
	May have abrupt mood changes.	

(continued on next page)

Developmental age	Regulatory issues	Keys to intervention
6–9 months	Unexplained crying stops. Takes regular naps several times a day. Can recover from distress within 10 minutes by being involved in social interactions (9 months).	Provide a structured routine, with naps at the same time every day. Use face-to-face games, motivating noises and actions to distract the child. Allow the child to go to sleep in the crib (without being asleep first). Use a set pattern of behavior each time the child goes down to sleep, so the expectation of sleep is established.
9–12 months	Can maintain security through social referencing (7–12 months). 90% of infants sleep through the night.	Provide comfort with looks, smiles, and soft voice. When the child cries in the night, provide calm touch and voice and encourage going back to sleep without being picked up.
12–18 months	May throw temper tantrum to get his or her way. Gets upset easily if routine is changed. Naps once per day.	Provide verbal reassurance, but set limits or the child will learn that tantrums are effective. Help the child anticipate changes with visual cues, props, and verbal warning. Give the child choices about how to do routines.
18–24 months	Uses objects to distract or calm self. Can use cues that assistance is needed (12–21 months). Has some rudimentary self-control to stop self from wrong behavior. Saying "no" is at its height (15–24 months). Has frequent tantrums (15–24 months). Gets upset if he or she cannot meet standards (15–24 months). Masturbation may be self-calming. Connects actions and consequences.	Use transition objects or comfort toys to help the child change routines or settings. Anticipate difficult times and suggest ways for the child to handle them in advance. Give the child time to self-calm when tantrum occurs. Give verbal assurance, and provide action choices for the child. Begin using simple words to describe the child's feelings and why he or she is feeling that way. Help the child understand how emotions and actions are connected. Provide options for expression of feelings.
24–36 months	Is able to talk about emotions and what elicits them. Is able to request adults' help to help the child handle emotions. May begin to recover from tantrums by him- or herself.	Encourage the child to use words to describe feelings, needs, and desires. Read the child's physical actions in relation to emotions and model the use of words the child can use. Praise the child when he or she is able to self-calm and point out what he or she did that seemed to help (e.g., sitting quietly, holding a doll). Remind the child of what helps him or her to calm. Provide activities to calm or arouse as needed.
36–48 months	Is occasionally aggressive with peers. May demonstrate extremes of emotions.	Help the child use words with peers to indicate his or her needs. Model actions and words. Point out the child's behaviors when excessive and suggest alternatives. Provide special place in environment for child to use for self-calming. Take materials that help the child self-calm along on excursions. Provide physical and verbal reassurance.
48–60 months	Is able to think about emotions and use discussion to help calm.	Talk about actions and consequent feelings for self and others. Help the child to think about alternative actions when needed. Encourage making choices between two acceptable actions. Have the child help think of ways to solve frustrating problems.
60–72 months	Can moderate emotions in different situations as appropriate (e.g., church, playground).	Talk about what various events or situations will be like in advance, and discuss options for behavior depending on how the child feels about what is going to happen. Encourage the child to ask for help when needed.

5

Facilitating Emotional and Social Development

IV. Strategies for Improving Behavioral Regulation

Goal Attainment Scale

1	2	3	4	5	6	7	8	9
Does not understand or respond to adults' requests to stop actions.		Beginning to understand what not to do, but does it anyway. Resists adults' input and control.		Understands right and wrong with adult input, so sometimes chooses appropriate behavior. Is beginning to look to adults for input on what to do.		Independently understands right and wrong and chooses appropriate behavior most of the time, but needs adult assistance to choose and manage behavior.		Chooses appropriate behavior and responds to adults' requests most of the time; tolerates a balance of control.

The subcategory of behavioral regulation examines the child's ability to understand and comply with the rules, values, and expected behaviors of both the family and the society in which the child lives. The ability to control impulses, monitor one's actions and interactions, and respond within the parameters of culturally accepted behavior develops concurrently with emotional regulation, discussed in Section III. In order to regulate behavior, a child needs to be able to 1) inhibit and control responses to an event, 2) remember previous consequences, 3) anticipate reactions, and 4) understand the social expectations for behavior. Throughout infancy, the ability to delay responses and understand consequences and expectations is developing, so that by 2–3 years of age children are able to follow rules.

Behavioral regulation is important because it helps children understand the need for compliance and a balance of control within the family, the school, and the larger society. Behavioral regulation is necessary for learning the values associated with social conventions and acquiring concepts of right and wrong within the child's culture and community. Behavioral regulation also is needed to control unusual behaviors or mannerisms that are not considered culturally appropriate and may have a negative impact on the child's social interactions.

Throughout life, whether within the child's daily routines, in school, in the community, or on the job, people will have expectations concerning appropriate behaviors, ability to comply with requests, and understanding of right and wrong. Problems with this area can have serious personal and societal consequences, including mental health treatment, school failure, and potential incarceration.

APPROPRIATE BEHAVIORAL REGULATION

Adults appreciate children who not only are aware of the "dos" and "don'ts," but who also are motivated to please adults by trying to learn the "rules" of what is acceptable and what is not. During the first 2 years of life, children are learning cognitive, social, and physical consequences of behavior. They are learning about their own personal limitations as well as social limitations. As language and cognitive understanding increase, children are beginning to make independent decisions about not only what they *can* do, but also what they *should* do. Caregivers provide the boundaries for children for what is and is not acceptable, and gradually children begin to understand the reasons for the limitations and develop an ability to delay gratification.

The capacity for self-control and ability to make conscious decisions about behavior typically is developed by the age of 3. In addition, the child's self-conscious emotions of shame and guilt also are developing, resulting in the establishment of internal motivation for compliance with rules. By the preschool years, the development of language and cognitive skills and the increasing sense of competence enable children to "argue" and negotiate regarding requirements and rules. Arguing is important, because it allows children to hear the reasons for the rules and enables them to learn how to negotiate outcomes.

Caregivers provide an important role model in this negotiation, because they model strategies such as compromise and also enforce outcomes for noncompliance. This is significant for children's social learning, because adults model behavioral outcomes when someone does not comply. For example, the child who is consistently hit when he does not comply may learn to demonstrate anger and/or aggression toward others when they do not act in accordance with his wishes. Parents who talk to their child and have the child correct his or her behavior may help the child learn to negotiate with words.

By the end of preschool, children have internalized many standards for behavior, which they then apply to their siblings, peers, and caregivers. In later years, they learn how rules can be applied differently in various situations, and how values and behavior may depend on numerous factors.

Ability to comply with adults' requests, control behaviors adults perceive as wrong, conform to social conventions, and inhibit off-putting behaviors are all part of behavioral regulation. The following depicts ways that typically developing children demonstrate behavioral regulation.

Appropriate Behavioral Regulation in Practice

▪▪▪▪▪ **IV. A. How well does the child comply with adult requests?**

Daily Routines (Home and Classroom)

- *Infant/toddler:* The infant takes dog food from the dog's bowl and starts to put it in her mouth. Her father says, "That's for the doggie. Give it to Daddy." The infant hands the dog food to her father. The toddler's mother asks him to pick up his clothes and put them in the basket. He does, smiles, and says, "I did it!"

- *Young child:* The young child's mother says it is time for bed. He responds that he wants to read one more book.

Play Routines (Home and Classroom)

- *Infant/toddler:* At the park, the infant starts to put a stick in his mouth and stops when his father says, "No. Don't put that in your mouth. It's yucky!" The toddler takes the truck from his friend, and when the caregiver says to give it back, he holds on to it and starts to cry.

- *Young child:* The young child is told to put her toy in her cubby. She replies, "Maria didn't put *her* toy in the cubby!"

Classroom Routines

During circle time, the teacher says, "I like the way Billy is raising his hand." Most of the children then raise their hands.

■■■■■ IV. B. How well does the child control behaviors that are perceived as wrong?

Daily Routines (Home and Classroom)

- *Infant/toddler:* The infant pulls her mother's hair. Her mother says, "Don't pull my hair; that hurts Mommy." The infant keeps pulling her hair. The toddler reaches for the glass bowl on the coffee table and says, "No, no!" He then picks up the bowl.

- *Young child:* The young child catches her younger brother dropping toys into the toilet. She runs to get her mother.

Play Routines (Home and Classroom)

- *Infant/toddler:* The infant crawls to the top of the stairs, smiles, looks down, then looks at her mother who is shaking her head *no*. The infant sits up and starts to cry. The toddler runs wildly around the room, yelling, "Don't run, don't run!"

- *Young child:* The young child and his little sister are playing with their cat. He tells her not to pull the cat's tail. "That's not nice."

Classroom Routines

At the literacy center, the child grabs the glue from another child, then stops and says, "It's my turn, okay? I'll give it right back."

■■■■■ IV. C. Does the child recognize and use social conventions of the home and mainstream culture?

Daily Routines (Home and Classroom)

- *Infant/toddler:* The infant waves goodbye to her grandma and leans forward to give her a kiss. The toddler reaches up for a cookie and says, "Cookie, please. Thank you."

- *Young child:* The young child runs to the corner and waits for his father to catch up. He then says, "Look both ways, Daddy."

Play Routines (Home and Classroom)

- *Infant/toddler:* The infant is playing Peekaboo and first covers his mother's head with his blanket; then laughs when she comes out. He then takes a turn and covers his own head. When her father says, "Let's pick up your toys so we can go outside," the toddler puts the toy car on the shelf.

- *Young child:* The young child is playing a board game with her caregiver. She says, "No, you have to spin first. Then you can have a turn."

Classroom Routines

During centers, the child starts to go out into the hall to put something in his cubby. He stops, comes back to the teacher, and asks permission.

▮▮▮▮ **IV. D. Does the child demonstrate unusual behavioral mannerisms that are not culturally meaningful and cannot be inhibited?**

Although many children display unusual behaviors, children who are developing typically can intentionally stop these behaviors. Some children with special needs, however, display unusual behaviors that they cannot control. Consequently, there are no examples for children who are developing typically in this section (see Planning Individualized Interventions for Improving Behavioral Regulation, below).

GENERAL PRINCIPLES FOR SUPPORTING APPROPRIATE BEHAVIORAL REGULATION

Adults use a variety of strategies to help children behave in ways that they feel support their values and culture. Not all cultures have the same beliefs in what constitutes right and wrong, what are considered to be acceptable social conventions and mannerisms, and what are appropriate strategies for adults to use to convey these to the children of a given culture. Even within individual families, the patterns of behavior that are considered acceptable may vary, which may lead to conflict within the family. For example, depending on the values and experiences of the family of origin, one parent may value independence, assertive behavior, and competition, whereas another may value following authority, acquiescence, and camaraderie. These different values may lead to contradictory parenting styles and confusion on the part of the children. Even within a given culture, the views about parenting values and styles change over time. For instance, within the United States the attitudes toward children's rights and corporal punishment have shifted many times in the last century. Therefore, family values not only reflect the culture, but also the time in which the family lives.

Most cultures have many values that are shared and passed on to the majority of the children. It is important for those who work with children and families to be familiar with the culture and the values of the families with whom they work. The following are examples of ways that many Western families may support the development of concepts of "right" and "wrong" that include 1) respecting and developing one's self-worth and not neglecting one's appearance, health, knowledge or talent; 2) caring for and not harming others; 3) sharing and not being selfish; and 4) protecting property and the environment and not being destructive.

Discuss What Is "Good" and What Is "Bad"

Adults discuss with children what others do and make comments on their behavior. For example, when a child is observed screaming and hitting his mother in the grocery store, the parent may take this opportunity to talk about why that behavior is not good and what would be a better way for the child to tell his mommy what is the matter. Observation of others provides emotional distance that is not possible when the child is involved personally in a situation.

Discussion with the child when his or her own behavior is involved also is important but requires the adult to get the child into a calm, listening frame of mind first. If behavior is out of control, the adult must first stop the behavior in question. Children cannot listen or negotiate when emotions are intense (see TPBI2, Chapter 5, Section III. Strategies for Improving Regulation of Emotions and Arousal States).

Explain What Is Right and What Is Wrong

Adults talk about what they perceive as right and wrong in many situations. Young children often are involved in religious activities that discuss values. Adults also read books to children that discuss values such as sharing, helping, being brave, and working hard. Children's movies such as *Finding Nemo* and television shows such as Sesame Street also present situations that illustrate values embraced by the majority culture. The adult can then use these illustrations as a basis for discussion of the characters' actions and whether the behaviors were "good" or "bad" and why. Discussion of various situations over time help children see patterns and develop a system for how they should view the world.

Model Valued Behavior

Adults teach through their own behaviors. When they are kind to others, children see the results. When they are patient and tolerant, the child experiences the effect. Even little acts, such as giving a toy to the homeless or splitting a cookie between two friends, can leave an impression on a young mind. Negative behaviors also influence the child. A child who is hit frequently as punishment or who often views violence at home, in the neighborhood, or on television may come to view aggression as an acceptable means of solving problems. Adults are thus monitors of the behaviors that children see modeled as right and wrong.

Provide Opportunities to Practice Desired Behaviors

Adults enable children to experience many different types of behaviors. Families from high socioeconomic environments are able to choose from a wide variety of experiences for their children. They may enroll them in sports, theater, computer, or science programs or camps. They typically enroll their young children in programs that they value and hope the children will come to appreciate as well. Children from lower income backgrounds may have access to a narrower range of opportunities, but parents who hold strong values will find community programs to encourage their children to pursue certain values. They may not have access to private classes and programs, but church, library, community recreation, and family activities all send a message to children about what is important and valued. Routines of the family also help establish behavior patterns and provide opportunities to practice specific behaviors.

Activities in the home and school also provide opportunities for children to practice values. Families can play cooperative or competitive games, talk out problems or dictate results, watch television or read books, show compassion or anger, celebrate holidays, and so forth. The degree to which each of these and other values are practiced and supported makes a difference in the behaviors children continue to exhibit.

Reinforce Desired Behavior

Adults consciously and unconsciously reinforce children's behaviors and values. By encouraging repetition of behaviors, applauding the child's efforts, arranging for classes or training, and other such actions, adults intentionally confirm children's conduct and values. They also unintentionally reinforce the child's actions when they pay attention to what the child is doing, comment positively on others' behaviors, and let children continue to do things they disapprove of without comment. Benign neglect may tell the child that whatever he or she is doing is acceptable.

Discourage Undesired Behavior

Adults use the words "no," "don't," "stop," and other such terms to discourage children from engaging in behaviors they do not like. They may mildly dissuade with a shake of the head or overtly oppose with punishment for actions of which they disapprove. Some parents might lecture a child for hitting a sibling, whereas others might send the child to the "time out" chair or even spank the child for this behavior. (This latter actually sends a mixed message, because it is modeling the same action that is being punished.) Adults also may deny the child opportunities to engage in activities of which they do not approve. For example, the parent who wants the child to focus on music skills may not let the child enroll in sports activities.

Replace Negative Behaviors with Positive Ones

Both reinforcing and discouraging behaviors can be done at the same time when the adult stops one behavior and replaces it with another, more preferred action. This is a powerful strategy because it not only helps the child know what not to do, but also shows the child what is a better behavior. For example, parents and teachers often encourage children who hit another child out of frustration to "Use your words." They may even give children words to replace the hitting: "Tell him you don't like it when he takes your toy."

THE PRINCIPLES IN PRACTICE

Daily Routines (Home and Classroom)

Feeding/Eating

The parent may try to get the infant to eat healthy foods that the child does not like by combining the food with a preferred food. For the older child who refuses to eat desired foods, the parent may use reinforcement, by saying, "Just try two bites and then you can have some fruit." Adults also model eating a variety of foods and enjoying them.

Diapering/Toileting

Toilet training is done at different times and in different ways across various cultures. Western cultures typically encourage "big boy" or "big girl" behavior and reinforce independent toileting with a variety of rewards, such as stars, hugs and kisses, and letting the child wear "big kid" briefs or panties. Parents often work to build the child's pride in accomplishment and independence. Many cultures use routines to build new patterns along with positive comments. They set an expectation, arrange for the event to occur, and then reinforce effort. For example, the parent may say, "It is time to go sit on the potty. I'll give you a book to look at." After the child gets off the potty, the parent may say, "You didn't go, but you tried! Maybe next time!"

Dressing

Values around cleanliness and types of clothing vary widely. The routines that parents put into place around dressing have an impact on the child's values and behavior around dressing. For example, routines can affect how often children bathe, how often they wear clean clothing, what type of clothing is worn, who selects the clothing, how much time is provided for dressing, and how much independence children are encouraged to have in the dressing process. The amount of latitude, support, and reinforcement of independence the parents give children related to these issues contributes to the children's compliance and behaviors related to dressing. Parents' comments provide a frame for behaviors. The parent may say, "You are all dirty. You need a bath so that you will be clean and smell nice. Let's pick out some nice clean clothes for you to wear." These comments provide the message that clean is good and dirty is not good. Baths are good and clean clothes are good. Such comments help shape children's ideas of what is acceptable behavior. The values supported in relation to dressing vary by cultures and individual family expectations.

Play Routines (Home and Classroom)

Face-to-Face Play

Most typically developing children enjoy face-to-face play. Culture, family values, and personal preferences play a role in the amount of this type of play in which children engage. Desire for and tolerance of this type of play also influences boundaries for face-to-face play. Parents model affect and interactions that reinforce this type of play. For example, the father may pull the child onto his lap and say, "Let's do 'Row, Row, Row Your Boat.' That's a good one!" As he begins to sing and pushes and pulls the child back-and-forth, he gives the child the message that this type of game is a positive behavior. As he models the movements, he gives the same message. When the child follows his lead and moves and sings, he reinforces her actions by saying, "You are such a good singer!"

Physical Play

As with face-to-face play, culture, family values, and personal preference influence how children respond to physical play. Families who value physical play often make opportunities for children within both the home and the community for movement games, outdoor play, and physical group activities. Reinforcement of successful actions also encourages children to view physical play as appropriate. Limits set by adults usually relate to not hurting others, taking turns, and being fair. The concept of cooperation and/or competition in physical play also may be reinforced by adults.

Manipulative Play

The type and importance of toy play varies across cultures and families as well. In some African cultures, toys may consist mostly of sticks and stones, whereas in the United States, toys consist primarily of commercial materials. The values of the family also influence what parents teach children about which toys are acceptable and which are not. For example, some parents do not allow children to play with toy guns because the parents disapprove of weapons; some families encourage play with "educational toys," whereas others encourage play with dramatic, artistic, or music toys. Gender also makes a difference in many families, with some toys being considered "off limits" for either girls or boys. Adults also set standards for *how* children play with toys. They may disapprove of aggressive or destructive play, encourage cooperative interaction, or enable children to play without adult limits. The types of toys parents allow and how parents reinforce or discourage toy play influence children's regulation of their behavior within this kind of play. For example, the parent may say, "You can play with these blocks and build something, but I don't like you to play with guns." When the child then builds a fort and cannons out of the blocks, how the adult responds also may influence the child's developing sense of right and wrong. If the reasoning is explained, the child can either accept or reject the adult's values. If behavior is punished or mandated, the child may either feel that the adult's values are right or he or she may feel that the adult is wrong and unfair.

Sensory Play

Children create messes! How much tolerance adults have for these messes influences how adults respond to children's messy play. Parents who appreciate their children's exploratory and artistic efforts not only may accept a mess, but encourage making one. Some children may resist this type of play due to anxiety or unpleasant feelings associated with various types of tactile input. Adults' provision of or lack of provision of such type of play experiences, in addition to their encouragement or discouragement of messy play, can have an impact on a child's acceptance of messy endeavors in the future. For example, the adult who says, "Put that playdough away! It makes a big mess!" is sending a message that the activity and the child's efforts are not valued and are to be avoided in the future.

Reading and Learning Routines

Circle Time

Circle time is a typical part of preschool that can last for several minutes to over a half-hour. Teachers require a great deal of behavioral regulation during this time. A variety of strategies may be used to help children attend to the desired activity. For example, the teacher may point out what behaviors are expected (e.g., "Sit with your hands in your lap"), tell a child what behaviors are wrong (e.g., "Sara doesn't like it when you poke her"), or reinforce good behavior (e.g., "I'll call on Molly because she is listening nicely").

One-on-One Book Reading

Reading a book to a child one-on-one enables the adult to discuss the actions and behaviors of the characters in the book. The adult can point out good and bad actions or discuss what is right and wrong in terms of how others are affected. They also can discuss the correct way to read books (e.g., front to back, top to bottom, and word to word), to treat books (e.g., gently and with respect), to read aloud (e.g., with expression and meaning), and to share a book (e.g., by taking turns talking about what is read).

Science and Math

Science and math activities involve exploration, comparison, analysis, and sharing of findings. Children can learn to respect careful looking, thoughtful investigation, and developing means of sharing results with others. Teachers play a role in this through modeling (e.g., "Watch how I mix the colors"), helping children to replace negative behaviors with positive behaviors (e.g., "Instead of throwing them, let's count how many there are"), and reinforcing positive actions (e.g., "I like how carefully you are taking that apart"). For young children, science and math can deteriorate easily into simple exploration or messy play. The adult can play a guiding role in helping children turn exploratory play into scientific investigation.

PLANNING INDIVIDUALIZED INTERVENTIONS FOR IMPROVING BEHAVIORAL REGULATION

All children struggle with compliance and issues of right and wrong at different times throughout childhood. Some children, however, have behavioral regulation concerns to a degree that interferes with their everyday functioning and social interactions. Children with emotional and social disabilities, autism spectrum disorders, fragile X syndrome, Prader-Willi syndrome, and mental retardation often have difficulty with impulse control, compliance, and understanding of right and wrong. Children with language disorders such as central auditory processing disorder or receptive language delays also may have difficulty understanding adults' requests and explanations. The strategies identified previously are often effective with children with behavioral regulation concerns. In addition, the following sections describe strategies that can be used to address specific behavioral issues.

▬▬▬ IV. A. How well does the child comply with adult requests?

In order to comply with adult requests, the child has to attend to what the adult is communicating, understand the request, and formulate the correct response. Attending to the communication requires the ability to focus on the person who is communicating as well as the capacity to hear, see, and/or touch the person conveying the message. Understanding the request requires conceptual abilities so that the child can interpret the meaning of the request. Formulating the correct response requires action. The child must be able to communicate a response through vocalizations, gestures, and/or physical actions. Children who have delays, disabilities, or disorders that affect their ability to accomplish any of these requirements effectively may have problems with compliance.

Compliance with adult rules is more difficult because it requires remembering the rule, understanding why the rule is needed, and then being able to control behavior that is not consistent with the rule.

Knowledge of which of these aspects of compliance is difficult for a child can help adults plan strategies to assist the child. Compliance with individual requests as well as group rules can be difficult for children with disabilities, particularly those who are functioning cognitively below the age of 3, who may have a lack of social cognition and empathy, attention deficits, and poor social skills.

Interaction Strategies

1. *Capture the child's attention.* Use sounds, touch, gestures, or other means to make sure the child is attending to the person who is communicating. If the child has a disability that makes it difficult for the child to give eye contact (e.g., fragile X syndrome, visual or motor impairment), look for body language or listen for sounds or words that indicate the child is listening (see TPBI2, Chapter 7, Section I. Strategies for Improving Attention). The position of the adult in relation to the child also is important (close and not out of sight). The speaker may need to touch the child gently or have a specific signal when a new comment or instruction is going to be given that the child needs to understand.

2. *Begin with requests about daily routines.* Children with disabilities need multiple opportunities to practice skills. Daily routines are events that recur, usually with a similar pattern, each day. They thus provide an opportunity for adults to teach children how to respond to requests with familiar actions. Once children have moved from having parents perform the daily tasks with the child to playing more of a guiding role, the parents can begin to request that the child perform the next action in the routine. The child then anticipates what comes next, and responding to the request is easier. For example, when the child is learning to dress independently, the child has been through the processes innumerable times. Thus, when the parent requests, "Now pull up your pants," the child knows what is involved.

3. *State requests and rules positively.* Tell children what *to do* rather than what not to do. In other words, say, "Walk" instead of "Don't run."

4. *Make requests slowly, with clear, short, and concrete statements.* Particularly for children with disabilities, requests need to be specific and to the point, containing only

necessary information. For example, a child with auditory processing problems, attention deficits, or cognitive delays may not understand a request that is stated like this: "It is getting late. You took a very long nap and now we have to hurry. I need for you to get ready to go so we can go to the grocery store and get something for dinner." Several things about this communication make it less effective than it could be. It is given too quickly, there is too much information, and the request is too general and is buried in the middle of less important information. The following, stated slowly, would be better: "We need to go to the store. I need you to get your coat." The reason for the request is given, and the important request is stated last in a short, concrete sentence.

5. *Make only one request at a time.* It is difficult for young children, especially young children with disabilities, to remember a sequence of commands. Give only one request, possibly two, at one time. For example, do not say, "Pick up your toys, go take off your clothes, get your pajamas, and meet me in the bathroom." Instead, try, "It's bath time. Pick up your toys." When that task is accomplished (with support and cheers when it is completed), give the next request.

6. *Use multiple means of conveying the message.* Children with disabilities may need more than words to help them comprehend a message. Gestures, picture cues, signs, and/or demonstration may be needed. If the child has routines that he knows how to perform, a picture schedule may be used, together with words, to let the child know that it is time to do that activity. For example, if the child has a picture schedule of the routines of his day, his mother can point to the picture of picking up the toys and say, "Time to pick up the toys." If the child does not yet know a routine, picture sequences can help the child see each step of a process (see TPBI2, Chapter 7, Section III. Strategies for Improving Problem Solving). The adult also may need to assist and demonstrate several times so the child has the physical experience of moving through the sequence correctly. This will help the child remember the sequence. If the child is not a visual learner, talking the child through the sequence in combination with performing the actions may support learning. The combination of seeing, hearing, and doing provides several channels for processing information.

7. *Make sure the message was received.* Just because the child heard the adult's request or saw gestures indicating what was needed does not mean the child understood the request. The adult may need to make sure the child understood. For example, the adult may ask, "What are you going to do next?"

8. *Help with the first step.* Frequently, all the child needs is support to get an action going. Once the first step is initiated, the event chain is set in progress. This is particularly true for routines and other activities the child has done frequently.

9. *Do not expect memory for all necessary steps.* Adults often expect children to be able to follow through on all of the steps necessary to fulfill a request. However children with memory problems, motor planning problems, and/or emotional problems may get started but then forget what comes next, be unable to perform a task, get distracted by something else, or lose motivation to continue. Adults may need to provide prompts or reminders of next steps, demonstration or guidance, or reinforcement for effort so children can follow through successfully.

10. *Provide supports if needed.* Children with cognitive or emotional disabilities may have difficulty monitoring their progress in complying with adults' requests, particularly when asked to do something without help or supervision. As mentioned previously, picture schedules or verbal supports can assist the child in remembering what comes next. Adult monitoring also can help, but the adult needs to support the child in moving toward independence by giving clues or prompts instead of telling the child

what to do or doing it for him or her. For example, if the child has been asked to go get her shoes, she may head to the bedroom and then not come back. Instead of yelling at the child, the adult may need to remember that she may have misunderstood, become more interested in something else, or forgotten the request. The parent could then go see where the child is and help her monitor her actions. For example, "You came in here to get your ____." If the child looks confused, the parent can give her another clue. "You came to get your sh . . . ," while signing SHOES or gesturing toward her feet.

11. *Teach children a response.* Some children with language delays or disorders, specific emotional problems, or conditions such as Rett syndrome have difficulty formulating a response, either verbally or motorically. When they are unable to respond, they may react with negative behavior. Children can be taught to say or sign a specific response when they are confused. Adults can use behavioral shaping strategies to get children to use signs or words such as "I need help," "I want," "Stop," and so forth. The point is to increase the child's communicative intentions in order to reduce noncompliance. The adult can then support the child in a variety of ways.

12. *Acknowledge efforts at compliance.* The adult needs to reinforce the child's efforts, not just the final successful response to a request, but the small steps that the child accomplishes. In the previous example, the child did not come to the parent with her shoes, but she did 1) respond to the request by moving in the right direction and 2) ended up in the place where the shoes were to be found. If the adult has a negative or punitive response, the child may get the message that she did something wrong by coming into the bedroom. This may actually reduce the child's attempts at compliance the next time the parent asks her to do something, because her efforts were discouraged. Instead, the parent can say, "Yeah! You made it to the bedroom! You are looking for something for Mommy. You came in here to get . . . " (see No. 10, above).

Environmental Modifications

In addition to interpersonal strategies that may support the child, environmental modifications often are useful. Depending on the findings from TPBA2, the team may want to consider some of the following environmental modifications.

1. *Make sure the environment supports seeing and hearing.* For children to actually understand the request, they need to be able to clearly hear and/or see what is being communicated. Eliminate extraneous noise if possible. Lighting also is important. For instance, shadows or back lighting, with the light behind the person speaking, can make it difficult for the child to see the adult's face.

2. *Use assistive devices if needed.* At particular risk for auditory difficulties that may require assistive devices are children who are experiencing temporary hearing loss from otitis media, children with mild to moderate permanent hearing losses, children with speech impairments, children who have learning disabilities and central auditory processing disorders, children for whom English is a second language, and very young children generally. Assistive devices such as hearing aids, frequency modulated (FM) systems, and sound field amplification systems may be helpful for these children. Individual amplification systems can improve auditory processing abilities for some children. Classroom acoustical amplification systems can improve sound field equalization. Sound field equalization is a classroom listening strategy that consists of creating an environment in which each child is at a favorable speaker–listener distance by routing the teacher's voice through small, wireless, high-fidelity public address systems self-contained in the classroom (Phonak Hearing Systems; Yahoo! Groups: Classroom

Acoustics, online discussion group/mailing list; see Additional Resources at the end of this chapter).

3. *Provide whatever assistive supports are needed.* In order for the child to comply with an adult request, he or she needs to be able to carry out the actions required. This may necessitate adult assistance or adaptive devices to enable the child to hold objects, move, or communicate. Adults should not make requests that require unreasonable effort on the part of the child.

4. *Use social stories.* Children who benefit from visual strategies, such as children with autism spectrum disorders or fragile X syndrome, often can learn to comply with adult requests when reminded by social stories. These are social skill lessons taught in brief (4–6 short sentences) lessons accompanied by simple pictures illustrating the desired behavior. The story is read to the child several times in a one-on-one situation immediately preceding the time when the problem behavior typically occurs. The pictures are used to emphasize what skill the child needs to remember. The child then keeps the social story and the reading is repeated until the social skill is learned (Gray, 1993). Social stories related to compliance issues concern repeated behaviors that are a problem; for instance, stopping play to go out in the car.

5. *Develop behavioral plans to address compliance issues.* A functional assessment can help determine why a child is acting in a certain way and how behaviors may be modified. Examination of the frequency, duration, and intensity of various behaviors is tracked. In addition, specific events that precede the behavior, what happens during the occurrence of the behavior, and what happens immediately after the behavior occurs are documented. Analysis of this information helps the adults in the child's life plan for environmental changes or interactional changes that may be needed to help the child behave differently.

IV. B. How well does the child control behaviors that are perceived as wrong?

In order to control behaviors, the child needs to understand what is expected of him or her and that communicating or acting in certain ways is considered wrong by significant adults. Children also need to understand why various behaviors are considered good and others bad. Behavioral regulation also requires that the child wants approval; cares about others; and can control the impulse to act, monitor his or her conduct, and correct actions if needed. Both cognitive and emotional capacities form the foundation for understanding right and wrong. Children with emotional or social concerns, attention-deficit/hyperactivity disorder (ADHD), learning disabilities, fragile X syndrome, autism spectrum disorders or Asperger syndrome, and other disabilities may demonstrate weak impulse control. Children with cognitive delays or disabilities affecting their conceptualization or social cognition, and children with various types of emotional issues, also may demonstrate lack of understanding of concepts relating to right and wrong or comprehension of principles and rules. Remembering previous consequences helps children anticipate the results of unacceptable actions. Children with memory problems, therefore, may repeat actions they have previously been told not to do or for which they have received negative consequences.

Rules often are established to help children learn right and wrong with regard to respecting others' rights and property, for preventing physical or mental harm to self or others, and for practicing fairness to others. The balance between who decides what behavior is appropriate gradually shifts as the child gains understanding of what is right and wrong and is able to assume more responsibility for his or her own behavior. For some children with disabilities, assumption of responsibility is delayed or may not be achieved. The child may stay at a cognitive level of not understanding something is wrong; follow certain rules but not understand the intent behind the rules; or lack empathy, which is necessary for understanding why something may be right or wrong.

Interaction Strategies

1. *Tell the child repeatedly what is right and what is wrong—and why.* Take time to explain expectations, decisions, and intentions each time a situation arises. Repetition is needed for learning. Be clear and concise. Talk about what should happen next.

2. *Be a role model.* Try to model the behaviors and values you want the child to display and be honest when you have made mistakes. Demonstrate how to "own up to" and correct mistakes. Discuss the consequences of your actions.

3. *Reinforce caring, unselfish, truthful acts and how they affect the feelings of others.* It is more common for adults to point out what is wrong than to acknowledge when the child is doing something right. However, children need to know when they are doing the right things. They also need to know *why* the act was the right thing to do. Saying, "I like that you shared," is important, but saying, "I like that you shared. You made her happy," lets the child know that caring for the feelings of others is important. In addition, label positive characteristics, such as persistence, bravery, truthfulness, fairness, honesty, patience, and so forth, so that the child learns these terms and is acknowledged for these efforts.

4. *Use books, television, and movies as opportunities for discussion.* All of these media provide opportunities for discussion of characters' choices, actions, and consequences. With some children, adults also can talk about "what if" certain situations or actions were changed. How would the results be different?

5. *Involve the child in problem solving about alternatives.* When situations occur that involve right and wrong behavior on the part of the child or others, discuss what should or could happen. Whenever possible, anticipate situations that may cause conflict or temptation for the child and discuss behaviors ahead of time. For instance, if the child is going to a birthday party where many new toys will be opened, discuss what the child may want to do in relation to asking, sharing, being thoughtful, and so forth.

6. *Take advantage of role play situations.* When children are able to play the role of others, they can assume another's point of view and see how they might feel or act. Dramatization also allows adults to support children in trying out alternative approaches in their play. Role play also can be used to teach children appropriate social responses and interactions. The adult can model and then have the child repeat the actions.

7. *Set a small number of reasonable limits.* It is important to not have too many rules for young children. Young children need a minimal number of rules, so adults need to focus on the most relevant ones.

8. *Enforce limits consistently.* Being firm is important, but showing affection, warmth, and respect for children is equally important. Listen to what they have to say, but keep predictable limits. Children need to know that rules will be enforced. For example, if the child hits another child one day and the adult says nothing, but the next time the child hits a child she is admonished, the child is getting a mixed message about whether hitting is acceptable.

9. *Increase freedom as the child shows responsibility.* Give the child opportunities to show responsibility. Give the child chances to show his ability to share, care for others and their things, be truthful, follow rules without being reminded, and so forth. If the child makes a mistake, give him a chance to take responsibility for the mistake and fix

the situation. For instance, if the child broke another child's toy, let him help glue it back together.

10. *Help the child express thoughts and feelings.* The adult should try not to react too quickly to acts perceived as wrong. Try to find out the reasons for the behavior. Reasons may include needing attention, peer pressure, not understanding something is wrong, or acting on impulse. Understanding the reason behind the actions can help adults know how to intervene. Adults need to help children develop the vocabulary to express their feelings, by giving them "feeling" words, such as *mad, sad, upset, angry, hurt,* and so forth. They also need to help children recognize the feelings they experience when they do something wrong as opposed to when they do something appropriate for the situation. Talk about how it is sometimes hard to do the right thing.

Environmental Modifications

In addition to interpersonal strategies that may support the child learning about right and wrong, environmental modifications often are useful. Depending on the findings from TPBA2, the team may want to consider some of the following environmental modifications.

1. *Provide a predictable environment.* Predictable routines are essential for children with many different types of disabilities, including children with autism, Asperger and fragile X syndromes, and various types of sensory dysfunction. If children know where items are to be found, what events are going to occur, what their role is in each event, and how adults are going to respond, they are less likely to react impulsively or with unacceptable behavior.

2. *Protect the child from bullying.* Children with disabilities may be vulnerable to bullying or may be the recipient of negative behaviors on the part of others due to their lack of social cognition or social skills. Adults can help prevent some of this by pairing the vulnerable child with a sensitive, caring peer and reducing the child's proximity to children who are verbally or physically aggressive. Adults also may want to teach children phrases to use or tell them how to respond should such events occur. For instance, children can be taught to say, "Stop. I don't like it," to move away from a teasing child, or to go to an adult for assistance. Help children develop repertoires of responses for different situations. Visual reminder cards, role play with puppets, or practice sessions with children may be helpful.

3. *Use interests and "fixations" to guide learning.* Some children with disabilities get fixated on certain toys, subjects, or actions. Arrangement of the environment can help children reduce obsessions. Topics on which a child perseverates can be used to teach other skills. For example, an obsessive interest in dinosaurs could be used to teach dramatic play sequences, new vocabulary, drawing, and writing skills.

Eliminate materials that tempt unwanted behaviors, or allow the behavior only at specific times or in specific places. For example, a child who masturbates excessively may be taught about when and where such behavior is acceptable and why it should not be performed in public. The child may be given a substitute object to play with or the adult may give the child an agreed-upon cue, such as holding up folded hands, to remind the child to do an alternative action with his hands.

4. *Provide "buddies" to model, guide, and support.* Many young children enjoy the role of teaching or helping others. After teaching the peer about a child's behaviors and why they occur, adults can pair the peer with the child with behavioral concerns, as a role model, coach, and peer tutor. The adult needs to train the peer and provide support for the interactions.

5. *Use social stories.* (See No. 4 in Environmental Modifications, under Compliance, above.) Social stories for learning right and wrong for a child who frequently hurts others at play time might involve behaviors such as biting or hitting.

6. *Develop plans for analysis of problem behaviors.* (See No. 5, Environmental Modifications under Compliance, above.)

IV. C. Does the child recognize and use social conventions of the home and mainstream culture?

Social conventions are behaviors that are determined informally by a culture or subculture to be preferred behaviors. Whereas behaviors that are considered right and wrong, as discussed previously, pertain to issues of harm, fairness, and rights, such as hitting or stealing, violation of social conventions is not harmful to others. Conventions usually are related to patterns of acceptable social interaction (e.g., greetings), appropriate appearance (e.g., wearing clean clothes), health and safety (e.g., washing hands before eating), or organization (hanging up clothing). The reasons for social conventions are more difficult for children to understand and typically are passed on through modeling or direct instruction.

Before parents expect children to understand right and wrong, they begin to expect children to comply with some social conventions. Conventions relating to using polite words such as "please" and "thank you" and safety issues such as not touching electrical outlets are expected as soon as the child starts talking and crawling. Children with disabilities may have social, cognitive, communication, and/or sensorimotor concerns that preclude them from understanding or being able to implement social conventions. This may be particularly problematic because children with disabilities may demonstrate characteristics that make them look or act different from their typical peers. Ability to adhere to social conventions is one way to help children with disabilities "fit in" and be more socially acceptable. For this reason, attention to this area is particularly important in early intervention and early childhood special education.

Social conventions are determined by culture, so they vary across groups. Issues such as conversational conventions—for example, wait time before answering, pace of response, and participation structure—are viewed by various cultures as showing respect, involvement, or cooperation. It is therefore important to understand the social rules, expectations, and conventions of the conversation of children from diverse backgrounds, especially as children move into a classroom environment.

Disabilities confound the issue of social conventions because the child may find it difficult to adhere to any social conventions, regardless of culture. Strategies to support children's functioning in the home and at school should include ways of teaching social conventions.

Interaction Strategies

1. *Model.* Bring the child's attention to what you are doing that is desired behavior. For example, the mother might say, "Watch Mommy. 'Daddy, can I *please* have a cracker?'" Dad might respond, "You said 'please,' so you can have one." If the child has a visual or hearing impairment, the adult needs to ensure that the child can understand the expectation using alternative learning channels.

2. *Prompt.* At the time the social convention is expected, the adult can prompt the action; for example, "If you have something to say, raise your hand." The adult should use the least amount of support needed to result in a correct response. For instance, some children will only need to observe the adult do the action; some will need a verbal or visual prompt (e.g., a sign or a gesture); some may need a physical assist (e.g.,

putting the eating utensil in the child's hand) or a cue such as the first sound of the word (e.g., "pl . . . " for "please"); others may need physical support through the whole behavior (e.g., hand-over-hand flushing the toilet). By using the least amount of support possible, the child acquires more independence in attaining the behavior.

3. *Reinforce appropriate actions.* When the child does use appropriate social conventions, comment on the behavior. This tells the child that the behavior was correct and encourages him to use it again. For example, "You used your napkin. Good for you. Your mouth is nice and clean." In this example, the adult also explained why using a napkin is important.

4. *Ask the child what is expected and wait for the response.* Help the child to think about the situation ahead of time, so the child has time to process the expectation. For example, "We are going to church this morning, do you think you should be quiet or noisy?"

Environmental Modifications

In addition to interpersonal strategies that may support the child's use of social conventions, environmental modifications often are useful. Depending on the findings from TPBA2, the team may want to consider some of the following environmental modifications.

1. *Arrange for observation of and/or discussion with peers.* Children learn social conventions from direct instruction from adults, but peers are a powerful influence. Through observation and discussion with peers, children learn social conventions. Adults can encourage children to observe other children's patterns during daily routines and activities. Peers also can be taught to instruct their friends in how to perform certain behaviors.

2. *Provide the materials or adaptive equipment the child needs to be able to demonstrate the behavior.* For example, independent hand washing cannot be practiced unless the child can reach the sink, manipulate the soap or soap dispenser, operate the faucets, and access the towel. For children with motor disabilities, this might mean having a support to enable the child to balance in standing at the sink. It might mean having adapted handles on the sink so the child can manipulate them. It could mean having an easily operated soap dispenser that requires only one hand and little pressure to activate. Cloth towels that are easy to maneuver and less irritating, or an air dryer, might be needed. Analysis of what is inhibiting the child's use of a social convention is important.

3. *Use social stories.* (See No. 4 under Environmental Modifications in Section IV. A, above.) Social stories for learning important social conventions might include behaviors such as washing hands after using the toilet.

▮▮▮▮▮ **IV. D. Does the child demonstrate unusual behavioral mannerisms that are not culturally meaningful and cannot be inhibited?**

Many children acquire habits that are not typically seen in all children. Unusual behaviors that cannot be controlled easily by the child, however, are more likely to be seen in children with disabilities. Sometimes these behaviors are associated with particular disabilities, such as hand-flapping by children with autism or constant eating by children with Prader-Willi syndrome. Occasionally, the unusual mannerisms are a result of neurological impairment, such as is the case with the uncontrollable vocalizations or motor movements that may occur with Tourette syndrome. Some mannerisms are acquired because they fulfill some physiological need; for example, children who must touch everything or lick everything may need extra tactile input to get sufficient sensory information. A wide range of mannerisms may be seen in children with disabilities, from severe self-injurious behaviors such as eye poking or arm chewing, to behaviors such as nose touching, body rocking, and object manipulation. Unusual fixations, such as picking up lint, also may be seen.

Unlike some behaviors that relate to right and wrong or lack of compliance, strange mannerisms usually are not harmful to others and do not interfere with others' rights. In some cases, the behavior may be contrary to social conventions, such as children who echo what someone else says. However, in most cases these unique mannerisms are unacceptable because they make the child "stand out" as being strange or highly bizarre. Such mannerisms also interfere with the child being accepted by others; may impede the child's engagement with people, objects, or events in the environment; and/or may interfere with acquisition of new skills and behaviors that foster development. For this reason, attention to reducing or modifying unacceptable mannerisms whenever possible is recommended.

As described previously, it is important to conduct a functional analysis of the behavior to try to determine what function the behavior serves. Observations of the child in several situations may be needed in order to ascertain the pattern of behavior. Determining the purpose of the behavior often is difficult, because there may be multiple functions: 1) the behavior may provide sensory input, either because of too much or too little stimulation from the environment, 2) it may occur when preferred activities are not available, and 3) it may serve as means to increase or reduce a particular type of stimulation or activity (e.g., gain social attention or stop engagement in a disliked task). The function of the behavior has implications for the type of intervention needed.

The following techniques, in addition to many of the recommendations noted previously, should be considered depending on the individual child. Many of these techniques should be implemented with the support of a specialist with knowledge in the specific approach. A behavioral specialist, occupational therapist, speech therapist, early interventionist or early childhood special educator, or psychologist may be able to offer training and support to caregivers.

Interaction Strategies

1. *Teach the child how to play.* Children often engage in strange behaviors because they do not know how to play in more sophisticated ways. They need to learn how to observe others, imitate, take turns, and develop internal motivation to explore and use materials functionally. Adults can learn strategies to help children learn to play (see TPBI2, Chapter 7, Section V. Strategies for Improving Complexity of Play).

2. *Focus on building a positive relationship with the child.* Many children with behavioral issues have problems with skills necessary for developing a mutually caring relationship with caregivers. They lack joint attention, social referencing, ability to share eye contact, and other behaviors that build communication and interaction (see TPBI2, Chapter 7, Section IV. Strategies for Improving Social Cognition). Adults need to have patience, observe and follow the child's lead, and motivate the child to share interaction in pleasurable ways.

3. *Ignore behaviors done for attention.* Ignoring many stereotypical behaviors does not result in the diminishment of the actions. Unless the behaviors are done in an effort to seek attention from the adult, other methods may be preferable.

4. *Teach replacement behaviors.* When the child is over- or understimulated by a particular type of input, the child may produce unusual behaviors such as rocking back and forth, covering his ears, or screaming. Once the function of the child's actions is de-

termined, adults can teach children compensatory behaviors such as playing with a "fidget" toy, putting ear plugs in or wearing a hat with ear padding, or providing a quiet place for self-calming, such as a bean bag chair.

5. *Reinforce gradual progress.* Many mannerisms are difficult to change. For example, it may take many steps to get the child to stop touching her nose every time she is stressed. The adult may need to start with teaching a response to a specific question, such as, "Are you ready to try?" The adult can model and prompt the response. After the child is able to answer "Yes" or "No," the child may be ready for completing a starter sentence, such as "I want . . . ," for which the child fills in the blank. The adult may need to model and prompt actions or behaviors as well with children who are lower functioning.

6. *Provide alternative means of communication.* Actions are another form of communication, although the meaning of unusual behaviors often is difficult to interpret. Adults need to help children develop a "readable" communication system. This may involve words, gestures, signs, or pictures, depending on the child. Using behavioral shaping techniques (e.g., the child is reinforced for each closer approximation of a communication), play strategies (e.g., face-to-face or reciprocal physical games), and teaching functional communication approaches (e.g., helping the child acquire two-way communication in daily activities) may be used individually or in combination.

7. *Provide consistent responses.* Once a plan of action is developed for reducing the child's unacceptable mannerisms, it is important for all caregivers, at home, at child care, or in preschool, to maintain a consistent approach. Support may be needed to ensure that all parties are able to implement the plan.

Environmental Modifications

In addition to interpersonal strategies that may help reduce unusual mannerisms, environmental modifications often are useful. Depending on the findings from TPBA2, the team may want to consider some of the following environmental modifications.

1. *Structure the environment.* Try to reduce the amount of stimulation in the environment, have objects in predictable places, keep the routine predictable, and assist the child with transitions (see TPBI2, Chapter 5, Section II. Strategies for Improving Emotional Style/Adaptability).

2. *Limit access to materials or toys that provoke perseveration.* Children may perseverate because they receive pleasurable input from a behavior or the behavior blocks out other unpleasant stimuli. They may find certain materials or toys (e.g., things that spin) that provide opportunities for both pleasurable input and enable the child to block out unwanted stimuli. Some children become obsessed with finding and using these materials. Adults should limit access to these types of toys in order to help children learn new skills. New skills will not come, however, just by giving the child new toys. The adult needs to provide the incentive for alternative actions. Using the desired toys as reinforcement for engaging in another activity is sometimes effective.

3. *Use visuals to structure actions.* Using pictures, symbols, or other visuals such as those in social stories, PECS, or picture sequences, can be a reminder to children with unusual mannerisms that they need to redirect their behavior.

4. *Find a positive substitute for the behavior.* As described previously, most peculiar behaviors serve some function for the child. Adults need to find a functional way for the child to direct his or her actions. If a child likes to throw toys, the adults may want to find objects that are meant to be thrown and add a goal, such as throwing a ball in a

basket, through a hoop, with another person, or toward a target. The goal is to enable the child to discover that this action can be purposeful. Once the child learns to enjoy accomplishing the goal, other actions can then be added that also are easy to do and have a big result.

5. *Desensitize systems that are hypersensitive.* When behaviors are hypersensitive, the child may react with avoidance, bizarre behaviors, or stereotypies. Adults, with the help of professionals, may be able to reduce the child's sensitivity through a program directed at the particular sensory area involved. For example, an occupational therapist may support the adults in implementing a program to reduce tactile sensitivity; a speech-language pathologist or audiologist may implement a program for auditory sensitivity; or a psychologist may help implement a program to desensitize children about specific anxieties.

ROUTINES FOR THE CHILD WHO NEEDS SUPPORT TO REGULATE BEHAVIOR

It is important for adults to recognize the difference between issues of compliance with social conventions or values, concerns with issues of right and wrong, and mannerisms that are not problematic in terms of social conventions or right and wrong but are impulsive mannerisms that hinder the child's functioning or negatively influence the perception of others. Each of these may be handled in different ways as the child goes through daily activities. Just saying "no" may help the child stop a behavior in a particular situation, but it does not help the child learn which alternative behaviors would be better and why. Some compulsive behaviors may not be influenced by verbal strategies alone, but require environmental modifications as well.

Daily Routines (Home and Classroom)

Feeding/Eating

Many children are picky eaters; do unusual things with food, such as not letting two different foods touch; or demonstrate poor manners. These behaviors may be irritating to parents, but they are not unacceptable or wrong. Parents may tolerate unusual eating habits or insist on following family values regarding how one eats. It may be hard to explain why it is important to use a napkin, but even saying, "Thank you for using your napkin and being so polite," tells the child what is expected. Issues of compliance often relate to sitting at the table for a period of time, eating a variety of foods, not being "silly," and so forth. More at issue are behaviors such as throwing a utensil at someone (except for infants) and sharing or stealing food (seen in children with Prader-Willi syndrome). Issues of right and wrong at mealtimes for children with special needs may be handled by modeling, shaping, rewarding good behavior, and teaching why certain behaviors are expected. Conditions such as Prader-Willi may require locking up food and other environmental changes in addition to interpersonal strategies.

Diapering/Toileting

As with mealtimes, many behaviors are culturally imposed and relate to health (e.g., washing hands) and socially expected actions (e.g., in most Western cultures, toileting in private, not in public). Unusual mannerisms may relate to rituals the child must follow, or behaviors with fecal material (e.g., smearing). Depending on the reason for the behavior, they may be dealt with using behavioral shaping, positive behavioral supports, or even medication (e.g., for some children with obsessive-compulsive disorder). Compliance issues concerning when and how to use the bathroom facilities develop as the child begins the independent toileting process. Behaviors of right and wrong may occur as children experiment with putting objects (or pets!) in the toilet. Discussion of alternative behaviors, reasons for the behaviors, and support of positive efforts is recommended; for example, "Toys go in the toy box, pee and poop go in the toilet. Let's put the toys in the box." After the child uses the toilet and starts to put wads of toilet paper into the toilet, the parent might say, "Just a little toilet paper. Too much will break the potty, and daddy will not be happy."

Dressing

Most of the conventions around dressing are social conventions related to weather, style, and cleanliness. Unusual behaviors might include only wearing certain types or colors of clothing, not allowing certain textures to touch the skin, or rigidity about how and where dressing takes place. As the child matures into preschool years, dressing behaviors that are considered wrong (in most Western cultures) involve exposing genital areas for others to see. Children who have been sexually abused may develop provocative behaviors with their clothing. Adults need to address appropriate ways for the child to get adult attention and at the same time address the issues of right and wrong and how even adults do bad things. Acknowledgment of adult wrongdoing is important and opens up opportunities for adults to discuss why certain behaviors are wrong. Adult modeling also is important in the area of dressing and grooming.

Going Out

Children with emotional and behavioral concerns often have difficulty when they go out to public places. In these situations, a child's routines are altered and his or her comfort zone is exceeded. At the same time, children are required to remember and follow rules for public places that may be different from their rules at home; for instance, they may be required to sit still and be quiet. Patterns are difficult to change and impulses tough to fight when one is young. A variety of strategies may help the child control behaviors: 1) prepare the child for going out by talking about how to behave before the behavior is needed, 2) provide something for the child to do that is an alternative to negative behavior (e.g., a coloring book or toy for a restaurant), 3) reward approximations of good behavior before the behavior escalates, 4) provide verbal and nonverbal cues to help the child remember what he is supposed to do, 5) point out when the child is behaving as expected and the effect (e.g., "Thank you for helping me find the right groceries. You are being so helpful! We will get to the park soon"). Use social stories to guide behavior.

Play Routines (Home and Classroom)

Face-to-Face Play

Face-to-face play involves conventions related to how close each partner gets to the other, whether and how touching can take place, and how much intensity is involved in the interaction. Right and wrong may involve interactions that are intentionally harmful, such as hitting the parent. Parents usually control this behavior by helping the child know what is or is not acceptable and physically moderating the child's actions. When hurtful behaviors such as hitting, head banging, or other harmful reactions occur, adults may begin to refrain from allowing this type of play. Because face-to-face play can support the development of attachment, eye contact, turn-taking, language, and playful social interactions, it is important to determine how to transform this type of play into a pleasurable activity for the child that is not stressful or harmful for the caregivers. The first step is to determine what aspects of the play (e.g., social distance, avoidance of eye contact, tactile interaction, control issues) are contributing to the child's negative behaviors. Moderation of these factors can help reduce negative reactions and behaviors in face-to-face play. Such one-on-one play can provide opportunities for the adult to introduce, monitor, and reinforce desired actions and responses.

Physical Play

Infants explore each other with physical play, crawling over each other, hugging, and playing. As they get older, they begin to discover that this type of play can have either a positive or a negative impact on their peers. As with face-to-face play, physical play can stimulate behavior problems. Physical play tends to arouse emotions and energy. Simple chase games can become aggressive and turn into fights or verbal or physical bullying for children with disabilities. Adults can support children in this type of play by having a few simple rules such as "Listen to you friend"; "Stop when the other person says, 'Stop'"; and "Share and take turns." The rules should tell children what to do, not just what not to do. Structure physical play through turns for children who have difficulty with impulse control or emotional regulation. Give children opportunities to practice impulse control with games requiring stopping and starting on command, such as the game Statue, in which the adult lets children run around and act silly and then stop where they are when the adult shouts, "Freeze!" They then stay that way until the adult says, "Go!" Social stories also are helpful for negative actions that recur in physical play.

Manipulative Play

Manipulative play presents many opportunities for caregivers to support the child in learning to respond to requests, understand right and wrong, control impulses, and reduce nonproductive mannerisms. Children with disabilities may not use the toys in traditional ways, and they may engage in more mouthing of the toys, throwing, or compulsive actions such as spinning, lining up the toys, and so forth. Here, the adult's challenge is to help the child transform these nonproductive mannerisms into actual play. Redirecting, modeling, or structuring the play may help give the child new patterns. Adult support is important while new skills are being acquired.

Another behavioral issue often seen with children with limited cognitive, language, and/or emotional and social skills is lack of understanding of the rights of others. Although all children struggle to learn sharing and respect for others' property, children with disabilities may not understand the reasons for rules relating to hurting others, stealing, or lying. They may become attached to favorite toys and see no reason why they should not take the toys home. They may want a toy with which another child is playing and just take it. The adult needs to use language and sentence structure that the child can understand in order to make requests and explain why certain behaviors are right or wrong, model use of language instead of negative actions, prompt appropriate interaction with toys and people, and reinforce the child's efforts to act appropriately.

Sensory Play

Sensory play presents many opportunities for children to control their impulses. Many parents have strict restrictions on what children can do in messy situations; for example, playdough can only be used at the kitchen table; the child can only play in the water in the play pool, not in puddles; and so forth. Family values tend to play an important part in how much sensory play is presented or tolerated. As sensory exploration leads to understanding of many concepts, environmental structuring can help children benefit from the experience but also keep within the boundaries of cultural expectations. Provide parameters for where sensory play takes place, and help children learn to stay within those parameters. As with physical play, sensory play can easily escalate into frenzied activity in which actions are difficult to control. Structure and guidance help keep it under control. In addition, it is important to involve the child in talking about why certain actions are necessary.

Dramatic Play

Dramatic play provides many opportunities for discussing reasons for actions, role playing appropriate actions and responses, and letting children be in control of social interactions. As early as 1 year, infants begin acting out routines such as eating. Adults can begin to help them think about their own actions as they play with dolls and act out routines. For example, during doll play, children reenact the social conventions of the home, such as changing diapers or sitting on a potty. They also reenact their understanding of right and wrong. For instance, the child might tell the doll to go to time out for "being naughty." As children begin to play with each other in dramatic play, cooperation is necessary, conflicts over toys and actions arise, and children have an opportunity to practice many behavioral patterns. Adults can use this time to help children think about their actions, role play using social conventions, respond to others' requests, and problem solve how to deal with conflicts and issues of right and wrong.

Reading and Learning Routines

Circle Time

Teachers often struggle with behavior during circle time, because the expectation is that children sit quietly, respond to the teacher's requests, refrain from bothering other children, and attend until circle time is over. This is challenging for all young children, but it is particularly challenging for young children who may have attention deficits, cognitive or language concerns that impair comprehension, sensory disorders that result in over- or understimulation during this time, or emotional and social issues that make participation in this type of structured activity difficult. Difficulties that may arise during this time include lack of adherence to social conventions such as interrupting, talking too loud, not waiting one's turn, or intruding on another child's space. Unusual mannerisms may include behaviors such as chewing on collars, making unusual noises or repeating the teacher's phrases, or flapping hands or fingers. Behaviors that are considered helpful or harmful to others during circle time fall into the right and wrong behavior category. Considerations for dealing with these issues include environmental modifications such as how the child is seated and where the child is seated in relation to adults and children, giving the child visual or auditory prompts as needed, reinforcing appropriate behavior, pairing the child with a peer for modeling and support, use of alternative sensory input (e.g., something appropriate to chew on), involving the child in a meaningful and developmentally appropriate way to divert attention from distractions, and so forth.

One-on-One Book Reading

Behaviors in one-on-one reading time usually relate to social conventions, such as attending to the whole book, to the child's behaviors with the book (e.g., tearing pages) or to the child's behaviors toward the person reading the book (e.g., hitting, head banging). One-on-one book reading provides opportunities to gradually increase the child's attention, increase appreciation of toys and materials as someone's property, improve listening and responding to requests (e.g., "Show me the duck"), increase turn-taking (e.g., "Now it's your turn to tell *me* what's happening on the page"), and reduce unusual mannerisms (e.g., licking the pages). The intimate nature of the reading process allows the parent to introduce requests, limits, and rules in a safe, nurturing way and to reinforce appropriate actions and responses on the part of the child.

Science and Math

Centers or activities involving investigation, explanation, or independent learning provide a challenge for children with attentional issues, limited problem-solving skills, lack of conceptual understanding, or lack of motivation. Teachers should ensure that activities can be modified so children can benefit at their own developmental level. Behavior problems often arise because the child does not understand the activity or is not motivated to participate. This means that some activities that involve analysis of concepts will be modified for lower functioning children to be more exploratory in nature and result in attainment of simple vocabulary comprehension, rather than a comparative or process analysis. For example, instead of asking the child to categorize which objects sink or float, the child might investigate the characteristics of the water (e.g., it is wet, it drips, it moves). Visual steps (action picture cards) or auditory aids (audiotaped assistance) may help the child reduce negative behaviors resulting from lack of understanding or interest. Peer pairing also can help the child learn through modeling, especially if the peer is trained in how to respond to the child's unusual or negative actions or responses.

BRICE

Brice is a 28-month-old boy who exhibits characteristics of Asperger syndrome. He reads some words, loves taking things apart and putting them back together, and is enthralled with books about machines. At the same time, Brice has little tolerance for doing what he is asked; rebels at changes in his routine; and shows displeasure by screaming, head banging, and pushing his fists into his eyes. When asked to do something he is not interested in, he starts flapping his hands and screaming. His parents are pleased with Brice's curious nature, but they are upset by his behavior. He is difficult to take into public places because of his tantrums, which seem to exceed the number, duration, and intensity of those of typical 2-year-olds. He shows no interest in other children and does not react to his parents' displeasure or unhappiness. His parents' priority at this point is for Brice to gain some control over his behavior and to begin to care about the feelings of others.

The following are environmental and interpersonal recommendations made as part of Brice's intervention plan.

Interaction Strategies

1. *Prepare for changes in Brice's routine (see strategies in TPBI2, Chapter 5, Section II. Strategies for Improving Emotional Style/Adaptability).*

2. *Capture Brice's attention and use exaggerated facial expressions; position yourself so that Brice can see your face.*

3. *Model using a soft, gentle voice and speak slowly. Use short, clear statements when making requests.*

4. *When you make a request, help Brice get started with the first action or word needed in the activity you want.*

5. *State what you want him to do in the positive. Rather than saying, "Brice, stop screaming," tell him what you want him to do instead: "Brice, tell Mommy what you want."*

6. *Reward Brice when he responds to requests and does not overreact. Acknowledge what he did (e.g., "Thank you, Brice. You brought me your coat" or "That was great! You used words and didn't scream").*

7. *Behaviors such as flapping allow Brice to avoid activities he dislikes. Redirect him when he begins flapping by introducing something he enjoys into the undesired activity; for example, if he does not want to take a bath and starts to flap, let him take his wooden screws and bolts with him into the tub.*

Environmental Modifications

1. *Maintain a predictable routine for Brice.*

2. *Introduce picture cues, picture sequences, signs, and gestures to help Brice when you are making a request for a new activity.*

3. *Use social stories with pictures or drawings to help Brice change his behavior. Introduce stories about screaming, head banging, and eye pushing one at a time. As changes in behavior stabilize, introduce a social story about another behavior. Include an alternative acceptable behavior in each story, so Brice has a way to express frustration or anger.*

4. *Introduce dramatic play with dolls during daily routines. Include short "scripts" including what to say in certain situations, such as mealtimes, toileting, meeting new people, and so forth. By modeling the actions and phrases used in social situations with a doll (e.g., "please," "thank you," "I'm finished," "I need the toilet"), Brice can practice using the terms. Dramatic play with an adult also will prepare him for play with peers.*

5. *Give Brice a wind-up toy, tiny Rubik's cube, or some small mechanical device that he likes to carry in his pocket. The object can be introduced when you anticipate a meltdown and can potentially replace negative reactions with functional play.*

6. *Use picture books and stories about emotions and behaviors. Relate them to Brice's emotions and behaviors as well as those of other family members.*

REFERENCE

Gray, C. (1993). *The original social story book.* Arlington, TX: Future Horizons.

RESOURCES

Web Sites

The Alliance for Technology Access
  http://www.ataccess.org

Early Connections: Technology in Early Childhood Education
  http://www.netc.org/earlyconnections

Phonak Hearing Systems
  http://www.phonak.com

Stokes, S. (2000). *Assistive technology for children with autism.* Cooperative Education Service Agency 7, Wisconsin Department of Public Instruction. Retrieved June 15, 2007 from http://www.specialed.us/autism/assist/asst10.htm

Yahoo! Groups: Classroom Acoustics (online discussion group/mailing list) http://groups.yahoo.com/subscribe/classroomacoustics

Books

Adams, S.K., & Baronberg, J. (2004). *Promoting positive behavior: Guidance strategies for early childhood settings.* Upper Saddle River, NJ: Merrill/Prentice Hall.

Chesebrough, E., King, P., & Gulotta, T.P. (2006). *A blueprint for promotion of prosocial behavior in early childhood.* New York: Kluwer Academic/Plenum Publishing.

Notbohm, E., & Zysk, V. (2004). *1001 great ideas for teaching and raising children with autism.* Arlington, TX: Future Horizons.

KEYS TO INTERVENTION BY DEVELOPMENTAL AGE

The following ideas are directed toward children who are functioning at approximately the following levels. The suggestions are not meant to be all-inclusive, but rather are indicative of potential areas for exploration.

Developmental age	Behavior	Keys to intervention
Birth to 3 months	Expects feeding and cries when hungry. Can be calmed by adult with voice, holding, and movement. Has eating routines. Stops actions to listen to adult.	Help the child anticipate results through consistent responses to needs. Talk to the child when interacting (feeding, diapering) and respond with increased affect when the child is listening.
3–6 months	Begins to self-calm. Protests when toys are taken. Resists unwanted actions or objects.	Watch for what helps the child self-calm. Provide those elements to help the child. Respond to child's protests when the situation allows (e.g., "You want to stay in the water longer? Okay. One more minute") and explain when it does not (e.g., "I know you like your bath, but it's time for bed. Tomorrow is another bath").
6–9 months	Cries or calls for attention. Begins to understand "no." Responds to adults' facial expressions meant to control behavior.	Initially, "no" with a facial expression is sufficient. Explanations will not be understood. Too much language may overshadow the issue.
9–12 months	Acts for adult attention. Reads adults' facial expressions to see if they are upset. Follows simple commands.	As the child begins to understand simple requests, add a request to the "no"; for example, "No. Give that to mommy." Then reinforce the response: "Thank you!"
12–18 months	Has awareness of results of own behaviors. Understands "no"; beginning understanding of "right" and "wrong." Throws temper tantrums to get own way. Will help someone who is hurt.	Children's growing language enables simple discussion of right and wrong by talking about other's feelings: "Tess is sad because you took her toy." Support activities that encourage turn-taking. "You can have it for one more minute, then it's Sophie's turn."
18–24 months	Tattles on self. Shows anger in physical ways. Can control emotions. Knows and verbalizes many behaviors he should or should not do.	Reinforce recognition of wrong behaviors (e.g., "That's right. The doggy was naughty to bite"). Help the child substitute words for anger (e.g., "Tell her, 'No, I don't like that'").

(continued on next page)

Developmental age	Behavior	Keys to intervention
18–24 months (*continued*)	Complies about 45% of the time. Can delay gratification.	Provide simple ways for the child to comply successfully (e.g., put out your hand while saying, "I'll take that cookie you took") and reward efforts with attention (e.g., "Thank you. You deserve a kiss for helping"). Reinforce waiting, but don't delay gratification for an extended time (e.g., "You have been quiet down two aisles in the grocery store. Here is a snack for you").
24–36 months	Knows rules, values, standards of family. Uses words to describe good and bad behavior. Shows remorse. Knows how to help others, share, cooperate. Begins to internalize rules, but has difficulty transferring them across settings. Needs adult to help control impulses. Tries to "fix" something done wrong.	Children of this age can begin to discuss behavior and why some actions are hurtful or helpful (e.g., "You helped pick up, so now we have more time to read"). State rules in simple, positive terms (e.g., "We share toys"). Repeat rules in different settings to help children transfer understanding. Help children anticipate situations that will tempt behaviors, give alternatives (e.g., "We are going to Sara's, and I know you will want to play with her toys, so let's take a few of your toys to share with her"). Allow the child to help "fix" situations rather than punish (e.g., "I know you didn't mean to break his toy, so let's see if we can glue it together").
36–48 months	Can discriminate acceptable behaviors, dos and don'ts, and right and wrong. Argues and negotiates what he can do with adult. Complies about 80% of the time.	Watch and talk about behaviors of others, and book and movie characters. Note when characters display good behaviors and when they do bad things; talk about what else they could have done. Begin to use examples to illustrate right and wrong.
48–60 months	Judges what is right and wrong by what gets punished. Knows what behaviors to show with a friend, although does not always follow them.	When someone does something wrong, ask the child why it is wrong or explain why it is wrong. Keep it brief. When rules are broken, ask the child to explain what happened, what rule was broken, and how things should change.
60–72 months	Has values related to right and wrong. Thinks justice is unchangeable. Can negotiate with an adult both actions and consequences. Begins to understand others' reasoning.	Talk about how actions can be right in one situation and not in another (e.g., noisy in the park, but not in church). Encourage discussion and negotiation, but keep limits consistent. Do not change the rules or consequences because you feel sorry for the child. Let children help determine what the consequences for misdeeds should be.

5

Facilitating Emotional and Social Development

V. Strategies for Improving Sense of Self

Goal Attainment Scale

1	2	3	4	5	6	7	8	9
Is dependent on others to meet needs.		Tries to access toys and people, shows adults objects, and smiles when others respond to his or her actions. Does not request assistance when needed.		Focuses on specific goals related to movement, objects, or interactions with people. Often requests help or needs reinforcement to maintain effort.		Is motivated to independently reach multiple types of goals, is persistent, confident, and pleased with successful efforts. Knows when help is needed.		Is goal-oriented, persists in the face of challenges, feels confident of success, and proud of accomplishments. Aware of own strengths and weaknesses.

As children gain the ability to move, engage their environment, and interact with others, they begin to explore the limits of their abilities and challenge themselves to learn and accomplish even more. They acquire a desire for independence, and, as they gain an understanding of their skills and their self-confidence increases, children also develop a desire to make decisions for themselves.

The term *sense of self*, as used in TPBA2 and TPBI2, includes autonomy, achievement motivation, and identity. Adults need to promote a positive sense of self—one in which children desire to do things independently, are persistent in trying to accomplish goals, and have a good attitude about who they are and what they can do. Children with disabilities, who have challenges with independence, achievement of mastery, or feeling capable in various roles, may need support to develop a positive sense of themselves.

APPROPRIATE SENSE OF SELF

Babies develop new capabilities with each passing day and increasingly become more aware of and pleased with their accomplishments. Infants first begin to do things to get a response from the special adults in their lives. Soon, however, they are practicing new skills, exploring, and trying out novel actions for the sheer joy of the feeling of accomplishment. By the second half of the second year of life, knowledge of a categorical self, or understanding of one's age, gender, physical characteristics, "goodness" and "badness," and things one can do begins to develop. Self-concept develops as children begin to place a value on these concrete attributes, their abilities, and their beliefs.

Children who have a positive sense of self generally feel good about themselves. They understand that there are things they can do and things they cannot, but they continually challenge these limits cognitively, physically, and/or socially. No one is good at everything, but a child with a positive sense of self understands that capacity for growth is not limited.

Appropriate Sense of Self in Practice

▓▓▓▓ **V. A. How does the child demonstrate autonomy and a desire to make decisions consistent with the culture of the family?**

Daily Routines (Home and Classroom)

- *Infant/toddler:* The infant turns his head away when the parent offers mashed peas, indicating his preference. The toddler is told it is time to leave the toys and go eat. She starts to scream, "No eat! I want to play more!"

- *Young child:* The young child independently goes to the toilet, washes his hands, and returns to the group.

Play Routines (Home and Classroom)

- *Infant/toddler:* The infant is throwing a ball at the television. Her father says, "Throw me the ball." The infant smiles and throws it at the television again. The toddler is playing with plastic kitchen toys. His mother says, "I'd like a hamburger." The toddler shakes his head and says, "We don't have hamburgers."

- *Young child:* The young child is building an elaborate airport tower with blocks. A peer starts to take some blocks down, but she says, "No. Control towers are tall. Leave it tall like I made it."

Classroom Routines

The young child chooses a center to go to and independently begins to construct his project. He looks at the other children's materials, picks some of the same materials and some different ones.

▓▓▓▓ **V. B. How does the child demonstrate achievement motivation?**

Daily Routines (Home and Classroom)

- *Infant/toddler:* The infant crawls to high chair and struggles to pull herself to standing. She then looks at her mother and smiles. The toddler is putting on his jacket and when his father tries to help, he says, "No, me do it."

- *Young child:* The young child comes to breakfast, saying, "Look, Dad, I got up and got dressed all by myself!"

Play Routines (Home and Classroom)

- *Infant/toddler:* The infant is hitting a toy that spins when hit. She repeats the action 10 times before shifting attention. The toddler is at the park and having difficulty going up the ladder on the slide. When his mother tries to lift him up, he pushes her away and goes back to the steps.

- *Young child:* The young child is acting out the story of the three little pigs. "Now you go over there and pretend to blow the house down. You have to blow real hard!"

Classroom Routines

The young child sits at the table with her drawing and laboriously, but carefully, writes her name. When she is not satisfied, she erases what she did and starts the letter over again.

V. C. What developmentally relevant characteristics related to self can the child identify?

Daily Routines (Home and Classroom)

- *Infant/toddler:* At bath time, the infant points to and says, "eyes," "nose," "mouth." While dressing, the toddler tells her mother, "You are a girl and I am a girl. Girls can wear dresses."

- *Young child:* The young child is running around the gym. He shouts at his teacher, "I'm really a good runner and I can jump really high. Watch me!"

Play Routines (Home and Classroom)

- *Infant/toddler:* The infant is climbing up and down the stairs. When she gets to the top, she turns her body around and goes down feet first. The toddler is running in circles, laughing and then falling down. She shouts, "I like to be silly!"

- *Young child:* The young child is in the dramatic play area. He says, "I am the father and you are the mother. And he is our baby. I have to go to work now. I'll be home soon."

Classroom Routines

The young child is sitting in circle time. The teacher asks, "Is anybody here afraid of something?" He responds, "I'm afraid of the dark. I get scared."

GENERAL PRINCIPLES FOR SUPPORTING APPROPRIATE SENSE OF SELF

Adults do many conscious and unconscious things that have an impact on the child's sense of self. Comments that make the child feel like he or she is not capable or competent are harmful to sense of self. Not allowing the child to experience challenge or failure build a false sense of self or make the child feel like he or she cannot succeed in challenging circumstances. Providing too much support or reinforcing minimal effort can do the same. Caregivers walk a fine line when trying to provide just the right amount of challenge, support, and encouragement.

Note Positives

Adults frequently make comments that influence a child's perception of him- or herself. Noting the child's positive characteristics and remarking on skills and abilities lets the child know his or her strengths. For example, the parent might say, "You are such a good artist!" If the child accepts the statement as true, this comment may contribute to the child feeling good about his drawing ability.

Praise Accomplishments

Children love to receive praise for their accomplishments. Caregivers of infants will clap, exclaim, show excitement, and give affection when new skills are seen. As the child grows older, verbal reinforcement becomes more common, and physical hugs and excitement become more subdued. The child begins to listen to what the adult says that acknowledges that the child is a good person, a capable person, and/or a worthy person. The adult may say, for example, "Good for you. You did it!"

Comment to Others

Children are always listening to the comments of others. As they grow older they become more sensitive to what others are saying about them. Adults may even make comments to others with the intention of conveying a message indirectly to their child; for instance, "I am so proud of Alejandro. He knows all of his letters and numbers and he loves books!"

Present a Slight Challenge

Children will make an effort if they feel they can do something. If they do not understand a task or feel they cannot do it, they will turn to something within their comfort zone. Caregivers typically know what the child can do and offer activities that are within the child's capabilities but still offer some challenge. For example, the parent might observe that the child is beginning to pull to stand. The parent will then provide incentives to encourage the child to try to do more. The parent may move a favorite toy from the floor up to the couch, which is higher than the child has pulled up before.

Provide Opportunities

Parents often try to provide opportunities for their child outside of the experiences they have at home. They may provide religious or social opportunities, lessons, or other types of adventures for the child to be able to acquire new attitudes, values, knowledge, or skills. For example, 3-year-old Jalaya's foster mother is sending her to preschool to give her social experiences, taking her to Sunday school to give her an understanding of her place in a spiritual world, and having her take a gymnastics class at the local recreation center to hone her advanced motor skills.

THE PRINCIPLES IN PRACTICE

Adults use a variety of strategies to support the child's attention for social and learning purposes. The following are examples of how caregivers use the previously described strategies during the day both at home and at school. These examples are approaches that most caregivers use naturally in their daily interactions with children. They are appropriate for most children with disabilities as well.

Daily Routines (Home and Classroom)

Feeding/Eating

Parents often use mealtimes as a time to let children choose what they like to eat, challenge them to try new things, and acknowledge their independent eating skills. For example, the parent may say, "Here is some chicken. You love chicken, and you can stab it with your fork."

Diapering/Toileting

Accomplishment of independent toileting is a major milestone for both a child and his or her parents. This is an area of development for which most children get much encouragement and reinforcement. The child typically feels a great sense of accomplishment and pride when this task is mastered. Adults support this process by having expectations that the child can accomplish the task, and by directing, helping, encouraging, and reinforcing the child's efforts and accomplishments. For example, "I know you can tinkle in the potty. Sit down here and I will listen for you to tinkle. Keep trying. You can do it! Yeah! I hear it. You did it!"

Dressing

Dressing independently often is initiated by the child and supported by parents. The child will offer a limb for placement in an article of clothing and the parent will then encourage the child to take the next step in terms of pushing the arm or leg in the garment. They will then move to having the child find the right "hole" for his or her head, arm, or leg by placing the object in such a way that the child has a clue to the correct response. Such gradual approximation helps the child learn to be successful in a step-by-step sequence.

Play Routines (Home and Classroom)

Face-to-Face Play

In face-to-face games, parents expect the child to respond with smiles, vocalizations, or actions. They position the child in such a way to ensure observation and interaction and then model, wait, and encourage the child to make a response. These games let the child know that turn-taking and social interactions are fun, and this encourages the child to watch others and imitate them. Such games also prompt children to initiate social interaction themselves and lead to children feeling confidence about their ability to interact. The adult promotes confidence by initiating, responding to, or supporting the child's efforts. For example, when the infant bounces on the bed and raises a finger to the parent, the adult may say, "Oh, you want to do 'monkeys jumping on the bed'? Let's sing it."

Physical Play

Physical play involves give-and-take and also enables the child to feel power and control. As the child sees the adult respond to his or her actions, the child begins to understand how one can influence the actions of another. For example, when the toddler runs away from her parent, stops, turns, looks back to see if her parent is following, then runs off again laughing, the child is learning that others care about what she is doing, that she can be a leader, and that successful interaction is emotionally rewarding.

Manipulative Play

Toy play can be done either in isolation or with others. In both instances, the child can enhance his sense of self. When the child plays alone, experiments, and finds solutions, the reward of accomplishment typically does not need adult reinforcement. The pleasure the child feels is reward in itself. Social play with toys involves other aspects, because the person playing with the child provides some type of feedback relating to how the play is going. With adults, this may be through directing, commenting on actions, or reinforcing successful play attempts. For instance, the adult might say, "Here comes my car. Oh, no! My car stopped. Where can I get gas? Oh, great, you have gas! Thank you for helping me! You are a nice person." This type of play enables the child to play out being competent, helpful, or knowledgeable and also lets the child play a leadership or collaborative role in play, contributing to a positive sense of self.

Sensory Play

Adult tolerance of messy play gives children the message that they can extend the boundaries of their play in many acceptable directions for self-expression. When messy play turns into creative, artistic endeavors, children then learn that these parameters can be contained and directed in another form of self-expression that others can understand and appreciate. Artistic expression in visual, physical, or auditory forms all can help children feel creative, appreciated, and powerful. The adult's response can tell children that they have talent and/or can communicate ideas or emotions. For example, "I love the way you made the sun orange. It reminds me of a sunrise or sunset."

Reading and Learning Routines

Circle Time

Teachers often use circle time as a time for children to express what they know, how they feel, or what they can do. During this time, the teacher can support each child's efforts at expression, level of understanding of a topic, and skill in various actions in which the group may participate. For example, the teacher may say, "Selina, that was a great idea," "Jeremy, thank you for telling us about your trip to Utah," or "Watch Brian. He can really dance fast."

One-on-One Book Reading

Whether looking at pictures in a book or helping the child try to sound out words on the page, one-to-one book reading provides many opportunities for supporting the child's feeling of accomplishment, reinforcing expression and social interaction, and acknowledging knowledge. At every level, from making sounds and labeling pictures, to describing actions and events, to telling stories and actually reading words, adults can help children feel good about what they know and how they express what they know. The parent of an infant says, "Yes, the cow says, 'Moo.'" The parent of a toddler says, "I think you are right. He is not a nice monster." The parent of the beginning reader says, "Sound it out. Yes! It says 'food.'" All of these comments tell children that they are competent and should feel good about their efforts.

Science and Math

Math and science involve the development of a conceptual system, from the very simplistic level of understanding single entities to more complex comprehension of interrelationships and systems. Adults typically help children learn certain concepts, such as counting numbers and stating the alphabet, through rote memorization. They also provide opportunities for children to use the skills they are acquiring in everyday life; for instance, "There are four of us for dinner tonight. Can you take four napkins and put one on each plate? Nice job of setting the table!" or "What letter is that on the stop sign? Yes, an 'S.'" Letting children demonstrate their knowledge and skills helps to build their confidence.

PLANNING INDIVIDUALIZED INTERVENTIONS FOR IMPROVING SENSE OF SELF

Children who have difficulty functioning in any developmental domain are at risk for having a more negative sense of self than children who are typically developing. Particularly if they have the ability to understand their limitations, children with developmental differences may compare themselves to others and feel that they are not "smart," "popular," "athletic," and so forth. In order to develop a positive sense of self, they need to discover and feel good about their abilities and understand how they can compensate for the areas that are more challenging. Adults play an important role in helping children to discover their capabilities, to become more independent, to be persistent in achieving their goals, and to feel good about what they *can* do. The following suggestions may be helpful when interacting with children who need to develop a positive sense of self.

▆▆▆▆ V. A. How does the child demonstrate autonomy and a desire to make decisions, consistent with the culture of family?

Children with disabilities may be more dependent on adults to assist them in their daily functioning. Adults may do anything from making small decisions for the child, such as picking what he will wear, to assisting with major tasks, such as feeding or helping him move through the environment. They may talk "for" the child or respond to any small gesture he makes by giving him what they think he wants or needs. Although this may seem necessary, it also can lead to the child feeling helpless and incapable.

Children who are more dependent on others also may be provided fewer opportunities to try new experiences or interact with peers. Adults may make the assumption that such occurrences will not be beneficial for the child and, therefore, are not worth the effort to plan and implement. However, reduced experiences with objects, people, and events mean fewer opportunities to make decisions and attempt independence. Children become used to the routines of home and school and how they are done. If others do things for them, this becomes an accepted pattern. Breaking out of that pattern requires effort on the part of both the child and the adults in the child's life.

Interaction Strategies

1. *Let the child make decisions.* Even infants have preferences and will look longer at the object in which they are interested. Children who cannot express their desires can be given visual options. If a child's eyes rest on one option longer, tell the child, "You want the blue shirt." Soon the child will begin to understand that his or her eyes are guiding the decision. For children who can communicate with gesture, sounds, or words, adults should let the child make choices at every acceptable opportunity. Even in situations in which the child does not have a choice (e.g., going out on errands, taking a bath), the adult can provide an acceptable option to enable the child to make a decision. For example, "Do you want to take a book or a toy in the car?" or "Do you want bubbles in the tub?" Being able to make decisions gives the child a feeling of control and is an important step toward building confidence.

2. *Break down the task.* Think about all of the elements of a given task from beginning to end and determine if the child can do some element. The child may be able to do the first step (e.g., picking up the spoon and holding it), a middle step (e.g., holding the toothbrush under the water), or a final step (e.g., pulling the end of the sock off). Every step the child can do provides motivation for trying to do another step. The adult's role is to determine what aspect the child could try, to encourage effort, and to give attention and affection for any, even partial, success.

3. *Model slowly.* Adults often do activities with children at the speed at which they ordinarily perform the task. For some children this may be too fast, and they may miss the process that is involved and only see the final result. For example, if the adult quickly builds a tower of blocks, the child sees the final tower but does not understand the subtleties of how it was constructed. The adult needs to break the task down, move slowly, describe what is happening, and give the child a chance to imitate each step. For instance, "Look. I am putting this block on top very carefully. Now it's your turn.

Yes! Let's just fix it so it doesn't fall off. Now it's my turn. I'm going to put another block on—very carefully."

4. *Model actions that are slightly challenging.* Children need practice with skills they are mastering, but they also need opportunities to try things that extend their skills. Adults need to monitor what the child can do and then model a slightly more difficult action or add one more step to the sequence. For example, if the child can pull off the last 2 inches of his sock, the adult might increase the challenge by having the child help to pull *on* the last 2 inches of a sock. This requires a little more strength and persistence on the part of the child. If the child is playing by putting things *in* a box, the adult might model taking things *out* or *throwing* them in.

5. *Expand your expectations.* Children often are limited by our expectations. We do not expect the child to communicate, so we take pointing toward an object as sufficient communication. If adults believe the child can produce more independent functioning, they will offer a model for the child, provide a minimal prompt, and/or increase their wait time. Children will have less to overcome if they do not have to conquer our limiting attitudes as well as their own developmental challenges.

Environmental Modifications

In addition to interpersonal strategies that may support the child, environmental modifications often are useful. Depending on the findings from TPBA2, the team may want to consider some of the following environmental modifications.

1. *Modify the child's position or the placement of materials.* Some tasks, such as putting on a pair of pants, require balance and coordination that are difficult for a child. By not requiring the child to stand to do the task, the child can participate more fully. For example, if the child is sitting on the floor and the pants are laid out in front of him or her and are facing the proper direction, the child will be able to pull the pants over both feet and may be able to position a foot into each leg of the pants.

2. *Allow opportunities for experimentation.* Children with developmental challenges may need to experience an activity or event many more times than a typical child in order to achieve understanding or mastery. For this reason, adults should introduce opportunities for practice in as many situations as possible. If the child only goes outside once a day, there is only one opportunity per day to practice putting on a jacket. However, if that jacket is available in a play area or near a mirror, the child may be motivated to practice "for fun." Have functional items such as spoons, wash cloths, combs, and so forth available where the child plays. Such items can then be included in dramatic play or just be used in practice play.

3. *Build mastery motivation first on highly motivating tasks.* All children have preferences for different types of activities. Some like sensory or physical play, some like manipulatives, some like dramatic play, and so forth. Children will persist longer on tasks that are motivating to them. Adults use motivating activities to get children started on goal-oriented efforts. They can then interject activities that are more challenging and encourage the same type of effort. Preferred activities also can be used as reinforcement for persistence on a less preferred activity; for example, "As soon as you finish washing your hands, you can go play with your baby."

4. *Provide opportunities for play with peers who are slightly higher functioning.* Young children with disabilities, particularly children with multiple disabilities, often spend most of their time with adults such as parents or therapists. Interaction with adults tends to be more adult directed and task focused. For this reason, it is important for all

young children to have peer interactions in addition to adult interactions. Peers are more casual and more interesting models for children and thus may stimulate children with disabilities to try to communicate, to imitate the other child's actions, or to participate in some way independently. Adults need to ensure that children have opportunities to play with peers as well as siblings. Peers who are slightly higher functioning will provide a model at a level that is just the right challenge for the child.

5. *Provide adaptive materials.* Adaptive materials and equipment frequently can enable children to perform independently. A child might not be able to tie shoes or button a shirt, but he can close a Velcro fastener. An adaptive spoon can enable the child to hold a spoon, correctly direct the spoon, and feed himself. A light box may enable a child to see shapes and figures for play, an adaptive chair may enable a child to sit independently for activities, a switch on a tape recorder may enable a child to activate the device independently, and so forth. Adults need to analyze the activities that are challenging for the child and determine what adaptations within the environment may enable the child to be successful more easily. Consultation with an expert in assistive technology may be helpful.

V. B. How does the child demonstrate achievement motivation?

Mastery motivation is the child's desire to reach a goal and the ability to persist through obstacles to enable him or her to reach the goal. Children can have a high level of mastery motivation and not be particularly successful, but it is unusual for mastery motivation to be maintained in the face of constant failure. For this reason, children with disabilities, who may encounter failure frequently, are at risk for reduced mastery motivation, giving up, and having a poor self-concept. All of the above strategies for increasing autonomy also are relevant here, because the more independent the child is, the more mastery motivation will be rewarded. In addition, the following strategies are suggested to build the child's motivation and persistence.

Interaction Strategies

1. *Show excitement.* Mastery motivation involves a high degree of internal interest or excitement about the activity in which the child is involved. Some children may not have that internal drive initially. Adults can model interest and excitement in their interactions with the child. If the child sees that persisting toward a goal can be fun and result in rewarding outcomes, he or she is more likely to keep trying.

2. *Reward the child's effort.* Mastery motivation is as much about the effort as it is about accomplishing the final goal. Even if the goal is not attained, the child should feel satisfaction in the effort and actions along the way. In sports, they say, "It's not whether you win or lose, it's how you play the game." For children with disabilities, the effort is key to feelings of satisfaction and self-worth. Caregivers need to be cognizant of this and not just comment on the "good job," the "pretty picture," or the "tall tower." Comments that reinforce the child's effort and persistence are critical. For example, the adult might say, "I love to see you working so hard!" or "Keep trying, you're almost there!" or "You should be proud of yourself for not giving up!"

3. *Provide minimal prompts.* As described previously, autonomy is important to the child's view of herself. If adults offer too much assistance, it detracts from the child's feeling of accomplishment and belief in her own capabilities. Therefore, adults should only offer help when they believe the child needs support to persist in her efforts. When assistance is offered, it should be the least amount of support that will enable the child to get to the next step. For example, for a child with motor difficulties who is try-

ing to draw, this may mean providing a little support at the wrist, help with the grasp of the pencil, verbal direction, or just encouragement to keep going.

4. *Set small goals within the larger goal.* As children get older, the activities that they engage in become more complex and involve multiple steps to reach a goal. The puzzle is no longer just a circle shape that gets placed in a circle form board—now it is a picture puzzle with multiple pieces. Understanding how to get to the goal of completing the puzzle may be daunting for a child, and it is easier to give up and shift attention to another toy. To build mastery motivation, the adult can break the task down into smaller goals. If the puzzle has 10 pieces, for example, the adult might put out just two corner pieces and see if the child can find which corner each goes in. Next, the last two corners are put out for the child. The adult comments on the child's effort and successes. "I can see you are looking carefully at where that should go. Wow! You figured it out. You got that one really fast!" At the same time, the adult can provide minimal prompts to help the child. "I see eyes on this piece. Maybe you could find the face they go in."

5. *Help children set personal goals.* As soon as young children begin to communicate with action words, they can begin to set goals for themselves by identifying things they want to learn to do. Children are more motivated to accomplish their own goals than the goals adults set for them. Even if the child picks a goal that is way above his present level, the adult can help the child set up intermediate goals to get there. For example, Charlaine, a 4-year-old with cognitive and motor challenges, wanted to learn to write her name. Because she was just making scribbling marks on the paper, she and her teacher made a chart that had steps for her to accomplish on the way to writing her name. The chart included things such as drawing a line, drawing a curve, drawing a circle, and so forth. Charlaine practiced every day and stamped a "happy face" next to what she had done. She proudly took each paper home to show her family she was learning to write.

Environmental Modifications

In addition to interpersonal strategies that may support the child, environmental modifications often are useful. Depending on the findings from TPBA2, the team may want to consider some of the following environmental modifications.

1. *Modify the level of activities.* Sometimes the level of the materials or activities presented to children is too high. When this occurs, frustration results and mastery motivation dies. It is better to modify the materials for the child than to present something that is bound to be frustrating. In the example of the puzzle (see No. 4, above), if the parent or teacher knows that the child cannot manipulate small pieces or cannot understand how to match part to whole, it would be better to provide a lower level puzzle, one with separate spaces for the pieces or only two-part part-to-whole puzzles. As the child sees that putting together a recognizable piece is fun, puzzles of increasing difficulty can be introduced.

2. *Provide variety.* As noted previously, practice is important for the development of independent skills. However, practice does not have to involve the same materials every day. In fact, if children see the same puzzles, books, or toys every day, they may develop mastery over those specific materials, only to find that they do not know what to do with new puzzles, books, or toys. Generalization of skills is important for maintenance of mastery motivation. In addition, boredom often sets in once something has been mastered, and children may lose interest in these types of activities.

3. *Modify presentation of activities.* Many activities can be modified to keep them interesting and motivating. Eating, dressing, bathing, and other functional activities be-

come routine and boring. Adult creativity can go a long way toward keeping the child motivated to work toward mastery. For example, eating is difficult for Adam and he always wants to quit soon after he sits down. He has a plate with many animals on it, and his mother uses various strategies to motivate Adam to eat a whole meal. One technique is to "hide" an animal of Adam's choice by covering it with food. Adam then tries to "free" the animal by eating what is covering it. On another day, they took turns eating bites of waffle and pretending the bites were silly things. His mother said, "I'm eating a bite and it tastes like butterflies." Adam laughed, took a bite, and said, "Bugs!"

4. *Use adaptive devices.* As described previously, the child needs to be able to be at least partially successful to maintain motivation. Use whatever assistive devices are necessary to enable the child to function more easily.

████████ V. C. What developmentally relevant characteristics related to self can the child identify?

Knowledge of one's own and others' characteristics demonstrates self-awareness. Children begin to notice first the obvious physical characteristics and differences between themselves and others. As they mature, they notice more abstract characteristics such as being nice, sharing, and so forth. Helping children to develop an awareness of how they are similar to and different from others is an important part of developing one's self-concept. For children with disabilities, seeing other children who can do things that they cannot, watching other children receive praise and affection, and seeing other children selected as play partners may have a negative impact on their developing sense of self. Adults can help children gain an understanding of their personal characteristics, emphasizing positive attributes while at the same time helping children see how they are similar or different from others.

Interaction Strategies

1. *Label positive characteristics in functional situations.* As soon as babies are born, parents start talking to them about their characteristics, their eye color, body parts, what they like and do not like, and so forth. Children with cognitive disabilities may need to hear these descriptions more frequently and in functional situations such as bath time or mealtime. As the child matures, description of more abstract characteristics is important. Children need to understand when they are being nice, respectful, caring, friendly, helpful, and so forth. Point out the positive instead of the negative. "Thank you for being helpful. That makes two times today that you were helpful—just now when you brought me your napkin and this morning when you took off your own pajamas." Note that this statement 1) points out a positive characteristic; 2) points out behaviors that are considered helpful; 3) does not describe the times the child was not helpful; and 4) reinforces the positive behaviors. After many such incidents, children often will begin to identify and classify their own behaviors. "See, Mommy, I'm being helpful."

2. *Talk about abilities.* In addition to talking about positive traits, adults need to help the child understand what skills he or she *can* do. Children with disabilities often have a self-image that is shaped by their *dis*-ability. Adults can help children see that they have many capabilities. As noted previously, having children identify their own goals helps build mastery motivation. Personal goal setting also can help children see the skills they have accomplished. In addition, caregivers and teachers can point out new skills to the child. "You are becoming so independent. You pick out your own clothes now, get dressed by yourself, brush your own teeth, go to the toilet alone. I am very proud of you for doing so many things all by yourself."

3. *Be honest about disabilities.* Unless they are severely disabled, most children are very aware of what they do well and what they cannot do. It does not do any good to pretend that the child is exactly like all other children. What the adult can do is point out the ways in which the child *is* like other children and then talk about ways the child is different. It is important that the differences not be referred to as things that are "wrong" with the child. The parent may say, "Your muscles have a harder time working, so it takes you a little longer to walk" or "Sometimes you have trouble thinking of what to do with a toy, so you go to lots of different toys." The adult also should help the child problem solve about what to do when frustrated by his or her challenges; for example, "If you want to get somewhere quickly, tell me or a friend and we will help you." Or "If you watch your friends and do what they do, it will help you have more fun with the toys." As the child gets older and hears other adults refer to labels, such as *CP* or *ADHD,* adults need to explain carefully what these terms mean so that the child does not feel that he or she is being labeled negatively by adults.

4. *Talk about learning and behavioral style with the child.* It also is helpful for children to understand how they learn best, or what can help them regulate their emotions or behavior. This can lead to the child seeking out assistance when needed, performing actions independently to improve behavior or learning, and helping others know what is needed. For example, if the child loses emotional control easily, the adult may help the child understand what helps him calm down. "Tyrone, you look like you need to go sit in your beanbag chair. It helps you calm yourself." After a period of time, Tyrone may need very little prompting to go to his chair; or if he remembers that it helped him, he may seek out the beanbag chair without prompting when he is upset. Children also can learn to ask for things that help them learn. If the child responds to visual schedules or picture cues, for example, the adult needs to help the child understand that this is the way she learns best; it is not a punishment because other children do not use them. As the child gets older, she may begin to ask for such assistance when she does not understand something; for instance, "Can you make me a picture so I can see what you mean?" or "I can think better when I have something to fiddle with in my hand," or "I can't see you when you stand there. Can you move over here?" Children need to learn that it is okay to ask for things that help them learn or interact better. It should not be a stigma, but merely a characteristic of how they learn best.

5. *Help children know how to talk to others about their differences.* Children also will feel better about themselves if they know how to deal with people who react to their appearance, behavior, or other differences. Teach children that others' behavior is a result of lack of understanding, rather than disapproval. They can learn to use the same words that adults have used with them to explain their differences. Explaining to other children in the class is a good place to start, because children do not typically ask many follow-up questions, but rather accept what is stated. Such discussions can help children feel more confident around others.

Environmental Modifications

In addition to interpersonal strategies that may support the child, environmental modifications often are useful. Depending on the findings from TPBA2, the team may want to consider some of the following environmental modifications.

1. *Make positive comparisons to characters in books and media.* There are many books available about children with special needs, and many television programs such as *Sesame Street* now have characters with disabilities. These can be used to help children identify with positive characteristics of children with various challenges and can provide suggestions about how to handle different situations.

2. *Let other children use special materials.* It is important that the child with special needs not be identified as the child who gets special attention and materials, because this can have a negative influence on the attitudes of the other children. If the child is using computer programs, a light board, earphones, a disco pillow (a round, textured, air-filled pillow the child sits on), a weighted blanket, picture exchange system, or other strategies, these should be available to other children to use as well. It will help them understand what the child with special needs is experiencing and how it helps him or her.

3. *Expose children in the class to children with special needs in a variety of ways.* In some inclusive classrooms, there may be only one or two children with special needs. It is important for all children to learn about the range of diversity and differences among people. All children should have opportunities to see, read about, and interact with a full range of diversity. Books, unit themes, movies, field trips, guest visitors, and so forth can all be incorporated into preschool experiences to increase the understanding, tolerance, and prosocial behaviors of other children in the class.

ROUTINES FOR THE CHILD WHO NEEDS SUPPORT WITH SENSE OF SELF

Daily Routines (Home and Classroom)

Feeding/Eating

Make sure the child is positioned in such a way as to be able to use his or her hands freely (i.e., is well supported). Provide utensils that the child can hold and manipulate easily. Give the child choices about what fruit, vegetable, and so forth is to be eaten. Respond to needs for eating foods separately rather than together, or eating certain foods first. Encourage the child to eat independently, even if it is messy, and commend the child for his or her independence and persistence.

Diapering/Toileting

Diapering always requires assistance, but children can learn to participate by lifting their legs, getting the diaper, or telling the parent when they have a "dirty" diaper. As the child becomes ready for independent toilet training, the adult can provide comments about the child's growing ability and independence. Desire to wear "big girl" or "big boy" panties can motivate children to become toilet trained. Having them choose their own first panties is a big incentive. (Once you've got them, you want to wear them!) Self-confidence can be reinforced as the child gets increasing responsibility for doing things independently. Picture cues of the various steps often are helpful for children with special needs, as is a chart on which they get to keep track of their progress.

Dressing

As noted earlier, even infants can begin selecting their own clothing just by looking at the one they like best. Early encouragement of choice making also motivates children to want to be involved in other aspects of the dressing process. Use positioning of the child and the clothing, adaptive fasteners, and practice opportunities to motivate the child to dress independently.

Going Out

Although often challenging for adults and children alike, going out can be an opportunity for children with special needs to engage with other people and encounter new experiences. Adults can support the child by preparing him or her for interaction with other people. Encourage the child to initiate or respond to conversation, especially if others frequently avoid the child or ask questions about the child's disability. Adults also should encourage the child to be an active participant in the community and to be as independent as possible, helping the family to choose food at the grocery store, selecting from the menu and ordering independently in a restaurant, picking out the clothes he or she likes in the department store, helping to pay at the cashier, and so forth. All of these experiences will help build the child's positive sense of self.

Play Routines (Home and Classroom)

Face-to-Face Play

Face-to-face play can help children feel confident in intimate social games. Because such games typically are played in close proximity, the child learns to initiate and respond to others. Caregivers can build the child's desire to master social games and feel comfortable initiating these games with others (first with relatives or friends and then with less familiar adults or peers).

Physical Play

Physical play often is more active and enables children to practice physical skills. Engaging in frequent physical play in a variety of settings, with and without play equipment, will allow the child to develop increased proficiency in physical activities and to feel confident in public play areas with other children. Children also can increase their mastery motivation if adults help them set small incremental goals for themselves in this type of play.

Manipulative Play

Manipulative play involves play with puzzles, blocks, clay, art materials, small action figures, and other small objects. It provides opportunities to help children learn how to solve problems, create objects or transform materials, and use their hands and fingers in precise ways. Children can draw, cut, build, play games, and so forth, all activities that can promote working toward a goal. Adults can help children set small goals, break down tasks, support their persistence, reinforce effort, and comment on their skills and positive characteristics during play.

Sensory Play

Sensory play can involve any of the senses and provides an opportunity for the child to learn about what types of sensory input are pleasurable for him or her. For example, if the child loves movement and proprioceptive input, gymnastic activities, dance or movement activities, or physical games may be arenas in which the child will enjoy practicing new skills. If the child likes tactile sensory input, exploration of creative endeavors, such as play with playdough or different types of media and glue, may allow the child to practice a variety of skills. He or she can draw with fingers and hands in fingerpaints; create action figures with playdough to dramatize a story; make birds from feathers, popsicle sticks, and glue; and so forth. Engaging the child's preferred sensory system enhances the child's motivation to master a task. With creativity on the part of the adult, children can practice many skills using almost any sensory system.

Dramatic Play

Dramatic play can assist the child in practicing daily routines, sequencing stories, and learning numerous other cognitive skills. Adults also can use dramatic play to help children practice social situations that are difficult for them. For example, the adult might act out asking another child to play, telling another child about her disability, or pretending to order in a restaurant. Dramatic play enables the child to practice social interactions in a safe context so that he or she will feel more confident about transferring those skills into real-life situations.

Reading and Learning Routines

Circle Time

Teachers can use circle time to point out positive traits, actions, thoughts, and behaviors that individual children produce. The teacher provides an important role model for other children, and they should hear the teacher use positive terms in describing *each* child. For example, the teacher might say, "Matthew is being very patient today" or "Ruby is working very hard to listen to her friends." It is important that the "good" children not be the only ones receiving positive comments. All children have positive traits and they need to hear them stated.

One-on-One Book Reading

Reading a book one-on-one with a child with special needs provides adults with many opportunities for discussion of areas related to the child's sense of self. With infants and toddlers, adults can point out and talk about characters in the books, comparing their physical characteristics with those of the child. As the child matures, discussion of actions, situations, events, and more abstract characteristics can be discussed. Books provide limitless possibilities for discussion of topics that might not arise naturally in the child's life. For example, the child might not have experienced teasing or being bullied before he enters preschool, but reading a book about a child who is teased and how he handles it can present a opening for the adult to talk about such situations, prepare the child, and practice responses.

Science and Math

Science and math activities should be presented in numerous ways so that children who learn in different ways can experience success. Manipulatives and sensorimotor, visual, and auditory activities can all be combined to reinforce learning. Let children set goals and help them see when they are making progress. Avoid use of worksheets (unless the child is highly motivated by worksheets), and use activities that are real, functional, and/or interesting to the children. A child might not be motivated to count blocks on a table, but she may be very motivated to count how long the dinosaur is on the class mural, using her own shoe to mark off the distance in "feet" versus how long the dinosaur is in feet on a ruler. Adults can build mastery motivation by making learning interesting and fun.

█████ *BENNIE*

Bennie is a 3-year-old with myelomeningocele (spina bifida). This condition is a result of malformations in the central nervous system, with lack of fusion of some bones in the spinal column and an accompanying protuberance of the spinal cord and the lining of the spinal cord.

Bennie is very small for his age, both in height and weight. He is not able to walk independently. He uses a walker to get around, is not toilet trained, and has gastric reflux problems and severe constipation. He is on a special diet and a regimen of laxatives. His language and cognitive skills are typical for his age. Bennie has undergone numerous medical procedures and his family is quite careful about what they allow him to do. They admit that they have "babied" him, both because of his small size and his medical issues. They would like to see him become more independent. Bennie is in preschool, where he mostly plays in isolation. He often is whiny about having to participate in activities and frequently asks for the teacher's assistance to do things that he could do for himself, because his hands and arms are not affected. The other children are curious about Bennie but do not seek him out for play. His teachers and family would like to see Bennie become more independent, understand his capabilities, feel more confident about what he can do, and be motivated to make friends.

Interaction Strategies

1. *Bennie likes the attention he gets when he asks for help. Reinforce Bennie's efforts to do things alone before he has a chance to ask for help. Say things such as, "Good for you. You are doing it all by yourself!"*

2. *Before giving assistance, ask Bennie to see if he can figure out the task himself, then give him a hug and attention when he does it independently.*

3. *Ask Bennie how it feels to do things without help. Use words such as "smart," "important," and "feel good." This will help Bennie notice the positive emotions that go along with independence and competence.*

4. *Point out positive traits and behaviors when they occur: "You are working hard!" "You are being a good friend." "You are a great helper!"*

Environmental Modifications

1. *Make sure that Bennie is well supported in his seat when at the table, with feet on the floor and materials at the correct height. Because he is small, the chair and table may not be the appropriate size for him. Use an adaptive chair that adjusts in height and has a foot rest, if needed.*

2. *Seat Bennie near other children who can model how to do activities. This may reduce his need to ask for help.*

3. *When Bennie asks for assistance, suggest that he watch his friends or ask a peer to help him. This will increase his interaction with peers and redirect attention-seeking behavior from adults to peers.*

4. *Once Bennie knows how to do a task, have him be the role model for another child. This will build his confidence and help him discover that knowing how to do things can be rewarding.*

5. *Have Bennie and his mother or father talk to the class about why Bennie uses a walker and why he eats special foods (in very simple terms). They could share pictures of him as a baby and with the family. This will show the class how Bennie is like them and their families. Have Bennie show the other children how his walker works and let them take turns trying it. This will take away the stigma of the walker.*

6. *Have Bennie set goals for what he wants to learn. Break these down into easily accomplished steps. Make a chart to help him mark progress.*

7. *Choose Bennie for the leader in some activities. This will allow him to show his skills to his peers and help him feel important.*

8. *Arrange a method to share strategies with Bennie's family, so that similar approaches are being used at school and at home (e.g., a back-and-forth notebook, a weekly phone call, or conversation at drop-off and pick-up times).*

KEYS TO INTERVENTION BY DEVELOPMENTAL AGE

The following ideas are directed toward children who are functioning at approximately the following levels. The suggestions are not meant to be all-inclusive, but rather are indicative of potential areas for exploration.

Developmental age	Characteristics	Key to intervention
Birth to 3 months	Studies environment.	Let children explore faces. Talk to them, call them by name, and name others in the family.
3–6 months	Discriminates among people, voices, tastes, proximity. Begins to recognize he can make things happen. Explores own face, eyes, and mouth with hand.	Let children see other children and adults. Exploring others' faces will lead the child to see differences. Let children use toys that can be activated easily. Place objects and materials on the child's body parts so the child will reach and explore.
6–9 months	Smiles at own mirror image. Discriminates between self and mother in mirror. Indicates need for help. Turns to own name.	Do mirror play with the baby at bath time. When the child is having a difficult time, wait for the child to request help and place a hand out for the child to see as a cue.
9–12 months	Touches or kisses mirror image. Claps when she does something she likes. Repeats actions if applauded. Fights for possessions. Shows delight in making toys perform. "Shows off." May demand help to get attention.	Encourage the child by giving positive feedback when the child does something special. Talk about the baby's things, bottle, clothes, diaper, as well as other people's things. Demonstrate how to make things happen and let the child try. Praise effort.
12–18 months	Says "no" to assert independence. Does something to help one in pain. Wants praise for good performance. Is assertive and independent, although will stay close to parent. Persists in tasks of moderate difficulty. Is aware of failure. Is able to represent self and others in dramatic play.	Allow the child to make choices to retain some control of the situation. Acknowledge what is done well. Encourage doing things independently. Break down tasks to help the child persist to the next step. Let the child try again when first effort does not work. Introduce dramatic play related to daily routines.
18–24 months	Recognizes self in mirror. Has interest in gender, body parts, and functions. Uses *me, I, mine.* Uses self-description and self-evaluation. Feels she can do anything. Can distinguish self in pictures. Has pride in accomplishment. May cry at failure to accomplish a goal. Wants to do things alone ("Me do").	Use a mirror for dressing if possible and talk about what the child is doing. Label body parts. Use pronouns when talking (e.g., *I, me, you, he, him* instead of *Daddy, Mommy,* and so forth). Make picture books for the child of his or her family and friends. Give the child small tasks he or she can finish quickly. Allow the child time and support to be able to complete tasks independently.
24–36 months	May get aggressive when others interfere with his actions. Has categorical knowledge of self (e.g., knows age, sex, physical characteristics, good or bad behavior, and competence). Talks about all the things he or she can do. May show shame at not being able to do things.	Encourage social engagement and joint problem solving. Talk about the child's concrete attributes, skills, and behaviors. Give the child many opportunities for trying different activities with adaptations to enable success. Talk about the need for practice to become better at skills, and introduce ways to practice in functional ways.

(continued on next page)

Developmental age	Characteristics	Key to intervention
36–48 months	Describes causes and consequences of her emotions. Is argumentative, proud of accomplishments (boasts). Knows what fears are (uses words "afraid," "scared"). Can go on errands around the house unattended.	Talk about individual differences and how people have things they do well and things they cannot do so well. Discuss the child's worries about success and failure. Give the child responsibilities to carry out tasks without direct adult supervision.
48–60 months	Judges own characteristics. Eager to learn new things. Can modify actions in different situations.	Discuss what the child is doing, what works, and what does not. Problem solve about options. Encourage trial-and-error learning and practice of new skills.
60–72 months	Desires acceptance of others. Can modify actions so others will like him or her. Uses attention-seeking behaviors.	Role play situations with the child to help the child initiate and maintain interaction and respond to others' comments. Talk about getting attention through completion of activities and positive behaviors.

5

Facilitating Emotional and Social Development

VI. Strategies for Improving Emotional Themes in Play

Goal Attainment Scale

1	2	3	4	5	6	7	8	9
Demonstrates limited range of emotions in play, and/or lacks awareness of or concern for emotions of others in the play situation.		Demonstrates a range of emotions in play through verbal and nonverbal means, but emotions reflect reaction to play itself rather than the meaning of the play.		Recognizes and labels own and others' basic emotions in play situations. Has repetitive, unresolved emotional themes in play.		Is able to attribute emotions to inanimate characters in dramatic play, and uses play themes to experiment with resolving emotional conflicts.		Is able to appropriately represent own and others' emotions, and can resolve emotional conflicts in interactions and themes within symbolic and sociodramatic play.

Children express emotions in play. Initially, they demonstrate how they feel about the play itself. Gradually, as they gain a greater understanding of emotions, they begin to be able to dramatize the emotions of the characters they play, or the emotions of the dolls or action figures they are manipulating in play.

In addition, children often have emotions of which they are not consciously aware. These emotions relate to their more global state of well-being. Such feelings as happiness, security, and nurturance may be demonstrated in their play through their affect and their actions. Less positive states of well-being also are seen in play. Worries, fears, and traumas are expressed through actions with toys and as language develops, their inner concerns often are articulated through the characters in their play. Understanding the inner world of the child is important, because early identification of concerns can lead to finding supports for the child and/or family to enable them to address the child's anxieties or fears.

APPROPRIATE EMOTIONAL THEMES IN PLAY

As adults, we want children's play to demonstrate their sense of security and contentment. However, play also is an important tool for children to use to work out their confusion about various situations or to problem solve about how to deal with specific life situations. For this reason, it is not expected that children's play will always be happy, with no conflicts or expression of negative emotions. Rather, play should reveal a range of emotions appropriate to the situations the child is representing, with exploration of various themes. Children's play will reflect what they see in their environment, their concerns and anxieties, as well as their joys and sense of security. What is desired is expression of more positive emotions in play than negative, and that when negative emotions are expressed, they are resolved in the play situation through socially acceptable means. For example, the 30-month-old who is playing with her baby doll may express a range of emotions related to her own experiences. She may rock the doll, kiss it, and feed it, saying, "Yum, good." She also may experiment with negative feelings: "You were bad. Go to your room." The balance of positive to negative feelings, however, will be weighted toward the positive. Negative actions and emotions are used as a means of discovering how to resolve these situations.

Although emotions are expressed in play beginning in infancy, themes begin to emerge as children start to represent actions and feelings in dramatic play. Thus, during the toddler period, when pretend actions are directed toward self, adults, and dolls, themes begin to emerge. As children begin to allow others into their play, emotions are directed not only at the toys, but also toward others. Themes relating to power and control, anger, or dependence can be seen. Again, what is important is the frequency and intensity of these emotions versus emotions that are more positive in nature. A child's ability to resolve emotional conflict in his play often is reflective of his ability to do so in his daily life.

Appropriate Emotional Themes in Play in Practice

▦ **VI. A. How logical and flexible are the child's patterns of thought in play?**

Daily Routines (Home and Classroom)

- *Infant/toddler:* While eating lunch, the toddler's mother spills food on the floor. The toddler says, "Bad, Mommy." When her mother makes a sad face, the toddler strokes and kisses her. (This demonstrates understanding of sequences and recognition of logical emotional responses.)

- *Young child:* The child is getting dressed for school. She is wearing a pink dress and tights. She says, "Look, Daddy. Today I am going to school as a princess."

Play Routines (Home and Classroom)

- *Infant/toddler:* The toddler picks up the baby raccoon stuffed animal and puts it next to the stuffed mama raccoon in the bed.

- *Young child:* While playing doctor, the young child says, "You have a temperature. You need an operation." His patient says, "No, I need soup." The doctor replies, "Okay. You can have soup first."

Classroom Routines

During circle time, the class is dramatizing part of the story that is being read. The teacher says, "How do you think the Big Billy Goat feels? What else could he have done?"

VI. B. What awareness of others' emotional roles and actions is reflected in the child's dramatic play?

Daily Routines (Home and Classroom)

- *Infant/toddler:* While bathing in the tub, the toddler puts her baby under the water and says, "Close your eyes" (imitating a phrase the adult uses when she is upset by water in her eyes).

- *Young child:* The young child is helping her mother put clothing in the washing machine. She picks up her brother's shirt, which has a red stain on the sleeve. "Look, Mommy. This is when Mikey fell down and got all bloody. He cried."

Play Routines (Home and Classroom)

- *Infant/toddler:* During playtime, the toddler takes another child's toy. When the other child starts to cry, the toddler hands the toys back.

- *Young child:* The children are playing school. The young child who is pretending to be the teacher points to another child and says, "You are not keeping your hands to yourself. Go to time out and stay there!"

Classroom Routines

During toileting time, one of the children runs to get the teacher, saying, "Elsa needs help. She can't get her pants down and she is crying."

VI. C. What emotional themes are expressed in the child's play?

Daily Routines (Home and Classroom)

- *Infant/toddler:* During naptime, the child takes all of the stuffed animals and lines them up along the edge of the crib. He then covers them with a blanket.

- *Young child:* The young child reenacts the sequence of cooking, feeding the baby, and putting it to bed. She uses nurturing words and speaks gently to the doll, kissing it goodnight.

Play Routines (Home and Classroom)

- *Infant/toddler:* The toddler takes the plastic lion and roars. He does the same with the tiger and the elephant.

- *Young child:* During play with action figures, the young child consistently has the good guy fight the bad guy, and the good guy always wins.

Classroom Routines

During book reading time, the child who is new to preschool consistently chooses the books about family, such as *Are You My Mommy?* and *The Kissing Hand.*

VI. D. How does the child integrate and match thoughts, actions, and emotions in dramatic play?

Daily Routines (Home and Classroom)

- *Infant/toddler:* The toddler wakes up from her nap and sits up in the crib. She starts to cry, then throws her blanket on the floor, then her doll. She shouts, "Mommy, I want out!"

- *Young child:* The young child puts her doll in the infant swing in the back yard. She pushes her and says, "Don't be afraid. I won't push you too high."

Play Routines (Home and Classroom)

- *Infant/toddler:* The toddler picks up the doll and says, "She's crying." She then holds the doll to her chest and pats the doll's back, saying, "No cry."

- *Young child:* The young child is dramatizing playing on the beach. He first pretends to dance in the water, laughing and splashing. Then, when another child comes up and says, "I'm a shark!" the child starts to scream and runs away.

Classroom Routines

After reading a book about firefighters, the children start to play in centers. One young child is playing a firefighter. He hears another child calling, "Help! Save me. I'm on fire." The child calls out, "Don't be afraid. I'll save you!" while rushing forward with his pretend hose.

GENERAL PRINCIPLES FOR SUPPORTING APPROPRIATE EMOTIONAL THEMES IN PLAY

From the time they are born, adults respond to children's emotions throughout the day. As children begin to represent feelings in their play, adults have additional opportunities to help children understand the relationship between actions and emotions. The following are some of the ways in which adults support children in gaining an overall positive sense of security and comfort.

Acknowledge Feelings

One of the important ways that adults help children around their emotions is just to acknowledge how they think the child is feeling (see Chapter 5, Section I. Strategies for Improving Emotional Expression) in their play. Talking about feelings that are evident through facial expression, body language, and verbalization is one way children come to understand emotions in themselves and others. It also is important for adults to acknowledge emotions that may not be evident physically—the ones that may be felt but not expressed clearly. For instance, when the parent is tired and becomes irritated easily by the child running a toy truck into her foot, the adult may say, "Honey, can you take your truck over there? Mommy is tired and grouchy." This explanation helps the child see how emotions may result in unexpected responses.

For example, if the child is playing with the family dog and it growls at her, the child may first exhibit fear and then get angry and try to kick the animal. The adult's first inclination may be to admonish the child not to kick, but the response should acknowledge both emotions, the fear and the anger, before talking about an appropriate response.

Connect Actions and Feelings

Adults help children see how actions are connected to their emotions. Infants smile or laugh when an experience is pleasurable. They cry when they are uncomfortable, irritated, or sad. Adults help children know why they are feeling what they are expressing, by telling them what is happening: "Oh, you like when I blow on your tummy! Here I come again!" "Are you hungry? Is that what's wrong?" "You don't need to cry. Mommy just went to get your bottle." These communications let children know that emotions people feel result in responses from others. Eventually, children will create their own explanations for emotions: "She's just mad because Sam ate her cookie." As children begin to engage in play activities, adults comment on the child's actions and feelings; for example, "The baby is crying. 'Waa! Waa!' What does she need?" They help children think about how to respond to emotions. Play enables children to explore these actions and feelings in a secure way.

Model Actions and Feelings in Play

Adults use play as a means for modeling problem solving around emotions. Action figures from popular television and movie characters often provide an opportunity for children to act out what they have seen in life and in the media. For example, the child may have seen a fight on a cartoon and then will reenact this event in his play. The adult who is playing one of the characters can then model how one of the other characters might react, talk about the characters' feelings, or problem solve about options; for example, "I'm Nemo. I'm lost. I'm scared! Oh, no! What should I do? My Daddy loves me. He'll find me."

Problem Solve About Feelings in Play

Adults support children in their play by helping to analyze and respond to the emotions they are feeling. This is particularly true when social conflicts occur. The parent typically points out what happened, how each child is feeling, and what needs to occur next. For example, when one child takes another child's toy and a fight breaks out, the adult might separate the children and say, "I know you are mad that Manola took your blocks, but he is mad because you are not sharing. Let's think about what could make you both feel better."

THE PRINCIPLES IN PRACTICE

Although adults support emotional development throughout the day, play presents many opportunities to delve into children's emotional world and support their thinking.

Daily Routines (Home and Classroom)

Feeding/Eating

Play often is incorporated into mealtimes. The child may feed a doll or pretend to be an animal. For example, the adult may say, "Here bunny. Here's a carrot for you. Bunnies love carrots."

Diapering/Toileting

Doll play related to diapering and toileting is common during the early years. Parents often let children use dolls as a way to let them express their anxieties around this routine. A napkin can serve as a diaper and a bowl as a potty chair. The child's actions and words reveal their feelings about this activity; for example, the parent may say, "Here is a potty for your baby." The child may then place the doll on the bowl and say, "You did it. You went all by yourself!" If the child is mean to the doll, saying, "You went in your diaper. You are bad!" the parent can reflect the child's anxiety. "Did the baby have an accident? That happens sometimes. It's okay. Maybe next time she'll go on the potty."

Dressing

Dressing a doll is another way for the child to deal with emotions around pride and frustration. The parent can model asking for help, "Do you need help with your zipper, baby?" or demonstrate building confidence, saying, "You did it, baby! You went potty all by yourself."

Play Routines (Home and Classroom)

Face-to-Face Play

When face-to-face games are too intense, children may fuss or cry. The adult then models recognition of the action's effect: "Ohh. Was I too loud? I'm sorry!"

Physical Play

Physical play often involves intense emotions. The adult can use this opportunity to reflect the child's feelings and model how to respond to the way others feel, saying, for instance, "Oops! Was I too rough? I'm sorry! Let me try that again."

Manipulative Play

All play with toys involves emotion, with some toys lending themselves to more aggressive play (e.g., cars, dinosaurs, action heroes) and other toys inspiring more nurturing play. The adult can lead the child into more of one or another by modeling, suggesting, commenting, or responding to the child's actions; for example, "Here comes the dinosaur. I'm afraid. Please don't eat me. Can we play instead?"

Sensory Play

Children's artistic creations reflect their inner feelings. How the adult responds to those creations is important. Adults can focus on what the child is trying to express, rather than the quality of the child's art. For instance, "That monster looks mad! He is black and has sharp teeth!"

Reading and Learning Routines

Circle Time

Reading with a group allows adults to compare children's perceptions of emotions. The adult can ask open-ended questions to elicit ideas about emotions; for instance, "How do you think he feels when someone laughs at him?" The adult can then compare the various responses without judgment, by talking about how people feel different feelings about the same situation.

One-on-One Book Reading

One-on-one book reading allows the adult to explore the feelings of characters in the book and compare them with the child's feelings; for instance, "Have you been lost? How did you feel?"

Science and Math

Although not typically thought of as a venue for play, math and science for toddlers and young children should involve playful investigation of situations and comparison of differences. Psychology is the study of thinking and feeling and also is a science. Adults help children compare how and when people feel certain emotions and how different people react. This can happen in dramatic play or in the science center when studying animal responses. The adult's role is to prompt making comparisons and thinking about responses.

PLANNING INDIVIDUALIZED INTERVENTIONS FOR IMPROVING EXPRESSION OF APPROPRIATE EMOTIONAL THEMES IN PLAY

▬▬▬ VI. A. How logical and flexible are the child's patterns of thought in play?

Children who have been in traumatic experiences or who have experienced inflexible, negative parenting styles often reflect rigid thought patterns and repetitive play patterns related to the emotions they have experienced. Children with developmental delays or disabilities such as autism spectrum disorders also may be rigid in their play patterns. There is a difference between limited play patterns that are due to developmental delays or cognitive disabilities and those that are related to emotional concerns. Children with emotional concerns often reenact traumatic experiences or actions related to their anxieties of fears. For example, a child who has a life-threatening illness or who has lost a parent may repeat play themes related to hospitals, or characters in his or her play may die. Children who have experienced or witnessed a great deal of violence may demonstrate aggressive themes in their play.

For children with cognitive and language delays, the adult needs to help expand their potential action sequences. Children with emotional reasons for their rigidity and inflexibility need adult support to help them understand their emotions, expand the emotional content of their play, and help them acquire ways to master their feelings.

Interaction Strategies

1. *Interest the child in new play patterns.* Children play in relation to what they are thinking about. For children with developmental delays, this often is what is familiar or what was done previously. For children with emotional concerns, play often reflects their predominant worries. For children who have limited ideas for play, the adult needs to help them expand their ideas and, therefore, their play patterns. Using the toys and materials the child likes, model new actions. Expand the emotional themes by introducing actions into the play that are associated with alternative emotions to those the child typically exhibits. For example, if the child typically plays violent games and kills action figures, the adult can introduce taking the character to the hospital and taking care of him so he gets better.

2. *Demonstrate and explain logical sequences.* Talk about alternative actions and the reasons for those actions. For example, one typical scenario that a child might play is crashing cars together and then repeating that action several more times. The adult can introduce the idea of consequences and at the same time add another series of actions: "Oh, no! (with sad voice) My guy got hurt in the accident. He needs help. I'm going to call 911 for help (excited voice). I want him to get better (nurturing voice)."

3. *Generate optional next actions.* Encourage the child to think of alternative actions. In the situation depicted in No. 2, the adult might say, "What do you think happens next?" If the child cannot think of a next action, the adult can prompt an idea such as, "Where can we find a phone?" or "We need an ambulance."

4. *Talk about feelings.* Play also can include talking about feelings, not just actions. When the child is dramatizing through role playing, the adult may say, "You look sad, what happened?" or "Your baby is happy now that she has a clean diaper," or ask, "How does your baby feel now?" In play with miniature characters, the adult also can relate to the feelings of the characters so that the child starts associating actions with emotional consequences.

Environmental Modifications

In addition to interpersonal strategies that may support the child in the development of logical and flexible thought patterns in their play, environmental modifications often are useful. Depending on the findings from TPBA2, the team may want to consider some of the following environmental modifications.

1. *Use props to prompt thoughts.* Introduction of a new prop can change both the action sequence and the emotional tone of play. In the previous example of the car accident, the introduction of an ambulance not only can expand the play to a new series of events, but also can shift the emotional tone from one of aggression to one of nurturance (see also Chapter 7, Section V. Strategies for Improving Complexity of Play).

2. *Use pictures to stimulate options.* Pictures can be introduced into play to prompt new ideas. For example, if a toddler is playing with stuffed animals, pictures of dogs or rabbits jumping or eating can prompt the child to add these actions. The adult might say, "Look, this puppy is jumping. Does your puppy do tricks? What can he do?" Pictures in play also can be used to discuss feelings.

3. *Use books to provide sequences.* Dramatize stories that you read to children which involve a series of actions resulting in emotions. Repetitive books such as *The Three Little Pigs* or *The Three Billy Goats Gruff* are easy to act out for developmentally younger children. Higher level children can act out more complicated stories such as *A Porcupine Named Fluffy*. This book involves emotions such as anxiety, embarrassment, and pride and provides an opportunity for the adult to relate these emotions to the child's experiences.

4. *Use games.* For children in preschool and kindergarten, simple games also can stimulate discussion of emotions. Games involving emotions such as Chutes and Ladders, Emotions Bingo, and others help children think about actions and emotions. Any game, however, could be used as an opportunity to talk about emotions. The competitive nature of playing a game, the need to share, and having to wait for your turn typically provide an environment in which emotions are experienced.

▬▬▬ VI. B. What awareness of others' emotional roles and actions is reflected in the child's dramatic play?

Although many emotional expressions are universal, the meaning of these expressions is not clear to all children. Understanding comes through observing facial and movement patterns that result after specific behaviors have occurred. Children with various types of disabilities may avoid eye contact, or they direct attention to their toys rather than to the people around them. In order to draw relationships between actions and emotional consequences, the child has to be able to attend to both the actions and the people involved simultaneously (see Chapter 7, Section I. Strategies for Improving Attention). Children may need adult assistance to help them attend to the relevant aspects of a situation. Other children need assistance to draw meaning from the emotions they are seeing. Children with autism, for example, may not understand emotions or motivations. In some cases, adults may need to teach children how to interpret various facial expressions or behaviors so that children can respond appropriately. Children who are blind will need to learn how to pick up on the nuances of the tone, pitch, and rhythm of the voice, just as children who are deaf rely more on the visual aspects of emotion.

Interaction Strategies

1. *Bring attention to faces, body language, and voices of others* (see Chapter 5, Section I. Strategies for Improving Emotional Expression, and Chapter 7, Section IV. Strategies for Improving Social Cognition). Point out the facial expression, the sound of the person's voice, and the movement of body parts. Avoid saying, "Look at me"; rather, point out the aspects that convey meaning: "My mouth is frowning"; "I am shaking my head 'no'"; "She is talking loud"; "He has tears in his eyes."

2. *Help the child interpret emotions in play* (see Chapter 5, Section I. Strategies for Improving Emotional Expression, and Chapter 7, Section IV. Strategies for Improving Social Cognition). Add to the previous comments the meaning of the action; for example, "I am angry that you broke that"; "Shaking my head means I am not happy"; "Her voice is loud because she is mad"; "His voice is shaky because he is crying."

3. *Help the child respond to emotions in others.* Adults should first see if the child understands appropriate responses to the emotions of others; for example, "She is sad that you bit her. What do you think you should do?" If the child has no response, give the child a choice of two positive responses: "Do you think you should help put on a bandage, or should you say you are sorry you bit her?" Then help the child carry out the action selected. If no choice is selected, have the child help repair the damage and talk about his or her feelings. After dealing with the other child, talk about why the child felt the need to bite, what his or her feelings were, and what would have been a better way to solve the problem.

4. *Model emotions in play.* Modeling one's own emotions is important. Children need to see a range of emotions in their caregivers to know that it is appropriate to feel a variety of emotions. Adults can model affect in play. When the child is demonstrating uncaring emotions, they also can give the child an opportunity to respond positively. Particularly in dramatic play, adults can interject situations in which their character is hurt, angry, lost, ashamed, and so forth. This gives the child the opportunity to respond to these emotions. If the child ignores the emotions or is confused about how to respond, the adult can provide suggestions. For example, while pretending to cook, the mother might accidentally "burn" her finger on the toy stove. "Ouch! I burned my finger! It hurts. What should I do?" In manipulative play as well, emotional situations can be introduced. When pushing the top down on the pop-up box, the adult might accidentally "pinch" her finger. The purpose of this is to stimulate nurturing behavior and positive responses to others' emotions. This is not necessary for children whose play is already nurturing and conveys primarily positive emotions.

Environmental Modifications

In addition to interpersonal strategies that may support the child learning to attend to others' emotions in play, environmental modifications often are useful. Depending on the findings from TPBA2, the team may want to consider some of the following environmental modifications.

1. *Teach emotional expressions.* Use pictures, dolls, books, and real situations involving one's own or others' emotions to teach children what emotional expressions mean. Show the child her face in the mirror when she is mad, happy, and sad. Take advantage of routines of the day during which children may demonstrate various emotions (e.g., tired before nap time, happy in chase games, mad at interruptions) to teach emotions in real-life situations. Let them know that it is okay to feel *many* emotions (see Chapter

5, Section I. Strategies for Improving Emotional Expression). Point out these emotions when they are seen in play situations.

2. *Structure time to discuss responses to one's or others' emotions.* In addition to incidental teaching that can occur throughout the day, structure time to talk about appropriate responses to the feelings of others. During dramatic play, the adult can suggest various responses be tried (see Chapter 5, Section IV. Strategies for Improving Behavioral Regulation).

3. *Structure time for puppet play or role play.* Dramatize situations that may arise relating to the emotions of others. This can be through role play, with puppets, or with action figures. This gives the child an opportunity to experience the situation and think about it before it occurs in real life. With enough practice and reinforcement, children will begin to apply the lessons learned.

4. *Use bibliotherapy.* Books can provide a basis for teaching children about others' feelings and what appropriate responses may be in different situations. Choosing books for one-on-one reading can help an individual child, whereas books chosen for groups can address issues the whole class needs to learn. Role playing during storytime also gives the child practice.

▆▆▆ VI. C. What emotional themes are expressed in the child's play?

All children express emotional themes in their play, project their feeling through actions with toys and other materials, and act out roles or actions they admire or worry about. Such play helps the child safely express emotions and fears and develop methods for dealing with his or her emotions. Play allows children a form of expression for complex emotions when words or an acceptable means of communication is not available. Adults should be concerned when the child's emotions and behaviors exceed the parameters necessary for adaptive functioning, when children are excessively withdrawn, lack delight and pleasure in play, or display seemingly unwarranted anger repeatedly and for an extended length of time in various settings. Parents, teachers, and caregivers can provide support to assist children with emotional and behavioral issues, but they also need to be aware that sometimes professional support is needed for the child and family.

Although evidence of psychological problems may be seen in children's behavior and play, the reasons for these concerns may not be clear. For children with severe psychological concerns, an outside professional may be needed to explore a child's belief system about himself and others and then provide therapy and resources for the family.

Regardless of whether the child is receiving outside treatment, however, there are supportive approaches that can be used in daily interaction with the child during play. The approaches outlined here are meant to support children with their conflicts related to five issues that children work through in their pretend play on a bipolar scale (Fein, 1989):

1. Connectedness (i.e., attachment versus separation)

2. Physical well-being (health versus bodily harm)

3. Empowerment (i.e., mastery versus helplessness)

4. Social regulation (i.e., support for social rules versus defiance)

5. Respect for or aggression against the material world

By viewing these as issues that all children explore, adults can support emotional development for children along the continuum for each factor. Children with emotional disabilities, however, may demonstrate a preoccupation with one or more of these themes. The play materials they select and their actions, language, and interactions with others all may reflect their emotional needs or conflicts. For example, the child who always selects aggressive toys such as dinosaurs or monsters, breaks toys on purpose, always crashes the cars, finds ways to hurt others in dramatic play, and seems always to be causing other children to cry may be struggling with several of the issues listed previously.

Children with a variety of disabilities, however, may show similar behaviors, not due to emotional conflicts but, rather, due to other disabilities such as sensorimotor concerns, developmental delays, or lack of awareness of others. Knowledge of contributing factors is important to ensure that all areas of development are addressed adequately. Such disabilities may require more directed intervention.

For children who do display emotional concerns in their play, the following interaction strategies are suggested. Although traditional play therapy techniques (usually started between the ages of 3 and 5 years) cannot be implemented in a classroom environment, some play therapy interaction strategies and materials are useful. Consultation with other professionals who may be working with the child is advised.

Interaction Strategies

1. *Comment on what the child is doing with the toys.* The adult can enter the child's emotional world by accepting and commenting on what the child is doing. Unless the child is causing harm, the adult watches and describes what the child (or his or her toy) is doing. For example, "Your cow is eating the farmer." When actions are repeated numerous times, the child may be emphasizing this for a reason. Interpreting the meaning of the action will take further exploration.

2. *Label and acknowledge the feelings that are exhibited.* Every action the child performs has some purpose for the child. The adult can help the child identify the purpose by acknowledging the feelings that accompany the child's behavior. Following on the previous statement, the adult might comment, "Your cow looks mad at the farmer." The adult waits after every comment to see if the child will offer more information. If the child hears the adult but is nonverbal, the child's actions following the comment may add meaning. For instance, if the child has the cow attack the farmer again, it may mean confirmation of the adult's remark. If the cow moves away, it may indicate lack of agreement or uncertainty. If the child's play is not harming anyone, recognition of the child's actions can help the child to feel that his or her feelings are being accepted.

3. *Explore the reasons for the feelings.* Trying to identify why the child is exhibiting certain actions in play is difficult, because merely asking "why" may not result in an answer. The child may not *know* why or may not feel comfortable talking about the topic. For example, Kalia repeatedly put her miniature doll figure in a box and angrily shut the lid, shouting, "And you stay there!" The adult said, "Someone is mad at that girl." Kalia answered, "Her Mommy put her in there 'cause she's mad at her." The adult said, "The little girl is crying." Kalia said, "It won't do her no good! She's bad." The adult also can try to distance the child from the experience by personalizing the emotions. For instance, "One time someone put me in a dark place, and I was really scared. I wonder if the girl is scared." Kalia then said, "She was really scared and cried." Further play and discussion led to the discovery that Kalia's mother punished her by putting her in "time out" in a dark closet. Kalia was conflicted by her fear and anger at her mother and her feelings of being bad and deserving punishment.

4. *Help the child master conflicts.* Children struggle with conflicts between wanting to be close to their parents versus wanting to be independent, wanting to be helpful ver-

sus wanting to be hurtful, wanting to be in charge versus wanting to have others do things for them, wanting to follow the rules versus wanting to make the rules, and wanting to protect versus wanting to harm. Adults can dictate or help children have power over their own decisions. The adult can guide thoughts by asking questions such as, "What do you think the Mommy should do now? The little girl is sad." The adult also can introduce new situations to the play to explore alternatives; for instance, "Here comes the little girl's daddy. What does the little girl tell him?"

5. *Provide support.* Children often do not understand what is right and wrong and what their own rights are. They view what all adults say and do as right, and therefore they are bad and deserve the treatment they receive. Adults can help clarify that everyone make mistakes and sometimes people all need help to know what is right or wrong. The adult may say, "It is not okay to hurt someone else—not even for mommies and daddies. Sometimes, mommies and daddies need help to do the right thing too."

Environmental Modifications

In addition to interpersonal strategies that may support the child, environmental modifications often are useful. Depending on the findings from TPBA2, the team may want to consider some of the following environmental modifications.

1. *Provide toys to allow children to express their feelings.* Let children choose from many different toys in their play. Although most toys can be used to express emotions in one form or another, miniature people and scenarios provide a means for children to act out all of the roles of the characters. This provides adults with an opportunity to observe how the child depicts relationships, power distribution, anxieties and fears, and so forth.

2. *Provide materials that enable children to create ways to express emotions.* Drawing and other art media provide powerful mechanisms for emotional expression. What and how children draw reveals something about their inner world. Media such as paint, crayons, markers, clay, playdough, sand and water, paper, glue, and a variety of other materials can be used to enable children to represent their experiences and feelings.

3. *Present a variety of themes in the dramatic play area.* Dramatic play is another form of representation. By having available props for daily routines, children can act out their daily experiences and relationships within those. It also is important, however, to provide alternatives to the "house" for dramatic play. Have props for dramatizing stories and creative situations that will enable children to problem solve around emotional issues. Stories involving heroes and heroines, conflicts between good guys and bad guys, rescue, loss, and so forth can help children gain mastery over their fears, insecurities, or negative past experiences. The adult can monitor the children's play and introduce comments or suggestions to clarify, expand, or guide the play toward resolution as described previously.

▩ VI. D. How does the child integrate and match thoughts, actions, and emotions in dramatic play?

Children with emotional conflicts may display one set of emotions overtly but feel something different inside. A child may have hurt feelings as a result of being teased, but will laugh instead of cry. A child may be angry at another child, yet hug that child with extreme intensity. Children often struggle with their feelings and their beliefs about what they *should* feel. As children learn the rules for social behavior and begin to understand right and wrong, they may try to display affect they think is socially acceptable, even though that is not what they are feeling. They also may display the true feelings they are experiencing, even though the feelings are not those expected for the situation. They may, for example, pretend to "kill" an action figure while laughing. Both situations are worrisome. In the first case, the child is not acknowledging true feelings but is presenting what others want to see. In the second case, accurate emotions are exhibited in a highly inappropriate situation, demonstrating lack of understanding of the relationship between emotions and consequences. Both need adult support to identify underlying issues.

Interaction Strategies

1. *Point out the emotions seen.* Children may not realize the emotions they are displaying. The adult might say, "You are laughing. Do you feel happy?" Reflection of what the child appears to be feeling enables the child to know how others are reading his cues and correct those interpretations if they are inaccurate.

2. *Explain the results of actions.* Children may not know how other children interpret their responses. Adults can help by mediating; for instance, "How did you feel when Marty said that to you? Did you feel happy?"; or "When you laugh, that tells Max that you liked what he said."

3. *Discuss the child's actions and the emotions.* Point out discrepancies between actions and feelings. Adults can help children by talking about situations, their reactions, and possible alternatives: "What Marty said was not nice. You said you felt sad, but he thought you liked it because you laughed. Is that what you want him to think? If someone else says something mean to you, what do you think you could say?"

4. *Use dramatic play to represent emotional situations.* Dramatize stories, role play situations, or use puppets to illustrate and explain what and why characters or people feel, how they show that, and how they act in response to those thoughts and feelings.

5. *Explore the reasons for feelings through safe venues.* Talking about what dolls or characters in books are feeling and why they feel that way, how the adult feels or has felt in similar situations, or how other children feel may give the child an opening for discussion of feelings without having to discuss his or her own. For example:

Adult: "Sammy is lost. He doesn't know where his mommy is. How do you think he feels?"

Child: "I don't know."

Adult: "One time, I couldn't find my mommy and I felt really scared."

Environmental Modifications

In addition to interpersonal strategies that may help children integrate and match thoughts, actions, and emotions in dramatic play, environmental modifications often are useful. Depending on the findings from TPBA2, the team may want to consider some of the following environmental modifications.

1. *Use picture sequences involving actions and resulting emotions.* Picture sequences using pictures from magazines, drawings, or actual photographs can be used with children to help them make a plan for action, recreate a sequence they saw or heard about, or follow a series of thoughts or actions. The pictures also can be used to help children match actions to thoughts, and feelings; for example, "How do you think he felt when she took his ball?"

2. *Talk about pictures in storybooks that reflect emotions.* Talk about what they think happened, what the character is feeling, and why. Books can be used for bibliotherapy, as a means of opening up discussion of emotions and problem solving how to deal with them (see Section VI. B, No. 4 under Environmental Modifications).

3. *Use pictures of the emotions of children in the class.* Take pictures of the children in the class expressing different emotions. When children are expressing emotions of discomfort or self-conscious emotions, have them match what they are feeling to the pictures of the children in the class. Help them label the feeling they have or those they see on other children.

4. *Introduce toys and materials that provide opportunities for emotional play.* Certain toys lend themselves to different types of thoughts and emotions. For example, puppets, plastic monsters, or dinosaurs may lead to expression of aggressive emotions; doctor kits and baby dolls with bottles and blankets may lead to more nurturing play. Children who are struggling with conflicted emotions or anxieties related to unresolved issues may find ways to insert angry emotions at every opportunity. They may, for example, "kill" the baby or spank it for being naughty. Provision of toys and materials (e.g., art materials, sand play, emotion-based games) that allow children to express and discuss emotions is important.

ROUTINES FOR THE CHILD WHO NEEDS SUPPORT TO DEVELOP COHESIVE, POSITIVE EMOTIONAL THEMES IN PLAY

Concerns related to daily routines for children with disabilities can result from characteristics of the child, expectations or feelings of the child or caregivers, or a combination of all of these. It is, therefore, important to understand the child's physical, cognitive, and communicative limitations as well as to be able to identify the child's feelings about the various routines. Adults also need to be able to identify their expectations for the child and their own emotions related to the child's abilities or actions. As these situations often are complicated, professional supports may be needed to get at the heart of the issue. Play therapy, filial therapy, parent counseling, positive behavioral supports, or other types of intervention may be beneficial. The following strategies are presented as options for adults to consider when interacting with children throughout the day. It is important not only to recognize the issues that children present, but also to acknowledge when further professional support is needed.

Daily Routines (Home and Classroom)

Feeding/Eating

Eating is usually a social situation and may involve many types of emotions, depending on the situation. For children with eating disorders—for example, those who have been tube fed, those who have been difficult to feed, or those who have syndromes such as Prader-Willi (which causes them to feel insatiate, as if they can never get enough to eat)—children may feel a range of emotions including embarrassment, shame and guilt, or anger. For parents, getting children to eat when they do not want to eat can be extremely stressful for the child and the family. Eating problems may involve medical, biological, psychological, and behavioral components. Adults who have children with eating disorders need to consult with professionals to adequately address these often-complicated issues.

Diapering/Toileting

As with eating, diapering and toileting involve social expectations that may lead the child to experience negative emotions. If toileting is difficult or painful, the child may avoid going. If the child has reduced sensations, he or she may not feel the need to go to the toilet, and if this persists, adults may get frustrated with the child's lack of success. This may result in feelings of inadequacy on the part of the child. Because independent toileting is valued by adults, children also may use this activity as a means of getting continued attention, maintaining control, or expressing anger. Adults need to understand which aspects of the child's toileting issues are related to developmental or biological concerns and which are related to emotions such as fears or anxieties. It is important to respond to the child's emotions and not just the successful outcome of independent toileting. Acceptance of concerns, discussion and problem solving, and patience are needed.

Dressing

Developing independence in dressing involves dependency and control in much the same way as eating and toileting. Children with disabilities may use this as a means of maintaining a closeness or dependency on their caregivers (or, conversely, adults may keep the child dependent longer). Children also may find certain materials or types of clothing to be aversive and may consequently resist wearing specific clothing. This may lead to conflicts with caregivers and negative emotions related to dressing. Adaptations can make independent dressing easier for children with disabilities. Velcro closures, slip-on shoes, zipperless pants, and so forth can reduce dependency and promote pride in accomplishment.

Going Out

Emotional issues are encountered frequently when children go out into public places such as stores or restaurants. Emotional concerns may result from anxiety about new people and situations (see also Chapter 5, Section II. Strategies for Improving Emotional Style/Adaptability); control or power issues related to the child getting what he or she wants (see also Chapter 5, Section IV. Strategies for Improving Behavioral Regulation); sensory concerns involving lack of ability to inhibit or moderate responses to sensory input, resulting in the child being overwhelmed; or attentional and behavioral concerns involving lack of impulse control (see Chapter 3, Section V. Strategies for Improving Modulation of Sensation and Its Relationship to Emotion, Activity Level, and Attention, and Chapter 5, Section IV. Strategies for Improving Behavioral Regulation).

Play Routines (Home and Classroom)

Face-to-Face Play

Children with emotional disabilities may find face-to-face play intrusive or frightening. For example, children with autism may avoid eye contact and find face-to-face play threatening or overwhelming. For this type of play to be tolerable, the adult needs to make the game highly interesting and motivating, rather than intrusive. Use the child's interests (e.g., body parts such as fingers, topics such as cars) to create turn-taking games. Do not force the child to look at you, but make face-to-face play rewarding for the child. For children who have experienced abuse or who have fears associated with extreme adult–child exchanges, the adult needs to reduce the intensity of the interaction, use subtle movements, and provide nurturing touch and communication. Talk to the child about what is happening and help the child anticipate pleasurable interaction.

Physical Play

As with face-to-face play, some children find physical play emotionally threatening. Other children seek out this type of play and find it emotionally exhilarating. Controlling the intensity of physical play can help children at both ends of the spectrum moderate their emotional response. In addition, adults need to be aware of fears that may be aroused by physical play involving pretend play related to monsters or other angry or aggressive characters. If the child does have such fears, physical dramatic play can enable the child to begin to master these fears and problem solve how to handle difficult situations. The adult's role is to monitor and interpret the child's reactions, stimulate discussion of feelings, and promote problem solving about optional responses. Taking turns in the role of aggressor and victim also enable the adult to model various approaches and responses.

Manipulative Play

Children with emotional problems often demonstrate their internal conflicts through play with small manipulative toys such as cars, animals, and action figures, or through play with sensory materials or art materials. Play with manipulative toys enables the child to gain distance from personal emotions by assigning actions and feelings to the toys and materials with which he or she is playing. Dilemmas related to issues such as power and vulnerability, aggression and victimization, independence and dependency, and control and loss are seen in the actions or emotions depicted with toys or materials, in the interactions between or among the toys or characters, and in the roles assigned to others in the play. For example, the child who is concerned about loss may continually depict characters dying or going away. Fears related to vulnerability may be seen in actions in which characters are repeatedly victimized. Power and control issues may be seen when the child must make all of the decisions about what happens with the toys and materials or when all of the child's actions relate to aggression or destroying toys and materials. The adult can explore what the child is feeling by discussing what is happening (e.g., "That driver is really mad. His car keeps hitting the other cars"), reflecting on what the characters are trying to do (e.g., "The baby is crying for her mommy to come home"), and asking questions to clarify what the child is expressing (e.g., "What happened to that guy? How did he get hurt?"). Adults also can imitate the child's actions as a means for eliciting discussion or problem solving; for instance, "My baby is crying too. What do you think is wrong with her?" or "My baby is sad too. What should she tell her Mommy?" Modeling also is possible as a means of helping children generate alternatives (e.g., "My baby says, "I need a hug, Mommy"). For children who are able to understand board games, a variety of games are available that enable adults and children to play and talk about feelings.

Sensory Play

Sensory materials, such as sand, playdough, or fingerpaints, provide the same opportunities as described previously for the child to move, create forms, and express emotions. The colors selected, forms created, and words used to describe the creations can lend themselves to understanding how a child is feeling. Sensitive comments and questions can provide clarification of what is happening for the child emotionally. With sand and playdough, action figures or other toys also may be introduced to enable more concrete expression of feelings and introduction of dramatic play elements.

Dramatic Play

Dramatic play can involve physical play, manipulatives, or sensory materials as described previously. Sociodramatic play involves the child in dramatizations with other children or adults and involves selection of what to dramatize, assignment of roles to each player, construction of action sequences and dialogue, and resolution of problems or conflicts encountered in the play situation. Each of these provides opportunities for adults to observe what the child is thinking and feeling. Who the child wants to pretend to be, for example, can provide insight into desired or perceived roles. Does the child choose to be the villain or the person who is controlled or nurtured by others? What roles does the child assign to others with whom he or she will interact in the play? Does the child engage in a logical sequence of play that reflects a variety of emotional situations, or does the child repeatedly reenact the same type of event (e.g., trauma, abandonment, aggression, or fearful situations)? What types of interactions are presented in the dialogue the child produces (e.g., bossing others around, using hurtful comments, nurturing others)? When problems arise in the play, how does the child choose to resolve them (e.g., with aggression, negotiation, dependence on adults)? Observation of these patterns can enable adults to intervene to explore reasons behind feelings, expand options, and support efforts at problem solving.

Reading and Learning Routines

Circle Time

Although many children are involved in circle time, books can be selected to be read that address the emotional needs of one or more children in the group. Discussion with the whole group about the characters, their feelings, and actions enables the child or children to hear the perspectives of their peers. Teachers also can integrate role play of alternatives or dramatization of the story. Puppets also can be introduced to discuss the story, act out various options, or prompt discussion among the children about actions, feelings, and choices.

One-on-One Book Reading

As discussed in previous chapters, use of books can serve a therapeutic purpose for children with emotional problems. Selection of books that are related to children's concerns can enable adults to talk about these issues from the perspective of the characters in the books. This provides some emotional distance for children, and they can then talk about the feelings of the characters rather than their own feelings. Often such discussions will then lead to children talking about their own feelings. Adults can use the situations in the book to prompt discussion of options for actions and reactions. They might discuss what characters might say or do differently, or what children would do or say in a similar situation. Such discussions about books can thus provide a means for children to compare their own situations with others and think about alternative viewpoints.

Science and Math

Psychology is a science. As such, children can "study" what makes animals and people act and react the way they do in different circumstances. They can study various needs for food, shelter, closeness, and love. Using animals, the class can discuss family relationships and care. The children can explore the life process from birth to death. Feelings related to home, being lost, being in fights, and so forth can be introduced and examined. Often, such discussions will elicit the perspectives of individual children with regard to their own experiences. Adults can sensitively explore these feelings with each child as they arise.

YURI

Yuri is a 2¹/₂-year-old who was recently adopted from Romania. He has had difficulty attaching to his adoptive family and demonstrates emotions of anger, control, and fear in his play. His favorite play themes include being the "parent" who disciplines the child; a mean, controlling adult; or a victim of harsh treatment. Yuri seems conflicted by being a victim and wanting control. His parents indicate frustration at his seeming lack of affection for them or his adoptive siblings. He also has had difficulty in his child care setting, where he often exhibits anger toward his peers and is aggressive in his manipulative play, often crashing cars, kicking others' toys, or knocking down their play structures. Yuri is verbally negative toward others, shouting negative words in Romanian or refusing to look at or respond to others' requests. The other children now avoid Yuri and often cry or complain to the adults in the room when he intrudes on their play.

The following were suggested for home and child care situations:

Interaction Strategies

1. *Reflect Yuri's perceptions of circumstances and his feelings associated with a given situation. Reserve judgment, and instead talk about options for reaction to the situation and feelings.*

2. *Share insights into how other children sometimes handle difficult situations.*

3. *Help Yuri think of options for how to respond to unique situations, and discuss how different responses might result in varying results for Yuri.*

4. *Comment on how Yuri's actions or words make others feel or respond. Provide examples of other statements that could result in more positive responses.*

5. *Provide numerous opportunities for nurturing Yuri throughout the day. Give him kisses and hugs at every opportunity. Model caring behaviors in real situations and dramatic play.*

6. *Ask Yuri to help you with tasks and give him opportunities to nurture you with adhesive bandages, pillows, kisses, and hugs to make you feel better.*

Environmental Modifications

1. *Provide opportunities for Yuri to observe others' play with adult comments and interpretation of actions and emotions. This will enable Yuri to see how others reenact situations with adult help for interpreting what is happening and why.*

2. *Read books to Yuri relating to developing a relationship with parents, siblings, and peers. Acknowledge how behaviors can be interpreted in different ways, and how the actions of the characters have an effect on how they are treated. Discuss the characters' and the child's feelings about different expectations and consequences of behaviors.*

3. *Provide props and materials for Yuri to express his feelings without judgment. Help him to verbalize his anxieties and fears and then help him think of alternative ways to approach these feelings so that he maintains control and security.*

4. *Provide materials, such as doctor or veterinary kits, that encourage nurturing play. Model nurturing behaviors with these props.*

REFERENCE

Fein, G.G. (1989). Mind, meaning, and affect: Proposals for a theory of pretense. *Developmental Review, 9,* 345–363.

RESOURCES

athealth.com: Filial Therapy
http://www.athealth.com/consumer/disorders/filialtherapy.html

Child Welfare League of America
http://www.cwla.org/

Family Enhancement and Play Therapy Center
http://www.play-therapy.com/index.html

Scholastic, Inc., Teacher Resources
http://teacher.scholastic.com/professional/bruceperry/index.htm

KEYS TO INTERVENTION BY DEVELOPMENTAL AGE

The following ideas are directed toward children who are functioning at approximately the following levels. The suggestions are not meant to be all-inclusive, but rather are indicative of potential areas for exploration.

Developmental age	Emotional expression and response	Keys to intervention
Birth to 3 months	Demonstrates interest, pleasure, distress through play. Responds to sensory input from others.	Read the child's emotional cues and respond sensitively to the child's needs.
3–6 months	Reflects extremes of emotion through play. Responds to social overtures from others with emotional response. Responds to meaning of emotional expression in others.	Give the child clear emotional cues with facial expression, gestures, words, and intonation. Touch can help the child experience facial expressions.
6–9 months	Vocalizes attitudes of pleasure and displeasure in play. Has negative response to unfamiliar people. Understands that adult signals convey information and emotion. Understands that own actions arouse emotions.	Respond to child's vocalizations and actions by stating what you think the child feels or desires. Support the child's anxieties by introducing new people and materials gradually. Give clear facial, gestural, and vocal emotional responses.
9–12 months	Communicates intentions and desires to others.	Let the child know that you understand his or her desires and intentions. This can be done with words, gestures, tone of voice, and touch or guidance.
12–18 months	Shows affection and nurturing in role play. Understands how self and others communicate feelings. May reveal worries through dramatic play.	Provide books about simple actions and events and consequent emotional responses. Introduce baby dolls, toy animals, and familiar costumes and props for dramatizing familiar routines.
18–24 months	Communicates needs, wishes, and feelings with words and gestures. Labels emotions. Represents feelings in play. Primarily demonstrates nurturing and self-care in dramatic play.	Read the child's nonverbal as well as verbal cues. Discuss emotions that are represented in play. Provide dramatic play opportunities for nurturing self and other characters.

(continued on next page)

Developmental age	Emotional expression and response	Keys to intervention
24–36 months	Role plays in isolated play related to nurturing, care, control, and independence. Can deal with complex wishes and feelings (play may reflect closeness, separateness, exploration, assertiveness, anger, pride, and showing off). Enjoys doll play, with attribution of emotion to dolls. Pretends to be a variety of characters with a variety of feelings. Play may be between "good" and "bad" characters.	Provide props and self-care materials for the child to practice independence and care of others. Expand dramatic play to new experiences that enable the child to express a range of emotions. Adults need to be present to monitor, comment, suggest alternatives, and support problem solving.
36–48 months	Enjoys pretending to be someone else. Can reverse roles. Able to discuss hypothetical situations. Often plays out aggression through "good" and "bad" characters. Enjoys role playing being afraid (chasing, scaring, laughing), being in control.	Examine what character the child chooses to be. Encourage child to play numerous roles. Do not discourage expression of various emotions. Discuss alternative responses to different situations. Help the child think of ways to be in control of the situations.
48–60 months	Coordinates actions with other players; able to verbally reflect on emotions. Engages in elaborate fantasy play, possibly reflecting inner feelings, fears, and nurturing.	When peers are involved, examine what role the child chooses to play and what emotions are exhibited. When appropriate, help the child try alternative ways of expressing a role or responding to others' actions.
60–72 months	Expresses sexual curiosity in doctor play. Increasingly plays out difficult emotional experiences. Plays themes of power, control, loss. Able to identify causes of emotion in characters from stories.	Help children determine limits for play actions, explore how to express various emotions, and maintain control of emotions without being domineering in the play. Question or suggest reasons for emotions.

5

Facilitating Emotional and Social Development

VII. Strategies for Improving Social Interactions

Goal Attainment Scale

1	2	3	4	5	6	7	8	9
Watches caregivers and reacts to their initiations with vocal or physical responses.		Is responsive to affection and initiates positive interactions with others. May have difficulty with separation from key caregivers.		Takes turns in prolonged interaction with family members and familiar people. May be shy or anxious with unfamiliar people. Plays alongside peers, but may have frequent social conflicts.		Primarily has positive reciprocal relationships with family members and peers in daily activities. Is able to initiate interaction and engage a peer for several minutes. Uses adults for conflict resolution.		Discriminates among familiar people and strangers, has close relationships with family, and maintains several friendships. Is able to initiate, and maintain interactions in reciprocal, goal-oriented play, and can negotiate conflict situations independently.

Social relations are the interactions that take place between a child and others, from simple observation to active engagement. Positive social relations are necessary for the development of important relationships, beginning with parents and other caregivers and expanding to siblings, peers, and other adults. Social relations are critical to development, because much of learning takes place as a result of social engagement. Although independent exploration of the world is important, the child learns a great deal through observation of and interaction with others. Other people provide models for positive interaction, exploration, and problem solving. People in the child's life often select activities that explain how things work, provide parameters for what is and is not appropriate behavior, model language and actions, and provide feedback on the child's efforts. How children view themselves and their competence also is partially derived from responses received during social interactions.

APPROPRIATE SOCIAL INTERACTIONS

The ability to initiate and maintain social relations results from the child's ability to attend to social aspects of play, read social cues, and interpret and communicate information. Socially competent children are able to get along with others, avoid negativity and conflict, regulate their emotions, and use good social problem-solving skills. Children who have positive social relations are able to *initiate* interaction by looking, touching, vocalizing, or offering objects to others. They are able to *maintain* interaction by continuing and taking turns with these same behaviors in a reciprocal fashion. They register positive affect and enjoyment in social engagement that encourages others to want to continue to participate in the social actions.

For infants, adults often initiate the interaction. Infants then respond with eye contact, noises, and, early in infancy, with smiles that prompt more interaction. As infants gain fine and gross motor control, they can reach for and touch others, offer objects, and crawl or walk to approach others. They begin to use social referencing to see how others are feeling and adjust their behaviors accordingly. As language comprehension and expression expand, children label things in their environment and respond to others' requests. They begin to initiate and maintain conversations about shared events. As children gain control over their bodies, they also begin to seek out others to participate in various types of activities (e.g., physical play, sharing a toy or book). As understanding of emotions increases, children also seek out interaction for emotional purposes (e.g., for comfort, excitement, reassurance, to share anger). By the preschool years, children have discovered the joy of sharing their play with peers, and they learn to play first near and then with other children. As social interactions in play increase, children learn how to play with others—to both lead and follow others' actions, to plan goals together, to negotiate disagreements with words, and to respond to the needs and feelings of others. Their social relations turn into friendship relationships that are mutually satisfying and supportive and can weather the occasional personal conflict. Young children also learn to adapt their play to fit the needs of children who are younger or older or have different play styles. They understand the social constellation of the classroom and can discuss other children's social abilities as well as their own.

Appropriate social interactions lead to positive social relationships. Integration of skills from all areas of development is needed.

Appropriate Social Interactions in Practice

▬▬▬ **VII. A. What emotions does the child respond to in others?**

Daily Routines (Home and Classroom)

- *Infant/toddler:* The infant holds her spoon over the floor and waits to drop it until her father is looking. The toddler sees her mother cry when she pinches her finger in the door, and she comes to comfort her.

- *Young child:* The young child sees his friend spill her milk at lunchtime. He says, "It's okay. It was an accident."

Play Routines (Home and Classroom)

- *Infant/toddler:* The infant sees her daddy laugh when she blows "raspberries," so she does it again. The toddler sees her sister get mad when she takes her toy, so she runs and hides.

- *Young child:* The young child sees her friend crying when her block structure gets knocked over and says, "I'll help you fix it."

Classroom Routines

During circle time, the teacher reads a story about a monster, and one child acts afraid. The child next to her says, "Don't be scared. It's just pretend."

▬▬▬ **VII. B. How does the child demonstrate a sense of pleasure and trust in his or her parents?**

Daily Routines (Home and Classroom)

- *Infant/toddler:* The infant opens her mouth and places it on her mother's chin to give her a "kiss." The toddler falls off the couch, looks startled, then runs crying to his dad.

- *Young child:* At the mall, the young child tells his father, "I know my phone number. If I get lost, I'll call you to come get me."

Play Routines (Home and Classroom)

- *Infant/toddler:* The infant lifts her shirt for her daddy to blow on her tummy. The toddler runs away from her mother, waits for her mother to run after her, then runs again, looking back to make sure she's still coming.

- *Young child:* The young child goes and gets a book and crawls up onto his father's lap. "Read this one, Daddy, and make the lion be loud."

Classroom Routines

During dramatic play, the child pretends to be the Mommy and tells the baby doll, "Oh, did you get hurt? Let me kiss it and make it better."

▬▬▬ **VII. C. How does the child differentiate among people?**

Daily Routines (Home and Classroom)

- *Infant/toddler:* The infant starts to cry when an unfamiliar adult tries to pick her up. The toddler hides under his mother's dress when being introduced to his mother's friend.

- *Young child:* At the grocery store, the young child is asked by a store employee if he wants help reaching the peanut butter. The child responds, "I'm not supposed to let strangers pick me up!"

Play Routines (Home and Classroom)

- *Infant/toddler:* The infant watches another infant in child care, but does not approach her. The toddler is playing with plastic food in the toy kitchen. She offers the baby a bottle and says, "Eat, baby! It's good for you."

- *Young child:* The young child is dressed up in a cowboy hat and boots. He tells his brother, "You be the bad guy. You rob the bank. I'm the good guy. I'll come chase you."

Classroom Routines

During a field trip to the pet store, the children ask the owner about what his jobs are with the animals.

▮▮▮▮▮ **VII. D. What types of social play are demonstrated with siblings and/or peers?**

Daily Routines (Home and Classroom)

- *Infant/toddler:* The infant is held on her older sister's lap. She smiles at her and reaches for her face. The toddler and his brother take turns playing chase around the backyard, then tackling each other and laughing loudly.

- *Young child:* The young child sits on a bench next to the potty where his little sister is sitting. He is "reading" her a book and encouraging her to pee. "Tell me when you're done and I'll get Mommy."

Play Routines (Home and Classroom)

- *Infant/toddler:* The infant crawls across the living room floor and up onto her older brother's face. He pretends to shout for help and the baby giggles. The toddler in child care waddles over to see what a peer is doing with the balls and ramp. She takes a ball from her and puts it down the ramp.

- *Young child:* The young children are outdoors on the climbing structure. One says to the other, "Let's see who can get to the top first. One, two, three, GO!"

Classroom Routines

During toileting time, a young child comes out and tells the teacher, "Sami can't get her pants down. She needs help."

▮▮▮▮▮ **VII. E. How does the child deal with social conflict?**

Daily Routines (Home and Classroom)

- *Infant/toddler:* When his dad says, "That's enough ice cream," the infant starts to scream. The toddler at the checkout counter grabs a candy bar from a shelf. Her mother says, "No. You can't have that." The child starts to cry, but calms when her mother gives her a cracker.

- *Young child:* The young child says, "If I eat all my food, can I have dessert?"

Play Routines (Home and Classroom)

- *Infant/toddler:* The infant is surrounded by toys. When another infant takes his toy car, he just reaches for another one. When a peer takes her truck, the toddler chases him and bites him.

- *Young child:* The young child on the playground is hit by a peer's shovelful of flying sand. She goes to the teacher and says, "Carlos is not being nice. He threw sand at me."

Classroom Routines

At the art center, two children want the same color marker. One says, "I'll use it first, then you can have it."

▮▮▮▮▮ **VII. F. How do other children react to the child in dyads or in group settings?**

Daily Routines (Home and Classroom)

- *Infant/toddler:* At the park, the toddler sees one child hit another and moves away from them.

- *Young child:* In the park, the young child is hiding in the "belly" of the park dinosaur. He shouts, "Hey, he ate me. Somebody come save me!" Other children come to join him.

Play Routines (Home and Classroom)

- *Infant/toddler:* The infant is observed playing with the ball and laughing. Another infant crawls over to investigate. The toddler is pushing her doll stroller. Another child goes to get a stroller and follows her.

- *Young child:* The young child tries to initiate play with a peer, but is ignored. He tells the teacher sadly, "Max doesn't want to play."

Classroom Routine

At the science center, two children are putting together three-dimensional plastic dinosaur bones. When one makes a mistake, the other offers a suggestion.

VII. G. How is the child's sense of humor demonstrated?

Daily Routines (Home and Classroom)

- *Infant/toddler:* The infant sees her dad's expression when she puts noodles in her hair. She then dumps the whole bowl on her head. The toddler pulls a long strip of toilet paper from the bathroom into the bedroom. "Look, Daddy! Big!" he giggles.

- *Young child:* The young child puts toilet paper on his head and says, "Look. I'm a poo-poo head!"

Play Routines (Home and Classroom)

- *Infant/toddler:* While sitting in the laundry basket, the infant pulls a towel over her head, says, "Peek!" and laughs. The toddler takes a sticker, places it on her mother's nose, and giggles.

- *Young child:* The young child plays Hide-and-Seek, popping out of the closet, laughing, and screaming, "Here I am!"

Classroom Routines

At the literacy center, the children are talking about words that rhyme with "me." The teacher is then writing them down. One child covers his mouth and giggles, then shouts, "Pee-pee!"

GENERAL PRINCIPLES FOR SUPPORTING APPROPRIATE SOCIAL INTERACTIONS

Most parents naturally support the development of positive social interactions with their young infants. As long as the parent is responsive to the child's needs and the child does not have a difficult temperament, most interaction patterns start out positively. Both infant and child contribute to pleasurable interactions. As the child develops, caregivers make both conscious and unconscious decisions about how to support the child's social competence. The following are common strategies that parents and other caregivers use to enhance social relations.

Read Cues

Parents quickly learn to read their child's cues and understand what needs are implied by different behaviors. They know the child is uncomfortable because he or she is wet, tired, or hungry. They understand what the child likes by facial expressions and body language. For example, they may note that the child laughs when tickled or tossed, or cries when the parent says, "No." As the child gets older, caregivers begin to help the child understand the cues he or she is giving others. They comment on behaviors that support positive social engagement. For example, the parent may say, "I see you looking at Sarah's cookie. Sarah would be sad if you took it."

Respond Immediately

When parents or other caregivers understand what a child is thinking and feeling, they can either respond or ignore the child's expression. Responding immediately teaches the child that their needs are understood. When done consistently, the child learns that initiating social interaction leads to adult response. When the adult responds, it also introduces an opportunity for further social engagement. For example, the child may hold up a ball to the parent. When the parent says, "You found a ball. Do you want to play?" the child's effort was acknowledged. The child can now decide whether to throw the ball to the parent, to play independently, or to take the ball somewhere else. Alternatively, consistently ignoring the child's attempts at communication may lead to reduced efforts to interact on the part of the child.

Follow the Child's Lead

Children often attend to their environment, or engage in vocal, physical, or manipulative play in isolation. When adults pay attention to what the child is attending to or doing, and then comment, imitate, or model additional behaviors, they encourage the child to engage in a social interaction. Paying attention to what is of interest to the child creates a "topic" around which social interaction can take place. For example, if the child chooses to throw the ball to the parent, this is an invitation to play ball, and the turns can continue. If, however, the adult ignores the child or says, "Let's read a book," the child may turn away. His desired topic was the ball, and his invitation, or lead, was not followed.

Balance Turns

Social engagement requires each party to take a turn in the exchange. The more equal the turns are with respect to number and length of initiations and responses, the more balanced the relations. Parents typically try to encourage play and conversational turn taking. In the previous example, if the ball gets exchanged every time it is thrown, there is balance in turn taking. If the parent comments, "Red ball," and throws it, and the child says, "Ball," and throws it back, there is balance in the turns. If, however, the parent takes the ball and says, "Look at the ball, Paulo. What color is the ball? It is red. Can you say 'red'?" The parent has taken over control of the interaction. The parent has made four statements. If Paulo responds "red," he is taking his turn, but the balance is still weighted toward the parent.

Scaffold

One of the ways adults keep turns going with a child is to scaffold, or help the child add higher level behaviors to his or her interactions. Scaffolding can be nonverbal or verbal. Scaffolding may be directed at cognitive, motor, or communication social skills, but it always requires social interaction. The following strategies are types of scaffolding used by adults. The examples provided are related to scaffolding of positive social relations.

Modeling

Adults play an important role in developing positive social relations when they model appropriate interactions themselves. How parents treat children and others is a way of telling children what is appropriate social behavior. We have all heard the adage, "Do what I say, not what I do," but children learn through observation and parents are powerful role models. For example, the parent who says, "Don't hit your friend" but then uses hitting for punishment is actually demonstrating that hitting is acceptable. Parents often recognize the importance of their own words and actions. When they do, they make a concerted effort to model the behaviors they want to see in their children.

Directing Interactions

Adults scaffold by telling children what to do and how to act. This is a necessary part of parenting and caregiving, because young children do not come into the world hard wired with this information. Adults direct children to perform social conventions (e.g., "Say 'please'"), how to treat others (e.g., "You need to share that with your brother"), and how to act in specific situations (e.g., "In church, you must be quiet"). Directing interactions is particularly necessary when the child is too young to understand consequences.

Explaining Consequences

Another way adults scaffold children's social relations is by explaining why specific social actions or responses are important. If children understand the benefit of their actions for themselves or others, they are more likely to engage in appropriate social behaviors. As children acquire more sophisticated language abilities, they are able to discuss actions and consequences and understand why positive social actions and responses are important. For example, the adult may say, "When you shared the book with Talia, it made her want to play with you. Now she wants to share a book with you too."

Prompting Social Problem Solving

Adults provide necessary mediation in children's social problem solving as social interactions with peers and other adults become more common. Adults set limits, offer suggestions, or provide solutions when needed. This enables children to see and hear how social dilemmas can be handled. As children mature, adult guidance should shift from more adult-directed guidance to more child-directed problem solving. Children will begin to remember and reenact previous solutions, model what they have seen others do in similar circumstances, or think of alternatives unique to the situation. For example, the 9-month-old may be told, "That is Macie's toy. Here is one for you." The 3-year-old may say, "This is my baby. Here is a baby for you."

THE PRINCIPLES IN PRACTICE

Adults use a variety of strategies to support the development of positive social interactions. The following are examples of how caregivers use the previously discussed strategies during the day at both home and school. These examples are approaches that most caregivers use naturally in their daily interactions with children. They are appropriate for most children with disabilities as well.

Daily Routines (Home and Classroom)

Feeding/Eating

Mealtime is a social event and presents many opportunities for social interaction. The feeding of an infant involves the adult offering something to eat and the child responding by eating it. Turn taking with infants in feeding begins when the child offers the mother or father a bite of food. The parent will either take the bite or pretend to take a bite and then say, "Thank you. Yum, yum!" This demonstrates response to child initiation, turn taking, modeling of a social convention, and affective response to a social gesture. With the older child, social interactions may be more conversational. Mealtimes offer an opportunity for discussion of food, likes and dislikes, events of the day, and plans for later.

Diapering/Toileting

Diapering is by nature a social act. Parents take time to talk to, tickle, and play with their child while they conduct the diapering. Toileting begins with social interaction and evolves into an independent act. Parents direct, guide, comment on, and encourage, and the child responds with feelings and actions.

Dressing

Dressing also begins as a social interaction and evolves into an independent event. Co-operation on the part of the child, while the parent manipulates and comments, leads to imitation and discussion as the child learns body parts and corresponding clothing pieces. Dressing offers an opportunity for direction, turn taking, questioning, discussion of preferences, and scaffolding as the child's skills increase.

Play Routines (Home and Classroom)

Face-to-Face Games

Face-to-face games are social by nature. Particularly in the early years, such games are important. Children learn to watch and imitate facial expressions, mouth movements and sounds, and songs. Adults often initiate these games with infants. As the child gets older, he or she may initiate a turn-taking game with words or actions. Face-to-face games are of two primary types: those that require turn taking, such as Peekaboo, and those that are done in unison, such as singing songs or doing fingerplays. Both types encourage children first to follow the adult in learning the interaction, then to get the adult to participate in the game.

Physical Play

Physical play can happen either in isolation or in social contexts. In social contexts, the child learns to be both an initiator and a responder. The nature of physical play tends to be more intense and starts with tickling in infancy, becoming chasing and more complex bodily play in preschool. In infancy, adults typically initiate such play, but as the child gets older, he or she begins to initiate the play and the adult scaffolds by making it more complex.

Manipulative Play

Toy play, when done in a social context with parents, provides an opportunity for turn taking and scaffolding. As infants discover and explore the characteristics of toys, parents imitate them, creating turn taking, and then model new actions. As the child moves into construction and dramatic play, the adult provides suggestions, introduces new ideas, responds to the child's feelings and thoughts, and helps with problem solving. All of these actions provide a role model for children's interactions with others.

Sensory Play

Messy play provides opportunities for the adult to share exploratory experience, to discuss texture and characteristics, and to respond to the child's reactions to the messy experience. Art is initially introduced and shared by adults, but also can become an individual experience. Sharing the child's feelings about his or her art and discussing the content of the art remains a socially important aspect of art for the child.

Reading and Learning Routines

Circle Time

Circle time can be either a social experience, with the adult directing comments toward the children; an exchange between the adult and a child; or a discussion among the adult and the children in the group. The adult plays the role of teaching socially appropriate conventions for this type of event, leading the communication, monitoring the social transactions, and managing the social behaviors.

One-on-One Book Reading

The sharing of books with adults is immensely important for social interactions with parents and other adults. During this time, the adult and child form a relationship. They share a prolonged focus of attention that enables them to engage in multiple social interchanges. They gesture, comment, question, answer, exclaim, and predict. They share words, thoughts, and emotions, both their own and those of the characters in the books.

Science and Math

Science and math activities focus on conceptual understanding. Adults encourage social interactions within these activities by facilitating joint problem solving and collaborative learning. Both adult–child exchanges and child–child interaction can support the development of positive social relations.

PLANNING INDIVIDUALIZED INTERVENTIONS FOR IMPROVING SOCIAL INTERACTIONS

The degree to which children learn appropriate social relations from the routines described previously is dependent not only on the adults and other children with whom they interact, but also on their cognitive, communicative, sensorimotor, and emotional development. Children who have delays, disorders, or disabilities in these areas may demonstrate difficulty with developing positive social relations. The following discussion addresses specific aspects of development that may have an impact on children's social interactions. Strategies to assist these children are suggested within each area.

VII. A. What emotions does the child respond to in others?

Children with attentional disabilities, vision impairment, mental retardation, autism, fragile X syndrome, and some emotional disorders may not be able to understand social overtures and/or the emotions and thoughts being expressed by others. For some, this lack of emotional and social understanding (see TPBA2, Chapter 7, Subcategory IV. Social Cognition) is due to lack of attention to these cues. Children with disabilities that affect their attentional focus may only attend fleetingly to other people, but they attend instead to objects or their own interests. Children with attention-deficit/hyperactivity disorder (ADHD), for example, may focus attention on objects of interest, flitting briefly from one play item to another, with disregard for other children. For children with attention disorders, other people may warrant only a brief focus of attention. People are "used" for the time needed to get their own needs met. They may not show interest in the emotional cues of others because their attention is directed elsewhere.

Children with vision impairment may not be able to see facial expressions or the subtle body language of others who make social initiations. They may rely instead on auditory cues, such as volume and inflection of the voice, touch, or body position. Understanding the social intentions of others may require increased effort on the part of children with visual impairments and additional strategies on the part of adults and peers.

For other children, lack of cognitive understanding of the meaning of emotional expressions or social behaviors contributes to their difficulties. Children with intellectual disability may be functioning at a cognitive level that does not enable them to accurately interpret the actions and emotions of others. As with children who have limited attention, their own needs may be of prime importance.

Children with autism spectrum disorders are known for their "mindblindness," or lack of understanding or concern for others' cues. They may seem to be in a world of their own and do not seek out social interactions except to get their needs met. These children and children with other disorders, such as fragile X syndrome and other XY-related syndromes, may not demonstrate interest in other people's social cues.

Psychiatric disorders also may influence a child's ability to respond to others' social cues. Children who become emotionally overwhelmed may not be able to think about others' needs when they are emotionally "out-of-bounds." Likewise, children suffering from emotional trauma, children with psychotic disorders, and children with attachment disorders also may live in an emotionally insulated world and are unable to respond to others' social initiations or emotional expressions.

Although each disability is treated differently, some of the following strategies may be helpful to consider in addition to those described previously (see also Chapter 7, Section IV. Strategies for Improving Social Cognition).

Interaction Strategies

1. *Help the child focus on people.* Children who avoid eye contact or feel anxious in social situations may focus their attention on objects rather than people. Adults can help children focus on people by positioning the child in relation to people or vice versa, by using exaggerated affect, by using gestures and unusual sound patterns to redirect attention, or by pairing the child's interest in an object with social interaction. For example, if the child is interested in a toy, the adult may pick up the toy and hold it near his or her face before interacting socially with the child and the toy.

2. *Interpret social and emotional cues.* Tell the child what you or others are feeling. Explain what facial expressions or actions mean in relation to feelings or intentions; for example, "Sahara is *crying*. She is *sad*." or "Sahara wants to *play with you*." Use exaggerated intonation to help the child understand the emotional words.

3. *Offer physical or gestural support in addition to verbal prompts.* Words alone may not be enough for some children with disabilities to understand social cues. Children with language or cognitive delays, for example, may not understand explanations about ab-

stract concepts such as emotions. Having a child touch your face when you are smiling or sad can bring attention to emotional expression. The adult can then add words to label the emotion. In the previous example, the adult might have the child gently touch Sahara's tears.

When another child makes a social gesture, the adult may need to help the child respond; for example, "Israel is trying to give you a picture (adult points to Israel). Let's look at it (supporting child's hand to reach for the picture). Let's tell Israel 'thank you.'" Here, the adult gave gestural, physical, and verbal support for a positive social response.

4. *Reinforce social responsiveness.* Respond immediately whenever the child reads and responds to emotional cues in others. This does not mean saying, "Good job," because this does not tell the child what he or she did that was good. Rather, acknowledge the child's responses by commenting on the emotional cues he or she read and why it was appropriate; for example, "You saw that Sahara was crying and gave her a hug. That was nice of you" or "You took Israel's picture. Israel is smiling."

5. *Point out consequences of positive responses.* When the child does respond to social and emotional cues, the adult can identify what happened as a result. This will help the child make the connection between social actions and behavioral consequences. For example, in the previous scenarios, if Sahara stops crying and starts to play, the adult might say, "Look, your hug made Sahara feel better. She wants to play now" or "Israel is happy that you looked at his picture."

Environmental Modifications

In addition to interpersonal strategies that may support the child learning social and emotional cues, environmental modifications often are useful. Depending on the findings from TPBA2, the team may want to consider some of the following environmental modifications.

1. *Use mirrors with the child and others.* Children can learn what expressions on others' faces mean by seeing their own expressions when they are happy or sad. Mirrors can help children make this connection. For example, when the child is upset, the adult might walk into the bathroom and show the child his face in the mirror. "Look at that unhappy face. You are really mad." When actions are taken to change these emotions, the adult can return to the mirror: "Look, no more tears. Let's see a smile" (modeling a smile).

2. *Reduce the distractors.* Lights, noises, or an abundance of toys or materials can all distract children from social observations and interactions. For children who have difficulty with social and emotional cue reading, have only one or two toys out, reduce the distraction of windows by closing window coverings, and reduce noises that might compete with conversation. Eliminating competing factors helps increase the chance that the child will attend to the people in the room.

3. *Use social toys and materials.* Many toys and activities lend themselves to social interaction and emotional expression. For example, bubbles, balls, and music can encourage the child to look to other people for interaction. Adults can moderate the starting and stopping of activities the child enjoys by controlling the materials and waiting for the child to look at the adult for more interaction. For instance, if the adult is blowing bubbles and the child is laughing, the adult knows this is an activity the child wants to continue. When the adult stops and waits, the child will then look to the adult for continuation of the bubble blowing. Once the child is looking at the adult, he or she can convey expression, gestures, and words back to the child.

4. *Use picture cues.* Babies typically love pictures of other babies, as do older children. Use of real pictures of people can help adults talk about social and emotional cues and what they mean. For example, when looking at a book of babies' emotional expressions, the adult might say, "Oh, look. This baby is . . . (the adult models the expression in the book and waits for the child to respond). What do you think happened?" Such pictures allow adults to talk about emotions objectively, without actual emotions being involved. This can be most effective when the book reading follows an actual situation involving the child and the emotions of the moment prohibited meaningful discussion about the situation and feelings.

5. *Use social stories.* Social stories (i.e., short, personalized books designed for specific children) can be used to point out how other people feel in specific recurrent situations. They also provide a model for a response on the part of the child. For example, Paulo had motor difficulties that caused him to frequently and unintentionally careen into others, causing them to get upset. A social story was written for him, showing him falling into another child. The next picture showed the child he knocked down with a mad face. The following picture showed Paulo saying, "I'm sorry" and helping the other child. This social story helped Paulo recognize his effect on others and learn an appropriate social response.

VII. B. How does the child demonstrate a sense of pleasure and trust in his or her parents?

Children and adults contribute equally to building a parent–child relationship that is characterized by primarily pleasurable interactions, predictability, reciprocity, and trust. Personality factors, physical characteristics, and interactional patterns all contribute to how the relationship forms, what patterns characterize the relationship, and how mutually satisfying the relationship is to both parties.

Children with disabilities may have characteristics that make interaction with their parents more challenging. Children with motor disabilities or social avoidance may not like cuddling; children with health or regulatory issues may be excessively fussy; children with cerebral palsy or various syndromes, such as Down syndrome, may not vocalize when expected or may not demonstrate pleasure in the same way as children without disabilities; children with autism may not respond to the parents' social efforts; and many children with disabilities also may be difficult to handle, feed, get to sleep, and so forth. All of these issues make parenting more challenging and, consequently, may place stress on the parent–child relationship.

On the parents' side, negative affect or depression, insecurity or lack of parenting knowledge, avoidance of interaction, unrealistic expectations for parenting, as well as other factors may contribute to parent–child relationships that are more challenging than pleasurable. Outside stressors on the parents, such as financial problems, health problems, a negative home or community environment, or marital strife, also can have a negative affect on the parent–child relationship.

Biological, environmental, and interpersonal influences contribute to the pleasure and security felt by both parent and child in their relationship. Because a strong emotional bond between parent and child promotes healthy social and emotional development, it is essential that early intervention address the quality of this connection. The following suggestions are directed to supporting parents in building a close affiliation with their child.

Interaction Strategies

1. *Read social and emotional cues.* Children with disabilities may give more subtle social and emotional cues. For instance, the smile may be only a hint of a smile, excitement may be indicated with a kick of one leg, or discomfort may be shown by a whim-

per or by turning away. Children with disabilities also may have unusual ways of demonstrating emotions. The child with cerebral palsy may grimace as a smile, the child with autism may flap fingers or hands when excited, and the child with fragile X syndrome may ask numerous questions when anxious. Learning how to read the child's cues and have the child read the parents' cues (see above) is the first step to building the relationship. Close observation of the child and what happens before the subtle or unusual cues are seen is important.

It is helpful to keep in mind that children seek out things that interest them, they repeat things they like, and they avoid things they dislike or that stress them. Watching these seeking, repetitive, and avoidance behaviors and matching these with the physical responses, or cues, shown by the child may give adults a way of understanding the emotions the child is expressing. If the same cues are used repeatedly in similar situations, the adult can then begin to assign meaning to these cues. For example, if the child consistently leans forward and takes a bite of chocolate pudding (e.g., seeking and repeating) and this action also is consistently preceded and/or followed by a particular grimace or facial expression, the adult can begin to assign a meaning of "pleasure" to this facial expression.

2. *Provide an immediate response.* The next important step after recognizing the meaning of a social or emotional cue is for the adult to respond immediately to what the child is thought to be communicating. For example, if the child consistently looks at a toy and then looks at the parent, the parent may interpret this action as an indication of desire for the toy on the part of the child. By responding, "Oh, you like that rattle" and handing the rattle to the child, the adult is teaching the child that his cues are being read. The child will then continue to use this method to get his needs met. Once the child knows the adult will respond, the adult can wait for a higher level response such as vocalization.

3. *Provide nurturing interactions.* Children who resist social interactions often do not appear to like typical nurturing efforts such as kissing or hugging or even, for some children, feeding. It is important for adults to find interactions that the child finds pleasurable and calming. For some children, this may involve the rocking of a swing, bouncing the child up and down on a knee, singing a certain song, rubbing the child's back, or using a vibrating toy on the legs. Children feel nurtured when they feel calm and safe, so it is important to find a way to connect with the child in a way that is non-threatening.

4. *Be consistent.* Another critical part of developing a trusting relationship is having consistent responses to the child's actions and feelings. If a behavior such as throwing food earns a laugh from the parent one day and punishment the next, the child does not know what to expect. The child may keep throwing food in the attempt to get that positive response again. Maintaining consistency is one of the hardest parts of parenting and caregiving, but it is extremely important because reliable, clear messages are reassuring to children. It teaches them that their interactions with their parents are predictable and dependable.

5. *Respect the child's interests and needs.* One way that adults can build a positive relationship with children is to respect what they like and want to do, even if it is not the adults' preference. Following children's interests and actions tells them that you accept them as a person and that their happiness and needs are important.

6. *Encourage mutual sharing.* Mutual enjoyment of the world is a great way to build a sense of connection with a child. Whether initiated by the child or the parent, any activity that is pleasurable to both will facilitate building the relationship. Turn taking

with actions, reflection of and sharing of emotions, and expressing delight in the interaction tells the child that this relationship is a positive one.

7. *Set limits.* Of course, the child cannot always get his or her way or be the decision maker regarding daily events or behaviors. Knowing what is expected and having restrictions about what, when, or how things will happen and what behaviors are acceptable gives children secure parameters for functioning. For children, having too much control over the events of one's life can seem overwhelming. Children may actually misbehave in an effort to have someone else take control. A balance between having too few and too many limits often is difficult for caregivers to find. Limits should be few when the child is very young and should be added as the child gains more independence and his or her environment expands into the community.

8. *Communicate love and a desire to keep the child safe.* Love can be communicated through all of the child's senses—through a loving look, comforting sounds, gentle touch, rhythmic movement, favorite tastes and smells, and calming holding. Children with disabilities may appreciate some of these types of input more than others. The adult can build a stronger relationship by understanding what types of input the child enjoys so that this can be incorporated throughout the day.

Environmental Modifications

In addition to interpersonal strategies that may support the child developing pleasure and trust in parents, environmental modifications often are useful. Depending on the findings from TPBA2, the team may want to consider some of the following environmental modifications.

1. *Use materials that require interaction.* Just as materials can be used to help children focus on others, they can be used to help develop a relationship. Materials that encourage interaction or activities in which adults can become involved provide opportunities for reciprocal play, nurturing engagement, and initiation, response, and turn taking by adult and child. Baby dolls, toy telephones, dramatic play situations involving more than one person, board or card games, and so forth all provide opportunities for adults to model; build give-and-take interactions; and demonstrate respect, trust, and nurturance.

Even activities that are usually done in isolated play, such as puzzles, drawing, or some cause-and-effect toys, can become venues for joint play. For example, when children are young, even simple shape puzzles can provide a means for supportive problem solving. Drawing a picture together can provide a way to direct each other, share ideas, and build confidence.

2. *Read to the child.* Reading to a child and sharing a book by discussing the pictures and actions is an important nurturing activity. Children usually sit on the adult's lap or next to the adult. The parent reads, comments, waits for the child to make noises or a comment, and then lets the child turn the page. Such interaction is particularly important for children with disabilities who—if they are children with cognitive delays, attention deficits, language impairment, visual impairment, deafness, autism, or cerebral palsy—may not be read to very frequently. All children can benefit from this social experience with significant adults, so it is important for adults to build reading into their daily routine. Modifications may be needed (e.g., short books for children with attention issues, tactile books for children with visual impairment, books with real pictures for children with cognitive impairment) to ensure that the child maintains interest and can participate in the book reading process.

Young children love books about relationships between parents and children, and about loving and being loved. These books offer adults the opportunity to talk about their relationship with their child and how much the child is loved.

3. *Stay within visual or vocal range.* When not participating in the child's play, it is important for adults to stay within close proximity to the child. Children who are developmentally younger frequently need to "check in" with the adult to make sure that he or she is still there. When the child is playing, the adult can sit nearby and be involved in another activity. Just looking up and commenting occasionally may be enough to help the child feel secure. The same is true if the adult is in another room. Talking the child and assuring him or her that you are close by can have a reassuring effect.

4. *Use technology.* Place the child's and other family members' pictures on the computer. This can function as another form of "book" that can be looked at and talked about together. A tape of the parent singing to the child may help the child feel comforted at bedtime.

5. *Use pictures and family books.* Children love pictures of themselves and family members. Making picture books for the child enables family members to name each other, talk about what they are doing in the pictures, talk about relationships (e.g., mommy, uncle, brother), and create a sense of family unity.

6. *Use parental materials for transition objects.* Children who have difficulty with separation may benefit from taking something that belongs to the parent with them to child care. Objects such as a handkerchief or scarf that a parent has held or worn will have the parent's scent on it, which may be comforting to the child. Children who have difficulty sleeping alone also may take or wear an item of the parent's clothing to bed. A T-shirt the parent has worn or a pillow case the parent has slept on also may be comforting.

7. *Use adaptive equipment to make interacting less challenging.* Positioning is particularly important for children with motor disabilities. Parents may be taught by therapists to carry the child in a position that breaks up the child's high tone, but also turns the child away from the parent. They may sit behind the child with high tone or low tone to provide more support for the child when playing. In both situations, the child is not getting face-to-face interaction with the parent. For this reason, it is particularly important to make sure there are times during the day when the child can play with the parent in a face-to-face position so that facial expressions can be seen and kisses can be exchanged. Special seating may be required to enable the child to be supported in such a way that he or she can interact without help from the parent.

8. *Create a safe environment.* Although a safe environment is necessary for all children, it is important to consider extra precautions that may be needed by children with special needs. For example, children who have no sense of fear may get themselves into unsafe or precarious predicaments on a playground or environment with high climbing spaces. Likewise, children who have a high pain tolerance or cognitive limitations may experiment with dangerous materials (e.g., fireplaces) without feeling or recognizing the harm. Supervision and child-proofing are another way children learn that parents can be trusted to keep them safe.

VII. C. How does the child differentiate among people?

Understanding the differences between family and strangers, familiar and unfamiliar people, males and females, and young and old are just a few of the differentiations that children learn as they encounter the world beyond their home. Social differentiations are important because children must learn to interact differently with varying categories of people. Young infants learn to understand who is mommy and who is not, who is familiar and who is a stranger. This understanding is important for developing the sense of trust described previously. Understanding who is a stranger also is important for safety reasons. As children come to understand age differences in the toddler years, they begin to interact with babies in a different way from their peers; they lower their language and play levels. Young children understand that boys and girls are different and that older people are different. They notice color differences, dress, accents, and language differences. They begin asking questions about differences and making inferences about what these differences mean.

Children with cognitive or social disabilities may not make these differentiations or may make them later in their development. Helping children understand the meaning of various characteristics and to appreciate individual differences is important for the development of appropriate social skills.

Interaction Strategies

1. *Point out differences.* Talk about characteristics of people and how behavior should vary depending on these characteristics. Some children with disabilities may not attend to personal characteristics or may not attach meaning to the characteristics they do perceive. Adults can help children focus on relevant social aspects and facilitate the child gaining an understanding of behaviors and characteristics of others; for example, "Jenny is a baby. She can't sit up yet. You have to put your arm under her head and be very gentle when you hold her"; "Grandpa has a cane to help him walk. Be careful not to run into him"; or "Ayana can't hear what you are saying. You need to get in front of her so she can see you. Then you can show her what you want."

2. *Prepare the child ahead of time.* Letting children know what is coming can alleviate some of the anxiety that some children with disabilities experience in social situations. Giving the child words to use in unfamiliar social situations may help: "We are going to a party. There will be lots of other children there for you to play with. Pick out a few toys to take with you. Then you can show them your toys and ask, 'Do you want to play with me?'"

3. *Discuss appropriate interactions in real situations.* Many children with disabilities cannot remember what they were told to do or do not generalize appropriate behaviors from one situation to another. Saying, "I told you before . . . " may be confusing to the child. Instead, the adult can use the real-life situation to explain what needs to be done and why. For example, when the child takes another toddler's toy, the adult might say or sign, "Play, please. I want to play too," introducing another toy and facilitating play together.

4. *Discuss appropriate interactions in hypothetical situations.* Ask, "What would happen if . . . ?" or "What would you do if . . . ?" For children who have the cognitive ability to hypothesize or think about possible social situations, adults can present various circumstances that the child might encounter and then talk about options for what the child might do. For example, with a young child, the adult might say, "What would you do if someone pushed you out of line?" The response can lead to a discussion of alternatives or reinforcement of ideas.

5. *Model or role play situations.* Modeling gestures, words, and actions is a powerful way to teach children social skills. Everything adults do is a model for children, but adults also can intentionally model specific social actions and responses. Infants and toddlers can potentially watch, listen, and imitate what they see adults do. For a child with disabilities, the adult may need to exaggerate his or her responses to make sure the child notices the adult's behaviors. For example, the adult may model using good manners: "THANK you! You SHARED with Mommy." With older children, role play of situations they may encounter can help children remember strategies to be used later. For example, adults might role play being approached by a stranger who offers the child candy. He or she may then model the response, "I don't talk to strangers."

6. *Give feedback.* All children need feedback about their behavior. Supporting positive social behavior rather than punishing negative social behavior is recommended. For instance, instead of saying, "Don't hit your brother!" the adult might say, "Ask him when you can have a turn. Then I will remind him when it is your turn."

Environmental Modifications

In addition to interpersonal strategies that may support the child making appropriate social differentiations, environmental modifications often are useful. Depending on the findings from TPBA2, the team may want to consider some of the following environmental modifications.

1. *Read books.* Books about different people can help adults talk with children about differences. Books about family members, grandparents, friends, strangers, and children with special needs can provoke discussion and comparisons to people in the child's life.

2. *Use social stories.* As described previously, social stories can help children understand how to treat different people. For instance, a social story for Benji, who had cognitive delays, was written to help him respect the other children and the teacher in circle time. The first page had a picture of Benji sitting in the circle with his hands in his lap listening to the teacher read a story. The second page had a picture of Benji raising his hand to answer the teacher's question. The last page had a picture of all of the children watching Benji answer the question.

3. *Use puppets and dolls.* For older toddlers and young children, dolls and puppets can be used to enact various scenarios involving different people. The puppets can show either positive or negative behaviors, and the children can help them figure out what they should do. For example, in a preschool class the teacher was having trouble with Marina, who was biting other children. The teacher used puppets to act out the situation, and the children then helped the puppets decide what to say. She then let Marina tell the puppets what to say and do.

4. *Expose the child to a variety of people and situations.* It goes without saying that children learn through experience. Having interactions with people of different ages, backgrounds, languages, and ability levels provides learning opportunities. With adult support, questioning and problem-solving, and practice, children can learn to interact appropriately with many different people.

▬▬▬▬▬ **VII. D. What types of social play are demonstrated with siblings and/or peers?**

Although at times all children have difficulties with social engagement with siblings and peers, children with disabilities may encounter social challenges more frequently. The types of social challenges that need to be addressed in intervention include extreme withdrawal or avoidance of social interaction, lack of ability to initiate interaction, inability to sustain interaction, use of inappropriate words, gestures or actions directed toward others, and hurtful actions toward others. Children may exhibit these problems for a variety of reasons. Children with ADHD or autism spectrum disorders may lack attention to or interest in siblings or peers. Children with cognitive delays, fragile X syndrome, autism spectrum disorders, or Asperger syndrome may demonstrate reduced social understanding. Physical limitations of children with motor impairments may restrict their access to other children and their ability to interact motorically in the same way that other children do. This inability to "keep up" also may lead to reduced motivation to play with other children. Much of interaction involves communication, and language delays or disorders can interfere with communication between play partners. Children with vision impairments or who are deaf or hard of hearing may have a difficult time following the play of others. Sensory, emotional, or behavioral regulation concerns can lead to actions or interactions that become out of control. Emotional difficulties that influence themes or social patterns within play with peers or siblings also can dominate play and inhibit children's response to the needs of other children.

For many children with special needs, social play with other children requires adult assistance. The following strategies frequently are helpful in scaffolding social interactions between and among children who need extra social support.

Interaction Strategies

1. *Make sure players are aware of each other.* Children who are focused on their own play may not even be aware that other children are near. The adult can bring attention to the other child by talking about what he or she is doing, telling the other child to watch, or engaging the other child in a way that the child with special needs cannot ignore; for example, "Look what Janella is doing! She's having fun with the cars!"

2. *Encourage interaction.* Children may not interact spontaneously without some assistance. The adult can promote interactions by drawing the children together. For example, "Janella, show Christian your cars." Giving the children a reason to interact is another way to encourage interaction; for example, "Christian has blocks over here, Janella. Bring your car over so you and Christian can build a car wash." Point to or make sure children know who is talking and, therefore, to whom they should be attending.

3. *Model interaction.* The adult also can entice children to play by modeling appropriate social interactions; for instance, "I need a block, Janella. Thank you so much! I need another block, Christian. Thank you! Now Janella needs a block, Christian."

4. *Prompt words and actions.* Children may want to interact but do not have ideas about what to say or do. The adult can prompt the child by suggesting words or actions; for example, "Janella, give Christian a car so you both have one. Christian, now you can drive your car through the car wash." Pictures of movements or signs for fingerplays can cue children how to respond.

5. *Use social temptations.* Give children a reason to interact. Social temptations lure children into interaction; for example, "Here is the water to wash the car. Who wants a brush to wash the cars?" Water is almost always an enticement, and having only one of the necessary brushes may encourage sharing.

6. *Comment on the peer's actions.* Talking about what the peer is doing and carrying on an animated conversation with the peer may attract the attention of the child with special needs and draw him or her into the play. This is particularly true when the child knows the peer and is interested in playing.

7. *Establish a relationship with the child, and then play with a peer.* If the child has had a fun interaction with the adult, he or she may not want to have that adult shift attention to another child. By playing with the peer, the adult can be the magnet that attracts the child to triadic play. Once the peers are playing, the adult can play the role of observer, commenter, and encourager.

8. *Be the "third party" who orchestrates interaction.* Triadic play with the adult or parent as the center of the triangle often can stimulate peer or sibling play. The adult can then use the strategies discussed previously with both peers or siblings to facilitate continued interaction.

9. *Provide only as much support as needed, and then back out.* It is important for adults to direct, guide, and support only as long as it is necessary. Playing with children is fun, and it is easy for the adult to become the center of the play. The goal is for children to be able to initiate and maintain social interactions independently.

Environmental Modifications

In addition to interpersonal strategies that may help the child engage in appropriate social play with siblings or peers, environmental modifications often are useful. Depending on the findings from TPBA2, the team may want to consider some of the following environmental modifications.

1. *Arrange the environment for social interaction.* Children who are uncomfortable with social interaction may play in areas away from other children. Arrange the environment in such a way that the toys with which children want to play are in close proximity. This will encourage parallel play and will enable the adult to facilitate interaction more easily.

2. *Pair children and use highly motivating social toys.* Knowing what motivates children and then matching children with like interests can encourage children to interact. Toys that involve movement, such as bubbles and balls, are engaging for children who like activity. Dramatic play involving a fun event with more than one character can be motivating to children who like creative play and talking. Children who like to solve problems may enjoy making a complex cause-and-effect toy work, such as a tape recorder and microphone.

3. *Provide games for positive social interaction opportunities.* Structured games can provide a means for teaching children to follow rules and take turns. Adult facilitation typically is needed as children learn how to play structured games.

4. *Use stories to provide a framework for interaction.* When peers or siblings like the same movies or books, adults can promote dramatic play by providing props and prompts for the children to reenact the story. Adult facilitation may be needed to get the play started.

5. *Train peers to request, suggest, and comment.* Peers who are sensitive and caring can be taught how to initiate play with peers who are less social. The adult needs to explain why the child needs assistance to be social and how the peer can use words or actions to engage him or her. Often, giving the child words to say, such as, "Can I play with you?" is helpful. The adult also can show the peer how to keep the play going by suggesting an action to the child or commenting on what is happening. With guidance and reinforcement for using social supports, peers can become effective social tutors.

6. *Pay attention to position.* Where children are positioned in relation to each other can influence interaction. In particular, children with vision and hearing problems need to be situated so that they are aware of their peers, can touch them if needed to get their attention, and can see and hear them as clearly as possible. For example, children who use sign language need to be facing their peers so that signs, gestures, lips, and facial expressions are clearly visible. Peers can be taught not to turn their backs to children who are deaf or hard of hearing. Children who have low vision need lighting that enables the child to see peers' faces and gestures; for instance, it is hard to see faces when children have light behind them from a window. Children who have motor problems may need to be positioned for social interaction. For example, children in wheelchairs may have difficulty engaging in dramatic play, floor play, or other types of social situations. Removing the child from the chair and positioning the child in an al-

ternative supported position may enable him or her to interact with other children more easily. Parents of infants with motor concerns often are advised to carry children in positions that "break up" high tone so the child is more flexed. Some positions, however, may not encourage face-to-face communication. Adults need to be aware of the impact of positions on social interaction and make modifications to enhance verbal, gestural, and physical interaction.

VII. E. How does the child deal with social conflict?

All children must deal with social conflict. The target of this discussion is the child who instigates significantly more conflict than most children. This may be because the child intentionally instigates conflict or because the child inadvertently initiates conflict. Children with emotional problems may find the attention received from causing conflict to be reinforcing, even if the result is negative attention. A few children get pleasure out of causing other children pain or unhappiness. On the other hand, some children cause conflict accidentally. Children with motor planning problems or sensory dysfunction may unintentionally irritate peers by poking, shoving, bumping into, or in other ways causing others to become angry. Children who are developmentally immature or cognitively unaware of others' needs also may pursue their own desires without thinking of the effects of their actions on others.

The following strategies are offered for working with children who need support for reducing or managing social conflict.

Interaction Strategies

1. *Model conflict resolution.* Make sure the child understands how positive conflict resolution takes place. This requires intentional modeling of behavior during specific conflict situations, as well as incidental modeling throughout the day. For example, the parent might say, "Did you see what Daddy did? Mommy and Daddy both wanted the last cookie, so Daddy broke it in half. That way we both got some." Adults are powerful role models for sharing, compromising, negotiating, appeasing, and placing value on other people's needs over their own.

2. *Point out positive conflict resolution.* When other children use words instead of hitting, for example, the adult can indicate that words worked to solve the problem. This can occur in a real-life situation, in a book, or on a television show. The parent watching *Angelina Ballerina* with a child, for instance, might say, "When Angelina didn't share with her friend Anya, she lost her friend and was sad. What did Angelina say to her friend to make her feel better? That's right, she said she was sorry and wanted to be friends. She even gave Anya her tutu."

3. *Provide choices that give the child some control.* Whenever possible, let the child make the determination of an appropriate decision. This gives the child the responsibility for actions, rather than making the adult the arbitrator. For instance, instead of saying, "Give the ball to your brother. It's his turn," the adult might say, "Your brother wants a turn with the ball. Do you want to give him a turn now or tell him he can have it in one more minute?" The child will most likely choose "one more minute," and the adult can then say, "Okay. Joshua and I will look at my watch and let you know when a minute is up." Often the child will relinquish the desired toy even before the minute is up, because control is in his hands.

4. *Provide two acceptable options.* Struggles often can be settled by showing children that there is more than one acceptable choice. For example, if two children want to sit on the teacher's lap to listen to a story, the teacher might say, "I need to hold the book

in my lap, but one of you can sit by me on this side, and the other one can sit by me on the other side."

5. *Make the second option as appealing as the first.* When two options are involved, present the options as equally appealing. For instance, if everyone wants to play in the water table, but there is not enough room for all of the children, the teacher might say, "The water table looks fun, but look over here! I've got glue and sparkles in shakers. Some of you will get to shake sprinkles and make it "snow" on your pictures."

6. *Let "fate" determine the outcome.* Children may become embroiled in fights over who gets to do something first or who gets a certain object when there is only one. Because there is bound to be an unhappy "loser," the adult can let an objective game, rather than a person, make the decision. For example, if both siblings want to have their bath "first" the parent might say, "I have a penny hiding in one hand. The child who picks the hand with the penny in it gets to take a bath first."

7. *Reinforce peaceful resolution.* Acknowledge children's efforts at sharing, compromising, negotiating, appeasing, and placing value on other people's needs over their own. Reinforcement can be in the form of a hug, verbal praise, or a special honor; for instance, "You were so nice to let Maggie play with your doll, I'm going to let you choose your ice cream flavor first."

8. *Use consistent, fair strategies to resolve conflict.* Although it is easy to give in to manipulation or whining, the adult needs to remain objective and aware of strategies that have been used in the past. If children learn that conflict gets them what they want, they will continue to use it. Adults also need to be cognizant of preferential treatment toward certain children and not fall into the trap of always letting a specific child have his or her way. Children pick up on this quickly and learn that the adult always makes decisions in someone else's favor.

Environmental Modifications

In addition to interpersonal strategies that may help the child deal with social conflict, environmental modifications often are useful. Depending on the findings from TPBA2, the team may want to consider some of the following environmental modifications.

1. *Remove objects of conflict from the situation.* Sometimes putting the object of the conflict in "time out" is effective. This removes the object of contention and, therefore, the need for conflict. It also teaches the child that without compromise, no one "wins." The adult might say, for example, "There is only one Superman figure. You can decide who gets to have it first. If you can't decide without fighting, Superman will go into time out until you decide how to share him." Once children realize that there is not going to be a "winner," they may decide to use negotiation or compromise.

2. *Use visual cues.* Many children with disabilities respond better to visual reminders than to oral directions or explanations. In addition to gestures and modeling, picture cues showing children sharing or talking together may be helpful in a classroom, where the teacher can point to the picture and say, "We share and talk, not fight." Visual cues can be helpful to prepare children for joint social tasks as well. Flashing the lights for cleanup, for example, helps all of the children understand what they need to do together. For children with hearing impairment, rules, the class schedule, and other activities should be shown in pictures as well as fingerspelling or signs. A poster of the fingerspelling alphabet also should be visible for children to see.

3. *Use social stories.* For children who have recurrent problems with social conflicts in specific situations, individual social stories may be helpful. As described previously,

drawings or actual pictures showing the child behaving positively are visual reminders to the child and can provide visual cues for a behavior sequence.

4. *Provide social supports for children with sensory limitations.* Children with vision or hearing concerns may have difficulty communicating their needs or frustrations or being understood by others. Their two-way visual and auditory communication is impeded, making conflicts more likely. Teach children specific ways to communicate key concepts that are needed when conflicts arise. For instance, signs or specific gestures may speed understanding. Teaching everyone the signs for *no, stop, want, play,* and *me too,* can increase comprehension among peers and reduce conflict with the child with a hearing impairment. Help peers understand that children with low vision may not see their attempts to communicate, and teach them to gently touch the child and get the child's attention before they talk. Children also can be taught to use objects in combination with their communication. For example, if a child who is blind wants a truck that another child is playing with, the peer can be taught that the child cannot see the other options available. Help peers to understand how to read the needs of the child who has a visual impairment and respond with concrete actions. For example, instead of fighting over one truck, the peer can hand another truck to the child.

▩▩▩▩▩ **VII. F. How do other children react to the child in dyads or in group settings?**

Children who are bullied frequently or are avoided by other children are more at risk for social and emotional concerns. Helping other children understand how to engage with these children is an important role for adults. Children who are excessively shy often avoid interaction. They play primarily in isolation, do not initiate play or conversation with others, and often will leave an area occupied by other children. Peers quickly learn to stay away from these children, and although they may not treat them negatively, they do not persist in trying to engage these children.

Another concern is children who have mannerisms or behaviors that make them the brunt of peers' teasing, abuse, and negative humor. These children may look different, have unusual mannerisms, talk in unique patterns, or behave erratically. Other children make them the target of either subtle or overt cruelty or mistreatment. Early intervention to increase positive social interactions is essential for such children. This must take a two-pronged approach, directed at both the child and the peers in the child's environment.

Interaction Strategies

1. *Discuss similarities and differences.* Adults can help children understand individual differences and appreciate different strengths. Talk about how we are all alike in some ways and different in others. Adults need to point out what children do well and that differences are to be appreciated. For example, a child who is shy may be described as "independent." A child who screams or hits may be one who "tells how he feels with actions instead of words" and he "needs us to help him use words."

2. *Help other children understand what the child likes and dislikes.* Tell other children what makes the child happy or unhappy, particularly if there are discernable patterns. Make suggestions for ways children can introduce preferred objects, activities, or play to the child to entice the child to interact; for instance, "Ricardo likes stacking the blocks. Maybe you could build a tower next to his." Do not force interaction, but encourage parallel play and attention to the same activity.

3. *Create social situations.* Some situations lend themselves to social interaction. The adult can create reasons for children to interact. For instance, it takes two children to

help tape up a large picture, help carry a basket of books, bring in the groceries, dramatize a story, and so forth.

4. *Create triadic play situations with adult intervention.* When children do not interact spontaneously, the adult can play a facilitating role. The adult forms the mediating role in a triangular interaction in which both peers are interacting with the adult but not interacting with each other. In this situation, the adult can create reasons for the children to engage each other; for example, "Sara needs a blue crayon" or "Can you get Clara's baby a bottle, Maria? Her baby is crying."

5. *Model caring and respect.* Children observe how adults treat other children. They may come to resent the "favored child," treat the "ignored child" with disdain, or be cruel to the child who is reprimanded frequently. Adults need to be aware of their own attitudes toward all of the children with whom they interact. They need to model and convey the need for respect, caring, concern, and fairness toward all.

Environmental Modifications

In addition to interpersonal strategies that may help other children understand how to interact with the child, environmental modifications often are useful. Depending on the findings from TPBA2, the team may want to consider some of the following environmental modifications.

1. *Create a respectful, caring environment.* In an environment where respect is expected and cruelty is not tolerated, children learn tolerance, acceptance, and prosocial behavior. Arranging the environment so that children are expected to share and interact positively is important. In preschool classrooms, pictures of positive interactions can be reminders. Teach children to appreciate individual differences and strengths. For instance, children can learn that Ben walks with a walker and cannot move quickly, but he loves to play and share toys when he is sitting comfortably. Teach children to look beyond appearance to the good things within each child. Practice commenting on positive characteristics and reframing behaviors, so children perceive them in a different light. For example, if a child has temper tantrums in class and makes others feel uncomfortable, the teacher should not describe the child as "naughty" or "stubborn" but rather "persistent" or "determined." Give children words to deal with the situation; for example, "Kyle is trying very hard to get what he wants by yelling. Let's help him learn to try hard with words instead."

2. *Arrange the environment to encourage cooperative interaction.* Place board games, card games, blocks, and other materials that encourage interaction out where they are visible. The adult may need to prompt joint interaction to get activities started.

3. *Train peers to be social tutors.* Peers can learn how to watch out for each other and to intercede if a child is being treated inappropriately. Again, giving children appropriate words or options for how to act in such situations is important.

4. *Use puppets, dolls, and other visual forms such as books or picture cues to remind peers about how to interact with each other.* Plan activities to allow children to see and discuss different types of interactions. Use of puppets who behave badly toward each other, for example, can enable children to gain distance and discuss objectively the consequences of words and actions on the feelings and behaviors of others.

▬▬▬ **VII. G. How is the child's sense of humor demonstrated?**

Humor is a wonderful social tool when it is positive and not denigrating to others. Unfortunately, some children with emotional or behavioral problems say things, in an attempt to be funny, that are hurtful or self-deprecating. This is not healthy for any of the parties involved. As children begin to learn the meaning and power of words, they also learn that words and actions can make others laugh. Most children enjoy getting others to laugh. Even in infancy, children repeat actions that result in making their parents laugh. Getting others to smile, giggle, or laugh is a rewarding experience. Getting others to laugh at the expense of others or oneself, however, has negative psychological results. The following suggestions are offered to help adults support the development of positive humor and discourage negative humor.

Interaction Strategies

1. *Engage in verbal and physical activities that are silly or contrary to what one expects to happen (e.g., putting a hat on your foot).* Encourage children to insert humor into their play and comment when something they do or say is funny. When the child makes noises or imitates funny sounds in infancy, adults laugh because the sounds are unexpected. When the infant dumps food on the floor, looks at the adult and laughs, he or she is laughing because the action was unexpected, not because he was trying to be naughty. Encouraging laughter is good. Adults need to help children set parameters around what is and is not funny. Their own actions and responses set the model for the child.

2. *Avoid laughing at things the child does that result in harm.* Help children learn to laugh with others, not at them. Young children are constantly doing things that make adults laugh. It often is hard to control oneself when one sees a child go down a slide and plop on his bottom in a puddle. However, laughing at something that causes another person discomfort gives a child the wrong message. If, however, the child who plops in the puddle also is laughing, it is acceptable to laugh with the child not at him. The adult needs to convey this message to children. Explain when it is okay to laugh and when it is not.

3. *Try to avoid laughing at things the child does that are not meant to be funny.* Children do many things in all seriousness that are hilarious to those who are watching. The child may dress up in a dramatic play costume and pretend to be a superhero, but what the adult sees is a little boy in tights and snow boots, with a towel around his shoulders and a bathing cap on his head. Laughing at the child conveys that the child's efforts and intentions were unsuccessful and worthy of ridicule. This is not a good message to give, because it also models laughing at others for inappropriate reasons. It would be better to comment on the child's creativity, take a picture, and then laugh hysterically later.

4. *Comment when others laugh inappropriately.* Children see things that are funny but, unlike most adults, do not yet have the cognitive skills to determine whether it is socially appropriate to laugh. Adults can help children develop this skill by talking about why things are or are not funny, and how laughing at someone may hurt their feelings; for example, "Kayla, that is a funny shirt that man is wearing, but it is not nice to laugh at him. I think he likes the shirt. If you laugh at him, it may hurt his feelings."

5. *Provide alternative statements or actions.* When the child wants attention from the adult and wants interaction that results in laughter, the adult can redirect the child to more appropriate humor. For example, when the child hits her sibling over the head with a foam bat and laughs, the parent can say, "I know you think that is funny, but your brother didn't think it was funny and neither do I. I think we could all laugh together if you tickled him instead."

Environmental Modifications

In addition to interpersonal strategies that may help the child develop socially appropriate humor, environmental modifications often are useful. Depending on the findings from TPBA2, the team may want to consider some of the following environmental modifications.

1. *Provide materials, activities, and situations that elicit appropriate humor.* Funny books, movies, toys, or games that create humorous results (e.g., wind-up or electronic toys that do funny actions), and materials that can create humorous situations (e.g., bubbles), give children legitimate reasons to cause others to laugh.

2. *Look for humor in all environments.* Funny things occur everywhere. Have the child help you look for and find situations that are funny. This will provide many opportunities to discuss what is funny and what is not, and why.

ROUTINES FOR THE CHILD WHO NEEDS
SUPPORT TO DEVELOP POSITIVE SOCIAL INTERACTIONS

Daily Routines (Home and Classroom)

Feeding/Eating

Mealtime provides opportunities for social interaction, conflict, and humor. Adults can help children with disabilities by ensuring that mealtime is a social event. Take time to talk about the day, the meal, and what is happening next. Take advantage of conflict situations (e.g., who gets more), involve the child in problem solving, give the child choices, and take time to be silly and laugh.

Diapering/Toileting

Diapering is a social event, but toileting becomes increasingly independent. The largest conflicts arise between adult and child because the child wants independent movement and control over his or her own body. Making diapering a fun, social time should be the goal. Talking, turn taking, helping with diapering tasks, and sharing games can make this a positive social time. Toileting becomes a conflict when the adult tries to assert control. Toileting is an opportunity for the child to assert independence and gain confidence and self-assurance. Give the child an opportunity to tell others about his or her accomplishments and model for other children.

Dressing

Dressing is more social when in infancy and toddlerhood. As children gain more motor and sequencing skills, the dressing task becomes less social. Children want to make their own decisions. For children with physical, sensory, or mental disabilities, this process may be delayed. However, if cognitive and emotional development are not delayed, some children may want more independence than they are capable of achieving. Conflicts may arise as children want control and are unable to be independent. It is important for adults to give children every opportunity to make choices and be in control of the situation. Deciding what to wear, what to put on first, and how quickly to dress can help children with disabilities have an important lead social role and can be used by adults for social problem solving. For instance, helping the child think about what clothing to wear, what to wear for the weather outside, and so forth can involve negotiation or compromise.

Going Out

Going out into the community usually is a social event, and it can be a challenging time for children with disabilities. People may treat them unkindly because of the way they look or act. They may have 1) behavioral issues that interfere with their ability to have successful social interactions with others, 2) language difficulties that make having social interactions difficult, 3) cognitive delays that may limit their understanding of appropriate social behaviors, or 4) other challenges that make "going out" complicated. Adults can help children with social interactions in the community by helping them to predict what the social expectations will be where they are going, providing suggestions for what they can say or do to interact, and reinforcing positive social efforts at each step of the way.

Play Routines (Home and Classroom)

Face-to-Face Play

In many ways, social interactions have their roots in face-to-face play, in which parents and infant exchange glances, smiles, talk, and games. Face-to-face play typically is based on achieving laughter or a humorous response. Children who do not like eye contact or who avoid close contact with adults may avoid this type of interaction because they may not find these games humorous or even pleasurable. For children with disabilities, face-to-face play offers opportunities for adults to build the foundations for social interaction: initiation, responding, turn taking, and enjoyment of another person's reactions. With sensitive cue-reading of the child's pleasurable reactions and stopping and pausing as the child needs, face-to-face play (e.g., Peekaboo) can help children who resist direct interaction find pleasure in this type of play.

Physical Play

Physical play is another form of play that some children with disabilities may resist. Children with sensory integration concerns, motor disabilities, or sensitivity to close proximity to others may not enjoy this type of play. Although roughhousing and physical games such as Chase are not necessary for the development of social skills, children do learn give-and-take skills in this type of play. Sometimes the child is the aggressor and sometimes the adult or peer is the aggressor. In both instances, the child has to learn to moderate her actions, communicate how she is feeling, respond to the other person, and be able to adjust her play in response to the needs of the other person. Such play can be useful in development of social skills. For children who do not find pleasure in active physical play, the adult or peers should begin with quiet, safe turn-taking play interactions. Only after trust has been developed should the person try more intensive physical play. The purpose of the play is to have fun and bring out the child's sense of risk-taking and exuberance; anything that does not produce this result should be modified or discontinued.

Manipulative Play

Manipulative play offers many opportunities for humorous actions, particularly when building silly structures, placing characters in funny situations, or exaggerating the actions in the play. For children with motor disabilities who cannot produce the manipulative actions necessary to perform maneuvers with small pieces, adults may be able to facilitate or support children's movements or move the pieces for them. The important aspect to remember when working with children with disabilities is that the goal is not just about acquiring new cognitive, language, or motor skills; the goal also is to find humor and enjoyment in all of play. Pretending to have action figures do silly things, making a humorous error, or making up funny stories can add an element to manipulative play that not only will make it more enjoyable, but also will contribute to the social foundations of a sense of humor.

Sensory Play

Most children enjoy sensory play and can create humorous situations with such things as bubbles, Silly Putty, playdough, water, and mud. Humorous play with sensory materials is almost always social and involves taking turns with building or doing something impractical with the materials that results in laughter. The humor that comes from messing with social conventions of neatness and cleanliness even extends into later years. For example, what is the high school food fight, if not sensory play? For children who have aversions to sensory materials, however, such play is not humorous. Children with sensory defensiveness need to be introduced to aversive materials gradually, in an exploratory—rather than a playful and humorous—way. Humor can be discovered only when the child feels safe and secure.

Dramatic Play

Dramatic play is probably one of the greatest venues for expression of sense of humor, because the child is free to create any actions or dialogue he or she can conceive. For this reason, children who have the ability to pretend—to interact with others in a representation of a real or imaginary sequence—can make dramatic play into a child's comedy club. They can act silly to amuse their peers, make up funny sounds or words, create outlandish stories, and involve their peers in ways prohibited by the rules of reality. The adult who understands the importance of this freedom can encourage and support the expression of humor in children. This can be done through modeling humorous actions as a way of showing acceptance, by laughing at things the child intends to be funny (even if they are not), and by generating funny plots together. For example, the adult might say, "I would like to have something funny for dinner. I want rocks for dinner tonight! What would you like to have that is funny?" The child might then catch on and add, "I want trees for dinner!" You can then enjoy the laugh. The child who does not catch on as quickly might need a suggestion: "Would you like to have bananas or rocks on your ice cream?" Exploration of the outrageous also promotes cognitive development because it takes the child out of the everyday patterns of thinking into new categories of comparison and deliberation about what is real, what is sarcastic, and what is just plain silly.

Reading and Learning Routines

Circle Time

As with one-on-one reading, circle time also offers an opportunity for children to share humor. Silly songs, fingerplays, books, and personal stories all provide methods for sharing humor. The influence of peers here is powerful, because they model laughing, explain what is funny to each other, and try to make others laugh as well. Adults can facilitate making circle time a joyful, sharing time by encouraging such exchanges.

One-on-One Book Reading

Many types of books for young children involve humor. Read books that involve funny sounds (e.g., Dr. Seuss books), unexpected actions or words (e.g., books in which an animal makes the sound of a different animal), or multimeaning language (e.g., "dressing" for salads and "dressing" meaning putting clothes on). All of these help children learn to share humor. For children with language, cognitive, or social delays, adult explanation may be needed for them to appreciate the nuances of language in the books.

Science and Math

Although math and science are not typically thought of as "funny," experimenting with various types of odd measurements (e.g., measuring with marshmallows), making outlandish comparisons among characteristics (e.g., comparing whales to guppies), and classifying things in humorous ways (e.g., all the children who can make silly faces) can teach children to think, compare, and group by similarities. There is no reason why science and math cannot be fun and funny.

▨▨▨▨ AMADOU

Amadou, a 4-year-old from Uganda, has been in preschool for a year. His English is good, his conceptual development is age appropriate, and his motor skills are above average. His parents report that he spends most of his time at home playing alone or with his 2-year-old brother. They say his lack of interest in interaction is not cultural and that they are concerned about his social interactions in his classroom. In class, Amadou avoids interaction with the other children. When a peer comes to the area where Amadou is playing or working, Amadou usually moves to another play area or center. When other children talk to him, he ignores them. He seldom gives eye contact to peers, but he will attend fleetingly to adults when they talk to him. Amadou's affect is serious. He seldom laughs or engages in silly actions, unlike his classmates. His teachers are concerned about his social and emotional development and would like to help Amadou develop better social skills.

The following recommendations were made for home and school:

Interaction Strategies

1. *Ask Amadou questions about what friends do, how they talk to each other, and so forth.*

2. *Prepare Amadou to be the "leader" of his peer partnership. Talk about and model how he can help his partner play, give his partner ideas, respond to his partner's ideas, and so forth. (See #1–4 under Environmental Modifications, below.)*

3. *Amadou's parents can support his play dates by teaching him card games and board games and having him teach his brother the games before he has a play date with his classroom partner.*

4. *When reading books about friendship, ask Amadou about what is happening, why, how friends interact, and so forth.*

5. *Role play situations involving friends. Focus on initiation and turn-taking interactions.*

6. *When dramatizing social situations, the adult can discuss, ask, suggest, model, and reinforce Amadou's social interactions.*

Environmental Modifications

1. *Conduct a unit on friendship within the class, and have children work in pairs on all projects, in games, and in play. Within the unit, have children work in pairs on*

drawing, doing science and math activities, playing together, reading together, and so forth.

2. *Pair Amadou with a child who is younger and also quiet, so that Amadou may take a leadership role (as he does with his sibling).*

3. *Have games requiring turn taking play an important part of the class.*

4. *When Amadou has interacted with his peer partner for several days, the parents can arrange a play date.*

5. *Read books about friendship and discuss what friends do.*

6. *Set up the dramatic play area in the classroom to involve a simple story relating to cooperation and working together, involving no more than three children at one time (so as not to overwhelm Amadou). A story such as "Friends" by Helme Heine can encourage interaction through the details of the story. The adult will need to facilitate the interaction through several dramatic play times. As Amadou begins to initiate interaction with peers, the adult should withdraw.*

7. *Use puppets, miniatures, flannel figures on a flannel board, computer games, and other avenues to allow Amadou to practice interactions through alternative figures.*

KEYS TO INTERVENTION BY DEVELOPMENTAL AGE

The following ideas are directed toward children who are functioning at approximately the following levels. The suggestions are not meant to be all-inclusive, but rather are indicative of potential areas for exploration.

Developmental age	Social characteristics	Keys to intervention
Birth to 3 months	Focuses on faces of people, especially the eyes; shows excitement in social exchange. Develops social smile. Recognizes caregivers. Produces indiscriminant smile.	Use face-to-face social interaction and play to build trust and pleasure in engagement with people. Position face in front of baby, read cues for starting and stopping.
3–6 months	Prefers familiar faces. Responds differently to new people. Vocalizes to initiate social interaction. Responds positively to social games. Recognizes photo of parent. Elicits and gives love.	Give baby wait time in interaction so he or she can watch the face and initiate or respond. Play games such as Peekaboo, tummy tickle. Play with toys that produce an effect.
6–9 months	Explores own and others' body parts. May cry with a stranger. Stays next to parent. Tries to get attention of other babies.	Play games with the fingers and toes, name body parts during bath and diapering. Take turns in simple play. Introduce to peers for observation.
9–12 months	Is beginning parallel play. Has separation anxiety. Moves away from adult but maintains eye contact. Engages in turn-taking play through 3 turns.	"Play dates" with other children allow child to observe and imitate play sequences. Encourage child to play independently as well as with other children and adults. Keep within sight of adult. Add additional turn when playing games. Introduce pretend play with dolls and routines.

(continued on next page)

Developmental age	Social characteristics	Keys to intervention
12–18 months	Imitates actions. Likes being around other children. Engages in parallel play. Is beginning dramatic play. Is beginning to share. Engages in turn-taking through 10 sequences. Sets limits on others.	Increase play dates. Adults may need to play as a facilitator at times. Have duplicate toys available to encourage parallel play. Provide opportunities for acting out routines with other children. Encourage turn-taking between children.
18–24 months	Is possessive, has difficulty sharing, but may make offer. Demands caregiver's attention. Alternates between clinging and resistance to adult. Pretend play directed toward others.	When child has trouble sharing, encourage turns. Provide real materials for dramatic play of routines. Encourage supervised exploration with a peer.
24–36 months	Plays with same toys, not cooperatively. Involves others in play sequences. Is beginning sociodramatic play. Relies on adults to make suggestions for alternative ideas.	Provide toys that encourage sharing, such as dramatic play materials. Suggest or model a new action or event in the dramatic play. Read books about sharing, helping. Encourage cooperative activities, such as cooking together.
36–48 months	Has separation distress. Prefers same-sex peers. Most play is cooperative. Can pretend with characters playing different roles. Engages in silly play with peers for humor. Is making friends.	Prepare child ahead for separation. Arrange "play dates." Dramatize books and media stories. Read funny books, sing silly songs, and engage in humorous antics.
48–60 months	Wants to please peers. Enjoys jokes and others' attempts at humor. Engages mainly in cooperative dramatic play. Is aware of others' emotions in play.	Encourage elaborate play by providing props and ideas (e.g., a lemonade stand). Encourage sociodramatic play of familiar themes and stories, and model or suggest social interaction as needed. Read stories of friendship, cooperation, collaboration, and others' feelings. Encourage child to see humor in words, stories, and jokes. Introduce board games and turn-taking games.
60–72 months	Constructs joint games such as puppet play, board games, cards. Is sensitive to others' responses and emotions in play. Is able to participate in group activities, wait turn, and contribute. Remembers and makes up jokes for others.	Provide opportunities for card and board games, group discussion and games. Discuss aspects of friendship and cooperation in real life and stories. Let children create their own group games and sociodramatic play with complex plots and interactions. Intercede only as needed to support interaction.

6

Facilitating Communication Development

I. Strategies for Improving Language Comprehension

Goal Attainment Scale

1	2	3	4	5	6	7	8	9
Focuses on speaker's face and reacts to sounds and voices.		Attends to or responds to own name and familiar gestures, signs, or words.		Understands gestures, signs and/or single words, simple one-step requests, and the early question forms, *yes/no, what, where.*		Understands familiar and novel two-step directions, *who* and *when* questions, and comments that are signed or spoken.		Understands age-appropriate basic concepts and vocabulary, *why* and *how* questions, grammatical structures, and multistep requests that are signed or spoken.

Language comprehension is the child's ability to attach meaning to sounds, words, gestures, signs, or actions that carry communicative intention. Children learn to attach meaning to the sounds they hear in their environment and to the words and actions people use to convey a message. Language comprehension is closely tied to cognitive understanding, because children learn about their world partially through the labels, descriptions, and explanations provided by others. Children hear a sound or see an action and gradually learn to associate that sound, sequence of sounds (as in words), or gestures with a person, object, or event. For example, the child who repeatedly hears the sound of a knock on the door, followed by the entry of a person, learns that the sound of a knock conveys meaning; that is, *someone wants to come in.* The child who hears the sounds *T-o-n-i* used in association with a sister learns that those sounds together constitute his sibling's name. Later, the child learns that those same sounds, used in a different context, mean *toe, knee.*

The ability to make sense of the combination of sounds, words, gestures, and actions enables children to share an understanding of the world with others. Without this shared understanding, knowledge may be idiosyncratic and fragmented, and the ability to communicate ideas with others may be difficult. Children who have difficulty comprehending what is being communicated also will have difficulty learning. For these reasons, language comprehension is fundamental to communication, social interaction, and cognitive skills.

APPROPRIATE LANGUAGE COMPREHENSION

Language comprehension begins with the child paying attention to the people, sounds, and actions in his or her environment. Several aspects support the development of good language comprehension. The child needs the ability to attend and listen; discriminate sounds accurately; make meaning of sound and word sequences provided in normal speech; associate sounds and words with their referents (mentally visualize); and coordinate these with facial expressions, intonation, sound emphasis, gesture, and body movements to obtain meaning. Later, pictures and symbols, in the form of graphics and print, will represent these sounds and words and convey meaning through writing. Language comprehension is a complex process involving many parts of the brain working together to enable the child to perceive, coordinate input, and make sense of what others are trying to communicate. Therefore, good language comprehension depends on the child's ability to accurately perceive visual, auditory, tactile, and other forms of input. Good language comprehension also requires the ability of the brain to accurately interpret this sensory input. Language comprehension also requires that the child has a sufficient number and range of experiences so that the sounds, words, and symbols can be related to existing mental representations in the child's mind. For example, the sound sequence that makes up the word "snow" may be heard accurately but will not have meaning because the child has no previous exposure to the referent for the word. Experience with actual objects and events, pictures, and stories helps the child build a base for knowledge and comprehension.

Appropriate Language Comprehension in Practice

▮▮▮▮ I. A. What early comprehension abilities does the child exhibit?

Daily Routines (Home and Classroom)

- *Infant/toddler:* The infant sees her father holding up the diaper and lifts her legs in preparation. The toddler holds spaghetti over her head and looks at her mother. Her mother purses her lips and shakes her head no. The toddler puts her spaghetti back in the bowl.

- *Young child:* The young child walks into the bedroom and his mother puts her finger to her lips and points to the sleeping sibling. The child tiptoes over to his mother and whispers in her ear.

Play Routines (Home and Classroom)

- *Infant/toddler:* The infant watches her father push the button on the pop-up box. She reaches over and tries to hit it. The toddler sees his brother holding out a cookie for him. He smiles and runs over to get it.

- *Young child:* The young child runs into the kitchen, calling for his mother. She is talking on the phone. She holds up her hand with her palm out toward him and her index finger up. He stops by her and waits.

Classroom Routines

During circle time, everyone is talking and the teacher raises her hand and holds it up. Soon, other children stop talking and raise their hands too. After a minute, all the hands are raised and the room is quiet.

I. B. What types of words and sentences are understood by the child?

Daily Routines (Home and Classroom)

- *Infant/toddler:* The infant is sitting on her father's lap. He says, "It's time for your bottle." The infant looks at the bottle on the table. The toddler is playing and his mother says, "Time to pick up. It's bed time." The toddler shakes his head and starts to cry.

- *Young child:* The young child is taking a bath. Dad says, "Okay. You're clean. Turn the knob to let the water out." The child leans over and turns the knob that adjusts the drain cover, so the water starts to drain.

Play Routines (Home and Classroom)

- *Infant/toddler:* The infant is playing with the ball. Dad says, "Roll it to me." The infant pushes it toward her father. The toddler is playing with her baby doll. Her mother says, "That baby looks hungry." The toddler picks up a toy cup and holds it to the baby's mouth.

- *Young child:* The young child is playing with her older sister. The sister says, "I'll be the doctor and you be the sick person. You have the flu." The young child lies down on the couch, pretends to cry, and holds her stomach.

Classroom Routines

The teacher describes the child's choices for centers. She says, "And who wants to make a book in the literacy center?" Two children raise their hands and say, "I do."

Types of questions the child comprehends

Daily Routines (Home and Classroom)

- *Infant/toddler:* The father is reading to the infant and says, "Where is the ball?" The infant points to the picture of a ball in the book. The toddler and his mother are driving down the road. Mother says, "Where are we going?" The child shouts, "McDonald's!"

- *Young child:* While shopping for clothes, Dad asks his young child, "Do you want shoes that tie or shoes with Velcro?"

Play Routines (Home and Classroom)

- *Infant/toddler:* Mother and infant are playing Peekaboo. The infant has the blanket on his head, and when his mother says, "Where's Josh?" he pulls the blanket off. The toddler and his dad are pushing cars across the floor. Dad says, "Can your car go faster than mine?" The toddler laughs and pushes his car ahead of his father's.

- *Young child:* The young child is pretending to be a waitress. Her father says, "How long will it take to get a hamburger?" The young child responds, "Ten minutes. Do you want fries with that?"

Classroom Routines

> The children are watching ice melt and turn into water. The teacher asks, "Why do you think the ice is melting?" One child says, "Because it's warm in here."

GENERAL PRINCIPLES FOR SUPPORTING APPROPRIATE LANGUAGE COMPREHENSION

In infancy, adults are aware of children's limited understanding and make efforts to enhance their comprehension of what is going on in the environment by showing and demonstrating. This also is true for toddlers, but as children's language becomes more complex, adults begin to talk to children in less deliberate and more natural ways. They tend to fall back on earlier patterns only when children do not appear to understand what is being said. The following are strategies most parents typically use when communicating with their child in order to increase language comprehension.

Make Sure the Child Is Attending

Early language comprehension requires the child to be attending to the adult and to what the adult is referring. When the bottle, blanket, or book is talked about, the adult makes sure the child is looking at or touching the object when it is labeled. As the child gets older and understands more words, the adult may not need to have the actual topic of discussion visible, but the child still needs to be listening to and paying attention to what is being said. Parents may first call the child's name and will even say, "Are you listening to me?" or "Look at me when I am talking to you." These are attempts to capture the child's attention so he or she will listen.

Show or Point to the Object or Activity Being Talked About

Adults naturally hold up, point to, or tap on what is being referred to in the conversation. This is to make sure the child understands the topic of the conversation. For example, when the child is first learning to comprehend words, the adult may hold up objects in which the child is interested, such as a rattle, a teddy bear, or a bottle. The adult then makes a gesture and comments "shake, shake, shake"; labels the object "teddy bear"; or describes the purpose, "You are so hungry" or activity, "bubble popped." Repeated presentation of these familiar objects or actions, help the child to relate the words, objects, and actions.

Emphasize Target Words to Be Understood

When talking to young children, adults frequently emphasize specific sounds or words they are using. By stressing specific words, the adult directs the child's attention to the most important part of a word or phrase. For example, the adult may say, "*Water.* Feel the warm water," "The cow says, 'MOO'!" "Put it *DOWN*!" or "Your name starts with *t* for *Tess*." Such emphasis on intonation highlights what the adult feels is the most important aspect for the child to understand.

Use Short Phrases or Sentences

Adults tend to use shorter expressions when trying to get a child to understand words or concepts. They identify key features or uses of items. For instance, the parent may say, "*You* do it. *Turn* it. That's it." Most parents do not give the child a long explanation when they are introducing something new. Rather, they hit the key elements, such as the name, the actions, or the use (e.g., "Key. It opens the door").

Talk Slowly and Distinctly

Another way of ensuring that children attend to key aspects of what is being communicated is to make sure they can attend to all of what is being said. By speaking slowly and clearly, adults know that children are not missing sounds or words.

Provide Gestures, Examples, or Explanation

Adults provide support for language comprehension by adding helpful information. Gestures, such as demonstrating how to turn a key, may give children additional visual information to support their understanding of how a key is used. Actual examples of objects or events are used with young children to illustrate what is meant. The parent will hold up the object (e.g., a cup), demonstrate an action (e.g., drinking), or use a picture of a concept (e.g., a photograph of a boat) to show the child what is meant. Particularly when the concepts being discussed are not present to explore, the adult uses alternative means such as pictures or explanation. Typically, verbal description and explanation alone requires the child to have a good basis for language comprehension in the first place.

THE PRINCIPLES IN PRACTICE

The strategies described previously are used by parents and other caregivers throughout the day to support their child's developing comprehension of language and communication. The following are examples of how adults integrate these approaches into various activities.

Daily Routines (Home and Classroom)

Feeding/Eating

For infants and toddlers, parents hold up and label various foods. They let the child touch, smell, and taste each item. For older children, parents may provide more information. For example, "Bananas are a fruit. They grow on trees. Monkeys like to eat bananas."

Diapering/Toileting

Diapering and toileting are sensory experiences, and adults use these opportunities to teach labels (e.g., *diaper, toilet, potty*); action words (e.g., *lift, sit, wipe, wash*); sensory descriptive words (*stinky, wet, dry, soft, hard*); and concepts (e.g., *elimination, pride*).

Dressing

Children learn to understand labels, action words, and prepositions (e.g., "Put your head through; put your leg in"). They also learn to comprehend a direction to do something (e.g., "Go get some socks").

Play Routines (Home and Classroom)

Face-to-Face Play

Face-to-face games teach children body parts (e.g., *hands, head, fingers, toes*), pronouns (e.g., *you, me, yours, mine*), prepositions (e.g., *on, up, on top*), and actions (e.g., *reach, touch, move*). Children also learn to read gestures and actions that carry communicative intent.

Physical Play

Because physical play involves movement, action words are easily demonstrated in this type of play to support the child's comprehension (e.g., *run, jump, catch*). Words of caution (e.g., "Be careful," "Watch out") often are used in active physical play. Adults also provide opportunities for the child to learn directions as they teach sequences of actions (e.g., "Lift your arm, pull it back, and throw the ball hard!").

Manipulative Play

As with other types of play, toy play provides opportunities for children to learn to comprehend the names of things, their functions, and descriptions of events. Adults use toys, especially in dramatic play, to illustrate real-life and imagined events. They narrate events and model language that is used in various situations to help children understand what is happening and why. For example, when pretending to cook with a battery-operated toy mixer that is not working, the parent can introduce new words, such as *mixer, broken, battery,* and so forth.

Sensory Play

Sensory and art play provide occasions for comprehension of descriptive words (e.g., *rough, smooth, wet, dry*). Adults illustrate the meaning of words through the child's sensory experiences with the materials.

Reading and Learning Routines

Circle Time

Teachers use circle time to help children comprehend a variety of concepts. Some use this time to talk about special or personal events, or to read and discuss concepts in stories. The teacher illustrates, explains, or discusses personal meanings of these concepts with the children in the group.

One-on-One Book Reading

One-on-one book reading provides a unique opportunity to help children acquire understanding of words and concepts that are out of their range of direct experience. Adults point out, describe, and talk about the pictures, sentences, print, story, and ideas presented in each book, thus helping children to understand a variety of aspects of language.

Science and Math

As children explore the characteristics of objects and events, they learn to categorize and systematically organize their ideas. Adults guide the development of conceptual understanding by relating how things are similar and different and how they fit into the larger system of relationships. For example, while planting seeds in a science experiment, the adult may explain how seeds grow, discuss different types of seeds, compare various types of fruits and vegetables, and so forth.

PLANNING INDIVIDUALIZED INTERVENTIONS FOR IMPROVING LANGUAGE COMPREHENSION

▓▓▓▓▓ **I. A. What early comprehension abilities does the child exhibit?**

Children may have difficulty understanding the meaning of nonverbal and/or verbal communications for a variety of reasons. If they have difficulty attending, perceiving sensory input, or interpreting sensory information, they may have problems understanding what others are trying to communicate. These children may need extra supports for making meaning out of communicative attempts.

Children who have a hard time attending to activities may have difficulty focusing on what adults are saying or doing, as their attention shifts quickly from one object or event to another. Children who have difficulty drawing relationships between words and actions or actions and consequences (e.g., holding out hands means, "I want to pick you up") also may have difficulty comprehending both nonverbal and verbal communication. Memory problems also may contribute to the child making sense of what is said. For instance, if the parent says, "Get your doll that Grandpa gave you," the child needs to remember the doll to which the parent is referring.

For children who are deaf, language comprehension requires the ability to read facial cues, body language, gestures, signs, lip movements, and also written symbols. They need to develop the ability to coordinate and mentally represent what these mean in various contexts as well. For children who are blind or have visual impairments, making meaning of the sounds they hear may involve coordination of other senses, such as movement and touch, to help them acquire a mental representation of what they are hearing. Adults need to analyze what is interfering with the child's comprehension skills and try various approaches to see what techniques help the child learn. The following strategies are recommended in addition to the strategies outlined previously.

Interaction Strategies

1. *Obtain the child's attention.* Eye contact is important because humans communicate emotional intent through their eyes and facial expression. The adult can gain the child's eye contact by being in the child's line of vision. Using exaggerated intonation or expression may attract the child's attention. Adults also should help children focus on other aspects of communication, such as gestures. Use of exaggerated affect or movements may help capture the child's attention. For children who are hard of hearing, teaching them to respond to tapping on their shoulder is recommended.

2. *Wait for the child to respond.* Provide enough wait time for the child to respond to directions, questions, or comments. Children with language delays or disorders benefit from enough wait time to be able to respond to the adult. Repetition also may be necessary. Often, children are already anticipating and wanting the adult to communicate something to them.

3. *Provide visual cues.* Adults often use gesture to accompany words. For children with special needs, gestures are particularly important because they provide a visual cue for meaning. Clear, emphatic gestures help the child focus. Gestures that illustrate what is meant, such as those used in sign language, are particularly useful. For example, the sign for *ball* is two hands shaping a ball. When paired with the object, the child learns the meaning of the nonverbal cue. The same is true for action gestures. The parent may model holding up the arms to be picked up while saying "up," pick up the child's arms in imitation, then pick up the child to show the consequence of using the gesture. Facial expressions also provide information to help the child understand.

4. *Provide repetition when necessary.* Repetition of the same gesture, paired with objects or actions, helps the child learn the meaning of the gesture. For example, parents of a young child who is deaf learn to tap on the child's shoulder to get the child's attention. At first, this gesture means nothing to the child, but soon the child learns that when tapped on the shoulder, he should look at the parent because something interesting is going to happen. Repeating a direction the second time as you help the child carry out the request also will facilitate the child's understanding of the direction.

5. *Incorporate songs into the day.* Using the same song to transition is helpful. The child will associate that every time he or she hears the clean-up song, it is time to clean up the toys and transition to a new activity. Fingerplays require reading and imitating gestures. They also encourage children to watch gestures carefully and do them in combination with specific words. This is good practice for watching others pair gestures with language.

Environmental Modifications

In addition to interpersonal strategies that may support the child's comprehension of language, environmental modifications often are useful. Depending on the findings from TPBA2, the team may want to consider some of the following environmental modifications.

1. *Make sure the child can hear as well as possible.* Hearing loss, either intermittent, such as that caused by an ear infection, or permanent, such as conductive or sensorineural hearing loss, has a negative impact on language comprehension. Monitor the child's health and pay attention to ear pulling or holding, complaints of pain, or apparent sudden inattention to sound. For children who have an identified hearing loss, consult with the child's health care professionals about the best options for improving hearing and learning potential.

2. *Make sure the child can see as well as possible.* Vision loss affects language comprehension, because the child cannot see what others are talking about. All children should have their vision checked, but children with disabilities are at higher risk for vision problems and may not be aware of or be able to communicate concerns. They therefore should be evaluated more carefully. Children who are blind must learn the meaning of words through other senses.

3. *Position the child or the adult in such a way that the child can clearly see gestures, facial expressions, and body language.* Children benefit when the adult is at the same eye level as the child. This provides face-to-face interaction that facilitates the child's ability to look at the adult's face, use of gestures, and body movements.

4. *Reduce auditory and visual distractions when communicating with nonverbal cues.* Provide an environment that does not have a lot of auditory and visual distractions that may affect the child's ability to respond to the adult and understand the language that is being used. Close proximity to the speaker also is important, especially in classroom environments where a child with special needs may benefit from preferential seating to facilitate language comprehension.

I. B. What types of words and sentences are understood by the child?

Children who have difficulty understanding nonverbal and verbal cues also may have difficulty learning what words and sentences mean. As noted previously, children who are deaf or hard of hearing, children with vision impairments, and children with cognitive delays often have reduced ability to comprehend language. In addition, children with frequent ear infections may get inconsistent or inaccurate auditory information, which has a negative impact on comprehension of words and sentences. Children who do not understand the meaning of words will have difficulty understanding what others are telling them. Some children may understand individual words but lose comprehension when words are combined. For example, the child may be able to look at his shoe when his mother says, "shoe," but he may not understand when she says, "Let's put your shoes on." The type of words (e.g., nouns, verbs, pronouns, adjectives) also may make a difference. The child may understand "shirt" but not, "Take off your shirt" or "Get your red shirt." Sentence length and complexity may hinder comprehension in some children. "Drink milk" may be understood, but "I'll put your glass on the table, so you can drink your milk" may not be understood. Also, some children understand more complex sentences when they are said in context or when visual cues are provided. For instance, if the father says, "Get your coat on so we can go," the child may look at him and not move. Yet if he points to the coat or picks it up and says the same words, the child may respond appropriately. Other children may understand part of a sentence but not all of it. For instance, if the parent says, "Take your toys to your room and bring me your pajamas," the child may disappear with the toys and come back empty-handed (or not come back!). This may relate to problems with language comprehension, memory, or both. Many children need to hear something several times for the message to "sink in." Some parents will say this is typical behavior and that their child "has selective hearing" due to the inconsistency in the child responding to the parent. The speed at which someone speaks also may affect comprehension.

What the child understands and the circumstances under which comprehension is greatest can be determined through observation in different contexts. Adults need to gradually increase the complexity of the child's language comprehension, including understanding of vocabulary, parts of speech, sentence type, word order, sentence length and complexity, and rate of speech.

The strategies listed in the previous section, in addition to the common approaches listed at the beginning of the chapter, are all useful. The following techniques also are suggested for increasing comprehension of words and sentences.

Interaction Strategies

1. *Enunciate.* Some children have difficulty hearing the individual sounds within words or making sense of the sounds when they are combined quickly. When introducing new words, make sure the words are stated slowly and clearly. Once the child understands a word, he or she will be able to interpret the word in natural speech more easily.

2. *Use short phrases and sentences.* Adults naturally shorten their phrases and sentences with infants and adjust their speech as the child gets older. This continues to be important for children with comprehension problems. Include the key words the child needs to understand. For instance, instead of saying, "Put the block in the box," "block IN" tells the child what is important. Emphasis on key words also can support comprehension.

3. *Encourage listening.* Whisper "secrets," listen to quiet noises, and try to hear birds chirping or an airplane overhead. In preschool, games such as Telephone, in which one person whispers something to the next person, and that person passes it on to the next, encourage listening. Singing songs and doing fingerplays encourage listening and comprehension of combined gestures.

4. *Use simultaneous multisensory input.* Children who do not hear well or who have difficulty comprehending words or sentences may need alternative forms of input to supplement words. Gestures, signs, pictures, and demonstration may help convey meaning. In addition children may need to touch objects, move through actions, or experience situations that otherwise might be explained with words. For instance, the child who is deaf may not understand the meaning of the word *dance* until it is observed and experienced. The child who has autism may need a visual picture to help her understand what she needs to do.

5. *Hold objects near the speaker's face.* Moving an object through space attracts a child's attention. Moving the object up close to the face of the speaker allows the child to attend to both the object and the adult's face at the same time. This will help the child see the relationship between the object and the word. It also will enable the child to see the affect of the speaker so that emotional meaning is understood as well.

6. *Provide a sequence of input.* Some children only can focus on one aspect of communication at a time. For these children, a sequence of multisensory input is recommended. The adult may bring the child's attention to an object by tapping on it, then letting him or her feel or explore the object, then holding the object near the mouth, as described previously, so the child can see the words being formed as the adult names the object or talks about it. The adult then may hand the object back to the child and label it again.

7. *Use repetition.* Children who do not have disabilities need to hear a word and how it is used many times in different contexts for the word to become a meaningful part of their vocabulary and to be understood in relation to other concepts. Children with special needs may need to hear the words or see the signs or gestures more frequently for the concepts to make sense to them. Instead of labeling an object or event once or twice, repeat the words several times. Also, limit what is being said to the essential words. For example, instead of saying, "See the cup. Lucy, this is a cup," say, "Cup" while tapping it and holding it near your mouth or in front of the child. This enables the child to focus on the word that is important to understand, rather than having to interpret a more complex phrase.

8. *Use consistent terms.* Although most items, actions, and events can be labeled in multiple ways, it is important to use the same term when trying to teach a child a concept. For instance, the "cup" named above also could be labeled with its contents. The adult might say "drink," "juice," or "milk." Adults should prioritize what concepts they want the child to learn. For instance, "drink" may be a priority at first, because it can mean both the contents and the action with the cup. Once the global term is learned, more specific labels can be taught.

9. *Provide varied opportunities for word use.* Adults need to consciously provide repeated exposure to situations that enable children to hear and experience many versions of the words they are learning in meaningful contexts. For example, the child may hear the word "pancakes" as Dad is making them and Mom and the child are helping. She may hear the word "pancakes" again in a restaurant when they are seen in a picture on the menu, when the waitress brings them out, and during the breakfast. She also may hear the word "pancakes" when pretending to cook with plastic food. Such repetition in different contexts helps the child develop a greater understanding of the meaning of words and how they fit in to her world.

10. *Keep directions short and clear.* Until the child can clearly understand complex sentences and remember multiple items, keep directions simple so the child is successful in competing the request. Directions involving familiar objects or routines also will be easier to remember.

Environmental Modifications

In addition to interpersonal strategies that may support comprehension of words and sentences, environmental modifications often are useful. Depending on the findings from TPBA2, the team may want to consider some of the following environmental modifications.

1. *See Environmental Modifications, under I. A. (p. 352)*

2. *Use assistive technology.* A variety of individual amplification devices are available. Based on the child's residual hearing, developmental level, and degree of independence, different approaches may be recommended. Professional and medical consultation is needed to determine the system that will best support the child's hearing and language potential.

3. *Use visual as well as auditory cues.* All children with vision problems can benefit from additional visual cues to help them learn about concepts. Pictures, books, real objects, and experiences support learning about the meaning of words and sentences.

4. *Use classroom technology.* Listening devices can promote better hearing in classrooms or noisy environments. Devices such as sound field systems help children cut out extraneous noises and focus on the important words being said.

▨▨▨▨ What concepts does the child understand?

Understanding concepts involves the child's ability to think about and relate simple words and form them into ideas about similarities and differences, groupings, and categories (see also Chapter 7, Section VI. Strategies for Improving Conceptual Knowledge). Children learn labels for individual things but then begin to organize these words into systems so that the world makes sense and is not just a compilation of millions of discrete word labels. For instance, the child learns that things have external characteristics that, although varying greatly, are all known as colors. The child learns to group characteristics that are similar into a specific color category, such as "blue." When the child is first learning the concept of color, he or she may assign the word for the known color to all items. Everything is "blue." Children also learn words for conceptual categories, such as "dogs," and then later learn to assign specific labels to various types of dogs. Learning about concepts then involves both grouping and building hierarchies or systems for words and also breaking down concepts into smaller components that comprise the concept. Children can encounter problems with either or both types of comprehension. For some children with disabilities, it takes more time and support to learn that a "ball" can be any color or size, that any toy that has a button or lever on it probably does something, that people who have a furrowed brow and a frown may be angry, and so forth.

Interaction Strategies

1. *Relate everyday objects by grouping them.* For example, show the child several similar, but not identical, items and name them, "shirts," "blankets," "stuffed bears," and so forth. Talk about the elements that are the same: "Look at the sleeves"; "These are warm and cozy"; "The bears say 'Grrr.'" This will help children learn characteristics of objects and help them to relate this to other ideas. For instance, after discussing the items, the child may begin to notice characteristics and make comparisons. She may say, "This shirt has long sleeves," "This coat is warm and cozy," or "Tigers say 'Grr' too."

2. *Point out differences.* Pointing out differences can help children begin to build a conceptual framework; for example, "Birds have wings to fly. People have legs to walk."

3. *Provide information.* Once children have learned basic labels for things, adults can provide information to help children classify objects and events. In the previous examples, the adult might follow up with information; for instance, "Yes, you have two feet. Boys have two feet; girls have two feet. Mommies and babies have two feet. People have two feet!" As the child's conceptual understanding grows, adults can provide information about things that are not present but have been seen or read about. For example, when talking about snow and ice, the adult might say, "Some Inuit people live in houses made of ice, called 'igloos.'"

4. *Emphasize opposites.* Showing children the difference between *big* and *little, up* and *down, in* and *out, wet* and *dry,* and so forth helps emphasize the basic aspect of various concepts. Children learn the extremes of a continuum before they learn the gradations.

5. *Imitate rhythms.* Rhythms help children learn sequences that are important for language. Imitating the emphasis in rhythms can help children learn to listen to patterns.

6. *Share books.* Reading books to children teaches them about "book language" or the patterns of intonation when reading. *Talking about* the content of books teaches children about concepts. Encourage children to comment, ask questions, and make comparisons about things or events in the books. Read the child's favorite books repeatedly, but also read related books to expand concepts, and introduce new books to expand topics and learn new concepts.

7. *Ask "thinking" questions.* Once children can answer concrete *what, who,* and *where* questions about the names and characteristics of objects, people, and events, begin to ask questions that require children to use reasoning. Ask questions that begin with *why* and *how.* Encourage children to discover the answers themselves whenever possible.

Environmental Modifications

In addition to interpersonal strategies that may support children in learning concepts, environmental modifications often are useful. Depending on the findings from TPBA2, the team may want to consider some of the following environmental modifications.

1. *Provide multiple ways to learn about a concept.* For example, learn the name of an egg by seeing and feeling one. Learn about the concept of an egg by seeing it, breaking it open, frying it, boiling it, or watching it hatch. The more varied experiences children have with people, objects, and events, the greater their understanding of the concepts involved.

2. *Identify concepts in multiple situations.* For example, identify body parts on the child in the bath, on dolls during play, on parents and siblings while they are using the various body parts, on the characters in books and on television, and so forth. The more opportunities the child has to hear terms used across situations, the greater the opportunity for concept formation related to these terms.

3. *Use listening devices.* A listening center in preschool or a tape recorder with earphones at home can help children focus on listening to stories or music. Children's books on tape or CD allow children to independently follow the pictures or print (depending on their level) in combination with the oral language. They also can listen as often as they want. Repetition of books enables the child to learn words, sentences, story sequences, and vocal intonation patterns.

4. *Visit the library.* Exposure to books is a critical way for children to learn about concepts to which they are not exposed directly. As noted previously, interaction with books is a foundation of learning.

5. *Use the computer.* Books and information also are available on the Internet. With adult support, children can access stories, games, videos, and information from all over the world that are designed for children of all ages.

What types of questions does the child comprehend?

Questions involve a restructuring of the simple sentence; for example, "You are going" becomes "Are you going?" In other instances, words are added that imply a question: "Where are you going?" Intonation of the words in a sentence also can imply a question; "You going?" said with rising intonation at the end also is a question. In order to understand questions, children need to understand how word order, word choice, and inflection influence meaning. Questions require a sophisticated manipulation of ideas that may be difficult for children with language disorders or developmental delays.

Most children learn to comprehend language in a predictable sequence, but that is not always true for children with language disabilities. However, in general, children learn labels for things first, then action and location words, and then descriptors and modifiers. They are, therefore, able to understand *what* and *where* questions first. Depending on the words parents have emphasized, children quickly add to the repertoire of words they comprehend.

When children are learning words, adults ask many *what* and *where* questions to see what they have learned. Children who do not comprehend the words *what* and *where* may be at a loss to respond or may answer with what they think the adult means. For instance, an adult looking at a book with a child may say, "What is this?" or "Where is the duck?" The child may look at the adult and say, "Quack." This response could indicate that the child does not understand the question; that he may be using "quack" for the label, *duck*; or that he thinks that is the correct response. After all, that was what the adult said the last time the book was read. Children need to hear the same information repeatedly to integrate it into their understanding of the world.

Children with disabilities also may have difficulty catching the intonational change that implies that a question has been asked. When we ask a question, voice inflection rises at the end of a sentence. This intonational shift carries meaning and tells the child that a response is desired. If the child does not hear or attach meaning to the inflection, he or she may not respond. The following suggestions are offered to support the child's developing comprehension of questions.

Interaction Strategies

1. *Teach the child to localize objects by looking and pointing.* This will enable the child to isolate something in the environment and refer nonverbally to the topic of conversation. Recognizing something is easier than coming up with the name for the object. When children are first learning to respond to questions, ask "Show me" questions. The child can then respond with a look and a point. *Show me* can then be paired with *where* to teach the meaning of *where*. For example, "*Show me* the cat. *Where* is the cat?" For children with severe motor involvement, eye-pointing can be used.

2. *Offer choices.* When the adult presents two objects to the child, the child typically will look at the one that is preferred for the longest amount of time or will reach for it. Present both objects and say, "Do you want milk or juice?" Give the child the one toward which she reaches, vocalizes, or looks at the longest. Then say, "You want milk," while nodding, giving the object, and saying "Milk." Hold up the other object and say, "You don't want juice," while shaking the head and saying, "No." Do the same thing with the question, "Which one do you want?" Once the child understands this game,

she will begin to choose more quickly. Once the child can vocalize, reach, or indicate *yes* or *no* with the head (nodding *yes* is harder than *no*), the adult can then start to present one object and say, "Do you want . . . ?"

3. *Ask developmentally appropriate questions.* Once children can recognize people, objects, and events in their environment, adults can help children comprehend questions relating to actions and characteristics. Questions relating to characteristics often start with *what* or *how many*; for instance, "What is he doing?" "What shape is it?" or "How many do you want?"

4. *Teach concepts.* As children develop more complex play skills, are able to manipulate toys, can study and figure out how things work, and can physically explore their environment, they can figure out how and why things happen. Higher level conceptual understanding typically is required to answer *why* and *how* questions. All of the strategies recommended previously for helping children understand concepts are, therefore, important.

5. *Model asking and then answering the question.* One way adults help children to understand questions is to model the asking and answering process. Ask the child the question, wait for a response, and then if the child does not answer, provide the question and answer again. "Where is your shoe?" Wait. If no response, say, "Where is your shoe? Here is your shoe." Also, for children who have limited language production, ask questions that can be answered by actions. For example, the previous question could be answered with a point.

6. *Emphasize the questioning intonation.* Putting more emphasis on the rising inflection may help the child recognize the shift in the adult's intention from a statement to a question.

7. *Use gestures that depict the object or action to which the words being used refer.* For example, use a gesture to indicate taking a drink when the child's cup is present.

Environmental Modifications

In addition to interpersonal strategies that may support the child's comprehension of questions, environmental modifications often are useful. Depending on the findings from TPBA2, the team may want to consider some of the following environmental modifications.

1. *Amplification may be needed.* Children who cannot hear clearly may not be able to hear changes in inflection. It is important to use appropriate assistive technology.

2. *Picture cues may increase comprehension.* In addition to words and gestures, pictures may help children understand what is meant. Children first use pictures in books as cues to what is meant when adults ask a question. This can be extended for children with special needs by creating picture books, or picture cues, of items about which the adult is most likely to ask. For example, the adult might point to the picture of the toilet, sign NEED, and make a questioning expression.

ROUTINES FOR THE CHILD WHO NEEDS
SUPPORT TO IMPROVE LANGUAGE COMPREHENSION

The following are examples of how the previous strategies can be incorporated into the child's routines at home and school. In addition to the strategies noted at the beginning of the chapter, used by caregivers of children who do not have special needs, these strategies may support increased proficiency in language comprehension.

Daily Routines (Home and Classroom)

Feeding/Eating

As adults teach children labels for food and utensils, comprehension can be addressed by requesting, "Show me what you want" or "Give me the cup." Provide choices to young children while pointing and waiting for a response; for example, "Do you want pears or peaches?" For older children, ask more conceptual questions; for example, "How do you want your egg? Hard? Or soft?" As children's conceptual development progresses, adults can add more information, explanation, and discussion related to foods, manners, eating situations, and so forth to increase comprehension of sentences and conceptual understanding.

Diapering/Toileting

As with feeding, there are numerous opportunities to develop comprehension during diapering or toileting. Understanding of specific words can be seen when the child looks or points to what is mentioned. Actively involving children in the process is important. For instance, "You need a clean diaper. Where is a clean diaper?" (Point to where the diapers are kept.) For older children, ask questions that can be answered with an action; for example, "What do you need to do next?" Conceptual development can involve many types of words—prepositions, such as *in, on,* and *under*; verbs, such as *lift, sit,* and *pull*; and descriptors, such as *stinky, soft, hard,* and *proud*. Giving a direction or asking a simple question can show whether the child comprehends the words. Modeling and gesturing can help increase comprehension. For instance, adults can gesture or sign IN as they put something in a drawer.

Dressing

As with the routines discussed previously, provide choices with a visual example for children who have difficulty comprehending; for example, "Do you want the red or the green shirt?" (while showing them). After the child can make choices in this way, provide more open-ended questions; for example, "What do you want to wear?" (while still laying out the options). As the child develops a memory for things that are not present, the adult can ask the question or request an action without having the choices visible.

Going Out

Going out on errands provides many opportunities for making statements, giving directions, and asking questions related to getting prepared to go, looking at things while in the car or stroller, talking about what is going to happen next, and reviewing what happened; for example, "We need to go. Please get your jacket"; "Do you want to take bunny or puppy with you?" "Let's sing a song. You pick one"; "We need to get cereal. Do you want Cheerios?" After shopping, the parent can ask questions to prompt memory and problem solving; for instance, "Can you find the Cheerios in the bag? Put them in the cupboard, please."

Play Routines (Home and Classroom)

Face-to-Face Play

One of the first games children play with parents is Peekaboo. "Where's baby?" is repeated with interaction and turn-taking many times. This is a great way to teach the child the concept of *where*. Fingerplays also promote comprehension, because they combine representational gestures with words and facial expressions. The combination helps children understand the words accompanying the actions. For example, the fingerplay "Where Is Thumbkin?" involves active participation and thus supports comprehension of questions. A dance and song, such as "The Hokey-Pokey" helps children understand body parts, actions, and prepositions.

Physical Play

Physical interaction often involves running, jumping, chasing, tickling, and so forth. Repetition of phrases helps the child learn meaning. Parents often initiate interaction by saying, "I'm gonna get you!" These words signal the child to anticipate an onslaught. The child thus learns that "I'm gonna . . . " will be followed by an action on the part of the adult. Adults also ask questions such as, "Do you want me to . . . ?" (e.g., get you, tickle you, chase you). Children learn words for body parts, action words, prepositions, and descriptors, such as *fast* and *slow, hard* and *soft,* during physical play. Asking questions such as, "Where do you want me to tickle you?" gives the child an opportunity to be in control and demonstrate comprehension without having to use words. Higher level questions might involve asking, "How do you want to . . . ?" or "How should we . . . ?"

Manipulative Play

Opportunities to demonstrate understanding of terms, actions, and concepts abound in manipulative play. The adult can determine whether the child comprehends by making statements such as, "I need a blue crayon." If the child gives the adult the wrong color, the adult can then demonstrate the correct response; for example, "That's a pretty red one, but I want blue, like this one. See, this is blue." As children learn to manipulate objects, adults ask many questions, ranging from "What is that?" to "How does that work?" Attention to the child's cognitive and fine motor abilities is important, so the question does not confuse the child or require a response he or she is incapable of providing. For example, if the child is nonverbal, asking, "What is that?" is too challenging. "What do you want to do?" is a question that enables the child to demonstrate his or her understanding by pointing or showing rather than requiring a verbal response.

Sensory Play

Play that involves sensory aspects may be enjoyable for some children and aversive to others. Either way, sensory play provides opportunities for understanding descriptive terms and related emotions. Questions related to likes and dislikes are appropriate during these activities (e.g., "Do you want to go fast or slow?"). Try not to ask too many yes/no or closed-ended questions that will stop the conversation; instead, ask open-ended questions. Higher level questions might include, "What does that feel like?" "What should I do next?" and "How can we clean that up?"

Dramatic Play

Dramatic play is a recreation of natural actions and events. For this reason, pretend play enables adults to reconstruct all kinds of situations that involve comprehension of language. When the child uses a term or action appropriately in play, it demonstrates memory and, probably, some level of comprehension. However, children can repeat what they have seen or heard without understanding what they are saying or doing—witness the toddler who repeats swear words! The more varied opportunities the child has to dramatize actions, stories, and events, the more opportunities the child has to use concepts and develop a deeper understanding of their meaning. Adults should support language comprehension in dramatic play by providing props, labels, and suggestions for actions or events and by modeling increasingly complex vocabulary and sentence structure for the child.

Reading and Learning Routines

Circle Time

Although circle time is not as focused as individual activities between a child and an adult, it provides opportunities for children to learn from each other. Children are particularly interested in watching each other. Listening to what other children say often prompts imitation. With repeated observation and discussion, children can learn concepts through social interaction with each other. The adult's role is to encourage exchanges among children that promote sharing information, demonstrating understanding, or supporting other's learning. For instance, when reading a book about winter to the children, the teacher asked, "Who knows what a 'snow angel' is?" Several children raised their hands. The teacher selected a child and asked the child to explain and show the other children how to make a snow angel. Then, all of the children laid on the floor and imitated the actions. Later, at outdoor time, they all made real snow angels in the new fallen snow.

One-on-One Book Reading

Aside from direct experience, books provide one of the best ways of learning to understand all of the components of language. Not only do the pictures support the words being said by offering a concrete illustration of meaning, but books also provide a variety of types of sentence structure in a logical sequence that supports comprehension. Books also provide an opportunity for adults and children to take the time to focus together on specific topics. The child and adult can point to pictures, label, discuss, question, and interact in a give-and-take exchange that supports quiet listening and learning.

Science and Math

Science and math concepts are best understood through actual experience—observing, touching, smelling, tasting, hearing, and experimenting. The adult's role is to help children notice characteristics, make comparisons, relate ideas, and draw conclusions that demonstrate understanding of the concepts being investigated. Comprehension of concepts goes beyond just understanding a word, but understanding bigger ideas such as *growth, measurement, time,* and so forth. Children will come to understand the concept of *number,* for example, not by doing worksheets where they practice counting items on a page, but by using counting in their everyday experiences. They can count the number of boots outside the door, the number of cups of popcorn needed for each child to have one, or even the sheets of toilet paper they use so it is not too much or too little! Number then is understood as *measurement of amount,* not just rote numbers. Adults can prompt comparisons to help children see the relationships between amounts, starting with *a lot* and *a little* and moving up to comparison of discrete amounts.

■■■■   ***THERESA***

Theresa is a 5-year-old with identified developmental delays with no identified etiology. She makes a variety of babbling sounds, which are occasionally interspersed with what sounds like a word. She uses about 10 recognizable words, including Mama, Dada, ball, doggie, here, *and a few approximations of names of familiar objects. Theresa sel-*

dom uses gestures but pulls her parents and teachers to what she wants. She has tantrums when frustrated by not getting what she wants. She gives people very little eye contact when they are speaking to her, and most of the time she does not respond to what she is told to do. She looks at pictures in a book but does not point to named objects.

The team believes that Theresa does not comprehend much of what is said to her, and because she is not looking at people when they talk to her, she also is missing non-verbal cues and gestures. To increase her communication and language production, reduce her negative behaviors, and improve her social skills, it is important to expand Theresa's language comprehension.

Interaction Strategies

1. *Make sure you are at Theresa's eye level. Hold the object you are talking about (or a symbol such as a car key for going out) up next to your mouth. Attract her attention.*

2. *Use gestures, exaggerated expression, and objects to convey meaning. Emphasize the words you want her to understand.*

3. *Use short sentences or phrases with Theresa so she has fewer words to decode.*

4. *Give choices instead. For example, say, "Do you want cereal or pancakes?" rather than, "What do you want for breakfast?" If she does not respond, ask the question again, this time holding up the cereal box and the box of pancake mix.*

5. *When Theresa does not respond to a request, repeat the request and physically help her do it. Label each step as she does it. Reward her with lots of attention for trying.*

6. *Play turn-taking games with songs and fingerplays, tickling, and so forth, and wait for Theresa to look at you before initiating your turn. When it is her turn, say, "Your turn. Do . . . " This will help her learn to participate in a turn-taking conversation and to follow directions.*

Environmental Modifications

1. *Because Theresa is beginning to look at pictures, pair words, pictures, and objects whenever possible to help her understand what you mean.*

2. *Reduce other auditory distractions, such as music or television, when talking to Theresa. Too much interference may hinder comprehension.*

3. *Use multisensory input to teach concepts. Look at it, feel it, smell it, move it, label it, and use it for its intended purpose.*

4. *Use picture sequences with familiar routines. Once Theresa knows the routine, just use the first picture and words to direct her actions.*

KEYS TO INTERVENTION BY DEVELOPMENTAL AGE

The following ideas are directed toward children who are functioning at approximately the following levels. The suggestions are not meant to be all-inclusive, but rather are indicative of potential areas for exploration.

Developmental age	Communication interests	Keys to intervention
Birth to 3 months	Differentiates between familiar and unfamiliar voices. Can distinguish sound segments and intonation, prosody, and stress of his or her native language from another language.	Talk to the infant during diapering, feeding, and so forth.

Developmental age	Communication interests	Keys to intervention
Birth to 3 months (*continued*)	Responds to voice by quieting. Can be comforted and calmed by touching and rocking. Stares at faces.	
3–6 months	Moves head side to side to localize sound. Differentiates and responds differently to sounds and voices. Demonstrates fear of loud or unexpected noises. Recognizes familiar sound patterns, such as in songs or face-to-face verbal games.	Initiate sounds from different places, not always right in front of the child. Read to the child (a reading voice is different than a talking voice). Identify sources of sounds for the child.
6–9 months	Learning meaning of "No" through tone of voice. Distinguishes between friendly and angry talking. Reacts to emotional displays of others. Enjoys listening to own voice. Likes complex sound stimulation. Listens selectively to sounds and words. Responds to own name. Bilingual child differentiates L1 and L2 words spoken in a speech stream.	Indicate what the child does that is acceptable or "good" from what is not acceptable with a different tone of voice. Use facial expressions to show emotions. Listen to a variety of types of music and songs, including those in other languages. Use all native languages of the home with the child. Illustrate what is being said with objects and actions.
9–12 months	Follows some simple commands paired with gestures. Understands some words. Dances to music. Understands some object names. Listens with interest to familiar words. Understands more commands paired with gestures (e.g., give me). Recognizes words and symbols for objects (e.g., *airplane*/points to sky; *doggie*/growls). Responds to "No."	Use short phrases when telling or asking the child to do something (e.g., "Give me"). Use gestures paired with the words. Point out source of all noises. Label objects and actions. Demonstrate sounds. Encourage imitation of sounds and mouth movements.
12–18 months	Moves head horizontally and downward to sound source (10–15 months). Identifies common objects when named. Shows intense attention to speech over prolonged time. Uses gestures in response to words (e.g., *up, bye*). Associates properties with objects (sounds of animals, location of objects). Responds to "Where is _____?" by searching for object or family member (12–16 months). Understands up to 50 words. Moves head directly to sound source (15–18 months). Sustains interest for 2 or more minutes looking at pictures named. Searches for objects named but not present. Follows simple directions with cues (e.g., "Give me the ball," "Get the shoes," "Show me"). Identifies an object from a group of objects.	Ask for familiar objects. Give choices without showing the object ("Do you want _____ or _____?"). Read books, look at pictures on boxes and cans, billboards, and so forth. Label and ask, "Where is the . . . ?" Hide objects in play and find them, labeling the location where they are found. Ask *what* and *where* questions about toys, people, and daily events.
18–24 months	Recognizes and identifies objects and pictures by pointing. Points at up to 3 body parts. Follows single-step directions. Understands the intent of questions. Responds to yes/no questions with head shake and nod.	Talk about what the child is doing; label body parts, steps in an action sequence. Do action songs with repetitive sequences the child can imitate, then leave out actions to see if the child understands the next step. Give a gestural hint if necessary. Tell the child what objects are needed without pointing or showing, to encourage listening.

(continued on next page)

Developmental age	Communication interests	Keys to intervention
18–24 months (*continued*)	Identifies 5 body parts. Listens to short rhymes with interesting sounds, especially with actions or pictures. Understands some emotion words (e.g., *happy, sad, mad*). Understands some personal pronouns, can distinguish "Give it to her," "Give it to him."	
24–36 months	Moves head all around to locate sound source. Recognizes and points to most common objects. Understands action words. Identifies and points to extended family members. Understands more than 300 words. Listens to and enjoys simple stories. Understands some pronouns (*my/mine, you, me*). Responds to *what* questions. Identifies actions in pictures. Identifies objects by their function. Knows difference between big and little. Points to smaller body parts. Follows two-step commands. Understands *one* versus *all*.	Identify what is needed by function. (e.g., "I need something to put on my feet"). When giving a command, ask the child what she is going to do, to see if she understands. Provide descriptions of objects and actions, then ask choice questions such as, "Is the towel wet or dry?" Do not ask yes/no or closed questions such as, "Do you want a blue crayon?" or "What color is it?" Instead, ask open-ended questions (e.g., "What color do you want?") or use the color words functionally (e.g., "I'd like a blue crayon, please"). Identify objects by location. Instead of "Go get your shoes" say, "You need your shoes. They are under the bed."
36–48 months	Understands descriptive words. Identifies gender. Identifies basic colors. Understands *why* questions. Understands spatial concepts (e.g., *in, out, on, off, under*) (33–36 months). Answers *where* and *what doing* questions. Understands categories. Understands *how many, who,* and *whose* questions (36–40 months). Follows two- to three-step instructions. Identifies most common objects and their pictures. Understands what others say. Understand terms for family relationships. Understands words for basic shapes and sizes. Understands descriptive concepts (e.g., *hard, soft, rough, smooth*). Understands *in front of, behind, top, bottom,* and *between*.	Watch interesting events during play and the day (e.g., the crane lifting beams) and ask and answer *why* and *how* questions. Describe characteristics of objects and then find other objects with the same characteristics. Make comparisons and label differences. Read books with descriptive vocabulary and rhymes about opposites. Relate time concepts to daily events (e.g., begin to use specific time numbers for routines). Use colors and shapes functionally, rather than asking questions (e.g., "You're wearing polka dots—little circles").
48–60 months	Knows opposites (e.g., *long/short, hot/cold,* and so forth). Differentiates between night and day. Shows understanding of time concepts (e.g., *before/after, yesterday/today*). Understands spatial concepts (e.g., *behind, in front, next to, above, below*). Identifies primary colors and shapes. Answers *how* questions. Answers *when* questions (52–58 months). Identifies coins. Understands about 13,000 words. Understands *some, more,* and *less.* Answers *what happens if . . . ?* questions.	Read many different types of books, including expository books about real things and events, to expand vocabulary and conceptual understanding. Let the child help with shopping and paying for single items, parking meters, and other small fares. Talk about quantities and make comparisons using global terms (e.g., "more/ less") in addition to numbers ("3 tablespoons").

6

Facilitating Communication Development

II.   Strategies for Improving Language Production

with Natasha Hall

Goal Attainment Scale

1	2	3	4	5	6	7	8	9
Expresses needs reflexively (e.g., crying, grimacing, body movement).		Uses eye gaze, facial expressions, body movement, gestures, and vocalizations to communicate.		Uses gestures, vocalizations, verbalizations, signs (words, word combinations, or phrases), and/or AAC to communicate.		Uses gestures, words, phrases, signs, and/or AAC to produce sentences (not grammatically correct) and to ask and answer questions.		Consistently uses well-formed sentences and asks and answers a variety of questions.

Language production is the process of communicating thoughts and ideas in a symbolic form. Language can be conveyed nonverbally or verbally in a number of different ways, including written, gestural, signed, body language and facial expression, and oral. Language production allows us to convey our needs, thoughts, wants, and feelings to others.

APPROPRIATE LANGUAGE PRODUCTION

Appropriate language production occurs when the message is transferred from one person to another and the idea of the speaker is understood by the listener.

Modes of communication: Children communicate using a variety of communication modes: eye gaze, facial expressions, body movement, gestures, vocalizations, or verbalizations. Based on the developmental age of the child, a child may use a variety of modes; some modes will occur with more frequency than others, depending on the communication partner and environment.

Level of communication: A child may communicate using vocalizations, verbalizations (words), phrases, or sentences to respond to and communicate with others.

Frequency of communication: The frequency and duration of a child's communications can be affected by decreased modes and level of communication as well as the child's social-emotional status (e.g., shyness, history of abuse or neglect, selective mutism).

Use of grammatical structures and syntax: What types of grammatical structures and sentence structures does the child use to communicate with others?

Use of language forms and concepts: What types of words and concepts does the child use when communicating with others (e.g., agent + object, agent + action + object).

Appropriate Language Production in Practice

II. A. What mode(s) of communication does the child use?

Daily Routines (Home and Classroom)

- *Infant/toddler:* During a diaper change, while lying on his back, an infant looks to the ceiling light and reaches toward it, simultaneously producing a word approximation (e.g., "aiy" or "aiyt"). The sign for light is the opening and closing of the hand when reaching toward the ceiling, which also is an easily taught early sign/word. The toddler brings his mom his juice cup and says, "Drink" while pointing at the refrigerator.

- *Young child:* The young child approaches an adult, points to her shoe, and says, "I need help, please."

Play Routines (Home and Classroom)

- *Infant/toddler:* To comment on a music and light toy, the infant looks to the adult and then looks back to the toy to share the experience. During play with her brother, the toddler grabs the toy from her brother and yells, "Mine."

- *Young child:* During a turn-taking game, the young child looks to the next player, passes the dice, and says, "Your turn."

Classroom Routines

During snack time, the child looks at his classmate, reaches for the pitcher, and verbally asks for the juice, saying, "Will you please pass the juice, Connor?"

II. B. What is the child's frequency of communication?

Daily Routines (Home and Classroom)

- *Infant/toddler:* The infant practices vocalizing throughout the day, especially when a parent is present. She squeals to gain attention and cries when tired, hungry, or in need of a diaper change. The toddler sits on her potty, talking to herself and singing. She makes noises, giggles, and makes more noises, experimenting with various sounds.

- *Young child:* The young child is working on a picture at the art area. He works intently without communicating for a few minutes, then talks to himself about what he did. He then calls other children and the teacher to see what he painted: "See, this is the fire house and this is the house on fire and it is red because it is on fire."

Play Routines (Home and Classroom)

- *Infant/toddler:* While playing in the sandbox, the toddler makes noises and says words while he stirs ("eee, stir"), pokes the sand ("hole"), and hits it with the spoon ("boom, bang"). He runs and laughs and makes silly noises as his father chases him.

- *Young child:* The young child and his friend are playing with Spider-Man characters. He says, "I'm gonna be Spider-Man. He climbs walls with his sticky, gooey fingers. Who do you want to be? You can be the bad guy. I'll chase you and when you get to the top of the building, I'll climb up to get you."

Classroom Routines

In circle time, the young children listen as the teacher asks if anyone had a fun weekend. Joey stands up and says, "Me and my dad and mom and my baby brother went to the zoo. It was free day, and my mom said next time we are going to pay, 'cause it is TOO crowded!"

II. C. What are the child's semantic abilities?

Daily Routines (Home and Classroom)

- *Infant/toddler:* When dad walks through the door, the infant says "Dada" in response, demonstrating that he differentiates between *dada* and *mama*. While playing with his brother, the toddler says, "Mine" to denote possession.

- *Young child:* The young child is able to communicate a variety of semantic relationships (i.e., "I want more milk please" → Agent–action–object). While helping with the laundry, the young child is able to label the different clothing items, verbally categorize them together, and describe different attributes about them (e.g., color, texture, shape).

Play Routines (Home and Classroom)

- *Infant/toddler:* The infant is sitting while her mother makes dinner. She sees a head of lettuce and says, "Ball." While playing a game of chase, the toddler says, "Run, Dad!" (i.e., action + agent).

- *Young child:* In preschool, the young child describes the "clean mud" in the sensory table using multiple describing words (e.g., *wet, white, soggy, looks like snow, squishy, soft*).

Classroom Routines

While cleaning up the play kitchen area, the young child notices that the pizza was placed in the vegetable basket and says, "Hey, that doesn't go in there! Those are all vegetables."

II. D. What grammatical morphemes does the child produce?

Daily Routines (Home and Classroom)

- *Infant/toddler:* The infant babbles a variety of consonant and vowel sounds in response to bubbles during bath time and points to share the experience with her mother. The toddler uses simple word(s) to describe the same activity (e.g., "bubbles"; "Mom bubbles").

- *Young child:* The young child uses phrases and sentences to describe bubbles in a sensory table (e.g., "This is like the bath tub at home. Let's give the baby a bath. We have bubbles at home, they spilled").

Play Routines (Home and Classroom)

- *Infant/toddler:* While looking at a book, the infant sees a picture of a duck and points to it while saying, "quack quack" and flapping his arms. While stacking blocks with her mother, the toddler knocks over the tower and says, "Uh-oh, mommy."

- *Young child:* While at the grocery store, the young child asks, "We are all out of cookies for my lunch, Mommy. Where are they?"

Classroom Routines

While reading a book during story time, the young child asks, "What's going to happen to the mouse, Ms. Sims? Is she going to be okay?"

▬▬▬ II. E. What are the child's syntactic abilities?

Please note that use of grammatical structures and appropriate syntax/grammar and appropriate language forms and concepts have been combined because strategies to address these areas are similar.

Daily Routines (Home and Classroom)

- *Infant/toddler:* A 6- to 8-month-old infant produces reduplicated babbling patterns (e.g., "ba-ba," "ga-ga," "di-di"). A 9- to 12-month-old infant begins to use variegated babbling (e.g., "ba-di-ga"). The toddler describes action by saying, "Mommy wash."

- *Young child:* While playing outside, the young child describes his play, saying, "I catched the ball with both hands."

Play Routines (Home and Classroom)

- *Infant/toddler:* Infants initially vocalize vowel sounds in exploration. Back consonant (i.e., gurgling, k, g) and bilabial consonant(i.e., p, b, m) sounds are typically the first sounds produced. The toddler attempts to use the plural form of a word, but incorrectly; for example, "fishes."

- *Young child:* While playing with toy cars with a peer, the young child says, "He taked my red truck."

Classroom Routines

The young child uses longer sentences but continues to make grammatical errors; for example, "I want more cheeses, please."

GENERAL PRINCIPLES FOR SUPPORTING LANGUAGE PRODUCTION

Caregivers typically engage in many behaviors to encourage more complex language production. Often this happens without conscious effort. The following are strategies that frequently are used to help children expand their ideas in play. These can be used with children of all developmental levels.

Imitate Sounds, Oral Motor Movements, and Words Produced

Infants are continually experimenting with sounds through vocal play. They learn new sounds and build their sound repertoire through this experimentation. Caregivers respond to infants during times of intense vocalizations by imitating the sound(s) produced by the infant. Face-to-face contact for these interactions is important for imitation and turn-taking purposes. Initially, sounds initiated by the infant may be non-speech sounds or just oral motor movements such as sticking out the tongue, raspberries, or blowing. As an infant's sound repertoire increases, sounds produced are more representative of vowels and consonants and then combinations. As the complexity of these imitation games increases, infants begin to imitate novel sounds, sounds in new combinations, or a pattern of sounds.

Capture the Child's Attention

It is important to first make sure that the child is attending before expecting him or her to respond. Adults often get on the child's facial level or make sure the child is attending to the adult's face, voice, gestures, and body language, in order to increase the probability of imitation and exchange.

Label Familiar Objects, People, and Events

Adults label objects, people, and actions within the environment to provide the child with knowledge and information about the world. Children typically understand a word before producing it verbally and require repeated exposures to the word before using it appropriately to communicate. When a child has a limited vocabulary, he or she may produce the same word to represent several different meanings (e.g., "baba" to label the bottle, "baba" to request milk, and "baba" to show possession when Mom has the bottle).

Encourage Multimodal Communication

Infants and toddlers use many modes of communication (e.g., gestures, body movement, eye gaze, vocalizations, words) to have their wants and needs met. Many times, adults expect infants and toddlers to imitate or use a word to communicate and mistakenly ignore or reject another form of communication. Adults who are sensitive to communicative attempts honor all efforts at communicating, even those that are not as complex or appropriate as they would desire. For instance, if a child reaches toward the adult and whines, the adult reaches toward him and says, "Up," thus demonstrating a higher level of communication (e.g., combining a gesture and a word instead of a gesture and vocalization). With an older child, an adult also may label feelings associated with the communication act. For example, if a child hits and says, "No," the adult may respond, "I see that you are mad because you wanted the ball. Try saying, 'My turn, please.'" This models a higher level of communication.

Scaffold the Child's Language to the Next Level

Most adults model language that is at a slightly higher level than the child is currently producing in hopes that she will eventually add new vocabulary, complex grammatical structures, and sentence structures to her language bank. If the child says, "Look, cow moo," the adult replies, "I see the big cow. He says, 'moo.'" Depending on the child's language level, the adult makes the reconstruction and expansion of this phrase as complex or as simple as needed. Repetition of these expanded utterances is not expected, but often the child imitates some portion of the expansion.

Repeat the Child's Utterances with Corrected Grammar

Even children who are developing language typically make grammatical errors, especially when experimenting with new verb tenses and plurals. For example, children often add –ed to verbs when learning past tense. The child may say, "I ranned fast."

When given an opportunity, adults repeat the phrase with the appropriate grammar change (e.g., "You ran very fast"), again not always expecting the child to repeat the corrected version.

Provide Simple and Correct Examples

Children learn language from the adults and other people who surround them. Adults modify their language with the intent of providing children with a little extra information. If a child is using 1-word utterances to communicate, such as "baba" and "doggie," for example, the adult keeps his or her language fairly simple by using short phrases and 2-word combinations. This naturally models the next natural step of language development (i.e., increase vocabulary and combine some simple words into 2-word combinations).

THE PRINCIPLES IN PRACTICE

Daily Routines (Home and Classroom)

The strategies described previously are used by parents and other caregivers throughout the day to support children's developing language production skills. The following are examples of how adults integrate these approaches into various activities.

Feeding/Eating

Adults offer verbal choices to toddlers and young children during mealtime; for example, "Do you want grilled cheese or spaghetti?" The child then responds with one of the choices, and the caregiver uses a scaffolding technique to increase the complexity of the request. For example, "You want a grilled cheese sandwich," adding a new label. Young children can be asked about the attributes of foods, such as color, size, taste, and type.

Diapering/Toileting

When a toddler approaches an adult and touches his diaper and says, "Stinky," the adult responds by first accepting and thanking the child for the information and then labeling it as a time to change his diaper. For young children, expanded comments may include directions.

Dressing

After eating dinner, a young child's mother makes the comment, "Time to get ready for bed. What do we need to do first?" The preschooler responds by saying, "It's time for a bath." The mother responds, "Which pajamas do you want to wear to bed, the dinosaurs or Sesame Street?" Child: "Dinosaurs." This interchange gives the child an opportunity to create a sentence and make a verbal choice.

Play Routines (Home and Classroom)

Face-to-Face Play

A mother waits until the infant attempts to imitate a new sound during a face-to-face babbling game. She says, "Ooh" as she softly rubs the baby's tummy. The young child tries to teach his dad the new song he learned at school. When he says, "Like a diver in the sky," dad says, "Like a 'diamond.' A diamond is a bright shiny stone that sparkles like a star."

Physical Play

While on the playground, the teacher will allow the swing to stop and wait for the child to initiate some form of communication before giving another push.

Manipulative Play

While participating in container play, the adult models prepositions by saying, "in" every time he places a shape in the container. The adult then waits for the child to say, "in" when it is his turn. For the older child, the teacher comments or asks questions such as, "How many blocks do you think will fit in there?" or "There's not enough room; what should we do?" This latter interaction encourages formation of a new thought and sentence.

Sensory Play

During an activity with dried noodles and glue at preschool, the teacher may comment that her art project looks like a girl's smiling face in order to elicit further symbolic language. The child may respond with, "Mine is going to be a mad face."

Reading and Learning Routines

Circle Time

During circle time, the teacher poses open-ended questions for the children to answer about an unfamiliar story, such as, "I wonder what will happen next?" and waits for the children to respond using visual support from the pictures in the story.

One-on-One Book Reading

The adult reads a familiar and repetitive book to the student, and as the child becomes familiar with the repetitive phrases, the adult pauses and waits for the child to fill in the missing words, sounds, and/or gestures.

Science and Math

At the science center, the teacher reviews the current month and discusses the season, talking to the child about what happens during this month outdoors. They brainstorm what will happen as the temperature gets colder.

PLANNING INDIVIDUALIZED
INTERVENTIONS FOR IMPROVING LANGUAGE PRODUCTION

▬▬▬ II. A. What mode(s) of communication does the child use?

Typically, as children develop, the number and complexity of the modes of communication increase as they acquire language, motor, social, and cognitive skills. There are many reasons why children may have limited modes of communication. Children with varying types of disabilities, language disorders, and delays often are unable to use multiple modes of communication. For example, children with autism spectrum disorders may use words and gestures to communicate but also may have difficulty initiating and maintaining eye contact. Children with cerebral palsy (CP) or other muscular disorders may exhibit a range of challenges that can have an impact on their ability to communicate; for instance, limited mobility, possible breath support issues, and decreased motor control affect expressive communication. Consequently, children with

CP may use idiosyncratic modes of communication, such as unusual facial expressions, gestures, or movements that convey meaning to a familiar adult. A child with spastic CP may have difficulty orienting his or her head to the speaker to maintain eye contact, limited control for use of gestures, and decreased breath support, which affects accurate vocalizations. For these children, augmentative and alternative communication (AAC) may be used to support expressive communication development and skills (see TPBA2, Chapter 5 for more information).

Interaction Strategies

1. *Bring the focus of attention to the desired modality.* By overexaggerating gestures, facial expressions, vocalizations, and words, the adult can bring attention to the desired modality. For example, when combining a known sign (e.g., MILK) with the spoken word, the adult needs to ensure that the child's attention is on his face and then overexaggerate the production of the word. The adult also can allow the child to touch his face to feel the airflow while the word is produced. For children with vision impairment, this may be particularly useful. Children who are hard of hearing or deaf may need to focus on both oral and gestural modalities.

2. *Model the mode for the child to imitate.* Depending on what mode of communication the child is currently using (e.g., gestures) and what additional modes are desired (e.g., vocalization), the introduction of a new mode should be incorporated with support. For example, if a child is reaching for the bubble wand to communicate continuation of the game, the adult can model the word "bubbles" as the child again reaches for the wand.

3. *Pair the new mode of communication with the old familiar mode to establish meaning.* Initially, an approximation of the new mode is acceptable as the child adapts to imitating and understanding the new mode. For example, when trying to expand from using a sign (e.g., BALL) to obtain an object, the adult continues to sign the word BALL while also saying the word. Given multiple repetitions, the adult will drop the use of the sign and use just the word, expecting the child to sign and say or approximate the word "ball."

4. *Use wait time.* When introducing new modalities, allowing extra time for the child to process and respond to the given model is necessary. Adults should expect and recognize multiple modes of communication but need to wait for production of the new mode before responding and reinforcing. After multiple turns during a Peekaboo game, the adult has modeled the word "boo" when coming face to face with the child. The adult then peeks but waits for the child to make a vocalization, body movement, or word approximation before the next turn. Children with disabilities often need extra wait time (5–10 seconds) in order to process a response.

5. *Adjust the timing of the response.* Children learn to communicate when they see that their efforts to communicate receive an immediate response. The adult's response time should be instant so the child knows he is understood. Later, as the child gets older, a delayed response time may encourage the child to provide more information to gain the adult's attention, depending on the child's language level.

6. *Incorporate new modalities into fun and interesting games.* It is important when introducing and incorporating new modalities that the child is motivated and receives appropriate reinforcement. Songs, fingerplays, dance, and movement to rhythm are some ways that children can practice vocalizations, gestures, signs, body movements, verbalizations, and eye contact in a fun and reinforcing way.

7. *Match the child's language level.* If the child is using vocalizations—for example, while holding a baby doll—the adult is encouraged to first imitate the vocalization and then interpret the meaning by providing the appropriate label and demonstrating the next level, "baby."

8. *Use augmentative and alternative communication (AAC).* It may be necessary to explore AAC options for children who are nonverbal or have limited verbal skills. AAC is a specialized area and requires the team to work together to address positioning, fine motor skills, cognitive functioning, language, hearing, and vision. Children with motor impairments may respond more readily when they can control the conversation using voice-activated or other AAC devices. Adults need to learn how to best interact with the child using these devices. All will require providing various levels of support, wait times, and types of responses.

9. *Encourage communication with a variety of different people.* Increasing the variety of modalities that a child can use helps him or her to communicate with a variety of people. It is important that a child can demonstrate appropriate use of different modalities with different people across environments. For instance, an infant may reach her arms up to communicate wanting to be picked up at child care or at home with her parents and other relatives. When toddlers and young children communicate with a variety of people, they learn to add modalities to help people understand them. For example, to clarify a point the unfamiliar adult does not understand, the child may demonstrate how a duck walks, move her fingers like a duck's bill, and make quacking sounds.

Environmental Modifications

In addition to interpersonal strategies that may support the child increasing the modalities of communication, environmental modifications often are useful. Depending on the findings from TPBA2, the team may want to consider some of the following environmental modifications.

1. *Ensure optimal positioning for communication.* Optimal positioning is essential for building communication modalities. Face-to-face contact should be established if possible. If the child has physical impairments, he may require special support to obtain appropriate breath support, trunk and head control, and eye contact. The adult may need to be creative to establish face-to-face communication. For example, placing a switch toy where a child with limited limb mobility can reach the toy allows the child to activate the switch and use AAC to communicate. Parents often hold infants facing out or over their shoulders. This prohibits seeing the face of the communication partner. Face-to-face communication is best whenever possible.

2. *Create a need to communicate.* Creating a problem so that the child needs to communicate is one way that adults can produce a communication opportunity. For example, taking the batteries out of a toy and discovering this problem during play is one way to create a communication opportunity. The child then has to communicate with the adult to solve the problem. Multiple modalities can be prompted during this problem solving process.

3. *Establish communication modes across environments.* Generalizing modalities across environments demonstrates understanding and proficient use of that modality. It is important to practice emerging modalities across environments. A child may be consistently using "all done" at the dinner table to communicate completion, but he needs to be encouraged to communicate "all done" when finished with reading a book before bed or after completing a task in preschool.

4. *Educate other people with whom the child communicates frequently about the child's unique communication style.* It is important for all adults working with children who use idiosyncratic forms of communication (e.g., idiosyncratic signs/gestures, AAC systems) to be educated about the child's communication system and intent. Making a list or book of the child's individual communication meanings to give to caregivers, teachers, therapists, and family members is critical so that the child's needs are met, she is understood, and she can participate.

II. B. What is the child's frequency of communication?

Reduced frequency of communication is reflective of both the levels and modes of communication. If a child has a reduced level of communication (e.g., uses vocalizations but no verbalizations), he may have difficulty initiating and participating in communication. The child's communication mode also may hinder the frequency of interactions. For example, a child using idiosyncratic gestures/signs may struggle to communicate with unfamiliar people. Reduced frequency also can be a result of social or behavioral concerns. For a variety of reasons, children with disabilities may not be motivated to communicate. For example, the child with no friends may be able to communicate but does not have a desire or opportunity to do so. The child with selective mutism only communicates under specific circumstances or with particular people. Children with motor difficulties may choose not to communicate often, because extensive effort is required to produce communicative sounds, words, gestures, or signs. Children with motor concerns also may be more isolated from social interaction. Children with verbal dysfluencies may avoid frequent communication in order to avoid the struggle to produce fluent speech and, thus, possible embarrassment. To increase the frequency of communication, adults need to set up a language-rich environment where there is constant communication occurring. Children who do not communicate frequently need a safe environment for communication and sensitive, responsive people with whom to interact (see also Chapter 5, Section III. Strategies for Improving State and Emotional Regulation, and Chapter 5, Section IV. Strategies for Improving Behavioral Regulation).

Interaction Strategies

1. *Be quiet and watch.* Observe the child for times when communication would aid his or her engagement with the environment or interaction with peers. For example, the child may need or want something but does not communicate this to anyone. Adults need to be alert for times they can meaningfully prompt communication.

2. *Read all actions as communication.* Children who communicate infrequently do communicate, consciously or unconsciously, how they are thinking or feeling through eye gaze (e.g., toward a desired object), movement (e.g., away from an unpleasant event), body language (e.g., pulling arms into body when anxious), and/or vocalizations (e.g., grunts, squeals, or other sounds to indicate level of interest). The adult needs to "read" these actions as communication and convey to the child what the action means to him or her; for example, "Jamie, you are looking at the cookies. I think you want one." This gives the child an opportunity to respond.

3. *Accept and support all communicative attempts and then model the next level.* To decrease frustration and provide reinforcement for the child's efforts to communicate, the parent can support the communication attempt and then model the next level. This encourages further communication attempts, which increases the frequency of communication.

4. *Create the need for communication.* In order to participate, the child needs to initiate some form of communication or respond to communication. By giving the child only a few blocks to play with but keeping more visible, the adult has set up the need for continued communication. Involve children in planning and setting up what is needed for various activities; for example, "Let's do some art. I'll get the paper. What do you want to get?"

5. *Reinforce any communicative intent.* Children need to be positively reinforced for attempting to communicate. If a child reaches for the cookie instead of asking for it, the adult then responds by saying, "Oh, you want a cookie?" to encourage verbalization. Do not reinforce by using nonmeaningful terms such as, "Good talking." "Good job" is another comment frequently used by adults; this comment also stops dialogue. Communicating back to the child tells the child that he or she is being understood. An appropriate verbal or physical response to the child's comment is reinforcing and encourages continued conversation. Do not pressure the child to talk, because this will increase stress and reduce the likelihood of meaningful communication.

6. *Reduce stress.* Because communicating is difficult for many children with disabilities, children may feel stress when they try to communicate. Reduce the child's stress whenever possible by not putting pressure on the child to talk. Have slow, relaxed interactions without placing demands.

Environmental Modifications

In addition to interpersonal strategies that may increase the frequency of communication, environmental modifications often are useful. Depending on the findings from TPBA2, the team may want to consider some of the following environmental modifications.

1. *Create a safe, accepting environment.* Children who struggle to talk, fear being made fun of, or are shy or anxious about talking need to feel accepted and their communicative efforts valued. Adults create this environment by giving every child an equal chance to communicate, accepting the child's feelings, providing activities the child feels good about and wants to share with others, and making communication an expected and encouraged part of every activity and routine.

2. *Create an environment where communication takes place frequently.* The expectation is that people naturally communicate to have wants and needs met. The term *vocal contagion* means providing a vocal environment for babies to increase vocalizations. For older children, a verbal environment also may stimulate more conversation.

3. *Use props and materials that encourage communication.* Use toys and scenarios that prompt communication (e.g., telephones, electronic toys that can be turned off, talking dolls, books); these types of toys promote language and communication rather than just manipulation.

4. *Provide social play opportunities with peers.* Children should be in an environment where they can see other children communicating and learn from them. Dramatic play, action figures, and board games are examples of social play opportunities. For young children, play games that require turn-taking, such as early board games (e.g., Candy Land) and card games (e.g., Go Fish). In addition, activities that are usually done in isolation (e.g., drawing, puzzles) can be done with a peer to encourage communication.

5. *Take advantage of problems in the environment.* Point out situations in which someone needs help, and encourage the child to assist the other child or adult. Ask about how to solve problems that arise, such as not having enough snacks for everyone.

When a jar lid is stuck, have two children work on the problem together. If no problem exists, the adult can always create one, for example, by not having paper to go with the markers, removing the chairs from the table, and so forth, so that children can talk about what is wrong.

▪▪▪▪ II. C. What are the child's semantic abilities?

How a child uses words both individually and in combination is referred to as *semantics*. The first words that a child produces typically are nouns that represent objects and events that are important to the family. Action words (e.g., *go*), location words (e.g., *up*), possession words (e.g., *mine*), agent words (e.g., *baby*), and reoccurrence words (e.g., *more, again*) are present within the 18-month-old child's spoken vocabulary. Once the child has a lexicon containing these different types of words, word combinations can be expected. As the child's lexicon grows, more complex semantic relations are produced. A child may have an extensive noun/object vocabulary, but if action and location words are not present, then few combinations can be created, delaying the child's expressive language development. A child with vision impairment uses fewer visual description words (e.g., *pretty*). A child with autism can perseverate on concrete feature descriptors such as color or number, but may not be able to describe the overall concept (e.g., pink hat, blue coat, purple boots → "She's ready to go outside in the cold"). Action words may not be as prevalent in the lexicon of a child with decreased mobility.

In infancy, children learn a variety of concepts related to objects, people, actions, places, events, and characteristics of these. Comprehension of the meaning of these concepts typically precedes expression of words related to these concepts. Children then begin to name familiar objects (e.g., "baba" for bottle), family members (e.g., "mama," "dada"), desired actions (e.g., "up," "eat"), and so forth. Children who have disabilities may have delayed conceptual development, meaning they produce these concepts later than their typical peers (e.g., children with language delays); they may have disordered conceptual development, meaning they develop concepts related to certain concepts but not others (e.g., children with autism may develop higher level abstract concepts but not concepts related to people); or they may have fragmented conceptual development (e.g., developing concepts that are "trained" or taught by parents or teachers but missing other concepts at the same or lower developmental level). Conceptual development requires that children not only learn the labels for objects, people, and events in their environment but also learn the relationships among these elements. The more concepts children acquire, the more they need to be able to see similarities and differences and form groups of related concepts to help organize thinking; otherwise, knowledge would be just a list of words. As children learn words and organize them into a subconscious structure, they begin to understand how to use these words to communicate their ideas. The grouping and structure of word meanings (i.e., semantics) and sequences into a predictable, intelligible pattern (i.e., syntax) is what communicates the child's comprehension of concepts.

Interaction Strategies

1. *Provide words for objects, people, actions, events, and descriptors.* Typically, children learn to express concepts in the following developmental sequence, with all areas overlapping as the child reaches toddlerhood. Strategies to promote higher conceptual expression include

Objects: The object should be present for the child to see and explore it. Different types of the object should be presented (e.g., basketball, Koosh ball, tennis ball) so the child understands the different features of the object.

People: Use pictures of different people.

- Label people when present (e.g., "Grandma's here").

- Use miniature figures to represent people (e.g., "Here's the mommy feeding the baby").

Places: Use associations with things that are familiar to the child (e.g., "We need to go to the store. We can get more apples").

- Use symbols or environmental print to represent a familiar idea (e.g., the golden arches means *McDonald's.*

- Provide objects or pictures that represent the place (e.g., a picture of a book means going to the library).

Events (actions, routines, activities): Provide objects or pictures that represent the event (e.g., keys for going in the car, a spoon for mealtime, a blanket for naptime).

- Recall a previous activity or visit to an event (e.g., "Remember when we went to the mountains and saw the deer?").

- Explain what will happen at the activity (e.g., "You will see your friend Annie").

Properties or characteristics (emotions, physical traits, descriptors): Use social stories to illustrate concepts (e.g., "Mary says, 'I want to play.' She is being nice").

- Interpret facial expressions and behaviors as they are seen (e.g., "You are making a mad face. Are you mad at Bobby?" "When Dora gave her friends a hug, she was being loving").

- Describe attributes or conditions that depict physical traits (e.g., "She has her hat, gloves, and heavy coat on, so it must be *cold* outside").

2. *Present a referent.* When emphasizing meaning, it is important to have the child use language in a functional context. Having the child say or sign "ball" to demonstrate that he can produce the symbol for *ball* when there is no ball present does not address meaning.

3. *Redirect tangential comments to the topic at hand.* If the child has limited use of language and decreased vocabulary, she may tend to perseverate on known words when introduced to unknown topics or environments. The adult can accept and then redirect these comments by modeling new and appropriate vocabulary to the child.

4. *Use commenting to elicit further language production.* Commenting on the topic at hand can elicit further language production and experimentation with use of new words and vocabulary. While looking at a book, the adult can comment on the targeted meaning: "Look, the kitty is on the chair."

5. *Provide the child with functional words that carry meaning, not overgeneralized requesting words.* When trying to establish meaning through the use of new words/signs, the child should be taught the word of the object, event, and so forth, rather than using nonspecific language such as, "more, please," "this one," or "that one." It is important to keep language specific in order for the child to fully understand meaning. When offering a child a choice, the objects should be named, for example, "milk or juice" rather than "this one" or "that one."

6. *Use multimodal cues.* When presenting unfamiliar language concepts such as prepositions, colors, or adjectives, it is important to have visual or other sensory representations of the concept being taught. To learn about what a feather is, the child needs to see feathers on many different birds, to touch them, and to feel them. Typically, a child understands a concept before he is able to produce a verbal representation of the concept. The child recognizes a feather and then learns to say the word. Consequently, concepts initially can be emphasized in a receptive task and then in an expressive task. For example, in teaching the concept of location, the adult might model and then suggest to the child, "Put the horse next to the barn." Then as the child begins to verbalize prepositions, he or she can tell the adult where to place the animals. To stress meaning, multimodal cues should be available for the child to see, touch, smell, hear, and taste. For example, when talking about different fruits such as bananas and oranges, having those items available for the child to explore helps the child understand the differences and similarities between the two.

7. *Demonstrate similarities and differences between objects and events.* To solidify meaning, grouping objects and events into categories can help children understand the meaning. For instance, sort shapes or stack same-sized blocks together and define the items' attributes as the items are placed, saying, "The circles are round," or "Let's count the number of sides a square has."

8. *Provide opportunities for new experiences and exposure to unknown concepts.* Children require exposure to unknown concepts and events to first understand them and then later to tell about them. Within a preschool classroom, children are exposed to a calendar—the days of the week and the numbers associated with the calendar—on a daily basis. They then are able to relate information about the calendar as the year goes on.

9. *Routine songs or rhymes.* Singing a song or saying a rhyme routinely to introduce an activity exposes a child to unfamiliar concepts in a fun way. It also provides structure within a preschool classroom that eases transitions from one activity to another. Examples of these songs are snack time, circle time, good-bye song, day of the week song, and so forth.

Environmental Modifications

In addition to interpersonal strategies that may increase the appropriate use of language forms and language concepts to express meaning, environmental modifications often are useful. Depending on the findings from TPBA2, the team may want to consider some of the following environmental modifications.

1. *Provide appropriate materials.* Materials should be chosen carefully when emphasizing meaning. Typically, a child will need concrete examples such as objects, pictures, or people to understand meaning.

2. *Use visual (objects/pictures) and environmental cues.* The use of visual supports in various environments (e.g., picture cards, objects, miniature objects, picture schedules) provides the child with a visual representation of the word meaning (e.g., picture cards with spatial concepts or a "stop" sign to indicate completion of an activity). Exposing children to both the visual representation of a concept along with the words that label that concept will increase understanding of the concept. Multisensory methods of presenting concepts are helpful because children experience different aspects of the concept. For example, when teaching colors, an activity could be to fingerpaint with the different colors. The children then get to feel, smell, and mix the colors to create even more colors.

3. *Comment on events as they occur.* Pointing out events as they occur is beneficial so that the child can see the action occurring. When other children are putting on their coats to go outside, the adult can point this out and say, "The kids are putting on their coats to go outside. What should we do?" This prompts the child to respond with an agent + action response.

4. *Group children by language concept level.* It is helpful to place children who have varying conceptual knowledge in the same group. This allows children with more conceptual knowledge to be peer models for those children who have less conceptual knowledge. For example, when completing a color-sorting activity at preschool, children with less conceptual knowledge could be placed in the same group with children who are proficient at color sorting.

II. D. What grammatical morphemes does the child produce?

Language development typically occurs in a predictable pattern within an age range. Children with disabilities often have delayed expressive communication. Imitation of motor and vocal behaviors is initially how infants and children acquire communication skills. Decreased imitation skills directly influence a child's language production and language level. For example, a child who has difficulty imitating syllable combinations and different consonant sounds will struggle to increase his language level to the single-word and multiple-word combination level. A child with vision impairment may have difficulty with the imitation of both vocalizations and signs and gestures. This child may require a multimodal communication system, focusing on the other senses and providing auditory, tactile, smell, and taste cues to build language production. To increase the level of communication, it is important for the facilitator to match the child's level and then build to the next level. For example, the child who looks to what he or she wants is ready to vocalize and/or point. The child who is capable of pointing and vocalizing is ready to formulate word approximations and/or words. This is "vertical" expansion, or moving the child to a higher step of development. At the same time, it is important to develop the depth and breadth of communication skills, or "horizontal" development. For example, if the child uses several single-word utterances, it does not mean he or she is ready for two-word phrases. Many more single words are needed for a language foundation. In addition, some children may use rehearsed or learned phrases appropriately (e.g., "I would like a turn, please") but are unable to produce an original sentence about a novel event. They are, in effect, using a multiple-word utterance as if it were one word: "Iwouldlikeaturnplease."

Interaction Strategies

1. *Demonstrate the desired modality.* Make sure to demonstrate the desired level of communication for the child. This occurs naturally when combining two modalities of communication. For example, when a child is reaching for her bottle, if the adult desires the child to say "bottle," the adult models "bottle" while the child is reaching.

2. *Play turn-taking communication games.* Communication involves turn taking. Children need to learn patterns of reciprocal exchange of words, gestures, facial expressions, and body language. Turn-taking games are one way of demonstrating an interactive exchange. At the infant level, the exchange of looks, sounds, and actions motivates the child to imitate the adult. As the child begins an exchange of words, he or she learns that turn taking involves initiating, waiting, watching and listening, and then responding. At this level, fingerplays and songs, word games, and jokes (e.g., "knock-knock") encourage this reciprocal exchange.

3. *Provide concrete cues.* Visual cues give the child a concrete example of the word. For a word to have meaning, children have to understand that a particular series of sounds (a word) always refers to the same meaning. For that understanding to develop, children need to hear (or see, in the case of children who are deaf; see Chapter 6, Section VII) the word many times in combination with its referent (e.g., object [*table*], action [*run*], descriptor [*pretty*]). The child learns the "name" of something by seeing the object (e.g., doggie), feeling it, hearing it, and, in some cases, tasting it, moving it, or experiencing its effect. Joint presentation of the word and its actual referent is critical to learning language. For example, while reading a book, a child points to different animals when the adult labels the animal and makes the sounds associated with that particular animal. The child has a referent for the label. Another example is giving the child a choice of two objects and naming them. The child has thus been prompted to use a word and a gesture to make a request. For children with vision loss or impairment and other disabilities, the use of tactile and/or other concrete input may be required (see Chapter 4).

4. *Exaggerate the type of communication you are trying to elicit.* By exaggerating the type of communication (e.g., intonation patterns, vocalizations, words, gestures) you are trying to elicit, the child's attention is brought to the desired level of communication. When playing a babbling turn-taking game with an infant, the adult can exaggerate the given consonant–vowel combinations for the infant to replicate.

5. *Emphasize the meaning by using multiple ways of demonstrating the meaning.* Using emphasis to enhance meaning allows the child to understand and then reproduce the desired level of communication. Signing while saying the word gives the child both auditory and visual input to raise the level of communication.

6. *Minimize the use of closed questions.* Closed questions require a yes/no or one-word response. These questions are appropriate when the child's level of expressive ability limits his or her communication (e.g., if the child does not have labels for objects or people); for example, "Do you need help?" However, for children capable of using words, the use of closed questions limits language production. The child uses one word instead of a longer communication. Another problem presented by yes/no questions is that when an adult offers the child a choice (e.g., "Do you want your bath now?"), the adult needs to be prepared to accept a negative answer. Instead, using open-ended questions such as, "What toys do you want to take to the bath?" does not give the child an option that he or she cannot have and also offers an opportunity for the child to produce a sentence or phrase.

7. *Use commenting.* Commenting on an event or activity is another way to elicit a higher level of communication. When an adult comments, rather than asks questions, a response is not demanded. The adult then waits for the child to integrate information and formulate a response to the comment. For example, while having a tea party the adult says, "I wonder what we could eat during our tea party." The child then responds with his or her own ideas.

8. *Imitate the child's vocalizations or words.* By imitating the child's vocalizations, words, gestures, or word combinations, the adult is setting up the expectation for the child to respond. The adult also can add to the child's production. For example, a child points to a picture in a book and says, "Look, a balloon." The adult says, "Look, there's a red balloon up in the sky."

9. *Provide choices.* Providing a verbal or visual choice is another way to scaffold a higher level of communication. If a child is primarily using single-word utterances when given a choice, the adult can scaffold the child by offering the choice using a two-

word combination to describe each choice; for example, "Do you want the big truck or the little car?"

10. *Combine wait time with an expectant look.* New challenges require additional time for processing and formulating an answer. Adults cannot rush a child when asking her to increase her communication level. The adult's attention should remain on the child, with an expectant look. For example, the adult may both wave and say, "bye-bye" and then look to the child for a response. Give the child several seconds before demonstrating again. As mentioned previously, a wait time of 5–10 seconds may be needed for some children with disabilities.

11. *Follow the child's lead.* When focusing on increasing a child's level of communication, it is important to follow the child's lead. Activities should be those that are motivating and interesting to the child, are fun, and involve age-appropriate toys. If a child gravitates toward a musical/light toy, the adult should use this toy to motivate and create communication opportunities. Forcing a child to talk about what the adult wants (e.g., "Tell me about the car"), requesting a performance (e.g., "Tell Grandma about your school"), or drilling a child on vocabulary ("What's this called?") may lead to resistance or a lower level response than desired.

12. *Use face-to-face communication.* The adult should bring him- or herself to the child's level. This helps the child develop appropriate social communication and allows him to see appropriate facial expressions, mouth movements, and eye contact that occur during conversation. Face-to-face communication also enables the child to see the adult's responses and, if the adult's responses are positive, will motivate the child to continue talking.

13. *Create anticipation.* Children learn to associate words, phrases, sentences, and so forth with familiar events and activities. While reading a familiar book, a parent can pause and allow the child to fill in the missing word, gesture, or phrase. Eventually, the child will be able to fill in more and more of the words. For example, when completing a routine activity at home (e.g., taking a bath), the parent can say, "Rub-a-dub-dub time" and the child will know what to expect and might say, "I want to bring ducky to the bath." Children need to hear words used hundreds of times in meaningful and varied contexts to be able to use them appropriately.

14. *Use repetition.* Children learn through repetition of familiar events, books, and activities. Reading the same story every night before bed may seem redundant to an adult; however, the child benefits from the retelling and can increase expressive language production when appropriately guided by the adult.

Environmental Modifications

In addition to interpersonal strategies that may increase the level of communication, environmental modifications often are useful. Depending on the findings from TPBA2, the team may want to consider some of the following environmental modifications.

1. *Place desired materials outside of the child's reach so the child has to request help.* Placing materials out of reach creates a situation in which the child is required to communicate. In doing so, the language level can be increased. If a child is only given a small amount of crackers at snack time and would like more crackers, her request for more becomes a teachable moment in which her language can be increased (e.g., "Crackers, please" → "I want more crackers, please").

2. *Create a problem.* Adults can create problems that the child can solve through communication. For instance, handing a child Legos in a sealed container prompts the

child to need help opening the box to start the activity; finding that the crayon box is empty elicits a remark.

3. *Position the child with proper support for an optimal communication environment.* If children have motor or positioning concerns, it is necessary for them to be placed in an optimal position for communication. Children with Down syndrome may require additional trunk support to participate in face-to-face communication and to give them proper breath support for practicing vocalizing. Children with cerebral palsy may need additional support for the head.

4. *Use visual cues.* Visual cues can be used to draw attention to the topic at hand so that the child has supplemental cues to increase the level of communication. Pointing to the speaker's mouth or touching the child's throat area is a way to draw attention to where the sound comes from when scaffolding to vocalizing. Picture schedules can be used to provide structure and predictability in a child's day as well as to expand expressive language skills. Adults can ask questions about the schedule to teach concepts, sequencing, and meaning. Children also can use augmentative forms of communication.

5. *Use augmentative and alternative communication.* Children with a variety of disabilities, including autism spectrum disorders and severe or profound communication, motor, and/or social impairments, may require picture or symbol boards, sign language/gestures, cued speech, objects, mini-objects, or high-tech devices such as body-activated speech devices. All options should be review by the family and a team of specialists to determine ease of use, cost, flexibility for lifestyle, and ability to communicate at the child's level of comprehension.

6. *Expose the child to a wide variety of experiences.* Exposing children to a variety of environments and experiences will help to increase vocabulary and concepts. Taking children to the park allows them to experience the different equipment and see new people. Pairing sounds with movement and then describing the movement can increase the level of communication (e.g., saying, "Whee," as the child goes down the slide and then describing the action, "You're going down the slide"). For older children, new experiences prompt questions, comments, comparisons, and new concepts. All experiences, whether from movies, books, television, field trips, community outings, or play and daily routines, need adult facilitation for children to maximize communication opportunities. Appropriate use of these strategies needs to be integrated into all environments.

▬ II. E. What are the child's syntactic abilities?

At 18 months of age, when children are beginning to combine words, they are beginning to produce various semantic relationships, grammatical morphemes, and syntactical structures and types. A morpheme is the smallest meaningful unit and can be a stand-alone word (i.e., free morpheme) or a bound morpheme. Examples of semantic relations may include the child's use of agents (e.g., *mommy*), actions (e.g., *eat*), recurrence words (e.g., *more*), location words (e.g., *down*), and possessives (e.g., *my*) and how the child uses them at the prelinguistic, one-word, and multiword stages. *Morphemes* are the smallest unit of meaningful speech of plurals, possessives, various verb tenses, subjective and progressive pronouns, and articles. *Syntax* is defined as looking at the word order a child produces in creating phrases and sentences, as well as the type of sentence structures (e.g., simple, compound, complex, compound-complex) and the classification of sentences (e.g., declarative, interrogative [type and complexity of question forms including *yes/no, what, where, who, why, which*], imperative, exclamatory).

Interaction Strategies

1. *Model appropriate grammatical structures.* Do not expect the child to always imitate the corrected version; just offer it. For instance, if the child says, "I felled down," the adult could respond with, "Yes, you fell down." Be aware of the developmental sequence of learning grammatical structures, and model both horizontal and vertical structures:

Present progressive (-*ing*)	Model a self-statement and give the child the format for imitating the structure (e.g., "I am jumping. What are you doing?" or "I am stirring and you are ____").
Prepositions (e.g., *in/on*)	Provide the space where the structure belongs for the child to fill in (e.g., "I'm putting your shoes ___"). Give a choice for the appropriate format (e.g., "Is it 'under' or 'on' the table?").
Possessives ('*s*)	Provide a model (e.g., "This is John's jacket and that is ___"). Challenge a response (e.g., "Is this mine?" [Point to child's snack]).
Contractible copula (e.g., "She's little")	Model using the contraction, and then add the extended version; for example, "He's big. He is big."
Uncontractible copula (e.g., "Who is happy? He *is*" [not contracted])	Emphasize the words being said to show the need for the word; for example, "He *is.*"
Regular third person (e.g., *reads*)	Model and encourage imitation, particularly when doing an action; for example, "Mommy reads books. Sara ____."
Irregular third person (e.g., *does*)	Correct the child with a model, rather than telling the child he or she was wrong. For example, when the child says, "He doed it wrong," say, "Yes, he *did* it wrong." Ask a question containing a model (e.g., "What did he do?")
Contractible auxiliary (e.g., "Mommy's running")	Demonstrate the change by using both forms; for example, "Billy is running. Billy's running fast." Ask a question: "What is Billy doing?"
Uncontractible auxiliary (e.g., "I am not going")	Provide the correct model. For example, if the child says, "I amn't going," the adult replies, "No, and I am *not* going either."
Sentence structure	Provide models for the child paired with the appropriate referent for each of the following structures: Phrase: "Nice try!" (while pointing at the child's legs, which are both inserted in the same pant leg) Statement: "You are doing it all by yourself." Question: "Do you want help?" Compound sentence: "Let's put on the pants first, and then we'll put on your shirt." Complex sentence: "While I'm getting your shirt, you finish pulling up your pants." Tense: • Present: "Daddy is in the car." • Past: "He went to the store." • Future: "He will be home soon."

2. *Overemphasize the structure being corrected.* When providing a correct model for the child, the adult can overemphasize the correct structure through vocal inflection. For example, the child may say, "We goded to the zoo." The adult responds with, "Yes, we *went* to the zoo."

3. *Provide suggestions in play.* While playing with action figures, the adult can prompt the child to use certain grammatical structures by modeling, "Tell him to go up the stairs."

4. *Prompt a desired structure through a question*. If the adult says, "What are you going to do next?" the adult has then prompted a future tense.

5. *Omit a word in a sentence for the child to fill in*. To demonstrate appropriate grammatical structures to a child, the adult can first model the sentence structure. For example, using a repetitive picture book, focusing on the *–ing* ending, the adult can start each sentence for the child: "The girl is _____ (swimming)."

Environmental Modifications

In addition to interpersonal strategies that may increase the use of appropriate grammatical structures, environmental modifications often are useful. Depending on the findings from TPBA2, the team may want to consider some of the following environmental modifications.

1. *Use ordered picture cards and/or cues*. Picture cues can be used to prompt appropriate grammatical structure. The adult can line up the pictures in order and point to each picture to cue the child. The pictures may be of actual objects or familiar signs; for instance, "I want cookies, please."

2. *Visual cues (signs/gestures/words)*. The adult can sign, gesture, or say the words in appropriate order to cue the child to imitate. The cues should be provided one word at a time in order to give the child time to imitate the word. As the child becomes successful at producing the appropriate structures, the cues can then be reduced.

3. *AAC devices*. Both low- and high-tech AAC devices can be used to construct appropriate grammatical structures.

4. *Choose children's books that emphasize appropriate grammatical structure*. Many children's books have repetitive concepts, words, phrases, sentences, and themes that focus on a particular language pattern. Look for books that target negatives, present and past tense, clauses, and so forth.

ROUTINES FOR THE CHILD WHO NEEDS SUPPORT TO IMPROVE LANGUAGE PRODUCTION

The following are examples of how the strategies outlined previously can be incorporated into the child's routines at home and at school. In addition to the strategies noted at the beginning of the chapter, used by caregivers of children who do not have special needs, these may support increased proficiency in language expression.

Daily Routines (Home and Classroom)

Feeding/Eating

During mealtime, there are multiple opportunities for a child to increase language production. Giving a child choices to respond to at mealtime encourages language production (e.g., "Do you want milk or juice?"). If the child is nonverbal, the actual objects or picture symbols can be used. Emphasis should be placed on having the child initiate the interaction by handing the juice box or a picture card to the adult to request the item. Once the child is using a variety of single words to request, label and comment; then, building two-word combinations and short phrases is the next goal. At preschool during snack time, a small pitcher of juice can be set in the middle of the table to encourage sharing and expressive language production. Initially, an adult will have to help facilitate passing and sharing among the children.

Diapering/Toileting

While diapering the infant, the adult can describe the actions both to model vocabulary and to reduce anxiety around the steps being completed and what is coming next. Diapering is a time when a lot of face-to-face interaction occurs, and the integration of a sensory-social game such as Peekaboo or vocal imitation games can be played. When a child is developmentally ready for toilet training, the adult can continue to label the vocabulary identified with toileting. It also may be necessary to provide the child who has decreased language production with a sign or gesture to initiate toileting. Verbally sequencing the steps associated with toileting (e.g., sit down, wipe, pull pants up, flush, wash hands) also encourages production of these words. A picture sequence chart that guides actions also can be used to talk about what is "next" and what just happened.

Dressing

Dressing provides many opportunities for a child to use expressive language to make choices, comment on actions and weather, and learn and produce sequencing words. Adults can support language production by setting the stage for the child to contribute to the conversation. The parent of a young child says, "Go look out the window and tell me if it is going to be hot or cold today." Once the child has answered, the parent can then address what types of clothes one would wear for that type of weather, asking questions of the child as dressing occurs. Choices about colors, clothing items, shoes, and outerwear also can be discussed. Sequencing words also can be modeled; for example, "We need to put on your underwear *before* we put on your pants." Action words such as *pull, step into, put, over, under, in, out, push, tighten,* and so forth can be emphasized during dressing activities. In addition, descriptive words (e.g., *pretty, frilly, stiff, blue, long*) can be added. Sentence structure can be modeled (e.g., "You are wearing a shirt, a vest, and pants"). Syntactical structures may be encouraged as well (e.g., "I wore a red dress yesterday. What did you wear?").

Going Out

When taking a child out to run errands, parents can offer their child a running commentary of the order of events. Older children (toddlers and preschoolers) can assist with grocery shopping by helping to label items, count, describe attributes, and predict how items are going to be used. Another motivating idea is to have the child generate a recipe for a special snack, talk about what he is putting in as he makes it, and describe the steps involved as they occur. The parent or adult can facilitate this interaction by slowing down the process. The child should be encouraged to talk about what is happening; what it looks like; and how it smells, tastes, and so forth (e.g., "I like this smell. What do you think it smells like?"). Adults can prompt the child by asking questions and even providing visual examples (e.g., cookbook illustrations, simple drawings, demonstration, verbal models).

Play Routines (Home and Classroom)

Face-to-Face Play

Face-to-face play occurs numerous times throughout a child's day. For infants, these opportunities present themselves at every feeding, diaper change, holding, and so forth. During these occasions, capitalize on the infant's full attention by smiling, cooing, babbling, or talking to the infant. As the infant matures, imitate vocalizations and verbalizations the child makes. Imitate the sounds, actions, or faces that the infant is making to encourage a back-and-forth game. These social-sensory games such as Peek-aboo or Pat-a-cake promote turn taking and anticipation of upcoming events. As the child matures, build on the child's interests to create verbal games, sing songs, and "read" to each other.

Physical Play

Physical play and outside time typically are when children are very vocal—even those who struggle with expressive language. For infants and toddlers, more language often is heard during swinging and gross motor play. As preschoolers, children are extremely motivated by certain playground activities, and these often are opportunities to emphasize turn taking and expressive language. Adults can wait for a child to initiate a game or try to take a turn, comment on what the child is doing and what the adult is doing, and ask about what should happen next. The request may be physical, vocal, or gestural; this pushes the child to initiate the communication to request further action (e.g., swinging).

Manipulative Play

During manipulative play, there are multiple topics that an adult can help to facilitate (e.g., categorizing, basic concepts, patterning, building, math concepts). Although fine motor skills are supported during manipulative play, language expression and concept development also are addressed. As a child completes a puzzle with farm animal pieces, imitation of sounds (e.g., "moo") and answering *Wh* questions can be facilitated. Other expressive language tasks could include counting, using prepositions (e.g., "in" and "out"), labeling animals, and requesting. Label objects, actions, and events; describe the play; and ask open-ended questions. Use problem-solving questions (e.g., "What would happen if?" "What should I do?").

Sensory Play

Sensory play allows the child to experience an event through multiple senses. This multisensory experience offers children with certain sensory impairments (e.g., visual impairments) to learn to use their other senses. This way, an event is meaningful to the child because he or she has touched, smelled, tasted, heard, or seen the activity. For example, during a preschool study of winter, the sensory table within the classroom may contain snow for the children to investigate. The adult can help to facilitate all of the descriptive words around snow (e.g., *cold, wet, white, light, fluffy, packed, hard, water, crunchy*). Sensory experiences also can encourage labeling of objects, actions, and sequences.

Dramatic Play

Dramatic play incorporates all of the routines described previously and, as such, can embody all types of language. Sociodramatic play, by nature, requires interaction while acting out play sequences and events. The adult can model language for various roles, ask questions about past or next events, and help children predict outcomes. In addition, the adult can introduce new vocabulary and illustrate concepts within the play (e.g., "I'm going to buy the baby a pair of new shoes. Look, I like these—two shoes that are alike—a pair"). Dramatic play can be a difficult area for children who have decreased expressive language skills, because this area requires advanced play and language skills to communicate in a meaningful way within the play schema. A child with poor expressive language may need help from an adult to act as part of the play schema rather than just completing perfunctory activities such as dressing up or washing the dishes. The adult needs to scaffold the child's language by asking questions and providing her with appropriate words/phrases to communicate with typical peers. The child says, "I farmer," and the adult responds with, "You are dressed like a farmer, so we better go feed the chickens. Where is the chickens' food?"

Reading and Learning Routines

Circle Time

Circle time is a prime time for children to share and express themselves. All children can participate during circle time if the adult facilitator is cued into each child's expressive language level. The adult facilitator can direct questions, assign specific circle time jobs, and create activities that are appropriate for each child's level and need. Rhyming, fingerplays, and singing also are activities that promote expressive language development. Children with poor expressive language can look to their peers for modeling and participate in a meaningful way even if they cannot participate verbally, by imitating body and motor movements. Songs, fingerplays, and rhymes are repeated throughout the course of the year, giving children multiple opportunities to practice and learn them.

One-on-One Book Reading

Book time can never be initiated too early. It is important that parents begin to incorporate book time at a very early age. Initially, book time does not have to include actual reading of a story but can instead look more like pointing, labeling, and demonstrating appropriate handling of books (e.g., holding right side up, turning pages, opening and closing the book). Books with noises, music, textured materials, and so forth are enticing to most children and can be motivating. For example, a farm book that, when touched, makes a sound for each animal can promote imitation of those sounds. Repetitive books also are useful, because children need repetition of one concept. Prereading to a preschooler is a strategy that will familiarize the student with the book. Later, that student will know how to answer questions appropriately and participate within a larger group storytime. As children become more familiar with a story that has been repeatedly read to them, higher level questions can then be asked (e.g., "What is going to happen next?"). (See Chapter 8, Strategies for Supporting Emerging Literacy.)

Science and Math

In the science and math center, the children are studying colors, shapes, textures, sizes, and kinds of fall leaves. The teacher facilitates a discussion of description, comparison, measurement, and categorization, asking the children to produce appropriate vocabulary in relation to the concepts.

ANN

Ann is a 2-year-old child with Down syndrome who is mildly to moderately deaf. She wears bilateral hearing aids inconsistently. She lives in a family with four brothers and sisters. Mom stays at home with her and the other children. She is primarily concerned about Ann's expressive language development. She is not yet walking and continues to scoot and crawl. She has just started to pull-to-stand on objects in the environment. Ann is a very social little girl and enjoys cause-and-effect toys such as bubbles and pop-up toys. She communicates with eye gaze, gesture, a few signs, and occasional vocalizations.

She is beginning to activate toys by pushing and pulling. Ann's family is motivated to teach her signs and has purchased a videotape that all members are using to learn to sign. They frequently play the tape for Ann to watch during the day. Ann has learned to imitate these signs in sequence as presented on the tape by an adult model without a visual representation of the object being signed. Ann receives her primary nutrition via a g-tube, but she has recently initiated some early oral feeding. She is currently receiving Part C services for all areas of development from an early interventionist, a speech-language pathologist, and an occupational therapist.

The following plan evolved from the follow-up discussion with Ann's parents and the intervention team.

Interaction Strategies

1. *Before communicating with Ann, gain her attention to your face and hands by tapping her on the shoulder, holding up an object, or making an exaggerated sound or expression that captures her attention. Wait until you have Ann's attention and then vocalize and sign in one to two words what you want her to attend to or do.*

2. *Provide direct communication around objects, events, or actions that are of most interest to Ann. When she reaches for an object, give it to her or hold it up and comment. When she turns away from something, interpret that as disinterest and need for a change.*

3. *Adults need to respond immediately and with exaggerated affect and movement to Ann's looks, gestures, signs, and vocalizations; interpret them as a communication; and react appropriately. Ann uses subtle movements, looks, and gestures to communicate intentions. If not responded to, she may stop attempts at communication.*

4. *Ann is capable of imitating signs and responding to signs spontaneously; however, she resists verbal requests to sign. Present visual and motivating reasons for Ann to request an action or respond to visual or verbal communication.*

5. *Use simple verbal, gestural, and signed labels instead of full signed or verbal sentences, because Ann is at the one-word level.*

6. *Ann responds to modeling of signs; however, the signs need to be paired with the actual object or event being represented, because signs in isolation are meaningless to her.*

7. *In order to learn the meaning of the word/sign, Ann needs to experience the meaning of the concept through all of her senses, by seeing, hearing, smelling, tasting, touching, and moving it.*

Environmental Modifications

1. *Encourage the family to promote consistency with Ann wearing her hearing aids. Because she enjoys music and has some residual hearing, allow Ann to listen to music with a strong rhythmic beat through headphones in order to help her acclimate to having something on her ears. Putting on the hearing aids in the morning should be part of Ann's daily routine, like brushing her teeth. Sequence her morning routine to include putting on the hearing aids every day after she puts on her clothes. Ann should wear her hearing aids throughout the day, whenever possible.*

2. *Due to reduced trunk control, tongue control, and breath support, Ann should be positioned so that she is well supported around her back and sides and under her feet. When working on speech and language activities, make sure that she is not expending energy stabilizing her body, so that she can focus on communication.*

3. *Move desired objects slightly out of Ann's reach to encourage her to make a request for the object. For example, move her favorite toy up onto the couch so she needs to pull to stand and make a request.*

4. *Start a face-to-face game with noise and sound turn taking, in which Ann touches your throat or lips to feel the sound and vibration. Ann can feel and understand where the sound originates. Then have Ann physically touch her own mouth and throat to prompt her to make these sounds.*

KEYS TO INTERVENTION BY DEVELOPMENTAL AGE

The following ideas are directed toward children who are functioning at approximately the following levels. The suggestions are not meant to be all-inclusive, but rather are indicative of potential areas for exploration.

Developmental age	Language production focus	Keys to intervention
Birth to 3 months	Produces vowel sounds/cooing. Uses pregestural motions. Looks. Vocalizes. Cries. Makes throaty sounds. Gurgles. Laughs.	Encourage face-to-face contact. Use calm, soothing speech. Vocalize. Use simple language to describe activities. Use exaggerated facial expressions.
3–6 months	Has differentiated cries. Uses continued cooing with introduction of early consonants. Produces vocalization in response to other's sounds. Squeals. Fusses. Babbles randomly.	Play social sensory games (e.g., Peekaboo). Encourage face-to-face interactions. Sing simple songs. Respond to speech and facial expression. Play vocal turn-taking games.
6–9 months	Cries/shouts to gain attention. Vocalizes consonants and vowels. Produces reduplicated babbling (*ba-ba-ba*). Uses gestures.	Play social sensory games. Imitate sounds. Provide "vocal contagion." Play music. Introduce the child to books. Use gestures/signs.
9–12 months	Gestures and vocalizes to communicate. Imitates sounds in back-and-forth game. Produces variegated babbling (*ba-di-gu*). Communicates need for help. Labels objects. Babbling becomes jargon.	Use gestures/signs. Imitate the child's sounds in verbal turn-taking. Provide verbal modeling of simple words and concepts within environment. Provide spoken words for what the child is commenting on or requesting. Overexaggerate words and sounds.
12–18 months	Waves *bye* and *hi*. Labels objects. Uses exclamations. Uses "mama" and "dada" meaningfully. Imitates animal sounds. Uses 5–20 words.	Pair verbal representation of object or person with gesture. Focus on labeling both objects and pictures. Provide verbal demonstrations of words and sounds across multiple environments.
18–24 months	Tells about experiences using jargon and words. Asks "What's that?" Names objects. Imitates and produces two-word combinations. Uses 50 different single words.	Expand the child's utterances and comment on objects/people + action. Provide experiences to boost vocabulary.

(continued on next page)

Developmental age	Language production focus	Keys to intervention
18–24 months (*continued*)	Uses words more than gesture and jargon. Uses intonation for questioning. Names pictures. Uses early pronouns. Names body parts.	Offer verbal and/or visual choices when introducing new question words (e.g., "Who eats all of the cookies on Sesame Street? Cookie Monster or Elmo?"). Use books to allow the child to comment on actions in pictures.
24–36 months	Communicates previous experience with prompting from adult. Names one color. Uses two- to three-word combinations. Asks yes/no questions. Requests adult help to handle emotions. Asks *why, how, what, where* questions. Uses some plurals. Gives first and last name. Uses pronoun "I."	Expand on the child's utterances by restating what is said and then adding information. Expose the child to the same concepts across environments. Model correct syntax and grammatical structures during conversation. Ask questions around play activities to encourage further language production. Provide opportunities for the child to play with same-age peers to practice language.
36–48 months	Produces hundreds of words. Uses three- to four-word combinations. Counts to 3. Produces pronouns. States gender and age when asked. Asks *why, who* questions. Retells the sequence of a story. Uses four- to five-word sentences. Knows songs/nursery rhymes.	Model complex sentences and syntax. Ask questions that require the child to predict and sequence information. Have the child retell past events. Incorporate songs, rhyming, and print into everyday conversations.
48–60 months	Recites verses, short stories, and songs. Names colors. Answers questions about a story told. Requests word definitions. Relays experiences without adult prompting. Uses six- to eight-word sentences. Uses correct grammar. Uses past tense.	Use new vocabulary and explain and relate it to known concepts. Require the child to "read" the bedtime story by explaining what is occurring on each page of the book. Request that the child share about the day's events at mealtime.
60–72 months	Produces past and future tense verbs. Produces irregular nouns and verbs. Names the days of the week in order. Tells opposites. Knows 2,000 words. States address. Produces all sentence types.	Challenge the child with questions that require him or her to relay information from the past and future. Use open-ended questions to acquire information and promote narratives. Use time concepts when talking about past and future events (e.g., tomorrow, yesterday).

6

Facilitating Communication Development

III. Strategies for Improving Pragmatics

Goal Attainment Scale

1	2	3	4	5	6	7	8	9
Does not understand or give "readable" physical, vocal, or verbal cues to communicate needs.		Uses and responds to eye gaze to share attention on an object/activity with the caregiver. Uses eye gaze, gestures, and vocalizations to send an intentional message to others.		Takes 1 or 2 turns on a topic of conversation, and uses eye gaze, gestures, signs, and/or words to request, comment, protest, greet, and regulate the behaviors of others.		Initiates, responds, and expands on topics in a conversation by taking extended turns, asking for information or clarification, and talking about things that have happened in the past with caregiver support.		Uses and responds to verbal and nonverbal communication for a variety of purposes, in a variety of contexts.

Pragmatics refers to social intentions in communication and the behaviors people exhibit that convey different types of meaning. Pragmatics is composed of using language for different social purposes, changing communicative behaviors to be appropriate for various social situations, and following the verbal and nonverbal "rules" for conversation.

Children acquire pragmatics skills through observation and interaction with others in their environment. They learn to jointly share a "topic" of conversation with another, whether that be through looking at the same object or talking about the same event. They begin to use nonverbal and verbal means to communicate various functions, such as greeting, making requests, making comments, asking for or providing information, and so forth. Children also learn to take turns in a conversation and that rules for interaction vary across people and situations.

Pragmatics skills are important because children need to know how to *use* the language they have in socially appropriate ways. They need to know how to initiate interaction, organize information that is to be shared so that others will understand them, take turns with others in conversation so that information is exchanged, and appropriately change a topic or terminate an interaction. They need to learn to wait until someone is finished talking before they start talking. They need to be able to understand what their communication partner needs to know for the conversation to be meaningful to him or her. For example, if the child blurts out "monkeys in tree" in the middle of a conversation about something else, the listener has no way of understanding the child went to the zoo that day and saw a monkey. In other words, children need to understand how to provide background information about a topic to someone who was not present for the event being discussed. Children also need to learn how to follow the lead of another person's topic and ask questions to gain more information. In addition, they need an ability to change the subject without being rude.

Children also need to learn about the nuances of the content of language and the social meanings of words. They need to understand when someone is teasing or when words used in a certain context tell a joke. They also need to understand when not to use certain words or joke themselves. For instance, it is not a good idea to tell someone that he or she has a "big nose" (even if it is true). All of these skills require learning the fine distinctions of communication and when specific forms of language are or are not appropriate.

Children may have good comprehension skills, a large vocabulary, and adequate syntax and semantics and still not have appropriate pragmatics skills. Pragmatics skills are the social foundation of communication, and without adequate skills the child will undoubtedly struggle in social communication.

APPROPRIATE PRAGMATICS SKILLS

Culture influences many aspects of pragmatics. How a person uses eye contact, gesture, proximity to speaker, and so forth is dependent to a large extent on the expectations of a certain culture. Knowledge of cultural and familial expectations is therefore important before professionals observe and interpret children's communication behaviors and also before consultation is provided regarding intervention. Intervention strategies should not be recommended that are counter to cultural norms.

Pragmatics skills are based on the social aspects of communicative interaction. Relating to another human being is fundamental to communication. Infants and parents both automatically seek to immediately make this connection. Through the parents' responses to nonintentional communication, children learn that adults can meet their needs. They begin to discover that adults respond to their sounds, facial expressions, and movements. As this awareness grows, infants begin to experiment with intentional means of communicating their needs. Children's intentional communication expands quickly to include more than getting their needs met and regulating their parents' behaviors. They begin to comment on the world, request and offer information, and understand how to modify their social interchanges in a variety of contexts. Parents and other adults mediate and guide children's communicative efforts to meet cultural expectations.

Appropriate Pragmatics Skills in Practice

III. A. Does the child understand and use joint attention (gestures, vocalizations, or words) to communicate intent?

Daily Routines (Home and Classroom)

- *Infant/toddler:* Dad points at the dump truck in front of the house and says, "Truck." The infant crawls over to the door and pulls up to look out. The toddler waves goodbye to his grandfather.

- *Young child:* The young child puts her hands on her hips and stomps her foot. "I'm not wearing that!" she tells her mother.

Play Routines (Home and Classroom)

- *Infant/toddler:* The infant bangs two blocks together and looks up at his mother, who says, "Bang, bang!" The toddler brings the doll to his mother and hands it to her. She says, "Baby. That's a nice baby!" He says, "My baby" and leans over and kisses it.

- *Young child:* The young child marches around the classroom pretending to play a horn. She comes up to the teacher and says, "Did you see me march? How did you like my music?"

Classroom Routines

During circle time, the young child stands up and says, "I brought a shell from the beach. Does anybody want to hold it?"

III. B. What functions does the child's communication fulfill?

Daily Routines (Home and Classroom)

- *Infant/toddler:* When the parent tries to change the infant's diaper, she cries and rolls over, trying to get away. When the caregiver places a new food in front of the toddler, he makes a face, pushes it away, and says, "No."

- *Young child:* When a new food is served to the young child, he asks, "What is that? It looks like green mashed potatoes."

Play Routines (Home and Classroom)

- *Infant/toddler:* The infant cries, "Mamamama," reaching for the toy her mother holds, clearly requesting that her mother give her the toy. The toddler asks, "Where is my train?" The adult responds, "On the couch." The toddler looks and says, "No. Not that one."

- *Young child:* The young child is playing with his friend and they are building a fort. He asks, "Does your cowboy want a horse? My cowboy is gonna have a horse and a big rifle."

Classroom Routines

During the lotto game at the science center, the young child says, "I have a spider, an ant, and a beetle. I just need a fly to win."

III. C. What conversational or discourse skills does the child demonstrate?

Daily Routines (Home and Classroom)

- *Infant/toddler:* Dad leans over the crib and says, "Who's my pretty girl?" The infant smiles and coos. Mom says, "Do you want to wear the red shirt or the blue shirt?" The toddler says, "Blue one." Mom says, "I like the blue one." He replies, "I want blue pants." "Okay. White socks?" asks Mom. The toddler answers, "Blue socks."

- *Young child:* "The young child asks her father, "Why do the clothes in the dryer go round and round?" Her father says, "Well, there is heat in there, and when the clothes go around, they get dry." She asks, "Why does it take so long?" "Good question!" her father exclaims.

Play Routines (Home and Classroom)

- *Infant/toddler:* The infant and mother look at and carefully watch each other. The mother sticks out her tongue and waits. The infant slowly sticks out her tongue. Mother opens her mouth and makes an "O," and the infant imitates her. It is a nonverbal conversation. The toddler and her brother are playing with a puzzle. He says, "What's this one?" The toddler says, "Cow, moo-oo." "Where does it go?" her brother asks. "Right here," she says. "That's right!"

- *Young child:* In the dramatic play area, the young child says, "I am going shopping." "I'll go with you," says his friend. "What should we buy?" "Hamburgers and french fries," replies his friend.

Classroom Routines

The teacher stops and looks at the young children drawing. "That is an interesting picture," the teacher says to a young girl. "It's me riding on the Ferris wheel," she states. "Oh, really. When did you ride on the Ferris wheel?" asks the teacher. "On the weekend."

GENERAL PRINCIPLES FOR SUPPORTING THE DEVELOPMENT OF EFFECTIVE PRAGMATICS SKILLS

Most parents interact effortlessly with their infant with genuine affection and interest. The infant responds spontaneously and makes his or her own initiations. Parents learn, by watching their infant's behavioral reactions to their facial expressions, vocalizations, and words, how to modify their approaches so that the child comprehends their intent. As the child observes and mirrors the parent, he or she learns how to have reciprocal communicative interactions. The following are strategies that parents use naturally in their communications with their child.

Talk to the Child's Face and Connect with the Eyes

Eye contact and facial expression are one of the principal means of sharing emotions. Most parents seek eye contact with their child by turning the child's face to theirs, moving their face to be in line with the child's, or waiting for the child to look at them. They use noises, visual signals, and words to attract the child's attention.

Use Gestures in Combination with Words

As indicated previously, parents and other adults use their own facial expressions in combination with objects to gain the child's attention. They hold up and later point to familiar objects in the environment. In combination with this gesture, they label the object, person, or event that is the topic of conversation. These actions not only help the child comprehend and learn to produce language, they help the child learn how to combine actions and words to get his or her needs met and learn about the world. For example, the father may hold the pet dog for the child to pet and say, "Doggie. Ruff! Ruff! Do you want to pet the doggie?" He labels the object, associates the object with a noise, and indicates that the child needs to reach for it or vocalize to get it. When she does this and then gets to touch the doggie, she is learning that her behaviors get a desired response.

Talk About Things in Context

For infants and young children, adults talk about what is in the immediate environment. This not only helps the child learn vocabulary, but also it helps the child see how communication is different in various contexts. For example, the father who said, "doggie" in the previous example would say the word differently and hold the child back if an unfamiliar dog approached them. The child is learning that words and actions change meaning in different situations, and therefore social responses need to be different.

Use Communication for Many Purposes

Pragmatics includes communicating for a variety of purposes. Adults model the use of different forms of language for different purposes. They make statements that provide information but require no response, ask questions and expect a response, respond to questions with information or a comment, and express feelings and opinions. They also prompt the child to produce language for various purposes. For instance, in a restaurant, the parent may say, "Tell the waitress what you want" or "Do you want a grilled cheese sandwich?"

Requesting Clarification

Adults often encourage children to continue providing information by requesting clarification. They want to be able to understand the child's meaning and when this is not clear, they ask for clarification. For example, if the child reaches for something and begins to fuss, the parent may ask, "What do you want?" or "Do you want a pretzel?" Asking for further explanation gives the child an opportunity to provide more information about his or her communicative intent. This approach also provides a model for the child of how to obtain clarification.

Correcting the Child

Parents encourage pragmatics skills by prompting social communication skills. For example, when the child is shyly looking down, the parent may say, "Look at Aunt Harriet. She is talking to you." In North American culture, eye contact is desired. In other cultures, eye contact would show lack of respect. Such behaviors are monitored and corrected by adults. Adults also correct the child's communication behaviors across contexts. For example, they quiet the child during church but encourage rowdy communication at the park. They point out what other people are talking about and how to read their body language. For example, "Watch out! He's pointing his squirt gun at you!"

THE PRINCIPLES IN PRACTICE

The previous strategies typically are used without conscious thought as parents, caregivers, teachers, and other adults interact with children. Teachable moments are not structured; they occur spontaneously throughout the day. The following are examples of how adults support the development of pragmatics skills throughout the day.

Daily Routines (Home and Classroom)

Feeding/Eating

During lunch, the child spits out what is in his mouth and says, "Yuck!" His mother says, "If you don't like it, say, 'I don't like it. No, thank you.'" Here, the child's mother is correcting a pragmatically unacceptable behavior, to hopefully prevent what others might perceive as a rude comment on their cooking. She gives him a more acceptable social comment with which to express his opinion.

Diapering/Toileting

Getting children to request a bathroom break is high on every parent's and caregiver's list of desired behaviors. Children do not want to stop playing and often communicate this need nonverbally, by bouncing up and down and holding their legs together. Adults help children learn to request an action by reading their nonverbal cues and then asking them, "Do you need to go to the bathroom? You have to tell me that you need to go, so you don't wet your pants."

Dressing

Children learn that adults can help them if they ask for assistance. Dressing is an area in which adults encourage children to ask for assistance. The adult might prompt the child to say, "Can you help me, please?" Dressing also is an activity in which adults encourage children to share information about body parts, colors, and other concepts; for instance, "What is that on your shirt?"

Play Routines (Home and Classroom)

Face-to-Face Play

Face-to-face games that take turns with actions, such as So Big, lay the foundation for turn taking in language. Children learn that actions, sounds, and words will be met with a reciprocal response. Adults encourage this by initiating the games, modeling a turn, prompting the child's turn, waiting for a response, and then reinforcing the child's behavior with the initiation of another turn.

Physical Play

Intense physical play encourages children to give commands such as, "Do it again." Children love to have parents roughhouse and tickle them, and parents love to oblige them until they scream for them to stop! Such play helps children experiment with controlling others' behavior by verbal and nonverbal means. For instance, the child crawls away from Dad and looks back, and then Dad comes after him and starts to tickle him. They laugh and roll around until the child screams and pushes away. Dad says, "Do you need a break? Say, 'Stop, Daddy.'" The child says, "Stop, Daddy." Then they start laughing and it starts again. In this interaction, the father is encouraging the child to control his (the father's) behavior through both verbal and nonverbal means.

Manipulative Play

Toy play offers an opportunity to encourage conversation. Adults promote conversations in toy play by talking about what the child is doing, asking open-ended questions, and extending the discussion. For example, when the young child is playing with action figures, the adult says, "Wow! Spider-Man is climbing the wall!" The child responds, "Yeah. He's got sticky stuff on him." The adult responds, "How does the sticky stuff work?" "It's on his hands and feet and sticks to stuff. And he can make these long strings and swing on them. Do you know what the sticky stuff is made of?" the child asks. The adult says, "No. I don't. What do you think it could be?" Here, the adult is encouraging the child to use communication both to provide information and to gain information by asking a question.

Sensory Play

Messy play and art provide adults with an opportunity to comment on textures and other characteristics of materials. Adults often prompt children to comment by asking questions such as, "What are you making?" or "How does that feel?" They also model and prompt offering an opinion, such as, "Red is my favorite color. What's yours?"

Reading and Learning Routines

Circle Time

Teachers use many techniques to get children to use a variety of pragmatics skills in group. They often ask questions, seeking information such as, "Who is missing today?" They may encourage a verbal exchange between children; for example, "Justin, tell us what you did this weekend." This may be followed with encouraging the children to ask questions; for example, "Justin said his family went to the beach. That must have been fun. Who has a question to ask Justin about the beach?"

One-on-One Book Reading

Adults use one-on-one book reading as an opportunity to provoke discussion. They ask about the characters and actions in the book and prompt the child to offer opinions and information and to ask questions. They also may use books as an opportunity to instigate a conversation by relating the book to the child's own experiences. For example,

Mom: "Do you remember when we went on an airplane?"

Child: "We went to see Grampa."

Mom: "Did you like riding in an airplane?"

Child: "I like when the plane made bumps!"

Mom: (laughing) "That's the part I didn't like!"

Science and Math

Science and math activities stimulate the child to ask questions and share information with others. The teacher promotes this by providing means for the child to investigate and see missing elements and to express ideas in many ways. For example, when studying dinosaurs they looked at many pictures of dinosaurs, looked at toy dinosaurs, and watched a movie. The children then listed in writing all of their questions about dinosaurs. When they found an answer (through books, asking others, or looking at informational videos), they shared the answer verbally with the class and also dictated it to the teacher to add to their question-and-answer chart.

PLANNING INDIVIDUALIZED INTERVENTIONS FOR IMPROVING PRAGMATICS SKILLS

III. A. Does the child understand and use joint attention (gestures, vocalizations, or words) to communicate intent?

Children with a variety of disabilities may have concerns related to pragmatics skills. Children with developmental delays, language processing problems, autism spectrum disorders, or fragile X and other syndromes may have difficulty with the social aspects of communication. Joint attention is the ability to attend visually to an object or event in collaboration with another person, sharing mutual interest. Joint attention is necessary for children to attain what they want or need, but also for gaining information about the world. Learning names for people, objects, and events is enhanced by joint attention. Learning new actions and relationships also is facilitated by joint attention. Children who have a reduced use of joint attention also can have reduced comprehension of language, as a result of lack of attention to the topic that is being discussed. The following strategies are suggested to help children develop an ability to use joint attention.

Interaction Strategies

1. *Encourage the child to focus on faces.* For the child to want to look at faces, the child needs an incentive. The adult's face needs to exhibit an interesting expression, and looking at the face needs to result in an appealing result. For example, face-to-face games such as Peekaboo, kissing and blowing on the neck, and singing songs may be motivating to the child. Although structured requests such as the adult saying, "Look at me," can result in the child looking at the adult, such prompts may result in the child only looking on request and not because looking at the adult results in reinforcing events. Adults should help children develop a natural desire to look at others because doing so is pleasurable.

2. *Respond sensitively to discomfort with eye contact.* If children find that eye contact provokes anxiety (as do children with fragile X syndrome), adults should not force eye contact but rather allow the child to use fleeting glances. Use of sunglasses or a hat with a visor also can enable the child to get used to looking at someone with eyes obscured or shielded.

3. *Establish turn taking through face-to-face games.* In addition to helping children focus on faces, face-to-face games can result in an increased ability to take turns in interaction. Adults can invent games that children can repeat, thus taking a turn. For example, taking turns making funny faces, repeating interesting gestures or fingerplays, and playing sound games can encourage children to imitate adults. Imitating children's sounds, facial expressions, or gestures can lead to games of imitation.

4. *Promote joint attention on objects.* The eye gaze of the adult, or the adult's gesture, often directs the attention of the child to important objects. It is important for the child to be able to focus on faces and the gestures of others to determine where he or she should direct attention. Children with special needs often have difficulty interpreting that the gesture of another person has meaning. Help the child learn this by closely associating the object with the gesture. For example, when the child looks at something he or she wants, go to the object and point to it, so the child sees the point and the object in close proximity. Then hold it up and wait for the child to indicate a desire for the object. Ask, while pointing, "Do you want the truck?" Point to objects and use gestures to accompany all object play initiations and requests by the child. Use wait time so that the child connects the gesture with the object he or she wants.

5. *Imitate the child's use of objects to prompt turn taking.* Once the child is aware of others' actions, the adult can try to introduce imitative actions. Children with special needs often are interested when the adult replicates their actions and sounds. Imitation often causes children to repeat actions in order to see if an adult will imitate again.

6. *Encourage the child to respond to gestures, vocalizations, and verbalizations.* A combination of words and gestures can help children direct attention to the desired focus. Sign language used to illustrate an action or an object also can attract children's attention and help them focus and attain meaning. For example, the adult can sign BALL (formed like the shape of a ball with both hands), point to the ball, and say, "ball." The sign may hold more meaning for the child than the pointing gesture alone and may therefore encourage the child to look toward the ball.

7. *Use sound effects and touch.* In combination with gestures, vocalizations, and words, sound effects and touch may attract the child's attention. For example, clicking

the tongue or snapping the fingers combined with a touch or tap on the child's shoulder may attract his or her attention. Once the child is attending, the strategies described previously can be used.

8. *Teach children to point or gesture.* Children need to use, as well as understand, gestures and pointing. Even if the adult understands what the child wants, the adult needs to encourage more specific communication. When the child vocalizes and fusses because she wants something, look confused and say, "Show me." If the child does not respond with a word or gesture, hold up something you know the child is *not* requesting and say, "Do you want this?" When the child fusses again, physically assist the child to point her toward the object you think she wants. This time, give the child the desired object. The adult is trying to get the child to see that by pointing or gesturing to the desired object, she can communicate a need more effectively.

Environmental Modifications

In addition to interpersonal strategies that may support the child in understanding the use of gestures, vocalizations, and verbalizations to communicate intent, environmental modifications often are useful. Depending on the findings from TPBA2, the team may want to consider some of the following environmental modifications.

1. *Have the focus of joint attention in close proximity to the speaker.* When talking about an object, action, or person, the child will more quickly draw a relationship if the target being discussed is close to the person talking. If the toy the adult is talking about is held next to the adult's face, the likelihood of the child relating the object and the word is increased. The same goes for using a pointing gesture. If the object is too far away, the child may mistakenly focus on the adult's pointing hand rather than the target of the point. By keeping the object in proximity to the speaker, the child can learn more easily that a point means, "Look at this." As the child starts to learn the meaning of pointing, objects can be moved farther away. For example, instead of pointing from across the room and saying, "There is your truck," go to within a foot of the truck, attract the child's attention, point to the truck, and say, "There is your truck."

2. *Select objects of interest to the child.* Motivation is the key to help children with special needs learn joint attention. They are much more likely to respond to gestures and words related to their favorite things. Use the strategies described previously using the child's preferred objects or actions to teach joint attention. For example, if the child loves to roughhouse, develop a sign or movement (e.g., the sign for PLAY or a movement representing tickling) that indicates that you want to do this favorite activity. Pair this with words such as, "Let's tickle." Once the child comprehends that the use of these gestures and words communicates the intent to do his favorite activity, he may start to initiate the words and actions himself.

3. *Use toys and materials that require the adult's assistance.* Use motivating toys that produce effects that are of interest to the child. This may be a toy that has moving parts or a toy that lights up or makes music. To establish joint attention, the adult activates the toy, waits for the child to show interest, activates it again, and waits for the child to come over to explore.

4. *Use duplicate objects to imitate the child and prompt turn taking with objects.* Joint attention also can be obtained by providing duplicate toys. The adult can create silly or interesting effects with his or her toy and entice the child into watching. The adult can then use gestures and words to help the child imitate these actions and establish turn taking.

5. *Use pictures and books.* Some children like pictures in addition to, or instead of, actual objects. Books, magazines, and pictures can serve as a focus of joint attention from which to build joint attention. Sharing books, for example, by pointing to, labeling, and discussing pictures can be a nonthreatening communication. Sharing books, particularly when the child is on the adult's lap, does not require eye contact, which can be difficult for many children with special needs. However, face-to-face interaction should be encouraged during book reading whenever possible.

▨▨▨▨ III. B. What functions does the child's communication fulfill?

Communication, both verbal and nonverbal, is used for many purposes: to get needs met, to control the behavior of others, to protest, to request objects and actions, to comment on events in the world, to request information, to provide information, to engage in social interaction, to express opinions, and so forth. All of these functions can be accomplished in many ways, with sounds, gestures, and words. All are important for learning about the world and having successful social relationships.

The earliest functions of language involve getting one's needs met and regulating the behavior of others. Children first reach for things they need, such as the parent, and things they want, such as toys. They also learn quickly how to control others' behavior. They bring objects to show the parents, point out interesting things in the environment, cry and use gestures to get parents to do what they want (e.g., pull the parent's hand to take him or her to the cookies), and so forth. Protests also are seen early in development. As language develops, children begin to comment by naming or describing things in their environment (e.g., "Mommy," "baby," "book"). They use both gestures and words to request information (e.g., "What's that?") and to provide information (e.g., "That's a yellow chicken"). They also begin to use language for social purposes (e.g., "Can I help you cook, Mommy?").

Children with disabilities often use their communication for a limited number of purposes. They may primarily communicate to get their own needs met and to control others' behavior to meet their own goals. They also may use other communication functions, but at a lower level. For example, a 4-year-old without a disability may ask, "Where does thunder come from?" or "How does a baby get out of your tummy?" The child with developmental delays may not have enough understanding of these concepts to ask higher level *how* and *why* questions. Instead, these children will ask for concrete information; for example, "What is he doing?" or "Where is the doggie?"

Children with pragmatics concerns also may offer information that is irrelevant to their current context. For example, they may talk about something that is off-topic and not related to the situations, activities, or routines in which they are involved. Although all children talk about what is on their minds, whether or not adults are on the same topic, a child with pragmatics issues may seem unconcerned about the adult's topic. The adult often may not be able to determine the association that triggered the child's comment or production of unrelated information.

Children with language issues related to pragmatics also may not use language for social interaction functions in the same way as children who are typically developing. For example, children with autism spectrum disorders may primarily approach adults to get them something, not for the purpose of sharing information, asking questions, or seeking interaction. Intervention for many children with special needs should focus on 1) expanding the range of functions of communication; 2) increasing the level of knowledge expressed (see Chapter 7, Section VI. Strategies for Improving Conceptual Knowledge); and 3) broadening the form of the production, including gestures, vocalizations, verbalizations, and complex language structures (see Chapter 6, Section II. Strategies for Improving Language Production). The suggestions that follow address expanding the range of communicative functions used by children.

Interaction Strategies

1. *Determine the child's goal or need.* The adult needs to determine what he or she thinks is motivating the child. If the child's intention can be established, the adult can assist the child to communicate his or her needs. Help the child use a gesture or sign before responding (e.g., model or assist the child to make a sign for what is wanted), or model a verbalization of what the child needs. For example, if the child is crying and the teacher determines the reason is because another child is sitting in "his" chair, the teacher might say, "Tell Maura, 'mine'" (also signs MINE). If the child does not imitate the teacher, the teacher can physically prompt the sign MINE and say to Maura, "Taylor is signing 'MINE.' He is telling you that you are sitting in his chair. He wants you to find another chair." Help the child see how communication can result in a desired outcome.

2. *Model commenting on objects and actions.* Try to think from the child's perspective. Read the child's cues to determine what the child is thinking. Then model a gesture, sign, and/or word for the child to communicate. For example, if the child is smiling and repeating an action, the adult might comment, "It turns. You like turning it." Then gesture and say "turn." If the child is looking out the window with interest, the adult might point and say, "Out? Do you want to go out?"

For the child who is verbal but does not share comments spontaneously, the adult can provide a verbal model. In the previous example, when the child is looking out the window, the adult might comment, "I like to go outside on nice days like this." Such a comment may inspire the child to comment in return.

3. *Request communication instead of crying or whining.* Encourage the child to protest with positive nonverbal communication (e.g., taking the adult to what is wanted or using gestures) or with words. Let the child know that others cannot respond if they do not understand what is needed; for example, "I can help you if you tell me what you want" or "Show me what you need." If the child complies and communicates without crying or screaming, his or her efforts should be reinforced. There are several key signs and words that are helpful for children to learn. These include *mine, give, again, play, thirsty, hungry,* and so forth. Most relate to helping a child accomplish a desire or goal (see the next sections).

4. *Encourage providing information in context.* Parents and other adults often drill a child on what he or she knows, asking him or her to count or label animals, shapes, or colors and so forth. Although children often do not mind "showing off" their knowledge, children who lack pragmatics skills need to learn more functional communication patterns. They need to learn to share information spontaneously, in the context of specific situations, rather than just in response to questions or solely in response to what is on the child's mind. For this reason, adults should try to discuss information in relation to current situations. Questions need to be relevant to the situation at hand. For example, when preparing for snack in a classroom or dinner at home, it is appropriate for the child to count how many people will need to eat. When outside, talking about the color of the trees and flowers is relevant.

When the child starts to share information that is irrelevant to a situation, the adult needs to determine how important it is for the child to stay with the current topic. For example, if the child starts to quote numbers she knows from license plates, it is probably better to redirect the child to the current topic. If, however, the child brings up information on a topic of interest to her, and the situation allows, the adult can take advantage of the opportunity to let the child share the information. For example, if the child is preoccupied about bats and brings up the topic of bats, the adult can encourage sharing this information, raise questions, and even help the child access even more information.

5. *Clarify the child's intent.* Children with pragmatics concerns may be unaware that others do not understand them, or they may have problems requesting clarification if they themselves do not understand something. When adults request clarification, children are asked to repeat or reframe their intent. Request for clarification can be gestural, such as a shrug of the shoulders or a sign for WHAT. It can be a simple word, such as, "What?"; a statement, such as, "Tell me again"; or a direct question, such as, "What did you say?"

Requests for clarification can occur because the adult truly does not understand the child, or they can be "fake" in order to get the child to expand on his or her communication. For example, if the child leans forward, reaches toward the toys, and vocalizes, the adult might say, "Which toys do you want?" or "Do you want the blocks or the ball?" If the child does not respond with a word or clear gesture, the adult can shrug, look at the child as if the adult is expecting an answer, and wait longer for a response.

Another benefit of requests for clarification is that the adult is modeling ways for the child to learn how to ask for clarification when the child is unclear what has been said or meant. Children can easily be taught the sign for WHAT—a gesture with both palms up and a questioning look (as many adults naturally use with a question).

6. *Encourage social games.* Social games are important because they involve paying attention to other participants, waiting and watching, and participating by taking a turn. All of these aspects are important components of pragmatics skills. Social games can be simple exchange games such as playing ball or blowing bubbles at each other; tickling bouts; pretending to talk on the telephone; or pretend play, which may be difficult for the child to do without prompting. Whenever the child initiates social play, the adult should respond positively and immediately with both words and actions in order to reinforce the child's effort.

Environmental Modifications

In addition to interpersonal strategies that may support the child using communication to fulfill multiple functions, environmental modifications often are useful. Depending on the findings from TPBA2, the team may want to consider some of the following environmental modifications.

1. *Provide interesting and novel experiences.* All children need exposure to a wide variety of experiences. For children with special needs, however, new experiences offer innumerable opportunities for expanding pragmatics skills. Novel objects and actions can provide opportunities for asking questions, commenting, and providing information. Sharing and turn taking often are needed in new environments as well. Children also are more socially dependent and less routine-bound in novel situations, which lend themselves to greater opportunities for adult–child communication. Trips to the zoo, the library, the museum, the airport, and other sites in the community can provide motivation to communicate.

2. *Create obstacles to problem solving.* Use environmental modifications to create communication temptations to encourage the child to make a request. A communication temptation is a situation that is created to motivate the child to communicate. The key to using communication temptations is to sabotage something the child really wants to do. For instance, placing the spinning top that the child wants out of reach encourages the child to ask an adult for the object or assistance. The request may be made with vocalization, gesture, and/or words. The inability to meet the goal without help prompts him or her to request. If the challenge is too difficult, however, or the activity is not

motivating, the child may give up and turn away or become frustrated and act out, rather than communicate a request. Other examples of communication temptations include making opening lids difficult by tightening them or putting tape over the top; leaving out some of the parts needed for an activity the child really likes (e.g., a missing puzzle piece from a favorite puzzle); leaving pants or shirt unbuttoned; and activating a toy, letting it stop, and waiting for the child to request that the adult activate it again. Creating a problem the child wants solved is a good way to motivate communication.

3. *Use toys and materials that require two people.* Toys that require two or more people increase the likelihood of both social interaction and communication. A good example is a teeter-totter or seesaw, which does not work without another person. The teeter-totter also provides an opportunity to create a communication temptation. Once the child's side is in the air, the adult can wait for the child to indicate what he wants (without getting the child frustrated!). Other toys and materials that require two people include swings (unless the child can pump with the feet); wagons; and, for young children, slides.

4. *When the environment presents a challenge, take advantage.* Stairs, highchairs, cribs, high cupboards, bathtubs, toilets, sinks, and many other aspects of the environment at home, school, and in the community present challenges for children to use independently. Adults can use these challenges as opportunities to encourage communication—to request help, to comment or question, to clarify, and so forth. Particularly for children with disabilities, adults too often leap to provide assistance, reducing or eliminating the need for the child to communicate to someone about the situation. This does not mean that the child should be made to struggle through life, but it will not take long for the child to learn what is needed for his or her needs to get met. It is then up to the adult to maximize communication opportunities.

5. *Use assistive technology.* Children who lack speech or who have delayed language abilities may benefit from one of several types of assistive technology:

Sign language can help children communicate for a variety of reasons.

Picture communication boards present a visual representation of words. Children can point to words they hear or want to express. Pictures can represent school and home routines with one or many pictures, depending on the child's abilities. Pictures can be changed, depending on the situation and curriculum needs at the time. Picture communication boards allow the child to express a variety of functions:

Answer questions by labeling familiar people, desired objects, or activities

Initiate a conversation by choosing a topic

Request a person, an action, or an object

Request social interaction in play or another activity

Change the topic or terminate an activity

Express an opinion or share feelings

Protest or agree

Voice output devices produce a prerecorded message when the child pushes a button or moves a switch. Devices vary in terms of how many messages can be recorded, whether messages can be sequenced, and how long the message can be. Vocal output devices can be programmed to allow children to participate in routines of the day, such as greetings, story telling, and singing songs. Depending on the child's level of functioning and typical day, the devices can be used for the child to express the previously listed pragmatics functions.

Storyboards or song boards can help children express narrative through pictures. The storyboard is another form of communication board, with pictures sequencing the words, actions, or events in a story or song. Use of the storyboard allows children to build a narrative sequence either independently or with other children.

Adults who interact with children using these materials first model the use of the assistive technology and then help the child use the materials in functional situations whenever the child has a perceived need.

6. *Use social stories.* Social stories are written for individual children to help them develop more appropriate social interactions (see Chapter 5, Section VII. Strategies for Improving Social Interactions). They also can help children learn more appropriate pragmatics skills, which are fundamental to positive social relations. The social story uses pictures and a script to tell children how to respond either in a common or a difficult situation. Social stories can help children learn to initiate an interaction, respond to a specific comment or action, or end an interaction.

III. C. What conversational or discourse skills does the child demonstrate?

Carrying on a conversation requires that someone initiates a topic; another person responds to the initiation; they maintain the topic of discussion through several turns; and then, someone either terminates the conversation or changes the subject. During the conversation, both parties participate in keeping the conversation going by commenting, asking questions, providing information, and all of the other functions discussed previously.

Another important skill in carrying on a conversation is the ability to successfully relate a narrative or story about one's experiences. This involves being able to tell about an event and what happened during that event (e.g., riding in the car to the zoo). It also includes being able to recount a story involving a sequence of events (e.g., all the things that happened at Grandma's house). Narrative requires the ability to organize thoughts in a meaningful way, with a beginning, middle, and end. For children, this can be seen when they recount their daily experiences, when they retell a story, or when they make up a dramatic tale.

Children with disabilities often have difficulties with even basic components of conversation, such as looking at the person they are talking to. Some children can use simple, concrete sentences through two to three turns. They may then not have anything else to say unless the adult carries the balance of the conversation by continuing to ask questions. Children with weak pragmatics skills may not understand what the other person would be interested in knowing. They may have information about a topic but not be able to organize thoughts in such a way as to share them in a logical fashion. Other children want to communicate, and they produce words or sentences out of context or unrelated to the topic at hand. Even children who are intelligent and have a strong vocabulary can lack pragmatics skills necessary for them to feel comfortable and to make others feel comfortable in discourse with them. Because pragmatics is so fundamental to successful communication and social interactions, these skills need to be addressed in intervention. The following suggestions are offered to help children develop successful pragmatics skills.

Interaction Strategies

1. *Wait for the child to initiate conversation.* Children with language and social delays often wait for others to initiate conversations. As a result, they have fewer conversations. To help children initiate conversation, use communication temptations described

previously. In addition, provide motivating toys that require assistance to operate or make the child want to show the adult, which can provide incentive for initiation. Then wait for the child to comment.

2. *Maintain conversational turns on topic.* Help the child learn how to have a conversation by continuing to expand information on the topic. Provide additional information, or comment on an interesting aspect of the situation. Offering information about the adult's own experience often prompts inquiries or comments. For example, when reading a book about a monster, the adult might say, "One time I had a dream about a monster," then wait for a reply. Do not provide too much information "for free"; make the child work for it!

3. *Ask open-ended questions.* Open-ended questions can have multiple answers and may lead the child to provide more information. For example, the adult might ask, "How did you fix that?" or "Why do you think that floats?" These questions require the child to use the higher level pragmatics function of providing information.

4. *Try to avoid asking closed questions.* Closed questions typically have only one answer (e.g., "What color is it?") or require a simple one- or two-word response (e.g., "Do you want . . . ," or "What's that called?"). They tend to end a conversation rather than extend it. The closed question prompts the pragmatics function of providing information but of a lower level, with a simple "yes" or "no" or a label.

Adults often bombard children who do not initiate conversation with closed questions. In an attempt to get a response, they ask a routine question such as, "How are you today?" or a question they know the child can answer, such as, "What is that on your shirt?" This type of question can break the ice but should be used in a limited way. Closed questions should be used when necessary or appropriate. For example, when the adult asks, "Is that too hot?" a conversation is not needed.

5. *Shift the topic to a related subject.* One way to extend a conversation when a topic has been exhausted is to shift to a related topic. The association with the previous topic makes shifting the focus easier. For example, if the child has been talking about animals he or she saw at the zoo, the topic could shift to animals on the farm or in the forest. This serves a double purpose, because it not only keeps the conversation going but it helps the child develop classification skills (see Chapter 7, Section VI. Strategies for Improving Conceptual Knowledge).

6. *Act confused.* Pretending not to understand, by making a face or asking for clarification, can prompt the child to add more information. The conversation then can be expanded. For example, if the child says or signs "more," the adult can say and/or sign, "More what?" with a perplexed face. If the child responds, "More milk," the adult can add, "How much do you want?" or "Do you want a little or a lot?" depending on the child's ability level.

7. *Build narration skills through conversation.* Talk about an activity that was just completed. Have a conversation that reviews what has been done, so it sequences the events that occurred. For example, the adult might say, "Let's talk about what we did, so we can do it again tomorrow. First we. . . ." (The adult can either start the sequence or let the child try to think of what happened first.) The adult and child then take turns commenting on the sequence. It is important to keep turns going to make it a conversation rather than a monologue by the child.

8. *Talk about the day's events.* Reviewing the day requires long-term memory. A good conversational routine to develop involves thinking about aspects of the day. For example, every day the adult and child can discuss one "good thing" or my "favorite thing" that happened that day, and one "bad thing" or "something that made me sad."

If done daily, the child will learn the routine and the pattern of the conversation as each participant shares, in turn, the events of his or her day that were memorable. Such a routine also prompts generative memory (see Chapter 7, Section II. Strategies for Improving Memory).

9. *Talk about planning future events.* Talking about the sequence of what the adult or child wants to do is a good way to build narrative and also prepares the child for a discussion of events during and after they occur.

Environmental Modifications

In addition to interpersonal strategies that may support the child in using conversational or discourse skills, environmental modifications often are useful. Depending on the findings from TPBA2, the team may want to consider some of the following environmental modifications.

1. *Present motivating objects, toys, and pictures.* For a conversation to take place, the child (not just the adult) needs to have something he or she wants to talk about. For this reason, building on the child's interests is particularly important for children who do not use conversational skills. Use toys the child loves or is intrigued by, find pictures of or books about things in which the child is interested, and participate with the child in nonroutine events that generate interest. The adult can then use the strategies listed previously to prompt discussion.

2. *Use computer and video for interactional discussions.* Computer games, live-action cameras ("webcams"), videos the child likes, and so forth can be the foundation for a conversation. Too often, television and videos are used as babysitters for the child; however, watching these in isolation only further restricts the child's social communication. If used as a topic for discussion, they can serve as a useful reason for communication. For example, the adult can watch part of a video, stop it, and talk about what happened. Live-action cameras on computers are great tools because they are typically silent and the adult and child can talk about what they are seeing.

3. *Use live action situations.* One does not need a live-action camera to see interesting things. Nature offers many interesting events to talk about. Whether it is the rain that is making puddles, the birds building a nest, the ants carrying food, or cows in a field, adults can build a conversation around those aspects of an event that are of interest to the child. Such situations also offer opportunities later in the day to discuss and build a narrative around. The child and adult can draw pictures, tell others about what they saw, or make up a story to go with the event.

4. *Use books to build narrative skills.* Storybooks relate a narrative; thus, they are perfect models for demonstrating to the child how to sequence events using words. Adults can use storybooks as a basis for conversation, but also to practice sharing a narrative. The adult can ask open-ended questions such as, "What happened to the little boy?" "What do you think will happen next?" and "What should he do?"

5. *Dramatize storybooks with props and materials.* Dramatization involves acting out sequences of actions. Acting out storybooks involves sequencing actions into events. The advantage of using a storybook as the basis for dramatic play, particularly for children with special needs, is that children can build on a structured sequence of events that are triggered by the memory of the pictures and words in the story. With the help of props and materials related to the story, they have a foundation for a conversation in dramatic play that is somewhat "scripted" by the story. For example, when the wolf says to the little pig, "I'll huff and I'll puff and I'll blow your house in!" the child does not have to create a response (although it would be great if he did!). Instead, he can re-

member the line in the story or be prompted by the adult with just a word or two to say the next line. Such semiscripted play gives children an opportunity to practice having conversations with the support of the story dialogue.

6. *Use social stories.* See #6 under III. B, Environmental Modifications.

ROUTINES FOR THE CHILD WHO NEEDS SUPPORT TO IMPROVE PRAGMATICS SKILLS

The following are examples of how the above strategies can be incorporated into the child's routines at home and school. In addition to the strategies noted at the beginning of the chapter, used by caregivers of children who do not have special needs, these may support increased proficiency in pragmatics skills.

Daily Routines (Home and Classroom)

Feeding/Eating

The picture schedule can tell the child that the routine of mealtime is next, for example, with a picture of the child eating. A communication board can help the child to choose foods by having pictures that can be changed as needed. It can allow the child to make choices; for example, "Do you want a sandwich (point to picture) or macaroni and cheese?" (point to picture). If the child has a physical disability, the adult can allow the child more control by pointing to what he or she wants a bite or drink of next.

Diapering/Toileting

A voice-output device can be used in many situations. For example, a child who is non-verbal is allowed more independence and is able to request assistance if the potty chair or toilet has a tray attached with a simple voice-output device on it. The child can then look at a book, or play with toys on the tray, and when finished going to the bathroom, he or she can hit the switch. The machine can be programmed to call out when the switch is activated, such as, "Mommy, I need you" or "I'm finished!" A general message such as these can be used in many situations and allows the child to make a request.

Dressing

One strategy for dressing is to encourage the child to request clothing and comment. The adult lays the child's clothes out in a line—first the underwear, then the pants, then the shirt, then socks, and finally shoes. The child is at the start of the line, by the underwear. The adult asks the child what she wants to put on first. The child may name, sign, point, or just lean forward and pick up the item. The adult then acknowledges the child's communication by saying, for example, "Okay. You want your underpants! I'll help you put them on." During this process, the adult can request or model a label for the item, body parts, or the actions the child is doing. Once the underwear is on, the next item is now further away and the child is asked what she needs next. Because the next items are out of reach, the child is required to use more effort to request what she needs. The adult can wait, model, or gesture or sign the request for what she needs. If this process is followed repeatedly, the child will learn the sequence as well as the means for requesting what she wants.

Going Out

Any trip out into the community provides an opportunity for conversation. Planning what to take, talking about what is seen and heard, and giving opinions about what is liked and disliked are all potential topics. In addition, the trip home provides a chance to review or build a narrative about what happened. For children with pragmatics difficulties, adults need to watch and listen for children's nonverbal and verbal responses to build the conversation. For example, most children in a store will reach for items they like. This is a nonverbal comment that adults can respond to; for example, "That is a pretty dress. I like red too." Let the child touch the item, if possible. Watch the response and what the child touches. Whenever the child looks at the speaker, the speaker should respond; for example, "Those are pretty buttons, aren't they?" As the child is allowed to explore, vocalizations are likely to increase.

Play Routines (Home and Classroom)

Face-to-Face Play

This is a good type of play for children who lack pragmatics skills, because the adult and child are facing each other and can learn to read and respond to each other's cues in a nonverbal or verbal conversation as part of play. Any turn-taking game that the child likes, even blowing spit bubbles, can be an opportunity for turn-taking interactions. Games can start at the child's level with regard to vocal ability, and the adult can add different or increasingly more complex actions, gestures, or words. Wait time will encourage the child to initiate and maintain the conversation. Up the "ante" by waiting for a higher level response. For example, if the child bounces up and down to get the adult to bounce her on the adult's knee, after a few successful turns, the adult can model "b-b-bounce, b-b-bounce" and wait for a sound before bouncing again.

Physical Play

In physical play, the same strategies apply as discussed in face-to-face play, but the cues may be tactile (in the case of roughhousing) or movement (in the case of chase or ball games). Eliciting a protest is easily accomplished in physical play, and the adult can try to give the child a sign or word to substitute for screaming or whining. The adult also can model comments such as, "I'm hot" while wiping his brow, or "I'm happy," with a sign or word.

Manipulative Play

Parallel play with manipulatives engenders imitation, which is a form of turn taking. Adding language makes it a conversation. Build on the child's actions and words. For example, if the child is stacking blocks and knocking them down, the adult can build a tower next to hers at the same rate as the child, so she is taking a turn and the adult is taking a turn. The adult can comment as he adds a block, "Block for Daddy," and comment as the child adds a block, "Block for Maddy." After several blocks, the child may begin to wait for her father to take a turn. This is now a "conversation," as she is acknowledging her father's part in the interaction. With this simple turn taking, the adult should not demand language. Modeling simple words like "block," names, or "you" and "me" is sufficient. What is important in this type of simple turn taking is getting joint attention on an activity and having the child acknowledge the role of another person.

Sensory Play

Varying types of sensory play can be fun, tolerable, or intolerable to different children. This presents the opportunity to request, protest, comment, offer opinions, provide information, and have discussions through conversation. Sensory play, as with physical play, can engender high levels of emotion. Adults should not avoid sensory activities the child does not like, for several reasons. First, because they heighten emotions, sensory play may encourage vocalizations, words, and expression of feelings. Second, the child may gradually become more tolerant of different types of sensory input. Third, sensory experiences provide an occasion to add descriptive information to help enhance the child's vocabulary comprehension and/or production.

Dramatic Play

Children with pragmatics concerns may struggle with dramatic play because they tend to engage in isolated or parallel play instead of sociodramatic play. Adults should first develop simple dramatic play sequences based on routines, using the same language interactions that they use in real life. Once the child is able to dramatize simple routines in interaction with the adult, the adult can become the facilitator to help the child interact in sociodramatic play. This may include

1. Suggesting a social statement (e.g., "You could tell Sara you want to drive to the store, too")

2. Modeling a sign (e.g., signing PLAY to another child to ask to play with him or her)

3. Modeling words that serve different pragmatics functions (e.g., a polite protest, request for a turn, a comment on what is happening)

4. Coaching other children to initiate or respond to something the child is doing. Children often will imitate what they hear other children say; help other children include the child with special needs. Having children who are verbal, outgoing, and sensitive to others is preferred over adult facilitation; as soon as possible, adult facilitation should be phased out.

Reading and Learning Routines

Circle Time

Teachers also should use the dialogic techniques described previously (and see Chapter 8, Strategies for Supporting Emerging Literacy) to encourage children to comment, provide information, ask questions, and so forth.

One-on-One Book Reading

With a child who does not speak much, it is tempting for the adult to just take over and read the book. The child enjoys it and it takes less of the adult's time. However, straight reading does not take advantage of a prime interactive time for the child and adult. The adult needs to use books as an opportunity to have a conversation. Books are a great model for pragmatics skills, and, once verbal children learn the book, adults can omit the words they want to emphasize for the child, wait, and then if the child does not offer the word, the adult can give a clue or gesture to help the child. Dialogic strategies can be used (see Chapter 8, Strategies for Supporting Emerging Literacy):

1. Ask *what* questions (do not use yes/no questions) about what the child sees (e.g., "What's this?").

2. Repeat what the child says or correct it (e.g., "Yes, it is a duck!" or "It looks like a duck, but it's called a 'goose'"). This reinforces the child's response.

3. Follow up with a question to expand the topic (e.g., "What is the goose doing?").

4. Respond to the child's gesture, vocalization, or comment (e.g., the child signs EAT and the adult says, "Yes, he is eating").

5. Expand what the child says, providing information and a model for language (e.g., "He is eating corn. Do you like corn?").

6. Use open-ended questions (e.g., "What else do you see?").

For lower functioning children, use interactive books with buttons and sounds to encourage turn taking and commenting. For children with motor problems, use books with pages that are easy to turn, such as board books, or adapt the book with "page fluffers" (i.e., a piece of sponge glued to the corner of each page to make it easier to get the fingers in between the pages to turn them) or one-half of a popsicle stick glued to the board book page to use as a handle to turn the page. These adaptations are important because the child's participation and involvement is key to turn taking and will encourage attention.

One-on-one reading also can involve peers. Have a time for "book buddies," in which each child shows a favorite book to a peer. This encourages initiation of conversation, and with prompting, children can learn to share books with each other by pointing, gesturing, signing, and using words and sentences.

Science and Math

Science and math activities provide opportunities for children to ask questions and share information they discover. At lower levels, science and math involve comparing, labeling, and developing categories for things. Caregivers and children can take turns finding things that are alike; for instance, finding all the cows. They can then talk about the cows—which ones are big, little, mamas, babies, brown, black, and so forth. The children can pretend to have the cows eat, talk to each other, and so forth.

With children at higher levels, teachers can prompt interaction and turn taking with games and activities such as lotto, construction of block structures, and other discovery activities. For some children, social stories may help give them the words and actions to use when playing with other children.

JAYMZ

Jaymz is a 5-year-old African American child who is in a foster home. His history is one of neglect and abuse. He has been in his current foster home for 6 months and has formed a close attachment with his foster mother and father and their biological 6-year-old son. The family is looking into adopting Jaymz, although they are concerned about his slow development and delayed language. They reported that he seeks them out when he needs or wants something but that he mostly plays by himself or next to, rather than with, his brother. They indicated that he is able to label many things in his environment, and he uses two-word combinations most of the time. Jaymz often appears to ignore others when they speak to him. The family has had his hearing checked and it is normal. They indicated that he has many more words than he did when they initially met him, and his teachers indicated that his skills have increased in school during the time that he has been in foster care.

Jaymz was assessed with TPBA2 to determine what strategies the family and teachers could use to help him develop language and better social interaction skills with his brother and his peers in school. During the assessment, Jaymz demonstrated a short attention span, flitting from one toy to the next. He seldom looked at either his family members or the play facilitator, although he would respond with a single-word answer when they asked him a simple question. Jaymz enjoyed cars and trucks and spent the longest time racing them around a track on the carpet. He used simple comments such as "truck go" and "broke" when the car stopped.

The assessment revealed that Jaymz was delayed in cognitive, language, and social skills, but that his progress in recent months was a good sign that the environment was having a positive impact on his development. The team determined that although Jaymz had increased his ability to get his needs met through communicating to others, one area he needed to improve, as a foundation for further progress in all developmental areas, was his pragmatics skills. They felt that improving the social aspects of his communication would enable him to have more positive interactions with others and thereby enable him to learn more concepts in his interactions at school and at home. He needed to increase his ability to reference others' eyes and faces to see what they were talking about, to share attention on objects and activities, and to expand the purposes for which he used language. The team talked about Jaymz's history and indicated that he had learned that paying attention to others did not pay off and that he had to fend for himself and stay out of harm's way. Because previously he had not had people showing him they cared about him and how others can help get one's needs met, Jaymz had learned not to look to others for love, information, or assistance. He needed to build the understanding that relating to and communicating with people was worth the effort. The following are possible suggestions for Jaymz's family and teachers:

Interaction Strategies

1. Go back to basics in building a relationship. Play fun games with Jaymz that require that he look at you for you to do something he likes. He likes to roughhouse with his father, so this is a good place to start. Do something Jaymz likes, then stop and wait for him to look at you before you do it again. His brother can be taught to do this too.

2. Learn to read Jaymz's nonverbal cues and give him words for what you think he is thinking or feeling when he moves away (e.g., "Oh, so you are finished?), comes close (e.g., "What do you need, Jaymz?"), glances at you out of the corner of his eye (e.g., "I'm right here watching you, Jaymz"), and so forth. Let him know that you care about what he is thinking and feeling. You also may be able to tell what he wants and needs by his nonverbal cues. Then, give him the words you think he might need; for example, "I see you standing by the refrigerator. Do you want juice or a snack?" This will help him learn with words and at the same time understand that someone is there to meet his needs.

3. Do lots of nurturing activities that involve taking turns. Jaymz is beginning to come to you and play near you. This is a sign that he is beginning to trust you. Build on that by playing games that he likes. Do not force your presence on him, just play next to him and mirror what he does. Comment on what he is doing and what you are doing. Read books together about families (people or animals) and friends, and label the characters and what they are doing. Ask Jaymz questions and help him participate in turning the pages, commenting, and so forth. Because his attention span is short, don't expect to finish a book. Just talk about the pictures and try to extend the time to look at the books and talk to each other. The important thing is spending time with him close to you, sharing something together.

4. When you want Jaymz to talk to you, get on his level. Squat down and get in front of him. Talk softly and smile. You want him to begin to look at you when you talk to him, but you need to start up close and work up to him looking at you from across the room. Once you have his attention, hold up what you want to talk to him about and point to it. We want him to start looking at things you point to after he starts looking at you. Once you get him to consistently look at you and the object you want him to see, you can stand up and do the same thing.

5. *Model key words and phrases relating to getting Jaymz's needs met, such as, "I need . . . ," "I want . . . ," "Can I . . . ," and "Will you. . . ." If he uses one of these phrases spontaneously or after you model it, try to give him what he needs as soon as possible. This will help him learn that adults do listen and respond positively.*

Environmental Modifications

1. *Jaymz has lived a life without many motivating experiences. Try to find ways to introduce him to fun activities and experiences. Include him in picking out food at the grocery store, go on a camping or fishing trip, or even go to a farm to see cows and pigs. All of these events are new to him and will give you things to talk about and label.*

2. *Create problems that will require your assistance. Jaymz is beginning to learn that you will support and help him. He can learn to communicate his needs faster when there are problems he needs you to solve. For instance, take batteries out of his favorite toy so he will come for help to get it to work. Hide one shoe so he needs to get you to find the other one with him. In other words, think about each daily activity and come up with ways that Jaymz will want to involve you. This will increase his communication to meet his needs. The next step is to talk about and model language once you have found what is missing or have solved the problem.*

3. *Dramatic play is important for Jaymz because it will allow him to act out how he feels and experiment with using language. He is currently struggling with conflicts among fears, anxieties, and desires and has difficulty with self-expression; therefore, he could benefit from professional help from a team that can jointly address social and emotional development, communication, and cognitive skills at Jaymz's level.*

KEYS TO INTERVENTION BY DEVELOPMENTAL AGE

The following ideas are directed toward children who are functioning at approximately the following levels. The suggestions are not meant to be all-inclusive, but rather are indicative of potential areas for exploration.

Developmental age	Pragmatics skills	Keys to intervention
Birth to 3 months	Smiles in response to high-pitched voice (0–1 month).	Immediately respond to the child's gaze with a smile and vocalization.
	Gazes on caregiver's face.	Respond to fussing and crying by trying to meet needs.
	Cries, undifferentiated.	
	Produce other sounds: burps, hiccups, sneezes, coughs.	Imitate sounds the infant makes.
		Play face-to-face games with mouth, lips, and tongue.
	Smiles back to familiar face (1–2 months).	
	Makes eye contact.	
	Enjoys responding to people and eye-to-eye contact (2–3 months).	
	Produces true social smile.	
3–6 months	Vocalizes to initiate socializing (3–4 months).	Respond immediately to vocal initiations.
	Responds differently to different people.	Point to and name familiar objects and people when they are in close proximity to the child.
	Laughs when socializing.	
	Shows anger or protest when frustrated (4–5 months).	Respond to anger with label of feeling expressed. Help the child resolve issues.
	Responds to social overture with an emotional response.	Play Peekaboo and other social games.
	Preference for familiar faces, smiles.	When the child rejects something, shake your head and finger and say, "no."
	Responds differently to stranger (may withdraw or frown).	Teach the child to recognize the signs and words for "want" (e.g., opening and closing hand, palm up).

Developmental age	Pragmatics skills	Keys to intervention
3–6 months (*continued*)	Enjoys social play and responds with an emotional response. Resists actions or objects he or she does not want (5–6 months). Objects to someone taking a toy away. Responds to meaning of specific emotional expressions in others.	Use exaggerated expressions to encourage looking at the face and recognizing facial expressions.
6–9 months	Plays games such as Peekaboo (6–7 months). Follows what someone points to (7–8 months). Points to objects to show others. Initiates intentional interactions (e.g., reaches for nose, hair, mouth) (8–9 months).	Increase face-to-face play, increasing the number of turns. Wait for the child to initiate after a few turns. Point to and name things that are not right near the child. Respond to initiations with sounds, actions, and words.
9–12 months	Vocalizes to request objects, people, and activities. Demonstrates fear of strangers (7–12 months). Enjoys turn-taking games. Vocalizes in response to others. Opens and closes three sequential circles of communication. Beginning social referencing (e.g., looking to adult for emotional information about situations). Vocalizes to request objects, people, and activities.	Imitate the child's vocalization and then label the desired object, person, or activity. Name new people; comment on child's emotional response. Increase turn-taking games to include play with objects, such as pushing buttons, pulling toys, stacking rings, and so forth. Add sounds and language to each turn. Notice how many turns the child is able to do before losing interest, and try to add one more by making it very interesting. Help child know that you are a source of comfort when he or she is stressed. Give clear facial cues about emotions, to help the child read your cues and encourage the child to continue to reference you. Wait for a vocal request in addition to a gesture.
12–18 months	Monitors adults' emotions to see how he or she should respond (by 14 months; social referencing, 12–14 months). Shares joint attention on an object with another (8–14 months). Likes to be around other children (8–14 months). Imitates actions of others (8–14 months). Shakes head "no." Consistently uses a far point to request actions and information. Uses rising intonation to request information. Makes verbal protests (10–18 months). Uses single words to request actions. Follows visual gaze of another outside of immediate visual field. Responds to a yes/no question. Shows ability to control own emotions/behaviors (by 18 months). Shows awareness of caregiver's wishes and expectations. Shows frustration. Uses protest words (e.g., "no," "don't"). Sets limits on other's behaviors (e.g., "stop"). A point accompanied by a representational word is used more than any other gesture. Responds to simple requests for clarification (e.g., "Huh?" "What?") (16–18 months).	Play together with toys, expanding the play and language simultaneously. Incorporate daily routines into dramatic play with dolls. Read books, using dialogic strategies. Build pragmatic functions with toys; for example, model requesting actions or objects, requesting information, providing information, protesting with words, and so forth. Facilitate peer play by offering words to accompany each child's actions. Point to and talk about objects, events and people that are distant and request a response. Model questioning using *what, where, who* (use gestures to support words). Eliminate the point and just use a gaze for objects that are in close proximity to encourage the child to watch facial cues to obtain joint attention. Encourage acquisition of emotion words to replace behaviors demonstrating frustration. Make simple requests for the child to follow, and encourage the child to use words and gestures to make a request, show frustration, or protest. Model the words needed and respond when the child uses an approximation. Respond to the child's verbal attempts to control your behavior with requests for more information or comments to encourage extending the conversation (e.g., "More juice"; "You are really thirsty!"). Request clarification to encourage providing more information (e.g., "Tell me more").

(continued on next page)

(continued from previous page)

Developmental age	Pragmatics skills	Keys to intervention
18–24 months	Begins to request clarification (e.g., "Huh?") 33% of time. Initiates topic with one word with shared attention. Uses gesture to clarify a word (e.g., representational gesture/cup to hand). Begins to narrate past events with adult help. Responds differently to a request for clarification by an unfamiliar adult. Takes 1–2 turns in conversation. Initiates a topic and responds with new information.	When child says, "Huh?" repeat the statement and also say it in a different way. This models clarification. Respond to the child's gestures and also give the child more information. When child labels an object, person, or event in view, use this as an opportunity to expand on the child's word and start a conversation with several turns.
24–36 months	Cooperates in games. Knows rules, standards, cultural values of family (24–30 months). Answers one-third of questions asked by adults. Internalizes rules and follows part of the time. Has some generalization of rules across time and settings. Regularly requests clarification (e.g., "Huh?" "What?").	Give verbal and gestural support for cultural norms and tell children why they are important. Get down on the child's level and obtain eye contact or face gaze before asking a question. Have a few rules that are talked about frequently. Children often ask for clarification, even if they heard and understood what was said. Clarify with a different statement than the initial one, and then ask, "What did I mean?" Discuss activities that were just completed. Read familiar books and talk with the child about what the book is about before and after it is read. This will help build conversational and narrative skills.
36–48 months	Discriminates appropriate roles and behaviors. Responds to request for clarification about 85% of the time (24–48 months). Combines two events in a narrative. Gestures and speech are paired similar to an adult level. Takes four turns in a true conversation.	Encourage the child to use different verbal behaviors in different contexts, and explain why (e.g., loud voice outside, quiet voice inside). When reading books, discuss why and how characters did things. Review daily activities and ask a range of questions to expand language functions. Create stories to act out in dramatic play, with characters talking in conversations.
48–60 months	Knows what behavior is needed to make friends. Begins to understand humor (enjoys jokes even when not understood). Begins perspective shift/understanding others' points of view. Sequences multievent story without a moral or meaningful outcome.	Encourage the child to initiate interaction with peers. Prompt with actual words if needed. Take turns making up and telling jokes, playing silly games, and rough housing. Understanding what makes others laugh is a pragmatic skill. Engage in dramatic play involving various characters and prompt acting like the character would act. Talk about why characters in books behave the way they do. Read and discuss longer stories with more complex plots and conflicts. Talk about "what would happen if . . ." to encourage the child to think of alternative narrative actions and outcomes. Provide opportunities for sociodramatic play with many children at one time. Provide simple board games with turns for 2–3 children.
60–72 months	Participates in group activities. Asks questions and exchanges information with others. Tells well-informed story with a climax.	Provide group games with turns for up to 4 children and structured play with turns for the class of children. Provide opportunities for discovery of novel situations with a peer. Encourage making up stories and telling them to other children. Act out complex narratives from story books.

6

Facilitating Communication Development

IV. Strategies for Improving Articulation and Phonology

Goal Attainment Scale

1	2	3	4	5	6	7	8	9
Coos, squeals, laughs, and engages in vocal play.		Produces strings of vowel and consonant sounds that are non-meaningful.		Produces word approximations, words, or phrases that may not be completely intelligible.		Speech often is intelligible to familiar and unfamiliar listeners in conversation and in a variety of activities.		Accurately and intelligibly produces the sounds of his or her language in conversation and in a variety of activities.

One of the most common concerns raised by parents regarding their child's early communication development is when their child's speech is not easily understood. When a child does not develop the ability to produce sounds appropriate to his or her age, the child may have a developmental articulation disorder or phonological disorder. The early identification of such a disorder may have future implications for school success, specifically in the areas of reading and spelling. In addition, children who are not easily understood by peers are at risk for developing negative behaviors as well as potentially being ridiculed and avoided by peers, thus decreasing the opportunities for appropriate social interactions with peers.

Most children develop speech sounds in the same, predictable sequence. Consonants produced anteriorly (e.g., *m, n, p, b, t, d*) typically are acquired first. Subsequently, sounds such as *l, r, s,* and *th* that require more complex coordination of the articulators (e.g., jaw, lip, tongue) tend to develop later as the child's system matures. Although children begin producing speech sounds in their first few months, it is over the next 7 years that they learn to produce all the speech sounds. This is due to the development required in the child's oral mechanism and the acquisition of refined and coordinated movement of the articulators (e.g., tongue, lips, palate, jaw). A child's ability to produce speech is dependent on his or her individual biological predisposition, physical structure, and neuromotor maturation, which is conditioned by experience and use. Any disturbance in any of these components may pose an obstacle for further speech development. A child's communication development also is affected by the simultaneous interactions of the cognitive, emotional, and physical areas of development. Consequently, a detailed background history can be crucial to making a diagnosis of a phonological disorder. Background history can include consideration of hearing acuity and the child's overall cognitive and language level. Additional information regarding motor presentation is essential to assess respiratory control which, in turn, affects phonatory control. Obtaining a broader picture of the child's overall presentation may clarify whether the child's articulation development is commensurate with the child's cognitive level.

As children develop the ability to produce speech sounds, some common mistakes can be observed. Specifically, omission of final sounds of single words can be seen as well as distortion of sounds or sound substitution; typically, the substitution of an earlier, easier-to-produce sound for a sound that is not in the child's present repertoire. Other patterns of sound acquisition involve the sequence of the production of sounds in various positions of words. Typically, consonants produced in the initial position of words are the easiest (e.g., *ba/ball*), followed by consonants in the final position of words (e.g., *up*). Consonants that appear in the middle of words are the most difficult (e.g., *mitten*). Furthermore, consonants that occur in a "blend" (i.e., 2–3 consonants combined) are particularly more difficult to pronounce (e.g., *star, school, play, broom, flag*).

APPROPRIATE ARTICULATION AND PHONOLOGY

Phonology is defined as the rules governing the sound system of a language. As children are learning to produce language and produce approximately 25 words, they are learning how the different sounds in their language are combined. This is the *phonological system*. As children are producing words, they simplify the adult language model into easier sounds and patterns also known as phonological processes.

Consistently mispronounced sounds are a concern as the child gets older. However, if she pronounces a sound correctly some of the time, she may be moving toward standard pronunciation on her own. Most children develop standard speech by the age of 6, although some children still have problems pronouncing the more difficult sounds at age 7—the age at which all speech sounds should be able to be produced. Errors with consonants are the most typical type of misarticulation. As with consonants, there is a developmental pattern in which vowel sounds are produced. Among English speakers, differences in vowel production usually are considered dialectic differences rather than misarticulations. However, there may be times when a child's production of vowel sounds may be distorted due to structural or functional problems of the oral mechanism. It is possible, therefore, to have a nasal or "gravelly" voice quality that is magnified during vowel production. For example, a hearing loss or cleft lip and palate may affect a child's ability to produce speech sounds. Also, a child who has difficulty with fluid movement and purposeful movement of the articulators also may exhibit difficulty with both vowel and consonant productions. Children with these conditions should be referred to a speech-language pathologist.

When observing a child's speech production skills, it is important to note the following:

- The sounds the child produces

- The sounds the child has difficulty producing (e.g., sounds made with the lips, teeth, tongue)

- The position of those sounds in a word (i.e., initial, medial, or final)
- The frequency/consistency of misarticulation

These observations can help determine the level of a child's articulation skills and whether he or she is delayed in this area.

A loosely drawn developmental scale for standard American speech production would look something like the following:

By age 3: vowels, p, b, m, n, d, g, h

By age 4: k, t, th, f, v, ng, j, ch

By age 5: sh, zh

By age 7: l, r, s, th

Appropriate Articulation and Phonology in Practice

IV. A. What speech sounds does the child produce (e.g., vowel and consonant repertoire)?

Daily Routines (Home and Classroom)

- *Infant/toddler:* The infant watches her mother's face during diapering and says "oo" and "ah." Out in the car, the toddler points to his stuffed animal that has fallen on the floor and shouts, "Doggie!"
- *Young child:* During snack time, the young child clearly announces, "I want another cracker, please."

Play Routines (Home and Classroom)

- *Infant/toddler:* The infant is blowing raspberries in a game with her sister. The toddler sings along to "Old MacDonald" "EE-I-EE-I."
- *Young child:* The child is playing with blocks and counting, "One, two, fwee, four, five, six, seben."

Classroom Routines

At the literacy center, the children are making a calendar. The children struggle to say "January" and "February," calling them "Janawy" and "Febwawy."

IV. B. What are the articulation abilities of the child?

Daily Routines (Home and Classroom)

- *Infant/toddler:* The child begins to string together vowels and consonants in babble during bath time. In the grocery store, the toddler points to the fruit and says, "Daddy, peeech."
- *Young child:* At bedtime, the child is able to recite the words to the book *Brown Bear, Brown Bear, What Do You See?* with only a few mispronunciations.

Play Routines (Home and Classroom)

- *Infant/toddler:* The infant picks up the baby doll, kisses it, and says, "Ba-ba." The toddler picks up the ball and says, "To ba (throw ball)."

- *Young child:* The child is able to imitate songs and fingerplays, but often misarticulates unfamiliar words. For example, "John Jacob Jingleheimer Smith" becomes "John Jako Jingle Hammer Smit."

Classroom Routines

At the science center, the child is able to pronounce most familiar words accurately but struggles with new multisyllabic words such as "hippopotamus," pronouncing it "hipotumes."

■■■■■ **IV. C. How intelligibile is the child's speech?**

Daily Routines (Home and Classroom)

- *Infant/toddler:* The infant reaches toward the bottle and says "ba." The toddler looks at the puddle forming at her feet and says, "Poddie, mommy, poddie!"

- *Young child:* During dinner, the young child tells a long story about a fight at school. His mother understands 90% of what he says without asking for clarification.

Play Routines (Home and Classroom)

- *Infant/toddler:* The infant's meaning is understood through the context of her play and is unintelligible in isolation. The toddler usually is intelligible out of context for simple labels and actions for her toys, such as "baby eat" or "car go."

- *Young child:* The young child carries on conversations that are understood by almost everyone, even out of context.

Classroom Routines

During sharing time, the child clearly announces, "I am going to fly to my Grandma's house in Arizona."

GENERAL PRINCIPLES FOR SUPPORTING EFFECTIVE ARTICULATION AND PHONOLOGY

Adults use a variety of strategies to promote articulation and phonology skills. The following are strategies often used by adults to help children support the movements for speech production. These strategies also are useful for children who have difficulty with accomplishing these skills.

Modeling

Parents like to talk to their young children and make sounds such as raspberries or sing familiar songs. Often the parent will make a sound, the child imitates it, and the parent repeats it. The back-and-forth sound game is the way the child explores making different sounds and imitating others. It begins with early sounds and later to words and then phrases.

Exaggeration and Emphasis

When children are learning how to produce new sounds and words, parents slow down their speech and exaggerate movements for their child to see. For example, for the child who deletes one consonant from a consonant blend, the parent models the missing sound for the child. For example, the little girl says, "Look, a nake," and the daddy says, "Yes, it's a ssssssnake." Parents also emphasize sounds that the child says incorrectly. For example, for the child who says "I want the boot," the parent says, "Here is the boo**k**," placing more emphasis on the "k" sound.

Using Visual Prompts

Some children may benefit from the use of gestural prompts to facilitate a child's ability to imitate sounds. For instance, the mother may press her lips together and exaggerate making the "m" sound in "mmmilk."

Practicing

Adults help children practice making sounds and words when reading repetitive books and singing songs. The rhythm and the repetitive nature of many books allow the child to practice the sound or word many times together.

THE PRINCIPLES IN PRACTICE

Adults use a variety of strategies to support children's articulation and phonological development. The following section provides examples of how caregivers use strategies described previously during the day at both home and school. These examples are approaches that most caregivers use naturally in their daily interactions with children. They are appropriate for most children with disabilities as well.

Daily Routines (Home and Classroom)

Feeding/Eating

During mealtime, Mother emphasizes the "m" sound by saying, "MMM, that's good. I like it!"

Diapering/Toileting

When pulling off his dirty pants, the toddler says, "Tinky, Mommy." She replies, "Yes. It is SSStinky!"

Dressing

Dad is pulling a t-shirt over his son's head. He says, "You are wearing a striped shirt. Can you say that? 'Striped shirt.'" His son says, "Stwipe sirt." "Close enough!" replies his father.

Play Routines (Home and Classroom)

Face-to-Face Play

Mom holds her son on her lap and bounces him to the rhythm as he sings the alphabet song. His mother slows him down and they sing "L-M-N-O-P" with pauses between letters.

Physical Play

During recess time, the kids take turns being the leader in Simon Says. The child says, "Simon says, 'Take seven tiny steps.'"

Manipulative Play

The child says, "Look, Mommy, my baby is cwalling." Mother gets down by the child and says, "She is c-r-awling." She talks slowly and exaggerates her mouth movements for the child to see.

Sensory Play

While fingerpainting, the teacher says, "Let's make funny noises while we paint. I'll make one first and you can imitate me. ZZZZIPPY! You try it. Now you make a funny noise, and I'll say it."

Reading and Learning Routines

Circle Time

The class is reading a rhyming book. Afterward, they all try to think of words that rhyme with *cat*.

One-on-One Book Reading

The child is "reading" to her teacher. She says, "Owivia wikes the cowuh wed." Her teacher says, "Yes. Rrred is her favorite colorrr. Try to make this sound: RRRRRed."

Science and Math

When the child is counting sticks, he says "sebun" instead of seven. His teacher point to his lower lip and says, "Put your teeth on your lower lip here and say, 'VVV.' Great! Now say, 'Se-vven.'"

PLANNING INDIVIDUALIZED INTERVENTIONS FOR IMPROVING ARTICULATION AND PHONOLOGY

IV. A. What speech sounds does the child produce (e.g., vowel and consonant repertoire)?

It is important to make sure the child's hearing has been checked. If hearing is intact, depending on the age of the child, the simplification of speech or substitution of one sound for another may simply be developmental in nature. As children begin to produce more complex and longer words and phrases, their speech may be naturally more difficult to understand. An important consideration then is how intelligible they are to familiar versus unfamiliar listeners and when the context of the subject is known versus unknown. Speech errors often are characterized as being one of the following:

- Omissions—when the child omits sound(s) from a word; these have the most adverse impact on intelligibility.

- Substitutions—when the child substitutes one sound for another in a word

- Additions—when the child adds a sound(s) in a word

- Distortions—when the child substitutes a distorted sound for a standard sound

For children who are producing phonological processes, it is best to consult with the speech-language pathologist to gain information as to how best to facilitate the child's speech. If articulation errors are determined through an assessment to be outside of the range of typical development, then suggestions may be made for speech therapy and additional activities at home with the parents. In addition to the previously described strategies used by parents of typically developing children, the following are interaction strategies and environmental modifications that may be used with the support of a professional.

Interaction Strategies

1. *Practice targeted sound.* Many articulation errors are due to forming an improper habit related to tongue or mouth placement. Practice is important for changing these habits, but drills can turn the child off. Make a turn-taking game of making the sound. This can be a silly game of imitation or a higher level game of Simon Says: "I'm going to say 'ss' with my eyes closed. Now, I'm going to say 'ss' with my hands on my head." Repeat the sound at least through 10 turns of the game and play the game a couple of times a day, during bath time, playtime, bedtime, and so forth. Once the sound is produced well, change the game to add the sound to the beginning, middle, or end of a syllable (practice only one at a time); then move to practicing words with the sound; and then sentences. These should be fun games, not drills.

2. *Play active games that incorporate the sounds being addressed.* Repeat actions with words; for example, "Bounce, bounce, bounce"; "run, run, run"; "throw, throw, throw." Make sure the child is saying the sound correctly before starting the game or he or she will be practicing the wrong sound. For some children, only have them say the word one time since they may have difficulty producing the word correctly in a repetitive pattern.

3. *Sing a favorite tune, substituting a sound for the words.* For example, substitute the *p* or *t* sound for the words to "Row, Row, Row Your Boat." This can be fun and very funny. Do it in the car while driving and take turns picking a sound. Another song to try is "I Like to Eat Apples and Bananas"; change the vowel sound throughout the song.

4. *Play Hide-and-Seek with pictures or objects that have the sound the child needs to practice.* The adult hides his or her eyes and cannot look until the child announces he has found the hidden object or picture. The adult gives clues to help the child find it. The child then announces what he found. Hiding many different pictures or objects containing a targeted sound gives the child a fun way to practice the sound.

5. *Model the targeted sound.* When talking about an object that contains the targeted sound, the adult should hold the object close to his or her mouth so the child will focus on how the sounds are made for the object, as well as the object itself.

6. *Play I-Spy-with-My-Little-Eye, and give the child clues to what is seen.* The first clue can be the first or last sound of the word (the sound that needs to be improved); for example, "I spy with my little eye something that starts with the sound 'ka.'"

7. *Identify functional words to focus on during daily routines.* For example, during bath time, identify those words with the target sounds that you can address, such as *bath, boat, baby, bubble,* and *ball.*

Environmental Modifications

In addition to interpersonal strategies that may support the child producing appropriate speech sounds, environmental modifications often are useful. Depending on the findings from TPBA2, the team may want to consider some of the following environmental modifications.

1. *Use online speech sound games to practice sounds.* These include pictures that are motivating to children.

2. *Play identification games.* Memory, card games, or board games encourage the child to identify animals, objects, and household items.

3. *Use mirrors to allow the child to have both visual and auditory feedback.* Play face-making games in the mirror that involve making and imitating sounds.

4. *Use computer animated programs.* Computer programs are available that use changing visual patterns when the child creates the correct sounds. These may be used in conjunction with a speech-language pathologist.

5. *Use computer animated programs (continued).* Computer programs for older children also are available that have a "talking" head that shows children where and how to place the mouth and tongue to make the sounds. These are motivating to children, and they can practice whenever they want for as long as they want. These programs have been shown to be effective with children with autism as well as other types of disabilities.

▨▨▨▨ IV. B. What are the articulation abilities of the child?
IV. C. How intelligible is the child's speech?

Children may be unintelligible for a variety of reasons. They may have poor control or musculature of the articulators; poor ability to plan, formulate, and sequence movements necessary for speech; or inability to control airflow for speech production. They may have physical problems such as poor dentition, nasal congestion, ear infections, or excess saliva due to lack of efficient swallowing. Children who are unintelligible need more than practice on isolated sounds. They may need physical, dental, or medical supports in addition to speech and language therapy. The transdisciplinary team is needed to ensure that all of the relevant issues are addressed.

Interaction Strategies

1. *Bring the desired or requested object up to the side of your mouth.* The child must see both what the object is and how the adult moves his or her mouth to produce the word. Focus on only one word, rather than a phrase or sentence, to reduce the numbers of sounds sequenced.

2. *Develop a picture book of words with target sounds.* Use real pictures or pictures from catalogs and magazines to make a book of the child's key words and favorite things. Read it together, with the child doing as much of the labeling as possible. Make this a sharing, comfortable time, not "therapy." This personalized book allows the child to learn the words that are important in her life first, making it easier to get her needs met. It also provides an opportunity to practice these words in a nonstressful, nurturing manner.

3. *Provide choices to the child whenever possible so that he or she will need to get more specific in the production of the word he or she is producing.* Mealtime, playtime, and getting dressed are daily routines in which choice making would be beneficial. Choices also allow the child to ensure that he or she is understood. Choose words that do not sound similar, so the adult is ensured of understanding the child, which reinforces future communication efforts.

4. *Use turn-taking activities as a way to model target sounds and words.* The child then has a correct model he or she can imitate. Turn taking may begin with making animal sounds, making faces (related to positions for sound production), and then sounds and syllables related to real words.

5. *Provide all caregivers in the child's life with the target sounds and strategies.* If the adults in the child's life are aware of the target sounds and words to elicit from the child, then the child will have a lot of opportunities throughout the day to practice.

Environmental Modifications

In addition to interpersonal strategies that may support the child improving intelligibility, environmental modifications often are useful. Depending on the findings from TPBA2, the team may want to consider some of the following environmental modifications.

1. *Computer programs.* Children can use computer-based activities, such as those described previously, in order to reinforce sound production through pictures and symbols.

2. *Use augmentative and alternative communication (AAC) devices.* AAC may be useful for children whose articulation is greatly compromised. These may be used on a short-term basis to augment and encourage motivation to produce speech or as an alternative for verbal speech production.

3. *Use sign language.* Signing may be useful as an adjunct to speech or a substitute for speech. Sign language may help the child feel less stress trying to communicate, leading to more successful verbal production.

ROUTINES FOR THE CHILD WHO NEEDS SUPPORT TO IMPROVE ARTICULATION/PHONOLOGY

The following are examples of how the strategies described previously can be incorporated into the child's routines at home and school. In addition to the strategies noted at the beginning of the chapter, used by caregivers of children who do not have special needs, these may support increased proficiency in articulation and phonology.

Daily Routines (Home and Classroom)

Feeding/Eating

Mealtime is a good opportunity to encourage children to produce speech sounds in words to request. Providing choices to the child will encourage him or her to be specific in the sounds and words he or she produces; for example, "Do you want a cookie or a cracker?" It is important that the child is not required to produce the target sounds throughout the meal.

Diapering/Toileting

During diapering, talk about body parts while emphasizing the name of each one. The variation of the different vowel and consonant sounds of the parts of the face (e.g., eyes, ears, mouth, nose) and major body parts (e.g., hand, head, toes, knee) are good for addressing early speech sounds. You also can talk about "peepee" and "poopoo," seeing if the child can imitate each word using the correct vowel sounds.

Dressing

Dressing is a time to use repetitive lines to help a child practice his or her speech sounds. For example, if a child has difficulty producing final consonant sounds consistently, focus on the word "on" or "off" as you help him or her put on or take off each piece of clothing.

Going Out

Going outside and to different places allows the sharing of many experiences. For the child who is learning to produce different sounds, talking about the different environmental sounds such as animals and vehicle noises would be enjoyable. For example, as you see the car, say, "beep" and the train, "choo-choo."

Play Routines (Home and Classroom)

Face-to-Face Play

Children learn to produce sounds by watching others' mouths and how they produce sounds associated with different objects and actions. While singing songs or playing other sensory social games, make sure the adult is in front of the child and at the same level.

Physical Play

It may be harder to focus on sounds consistently during physical play because the child also is focusing on his or her motor skills. However, if there are opportunities for turn taking and there is a break in the motor movement, such as requesting objects or turns to continue the activity, then eliciting speech sounds is an option.

Manipulative Play

Fine motor activities are a great time to elicit speech sounds since often the child is seated and the activity can be set for requesting required or desired objects or pieces of objects, such as a shape sorter or puzzle pieces. As mentioned previously, for some children who are focused on fine motor tasks, care is needed not to require the child to produce target speech sounds when he or she is fully involved with executing the fine motor movement. Once again, take turns and model the correct production and then have the child take a turn to request an object or turn. These types of activities also allow for lots of practice of the sounds and words.

Sensory Play

Talk about what the adult or the child is doing using different sounds and words that the child can imitate (e.g., *swish, push, w-h-e-e*).

Dramatic Play

This type of play allows the child to practice using the names of familiar objects as well as producing functional language that he or she may use day to day. Peer models allow the child to imitate others.

Reading and Learning Routines

Circle Time

Practicing different speech sounds during circle time is a great opportunity for a child to hear a model of sounds or words from adults or his or her peers. Songs with repetitive lines or environmental sounds are best, including "The Wheels on the Bus" and "Old MacDonald."

One-on-One Book Reading

Find books that target certain sounds or have a melody or repetitive line for practice. Make sure to pause and allow the child to produce the sounds or words. Reading the book verbatim may not be as important as talking about the pictures.

Science and Math

Talk about the different materials, what they look like, feel like, and so forth. You can use carrier phrases to help the child practice the correct production in phrases, such as "I see a ___" or "I need ___."

ALI

Ali is a 28-month-old girl who was referred for an assessment due to concerns about her speech and frustration level. Her parents reported that she had a history of chronic otitis media and in the past month had pressure equalization tubes (PE tubes) put in her ears. They feel that she has started talking more and is producing different words but that she is difficult to understand. Ali is approximately 60% intelligible to her parents and less than 50% intelligible to others when the context is known. She repeats herself when others do not understand her and sometimes cries. According to her parents, it is sometimes a guessing game to try and figure out what she wants.

During the assessment, it was noted that Ali produces age-appropriate vowel and consonant sounds but deletes all final consonants from words. For example, some of her productions included the following: "po bubo/pop bubbles, mo ju/more juice, my boo/my book." Because she is combining words, it is more difficult for her parents to identify words in phrases.

The team determined that Ali could benefit from early intervention to support her learning and development. The following are ideas related to the concerns Ali presented.

Interaction Strategies

1. *Model the correct sounds in words. Do not reinforce Ali's misarticulations by repeating what she has said.*

2. *Emphasize and prolong those target sounds for correct production as you say them; for example, "Bussss go/bus go."*

3. *Work with the speech-language pathologist to identify functional words that are important words in Ali's life and include these sounds. It is important to keep in mind the vowels and consonants in her current sound repertoire and her ability to produce the sounds in different words. Start with the target sounds and words and add to her repertoire. It is important to focus on words that are functional and that Ali can practice throughout the day in different daily routines.*

4. *Try to elicit speech alone. Do not make demands of Ali to correctly imitate or produce target sounds when she also is doing a fine motor task. For example, if Ali is playing with a puzzle, model the name of the requested puzzle piece for Ali to imitate before handing over the piece for her to place in the puzzle.*

Environmental Modifications

Develop an individualized word book with pictures of objects, people, and actions in Ali's environment. Start with pictures of words that contain the sounds Ali uses already. Talk about the book and pictures every day at a nice, quiet time for interaction. Use rhythmic reading and emphasize sounds within words to encourage imitation of sounds.

KEYS TO INTERVENTION BY DEVELOPMENTAL AGE

The following ideas are directed toward children who are functioning at approximately the following levels. The suggestions are not meant to be all-inclusive, but rather are indicative of potential areas for exploration. Identified concerns with the structure or function of the oral mechanism may adversely affect the production of speech. It will be important to consult with the speech-language pathologist on the team for guidance.

Developmental age	Articulation abilities	Keys to intervention
Birth to 3 months	Imitates tongue and mouth movements. Produces sounds in the back of mouth (2 months). Defers imitation of facial movements. Brings hand to mouth. Takes object to mouth (3 months). Sucks on hand and fingers. Produces little saliva.	Talk to the child, letting him or her see your face and mouth. Encourage oral exploration of objects and hands.
3–6 months	Attempts imitation of sounds (4 months). Produces vowel "ah." Plays with sounds and patterns of sound (5 months). Makes consonant sounds (e.g., *p, b, n, k, g*). Often puts objects in mouth (6 months). Makes different vowel sounds (e.g., *ah, eh, ee, oo*) and early consonant sounds (e.g., *b, m, g*). Makes raspberries.	Play face-to-face games with mouth movements and vowel sounds. Model making noises with lips and tongue. Model and imitate sounds such as raspberries, vowels, and with frontal (*b, m*) and back (*g*) sounds.
6–9 months	Control of saliva in all positions unless feeding, actively playing with objects, or teething. Produces consonant–vowel (CV) syllables (e.g., *ba*) (7 months). Produces syllable chains (e.g., *bababababa*) (8 months). Imitates speech sounds (9 months).	Imitate the sounds the child makes. Sing tunes with just one syllable or sound emphasized (e.g., *la-la-la; ba-ba-ba*). Say words with frontal sounds slowly (e.g., *ma-ma; da-da; ball*) and let child watch your mouth. Pay attention to positioning for appropriate head, and neck support.
9–12 months	Less drooling occurs during mealtime. Produces first word (12 months). Articulation may be understood by familiar listener. Produces a variety of consonant and vowel approximations during babbling.	Use simple one- to two-word phrases so the child can try to imitate you separately. Read books with animal sounds.
12–18 months	Drooling may occur during teething and some fine motor tasks. Produces a variety of early consonants: *b, m, n, t, d, w*. Says "muh" for *milk*. Imitates sounds and words (18 months). Omits most final consonants in words. Omits some initial consonants in words. Produces sentence-like intonation.	Read books with simple words and phrases. Introduce the child's individual word book, and add pictures as the child adds words. Sing songs with repetitive patterns. Label objects and actions. Repeat the child's production to reinforce them.

Developmental age	Articulation abilities	Keys to intervention
18–24 months	Produces speech that is less than 50% intelligible to unfamiliar listeners (21 months). Inconsistently deletes final consonants in words. Approximately 50% intelligible (24 months). Produces consonant–vowel–consonant (CVC) structures (e.g., "mo mick"/*more milk*) using early consonant sounds: *p, b, m, n, t, d, h, w.*	Prolong and emphasize sounds the child may have a hard time producing. Model words that have new sounds. Encourage the child to imitate other environmental sounds.
24–36 months	Drooling should not be present. Speech is 50%-70% intelligible to familiar listeners (30 months). Deletes one consonant from a consonant blend (e.g., "_top"/*stop*). Repeats syllables in words (e.g., "wawa"/*water*). Simplifies words that are multisyllabic (36 months). Substitution and distortion of consonants still present. Speech is 70% intelligible. Produces sounds made in the back of the mouth (e.g., *c, car; g, go; -ing, eating*).	Correctly produce words to be a good model for the child. Using dancing and singing to put sounds and words to rhythm. Use books with sounds included in the story. Do simple songs and fingerplays. Omit words and phrases from favorite books and songs for the child to fill in.
36–48 months	Speech is intelligible to unfamiliar listeners (42 months). Produces the consonants *l, f, s,* and *y* in some positions of words. Speech is approximately 80% intelligible (48 months). Produces faster speech. Produces a few consonant substitutions and omissions. Consonant blends may still not be completely present with all consonants. Produces more consonants: *z, v, sh, ch, j.*	Do dramatic play activities involving words that are part of the child's sound repertoire. Say names of letters and sounds the child makes. Talk about the day's events.
48–60 months	Produces most consonants accurately in all positions. Speech is intelligible to unfamiliar listeners.	Write letters and say sounds for familiar words from the child's word book. This will provide an added visual cue to match auditory output. Involve the child in storytelling to develop narrative skills. Let the child make up words or sentences in the story. Make up songs to go with the stories. Read poems for children with rhymes and rhythm. Learn simple ones by heart. Incorporate props and language from favorite books into dramatic play to encourage reproduction of the language and story sequence.
60–72 months	Produces all sounds in all positions by age 7.	Have the child generate words he or she wants to learn to write. Then write down these words and let the child copy them with magnetic letters, stamp letters, writing, or other means. Have the child read the words back to you. Use language and storyboards, puppets, and flannel board stories. Develop dramatic play with scripts based on storybooks.

6

Facilitating Communication Development

V. Strategies for Improving Voice and Fluency

with Renee Charlifue-Smith

Goal Attainment Scale

1	2	3	4	5	6	7	8	9
Breath support is adequate for crying, grunting, cooing, or laughing, but not for voice production.		Breath support and voice production (phonation) are adequate for sound, but the child does not yet babble or make single-word approximations.		Breath support is adequate for voice production, but any of the following behaviors are chronic, noticeable, and interfere with the child's communication: *Pitch:* very high, very low, or monotone *Quality:* very breathy, harsh, hoarse, nasal, or stuffy *Loudness:* inadequate or very loud *Fluency:* very choppy rhythm, and/or frequently occurring disfluencies (sound or syllable repetitions, e.g., "c-c-c-cat"; prolonged sounds, e.g., "sssssssat"; or silent blocks) *Speech rate:* very slow or very fast		Breath support is adequate for voice production. Any of the following behaviors are noticeable, but do not markedly interfere with the child's communication: *Pitch:* slightly high, slightly low, or monotone *Quality:* slightly breathy, harsh, hoarse, nasal, or stuffy *Loudness:* slightly soft or slightly loud *Fluency:* slightly choppy rhythm, and/or occasionally occurring disfluencies (sound or syllable repetitions, e.g., "c-c-c-cat"; prolonged sounds, e.g., "sssssssat"; or silent blocks) *Speech rate:* slightly slow or slightly fast		Pitch, quality, and loudness of the voice and speech fluency and rate are appropriate for the child's age, size, gender, and culture.

Complex interactions among the lungs (respiration); the larynx or voice box (phonation); and pharyngeal (throat), oral (mouth), and nasal (nose) cavities (resonation) result in the unique voice of each child. When the child exhales, the vocal cords vibrate in the larynx as air passes through, altering the sound wave as it travels out the oral and nasal cavities.

Children's first vocal communication is through crying, cooing, and vocal play with the adult. Adults interpret these vocalizations as carrying communicative intent. As the child develops, his or her sound repertoire, range of pitch, and intonational patterns become important for effective communication and social interactions. The loudness, quality, resonance, rate, and pitch of the voice all influence the child's intelligibility and others' social perceptions of the child.

Fluency is the ability to produce and combine the sounds, phrases, and words needed to convey thoughts in a smooth and rhythmic manner. Stuttering is the repetition of sounds and syllables (e.g., "p-p-p-p-push it"), prolongation of sounds (e.g., "mmmmy car"), or blockages in producing sounds or words (e.g., no sound). Fluency is important for others to be able to comprehend what the child is trying to communicate. It also is important for the child's developing sense of self in being an effective communicator. An inability to communicate with fluency can be extremely frustrating and self-defeating.

APPROPRIATE VOICE AND FLUENCY

Both voice and fluency change over time as the child's physiology changes and he or she acquires the ability to create new sounds and words. A child's voice is considered normal when its loudness, pitch, and quality match the child's communication needs and do not overshadow what the child is saying. Voice changes occur as the child's larynx, vocal cords, and the oral and nasal structures grow with the child.

In terms of fluency, the development typically proceeds in a predictable fashion, with sounds, sound combinations, and words developing in rapid progression during the first 18 months of life. Children begin with crying and vocalization of vowel sounds and then begin to combine vowels and consonants, repeating them in reduplicated patterns. These patterns begin to increase in variability and complexity of sounds, length of sound patterns, and approximations to real words. Words are produced first singly, then combined with other words to convey more sophisticated thoughts. For most children, even if the sounds produced are not accurate, they can combine sounds easily and fluidly.

Young children between 2 and 5 years of age often repeat words or show difficulty producing words in the course of normal language development. As they are trying to produce longer and more complex productions of their thoughts, sometimes their articulators just cannot keep up. These disfluencies may occur when the child is excited, anxious, or uncertain about a situation and may take several forms: whole-word repetition (e.g., "my, my, my train"); phrase repetition (e.g., "my doll, my doll is dirty"); a revision, when the child changes the course of the sentence midstream (e.g., I want juice-[pause]-milk); or an interjection, in which the child uses a "filler" word, such as "um." The appearance of these disfluencies may occur for days or weeks and resolve without assistance.

Appropriate Voice and Fluency in Practice

▨▨▨▨ **V. A. How are the pitch, quality, and loudness of the child's voice?**

Daily Routines (Home and Classroom)

- *Infant/toddler:* The infant cries loudly, with a clear, high, prolonged wail. The toddler whispers in her mother's ear, "I love you."

- *Young child:* The young child is singing in the tub. He lowers the pitch of his voice to be the bull frog and then raises it to be the lady frog.

Play Routines (Home and Classroom)

- *Infant/toddler:* The infant is lying in her crib and is making sounds. She squeals in a high-pitched voice, then blows bubbles, then squeals again. The toddler screams with excitement while running around the playground, chasing his puppy.

- *Young child:* The young child sings a familiar song, changing the pitch and rhythm of his voice in time with the music. His voice is clear.

Classroom Routines

Three children are playing at the water table. Their voices get increasingly louder as they start washing their cars, making noises like a car wash. The teacher tells them to use their "inside" voices. They all lower their voices.

▬▬ V. B. How fluent is the child's speech?

Daily Routines (Home and Classroom)

- *Infant/toddler:* The infant vocalizes, running together strings of sounds in a speech-like intonation. The toddler says, "Me go" without hesitation as she sees her parent get his coat on.

- *Young child:* The young child carries on a long dialogue about a television show. He rambles on about the characters and the action, only occasionally saying, "and, um, then the . . . "

Play Routines (Home and Classroom)

- *Infant/toddler:* The infant looks at herself in the mirror and begins to babble a string of consonant–vowel sounds. The toddler takes the plastic banana from the basket and offers it to her friend, saying, "You want nana?" (this is a normal omission of a syllable, not a disfluency).

- *Young child:* The young child asks his friend, "Will you play with me? I want to build a castle and you can help me." His sentence is said rapidly, with no pauses.

Classroom Routines

During circle, the young child is asked what she did over the weekend. She responds, "Uh, I went to the, um, zoo with my brother." (This is a normal disfluency, used to give the child time to formulate her thoughts.)

GENERAL PRINCIPLES FOR SUPPORTING EFFECTIVE VOICE AND FLUENCY

Model

Adults model both fluent speech and voice modulation for children. For example, they often lower their own voices when the child is being too loud. When the child is searching for a word, the adult may say the word for the name of the object that the child might say. For example, if the child says, "I want a um . . . " the adult waits and may offer a choice or label the object the child is looking at, such as, "You want a banana?"

Direct

Adults direct children to modulate their voices. For example, in the previous example, the teacher tells the children to use their "inside" voices. This is understood by the children to mean that they are being too loud.

Wait Time

For children who produce disfluencies in their speech, adults often just wait for the child to produce the correct word or words, giving their full attention to the child, listening intently, and not interrupting.

THE PRINCIPLES IN PRACTICE

Daily Routines (Home and Classroom)

Feeding/Eating

Adults encourage sound and word production during meals. They label and describe what the child is eating. The mealtime or snack allows everyone to take a turn in the conversation and talk about the day or an event.

Diapering/Toileting

Adults model language during diapering and toileting and encourage quiet interactions.

Dressing

Dressing is a sequential action, so adults use repetitive sentences to encourage children to link words (e.g., "Pull off your socks") as well as to use sound effects (e.g., "zzzip" as the pajamas or coat is being zipped up).

Play Routines (Home and Classroom)

Face-to-Face Play

The songs and actions done in face-to-face games encourage imitation and fluency of sounds and words, intonation, and voice modulation.

Physical Play

Physical play is an area in which adults allow and encourage loud play, squealing, and laughing.

Manipulative Play

Adults prompt imitation of a variety of noises—animals, trucks, planes, trains, sirens, and crashes. These enable children to experiment with voice modulation. In addition, children practice fluent sentence development as they imitate adults' comments.

Sensory Play

Adults encourage playing with sounds that match actions (e.g., "Zoop!" "Swish!" "Plop!"), and children often express exuberance in this play with a range of pitch and loudness.

Reading and Learning Routines

Circle Time

During circle time, adults request students' participation by directing them to respond to questions, comment on the routine, or interact with a peer. They prompt appropriate voice for the situation and encourage peers to wait while the child completes his or her thoughts.

One-on-One Book Reading

Adults model fluent reading language and encourage child participation through imitation and filling in missing sentences in familiar books. Memory for book passages encourages fluency.

Science and Math

Adults encourage fluent sequencing of counting. Science activities also involve sequencing of thoughts. Adults encourage children to recount what they did, what happened, and what will happen next.

PLANNING INDIVIDUALIZED INTERVENTIONS FOR IMPROVING VOICE AND FLUENCY

▆▆▆▆▆ V. A. How are the pitch, quality, and loudness of the child's voice?

When the child has a deviation in the pitch, loudness, or quality of the voice to the extent that it interferes with communication or is inappropriate for the child's gender, age, or cultural background, a voice disorder may be diagnosed. Problems with any of the physical contributors to voice—respiration, phonation, or resonation (nasal or oral cavities)—can affect voice quality. Children may present with a voice disorder for a variety of reasons. Genetic, neurological, physical, or environmental issues may be the underlying cause. Children with disabilities, including hearing loss, Down syndrome, cerebral palsy, and emotional and behavioral concerns, and other language and cognitive issues, may demonstrate more concerns with voice quality at a higher rate than children who have no additional developmental concerns. Other factors that may contribute to poor voice quality are inappropriate breath support and rate of speech. The following are the most common voice problems:

- *Resonation:* hypernasal (i.e., excessive nasal resonance) or hyponasal (i.e., sounds like the child has a cold, too little nasal resonance, especially with nasal consonants, /m/, /n/, /ng/)

- *Quality:* hoarse, harsh, or breathy voice

- *Loudness:* too soft or too loud

- *Pitch:* too high, too low, or monotone

Hypernasality can be caused by health issues such as congestion or sinus problems or physical problems such as craniofacial disorders (e.g., cleft lip and/or palate). Children with neuromuscular involvement, such as cerebral palsy, may have difficulty with respiration for speech as well as difficulty with vocal quality, loudness, and rhythm. Children with autism spectrum disorders also may have problems with voice rhythm and volume when talking.

A hoarse, harsh, or raspy voice may be caused by medical etiologies such as allergies or irritation from gastroesophageal reflux or abuse of the vocal cords due to constant yelling or screaming, or talking with too low a voice or inappropriate breath support over an extended time. Vocal abuse can result in swelling of the vocal cords or the development of vocal nodules or polyps, which are small growths that develop on the vocal cords. These conditions require a medical consultation by an otolaryngologist (ear, nose, and throat [ENT] doctor) to assess, to identify any medical causes, and to develop a treatment plan. In some cases, surgery may be required. However, depending on the severity of the presenting problem, voice therapy often is the first choice to address the problem.

Interaction Strategies

1. *Encourage talking in an appropriate voice.* Discourage use of a rough voice, as in making animal sounds (i.e., growling) or truck sounds, over an extended period of time.

2. *Model appropriate rate of voice, talking in a relaxed and calm voice.* If voice rate is too fast, it may contribute to disfluent speech.

3. *Teach the older child how to breathe.* With the support of the professional team, teach thoracic and abdominal (diaphragm) breathing, rather than clavicular (shoulder) breathing, which is not efficient for speech. Have the child feel her lower ribs expanding as she breathes with this pattern. Easy, relaxed breathing supports the voice.

4. *Learn how to help the child relax.* Practice relaxation of the body and face with the child. Children respond well to deep breathing and relaxation strategies. Do the exercises together in a calm and relaxed environment.

Environmental Modifications

In addition to interpersonal strategies that may support the child in moderating the voice, environmental modifications often are useful. Depending on the findings from TPBA2, the team may want to consider some of the following environmental modifications.

1. *Consider postural needs.* The chest, neck, and head need to be upright and supported to achieve good breath control for speech.

2. *Maintain a relaxed environment.* A relaxed environment can help the child relax as well, supporting breathing and speaking.

3. *Be a good model of how to use one's voice.* Instead of screaming for children to come into the classroom, the teacher can ring a bell.

4. *Provide a quiet environment that has a lower vocal demand.* Competing noises such as the dishwasher, vacuum, and television require the child to increase his or her volume. In a noisy environment, do not require a high vocal demand (i.e., need to raise vocal volume and/or talk for long periods of time).

▨▨▨ V. B. How fluent is the child's speech?

Children who have difficulty producing fluid speech may demonstrate disfluencies, or stuttering. Stuttering may take the form of repetitions of sounds or syllables (e.g., "g-g-g-ive me" or "gi-gi-gi-give me"), prolongations of sounds (e.g., "mmmmm-ine"), unexpectedly long pauses or blocks (e.g., no sound), revisions of what was said, or interjections of sounds or syllables (e.g., "um," "uh"). Children who stutter also may demonstrate struggle behaviors, or actions that indicate that producing speech is difficult. These may include struggle and tension in the face or body, movement of all or part of the body, or looking away while stuttering. When a child is excited or nervous, the stuttering behaviors may increase. The child also often shows changes in loudness and pitch during repetitions.

Another kind of fluency disorder is called *cluttering*. Cluttering is speech that is hard to understand because it is too fast and many sounds of speech are left out or slurred. Sentences also may be disorganized. These children often do not display struggle behaviors because they may be unaware that their speech is difficult to follow.

Views about treatment for young children who stutter have been evolving over the years. Early intervention with the child and beneficial and ongoing collaboration and communication with the family and staff (i.e., child care providers and teachers) is recommended. Ongoing consultation with a team is needed because the child's stuttering may have an adverse effect on other developmental areas such as social-emotional.

Interaction Strategies

1. *Do not tell the child to slow down or take a breath.* This brings attention to the disfluency and causes stress that can increase rather than decrease the behavior.

2. *Provide full attention to the child when he or she is talking.* The listener should give eye contact to child and stop any other activity he or she may be doing.

3. *Model a normal rate of speech.* Watch the rate of speech when talking to the child. Pause at the end of sentences and use good inflection. A slow rate of speech tells the child there is no hurry.

4. *Model back what the child said, in a relaxed and slow manner.* Do not correct the child if he or she is disfluent. Correctly repeat what the child said. For instance, if the child says, "I wa-wa-wa-want a cracker," the adult can say, "Okay. You want a cracker? I'll get you one."

5. *Provide turn taking in conversation.* If there is a group activity and every child is going to take a turn, do not make the child who is disfluent wait for a long period of time before he or she takes a turn. At mealtime, let everyone take turns communicating, allowing time for each person to express his or her thoughts without being interrupted.

6. *Provide wait time.* Even if you know what the child is going to say, wait for the child to complete his or her communication before responding. Do not interrupt the child while he or she is talking.

7. *Reduce requests for information or performance.* Get the information you want in a conversation rather than a direct request; for example, "I wonder what squirrels eat for breakfast." Do not ask the child to perform or recite in front of others. Also, if the child is going to need to respond verbally to a request in front of a group, try to request information that is familiar to the child. Decrease the use of questioning for the purpose of performance. For instance, do not tell the child to "Show us how you can count to 20." Give alternatives such as, "Do you want to play in the dramatic play area or the science area?"

8. *Speak on the child's level.* It is important to connect with the child, so speaking on the child's physical level, using face-to-face interaction, and interacting on the child's developmental level can reduce stress.

9. *Comment on what is causing stress.* Disfluencies increase with stress, so try to reduce the stress; for example, "It's very noisy in here. Let's turn down the music so I can hear you."

10. *Remain calm.* Be supportive, encouraging, and approachable so the child will want to communicate. Do not show pain, concern, or frustration on your face.

11. *Provide verbal praise.* When the child is talking, comment on his or her talking, "You are doing such a nice job of describing your trip."

Environmental Modifications

In addition to interpersonal strategies that may support the child improving his or her fluency, environmental modifications often are useful. Depending on the findings from TPBA2, the team may want to consider some of the following environmental modifications.

1. *Try to structure time for the child to talk.* Having special times for just the child and parent to interact is important.

2. *Incorporate familiar books, songs, poems, and fingerplays into the day.* Familiarity reduces stress and increases fluency because known patterns flow more easily. Fingerplays and movements with songs also decrease the child's concentration on speech.

3. *Keep a record of when speech is most disfluent.* Some of the following may contribute:

- Feeling pressure to speak in front of others
- Competing to speak
- Fearing the consequences of what is being said
- Expressing complex ideas or using new vocabulary
- New situations or people
- Being hurried

4. *Use visual aids.* Encourage children to use visual aids such as pictures to help them explain what they want to share. The pictures may help guide thoughts.

5. *Give children time to talk about what is of interest to them.* Children are less disfluent when they know what they are talking about.

6. *Explore assistive devices for older preschool-age children.* Assistive devices that alter the way a child hears his or her voice have been shown to be effective with some children. Consult with the speech-language pathologist working with a child.

ROUTINES FOR THE CHILD WHO NEEDS SUPPORT TO IMPROVE VOICE AND FLUENCY

The following are examples of how the strategies discussed previously can be incorporated into the child's routines at home and school. In addition to the strategies noted at the beginning of the chapter, used by caregivers of children who do not have special needs, the following may support increased proficiency in voice and fluency.

Daily Routines (Home and Classroom)

Feeding/Eating

Structure mealtimes and other "talk times," and make sure siblings or peers understand that each person needs time to share ideas and thoughts. These should be unhurried, relaxed times for sharing, and individuals should not be interrupted. Initially, pass around an object and indicate that whoever is holding it is the person who has a turn to share.

Diapering/Toileting

The caregiver takes turns talking to the child as the diaper is being changed.

Dressing

The parent provides choices in clothing items and lets the child try to help getting dressed. The activity is not rushed, and the child has an opportunity to talk.

Going Out

The caregiver models appropriate volumes and tones during outings.

Play Routines (Home and Classroom)

Face-to-Face Play

Sing songs and play turn-taking sound games to enable the child to practice a range of sounds, loudness, and tones.

Physical Play

This type of play often elicits screaming. Try to decrease too much loud and rough vocal play on a consistent basis.

Manipulative Play

Children often enjoy making animal sounds and vehicle noises. Monitor the production of too many rough sounds, and model other tones and pitches.

Sensory Play

Adults can model different sounds with their voices as they play with different objects.

Dramatic Play

Provide opportunities for each child to take turns in the play and communicate his or her thoughts.

Reading and Learning Routines

Circle Time

Make sure there is structure to the circle time activity in order to decrease interruptions. Everyone should have an opportunity for taking a turn during the activity.

One-on-One Book Reading

Let the child participate and fill in words at the end of a phrase. Model different tones of voice for different characters.

Science and Math

Study and imitate the sounds associated with various aspects of nature (e.g., animal sounds, nature sounds, environmental sounds). Identify loud and soft sounds in the environment or sounds that are made with objects. For older children, talk about the importance of good health including drinking a lot of water throughout the day.

MICHAEL

Michael is a 3-year-old boy who was referred for TPBA2 by his preschool teacher because he is easily frustrated. His parents would like to know how they can further his development in speech. Generally, Michael had typical development except that his speech and language development was slow compared with his twin brother and friends. Michael does not talk frequently, but when he does talk he usually is intelligible to his parents. However, they reported that others often do not understand him. According to his parents, Michael is not as social as other children his age. He does not like big crowds or noisy environments and "he seems to need more attention." He gets cranky easily, loses his temper quickly, and can be very hard to calm down. During TPBA, Michael's speech was characterized by sound substitutions that were developmental in nature. However, Michael often was unintelligible during the assessment due to whispering and the lack of pitch variation or the monotone quality of his voice. Attempts were made by his facilitator to elicit from Michael a typical volume, a voice to tell his parents something across the room, and a yelling voice (in the playground with his brother) and different inflections. During the assessment, Michael spontaneously used a high pitch while talking; this behavior lasted for a few minutes. His teacher reported these vocal behaviors as typical of Michael in the classroom.

JESSICA

Jessica is a 4-year-old girl who lives at home with her parents, older brother (age 7 years), and infant sister (age 6 months). The family moved a few months ago; Jessica has since shared a room with her sister. Her parents stated that she started repeating the first sounds in words at approximately the time the family moved. They are concerned that she is stuttering. She is not aware of the disfluent behavior, but her older brother has been teasing her about it. During the assessment, Jessica exhibited struggling behaviors and often repeated the consonants /m/, /b/, and /p/ in words.

Interaction Strategies/Environmental Modifications

1. *Concerns about a child's voice quality should be referred to an otolaryngologist for further examination.*

2. *The child with voice or fluency concerns should be seen by a speech-language pathologist for intervention. In some situations it may be beneficial for the child to be seen by a speech-language pathologist with specialization in the area of voice or fluency. The family should be involved in the intervention process.*

3. *Minimize the amount of stress and conflict at home.*

4. *Provide an environment that is quiet, relaxing and allows the child to speak without distractions.*

KEYS TO INTERVENTION BY DEVELOPMENTAL AGE

A child's voice quality and fluency do change over time as the child's neurological system matures and the structures and functions of the oral and nasal cavities develop. With the exception of typical disfluencies that occur between the ages of 2 and 5 years, voice and fluency interventions should be individualized to the child, with education and support to the family, to address the child's voice and fluency.

6

Facilitating Communication Development

VI. Strategies for Improving the Function of the Oral Mechanism for Speech Production

Goal Attainment Scale

1	2	3	4	5	6	7	8	9
The structure and/or symmetry of the palate, lips, jaw, tongue, or bite interfere with functional speech.		Structures are adequate, but speech is made primarily with gross jaw and lip movements. The range of movement may be excessive or limited.		Structures are adequate for speech. The child can round and retract the lips with good contact, move the tongue up, down, and front to back, and use finely graded jaw movements to produce sounds and simple words.		Structures are adequate for speech. The child moves the lips, tongue, jaw, and palate independently but has some difficulty integrating movements to say complex words (e.g., *potato, buttercup*) or phrases.		Structure and function of the oral mechanism is adequate for age-appropriate speech.

The oral mechanism is the physical component necessary to produce speech, including the development of coordinated movements of the respiratory and phonatory systems and the actions of the articulators for communication. The oral mechanism includes the physical structures of the mouth and jaw, including the teeth, and the musculature of the lips, tongue, and cheeks. Sensory processing of touch, pressure, and movement are needed. Postural support, including trunk and head control, also contributes to the child's ability to speak.

APPROPRIATE STRUCTURE AND FUNCTION OF THE ORAL MECHANISM

Observe the overall appearance, symmetry, and mobility of the lips, tongue, and jaw at rest and while talking. How is the child's dentition? What is the shape of the palate? Is there a history of a cleft lip or palate? Does the child have missing or misaligned teeth that may affect speech production? All of these questions should be considered when providing support around the child's ability to use the oral mechanism for speech production.

Appropriate Structure and Function
of the Oral Mechanism for Speech Production

VI. A. What is the overall appearance of the articulators at rest?

Daily Routines (Home and Classroom)

- *Infant/toddler:* The infant lies in the crib, sticks out his tongue, and blows raspberries. The toddler puts her teeth together and smiles widely to brush her teeth.

- *Young child:* When the teacher reads a book about a frog, the young child sticks out his tongue in imitation.

Play Routines (Home and Classroom)

- *Infant/toddler:* The infant watches the father blow spit bubbles, puckers up, and imitates him. Dad blows bubbles on the toddler's tummy. The toddler then tries to do the same. He opens his mouth, puts it on his dad's stomach, and tries to blow, but instead hums and leaves a circle of saliva.

- *Young child:* The young child is pretending to be a puffer fish. She puffs out her cheeks, pinches her lips together, and holds her breath.

Classroom Routines

During circle time, the children take turns making noises like various objects. The other children then try to guess what object the child was pretending to be. One child stands up and makes swishing noises, opening and closing his lips rapidly. When no one guesses, he laughs and shouts, "I'm a toilet!"

VI. A2. What degree of control of the articulators does the child demonstrate during speech?

Daily Routines (Home and Classroom)

- *Infant/toddler:* The infant sees his father and says, "da-da." In the bathtub, the toddler rattles off a string of vowels and consonants into jargon that sounds like speech. The words "duck" and "bubble" are intelligible within this jargon.

- *Young child:* At the dinner table, the young child tells his family, "It was Apwi's (April's) buday (birthday) today. Her mommy bwot (brought) cupcakes."

Play Routines (Home and Classroom)

- *Infant/toddler:* While kicking at her mobile, the infant makes guttural sounds, trills, and squeals, playing with sounds. The toddler picks up the toy phone and says, "Hi, Daddy. Bye, Daddy," and hangs up.

- *Young child:* While in dramatic play, the young child makes zooming and crashing noises as he and his friend race their cars around the track. He says, "Watch out, buddy! I'm comin' fast."

Classroom Routines

During circle time, the young child stands up and sings the "Itsy Bitsy Spider" all by herself, with no mispronunciations.

GENERAL PRINCIPLES FOR SUPPORTING EFFECTIVE FUNCTIONING OF THE ORAL MECHANISM

Adults use a variety of strategies to promote oral motor skills related to speech production. The following are strategies often used by adults to help children support the movements for speech production. These strategies also are useful for children who have difficulty with accomplishing these skills.

Modeling

From the earliest days of infancy, adults model sounds and words for the child to imitate; for example, the mother blows raspberries for the child to see and imitate. When the child coos, the parent imitates the sound back and the child then sees the shape of the mouth that made that sound. Back-and-forth sound games continue, with the child becoming increasingly more adept at imitation, and eventually sounds become words. The adult continues to model sound and word production throughout the early childhood years, particularly if the child is having difficulty with imitation.

Using Slow Motion and Exaggeration

Both when the child is initially learning a sound or mouth movement and when the child is having difficulty producing sounds, adults slow their speech and mouth movements so the child can see more clearly. In addition, they exaggerate the position of the mouth, lips, or tongue. For example, when trying to get the child to say a difficult word such as *spaghetti,* the adult might exaggerate the *s* sound and emphasize the *pa* when putting the syllables together and showing the child how to say the word.

Using Gestural Prompts

Some children might benefit from the use of gestural prompts to facilitate their ability to imitate sounds; for example, pinching the lips together to show the m sound.

Practicing

Adults help children practice making sounds and words when they sing together, when the adult asks the child questions requiring the use of certain words in a response, or when they read books together and the child learns the sounds and rhythms of the words in the books. When children are learning a new sound, adults often use the word several times in a row to encourage practice.

THE PRINCIPLES IN PRACTICE

Adults use a variety of strategies to support the child's development of the oral motor mechanism for production of speech. The following examples explain how caregivers use the strategies described previously during the day both at home and at school. These examples are approaches that most caregivers use naturally in their daily interactions with children. They are appropriate for most children with disabilities as well.

Daily Routines (Home and Classroom)

Feeding/Eating

Adults not only offer a model for movements of the mouth when eating, but also model sounds and words during feeding. For example, the adult says, "Mmmmm. Good! Do you want more O's?" (for Cheerios).

Diapering/Toileting

Adults use descriptive words and sounds during these processes, making faces while emphasizing the meaning of the words; for example, "Oooh. That's a *stinky* one!" or "Tinkle, tinkle. Good for you!"

Dressing

Adults often exaggerate sounds that accompany actions when they are getting children dressed; for example, "ZZZip!" or "Puull the pants *up*!"

Play Routines (Home and Classroom)

Face-to-Face Play

Face-to-face games frequently involve imitation of each others' facial movements and sounds. Early games involve physical play (e.g., pulling the blanket off the face) accompanied by a sound (e.g., "Boo!"). Sound imitation games with vowels and early consonants typically follow soon after. These games become more complex as children start to understand more vocabulary.

Physical Play

In physical play, adults use sound effects (e.g., "Zzap!"), word emphasis (e.g., "I'm gonna *get* you!"), and exaggerated facial expressions to get children's attention and convey the intent of the play. Children often imitate these sounds and actions in return.

Manipulative Play

Toy play frequently involves sounds. Toys make sounds that adults then imitate, or adults add sounds to the toys. For instance, a battery-operated car may make a honking noise. The adult imitates that to encourage the child to do the same. A small toy car does not make sound, but the adult may add sound such as "oo-oo" to simulate the sound of a train or pretend to honk a horn by saying, "Beep! Beep!"

Sensory Play

In the same way that adults add sounds to toy play, they also can add sounds that accompany the child's movements or the actions of the materials being used by the child. When playing with fingerpaints, for example, the adult may model drawing a circle with a finger and say, "Rrround and rrround." When filling up a container in the water table, the adult may make an escalating sound (e.g., "ooOOOO") to accompany the rise in the water in the bottle. The intent is for the child to replicate these actions and sounds. The actions serve as a motivator to make the sounds.

Dramatic Play

When adults are involved in dramatic play, they have many opportunities to model sounds, phrases, and words. When playing fireman, for example, the people cry, "Help!" the fire truck sounds, the pretend water "sshhshss," and the adult models language such as, "Save me. I'm hurt."

Reading and Learning Routines

Circle Time

Teachers use songs and fingerplays in circle time to encourage imitation. The rhythm and rhyme motivate children to imitate the teacher and each other.

One-on-One Book Reading

Children love the rhythm of reading language and want to learn the words. They soon learn the patterns and are motivated to repeat them each time the book comes out. In one-on-one reading, the adult can lead the child through recitation of whole books.

Science and Math

Adults use the study of animals and books about animals to make animal sounds and talk about animal food, homes, and so forth. Children's first sounds and words often are related to animals. Children imitate the sounds and words adults make when looking at pictures, animal toys, or puzzles.

PLANNING INDIVIDUALIZED INTERVENTIONS FOR IMPROVING FUNCTION OF THE ORAL MECHANISM

▰▰▰▰ VI. A. What is the overall appearance of the articulators at rest?

Two basic types of oral motor problems are seen in young children. The first is structural, resulting from physiological concerns including, for example, the presence of asymmetry in the oral structures. The second type of oral motor problem is functional, in which the child has difficulty initiating and/or coordinating the movements of the jaw, lips, tongue, and cheeks spontaneously, in imitation, or on request. The first concern is addressed in this section and the second in the following section. These issues also may overlap, making it difficult to discern the primary problem.

Children with a variety of disabilities and health care and dental issues may have physiological concerns that may negatively affect speech. The following factors may affect the function of the oral mechanism or articulators for speech production:

1. Children with low muscle tone, or *hypotonicity,* may have reduced trunk, head, neck, and shoulder girdle control, and this lack of stability may affect movements and/or respiration and breath support for talking. Low tone may contribute to reduced jaw control and, consequently, cause an open-mouth posture, mouth breathing, and/or a tongue thrust that inhibits making precise sounds and contributes to drooling.

2. Increased muscle tone, or *hypertonicity,* also can restrict movement. The child's lips may be retracted or the head and neck contracted to one side.

3. Abnormal reflex patterns may inhibit voluntary movements needed for speech.

4. Decreased sensitivity to tactile input can reduce the child's awareness of saliva in the mouth, which may in turn reduce efforts to swallow saliva and contribute to drooling. The child with hyposensitivity may be unaware that he or she is drooling. The child also may be unaware of the position of the tongue and lips, making sound production more difficult.

5. Increased sensitivity may result in avoiding the use of speech sounds that produce certain vibratory or irritating sensations in the mouth.

6. Poor dentition or changes to the appearance of the lips, palate, or tongue (e.g., cleft palate, an extremely high palate, mouth structure change from behaviors such as thumb-sucking or teeth grinding) can contribute to difficulty producing certain sounds.

7. Allergies, enlarged tonsils or adenoids, or other respiratory issues can cause open-mouth breathing.

Children with the aforementioned difficulties with the oral mechanism may have difficulty formulating sounds, and when they do put sounds together in speech, the speech may be unintelligible or only partially intelligible. Children with concerns of the oral mechanism may possibly have difficulty with feeding and eating (see Chapter 3, Section VI. Strategies for Improving Sensorimotor Contributions to Daily Life for ideas related to this area). Suggestions related to the oral motor mechanism and speech production are presented in the following section. Consultation with health professionals, a speech-language pathologist, and other team members is important to determine what is appropriate for individual children.

Interaction Strategies

1. *Play kissing games.* Kissing requires puckering the lips and is fun as well. Take turns kissing each other's neck, cheek, lips, and hands. With each turn, say, "I'm going to *kiss* you."

2. *Help the child become orally aware.* Give the child a cue, such as touching the chin to cue the child to close his or her mouth or under the chin to signal a need to swallow. This initially can be done directly on the child as a touch cue, then on the adult as a visual cue for the child, and then phased out as the child gains motor control.

3. *Make brushing teeth an interactional time.* Brushing teeth is important for oral health and also is a great way to practice functionally moving the tongue, lips, and mouth. In this way, the adult can model the movement of the mouth and lips. Let the child do as much as he or she can independently; otherwise, this feels like a "chore" rather than a fun interaction. Make brushing teeth into a game by making faces, smiling broadly, spitting at a target in the sink, or gargling.

4. *Repetition is important.* For neurological patterns to develop so that actions become automatic, repetition is crucial. Try to find as many ways as possible to incorporate oral motor movements into daily routines and games. For example, play Simon Says face-imitation games during bath time. Use a mirror and try to make each other laugh by making silly faces before lunch. While playing the game, emphasize movement of the lips, tongue, and cheeks. The next time, add hats, and the following time, add face paint to make it even more fun. Interaction should be reciprocal and not feel like something is being done *to* the child.

5. *Provide encouragement and reinforcement for effort.* Comment when the child remembers movements such as closing his mouth; for instance, "Your lips are closed. Good for you. Your shirt is dry!"

Environmental Modifications

In addition to interpersonal strategies that may support the child in the normalization of oral mechanism function, environmental modifications often are useful. Depending on the findings from TPBA2, the team may want to consider some of the following environmental modifications.

1. *Make sure the child is positioned properly.* Good head and trunk support, with head in midline and the neck neither extended backward nor flexed, promotes use of oral mechanisms for speech. For children with motor involvement, modified seating with head and/or neck stabilizers may be needed.

2. *Introduce augmentative and alternative communication (AAC) to aid intelligibility.* If children are unintelligible, they may become frustrated when others do not understand what they are saying. Total communication and other AAC systems may help to reduce the child's frustration and increase communicative attempts. The type of augmentative system should be determined based on the child's cognitive, motor, and social abilities.

3. *Orthodontic appliances may be helpful for some children.* See a dentist or specialist for consultation.

4. *Use an appropriate drinking cup.* Decrease use of a bottle, sippy cup, and pacifier past a developmentally appropriate age, because these can negatively affect the development of the oral structures. For example, prolonged use of a pacifier may contribute to an open bite of the teeth and jaws. Prolonged use of a bottle or sippy cup can contribute to a frontal position and movement of the tongue during some speech sounds.

▨▨▨▨ VI. A2. What degree of control of the articulators does the child demonstrate during speech?

Speech requires that the child be able to formulate fine motor movements in an organized way to create specific sound patterns and sequences. At first, sounds are emitted with little conscious thought. As the child gets older and begins production of speech sounds, language becomes increasingly more complex, requiring conscious production of sound sequences. The child must quickly move the jaw, tongue, and lips in a sequence that is coordinated with breathing patterns. Sounds are combined into words, words into phrases, phrases into sentences, and sentences into conversations to express ideas and feelings. Children with childhood apraxia of speech (CAS), a form of motor dyspraxia, have difficulty organizing the movements of the oral motor mechanism for speech production. Instead of the movements becoming automatic with the natural practice of various movement patterns, as is the case with children who show typical development, children with CAS struggle to rapidly formulate the needed sound sequences. In addition, children with CAS also may have difficulty with organization of thoughts and movements in general, thus compounding the impact on language (see Chapter 3, Section IV. Strategies for Improving Motor Planning and Coordination). Emphasis in intervention is not focused on isolated sound production (see Chapter 6, Section IV. Strategies for Improving Articulation and Phonology) but on the sequencing of sounds, or "hooking sounds together," to make words, phrases, and sentences. The following strategies, used in consultation with a team of professionals, may be helpful for children who have difficulty organizing the movements of the oral mechanism to produce speech.

Interaction Strategies

1. *Use multisensory cues.* Children with CAS have difficulty learning the sequencing of speech sounds with auditory input alone. They need multiple and multisensory cues for sound production. Sign language, touch cues (e.g., showing where to position the tongue), prompts, and picture stimuli provide cues to help children start speech and formulate the next sounds or words. These cues offer supports as children learn speech, but the cues do not replace speech. For example, the word *ball* is signed and said, and

then a physical prompt is given, such as touching the lips to indicate a *b* sound. Each of these would be faded out as the child learns the sounds, and only used as needed. For older children, use of picture sequences, for example, can facilitate the construction of longer speech productions (see also #3 in this section).

2. *Model and encourage a slower rate of speech.* Although imitation of speech alone typically is not effective, it is still important. Adults need to slow the rate of speech and model exaggerated placement of lips, tongue, and jaw. When children hold the sound positions longer, it enables them to "feel" the position of the tongue, lips, and other structures in a more pronounced way. Children who are stimulable for imitation of words progress faster in the development of language.

3. *Teach early developing and frequently occurring sounds first.* Some early-developing consonant sounds are *p, b, t, d, m, n, h,* and *w.* Identify words that use these sounds and use them in daily routines as frequently as possible.

4. *Associate visual and tactile cues with sounds.* Hand signs (not sign language) and tactile cues can be developed to prompt particular sounds. They may indicate the shape, placement, or movement of the articulators. Once children learn these signals, they can provide an anchor from which children can build sound sequences.

5. *Practice sounds and words relevant to the child's life.* Make a list of the words that are important to the child in his or her life (see #3 under Environmental Modifications in the next section). Next, select words that contain sounds that are already part of the child's sound repertoire. Then play sound games with the sounds in these words. For example, if the word *blanket* is important to the child, and the "b," "a," and hard "k" sounds are part of the child's repertoire, this would be a good word to practice. The blend *bl,* however, is hard to produce, so create a shorter, easier word for blanket; for example, *banky.* Play music and sing the tune with the "b" sounds first; then make nonsense sounds with the *b,* such as "bo" and "ba," to the rhythm of the music. Finally move to the use of the word *bank* to the rhythm of the music, while waving the child's "banky" along in time. In general, practice vowels, then consonants, then syllables of consonants and vowels, and then single-syllable words. Make sure the game is fun, not pressured, and the child achieves success before trying more words. Use the word *bank* or *banky* frequently throughout the day so the child practices the sound sequence.

6. *Teach multisyllabic words separately.* Diphthongs, consonant blends, and progressions between syllables and between words in conversation are the most difficult for children to master. These may be taught using *successive approximations*—shaping the child's productions by reinforcing each step of sound production.

7. *Wait for communication.* Let children take their time. Do not pressure them to talk quickly or become impatient and talk for them.

8. *Try to interpret what the child is saying.* Listen to the sounds produced in unintelligible sequences and assign meaning to the words or phrases. Say what you think the child meant. For instance, if the child jumbles together sounds while stacking green blocks, and you hear the sound "gee," you might say, "Yes, *green* blocks." This often prompts the child to try to repeat that word again, particularly if it *is* what the child was attempting to say.

9. *Use "carrier phrases" and "power phrases."* Once children are producing word combinations, give them ways to produce multiple sentences using a simple phrase they can attach to multiple words or situations. The *carrier phrase* allows the child to communicate many ideas more easily and, at the same time, focus solely on the production of the word at the end of the phrase. For example, "I want ____" and "Give me ____" are carrier phrases. The blank can be filled in in innumerable ways.

10. *Power phrases,* on the other hand, are complete in themselves. They can be used in multiple situations to convey a major idea. For example, "No way!" "Not now," and "What's up?" are power phrases. They can help children communicate while they are learning to produce more complex sequences.

Environmental Modifications

In addition to interpersonal strategies that may support the child using the oral mechanism for speech, environmental modifications often are useful. Depending on the findings from TPBA2, the team may want to consider some of the following environmental modifications.

1. *Encourage gestures and AAC as a bridge to verbal communication.* Gestures, personal signs (ones made up for the child), sign language, communication boards, picture schedules, and so forth are helpful, not as a replacement for verbal production but as a support for communication, while the child acquires speech production abilities. As indicated in the previous section on structural issues of the oral mechanism, lack of intelligibility can be extremely frustrating for children. Encourage the child to use alternative means to supplement speech. This reduces the stress on the child and, consequently, can actually help the child formulate speech sequences more easily. (Note: use a sign system that is matched to oral language [Signing Exact English or signed English], not a sign language system, because the goal is not for the child to learn sign language as used in the Deaf culture, but to use signs to aid oral speech.)

2. *Use universal gestures rather than signs when possible.* Use simple gestures, such as a head nod or shake, rather than a sign or symbol when possible, so that everyone can understand.

3. *Develop a list of most-needed and functional vocabulary.* Although some frequently needed vocabulary will be the same for most children (e.g., want, stop, more), cultural and family lifestyle differences will make each list unique. This list can help the adults in the child's life focus on priorities for the child's language. There is no point in working on a word that is not something the child sees and wants to talk about frequently. Because speech requires much effort and practice for the child, choose words the child will want and need to say, such as favorite foods. Include on the list

- Names of important people

- Names of daily routines

- Favorite foods

- Favorite toys

- Favorite activities

- Words for location (e.g., *in, on, under*)

- Words for requesting objects, people, and activities (e.g., *more, want, what, where, who*)

- Words for requesting actions (e.g., *help, go, do*)

- Simple words for protesting (e.g., *stop, don't*)

- Common words for describing (e.g., *big, little*)

- Questions that can be answered with a simple yes/no

- Words to initiate social interaction (e.g., *play, come, hi*)

4. *Develop a picture book of frequently used words.* Use real pictures or pictures from catalogs and magazines to make a book of the child's key words and favorite things. "Read" it together at night along with the child's regular books, with the child doing as much of the labeling as possible. Make this a sharing, comfortable time—not "therapy." This will provide an opportunity for practice of these words in a nonstressful manner.

5. *Use music and rhythm.* Singing provides fluidity for speech. The rhythm helps the child connect the sounds. Singing or chanting also provides practice in a fun way. Make up songs using favorite tunes that incorporate the child's most-needed vocabulary and sing them together; for instance, the children's song "This Is the Way We . . . " can be modified for many different actions (e.g., "open the book," "brush our teeth").

6. *Use technology, if available.* Monitor the Internet for developing technology that provides feedback on oral movements and speech production.

ROUTINES FOR THE CHILD WHO NEEDS SUPPORT TO IMPROVE THE FUNCTIONING OF THE ORAL MECHANISM

The following are examples of how the strategies discussed previously can be incorporated into the child's routines at home and at school. In addition to the strategies noted at the beginning of the chapter, used by caregivers of children who do not have special needs, these activities may support the increased proficiency in functioning of the oral mechanism.

Daily Routines (Home and Classroom)

Feeding/Eating

It is important for children with speech difficulties related to oral motor sequencing issues to have a relaxed, slow conversation about the meal, the day's events, upcoming activities, and so forth. For children with oral difficulties, talk about the day and the meal. Use emphatic mouth movements as the words are enunciated; for example, "ma*SH*ed p*O*-t*A*-t*O*es," "p*Ut* the juice away," "di*P* your chicken."

Diapering/Toileting

Diapering is an ideal time to play face-to-face games. While the child is sitting on the toilet, give him or her a favorite book and have the child "read" it to you or talk about the pictures. You also can use the child's picture book of key words, described previously. Toy catalogues are particularly popular with children and may motivate talking.

Dressing

Dressing involves a sequence of actions; therefore, talking while the child is getting dressed provides support for thinking and talking about that sequence. Dressing also can be accompanied by singing. Make up a "This is way we . . . (put on our shirt)" song. Action songs such as "Head, Shoulders, Knees, and Toes" or "This Old Man" also can be integrated into dressing, in order to practice saying body parts. Use carrier phrases such as, "Next I put on . . . " and power phrases such as, "That's done."

Going Out

Use picture sequence cards, coupons, a picture grocery list that was made with the child, or other visual supports to help the child generate words and phrases. Use a carrier phrase that the child can learn when grocery or clothing shopping, such as, "We need . . . " or power phrases such as, "What's next?" These will help the child participate in the process and initiate some comments.

Play Routines (Home and Classroom)

Face-to-Face Play

Play games with the child, such as blowing raspberries, making noises with the fingers and lips, making funny faces in a mirror, and so forth. Sing songs together and do fingerplays, such as pretending to pop corn or bubbles with the fingers while saying "pop."

Physical Play

A variety of sounds can be incorporated with physical actions. Involve the child in blowing raspberries, making environmental sounds, and so forth. Dancing to music encourages singing or just rhythmical repetition of sounds to the beat. Incorporate words the child is learning to say so that the word is being repeated to the beat of the music.

Manipulative Play

Play musical instruments with the hands (e.g., drum, tambourine, triangle) that allow the child to sing along and imitate the sounds of the instruments.

Sensory Play

Sensory play with the oral mechanism can involve blowing raspberries or playing animal sound games (e.g., making sounds of snakes, pigs, chickens).

Dramatic Play

Dramatic play can provide many opportunities for dialogue. Dramatizing stories that have been read repeatedly is a good way to help children with disabilities, because they can incorporate learned phrases from the story. For example, *Goldilocks and the Three Bears*, *The Three Billy Goats Gruff*, and *The Three Little Pigs* all have repeated lines that are emphatic, can be stated rhythmically, and are supported by gestures.

Reading and Learning Routines

Circle Time

As with one-on-one reading, reading the same book repeatedly in a group helps children learn the words, sequence, and rhythm of the book. The children can then fill in words, phrases, or lines the adult leaves out. Choose books that have repeated phrases such as *Are You My Mother?* or *Brown Bear, Brown Bear, What Do You See?* so the children anticipate what is coming and can say it together. Sing songs and do fingerplays in circle. The presence of the group takes the individual pressure off of a child. (Do not ask the child to perform alone in front of the group!) Fingerplays are an alternative form of communication that supports the use of the words in the song. Make up gestures or signs to go with the children's favorite songs.

One-on-One Book Reading

Read books with predictable patterns, rhythm, and rhymes. Books with alliteration allow practice of a particular sound. Books with onomatopoeia (i.e., words that sound like what the word means, e.g., "crunch") help the child connect production of sounds and meaning. Choose books that are simple and fun to repeat together. Read the same favorite books repeatedly, so the child can say the words simultaneously with the adult as the book is read. Use a sing-song voice when reading together to aid fluency. Also, make a book of the child's favorite words with actual photographs or pictures from magazines. Read the child's word book daily.

Science and Math

Study the mouths (or beaks) and tongues of different animals in pictures in books and on the computer. See how they use them to communicate. Bring different animals to class or go to the zoo and watch the animals make noises. Try to imitate the animals' sounds.

▬▬▬ RUBEN

Ruben is a 3-year-old who was referred for assessment due to his lack of language. Ruben demonstrated use of some vowels (e.g., ah, eh, uh) and a few consonants (e.g., m, d, b) and produced "na" when he wanted something. He exhibited a slight tongue thrust, excessive drooling, and an open-mouth posture the majority of the time. Ruben demonstrated frustration at his inability to make himself understood and whined and pointed when he wanted his mother's help. Ruben also demonstrated reduced ability to organize his play activities. His mother reported that Ruben has emotional breakdowns at least once per hour, and these tantrums appear to be getting worse as he gets older. She wants help to understand how to "get him to talk."

The team determined that Ruben has low muscle tone and difficulty imitating sounds. He needs ongoing support from a transdisciplinary team to support his learning and development. The following are ideas related to the concerns Ruben presented.

Interaction Strategies

1. *Model speaking slowly and use exaggerated mouth movements to make sounds. Emphasize and prolong those target sounds for correct production as you say them.*

2. *Begin using signs with Ruben to give him an alternative way to communicate, so he will be less frustrated as he learns to use speech. See http://www.signwithme.com to find simple signs for Ruben to use.*

3. *Ruben uses a few vowels and consonants. Work with the speech-language pathologist to identify functional words that are important in Ruben's life and that include these sounds. It is important to keep in mind the vowels and consonants in his current sound repertoire and Ruben's ability to produce the sounds in different words. For instance, "dog," "mom," and "ball" might be possibilities. Start with the target words and add to his repertoire. It is important to focus on words that are functional.*

4. *Ruben loves music. Sing songs with the names of family members, favorite toys, and so forth. The team will help generate ideas.*

Environmental Modifications

1. *Ruben is unaware of his drooling and has reduced sensitivity around his mouth. He needs to develop increased sensitivity around his mouth and to learn to close his lips, swallow, and make frontal sounds. Tips to help him with this include*

   • *Use a touch cue to Ruben's chin to remind him to close his mouth; then fade the cue to your chin to remind him.*

   • *Use a touch cue under Ruben's chin to remind him to swallow, then fade the cue to yourself. The speech-language pathologist will help you think of other touch cues for Ruben.*

2. *Develop hand signs and/or touch cues to show Ruben the shape of the mouth, the placement of the tongue, or what the sounds does. The speech-language pathologist will assist with this.*

3. *Develop "Ruben's Word Book" with pictures of objects, people, and actions in Ruben's environment. Start with pictures of words that contain the sounds Ruben uses already. Talk about the book and pictures every day at a nice, quiet time for interaction. Use rhythmic reading and emphasize sounds within words to encourage imitation.*

KEYS TO INTERVENTION BY DEVELOPMENTAL AGE

The following ideas are directed toward children who are functioning at approximately the following levels. The suggestions are not meant to be all-inclusive, but rather are indicative of potential areas for exploration. It should be noted that oral motor problems first may be identified for some young children who present with structural or functional problems due to motor control or tone issues or other neurological concerns.

Developmental age	Oral abilities	Key to intervention
Birth to 3 months	Imitates tongue and mouth movements. Produces sounds in the back of mouth (2 months). Deferred imitation of facial movements. Brings hand to mouth. Takes object to mouth (3 months). Sucks on hand and fingers. Produces little saliva.	Play face-to-face games with mouth movements and vowel sounds. Encourage oral exploration of objects and hands.
3–6 months	Attempts imitation of sounds (4 months). Produces vowel "ah." Plays with sounds and patterns of sound (5 months). Makes consonant sounds (e.g., *p, b, n, k, g*). Often puts objects in mouth (6 months). Makes different vowel sounds (e.g., *ah, eh, ee, oo*) and early consonant sounds (e.g., *b, m, g*). Makes raspberries.	Play face-to-face games, making noises with lips and tongue. Imitate the sounds the infant makes.
6–9 months	Has control of saliva in all positions unless feeding, actively playing with objects, or teething. Produces consonant–vowel (CV) syllables (e.g., *ba*) (7 months). Produces syllable chains (e.g., *babababababa*) (8 months). Imitates speech sounds (9 months).	Sing tunes with just one syllable or sound emphasized (e.g., *ba-ba-ba*). Say words with frontal sounds slowly (e.g., *ma-ma; da-da; ball*) and let child watch your mouth. Pay attention to positioning for appropriate head and neck support.
9–12 months	Less drooling occurs during mealtime. Produces first word (12 months). Articulation may be understood by familiar listener. Produces a variety of consonants and vowels approximations during babbling.	Use simple one- and two-word phrases so the child hears the words separately. Prolong and emphasize sounds. Read books with animal sounds and other environmental sounds.

(continued on next page)

(continued from previous page)

Developmental age	Oral abilities	Key to intervention
12–18 months	Drooling may occur during teething and some fine motor tasks. Produces early consonants: *b, m, n, t, d, w.* Says "muh" for *milk.* Imitates sounds and words (18 months). Omits most final consonants in words. Omits some initial consonants in words. Produces sentence-like intonation.	Use books with simple words and phrases that contain early sounds. Introduce the child's word book, and add pictures as the child adds words. Sing songs with repetitive patterns.
18–24 months	Produces speech that is less than 50% intelligible to unfamiliar listeners (21 months). Inconsistently deletes final consonants in words. Approximately 50% intelligible (24 months). Produces consonant–vowel–consonant (CVC) structures (e.g., "mo mick"/*more milk*) using early consonant sounds: *p, b, m, n, t, d, h, w.*	Signs of motor planning difficulties may begin to be seen when the child has difficulty imitating sounds and words. Begin to use physical prompts and touch cues to assist sound formation. Use gestures and common signs to aid communication.
24–36 months	Drooling should not be present. Speech is 50%-70% intelligible to familiar listeners (30 months). Deletes one consonant from a consonant blend (e.g., "_top"/*stop*). Repeats syllables in words (e.g., "wawa"/*water*). Simplifies words that are multisyllabic (36 months). Substitution and distortion of consonants still present. Speech is 70% intelligible. Produces sounds made in the back of the mouth (e.g., *c,* car; *g,* go; *-ing,* eating).	Listen to the child's sounds and find words in his or her environment that use those sounds. Add these words to the child's picture book. Add signs and picture sequence cues for aiding the child. Using dancing and singing to put sounds and words to rhythm. Use books with sounds included in the story. Do simple songs and fingerplays.
36–48 months	Speech is intelligible to unfamiliar listeners (42 months). Produces the consonants *l, f, s,* and *y* in some positions of words. Speech is approximately 80% intelligible (48 months). Produces faster speech. Produces a few consonant substitutions and omissions. Consonant blends may still not be completely present with all consonants. Produces more consonants: *z, v, sh, ch, j.*	Do dramatic play activities involving mouth actions and words that are part of the child's sound repertoire (e.g., birthday party). Do group games with repetition of words and actions (e.g., "Duck, Duck, Goose"). Use augmentative communication individualized for the child's abilities. Say names of letters and sounds the child makes. Talk about the day's events to encourage production of sequences of sentences. Omit words and phrases from favorite books and songs and let the child fill them in.
48–60 months	Produces most consonants accurately in all positions. Speech is intelligible to unfamiliar listeners.	Write letters and say sounds for familiar words from the child's word book. This will provide an added visual cue to match the auditory output. Involve the child in storytelling to develop narrative skills. Let the child make up words or sentences in the story. Make up songs to go with the stories. Read poems for children with rhymes and rhythm. Learn simple ones by heart. Incorporate props and language from favorite books into dramatic play to encourage reproduction of the language and story sequence.
60–72 months	Produces all sounds in all positions by age 7.	Have the child generate words he or she wants to learn to write. Then write down these words and let the child copy them with magnetic letters, stamp letters, writing, or other means. Have the child read the words back to you. Use language and storyboards, puppets, and flannel board stories. Develop dramatic play with scripts based on storybooks.

6
Facilitating Communication Development

VII.   Strategies for Improving Hearing and Communication

with Jan Christian Hafer

Goal Attainment Scale

1	2	3	4	5	6	7	8	9
Not aware or only minimally aware of sounds in the environment.		Distinguishes that one sound is different from another with or without adaptive support.		Differentiates environmental and some speech sounds with or without adaptive support.		Inconsistently responds to sounds and spoken language with or without adaptive supports.		Attends to and localizes to sounds and speech, and uses hearing functionally in conversation with or without adaptive support.

Hearing involves sound waves being conducted through the hearing mechanisms of the ear and nervous system to various areas of the brain, where neurological signals are registered and then interpreted for meaning. Once the meaning is understood, the child can respond appropriately to the situation.

A *decibel* (dB) is the unit used to measure sound intensity. The softest sound a typical person hears is designated as 0 dB. The sound of a jet is about 120 dB. Normal hearing for children involves a range from 0 dB to 25 dB. The speed of the vibration that causes the sound is measured in a unit called the *hertz* (Hz), resulting in what we call the *pitch* of the sound. The human ear can respond to vibrations between 20 and 20,000 Hz, with most speech sounds occurring between 250 and 8,000 Hz.

Note: In this section, "deaf" with small "d" is used to refer to an audiological status, whereas "Deaf" with a capital "D" is used in reference to the linguistic minority that makes up the Deaf community, shares Deaf culture, and is composed of individuals who identify themselves as Deaf people (Marschark & Spencer, 2003).

For more information about language and communication approaches used by people who are deaf and hard of hearing, go to the Laurent Clerc National Deaf Education Center of Gallaudet University, http://clerccenter.gallaudet.edu/infotogo/index.html

Although hearing is just one of many important senses, typical hearing enables the child to acquire meaning more easily from his or her environment (e.g., *I hear a siren; there must be a fire*), understand relationships between sounds and other characteristics of situations (e.g., the movement of the trees and the sound of the wind), and participate more fully in communication (e.g., hearing the nuances of affect in a person's voice). Of course, one of the most valuable aspects of normal hearing is that one can hear speech sounds and then learn to produce and combine these sounds to make words that are understood by others. Hearing, in combination with other skills, helps children learn to speak. All speech sounds are louder than the softest sounds that children can hear, ensuring that they will be able to hear the sounds that are part of their language. Typically, by 1 year of age, children are producing sounds with the intent of conveying meaning. Without normal hearing, children's language development, and consequently their social interactions, may be negatively affected.

Hearing also helps children learn to listen. Listening encourages understanding. Listening to others' thoughts, to books being read, to the nuances of music, and to the sounds of nature provide some of life's greatest pleasures. Helping children learn to listen can enrich their learning and their lives.

Being able to hear helps us participate more safely and fully in all aspects of life. It gives us information about where we are in relation to other people and things in the environment (e.g., where things are, how far away they are, and their direction in relation to us). Hearing enables us to understand the cause-and-effect relationship between sounds and actions (e.g., when the doorbell rings, someone is at the door). Hearing also serves a regulatory function. When we hear threatening sounds, we alert and prepare to respond defensively. When we hear comforting sounds, we calm. Sounds also can arouse us to positive actions, causing us to pay attention or inciting us to dance or sing.

APPROPRIATE HEARING CHARACTERISTICS

Children should be able to hear a full range of different types of sounds, from low pitch to high pitch and from loud to soft sounds, in both ears. They should be able to listen, isolate the source of sounds, and attach meaning to sounds so they know how to respond.

Babies will quiet and react positively to familiar soothing sounds. They will startle to loud noises or cry when alarmed by an unusual sound. They want to know the source of different sounds, which causes them to begin to explore their environment, first visually and later physically. As babies experiment with sounds and the feel of making sounds, they also begin to pay attention to the sounds other people make and start to try to imitate the sounds they hear. Sound combinations that are heard repeatedly and are always associated with the same object come to be known by those sound patterns, or "words" (e.g., *bottle, blanket, Daddy*). Hearing their own names repeatedly when others call them helps children learn they have their own special identity. Soon, children understand the words for many objects, actions, people, and events. They begin to produce these words by imitating the sound patterns they hear. Speech evolves quickly once the child is able to imitate sound sequences and associate words with their referent, thus increasing their vocabulary.

At the same time that children are learning to make sense of speech sounds, they also are learning to make sense of other environmental sounds. Animal noises, mechanical noises, sounds of nature, and many other sounds come to acquire meaning as children hear them and adults help explore their meaning. As language increases, children will begin to ask questions about sounds (e.g., "What is that noise?" "How does the frog make that sound?"). Such questioning leads to greater investigation of sounds and understanding of the characteristics and relationships of objects and events in the environment.

As children learn to read, they also experiment with the various sounds of language as they appear in print. The rhythms of reading are different from those of everyday speech. Hearing others read helps children learn reading strategies.

Appropriate Hearing in Practice

▬▬▬ VII. A. Child's ability to hear voices and sounds

Daily Routines (Home and Classroom)

- *Infant/toddler:* The infant quiets when mother talks softly to her. The toddler hears his mother call him to come eat lunch, and he goes to the kitchen.

- *Young child:* At lunch the teacher asks, "Who wants to be first to wash hands?" and Miranda raises her hand.

Play Routines (Home and Classroom)

- *Infant/toddler:* A bell sounds when the child pushes a lever on the toy. She pushes it again to make the sound recur. The toddler punches the buttons on the toy phone to make the ringing sound, and then she says, "Hello."

- *Young child:* During dramatic play, the child activates the toy cash register, but no sound occurs. She takes it to the teacher and says, "It's broken."

Classroom Routines

The children are studying transportation. They are sitting in a circle. As the teacher plays the sounds of different vehicles, the children try to guess which vehicle sound matches the pictures of various vehicles.

▬▬▬ VII. B. Tracking of sounds to their sources

Daily Routines (Home and Classroom)

- *Infant/toddler:* Father turns on the music box, and the baby turns to look. The toddler hears a dog barking outside and goes to the window to look.

- *Young child:* At rest time, two children are whispering. Joshua sits up, looks toward them, and puts his finger to his lips, saying, "Shhh."

Play Routines (Home and Classroom)

- *Infant/toddler:* The infant hears a tinkling sound and shakes the ball to see if it happens again. The toddler recognizes the sound of the toy fire truck and goes to find out who is playing with it.

- *Young child:* The children are playing "picnic." The child puts pretend hot dogs on the grill, turns the switch on the toy barbecue, and when it makes a sizzling noise, he says, "Now it is cooking."

Classroom Routines

The children are playing a Hide-and-Seek game in the floor play center. Four children hide their eyes while the teacher hides the tape recorder that is making vehicle sounds. They then try to identify and find the sound.

▨▨▨▨ VII. C. Meaningful response to sounds or words

Daily Routines (Home and Classroom)

- *Infant/toddler:* The infant hears the bedroom door open and starts to bounce and squeal. The toddler hears the doorbell ring and goes to the door.

- *Young child:* On the playground, Marie hears a child crying and runs to help her.

Play Routines (Home and Classroom)

- *Infant/toddler:* When the dog barks at the pop-up toy, the infant looks at the dog and starts to cry. The toddler hears the phone ring and runs to pick it up.

- *Young child:* While playing house, one child is playing "Mommy" and the other is playing "Daddy." Mommy puts the doll in the crib and says, "Shhh." Daddy then starts to whisper and walk on his tiptoes around the play area.

Classroom Routines

When a loud crash occurs in the block area and a child starts to cry, Michael drops his toy and runs to see what happened.

▨▨▨▨ VII. D. Immediate response to sounds

Daily Routines (Home and Classroom)

- *Infant/toddler:* When the child reaches toward the hot cup of coffee, his mother says sharply, "No, no. It's hot. Burn." The child withdraws his hand. The toddler hears the sound of the tea kettle whistling and runs to his mother, points to the stove, and says, "All done, Mommy."

- *Young child:* The bell rings for "cleanup time" and the young child immediately starts picking up his blocks.

Play Routines (Home and Classroom)

- *Infant/toddler:* Mommy says, "Where's Keesha?" The infant immediately holds her blanket up in front of her face. The toddler and her Mommy are dressing her doll. Mommy says, "She needs shoes," and the child immediately picks up a shoe.

- *Young child:* On the playground, children are riding tricycles around the path. Alex is standing on the path facing away from the traffic. A child on an oncoming tricycle pushes his bell and shouts, "Move, Alex!" Alex jumps out of the way.

Classroom Routines

When the fire alarm goes off during center time, the children immediately stop what they are doing and go line up at the door.

▨▨▨▨ VII. E. Accurate imitation of sounds

Daily Routines (Home and Classroom)

- *Infant/toddler:* Mother is dressing the baby. She says, "Say, 'Ma-ma.'" The infant replies, "Ma-ma." Dad is reading the toddler a book. He says, "The cow says, 'moo.'" The toddler responds by saying, "Moo."

- *Young child:* The teacher introduces a new song, and Charlie repeats each line after the teacher sings it.

Play Routines (Home and Classroom)

- *Infant/toddler:* Mommy pops out from behind the blanket and says "Boo!" Keesha says, "Boo!" and laughs. The toddler pushes the button on the toy chicken. It says, "Cheep, cheep," with a high-pitched sound. The toddler says, "Eep! Eep!"

- *Young child:* The children are playing house and the Daddy scribbles on a piece of paper and hands it to the Mommy, saying, "We are out of bread and peanut butter. Here is your list. Go to the store." She takes the list and says, "Okay, bread and peanut butter."

Classroom Routines

In the literacy area, Josie is telling the teacher the words she wants to write about her favorite things. The teacher is helping her sound out the words and figure out what letters she needs to write. Josie wants to write her favorite color, blue. She imitates the teacher making the sound "b," then thinks and asks, "B?"

GENERAL PRINCIPLES FOR SUPPORTING HEARING

Adults are interested in children learning to listen to what is being said, imitate sounds and words, follow directions, and comply with requests. Adults also naturally use visual supports to help them get their messages across. They typically do not consciously practice listening or looking skills, but rather naturally incorporate activities that require listening/watching. The following are strategies that adults naturally use. Many conventional strategies involve the combination of auditory and visual strategies. The following often are incorporated into communication with children with normal hearing, but most are appropriate for children who are deaf or hard of hearing as well, with the use of visual aspects emphasized.

Shared Mutual Regard and Joint Referencing

Parents naturally seek to engage the child in eye contact and face-to-face interaction. They do so during feeding, talking, and playful interactions. Caregivers play games with noises, facial expressions, and songs. Adults capture the child's attention, exchange communication, and direct the child's attention to things of interest or importance. Joint referencing, or regarding the same objects or events, leads to sharing a common topic for communication. The early infant–parent relationship, based on both meeting the child's needs and mutual enjoyment, builds the foundation for the child to look to the adult for nurturance, guidance, and information.

Point Out Sounds in the Environment

Parents help children to notice sounds in the environment. When a noise occurs, they often show a surprised expression and point to the object or person making the noise.

Vary Pitch and Loudness of Sounds

Children are naturally exposed to varying pitches and volumes of sound. For example, adults use different pitches of voice for different purposes. They talk in a higher voice when they are trying to get the infant's attention and a lower voice when emphasizing something. They talk softly when they want to quiet the child and loudly when they want to ensure that the child hears. They also change the rhythm of speech when talking in order to emphasize different aspects of what they are saying. Adults also introduce sounds of different pitch and loudness. For example, they may play a soft, slow melody for quiet times and faster, louder music for arousal. A musical toy may play a high-pitched tune, whereas a toy drum may make a lower sound.

Demonstrate and Model

Parents and other adults demonstrate and model many different kinds of sounds for children. They make sounds with their mouths, such as making raspberries with their lips. Adults enunciate the sounds of words so children can see the shape of the lips as well as hear the sound being made. This makes it easier for children to imitate adults. They also demonstrate sound-making mechanisms such as switches, buttons, levers, and squeeze toys. As children imitate the adults' actions, they produce the sound themselves. This creates a sense of power and control in children that leads to repetition of the actions and creates memory for the relationship between the action and the resulting sound.

Exaggerate Sounds

Adults also exaggerate sounds, syllables, and words to emphasize what they want children to hear. For example, the adult may say, "*BRRR*. It's cold," "Give it to *MOM*my," "*NO*. Don't put it in your mouth," or "*UP* you go!" The emphasis on the specific sounds helps the child focus on the important sounds or words. Such exaggeration also helps prompt imitation.

Explain Meanings of Sounds

Children begin to attach meaning to sounds as they see the source of the sound. They see the rattle and hear the sound and relate the two. They hear a voice and see the parent's mouth move and relate the two. As the infant develops understanding of language, adults use language to explain what sounds mean. When the toy spinner rotates toward the picture of an animal and makes that animal's sound, the parent points to the picture and says, "Duck. The duck says, 'Quack, quack'!" When the wind howls outside, the parent says, "That's the wind blowing through the trees." The adult also clarifies sounds for the child. When the child hears a bird tweet and says, "Duck," the parent says, "That's not a duck. It's a robin. It's a different kind of bird." As children get older, adults discuss various types of sounds: human sounds, animal sounds, mechanical sounds, and sounds of nature. Over time, children learn to distinguish these sounds and predict related or resulting events. For example, they will hear thunder and predict it is going to rain.

Request Sound Imitation

As children begin to put sounds together, adults begin to request imitation. They prompt children to make certain sounds or words. They first imitate a child's own vowel sounds, prompting the child to repeat the sounds. They then prompt imitation of consonants, reduplicated sounds such as "mama" and "dada" (which, of course, parents attribute to naming themselves!), and finally words. By slowly modeling lip and tongue movements, the child sees how sounds are produced. Adults love to hear the child produce spontaneous sounds, but when the child begins to imitate adults' sounds on request, they know that language is emerging. Adults reinforce imitation, and success leads to more modeling, resulting in an ever-increasing cycle of speech and language learning.

As children begin to produce words with multiple syllables and have difficulty with pronunciation of blends, adults slow down their speech and break down words children cannot produce into syllables. This helps children hear the individual sounds within the words. Again, adults visually model how the sounds are produced. Later, adults help children relate the different sounds or spoken words to the sounds represented in written symbols.

Request Repetition of Words

As vocabulary grows, adults present new words, define them, and often ask for repetition so they can hear children pronounce the words accurately. For example, Dad may say, "We are having spaghetti for lunch." Adam looks at Dad with a questioning expression. Dad says, "Spaghetti. Like noodles" and shows Adam a strand of spaghetti. Adam says, "Ba-ske-tee." Dad gets down in front of Adam's face, "Say, 'spa-GET-ee.'"

THE PRINCIPLES IN PRACTICE

Adults in a child's life use different strategies throughout the day. Their goal is to encourage listening (with eyes as well as ears), understanding, and language. Presented next are examples of how caregivers use the previously discussed strategies during the day both at home and at school. These examples are approaches that most caregivers use naturally in their daily interactions with children. These strategies are appropriate for most children with disabilities as well.

Daily Routines (Home and Classroom)

Feeding/Eating

The parent makes noises associated with enjoyment and pleasure in eating, such as smacking the lips or saying, "Mmm" or "Yum, yum." Older children may listen to the "snap, crackle, and pop" of cereal or become intrigued by the sound of the spoon stirring in the bowl.

Diapering/Toileting

There are many sounds associated with elimination! Early sounds include the comments of the parents as diapers are changed (not always pleasurable!). As the child begins toilet training, the adult often encourages progress by listening for the sounds of "tinkling" or "plunking." The ability to cause the toilet to flush is a big reward.

Dressing

While dressing and undressing, adults point out the sounds of zippers and opening Velcro and name the body parts and pieces of clothing that are worn.

Play Routines (Home and Classroom)

Face-to-Face Play

Face-to-face play almost always involves sounds. It may include noises, singing, words, or sounds of surprise or glee. Adults use this type of play to model turn taking with sounds and actions. Whether the adult is humming while pulling the child back-and-forth, or singing, "Row, Row, Row Your Boat," the child listens and engages in physical and vocal imitation.

Physical Play

Physical play often involves tickling, wrestling, or chasing, all of which elicit giggles and laughter. Just as adults initiate this play to hear these joyful sounds emanating from children, children begin to reciprocate in order to elicit the same sounds from their caregivers, siblings, or peers.

Manipulative Play

Many toys involve sounds. Infant cause-and-effect toys often include sounds that encourage children to investigate and initiate the actions needed to produce the sounds. Adults seek out these toys and then model how they are used. They comment on the sounds and encourage imitation. Even toys that are not meant to emit a sound often are used in play to produce sound. Children, for instance, love to stack blocks and knock them down to hear the crash of the blocks. They like to crash cars and make car noises. When toy animals are brought out, children like to make animal sounds. In dramatic play, children imitate the sounds they hear in their own lives. Adults encourage listening by showing, modeling, prompting, and reacting when the child responds.

Sensory Play

Messy play involves the noises of squirting, squishing, squeezing, popping, and other intense actions. Adults comment on sounds (e.g., "Listen, out comes the shaving cream!"), use sounds (e.g., "Let's get the bubbles! Pop! Pop!"), and encourage the child to make sounds (e.g., "Make your fingers go 'zooop!' through the fingerpaint").

Reading and Learning Routines

Circle Time

Circle time is an opportunity for teachers to share ideas with a group of children. Teachers may use this time to play listening games, share stories, talk about a topic such as animals of the forest, or investigate aspects of the environment. Certainly, circle time typically involves listening and following directions, but it also can involve sharing perceptions related to meanings, including those of sounds.

One-on-One Book Reading

When adults read to children, they model the articulation of words, the rhythms of reading, the sound effects in stories, the changes of voices of characters, and the intonation of feelings. This is important for children's own natural language as well as their emerging literacy skills.

Science and Math

Comparing and classifying aspects of nature is part of science and math. For toddlers, this may mean investigating animal sounds, and for young children, other sounds of nature such as falling rain, cracking ice, or sucking mud sounds.

PLANNING INDIVIDUALIZED
INTERVENTIONS FOR IMPROVING HEARING

▰▰▰ **VII. A. What behaviors indicate that the child hears voices and sounds?**

As noted previously, children can have difficulty hearing all sounds or just certain sounds. Children who have difficulty hearing sounds rely on the environment (including people in their environment) to provide auditory input at the pitch and loudness that they can hear, visual cues to aid understanding, face-to-face interaction to support lipreading, or object-to-face engagement to facilitate tactile (vibratory) input. Children also need to learn to listen carefully in order to take advantage of the hearing they do have. Listening skills are important for all children, but they are especially important for children with hearing loss who can benefit from technical support (e.g., hearing aids, cochlear implants) in this area. Careful evaluation is important to determine how much and what kind of interactional and environmental supports are needed. For some children, cochlear implants, hearing aids, or other augmentative devices may be useful.

Children who are deaf or hard of hearing may increase their ability to listen and hear various sounds through the use of technology or training. Experts disagree about the best communication approach to use with children who are deaf or hard of hearing, and this also includes the debate about whether amplification should be used.

Two out of the three most widely used approaches to teaching communication to children who are deaf or hard of hearing incorporate improving listening as an important component. The primary communication alternatives include 1) an auditory-oral approach, one that emphasizes developing the child's residual hearing abilities and developing oral speech; 2) a total communication approach, incorporating all modes of communication including hearing, speech, lipreading, facial expression, gesture, sign involving a manual form of English, and fingerspelling; and 3) a bilingual approach, which emphasizes teaching American Sign Language (ASL; a visual gestural language with its own grammar and syntax) as the primary language and English as the second language. ASL is taught through reading, writing, and spoken language in varying degrees, depending on the child's abilities and needs. Another approach that is not used as widely is Cued Speech. Cued Speech is a system used to assist in clarifying speechreading information for a child. Hand-based cues are provided to help a child differentiate the various phonemes of speech that look similar on the lips. This approach aids comprehension of spoken language but does not necessarily assist the development of expressive language. For all of these approaches, spoken language instruction (i.e., speech therapy) and amplification are optional and may be helpful. Discussion of the advantages and disadvantages of these approaches is beyond the scope of this chapter (see the web site for the Laurent Clerc National Deaf Education Center of Gallaudet University, http://clerccenter.gallaudet.edu/infotogo/index.html). Studies on these approaches have not revealed any one to be appropriate for all children with hearing loss (Carney & Moeller, 1998; Erting, 2003; PARA, 2007). The degree of hearing loss, whether parents are hearing or deaf, the values of the family, other disabilities that may have an impact on the child's skills, and available resources are all important considerations when selecting a communication approach (Rushmer, 2003).

The ability to hear and make sense of sounds requires focused listening. Most children with hearing loss have some residual hearing that can be enhanced through technology or training. Regardless of the communication approach used, important adults in a child's life can implement strategies such as those suggested here to increase the child's attention to and ability to discriminate speech sounds as well as sounds in the environment.

Visual communication reinforces auditory learning, and it is particularly important for children who are deaf or hard of hearing. Although there are children who are both deaf and have visual impairment, most children with hearing problems can use their vision to supplement their understanding of what they can hear, or, if they cannot hear, they can replace auditory with visual forms of meaning. For this reason, it is important to understand how children typically use visual strategies.

Interaction Strategies

1. *Speak near the infant's ear.* This helps the infant discriminate speech from other environmental sounds. This is particularly important if the infant has a slight hearing loss or middle ear infection.

2. *Bring attention to sounds.* Children who are hard of hearing may not notice all of the sounds in their environment. Adults can point out noises by saying, "Listen" and pointing to their ears, "The phone is ringing." They also may point to something that is making a sound and emphasize the noise: "Look, Samantha, a bird is singing."

3. *Gain the child's attention before speaking.* Children will be more attuned to the sounds and words that are being produced if they are looking at the face that is communicating to them. Get the child's attention by tapping her on the shoulder or gesturing to get her attention. Once the child is looking at the speaker, maintain direct face-to-face contact. This will enable the child to see the way sounds are formed, read facial expressions, and focus on listening to the message. (In the auditory-oral approach, observing lip movements may be discouraged so the child can focus on the sounds.)

4. *Speak at a regular volume.* It is important that children learn to use their remaining hearing. Speaking at a regular volume will encourage listening, but use simple sentences and do not speak too quickly.

5. *Use the pitch that is easiest for the child to hear.* Some children hear better at a certain pitch. Infants normally tune in to higher pitch, and adults naturally use a higher pitch when they address an infant. Once the child's hearing is evaluated, adults will have an idea of the types of sounds the child will be better able to hear. Toys can be selected that incorporate appropriate pitch and loudness, and adults can modulate their voices.

6. *Use acoustic highlighting techniques.* Use sentences that are rich in intonation, melody, and expression. Children are better able to pick up on sounds when there is variation in intonation and a rhythmic cadence. Varying the typical sentence pattern to include more of a singsong rhythm can make children want to listen. Use occasional whispering to encourage listening, and emphasize varying elements of syntax to highlight important aspects of words or phrases.

7. *Encourage listening to one's own voice.* Children like to hear their own voices. Adults can reinforce children's noise making and talking by commenting, "I hear you talking!" "You have such a pretty voice, sing some more!" This encourages both verbal production and practice in listening, as well as the vocal turn taking necessary for conversation.

8. *Pair sounds with meaning.* Children like to know what sounds they are hearing. Help children understand what is making sounds by demonstrating (e.g., animal sounds), pointing out environmental sounds (e.g., the flushing toilet), and having children produce the sound (e.g., pushing the "on" button on the clothes dryer). After repeated exposure to such pairings, children begin to attach meaning to the sounds they hear.

9. *Play listening games.* Help children learn to listen for and discriminate sounds by playing games involving sounds. After the child has seen an object and event paired several times (see item #8), try having the child identify sounds without the visual referent. For example, play the sound of a drum, a horn, or a guitar (on tape or while the child is blindfolded or turned away). The child can point to the picture of what was heard, gesture, sign, or say the word. This is the "I hear a _____" game, and letting the child choose sounds for the adult to guess as well makes it more fun.

10. *Follow the child's lead.* All children are more likely to listen to something that is of interest to them. Pay attention to those things toward which the child looks, items with which he or she plays, events about which concern is displayed, and so forth. Help the child identify sounds associated with things of interest.

11. *Incorporate listening to key sounds.* Six sounds, representing low-, medium-, and high-frequency sounds found in spoken language, often are incorporated into a "test" of hearing; they are "ah" (as in *father*), "oo" (as in *moon*), "ee" (as in *key*), "sh" (as in *shoe*), "s" (as in *sock*), and "m" (as in *mommy*) (Ling, 2003). If the child can respond to these sounds (with or without listening devices), he or she should be able to hear the sounds of human speech.

Environmental Modifications

In addition to interpersonal strategies that may support improving the child's listening, environmental modifications often are useful. Depending on the findings from TPBA2, the team may want to consider some of the following environmental modifications.

1. *Sit on the side of the child's better-hearing ear (within earshot).* If the child has a cochlear implant or wears a hearing aid, move closer to the microphone or hearing device.

2. *Provide a clear line of sight to people and objects making sounds.* Children will be better able to understand what they hear if they see the facial expressions and lip movements of the speaker. For children in a group, sitting in a circle allows the child who is deaf or hard of hearing to see everyone.

3. *Reduce background or conflicting noise.* Turn off the television, radio, or stereo and reduce other background sounds such as fans, so the child can focus on spoken language. Shut windows or doors to reduce street noise or sounds from other rooms. Speech must be at least 30–40 dB louder than the background sounds in order for the child to be able to attend to it. Draperies, carpeting, upholstery, and acoustical tile can all help absorb background noise.

4. *In the preschool classroom, lower visual barriers such as bookshelves.* As noted previously, it is important for children to have face-to-face communication; thus, dividers in a classroom should be low so children can see over them and sound is not obstructed.

5. *Before giving auditory input, give a visual warning to alert the child to listen.* Use a visual signal such as a gesture or, in the classroom, a flicker of the lights to bring the child's attention to the speaker.

6. *Practice listening to environmental sounds.* Make a listening game out of everyday sounds by trying to identify sounds in the house and outdoors. For example, try to identify running water, the doorbell, the washing machine, or the dishwasher in the house. Outdoors, listen for birds or other animals, the sound of a river, cars or buses, and so forth.

7. *Record voices and sounds.* Make a recording of the child's vocalizations or talking and play it back to him or her. This will stimulate infants to imitate the sounds they hear and older children to comment on what they hear.

8. *Use sound-producing devices with a pitch and loudness that increase the potential for being heard.* Use toys that produce sounds that the child can hear as well as sounds that challenge the child to listen.

9. *Use technology to improve hearing.* Use state-of-the-art technology to amplify sounds and maximize residual hearing. A frequency modulated, or FM, system with a microphone and wireless transmitter worn by the speaker and a transmitter worn by the listener can help the child hear when he or she is not close to the speaker; it also can reduce the background noise the child hears in a classroom. External hearing aids or cochlear implants, which require surgery, also are options. Numerous types of hearing aids exist, and a specialist should be consulted to help the family identify the best individualized option for their child. Make sure all devices are monitored and kept in working condition.

VII. B. Does the child look or turn to the source of sound?

Sound localization is the child's ability to identify the source or origin of a sound. It requires comparing sounds through the two ears and filtering the sounds through the external body and ear structures. The ability to localize sound may be negatively influenced by hearing loss in one or both ears or by physical abnormalities that affect the filtering of sound. Hearing aids improve hearing but not sound localization. The child may be able to hear the approaching car but does not know from which direction it is coming. Sound localization is important for safety and for everyday functioning. Anyone who has ever tried to find a ringing cell phone can attest to the importance of sound localization for everyday routines!

Interaction Strategies

1. *Speak immediately after a visual, vocal, or tactile cue.* Once the child has had a cue to look to the speaker, it should be followed immediately by a vocal communication. For example, if the parent calls the child's name and the child turns to look, the parent should respond immediately with a comment.

2. *Pair visual regard of a sound-making toy or object with a sound from that object.* For example, if the child hears the sound of a musical toy and looks in the direction of the toy, repeat the sound of the toy and comment, "Yes. It makes music!"

3. *Play "find the sound" games.* Use noise-making objects and make a game out of searching for the sound. Start with sounds that are close and fairly loud, such as shaking a tin of beans under a table. Ask, "Do you hear that? Where is it?" Once the child starts to understand the listen-and-search sequence, try noises of different loudness and timbre, such as a whirling birthday noisemaker, a sack of rice, or other varied sounds. When the child can easily locate closely placed sounds, record various sounds on a tape recorder and hide it in different spots around the room for the child to find it.

4. *Provide cues.* Whenever an unexpected noise is made in the environment, say, "Listen, I hear a . . . " and look toward the sound. Have the child watch you approach the sound (e.g., a kitchen timer) or show the child the cause of the sound if possible (e.g., the neighbor's lawnmower). This will encourage the child to look for the causes of sounds.

5. *Search together, following the child's lead.* When a repeated or recurrent noise is heard that allows time for a search, talk about the sound and search for it together; for example, "I hear a siren. Let's look for a fire truck" or "I hear the phone ringing; let's go answer it." Go where the child points or directs until the sound is located.

6. *Allow wait time for the child to process auditory information.* The child may take more time to take in auditory input and interpret the meaning and location of the sounds. Wait for the child to respond before directing his or her attention.

Environmental Modifications

In addition to interpersonal strategies that may support the child looking for the source of sound, environmental modifications often are useful. Depending on the findings from TPBA2, the team may want to consider some of the following environmental modifications.

1. *Noises are easier to locate when they are on the side of the better hearing ear.* When playing listening games, make noises or place sound-making objects first on the child's "best listening" side.

2. *Sounds are easier to locate when they are closer than when they are farther away.* Start identification games in close proximity to the child and gradually move the sound-making objects to more distant locations.

3. *Pay attention to the sounds in the environment.* Most people ignore many of the background noises in the environment. This is a good thing, because it allows us to focus on the important sounds we need to hear. Help the child learn to focus by eliminating all but two or three sounds; for instance, the television and the dishwasher. Play "hide at this sound" and take turns telling the other person which sound to go to, then count to 10 and go see if the person is waiting at the right place.

4. *Help the child follow a conversation.* When a conversation is taking place between other people, use a gestural cue, pointing to who is talking to help the child follow the vocal interchange between speakers.

▨▨▨▨▨ VII. C. Does the child respond meaningfully to sounds or words?

Children not only have to hear sounds, they also need to attach meaning to those sounds so that they can respond appropriately. Children who are hard of hearing, have auditory processing problems, or have attention deficits may find it difficult to associate accurate meaning to the sounds they hear. Accurate understanding is demonstrated by an appropriate response to the sounds heard. Children who do not respond appropriately may ignore the sounds (e.g., keep doing what they were doing before the communication or sound); have an approximate but incorrect response (e.g., the adult says, "Give me your hand" and the child gives the adult his hat); or have a totally incorrect response (e.g., the child hears a timer go off and goes to answer the door). Depending on the child's concerns (e.g., hearing versus auditory processing issues), the following suggested strategies might be helpful.

Interaction Strategies

1. *Talk about what is important to the child, what interests him or her, or what concerns the child.* Read the child's cues related to sounds. Look for facial expressions following a sound, such as a curious look or a vocalization that rises in intonation, indicating a question; a look of surprise shown by the raising of eyebrows; or a look of distress demonstrated by a furrowed brow. Then use concrete means to explain or demonstrate

the meaning of the sound. Of course, there are times when the adult needs to direct the child's attention, but following the child's lead will teach the child that the adult can provide interesting information.

2. *Reword to help the child understand.* When faced with complicated sounds, words, or sentences, the child may need to hear an alternative as an aid in understanding. For example, another word can be substituted; a simile or definition of a word can be given; a sentence can be reworded; or the word, phrase, or sentence can be restated. The adult needs to determine which of these is most likely to help the child interpret accurately and respond appropriately.

3. *Provide wait time.* Many children need time to process what they have heard and translate sounds into meaningful information. Give children who are hard of hearing or have auditory processing difficulties time to think. Some children may need at least 10 seconds.

4. *Make sure that the speaker's face is clearly visible.* Children may misinterpret what they hear if they cannot see the lip movements and facial expressions that accompany the words. For example, in the previous example of the child hearing *hat* instead of *hand,* if the child could see the adult saying the words, he or she might have been able to see the adult forming the "nd" sounds on the end of *hand.* Adults should keep their hands away from their face and mouth while speaking, so the lips can be clearly seen. (In contrast, for the auditory-oral approach, adults may at times intentionally obscure the mouth to ensure the child is using *hearing* and is not lipreading.)

5. *Use physical prompts to help the child make sense of rhythms and music.* For example, the adult can hold an infant against his or her chest, and rock in time to the music or vocalizations to help the infant make a connection between sound and movement. For the older child, helping the child beat out a rhythm or dancing to music will bring the sounds to life.

6. *Teach siblings and peers to use gestures and signs to accompany language.* For all children, gestures in addition to sounds and words can clarify meaning. For children using a total communication approach or a bilingual approach, teaching peers the key signs for daily routines and interactions is important to support understanding communicative intent.

7. *Encourage exploration and experimentation.* Children who have difficulty hearing need to have opportunities to discover and learn by doing. They need to explore their environment and find out through tactile and movement experiences the differences between various types of vibrations and movements and sounds. They need to learn the various associated meanings of things, such as *hard* and *soft* through experiential learning. For example, *soft* can mean a light pressure or a quiet noise. Language and conceptual understanding grow with the child's ability to compare and categorize various experiences.

Environmental Modifications

In addition to interpersonal strategies that may support the child responding appropriately to sound, environmental modifications often are useful. Depending on the findings from TPBA2, the team may want to consider some of the following environmental modifications.

1. *Use assistive devices.* Common accommodations for children who are deaf or hard of hearing include using sign language or gestures to support communication or ex-

plain sounds, assistive listening devices in the classroom, and signaling devices (e.g., a flashing light to alert children to a door knock or ringing bell).

2. *Use picture cues.* Picture cues related to routines such as dressing and eating, or classroom assignments, activities, or centers, can support the use of gestures, vocalization, or sign language. A picture schedule can explain the sequence of events in an activity and help the child understand verbal directions. A list of classroom rules with pictures associated with the words can be used along with language when a child breaks a rule. Pictures of family members and class members can ensure that the child identifies the person who is being discussed.

3. *Label areas of the room with pictures, signs, and fingerspelling for children who use sign and aural language.* Labeling can be done both at home and in the classroom. This allows the adult to say a word or talk about a routine and make sure the child understands the context. The child is then more likely to understand the conversation about the topic.

4. *Use books with signs or visual symbols.* When reading to an individual child or a group, the child with a hearing impairment who is learning sign language can benefit from books that have the signs included with the words. For children who can hear and children who are using an auditory-oral approach, books with symbols for the words (e.g., Writing with Symbols; Mayer-Johnson, LLC) support their listening and their emerging literacy understanding.

5. *Read books and create situations for play that have opportunities to recreate sound effects.* Show pictures and have all the children make the noise (e.g., the wind, a howling wolf, clapping hands). Use props to produce the sound effects (e.g., a bag of corn flakes to crunch for the sound of "crunching" snow, popping bubble wrap for the sounds of branches "snapping"). Let the children dramatize the stories in the dramatic play area and use the sound effects in their play.

6. *Pay attention to lighting.* The light source should be on the face of the speaker and not in the eyes of the child. Do not position the speaker in front of a window because that will throw shadows on his or her face and make lip movements, facial expression, or signs more difficult to see.

7. *Pair a sound with a visual cue.* A visual cue such as blinking the lights can be used to tell the child who is hard of hearing that it is time to clean up. When that signal is paired with the sound of the cleanup bell over time, the child may learn to respond to the bell alone.

▨▨▨ VII. D. How quickly does the child act in response to sounds and words?

Processing auditory information involves both listening and understanding what is heard. To respond quickly, the brain has to convert sound signals into a useful message. Children who do not respond quickly may have problems with attention, ability to listen, hearing, or ability to make sense of the information received. A child who has difficulty discriminating, identifying, and retaining sounds after he or she hears them may have a central auditory processing disorder (CAPD). People with CAPD have difficulty attaching meaning to sound groups that form words, sentences, and stories. They may experience similar problems with processing and organizing written language during reading.

CAPDs are not the result of a hearing loss. The brain may receive only parts of the message accurately, causing people with CAPD to have incomplete information. Children with this type of language processing problem often demonstrate delayed responses to questions or directions, and they may need to practice or review new information several times. Determination of CAPD typically requires a specialized assessment by a team of professionals.

Children with hearing loss may hear distortions in sounds or may not hear sounds at certain loudness or pitch levels. Although a different issue than CAPD, hearing loss also can result in children having delayed processing time, as they try to interpret the message. Intuitive strategies can assist children who have CAPD by organizing information before they need to listen, which helps them to understand what they are hearing and to retain information after it has been heard.

Interaction Strategies

1. *Make sure the child is attending to the speaker before talking.* The entire message may be lost if the child is engaged in something else that is capturing his or her attention.

2. *Use facial expression, body language, and gestures to support comprehension.* For example, a raised eyebrow denotes a question. A relaxed face typically indicates a statement.

3. *Break down directions into specific aspects rather than general statements.* For example, say, "Put all the trucks in this box," rather than "Go find something to put your toys in."

4. *Give instructions one or two steps at a time, rather than all at once.* This will allow the child to comprehend and respond accurately to each step. If given all at once, the child may not be able to retain or understand all of the necessary actions. For instance, "Go put on your pajamas, brush your teeth, and get a book to read. It is time for bed" requires the child to process and retain too much information at one time.

5. *Provide key information without unnecessary details.* State the topic of conversation, providing just the main ideas. Then restate important points. For example, in the following statement, the teacher is providing too much information: "Landon, it is going to be a really busy day, because we are going to do our centers and then go on a fun field trip to the veterinarian. The vet has lots of sick animals and we will get to watch her examine the animals, find out what is wrong with them, and then make them better." A child with CAPD or a hearing loss may struggle to understand all or part of this message. A better approach with children would be to tell them slowly, "We are going to visit a veterinarian today." After a pause, the teacher could add, "We will do centers first. Then we will go on the field trip."

6. *Use visuals to support learning.* Children with CAPD and with hearing loss benefit from learning to visualize what is being said. This gives them a referent that is understood more easily. In the previous example, the teacher could show the children a book about a visit to a veterinarian, to help them learn what to expect and what to look for on the visit. This process is helpful for all children and ensures that they all have the same basis of understanding.

7. *Restate important information in more than one way* Use phrases such as "that means" or "another way to say that is." In the previous example, the teacher might say, "Another way to think of a veterinarian is an 'animal doctor.'"

8. *Allow time for the child to think about what has been said.* Children need time to think about what was said and process the information so that it makes sense. When asking a question, provide 5–10 seconds before expecting a response.

9. *Ask the child to tell you what he or she understands about what was said.* For example, the query, "Landon, what do you think will happen today?" will enable the adult to determine what the child has understood. The adult can then correct errors or clarify misperceptions.

10. *Teach the child to ask specific questions.* Many children who do not understand what has been said will not want to admit that they are unclear. They may say nothing, nod, or watch their peers for clues for what they should do. Asking questions is an important way to gain information. Parents and professionals can model asking questions and build in a time during each discussion during which each child is expected to ask questions. The adult can say, "What questions do you each have?" and then call on each child. Once this is a routine, the child who is befuddled will not feel embarrassed to ask a question for clarification.

11. *Repeat the comments and questions of other students.* The child who does not hear or understand the other children will most likely not indicate this aloud. Instead, he may stare vacantly at the other children or be distracted by some other activity.

Environmental Modifications

In addition to interpersonal strategies that may support responding immediately to what is heard, environmental modifications often are useful. Depending on the findings from TPBA2, the team may want to consider some of the following environmental modifications.

1. *Provide technological supports.* Use an FM amplification system in the classroom and reduce extraneous noise, as described previously. Use materials that reduce reverberations of sound.

2. *Provide visual supports in a variety of ways.* Puppets, flannel board characters, and props can be used during story time to illustrate characters and actions. Slides, overheads, pictures, computer graphics, and other visual aids can emphasize important concepts. Films, videotapes, DVDs, and visual Internet sites also can reinforce information when used with appropriate adult support.

3. *Make sure children speak one at a time.* It is hard enough to concentrate on what one person is saying. If several children or adults are talking at the same time, the child will likely become very confused.

4. *Avoid environmental factors that will confound what is heard.* For example, chewing gum, biting on a pencil, resting the chin in the hand while talking, or smoking a cigarette all interfere with giving a clear message and prohibit the child seeing accurate production of sounds with the lips.

5. *Assign a buddy to the child for activities involving listening and following directions.* The child can then observe the buddy and ask him or her questions to help ensure that the child with a hearing loss knows what will happen next (e.g., moving to the story circle or art area).

VII. E. Does the child accurately imitate sounds?

Imitation is a fundamental skill for learning in all domains of development (see also Problem Solving in the cognitive domain, TPBA2, Chapter 7, Section III). Accurate imitation of sound production is crucial for speech development. Imitation of sounds requires the child to be able to mimic the placement of tongue, lips, and teeth. This necessitates the ability to watch another person, feel the placement of these structures, and reposition as needed to make an accurate sound. In addition, the child needs to imitate the loudness, intensity, pitch, and timbre of the sound being emitted. This requires precise hearing, breath control, and subtle movements of the oral structures. Clearly, more than hearing is involved in imitation, and although hearing is critical, children who are deaf or hard of hearing can learn to speak.

Adults need to make sure that interactions with children to increase imitation of speech sounds are integrated into daily routines and play activities. By observing children's interests and spontaneous behaviors, adults can build sound production and imitation as part of pleasurable and playful interactions. Internal motivation is key to continued development of children's skills.

Interaction Strategies

1. *Make sure the mouth of the speaker is clearly visible.* Avoid obscuring or covering the mouth while talking.

2. *Imitate the infant's own vocalizations or actions.* Infants will imitate sounds in their own repertoire before they imitate novel sounds modeled by adults. Even infants who are totally deaf will make noises and babble until about 6 months of age. Take advantage of this time to encourage production of sounds.

3. *Provide wait time.* Wait for the child to look at you. Once the child looks at the adult, the adult can make a sound or comment on what is happening. Many children need time to think about how to make sounds or words. Therefore, wait time is needed again before repeating the sound or word. Waiting is difficult but very important! When the child initiates a look, it means that the child is ready to engage. If the child does not look, a gentle tap on the arm or leg may attract attention. In the Deaf community, touching the face is not acceptable. The adult may then tap an object or point to an object and name it. The association with the word being used is critical, so the child is learning to listen to the meaning of the sound, not just imitating random sounds and syllables.

4. *Ask the older child, "What did you hear?" before repeating sounds or words.* This will prompt the child to imitate.

5. *Provide many opportunities for repetition in context.* Children typically need to repeat the use of a word more than 200 times in context for it to become part of their repertoire. This is important to remember because children with hearing loss may need additional practice. Just having children imitate sounds is not motivating and will, in all likelihood, lead to resistance. Rather, it is better to use sounds and words that children can learn in meaningful situations. The first consonant sounds children learn, for example, are sounds using the lips together, as in *b, m,* and *p.* Look around the child's environment and find simple, meaningful words that start with these letters, such as *baby, bottle, binky, mama, puppy,* and *papa.* When an object is held up, the adult can repeat the word several times in a row, with wait time in between each repetition.

6. *Prioritize key words for the child's routines, favorite objects, and activities.* When working on imitation, it is important not only to choose words that have sounds the child is developmentally ready to make, but also words that are important to the child. This will ensure that the child is motivated to use the words. Initially start with low- and mid-frequency vowel sounds; for example, play games that tempt the child to use the words. For example, show the child something she likes, and then hide it under the blanket. When the child looks at you to see what happened, say the word slowly and clearly. At first, for any sound the child makes, bring the toy out and give it to the child to play with, and then increase the demand for a closer approximation before giving it to the child.

7. *Read to the child as often as possible.* The rhythm of reading and the opportunity to use exaggerated tones and facial expressions provide incentive for children to listen and imitate. Children love to read the same book over and over, and this is true for children with hearing impairment. Read books with repetitive sounds and phrases,

rhymes, songs, and fingerplays. Take turns making sounds of the animals and characters. Give the child the opportunity to initiate "reading" to the adult by pointing to pictures, vocalizing, and so forth.

Environmental Modifications

In addition to interpersonal strategies that may support the child imitating sounds, environmental modifications often are useful. Depending on the findings from TPBA2, the team may want to consider some of the following environmental modifications.

1. *Amplification can help children hear the sounds better.* The younger the child is when he or she gets an assistive hearing device, the better it is for the child's sound imitation and language production.

2. *Create an "experience book" with the child.* Collect pictures of the child's family and friends doing familiar activities; pictures of the child's favorite objects, toys, and activities; and examples of items from special experiences the child has had. The experience book can include scraps of cloth from a favorite blanket, a wrapper from a favorite food, and so forth. As the book is shared and added to, the adult and the child can name and label people, objects, and events of importance to the child. The book allows repetition of words that are familiar and important to the child. Familiarity also enables the child to look at and produce sounds and words when the adult is not present.

3. *Find a quiet spot for talking, reading, and playing imitation games.* A quiet environment with few visual and auditory distractions will enable the child to be more focused on speech sounds.

4. *Place mirrors in several rooms at the child's level to encourage vocal play in the mirror.* Bath time and playtime are natural times to engage in mirror play. Young children love to see themselves in the mirror, so turn taking around imitating faces and noises can be introduced. This should be silly and fun, rather than "therapy."

5. *Provide toys that trigger imitation.* The child can activate toys that imitate animal sounds or speak words or phrases. Make sure the toys selected provide clear sounds and are loud enough for the child to hear.

6. *Provide props and opportunities for pretend play.* Children imitate others' actions, speech, and interaction patterns. Use of action figures and dress-up outfits, along with materials from common routines, encourage children to recreate scenarios and narratives. Adult participation can provide opportunities for modeling and expanding children's speech.

7. *Provide a variety of experiences outside of the home.* Challenge children's curiosity and imagination. When the child questions what something is or does, why or how something occurs, and requests more information, the adult can provide new vocabulary and build concepts. Exposure to new objects, materials, events, situations, people, and problems stimulates the child to want to learn new concepts. The child with hearing loss will then imitate words and phrases the adult uses and over time will apply them in new situations.

General Suggestions

Strategies recommended for working with children who are deaf or hard of hearing depend greatly on the philosophical approach adopted by the family. Strategies selected are guided by family preference, needs of the child, and community resources. Most of the strategies explained in the previous section are appropriate for the three major approaches—auditory-oral, total communication, and bilingual/bicultural. *Note:* Visual attention is sequential, so the child must be allowed to attend to the object first and then shift his or her vision to the adult's face for spoken or signed words, or both (in simultaneous communication).

However, the more hearing the child has, the more emphasis should be on listening and understanding spoken language. The more severe the hearing loss, the more likely the child will need to use ASL or a sign system (Seeing Essential English [SEE-1]) or Cued Speech. If emphasis is placed on the spoken word, then gestures and eye gaze can be used for support of speech and auditory skills. If a child needs a visual form of communication, Cued Speech or a form of manually coded English (Signing Exact English [SEE-2]) may be used along with spoken English. *Note:* The adults in the child's life will make decisions about how to communicate with the child with a hearing loss. This should be a decision that is implemented across home and school environments. They may decide to speak only, at all times, or to speak only when a word or phrase is emphasized, whether auditorially or in combination with speech reading. Adults may decide to speak and sign simultaneously or sign only. Any one of these options can be used at any time, depending on the goals of the adult.

If a bilingual system is implemented, ASL is taught as the child's first language. The strategies selected vary, depending on the approach to teaching communication that is selected by the family. It should be noted that families using an auditory-oral approach would not use sign, gesture, or lipreading, as some strategies suggest. A bilingual approach, on the other hand, would emphasize these elements rather than speech.

The Visual Mode—Strength for Deaf Children

When a child is exposed to a visual-manual language such as ASL from a very early age, he or she develops language through this visual-manual mode naturally and effortlessly. If a hearing child is born to Deaf parents who sign, that child's first language will be ASL (in the United States); if a deaf child is born to hearing parents, and those parents learn and use ASL in their child's early years, that child's first language will be ASL. Children learn the language that is presented to them in a clear, accessible, and fully developed model, when they have infinite opportunities to interact with other users of that language.

Just as children with normal hearing value and learn to use their hearing abilities to develop language, children who are deaf or hard of hearing use their visual skills to monitor their environment and to communicate. When a child sees the door light flash, she goes to the door or alerts her parents. When the baby cries and the baby-cry light flashes, the child responds appropriately—just as a hearing child does who hears the sound. Just as a child babbles with his voice, a child who is learning to sign will "mabble" or manually babble with his tiny hands. Hand shapes combined with movements and position in space, when associated consistently with their referent, will be learned as words (signs), and signs modified by movement and facial expressions and combined with other signs form a complete language. Anything that can be said in spoken English can be signed in ASL.

ASL also provides the means of expressing, in a visual way, sound in our environment. Deaf adults use the elements of facial expression (including lip formations and movements), gestures, body movements, and hand shapes to create the visual equivalent of sounds.

Demonstrating and modeling accurate, articulate signing for children is essential to their complete language development. Deaf adults (and other fluent signers) use techniques such as getting down at the child's eye level, signing in close proximity to the child and providing an opportunity for the child to copy the sign to aid in "articulation." Imitation of things that move (e.g., animals, machines, people) in the environment is fun for children and helps them refine their visual-motor expression, which is an important element of communicating in a visual environment. ASL storytellers are masters at this skill and can help parents and teachers develop it as well.

When signing, a person can change the rate (speed) or size and intensity of signing to indicate differences in meaning. For example, to say, "He walked slowly," the signer could sign the sign for WALK in a slow manner. To say, "I live in a small house," the signer could sign the sign for HOUSE in a smaller space. Indicate intensity by signing more loosely or firmly. To really get someone to STOP, it would be signed firmly. Adults can encourage children to play with their language and modify their facial expressions accordingly. As always, fluent sign models for children are essential.

Children who are deaf learn to read without hearing the sounds of language, although the ability to use phonics may enhance a child's reading abilities. In programs for which ASL is the primary language of discourse, a bilingual approach to learning English literacy (reading and writing) is used.

If parents and teachers use some form of signing, there are specific strategies that research shows to be effective in maximizing visual communication (whether ASL or some variation). The following are examples of strategies used by Deaf parents.

Interaction Strategies

1. *Use nonverbal communication.* Smiling, facial expressions, and gestures support the development of looking patterns that are essential to communicating in a visual mode.

2. *Use touch to gain visual attention.* Touching, patting, or stroking is an effective strategy used by Deaf parents to train their child's attention. Deaf parents also use touch to provide positive feedback and reassure the child when parents are out of the child's visual field.

3. *Gain visual attention.* Waving a hand or moving an object into the child's line of vision, or swaying back and forth, will train the child to attend to the adult's face.

4. *Use pointing to direct attention while still permitting language input.* Visual attention is sequential, not simultaneous. Deaf parents gain the child's attention, tell him what he will see, and then direct his attention to the topic. They also displace the sign near the object under discussion so the child can see both the object and the sign.

5. *Reduce the frequency of communication so that it is recognized as important.* Children who are deaf must switch attention between activities and the person with whom they are communicating. Deaf parents typically communicate less often and wait for the child to look at them in order to ensure that the child will see his or her parents' communications as important.

6. *Use short utterances.* Using short utterances minimizes disruptions of children's activities and the demands on memory as they shift visual attention from one focus to another.

7. *Position self and objects in the child's visual field.* Deaf parents conserve the child's energy by placing themselves behind or next to their child, curving their bodies around so the child can see both them and the object of interest.

8. *Move hands, face, or both into the child's visual field.* Making signs on the child's body or displacing the sign into the child's field of vision helps the child reduce the need to redirect attention from activities to the parent (when the parent is attending to something).

9. *Use bracketing.* Deaf parents name an object, then point to the object, and then sign the name for the object again, thereby clarifying the meaning of the language.

10. *Modify signs.* Deaf parents modify signs by repeating, enlarging, prolonging, and placing them close to the object of attention. This promotes understanding by allowing the child a longer period of time to internalize the language.

Environmental Modifications

In addition to interpersonal strategies that may support improving the child's visual attention, environmental modifications often are useful. Depending on the findings from TPBA2, the team may want to consider some of the following environmental modifications.

1. *Make sure that the adult is in the direct line of sight for the child during all communication acts.* Before communicating, check to see that all children with a hearing loss can see the speaker clearly, so that the message is unambiguous.

2. *For group instruction, place children in a circle or semicircle for clear sight lines.* Children with a hearing loss need to see each other in order to participate in group discussions and other group activities.

3. *Reduce visual distractions in the classroom that may block sight lines for communication.* Analyze the visual environment and relocate furniture or materials that make it difficult for the children and teachers to see each other in all areas of the classroom.

4. *Acclimate the child to visual alerting devices in the classroom (e.g., visual fire alarms, door alerts, visual message boards).* Just as adults would explain a public address system for announcements or an auditory fire alarm to children with normal hearing, children who depend on their vision should have the same experience in order to function as independently as possible.

5. *Make video recordings of interactions in the classroom and discuss with children.* Use videos as a tool to develop clear communication skills such as making signs clearly, correct placement of signs, and so forth.

6. *Use technology to enhance visual learning.* Multimedia CD-ROMs that contain material such as movies and graphics (in ASL/English); SmartBoards; and digital video cameras and/or still cameras are effective tools for supporting learning.

ROUTINES FOR CHILDREN WHO NEED SUPPORT TO USE HEARING

The following are examples of how the strategies discussed previously can be incorporated into the child's daily routines at home and at school. In addition to the strategies noted at the beginning of the chapter, which are used by caregivers of children who do not have special needs, these strategies support increased proficiency in using hearing.

Daily Routines (Home and Classroom)

Feeding/Eating

During snack or mealtimes, the adult can pass an item of food across the child's field of vision. This will bring the child's attention to the topic of conversation. As the child visually follows the bowl, the parent can hold the bowl up beside his mouth. Once the child is attending, the adult can make an exaggerated expression and label the item, "Peas!" Encourage the child to repeat the word by saying, "I want ____." Let the child fill in the blank: "Peh." "Yes. *Peas!*" Use short phrases and make sure the child is attending to whoever is talking. Remind people at the table to use a gesture to show they are talking now.

Diapering/Toileting

Diapering is an ideal time for rhythmic activities and face-to-face communication. Take advantage of this time to introduce words related to body parts, location, actions, and so forth. While the child is lying quietly on the table and is a captive audience also is a good time to point out sounds in the environment. For example, during diapering, Mom picks up Alex's feet and sings a song while rocking his feet back and forth to the music. He laughs and moves his feet. She takes his hands and claps them to the rhythm as she sings. She then puts his diaper on while labeling each action: "Legs *UP.* Diaper *ON.* SNAP pants! All done!" She holds Alex up so he can see and says, "Listen, Alex." She steps on the diaper pail pedal and imitates the sound it makes, saying, "Clunk! All gone!" As children become more independent and start moving into toilet training, adults can have children listen to the sounds in the bathroom, such as water running, the toilet flushing, the toilet lid klunking, and so forth. Attention to these sounds is important so that children remember to flush, know when the water is off, and so forth. Adults also can use this routine to expand vocabulary to include labels for the action steps and so forth. Signs and words can be combined.

Dressing

As with the previous routines, dressing provides an opportunity for increasing vocabulary through imitation of words in a functional context. Use of signs, gestures, and vocal prompting may be needed. For example, while dressing Dustin, Dad taps him on the shoulder. Dustin looks at his Dad. "Foot," his father says. Dustin lifts his foot and says, "oot," and his father helps him get his foot in. Dad taps his shoulder again. Dustin looks at his father, who says, "Arm." Dustin stands looking at his dad without moving. His father points to Dustin's arm and says, "Arm." Dustin then lifts his arm and says, "Am." His father puts on his shirt. Dad gives Dustin a big hug, waits for Dustin to look at him, and says, "All done, Dustin." Notice how wait time was used, along with modeling, gestural cuing, and reinforcement of vocalization.

Going Out

Doing errands involves going out into the community where there is much background noise. It is important for children with hearing loss to learn to distinguish various noises, especially what is a background noise compared with a sound that should be the focus of attention. Community activities are a good time to point out various sounds in the environment so that the child recognizes what they are. For example, Mom holds Kobi's hand as they walk out to the car. She stops, sits on the front steps with him, and points to her ear. "Listen, Kobi. What do you hear?" Kobi turns his head both ways, then shakes his head. Mother points up in the air. Kobi looks up. He points to the white trail of an airplane and says, "Ayplane." Mother points to her ear again. Kobi tips his head so his ear points toward the sky. He smiles and says, "Ayplane."

Play Routines (Home and Classroom)

Face-to-Face Play

Face-to-face play often involves movement, singing, or taking turns in a game. It presents an opportunity for eye contact, imitation, and movement to sound. The interpersonal nature of this type of play is motivating to children and encourages conversational patterns and imitation. For instance, Mother is holding Hunter's hands and rocking him back and forth on her lap. She is chanting, "Baa, Baa, Black Sheep" to the rhythm of her movement. She rocks him backward and waits. He looks at her and she keeps waiting. She says, "Baa." He says, "Ba," and mother laughs and pulls him up, chanting, "Baa, baa, black sheep, have you any wool?" She repeats the action again, waiting for him to vocalize.

Physical Play

Unlike face-to-face play, physical play often involves separate movements or interactions that do not involve direct eye contact. It is important for adults to modify their interactions with children who are deaf and hard of hearing in order to enable increased face-to-face exchanges. For example, Dad is chasing Darla. He hides behind the couch waiting for Darla to look for him. When Darla runs around the corner, her father shouts, "Gotcha!" and hugs her. Darla screams with laughter, then wiggles away and starts to run. Dad pulls her back, waits for Darla to look at him, and asks, "Again?" Darla nods and shouts, "Aga!" while running away. Dad catches her and holds her, asking, "What should I do?" Darla tries to get away. Dad taps her on the shoulder and she looks at him. Dad raises his eyebrows and says, "Should I run or chase you?" He points to himself, then Darla. She pauses, thinks a few seconds, and then says, "Run." Dad lets go of her and starts to run away. In this example, the father manipulated the child into a face-to-face dialogue but gave the child the choice of what actions would follow. Language was modeled, an opportunity for initiation was given through gesture and words, and Dad followed his daughter's lead, increasing the chances that another opportunity for dialogue will occur.

Manipulative Play

It is important for adults to encourage creative thinking and imaginative play. Introducing new materials to a play situation can increase problem-solving opportunities and provide new vocabulary for objects, descriptions, and actions. For example, Jennie is playing with a small doll. She puts her in the bed and says, "Nye-nye." Then she picks the doll up and starts to dress her. She labels, "Shoes, dress." Mother enters the room and sits down next to Jennie. Jennie looks at her. Mom says, "Baby is all ready." Mom smiles and pats Baby. She waits for Jennie to look at her. Jennie says, "Ready." "Where is she going?" asks Mom. Jennie does not respond. Mom goes to the kitchen and returns with a pan of water. Jennie looks at her with a questioning look. Mom smiles and says, "Does Baby want to go swimming?" Jennie laughs and says, "Baby likes swim." In this situation, the child had repeated the actions with the doll many times in the past. Although she was using familiar vocabulary, she was ready to expand her actions and words. Her mother introduced new play and language opportunities just by bringing in a motivating prop to add to the play. They can now create a whole new scenario with new sounds and words.

Sensory Play

Facilitation of peer interaction is important, especially when children who can hear are playing with a child who is hard of hearing. The adult needs to help peers understand how to communicate through getting the child's attention, using gestures, and talking directly to the child. For instance, Luilia is playing in the sensory center with her friend Rhonda. The teacher comes over and kneels down next to them. Rhonda is talking, but Luilia is looking down at the materials in the sensory table—soft, fluffy pillow stuffing mixed with prickly items such as toothpicks and pine cones. The teacher comments to

Rhonda, "Luilia can't hear you very well. You need to make sure she is looking at you when you talk to her. Tap her on the shoulder nicely, and when she looks at you, then hold up what you want to show her." Rhonda taps Luilia on the shoulder. When Luilia looks at her, Rhonda smiles and looks at the teacher. "That's right. Now she is looking at you. What do you want to show her?" Rhonda holds up a pine cone in front of Luilia and says, "Look, Luilia, it comes from a pine tree. I have a pine tree at home." The teacher gives Luilia a pine cone, holding it next to Rhonda's. When Luilia looks at her, she slowly says and signs, PINE CONE. TWO PRICKLY PINE CONES. Luilia imitates the sign for PRICKLY and says, "Puh-lee." The teacher repeats the word, emphasizing how to position the lips to make the "pr" sounds. Rhonda does the same, saying, "Look, Luilia. Like this." In this instance, the teacher has guided and demonstrated in order to increase communication among the peers.

Dramatic Play

Dramatic play enables children who are deaf or hard of hearing to play out what they have seen and heard. It provides a safe arena for practice of language, actions, and expression of emotions. The teacher should incorporate themes that build on children's experiences both with literacy and in real life. In the following example, the social interactions in dramatic play encourage children with hearing loss to communicate.

> The children are in the dramatic play area. Luilia is dressed in the white doctor's coat and is checking the heart of a stuffed puppy. Rhonda comes over with another stuffed animal and says, "He's sick too." Luilia signs, SICK, placing the middle finger of one hand on her stomach and the middle finger of the other hand on her head, while making an unhappy expression. Rhonda laughs and imitates Luilia. Rhonda says, "Sick." Luilia says and signs, "Sick. Puppy sick." The language used when reading books about the veterinarian, knowledge gained from a field trip to the local veterinarian's office, and dramatic play props give both children a common language and set of experiences on which to build. The teacher needs to monitor the play to see whether facilitation of interaction is needed to prompt new ideas or communication.

Reading and Learning Routines

Circle Time

The teacher needs to make sure that the child who is deaf or hard of hearing benefits from all aspects of activity. Placement of the child in relation to the teacher, the circle activities, and the other children is important. The child needs to be able to see all faces, picture cues, books, signs, and gestures. Use of visual aids is important. If the child uses sign language, teach the rest of the class key signs that are related to routines, and add new ones for each new book the class reads. Make pairing signs and words a memory game for everyone. The following example demonstrates how some of these principles can be incorporated.

> The children are sitting in a circle, all talking about their field trip. The teacher raises her hand and signs for them to be quiet. She says, "It is important for you to raise your hand [demonstrates] and speak slowly [signs]. We want everyone [gestures] to be able to see [signs] and hear [signs]. John, [she points to John] show us and tell us what you like best about the visit to the vet [holds up the book about going to the veterinarian]."

One-on-One Book Reading

The adult needs to make book reading a two-way process with the child with hearing loss. If the adult just reads the book, he or she has no idea of what the child comprehends. By making the book reading interactive, the adult can monitor what the child sees and hears, and build turn-taking skills. For example, while sitting on the teacher's lap, the toddler is looking at a book about baby animals. The teacher puts her mouth close to the child's better-hearing ear and talks slowly. She points to the picture and says, "Sheep." She waits; when the child does not respond, she says, "Sheep. Sheep says, 'Baaa'!" The child points to the picture and says, "Baa." The teacher touches the child's fingers to her lips while she repeats, "*SHEEP* says 'baa.'" The child tries, "Cheep."

Science and Math

Complicated directions often are hard for children who are deaf or hard of hearing to follow. A picture sequence chart can give guidance to support verbal and signed directions. The child who is deaf often will pick up cues by watching other children, so make this an acceptable and expected behavior by pairing children with a "work buddy" or appointing an "activity leader" or "center helper." The following example illustrates these points.

> The teacher tells the children at the science center how to mix the recipe to make "dirt dough" to make an African village hut. She places picture sequences on the table that show what to do. She assigns a child who has made the recipe the day before to be the center helper and has him sit across from Luilia so she can see him. The teacher then tells everyone, "Ask Charlie if you need help."

ROUTINES FOR INFANTS AND VERY YOUNG CHILDREN WHO COMMUNICATE USING ASL

Daily Routines (Home and Classroom)

Feeding/Eating

While holding your baby or placing her in a high chair, introduce her favorite foods to her as you smile and sign. Bring the food item up to your face as you sign so your child can see both your facial expressions and signs.

Going Out

Always tell the baby where you are going as you leave the room. Using a baby harness (e.g., Snugli), position the baby facing out so she can see around her and sign out in front of her as you comment on things she sees. Position a mirror in the car and adjust it so the baby can see your face while you drive. Tell the baby about things that happen outside her visual range. For example, tell her that you see Daddy walking outside or you hear her brother crying or a fire truck approaching.

Play Routines (Home and Classroom)

Face-to-Face Play

Imitate baby's hand shapes and movements (i.e., "mabbling" or manual babbling). Share simple ASL stories using repeated words (2–3 signs). For example, you can sign EYES, EYES, BLUE, BLUE, BLUE. Sign simple ASL poetry using one hand shape (e.g., LEAF) and vary the movement to show LEAF FALLING, FALLING, DOWN. Play visual imitation games; for example clap a simple rhythm (clap, clap, clap) in front of the baby, or tap the baby on her head three times and then smile, and repeat. Use the FIVE hand shape, sign SUNSHINE shining down on the baby's face, AND then sign SLEEP gently on the baby's face. Repeat a few times, or sign LEAF, then SLEEP; then sign LEAF FLUTTER AWAY, and then sign DREAM. Repeat. Play the lights on/off game. As you hold your baby with one arm, turn the light switch on and off. Point to the light and sign LIGHT ON, then point to the light. Turn the light off and sign LIGHT OFF. Repeat. Make sure that you allow adequate time for the baby to look at the light and back at you as you continue the game. Sign one hand shape or ASL word. For example, sign the I LOVE YOU hand shape and then have it "take off," "fly around" as an airplane does, then "land" on the baby's tummy. Sign BUTTERFLY and have it fly in the baby's visual space, landing on different objects and finally on the baby.

Manipulative Play

Introduce the play vocabulary found in the manipulative play area with a story, a demonstration, or both. Take pictures of the children playing and then discuss in circle time. During circle time, take pictures of the children signing the appropriate ASL sign, such as WATER, POUR, and so forth. Post sign photos next to the photos of children playing with the manipulatives; label each with a short narrative describing the picture.

Dramatic Play

Provide play items that are part of the child's experience, such as pagers used by Deaf adults to communicate through text messaging. Expand the child's language abilities as they act out events and scripts through gesture and movement by providing the ASL vocabulary. Explain any iconic characteristics of the signs; for example, the sign for TIGER is made with claw hand shapes drawn across the face to represent stripes on the face.

Reading and Learning Routines

Circle Time

Use conversation about events and things in the child's world to develop increasingly sophisticated language use and literacy skills (dialogic inquiry). Use visual and tactile signals to ensure children's attention. Use eye gaze as a technique for managing classroom discourse. Produce signing close to the object of attention to support eye-gaze coordination. Seek opportunities for deaf adults and older deaf children to interact with the deaf child for language and communication growth. Sign ASL hand shape stories and visual rhymes with the class. Ask a Deaf adult for examples.

One-on-One Book Reading

Demonstrate multiple and complex links between ASL and the English text. Use role playing when interacting with the story. Sign on children's bodies when highlighting a particular vocabulary word or concept. Use "sandwiching" and "chaining" to teach vocabulary; for example, sign the word, fingerspell it, point to the object, or point to the print (or some combination of these). Show the child ASL story videotapes and have fun practicing the signing you both see. Use *child-directed signing* to ensure attention and comprehension. Make sure book sharing is visually accessible for the child. Translate the text into ASL first. Model a hand shape, pretend to think, and then sign a sign using that hand shape. Example, make the hand shape for "5," then sign MOTHER, FATHER, and TREE from vocabulary in the book you are sharing. Adults often mold the child's hand into the correct shape. Adults slowly sign the target word so the hand shape, movement, and placement are easier to see. Of course, as in speech, approximations are accepted because some signs are more complex motorically and therefore are more difficult to sign. Babies who sign from birth manually babble or "mabble," and parents imitate their babies' hand movements and provide assistance to form the correct hand shape, just as parents who use spoken language imitate their babies' babbling and emphasize target sounds and mouth movements.

Science and Math

Ensure that children have the appropriate ASL signs for science and math vocabulary. A great resource online is http://www.needsoutreach.org.

TALIA

Talia is a 4-year-old girl who has moderate hearing loss. Her parents involved her in an auditory-oral program soon after she was diagnosed. Consequently, Talia's parents have emphasized learning to listen in order to develop her residual hearing. Talia attends an auditory-oral therapy session twice per week. She is now being integrated into a regular preschool program. Talia uses her speech to communicate, but often it is difficult to understand her.

Talia's parents selected a preschool that was using the Read, Play, and Learn! *curriculum (Linder, 1999) because this curriculum has a heavy emphasis on language and literacy development in a play-based context. Talia would be able to learn in a program that incorporated thematic concepts throughout the day in functional, applied activities. The emphasis on learning through social interaction also was important to her parents, who want Talia to learn to communicate with her peers as well as with adults. The following environmental and interactional recommendations were developed to support her teachers' efforts to provide an appropriate education for her.*

Interaction Strategies

1. *Talia's teacher should use clear speech, a moderately loud level, precise articulation, and a slightly slower rate. Also recommended is acoustic highlighting, in which the teacher prompts the child to listen before conversing, stresses the key words in a sentence, and uses animated intonation.*

2. *The teacher and/or teaching assistant should engage Talia in one-on-one conversations daily to reinforce vocabulary and concepts as well as provide a clear speech model for her. These conversations should take place in a quiet area of the room.*

3. *The teacher should model correct pronunciation of a word in a short sentence but not correct it when Talia mispronounces or misuses a word.*

4. *The teacher should reinforce key concepts and vocabulary throughout the day so Talia hears and understands the words in a variety of contexts.*

Environmental Modifications

1. *Hearing aid checks should happen throughout the day to ensure that Talia is hearing what is happening around her. The audiologist should instruct the teacher on basic troubleshooting strategies as well as how to conduct the Ling Six-Sound Test (Ling, 2003) for speech reception.*

2. The teacher should use an assistive listening device (ALD) or FM auditory trainer consistently, as prescribed by the audiologist.

3. The classroom should have carpet and acoustical tile on the ceiling to absorb sound so Talia will have an easier time hearing speech. The classroom door should be closed to keep out unwanted noise.

4. Children should be taught to cue Talia to direct her attention if needed.

5. Talia should be placed close to the teacher, near the front of the group, to maximize visual and auditory information during storybook reading or group activities.

6. Talia's teacher should maintain a communication book that goes home every other day with Talia to inform her parents of classroom activities and topics that they can discuss with her. The parents should write back to inform the teacher of what happens at home so concepts and vocabulary are reinforced.

STACY

Stacy is a 4-year-old profoundly deaf child who has been in an auditory oral classroom. She has not been fully successful in acquiring spoken English as her parents and teachers had hoped, so she is now placed in a bilingual/bicultural program that emphasizes ASL and written English. Her parents made this decision after meeting a Deaf adult who was a cousin of her neighbor. The Deaf adult spent many hours explaining (with the help of her cousin, who was fluent in ASL) about sign language and how Deaf people communicate with hearing people, and she listened empathetically to Stacy's parents about their concerns, fears, and hopes for their daughter's future. Stacy's parents decided to try a placement in the bilingual/bicultural preschool program at the school for the deaf in a nearby town. Her parents want her to continue speech and auditory training but realize that the path to language, cognition, and socialization is a visual one. The program has assured the parents that speech and auditory training will be provided as an ancillary service.

Stacy's parents will be provided instruction in ASL through home visits that focus on functional communication within the family and through group instruction offered at the school, which has a more structured approach to learning ASL. They also will learn about Deaf Culture with other parents. The family will be matched with a Deaf family (parents and children) who will serve as cultural and communication guides as they interact in various family activities.

Stacy's school also will provide her with additional supports outside of the classroom that will support her immersion in a bilingual/bicultural environment. The following environmental and interactional recommendations were developed to support her teachers' efforts to provide an appropriate education for her and a smooth transition to a new way of communicating and learning.

Bilingual/Bicultural Interaction Strategies

1. Teachers will provide both group and individual contingently responsive conversations with Stacy to support both her cognitive and her communication development.

2. Discourse strategies such as code switching, chaining, sandwiching, and fingerspelling will be used to provide multiple forms of a message.

3. Teachers will respond to the content of Stacy's communicative attempts first and then model the correct sign formation, at times matching their hand shape to Stacy's or molding Stacy's fingers into the correct hand shape in a playful manner.

4. *Teachers will introduce Stacy to various forms of ASL literature—poems, ABC sto-ries, and rhymes—to move beyond functional language.*

Bilingual/Bicultural Environmental Modifications

1. *Direct line of sight is provided for each student during instruction. Stacy will be shown examples of obstructed and unobstructed views and instructed how to signal to the teacher in either case. This helps to teach her that she is responsible for ensuring that she has access to events and conversation in the classroom.*

2. *Stacy will be introduced to the visual environmental elements (e.g., visual fire alarm, message boards). Use of gesture, role playing, and child-directed signing will be used to convey the purpose of these technologies and the students' appropriate use of and response to them. This helps Stacy see the importance of these tools and also helps her have a feeling of security in her environment.*

3. *Children and adults throughout the school will be introduced to Stacy as "Deaf" or "hearing" and demonstrate how, for example, each responds to sound (i.e., some react, some do not) and how all respond to a visual signal. This strategy will help her develop an understanding of how to use different strategies when communicating with deaf or hearing people as appropriate.*

4. *Speech and auditory training will maximize visual strategies and technologies that help Stacy understand the activities and motivate her to participate.*

5. *Videotape will be used to document Stacy's acquisition of ASL. These tapes can be used as parent education materials as well.*

6. *Teachers will use many visual resources in providing support for Stacy as she learns ASL. Pictures, video recordings of events and interactions, still pictures, or real objects will be paired with child-directed signing to provide an array of information during conversation and/or instruction.*

REFERENCES

Carney, E.A., & Moeller, M.P. (1998). Treatment efficacy: Hearing loss in children. *Journal of Speech, Language, and Hearing Research, 41,* 561–584.

Erting, C.J. (2003). Language and literacy development in deaf children: Implications of a socio-cultural perspective. In B. Bodner-Johnson & M. Sass-Lehrer (Eds.),, *The young deaf or hard of hearing child: A family-centered approach to early education* (pp. 373–398). Baltimore: Paul H. Brookes Publishing Co.

Linder, T.W. (1999). *Read, Play, and Learn!®: Storybook activities for young children. The transdisciplinary play based curriculum.* Baltimore: Paul H. Brookes Publishing Co.

Ling, D. (2003). The Six-Sound Test. In W. Estabrooks & L. Birkenshaw-Fleming (Eds.), *Songs for listening! Songs for life!* (pp. 227–229). Washington, DC: A.G. Bell Association for the Deaf and Hard of Hearing.

Marschark, M., & Spencer, P. (2003). *Deaf studies, language, and education.* New York: Oxford University Press.

PARA. (2007). *Reading and students who are deaf or hard-of-hearing.* Retrieved June 15, 2007, from http://www.readingassessment.info/resources/publications/deaforhardofhearing.html

Rushmer, N. (2003). The hard of hearing child: The importance of appropriate programming. In B. Bodner-Johnson & M. Sass-Lehrer (Eds.), *The young deaf or hard of hearing child: A family-centered approach to early education* (pp. 223–251). Baltimore: Paul H. Brookes Publishing Co.

7

Facilitating Cognitive Development

I. Strategies for Improving Attention

Goal Attainment Scale

1	2	3	4	5	6	7	8	9
Inattentive, unaware of surroundings, or distractible and unable to focus on one object or person for a sustained time.		Selective focus of attention. Has difficulty sharing a focus of attention with another person and pays attention only to specific interests. Alternatively, focus of attention shifts rapidly from one thing to another.		Attends to relevant people, objects, and events with prompts. Can share a focus of attention with someone, but needs verbal and physical support to maintain or shift attention.		Independently attends to relevant people, objects, and events. Needs occasional verbal or gestural suggestion to maintain attention.		Is able to select focus, maintain attention, and shift focus from objects to people, and person to person, appropriately.

Attention is the ability to select and focus on stimuli, sustain concentration, shift focus when needed, and ignore distractions. Attention is important for all aspects of social engagement, learning skills, acquiring knowledge, and meeting one's own needs.

For successful social interaction, a child must *select* the person on whom to *focus attention* for communication purposes. He or she must then be able to *maintain attention* to the person while interaction is taking place. If more than one person is involved in the interaction, the child must be able to *switch attention* from one person to another as the conversational or interactional turns are exchanged. In the case of interactions involving people and objects, materials, or situations, the child must be able to *shift the focus* of attention from the person talking to the subject of the conversation as needed for learning, responding, or clarifying information. For example, if the child is looking at the parent while the parent is talking and the parent says, "What is that outside the window?" the child must look away from parent and out the window in order to be able to respond. Being able to *share attention* with another person is also important. When an adult shares a book with a child, for instance, the child needs to attend to the words, the pictures, and the meaning represented by both. Another aspect of attention needed for social interaction is the ability to *divide attention*, or to be able to attend to two things at once. The child needs to be able to attend to the castle that he is building, but at the same time attend to where his little brother is driving his truck nearby, and also attend to his mother when she calls for him to come to dinner. Being able to *ignore distractions* that are not relevant, however, also is important. If the child who is building the castle must stop to attend to the cars going by, shift to look at another toy he spots across the room, and then get up to go see why his brother is making noises, he will never complete his goal of building a castle. Another aspect of attention is being able to moderate the level or intensity of attention directed to different aspects of a social situation. For instance, if several conversations or social interactions are taking place in a preschool classroom, the child needs to be aware of what is happening around him, but also be able to pay more intense attention to the interaction in which he is engaged.

All of these aspects of attention also are critical for learning. The child must be able to focus his or her attention on the most significant aspects of the environment in order to learn and participate fully. Attention is essentially for every aspect of life, including meeting one's own needs, gaining knowledge and skills, and having positive social interactions.

In the following sections, attention for all of these purposes is addressed, because they overlap and the methods for supporting attention for all three purposes are similar.

APPROPRIATE ATTENTION

The attentional abilities discussed previously become more sophisticated as a child's brain develops. Routines and events involving other people are always important in a child's life, and all of the elements of attention are necessary for successful social interaction, learning, and becoming independent. Young infants focus on the face and mouth and, thus, learn to imitate movements and expressions and to read social cues. As motor skills develop, children focus on manipulation of toys, notice others respond to their actions, and observe and imitate what others do with objects. Attention is directed toward both people and objects. Children explore various characteristics, imitate behaviors of other adults and children, and experiment with cause and effect. By preschool, maintaining social interaction with peers should become an important attentional focus. Children are able to carry on conversations, carefully investigate objects and events, explore in collaboration, and plan and carry out elaborate play sequences both independently and with others. Children also attend to what behaviors result in getting positive social responses and what behaviors result in negative or punitive responses. Combined with increasing understanding of why actions are considered right and wrong, attention to behavior increases. By the end of preschool, children should be able to choose appropriate aspects of situations on which to focus attention, maintain attention to completion of a task requiring 15–30 minutes, shift their attention between people and objects as needed, and divide attention intermittently between two things. The following examples provide appropriate attentional behaviors for infants, toddlers, and preschoolers for selecting and focusing attention, maintaining attention, shifting focus, ignoring distractions, and dividing attention.

Appropriate Attention in Practice

I. A. How well can the child select, focus, and maintain attention to a task?

Daily Routines (Home and Classroom)

- *Infant/toddler:* The toddler walks to the refrigerator, points, and says, "Milk," then walks to the counter and waits for her mother to pour and hand her the milk.

- *Young child:* The young child goes to the cupboard, picks out a cereal, and takes it to the table where she pours some in her bowl. With her mother's assistance, she pours milk on the cereal. She then sits at the table and eats her breakfast along with her sister.

Play Routines (Home and Classroom)

- *Infant/toddler:* The infant stops at the ball, picks it up, looks at it, and throws it. She chases it and throws it again.

- *Young child:* The young child is making a spaceship from a round oatmeal box. He colors the outside, cuts paper to make a cone on the top, goes to find tape, and attaches the paper to the top of his rocket. He then gets out his space action figures and puts them inside the rocket and does the countdown for takeoff.

Classroom Routines

During the reading, the child next to her shows the young child a toy and begins to talk to her. She looks at the toy, then looks back to listen again.

▬▬▬ I. B. How well can the child inhibit external stimuli?

Daily Routines (Home and Classroom)

- *Infant/toddler:* While the toddler's milk is being poured, his older brother comes into the kitchen and talks to their mother. The toddler notices his brother, but keeps paying attention to the cup of milk being poured.

- *Young child:* The young child is helping her father build a bird house. She hears the neighbor children playing next door, but she keeps her focus on holding the nail for her father.

Play Routines (Home and Classroom)

- *Infant/toddler:* The infant's sister asks her father to read her a book. The infant ignores her and continues to play ball with her father.

- *Young child:* The young child is climbing on the outdoor play equipment. Other children are laughing and calling out to each other, but the child concentrates on placing his feet carefully on the heavy chain ladder.

Classroom Routines

During circle time, a child is heard crying in the hall. The girl answers the teacher's question and does not appear to notice the noise in the hall.

▬▬▬ I. C. Can the child shift attention from one aspect of a stimulus or problem to another?

Daily Routines (Home and Classroom)

- *Infant/toddler:* The toddler gets his milk and stands drinking from his cup. His brother says, "Wanna see my castle, Max?" The toddler follows his brother, drinking from his cup and stating, "My blocks."

- *Young child:* The young child is looking for a specific shirt he wants to wear. It is not in his drawer, so he looks under the bed and then in the dirty-clothes basket.

Play Routines (Home and Classroom)

- *Infant/toddler:* When done playing ball, the infant's father gives her a bottle. She drinks from the bottle, looks at her father, and sticks her fingers in his mouth.

- *Young child:* While trying to figure out how to make a new toy work, the child turns the toy around, looking for a knob or lever. He finds a button and presses on it. When nothing happens, he takes it to his father and says, "I think it needs a battery."

Classroom Routines

At the end of circle time, children begin to pick their centers. As the teacher explains what is happening at each center, the young child listens and then looks at each center to decide what to choose.

GENERAL PRINCIPLES FOR SUPPORTING APPROPRIATE ATTENTION

Adults have many strategies they use naturally to help children attend to various aspects they believe are important. The following are strategies often used by adults to help children attend. These strategies also are useful for children who have difficulty attending.

Emphasize What Is Important

Most adults naturally use gestures and pointing to help children attend to people, objects, events, or specific aspects of these. For example, a father may point to a dog and say, "Look, Anna, a doggie." The teacher may hold her hand high and say, "Look how high it is!" Adults also may point out specific aspects of a situation. For instance, a mother may say, "See the bunny's nose. He is wiggling his nose."

Along with the use of gestures and pointing, adults also exaggerate their voice or movements. After pointing to the water and soap, a mother may, for example, say, "Wash your *hands,* Kelly. Use the soap." She may then pretend to wash her hands vigorously. Exaggerated affect also helps children to focus attention. A teacher may say, "Oh, look what is happening!" This exclamation is typically combined with pointing to the event the teacher wants the child to see.

Another strategy frequently used by adults with young children is moving the object the adult wants the child to attend to into the child's field of vision. By raising the object in front of the child's eyes or moving the object back-and-forth in front of the child, the adult attracts the child's attention.

Redirect Attention

Using visual or auditory distractions, adults frequently can distract the child from one person or object to another. When the infant is playing with a toy and the parent wants him to come to her, the mother may call the child's name and hold up a different toy, saying, "Look, Caleb! Want your ball?"

When the child does not respond to the adult's attempts to redirect the child's attention using gestures, pointing, or interesting objects, physical manipulation is often the next step. The parent may turn the child toward the desired target or pick the child up and move him or her to look at something else. For example, a frequent ploy used by babysitters when parents leave and the child starts to cry is to take the child to another part of the room and find something that has motivational value. The sitter may take the child to pet the kitty, look out the window, or play physical games.

The strategies discussed previously often are combined with using something of higher interest to the child. For instance, if the child loves dinosaurs, redirecting the child to the plastic dinosaurs or a dinosaur book may be successful. Understanding the child's interests and actions that result in pleasurable responses is the key to this strategy.

Minimize Distractions

A key to helping children focus is to eliminate competing sensations. If the adult wants the child to attend to a book that is being read, is important to eliminate the sounds of the television and the visual stimulation of toys that may compete for attention. Distractions are usually visual or auditory, but also they can be physical distractions. A chair that is uncomfortable can cause a child to want to get down and do something else. Parents who are good at reading cues often can figure out what is distracting the child and change the environment to help the child attend.

Demonstrate

Sometimes children do not attend because they are not aware of what they should attend to or what they should do in a given situation. When a child is given a new toy, for instance, the child may investigate the toy briefly, then if nothing interesting happens, he or she may return to familiar toys or activities. In this situation, adults often will demonstrate how the toy can be used or how it works. Adult demonstration also can raise a child's interest and attention. Demonstrating such things as jumping, singing, or activating cause-and-effect toys are actions that are almost sure to attract the child's attention, and often elicit an imitation.

THE PRINCIPLES IN PRACTICE

Adults use a variety of strategies to support the child's attention for social and learning purposes. The following are examples of how caregivers use the previously described strategies during the day both at home and at school. These examples are approaches that most caregivers use naturally in their daily interactions with children. They are appropriate for most children with disabilities as well.

Daily Routines (Home and Classroom)

Feeding/Eating

While feeding an infant, a caregiver often takes advantage of the infant's interest in the face by modeling opening the mouth. For older children, attending to eating often is less interesting than playing. Caregivers frequently use verbal prompting or reinforcement with dessert; for example, "After you eat your dinner, you can have ice cream."

Diapering/Toileting

The caregiver often tries to get the child to attend to something other than the diapering process. A mobile hanging above the changing table attracts the child's attention. For older children, caregivers may try a book or toy to keep them sitting.

Dressing

The caregiver plays games such as, "Where's your arm? Here it is!" He or she helps the child break down the task so the child can attend to one step at a time. For older children, picking their own clothing may help them attend.

Play Routines (Home and Classroom)

Face-to-Face Play

The caregiver often experiments to find the child's favorite turn-taking game, such as Peekaboo or making faces. For older children, songs and fingerplays often are used.

Physical Play

As with face-to-face games, the caregivers experiment with what the child likes. Some attend to chase games, tickling, tossing, or roughhousing.

Manipulative Play

To help children attend to play with toys and household items, caregivers typically demonstrate what to do with an object. They also may comment on what the child is doing or ask questions to encourage the child to experiment.

Sensory Play

Although many caregivers discourage messy play, caregivers may demonstrate and direct such play. Preschool teachers may provide a variety of materials and encourage experimentation.

Reading and Learning Routines

Circle Time

Preschool teachers use strategies such as individual carpet squares to delineate space, big books that are visually appealing, verbal reminders, and questions.

One-on-One Book Reading

Holding the child on the lap, pointing, labeling pictures, and asking questions are common strategies used by caregivers when reading to young children.

Everyday Literacy

Caregivers often point out signs and symbols they want the child to see as they go on their errands in the community.

PLANNING INDIVIDUALIZED INTERVENTIONS FOR IMPROVING ATTENTION

Attentional issues are commonly seen in children with disabilities. For this reason, it is important for parents and professionals to be knowledgeable about a variety of strategies to help increase the child's ability to attend to relevant aspects of the environment. In addition to the common strategies typically used by caregivers and teachers outlined previously, the following techniques may be used to individualize programs for children with concerns relating to various aspects of attention.

▇▇▇▇ **I. A. How well can the child select, focus on, and maintain attention to a task?**

Children with attention-deficit/hyperactivity disorder, certain types of sensory dysfunction, hyperactivity, severe cognitive delays, or other related disorders may demonstrate high distractibility. Everything looks interesting or nothing looks interesting. The child may thus "flit" from thing to thing or wander aimlessly. Children attend to activities that are interesting and motivating. The adult's role with children is to help them find enough interest in a person, object, or event that they want to engage in an extended interaction.

Different characteristics are appealing to different children. A spinning top may attract one child and scare another away. Some children love messy play, whereas others avoid it entirely. Some children prefer quiet play, whereas others like movement and action. The information gained from the family and the TPBA2 process should help the team understand what characteristics are most motivating to each child. This knowledge is then transferred to each aspect of the day. Because attention is the fundamental aspect of engagement, capturing the child's attention is critical.

Just as important, however, is for the child to select an appropriate focus of attention. For example, the child may be entirely focused on the truck he is playing with, but he only attends to the spinning of the wheels. Another child may be focused on an adult who is talking to her, but she is focused on the buttons of his shirt rather than on his face. A baby may attend to the bright colors of a toy but not attend to what the toy can do. Thus, it is critical to consider not only whether the child can focus attention on one thing, but also on whether he or she can focus on the relevant aspect of the object or event.

During each activity, routine, or event of the day, different elements require attention. Which elements are most important is partially dependent on the developmental level of the child. Take a book, for example; for a young infant, the book is an interesting object because of its colors, its shape, and the turning of pages. For a 10-month-old, the same book is interesting because of the pictures and the recognition of familiar objects. For a 2-year-old, the same pictures in the book are interesting, but being able to name the objects and identify aspects of the pictures holds the attention. For a 4-year-old, pretending to read the book and recognizing some of the printed letters is captivating. For a 6-year-old, the print and pictures in combination holds attention as the child uses the pictures to provide clues to aid in recognizing familiar words. Part of the task of the adult is to determine what element of each situation needs attention for an individual child, based on both interest and developmental level.

The key is to start with the element that is motivating to the child and then use that aspect to direct attention to developmentally appropriate interactions. Once the child has focused on an activity, maintaining attention is important. Completing a task, solving a problem independently, and carrying on a conversation all require sustained attention. Numerous issues may contribute the child's inability to sustain attention; lack of interest is one. Some children are only interested in engaging certain people, toys, or materials. Other options do not hold their attention. Children with autism spectrum disorders, for instance, may have limited interests and may only maintain attention to certain preferred objects or events. Lack of ability to maintain attention also may be related to cognitive concerns such as not being able to determine what aspects of a situation to address, not understanding options for using materials, not having a goal in mind, or not understanding how to sequence actions toward a goal (see Chapter 7, Section III. Strategies for Improving Problem Solving). Physical limitations also may contribute to the child attending only briefly to certain types of activities. Children who have fine motor difficulties, for example, may not attend to toys requiring precise manipulation, such as puzzles or small Legos (see Chapter 3, Section III. Strategies for Improving Arm and Hand Use). Children who feel uncomfortable or unsure of maintaining control of their bodies may avoid gross motor tasks (see Chapter 3, Section II. Strategies for Improving Gross Motor Skills). Older children who have difficulty communicating may have brief social interactions and may avoid social play (see Chapter 6 for communication strategies sections). It is thus important for the team not only to try to help the child sustain attention, but also to address the underlying reasons that the child may be having difficulty.

Interaction Strategies

1. *Obtain eye contact.* When adults want the child to attend to social interactions, they should be close to the child's eye level. Talking to a young child from another room, or even across the room, is much less likely to result in engagement. If the child has a visual impairment, use sounds or touch and read the child's body language to make sure his or her attention has been secured before communicating with the child.

2. *Encourage the child to explore objects.* Encourage children to explore objects visually, tactually, auditorially, or with their preferred senses. As mentioned previously, children have preferred means of engagement. If the adult understands those preferences, he or she can emphasize those elements of objects or situations when engaging children. For example, for the child with a visual impairment, exploration of the sounds, smells, texture, and even taste should be encouraged.

3. *Model interest in an object, person, or event using exaggerated affect.* As children become aware of what others are thinking and feeling, they also become interested in what elicited the observed emotions. Adults can capitalize on this interest in emotions by directing their emotions to the objects, people, or events to which they want the child to attend. If it looks like the adult is enjoying it, the child may want to investigate it as well.

4. *Model actions for the child.* Young children learn through imitation. They want to emulate what they see adults do, particularly when the adult is demonstrating positive affect, as described previously. In the same way that exaggerated affect can draw attention, exaggerated actions also can increase the likelihood of children attending to the same actions. For example, if the adult picks up a peg and taps it gently into a hole, the child may pick up a peg and do the same. However, if the adult has a big smile, uses large pounding movements, and says, "Bang! Bang! Bang!" The child may be even more attentive and is likely to imitate the adult because it looks like great fun.

5. *Point to objects, people, or events.* Point to objects, people, or events or to aspects of objects, people, or events that the child may not have noticed. Pointing is probably the most frequently used method to compel a child to attend to something. Pointing also is a method of getting the child to notice a specific *aspect* of something. For example, when the child is trying to put the square block in the round hole, all that may be necessary is for the adult to point to the round hole in order to redirect the child's attention.

6. *Use the object of interest in an unusual way.* As children begin to understand the functions of objects and how things go together, they learn how to use toys and materials in traditional ways. They can become enticed to attend to old, familiar things when these items are used in unusual ways. For example, when the bench the child typically sits *on* is turned over and the bench becomes a sled the child can ride *in*, the child may now attend to this object in a totally new way. In addition, the child may become more interested in attending to the interaction that needs to occur to get the sled to slide.

7. *Connect the object, person, or event to which you want the child to attend with something that shifts the child's attentional preference.* For example, if the child is repeatedly stacking and knocking down blocks and the adult wants to modify this perseverative activity, the adult might dispatch a truck to knock down the blocks, present a bucket of beans

(or shredded newspaper) to play Hide-and-Seek with the blocks, or introduce action figures to jump off of the block tower into a "pool" of water.

8. *Introduce objects and actions that require more than one person.* To increase a child's attention to and interaction with people, introducing motivating activities that cannot be done alone is important. As in the case of #6, the child cannot "ride" in the "sled" if someone does not push it. Making interaction a fun game, then waiting for the child to make the adult interact, forces the child to attend to the adult. If the adult is too willing a participant, the child can just enjoy the ride and still not attend to the adult causing the fun to occur. With almost any activity involving a turn-taking game that is motivating to the child, the adult can use this strategy to get the child to attend to the other person in the game.

9. *Point out one step at a time or one aspect of a situation at a time.* It is important that the child does not become disinterested or frustrated because of lack of understanding. For instance, if an infant is playing with a pop-up toy and banging on a knob that needs to be turned, she may give up quickly if the toy does not respond as expected. The caregiver can help the child by 1) demonstrating the movement of the wrist (signing TURN), 2) actually demonstrating how to turn the knob, or 3) using hand-over-hand to assist the child. These approaches are in order from least support to most support; thus demonstrating in this sequence will give the adult clues about how much support is needed.

10. *While sitting next to the child, use a second similar object or activity and use "self-talk" to show the child how the problem is being solved.* Self-talk is talking about what one is doing; for example, "I'm putting the baby's arm in her sleeve." This approach enables the child both to see a demonstration and to hear an explanation.

11. *Talk the child through the task one step at a time.* For instance, say, "The baby wants to put her hand in the shirt sleeve. Now she wants to move her arms back so she can put her other hand in the other sleeve." This strategy requires a high level of language comprehension if it is used without actual demonstration or assistance.

12. *Comment and ask questions to help the child think of the next step.* Say, for example, "You made the walls with blocks. It looks great! What can we use for a *big* roof?"

13. *Encourage the child who is verbal to use self-talk to explain what he or she is doing.* This helps the child "think out loud" about the goal; for instance, "Tell me about the picture you are coloring. What are all the things you want to put in it?"

14. *Use questioning expressions and gestures to indicate that you are waiting for the child to try something else.* When the child looks to you for help, you might shrug, make an "I'm not sure" face, and point back to the activity, waiting for the child to try again.

15. *Help the child want to do the activity independently.* Do not solve children's problems for them. This only teaches children that they cannot do it themselves, and they will quickly turn their attention to adults for help in the future, instead of persisting with the task. Provide enough assistance to help the child stay focused on the task.

Environmental Modifications

In addition to interpersonal strategies that may support the child selecting and focusing on specific activities, environmental modifications often are useful. Environment adaptations and assistive technology also can help the child maintain attention. Children who have more severe cognitive, language, and motor limitations may need assistance to persist in attending to various aspects of the environment. Various types of environmental supports can help them maintain attention. Depending on the findings from TPBA2, the team may want to consider some of the following environmental modifications.

1. *Place or hold objects at the child's eye level and within reach.* Children are more likely to attend to objects and events that are easily accessible. In the same way, moving an interesting object into the child's line of vision can also help shift the child's attention when a change of focus is desired.

2. *Provide materials that take advantage of the child's interests and sensory preferences.* For example, a child who likes to touch everything may like books with textures on the pages.

3. *Highlight aspects of the object deserving attention with another color, texture, or sound.* For many children, multiple types of sensory input make an activity more captivating. Toys with lights and sounds often are of interest to young children. This same principle can help children focus on specific aspects of objects or events. For instance, if the tape recorder has a piece of green felt glued to the *on* button, the child is more likely to attend to that button. If a board book has a red wooden tab attached to the page, the child is more likely to turn the page. If bells attached to a string are hidden under a blanket and then shaken by pulling the string, the infant is more likely to continue to look for the bells.

4. *Reduce the number of distractions.* Limit the number of toys and other visual distractions. For some children, reducing the intensity of lighting or noise, or even modifying the room temperature, is helpful. Uncomfortable clothing also can be a distraction. Some children are bothered, for example, by tags on the inside of their clothing, tight neck holes or waist bands, and so forth.

5. *Switch toys are easily activated and assist children who lose attention due to difficulty with physically causing something to occur.* If children feel they can control aspects of their play and interaction, they are more likely to continue engagement. For children at the infant level developmentally, toys that can be activated with a swipe can hold the child's attention. Computer modifications that allow children to create effects without having to isolate tiny buttons also are helpful for many developmental levels.

6. *Breaking down an activity into smaller steps can help a child who becomes easily overwhelmed to continue to attend.* For example, when putting together complicated dinosaur bones, some preschool children may give up easily just from looking at all the pieces. However, if the task is broken up so that the child only has a few pieces at a time to assemble, he or she may complete the whole task without adult assistance.

7. *Visual cues are helpful for children who lose attention due to lack of awareness of what comes next.* Picture cards of sequential steps in an activity can cue the child who has difficulty maintaining attention. Just as adults look at the lid of a jigsaw puzzle for clues as to how to proceed, children often need a model of what possibilities exist.

8. *Provide peer models that demonstrate and encourage the child to interact with toys and materials.* Peers also can function as "learning facilitators" if taught how to support their friend's attention. Peers can be taught to model, reinforce, and encourage.

I. B. How well can the child inhibit external stimuli?

In order to be able to learn, children need to be able to focus their attention and not be distracted by all of the other information that is coming into their sensory systems from the environment or even from their own thoughts. Children with a variety of special needs may have difficulty screening out the relevant from the irrelevant. For example, children with sensory processing difficulties may have difficulty focusing because they are getting too much sensory information to adequately process and make sense of where they should be focusing their attention. Children with attention-deficit/hyperactivity disorder, as well as certain syndromes, also may have difficulty focusing attention, shifting their attention to what is most important to attend to, and maintaining attention for long enough to complete an activity. Their minds may wander easily to other topics. Children with autism spectrum disorders may have a different type of attentional concern. They may screen out relevant external information and focus intently on a specific stimulus of special interest. The adult's challenge then is to expand the child's world by reducing inhibitory responses.

Interaction Strategies

1. *Use the strategies noted previously, because distractibility is related to inability to focus.*

2. *Stand close to the child when talking to him or her.* This will make the adult's voice stand out against background noises.

3. *Avoid giving more than one direction at a time.* Children with attention issues, auditory processing concerns, and motor planning problems may not be able to integrate all of the information and thus will direct their attention to something else.

4. *Talk about what the child is doing.* Verbal support from an adult can help a child stay focused and less distracted. The adult can comment on what the child is doing and give supportive ideas for next steps.

5. *Position materials and the child.* If the materials are close to the child and at an angle so that other visual distractions are blocked, the child may be able to attend better (see Chapter 4, Strategies for Working with Children with Visual Impairments). Seating the child in a stable position, with feet, bottom, and back supported, can reduce fidgeting and thus distractibility (see Chapter 3, Section I. Strategies for Improving Functions Underlying Movement).

6. *Provide heavy work.* Activities that require more effort may reduce distractibility; for instance, cutting heavier paper, pushing or carrying heavy materials, and so forth (see Chapter 3, Section V. Strategies for Improving Modulation of Sensation and Its Relationship to Emotion, Activity Level, and Attention).

7. *Use computers in the classroom.* Children with attentional issues often focus better when working or playing games on the computer. The vision is directed straight ahead, there are boundaries to the screen, and motion on the screen focuses the child's attention.

Environmental Modifications

1. *Provide a nondistracting space.* As noted previously, the characteristics of the environment are important to consider. It is difficult to inhibit external stimuli in a noisy or chaotic environment. Classrooms that are loud or have poor acoustics, walls with too many materials on them, or spaces that are crowded have a negative impact on children who have difficulty inhibiting distracting input. Limiting the number of distractions can help children maintain attention.

2. *Provide a private space when needed.* Children with attentional issues should not be isolated from their peers, but when a task or activity is being done on which the child needs to focus independently, a separate quiet space is needed.

3. *Use earphones.* Some children benefit from wearing earphones that block sounds when they are engaging in a quiet activity such as reading a book.

4. *Investigate sound field systems.* Sound field systems use a wireless microphone to amplify the teacher's voice, which helps children attend to what is being said over other distractions. Both classroom and individual systems are available.

5. *Prepare the environment ahead of time if the child needs to perform a specific task.* Children with special needs can be distracted easily if they have to search for what is needed. It is better to have the clothing, materials, or other necessary items in close proximity to the child.

6. *Use visual cues.* Highlighted lines, a spot on the area to which the child needs to attend, or a picture sequence of actions can be used as a reminder of what needs to be done.

▣▣▣ I. C. Can the child shift attention from one aspect of a stimulus or problem to another?

Choosing a focus of attention and maintaining attention are important, but one aspect that is frequently overlooked in intervention is the ability to *shift* the focus of attention. This means shifting attention from one activity to another or one aspect of an activity to another aspect of the same activity. Another important skill is the ability to shift attention between objects or activities and the adults or children who also are interacting with the child and materials. Children visually refer to others for information, suggestions, feedback, and confirmation. Inability to do so limits communication, learning, and interaction.

Some children with disabilities have difficulty knowing where to shift their attention or even understanding why they need to shift attention. Children with autism, for example, may perseverate on one toy or action for an indefinite period of time, as if their attention is "stuck."

Children with attention deficit disorder may shift their attention frequently, but without purposeful intent. Children with cognitive delays may not understand that they need to shift their attention back and forth between objects, between adults and objects, or from one aspect of a situation to another in order to follow events or obtain information to make their efforts more successful. Some children also may have delayed responses so that the timing of their attentional shifts is slowed, making actions or responses appear out-of-sync.

Being able to control attentional focus also is needed to be able to divide attention between two things at once. Listening to music such as "The Hokey-Pokey" and dancing at the same time requires the child to be able to think about what she is hearing and match her movements to the rhythms and the actions in the song. The ability to do "two things at once" becomes more refined as children get older, and in adults is known as "multi-tasking."

The following interpersonal strategies are suggested for children who have difficulty shifting attention.

Interaction Strategies

1. *Provide adequate wait time.* When the child needs to shift attention, give plenty of wait time to allow the child to process and refocus attention.

2. *Use visual cues.* Use visual cues for where the child needs to be looking. Pointing at an object, person, or event, or holding up an object of interest, may draw the child's attention.

3. *Use verbal emphasis or sound cues.* For instance, if the child is kicking a ball and you want him to throw it, slap the side of a container to get his attention, and point to the inside while saying, "See if you can throw it in here!"

4. *Change the typical rhythm of your voice.* Singing or emphasizing words in an unusual way may draw the child's attention to your face or what you are saying.

5. *Imitate the child.* Imitating the child's actions can help shift the child's attention to the adult. The child is curious about why you are doing what he is doing! Once turn-taking in imitation of the child occurs through several turns, the adult can interject a new action to help shift the child's focus.

Environmental Adaptations

1. *Position the objects of attention close to each other so the child does not need to reposition to be able to look back and forth.* For example, if the child is learning to put on shoes and he needs to look down toward his shoe and then reference you for more information, crouch down next to the child so your face, feet, and hands are close to the child. Now you can demonstrate, give suggestions, and reward effort so that the child can easily attend to both you and his task.

2. *Take advantage of lights and sounds.* Many fun children's software programs have lights and sounds that help the child shift focus from one aspect on the screen to another; for instance, following the actions of a character in a game or a bouncing ball for a song.

3. *Use light to point.* A laser pointer or flashlight can be a motivator to get the child to follow the light from one object or person to another.

4. *Use picture cues or object cues to help the child understand what is happening next.* This can help shift the focus of attention. For instance, at bath time, bringing out the towel and a bath toy prepares the child to shift attention to the next activity. Once in the tub, holding up the wash cloth and soap next to each other allows the child to look from one to the other before they are combined. This helps the child understand the relationship and the sequence of activities. Sequence cue cards with pictures, symbols, or simple words also can help.

ROUTINES FOR CHILDREN WHO NEED SUPPORT WITH ATTENTION

Daily Routines (Home and Classroom)

Feeding/Eating

Not all children love to eat. Some would much rather play with the food than eat it. Some children are easily distracted by more preferred activities. To help children attend to eating food, the following strategies are suggested:

- Give the child a reason to attend to the food rather than to other things. For example, make the food into the shape of a face or point out the parts.

- Focus on an aspect of the food; for example, "Let's find the green pieces."

- Help the child shift focus by attending to turn taking. For example, say, "It's my turn to take a bite. Now it's your turn" or " I'm going to eat a little bite. What size are you going to eat?"

- Help shift focus by supplying choices such as, "Do you want a bite of something soft or hard?" or "Do you want this green one or this yellow one?"

Diapering/Toileting

For infants, diapering is not the most interesting activity. In fact, doing anything else is more fun! The adult needs to determine what he or she wants the child to attend to at this time. For young infants, distracting them from the uncomfortable aspects of diapering is key. Presenting a toy or an object to explore, such as a bottle of baby lotion, may keep the child interested. A mobile that the child can look at, kick, or bat can be another option. For older infants who are ready to crawl off the table, keeping them engaged in something that requires them to lie flat is desired. Sometimes a book, a toy, or a mobile can attract attention. Face-to-face games such as Peekaboo with a blanket, an imitation of blowing raspberries, or singing songs while diapering can help the child focus on something other than the diapering experience. On the other hand, engaging the child as a participant in the process is sometimes an easier and more adaptive approach. For instance, talking the child through the process and engaging her not only can help get the task done, it can teach the child the sequence of the activity and help her be more independent; for instance, "Who can lift up those legs? Whoa! Look how high you lifted! Now who can help me hold the diaper so we can push down the tabs? All right!" This latter sequence not only holds the child's attention, but also encourages independence.

Dressing

As in the previous example, dressing needs to direct the child's attention toward performing the task independently. Although distractions can be used to allow the caregiver to dress the child, the ultimate goal is for the child to attend to this task independently. For this reason, having the child attend to the process of dressing and undressing is desired. To maintain the child's attention, it is important to give him or her as much control over the process as possible. Let the child pick up the piece of clothing and do as much as possible independently. The adult can suggest, hold, assist, and encourage. Although time consuming at first, having the child feel pride in dressing will lead to more attention on the child's part and less intervention on the part of the adult.

Going Out

Going out for shopping or other errands often is difficult, either because the child does not want to go and is upset or because the child is distracted by items the adult does not want to deal with. Grocery shopping is a particularly notorious event. Making the child not only a willing but a helpful participant is a priority. One of the problems with shopping is that everything is a distraction. Finding a way to have the child participate and focus on desired items is important. One way to do this is to have the toddler or preschool-age child take a "shopping list" with pictures of or coupons for items on the list. The child can then help look for the items in the pictures.

Play Routines (Home and Classroom)

Physical Play

Most children love physical play, even if they are not skilled in motor tasks. Attention to motor tasks is most difficult for children who dislike movement or for whom motor play is too hard. Helping children focus on motor activities can be done in several ways:

- Have a favorite friend initiate and lead the actions.

- Involve a preferred toy in the motor play (e.g., take the baby doll for a ride, swing the baby, help the baby jump over the rocks).

- Make the play so much fun that the child cannot resist.

- For some children, verbal suggestions along with tactile cues help them understand what body part to attend to and what to do with it (e.g., "Lift this leg up and over the fence").

Manipulative Play

Some children need to expand their play repertoires by

- Attending to the characteristics of objects (see suggestions for focusing attention under I. A)

- Shifting attention from familiar toys to new types of toys or materials (see suggestions for shifting attention under I. C)

- Shifting attention to new actions with familiar toys (see suggestions for shifting attention under I. C)

Sensory Play

Young children typically love sensory play of all kinds, but some children avoid certain types of sensory play (see Chapter 3, Section V. Strategies for Improving Modulation of Sensation and Its Relationship to Emotion, Activity Level, and Attention). Exploration and labeling of experiences is critical for learning about the characteristics of objects and events. For this reason, adults need to ensure that if children avoid certain aspects of sensory play, alternative exploratory means can be used. For example, if the child does not want to touch a material, he can examine it with his eyes (or a magnifying glass), smell it, or examine it in other ways. After the child has experienced the object of avoidance in many different ways, attention may gradually increase and desensitization can take place.

Dramatic Play

Dramatic play is important for development in all domains. Children who do not enjoy dramatic play can be helped to attend longer to this type of play once they are capable of understanding and implementing simple daily routines and they can combine objects in meaningful ways. The adult can use the following strategies:

- Model simple familiar routines using real objects (e.g., pretend to eat or sleep).

- While the child is doing the actual routine, pretend to be doing the same thing while explaining what you are doing (e.g., "You are drinking. I'm going to pretend to drink too").

- Suggest reasons to use objects in a pretend fashion (e.g., "This baby looks dirty. Here is a wash cloth to give her a bath").

- Request pretend play in a purposeful situation (e.g., "Let's pretend to have a snack").

- Act out parts of favorite stories as they are read.

Reading and Learning Routines

Circle Time

It is a challenge to keep all children attending during circle time. Some ideas include

- Choose motivating books or activities.

- Do not do the same sequence every day. Keep an element of the unexpected.

- Do "crazy" or unexpected things (e.g., dress up as a character, act out a part).

- Give each child a role or a way to participate without having to wait.

- Provide supports for children who need verbal (e.g., signs or personal pictures), sensorimotor (e.g., positioning or proprioceptive input), emotional or social (e.g., sitting with an adult), or cognitive (e.g., actual objects or actions) supports to aid attention.

One-on-One Book Reading

Depending on the developmental level of the child, the adult can bring attention to the most relevant aspects:

- Point to and label pictures, details within pictures, actions in pictures, why things are happening, and what will occur next.

- Ask questions at the child's level.

- Encourage the child to comment or "read" the book to you, a sibling, or a friend.

Science and Math

When manipulative and discovery techniques are used to teach science and math, children may be very motivated to attend. Activities involving experimenting, however, often include multiple steps, and children with attention issues may lose focus. Some ideas include

- Use pictures of the sequence of actions the child needs to perform. This will remind the child of the next step in the sequence.

- Pair the child with a peer who can be a mentor. The peer should not conduct the activity independently with the child watching, which may happen if an adult does not prepare the peer ahead of time. Teach peers how to model, watch, and support their friends.

- Computer games can be educational and motivating and can hold the child's attention because active involvement is necessary. The following web sites review computer programs for young children:

Common Sense Media
    http://www.commonsensemedia.org/reviews/Video+Game/
        Computer-Software-Preschool/

Edutaining Kids
    http://www.edutainingkids.com/

Electronic School
    http://www.electronic-school.com/199909/0999poweruser.html

Review Centre
> http://www.reviewcentre.com/products2044.html

CHARITY

Charity is a 4-year-old who has been identified as having severe developmental disabilities. Social interaction is a strength for her. She smiles at both adults and children and enjoys looking at toys and books. Due to sensorimotor difficulties, she is unable to physically explore toys beyond simple swiping and minimal mouthing. Although becoming physically more independent is a goal, a more immediate goal is to increase Charity's ability to communicate what she wants and needs through visual, auditory, and tactile attention to objects and people.

Developmentally, Charity is able to shift her gaze from object to object and from an object to a person; she is able to show a preference by using a prolonged gaze for preferred objects. Her intervention team, parents, and child care providers planned ways to incorporate into her daily routines intervention strategies to increase her attention and focus and use her attentional focus as a means for communication and more advanced play. The following strategies were suggested for a few of her daily routines:

Interaction Strategies

1. *Use Charity's eye gaze as a means to give her some control over her activities. During meals and other daily routines, give her a choice between two options held at her eye level, so that she can choose what she wants to eat, drink, wear, and so forth.*

2. *During play routines, give Charity options between two toys, or pictures of actions she would prefer to do.*

3. *Because fine motor control is extremely difficult for Charity, let her control play sequences by having an adult or peer act as her hands. Have a series of objects, such as a doll, dress, bottle, and sponge, laid out for her to see. Let her visually guide what play should happen first, second, and so forth with her eyes, while her play partner acts out the sequence and adds comments.*

4. *Use exaggerated affect to attract Charity's attention to your face for communication or "big" actions to increase her attention to gestures or movements.*

Environmental Modifications

1. *Position Charity in such a way that her head and neck are well supported but she can easily track with her head and eyes (a slight backward incline with trunk in supported seating).*

2. *Adapt action toys with switches to enable Charity to activate them easily; for instance, add a switch to enable her to activate a tape recorder or a video/DVD player.*

3. *Add a large adaptive mouse pad to a computer to enable Charity to "turn pages" on a book that has been scanned onto the computer or to use simple software that incorporates cause-and-effect actions on the computer screen.*

KEYS TO INTERVENTION BY DEVELOPMENTAL AGE

The following ideas are directed toward children who are functioning at approximately the following levels. The suggestions are not meant to be all-inclusive, but rather are indicative of potential areas for exploration.

Developmental age	Attentional interests	Keys to intervention

Birth to 3 months	Attends to:
	  Faces
	  Black and white contrast
	  Movement of objects
	  Circular patterns
	  Sensory input (e.g., sounds, music, movement)
		Emphasize face-to-face interaction.
		Use slow movements of objects at close range so the child can track and focus.
		Introduce clear, rhythmic voices and sounds.

3–6 months	Attends to:
	  Own face, body, hands, and fingers
	  Interior aspects of figures
	  Familiar routines and objects
		Assist to explore body parts by touch, in mirror.
		Explore familiar objects in more detail.

6–9 months	Attends to:
	  Preferred toys, new objects
	  Parts of objects
	  Smells, sounds, and new movements
	  Familiar words
	  Pictures
		Introduce new objects from home.
		Let child smell foods, lotion, and so forth.
		Use irregular movements for attention.
		Point to objects, pictures, and aspects of toys at varying distances.

9–12 months	Shifts interest in object to adult responses. Has preferred toys. Has increased interest in action toys. Attends to speech sounds made by adults.	Exaggerate facial and vocal responses to encourage looking at adult for response; look at books. Demonstrate cause-and-effect with household objects and toys. Exaggerate making noises using lips and tongue.
12–18 months	Focuses on specific physical aspects of objects and what they do. Looks into distance. Likes naming or identifying pictures in books.	Point out and talk about characteristics of objects. Look for and talk about events. Have frequent one-on-one book time.
18–24 months	Focuses on others' actions. Looks at books. Has intense interests in own play.	Encourage dramatic play, imitation of complex actions. Interactive book reading and investigative play.
24–36 months	Attends to stories in books. Likes problem solving with small objects and figuring out how things work. Pretends in social interactions. Combines objects in unusual ways and experiments.	Ask open-ended questions about books, cause and effect, pretend play. Set up opportunities to explore, experiment, and combine objects in new ways.
36–48 months	Attends to amount, likeness and difference, symmetry, balance, directionality, classification. Engages in visual-motor problem solving. Engages in dramatic play sequences. Attends to multiple sensory characteristics of objects and events. Analyzes behaviors and situations.	Present opportunities for construction, comparison, description, figuring out why thing happen and how they are alike, sequencing actions. Describe and question about characteristics. Assist in analysis of situations. Encourage comparison. Encourage planning sequence of actions.
48–60 months	Focuses on multiple attributes of objects. Orientation and identification of letters and numbers. Complex sociodramatic play with storyline. Attends to difficult tasks.	Encourage use of letters and numbers for functional purposes. Make up stories; dictate, illustrate, and dramatize as motivated. Provide challenging experiments, discovery.
60–72 months	Attends to long stories, complex tasks. Can plan, implement, and evaluate own efforts.	Provide opportunities for extended exploration, questioning, experimentation, and documentation of thoughts and actions.

7

Facilitating Cognitive Development

II. Strategies for Improving Memory

Goal Attainment Scale

1	2	3	4	5	6	7	8	9
Shows memory by looking longer at novel items.		Anticipates what to do or how to react with familiar toys, people, or events. Imitates simple actions after demonstration.		Verbally or non-verbally shows recognition of names of simple objects, people, places, actions, and routines.		Demonstrates ability to accurately recognize, recall, and reconstruct routines, skills, concepts, and events after both short and long periods.		Relates complex classification and rule systems, conceptual processes, physical skill sequences, and multifaceted events in detail.

Memory is the ability to recognize sensory information that was previously encountered or to generate a representation of information that was previously perceived. Memories can be expressed verbally or nonverbally. The information retained and retrieved may be simple (e.g., names of things, places, dates, routines) or complex (e.g., classification and rule systems, conceptual processes, physical skill sequences, multifaceted events). All sensory systems contribute to memory abilities, as does attention, previous experience, and intensity of emotional involvement. Memories can be retained for a short time (e.g., just a few seconds, hours, days) or long term (e.g., weeks, months, years) and can be recalled in great detail or in a vague "gist."

Memory is critical to learning because it is involved in every aspect of behavior and development. Learning is based on building a coordinated system of interrelated memories. Without memory, learning would not occur.

APPROPRIATE MEMORY

Memory can be observed in every aspect of a child's day at every age level. Infants quickly learn to recognize familiar faces, smells, objects, and movements. Within a few months, they recall what happens when they swipe at a mobile or giggle at their par-

499

ent's tickles. They acquire habits, such as thumb sucking, as they recall actions that are self-soothing or yield desired results. Infants learn procedures, such as how to move their bodies to get into different positions, and they observe and remember how to reconstruct action sequences they have seen, such as pulling a switch to turn on a light.

Toddlers demonstrate memory in increasingly sophisticated ways. They recognize favorite foods, games, toys, and events. Toddlers can recall words and sentences and formulate new sentences using their memory of rules for how to put sounds, word segments, and words together (e.g., "I *falled* down"). They have acquired habits that include complex routines (e.g., their individual sequence for going to bed). Increasing memory skills enable toddlers to remember the steps for complex procedures such as learning how to ride a tricycle. Dramatic play also becomes more complicated as toddlers reconstruct the routines of their day and events they have observed.

Young children integrate sights, sounds, tastes, smells, and a myriad of experiences into an increasingly organized memory structure that enables them to fit new concepts, actions, and experiences into a foundational categorization and classification system. The broader and deeper the experiential memory foundation, the easier it is for new material to be integrated. Combined with memory of consequences related to their experiences, they can begin to establish increasingly diverse approaches to problem solving.

Appropriate Memory in Practice

▨▨▨▨ **II. A. What short- or long-term memory skills are evidenced through the child's spontaneous actions and communications?**

Daily Routines (Home and Classroom)

- *Infant/toddler:* The toddler recognizes the sound of the doorbell and runs to see who is there.

- *Young child:* The young child at bedtime says, "No, Daddy, I want the blue *blanket!*"

Play Routines (Home and Classroom)

- *Infant/toddler:* The 10-month-old wakes from a nap each day and lies in her crib creating noises and babbling.

- *Young child:* The young child dramatizes the story the teacher read, and reminds his peers what to do next.

Classroom Routines

During the science center, Maria watches Julio mix blue and red paint and then paint a purple square. She then mixes blue and red paint and paints a purple square.

▨▨▨▨ **II. B. How long does it take for the child to remember concepts, action sequences, or events?**

Daily Routines (Home and Classroom)

- *Infant/toddler:* In the grocery store, the adult points to an apple and the toddler says, "I want apples" (demonstrating memory for the word *apple*).

- *Young child:* The young child at the dinner table says, "My teacher said green food is good for you, and I told her you say the same thing."

Play Routines (Home and Classroom)

- *Infant/toddler:* The toddler sees the Elmo doll and says, "That's Elmo. He laughs."

- *Young child:* The young child looks at the picture of the block structure on the box, then places the blocks to try to match them. He then looks back at the box to see if his looks the same.

Classroom Routines

Alex picks up the book and without hesitation begins to "read" the story from memory by looking at the pictures on each page.

GENERAL PRINCIPLES FOR SUPPORTING APPROPRIATE MEMORY

Most adults use instinctive methods to help children remember things the adults think are important. The following are approaches commonly used by parents, caregivers, and teachers to support memory development.

Repetition

One is more likely to remember the person, object, or event that is heard, seen, felt, or smelled frequently. The first long-term memories for babies are of the people they see frequently during the day; the objects they repeatedly see, hear, smell, or touch; and the routine events that happen periodically each day. These experiences are not repeated for the *purpose* of helping a child remember; they just recur naturally. Each stimulus creates a neurological memory trace. Each time the stimulus is repeated, the neurological path for that memory is strengthened. Think of it as drawing a line on paper and then repeatedly tracing over that line. With each stroke, the imprint of that impression is intensified. Repetition of experience acts in the same way.

Multisensory Experiential Learning

Just as repetition of a particular stimulus strengthens memory, input from various types of sensory stimuli reinforce memory. Each type of sensory input—visual, auditory, olfactory, gustatory, tactile, proprioceptive, and vestibular—leaves a different type of neurological "marker" in the brain related to a given experience. The number and intensity of each of these sensations is important for retention of memories. For instance, if a child sees a dog, hears it bark, smells its breath as it licks her face, feels the fur when she pets the dog, and is bumped by its wagging tail, she is more likely to remember the word *dog*, the event of encountering a dog, and the aspects or characteristics of a dog than if she sees a picture of a dog in a book and the adult labels it as a "dog." Without understanding the underlying science, most adults commonly try to make experiences multisensory for young children. Adults point out different features and encourage exploration of different sensory aspects of each situation.

Intensity of sensory stimuli also has an impact on memory. Intense smells; vivid colors; unusual sounds, tastes, or textures, and so forth are remembered more easily. Intense stimuli also may result in an amplified emotional response. Increased emotional responses, both positive and negative, also are associated with memory retention. For example, a child who is bitten by a dog may recognize the picture of a dog or an actual dog immediately and have a negative emotional response to that memory for many years. On the other hand, a child who had a giggling, rough-and-tumble encounter with a puppy also may immediately recognize a picture of a dog, the sound of a dog barking, or an actual dog; recognize and label it as a "doggie"; and have a positive emotional response to dogs. Adults typically attempt to make young children's experiences either emotionally positive or neutral. Positive emotional responses are more powerful than neutral ones, and are obviously preferred by children to equally memory-enhancing, emotionally imbued experiences that are negative.

Generalization

Memory is enhanced by engaging what is to be remembered in numerous ways, in various settings, and across different people. Using concepts or actions many times in different contexts not only enhances memory, but also expands applications of the knowledge or skill. For example, parents teach toileting in a variety of settings; they point out vocabulary at every opportunity (e.g., a monkey in the zoo, on television, in a book); they help the child climb stairs at home, at the park, at school, at friends' homes, and so forth. Using specific concepts and skills in many contexts, including across people, places, and situations, reinforces memory acquisition of the particular concept or skill. Adults often ask questions or remind children of how concepts and actions should generalize; for example, "Jack, what are you supposed to do after you go to the bathroom? That's right. Wash your hands."

Emphasis

What is emphasized in a given situation helps guide what is remembered. Emphasis can come in many forms. When the parent is talking to a child, the parent frequently emphasizes the words he or she wants remembered. For example, when looking in a pond, the parent may say, "The fish is *swimming*" (emphasizing the action word), or when crossing the street, "Look *both* ways!" (emphasizing directions). Adults also use visual emphasis. They hold important objects up, demonstrate actions, or use gestures to accompany words. As pointed out in the section on attention (Chapter 7, Section I. Strategies for Improving Attention), such visual supports increase attention, and focused attention enhances memory.

Associations

Parents and other caregivers often use reminders or associations to help children remember. They will use reminders such as, "Remember when we saw the giraffe at the zoo?" Adults help children make connections such as, "This doll is just like your baby at home." In preschool, teachers often use associations with an easily recalled item to help a child remember a new concept; for example, "Anita, look, the word *apple* starts with the letter *a* just like the *a*'s in your name." Parents will use associations such as, "Tessie, remember Auntie Marge? She gave you that pretty pink dress." Children also use their own associations as aids to recall. For instance, a child may remind himself, "The tiger is the one with stripes, and the leopard is the one with spots." Questions frequently are used by parents and preschool teachers to stimulate recall; for example, "Who remembers the name of the other book we read about a snowman?"

THE PRINCIPLES IN PRACTICE

Adults use many of the strategies discussed previously to help children remember. The following are examples of how caregivers use these approaches during the day both at home and at school.

Daily Routines (Home and Classroom)

Feeding/Eating

While the child is eating, adults often will ask questions or prompt recollection; for example, "What is your favorite cereal, Mark?" The teacher may say, "Guess what we are having for snack. They are orange, and bunnies like them."

Diapering/Toileting

Diapering is used as a time to stimulate recall of names of body parts and procedures. For instance, the parent may give an older infant the diaper and wait for the child to place it on the right body part. Toileting is frequently used to help children remember sequences, procedures, and social rules. For example, the parent may say, "Maya, you remembered to wipe and wash your hands, but you forgot something. What goes on your bottom? Yes! You forgot your underpants! Little girls need their underpants."

Dressing

Dressing is a good time for adults to help children remember names of body parts, types of clothing, concepts such as colors, procedures for dressing, and functions of objects. As part of the dressing process, early in infancy adults label these ideas. As infants acquire language, adults begin to ask questions requiring children to come up with the required label or action. With toddlers and young children, adults often ask higher level questions, requiring not only recall but problem-solving skills; for example, "It's cold today. What do you think would be a good thing to wear?"

Play Routines (Home and Classroom)

Face-to-Face Games

For infants, parents often stimulate recall of physical games. They will poise their fingers above the child's tummy and say, "I'm gonna get you!" and wait for the child to anticipate the game and start to giggle. Young children love to sing songs and fingerplays. Adults may get them started and then pause to see if they can remember the next phrase or movement.

Physical Play

For infants, play at the park or in the backyard typically involves imitation of actions seen or performed previously. As the child gets older and has increasingly adept motor skills, repetition of favorite games or sequences becomes predominant. Adults may also prompt memory for actions; for example, "Remember how you climbed on the dinosaur yesterday? Can you do that again?"

Manipulative Play

Adults use toy play to primarily encourage memory for labels and actions. They often ask what an object is, what color it is, what it is used for, and so forth. For young children in preschool, toy play often involves reproduction of actions seen previously, such as drawing pictures, building structures, or engaging in dramatic play involving representation of others' actions and behaviors.

Sensory Play

With infants, messy play requires memory of what happens when one does certain things with the materials (e.g., remembering the paint feels cold, makes marks). Caregivers of infants frequently model actions, which the child then imitates. Older children engage in reproduction of previously seen objects or actions, and adults frequently suggest topics from children's experiences for them to draw, build, or create.

Dramatic Play

Memory clearly is seen in dramatic play. Caregivers of infants prompt memory of routines by stimulating recreation of eating, drinking, sleeping, washing, and so forth. With older children, adults may stimulate memory for more complex events. For example, after reading a story, a teacher may provide some props from the story to encourage the children to remember and reenact the story sequences.

Reading and Learning Routines

Circle Time

During circle time, teachers may ask questions such as, "Does anyone remember the author of this book?" or "Who remembers what happens to the bear?" The teacher may leave out words while reading a story and have the children supply the missing word, phrase, or action; for example, "Then the wolf said, 'Little pig, little pig. . . .'" Children may be asked to recount the story for other children.

One-on-One Book Reading

The strategies discussed previously often are used by adults in one-to-one reading as well. In addition, the adult may make reference to the child's own life, triggering associations such as, "Have you ever been lost?" The adult may use knowledge of the child's awareness to stimulate memory; for example, "Bobby, look, all the words on this page start with *b*. What other words do you know that start with *b*?"

Everyday Literacy

As parents and other caregivers encounter pictures or symbols that are known to be familiar to the child, they often will engage the child in a discussion about the meaning of the symbol; for instance, "Look, Lacey, at what's on this box. What do you think we are having for lunch?" or while driving in the car, the parent might say, "There is a red light. What does that mean?"

PLANNING INDIVIDUALIZED INTERVENTIONS FOR IMPROVING MEMORY

II. A. What short- or long-term memory skills are evidenced through the child's spontaneous actions and communication?

Many types of short- and long-term memory are needed for successful functioning, including recognitory memory (i.e., recognizing something from memory), recall or generative memory (i.e., being able to produce something from memory), simple and complex procedural memory (i.e., being able to remember specific physical and mental sequences), and both simple and complex reconstructive memory for events (i.e., being able to physically, visually, or verbally reconstruct situations or events from memory). These are all discussed in more detail in TPBA2, Chapter 7. Strategies related to the development of each of these memory functions are described here.

Recognition is the most basic form of memory. The child needs to be able to call to mind that something has been encountered before and identify the meaning of the object or situation before more active recall through labeling or actions is possible. This requires encoding information in neural networks throughout various areas of the brain so that when stimuli are reengaged, the same neural networks are activated and recognition takes place.

Recognition begins in utero as the baby's brain processes sounds and movements. It is demonstrated shortly after birth as children recognize the familiar smell of the mother's breast milk and the sound of parents' voices. Most infants soon recognize familiar elements of their environment and move quickly into seeking new experiences and then relating these experiences to the familiar categories. Some children, however, require more support to build the foundations needed to process complex and long-term memories.

Being able to recall or generate actions, words, or sequences seen before is a higher level of memory than just recognizing something from past experience. As children begin to physically and verbally recall actions and words and use them in meaningful contexts, conceptual understanding is enhanced and behaviors are reinforced.

Memory for procedures requires ordered or sequential recall of actions. As infants begin to combine thoughts and actions, they lay the foundations for learning how to acquire complex skills. When combined with memory for the consequences of actions, memory for procedures leads children into goal-directed behaviors and problem solving. Therefore, supporting the development of procedural memory is fundamental to learning.

Reconstructing events through various forms of representation, such as doll or puppet play, dramatic play, manipulative play, construction, movement and dance, drawing, writing, and storytelling, requires integrating all forms of memory. All of the memory strategies outlined previously help the child be able to reconstruct. Early reconstructive memory is seen when children recreate the actions they have seen their parents perform. As neural structures become more complex, this reconstruction can be carried out in a variety of increasingly complicated reproductions.

The strategies mentioned previously are all applicable, as are the following interactional supports that may assist children who have difficulty remembering sequences or procedures.

Interaction Strategies

1. *Use predictable action patterns.* Do routines in the same way so the child recognizes what is happening. This means initially having a consistent caregiver for the child, because even diapering and feeding is done differently by individual people. For some children with disabilities, the use of a specific touch cue, sign, or gesture can be added to steps of a routine to help children recognize what is happening. Predictable patterns or sameness to routines also helps children recall and produce them on their own.

2. *Pair the unrecognized with something that is associated and known.* Because the familiar sparks memory, pairing the familiar with something else that is in some way associated with the familiar memory helps the child remember the new mental structure. In other words, it is just a little diversion from the main memory trace to establish a new one. For children who have visual impairment and cannot see what is being felt or talked about, using a recognized object can help children learn a new concept. For example, once the child feels the bottle and recognizes the shape and the actions that follow, touching other objects that are shaped like a bottle will indicate that drinking most likely will be occurring soon. In a similar way, children who are deaf learn a sign or movement of the lips associated with a label when the real object or picture of the object or action is presented consistently along with the sign, lip movements, or actions. Children who are neither visually impaired nor deaf also can learn to recognize objects and events in the same way.

For example, the child who likes to ride in the car may not recognize the meaning of the words *car* or *ride*. However, if each time the parent takes the child for a ride in the car the child holds the car keys, very soon the repetition of this association will lead the child to understand that when the car keys are presented, a car ride will follow. Such concrete associations can help the child to recognize and anticipate routines.

3. *Modify routines and introduce new materials.* Once the child shows recognition (e.g., through a change in facial expression or alteration in body tension, vocalizations, or movement), the adult can begin to introduce modifications. When another toy or object is presented, the child will probably choose the now-recognized toy, but interest soon will shift to the novel. Thus, learning can be transferred to new situations as the child recognizes an increasing number of events. For typical infants, this gradual transition is not needed. For children with significant delays, however, modification after recognition is established through consistency has been found to work best.

4. *Model or suggest next steps.* After the child initiates an action, the adult can model a next step. For instance, if the infant pushes down the lid on a pop-up box, the adult can model opening it. If the 30-month-old points to a toy he wants, the adult can suggest pushing over the step stool so he can reach it. If the 5-year-old is experimenting with a musical instrument, the adult can model producing a sequence of notes.

5. *Use rhyme and rhythm.* Children love music and rhymes. Lines from songs or fingerplays often are some of the first full sentences they remember. Singing the steps of a routine to the tune of a familiar song can help children remember the sequence; for instance, to the tune of "The Hokey Pokey"—"You put the soap on this hand, you put the soap on that hand, you put the soap on both hands, and you rub it all around." Chanting (e.g., "First, rub, rub, rub; then scrub, scrub, scrub!") or using an unusual inflection when performing a sequence can have a similar supportive effect on memory. For instance, emphasizing words in a sentence that are not usually emphasized helps the child attend to those words. If the adult says, "Let's wash those *dirty hands* and dry them," the noun and adjective are emphasized. If instead the adult says, "Let's *wash* those dirty hands, then *dry* them," the desired action sequence is emphasized and the unusual intonation captures the child's attention.

6. *Break down the procedure.* Children do not learn to navigate their community by being told to "Go to the store, buy a loaf of bread, and come home." They learn about space, direction, and distance by first learning how to make their way around a room, then their home, their yard, and their block. In the same way, children can learn to do complicated procedures by breaking the processes into smaller sequences. For example, the total process of bathing involves several smaller sequences. Taking clothing off is one sequence; getting into the tub is a second sequence; washing hair is a third sequence; washing the body is a fourth sequence; playing in the tub can involve several more sequences; getting out of the tub and drying off is another; dressing is another; and combing hair is a final sequence. If each of these is viewed as a separate set of steps, the overall process is accomplished more easily. A similar breakdown can be done with almost any task.

7. *Encourage the child to use self-talk.* Adults can model how to use "verbal mediation," or words to talk oneself through a series of actions. For instance, when making breakfast together, the parent might say, "First let's get out the eggs and butter. Then let's get out the pan. What should we do next?" When the child is making a drawing, the teacher can say, "Tell me what you are drawing first." When the child has completed that, the teacher can prompt more drawing by saying, "That's a mean-looking dragon! What else are you going to add?" Many children are "done" after making a simple drawing because they have not yet thought of drawing as a sequential activity. With a little encouragement or stimulation of memory, the teacher can expand drawing into a more complex activity. If the child has no idea what to add, the teacher might add, "Let's think about what else was in the story about the dragon."

Environmental Modifications

In addition to interpersonal strategies that may support the child's developing memory, environmental modifications often are useful. Depending on the findings from TPBA2, the team may want to consider some of the following environmental modifications.

1. *Present consistent sensory input.* Children recognize objects and situations by the "sameness" of the object or event. For instance, a bottle is recognized by its shape, a dog by the four legs and wagging tail, and a doctor by the white coat. Keeping the environment consistent and not introducing variations too quickly can help children recognize familiar objects and events. For children who are lower functioning developmentally, caretakers should present a consistent image (e.g., wearing similar clothing, hair style, the same perfume each day). As mentioned previously, before introducing variations, use the same toys until they are recognized and their functions are understood.

2. *Children are more likely to recognize and remember things that have unusual or unique characteristics or somehow capture their attention.* See Attention (Chapter 7, Section I, p. 490) for examples of environmental means of capturing children's attention. A special cue (e.g., color, texture), symbol, or aroma can help children recognize objects or people.

3. *Expose children to as many varied situations, events, and experiences as possible.* Take advantage of community venues, many of which are inexpensive (e.g., go to the park, take advantage of "free days" at zoos and museums). Experiences such as riding the bus, going hiking or camping, or just seeing the sights of the city all provide valuable memories for children to build on.

4. *Books can take children to places they cannot physically go and let them in on experiences they have not had.* Children in the desert learn about the ocean and snow through books, television, movies, and the computer. Judicious use of these latter media can open new worlds for children, particularly when they are not in a cartoon format.

5. *Use adaptive equipment to enable children to access these media more easily in order to acquire information.* (See Chapter 3, sensorimotor sections.)

6. *Use adaptive devices or assistive technology to enable children with special needs to express their thoughts and actions more easily.* Approaches may include gestures, signs, symbols, pictures, or voice output technology.

7. *Provide multisensory input when presenting an account of an event, a story, or other information that you want the child to be able to reconstruct or represent in some way.* For example, if a child sees, hears, feels, smells, tastes, and moves through aspects of an event (e.g., a trip to the circus), she is more likely to be able to reconstruct a more accurate, comprehensive representation of that experience than if she just reads a story about going to the circus. The story would give the child some knowledge of the circus, but not the sensory memories that contribute to constructing an experiential memory. Because children cannot always have the opportunity to participate directly in all possible experiences, the next best thing may have to suffice. Especially for children who have limited experiences due to their backgrounds or disabilities, it is necessary to ensure that children come to understand concepts and events through as many senses as possible. In the previous example, if the teacher reads *Olivia Goes to the Circus* and wants children to understand more fully what a circus is, the teacher may provide numerous experiences to accompany the book:

- Sounds on tape of animals in the circus

- Tactile experiences of sawdust, animal fur, sequins, and taffeta

- Smells of popcorn and cotton candy

- Dress-up costumes for clowns, animal tamers, and trapeze fliers

- A circus dramatic play area in the classroom with stuffed animals, a circus "ring," and a swing or mock trapeze

In the same way, a caregiver of infants or toddlers may read a book about a dog and bring a dog to the classroom along with its bowls, leash, and so forth. The next time the book is read or dogs are mentioned, a broad range of sensory memories will be elicited, bringing with them a variety of means of reconstructing the children's experience of playing with a dog.

8. *Use picture cards and objects to aid memory.* Picture cards and actual objects such as described in the previous scenario can help with reconstruction of memory, especially when arranged in the order in which events occurred. For example, the teacher might lay out 1) a stuffed dog, 2) a leash, 3) a bag of dog treats, and 4) a bowl. The toddlers could not recreate the whole event spontaneously, but they could act out the whole event with the objects as cues for the required words and actions.

II. B. How long does it take for the child to remember concepts, action sequences, or events?

Recall implies expressing what one knows through some type of behavior. This behavior may be sounds, gestures, words, signs, actions, pictures, or other means of representing understanding. In infancy and throughout early childhood, immediate imitation and then deferred imitation (without a model present) is an indicator of short-term and long-term memory, respectively. As the child integrates various types of information, behaviors reflect recall, generalization, and adaptation of information to meet individual needs.

Finding ways to increase the child's ability to quickly recall and express what is known often is a challenge for children with special needs. Attention, comprehension, and ability to process information and functionally use information is essential (see also Chapter 7, Section I. Strategies for Improving Attention; Chapter 6, Section I. Strategies for Improving Language Comprehension; and Chapter 3, Section IV. Strategies for Improving Motor Planning and Coordination). Both interpersonal and environmental strategies may be useful, including some of the following.

Interaction Strategies

1. *Provide time for recall.* Many children need more time for processing of information to take place. Adults should give children adequate time to respond before providing cues or scaffolding. This is true for both verbal and nonverbal behaviors.

2. *Use cues.* Children who have difficulty with recall often need a little clue to help them recall what is needed in a given situation. These cues or clues can come in many forms. For instance, a visual cue may assist some children. Real objects or simulations may function as cues. The caregiver may hold up two shirts and say, "Do you want to wear the red one or the blue one?"

Structuring the interactions to scaffold recall also is possible. For example, before going to the grocery store, the parent might sit down with the child's book with pictures of different foods and talk about what they want to get at the store. They could take the book along and then use the pictures to help the child recall what they want to get. A sound cue may also help. While in the fruit section of the grocery store, the parent might ask, "What fruit did you ask for?" When the child cannot remember, the parent might prompt with, "You said you want p-p-p . . . Right, pears!" A higher level child might respond to a game of clues such as, "It's yellow. It has a stem at the top. It's a little fatter on the bottom. And, it's your favorite fruit."

3. *Provide choices.* When asked a question, some children have difficulty because they cannot think of a response. If, however, the adult asks them to choose one of two choices, the child only has to recognize and recall those two ideas and then select a response. For example, if the parent says, "What do you want for breakfast?" the child may say, "I don't know." That question requires the child to remember all the possible options and then pick one. If, however, the parent says, "Do you want pancakes or cereal for breakfast?" the child now can envision those two options and think about which is preferred.

4. *Model various forms of reconstruction.* Children are born imitators. They want to do what adults do. If the adult says, "I had a taco for dinner," the young child is immediately prompted to talk about what he or she had for dinner.

Modeling dramatization is another form of support. The adult should select the events and sequences, the language, and the props to use in the reenactment based on the child's ability to reproduce sequences of actions. The adult can 1) model the role play; 2) facilitate the child's or children's role play; and 3) after the child has the sequence with facilitation, let the child reenact the sequence alone or with other children. Children with special needs may need more demonstration, suggestion, or turn taking to internalize the event being dramatized, and the adult may need to dramatize short sequences first, adding more actions as the child begins to remember the practiced actions.

5. *Elicit reconstruction.* Children with delays or disabilities may get "stuck" in one aspect of a reconstruction; for instance, stacking blocks or lining them up. Adults can help children think of other aspects of a construction by giving them prompts or reminding them of other ideas. For example, the child who starts to construct a road and then gets carried away with the road and forgets the purpose of the road can be reminded by the adult interjecting actions or questions such as, "Here comes the police car down the road. He has on his siren. Here is your car" or "I'm putting a house at the end of the road so the car can drive into the garage."

Reconstruction can be elicited through storytelling, with the adult encouraging the process by saying, for example, "Oh, my goodness! And then what happened?" Reconstruction can occur in puppet play, with the adult playing one character and extracting the story and actions from the child's puppet; for instance, "You were so nice to ask me over. Can I have some cookies?"

Drawing can tell a story. As described previously, by commenting or suggesting, adults can help children remember another aspect of the story the picture tells.

Dance and music can help children remember stories or narratives. Adults can put stories to music and then move with gestures, words, and dance to depict the actions. For example, with classical music and filmy scarves, the children can portray the wind blowing the clouds and the leaves, the leaves falling down, and the new plants growing in the spring.

6. *Prompt extension of ideas.* Use verbal strategies such as

Comments: "That flower seems to be missing something" (on a child's drawing); "I brought you a present" (in dramatic play)

Suggestions: "It looks like a happy flower. I'll bet the sun is shining" (on a child's drawing); "We could make a cake for the party!" (in dramatic play)

Questions: "How is the little girl going to get into the house?" (on a child's drawing); "What can we use for candles?" (in dramatic play)

Prompts: "It looks like he is. . . ." (on a child's drawing); "I think the baby needs something to eat" (in dramatic play)

Environmental Modifications

In addition to interpersonal strategies that may support the child's memory, environmental modifications often are useful. Depending on the findings from TPBA2, the team may want to consider some of the following environmental modifications.

1. *Use picture cues for choice making.* Pictures of objects or actions can help children make choices or communicate wants and needs. A variety of assistive devices exist for aiding children in generating responses when oral means are difficult (see Chapter 6, Section II. Strategies for Improving Language Production, for picture communication devices). Pictures also can stimulate recall of ideas. For instance, the toddlers' teacher may hold up two different books and ask, "What is the name of the book we read before lunch?" This is not giving children a choice between two provided answers, as pointed out previously, but it helps children generate a response using a visual reminder.

2. *Use picture or symbol cues to guide actions.* Pictures can help children understand what event or action should happen next. These cues are particularly helpful for children who have trouble remembering rules (e.g., *share* illustrated by two children playing with one truck) or recalling a sequence of events (e.g., first circle time, then centers), or a sequence of actions (e.g., first put the flour in, then pour in the milk, then stir). Children with autism spectrum disorders, who often perseverate on an action, may benefit from seeing a picture or visual symbol to remind them of what comes next. Pictures of items also often are placed in classrooms next to where the items belong (e.g., picture of blocks on the block shelf).

3. *Use consistent patterns of associations.* Just as adults come to expect the keys on the computer keyboard to be in the same place every day, children use consistent environmental cues to help them remember. Although the toys, materials, and activities may change from day to day, the schedule, location of centers, and expected interactions stay predictable. As changes are introduced, caregivers and teachers need to provide visual, auditory, and tactile supports to help children recall needed information, actions, and events.

4. *Establish routines.* Procedures are easier to remember if they remain consistent from one time to the next. Let the child help establish the routine, deciding what should happen first, second, and so forth. For example, at bedtime the parent can let the child decide if he or she should read in a chair or in bed, which animals should sleep with the child (or how many), or if music will be left on while the child goes to sleep. Keeping this routine helps the child know what to expect and helps the child feel safe and in control. It also builds procedural memory. In the same way, if picture cards are used to cue the child about a sequence of actions, present them in the same space and order each time.

5. *Present smaller segments for complex procedures.* Complex procedures can be overwhelming for children who have difficulty sequencing ideas. For them, it is important to present smaller segments that can then be combined to accomplish a larger goal.

Building a whole town of blocks, for instance, requires a long-term plan. If the teacher leaves the blocks out in a special space, the children can add to their "town" each day, building different parts, adding props, signs, and so forth. Seeing the old construction each day helps them recall the sequence. They can then recount the sequence each day as it comes together and then determine what is still needed.

ROUTINES FOR THE CHILD WHO NEEDS SUPPORT WITH MEMORY

Daily Routines (Home and Classroom)

Feeding/Eating

For infants, recognition and recall of food, and anticipation of the sequence involved in eating, is important. Parents hold up bottles and jars of baby food, model opening their mouths, and label the foods and actions of the baby. For babies who are not as quick to respond, these actions can be slowed and exaggerated, with plenty of wait time for a response demonstrating memory. For children with visual impairments, using object cues for them to feel may prepare them for what is happening. For older children, eating is a time to learn to remember manners, consequences of different table behaviors (e.g., spitting milk), and the whole sequence from setting the table to cleaning up. Caregivers can support the child by asking questions such as, "What else do we need?"; "What should we do next?"; "We are having hamburgers, what else should we have with them?"; or "What would happen if I spit my milk on Daddy?"

Diapering/Toileting

Early in infancy, caregivers begin to prepare children for the sequences involved in independent toileting. Infants experience the undressing, cleaning, and redressing. They begin to anticipate the next action in the sequence and move their body parts to assist. All of this contributes to the memory base they will need for learning independent toileting. If this time is made into an interactive time, by labeling body parts, playing face-to-face games, and encouraging and reinforcing initiation and participation on the part of the child, the experience of toileting later is more likely to be imbued with positive memories and motivation for recreating this feeling of independence. Adults need to break down the steps for children with delays, ask children to label various aspects of the task, and ask them to remember what they need to do next. Picture cues in the bathroom may be helpful for some children.

Dressing

Dressing involves motor skills as well as memory for what to wear and how to dress. Using small cues, the adult can provide reminders. For example, holding the neck of a shirt open and positioning it for the child to put her head in is a reminder cue of what the child is supposed to do. Asking, "What goes in this hole?" is another prompt for remembering the names of body parts. Requiring the child to recall and initiate a procedural response provides opportunities for repetition, eventually leading to dressing habits. For children with disabilities, who may take longer to dress, it is particularly important not to control the dressing, or "do it for them."

Going Out

Excursions into the community provide many prospects for adding experiences to the memory pool. In addition, the child has the opportunity to recognize, recall, and enhance memories by enriching them with personal meaning. Adults should point out familiar items, encouraging recognition; ask questions, encouraging recall; and help the child make associations to previous experiences, encouraging episodic or personal memory.

Play Routines (Home and Classroom)

Face-to-Face Play

Face-to-face play can involve several types of memory. If the child sees the adult get in position to play and smiles, she recognizes or anticipates that a game is coming. If she imitates the faces or actions of the adult, she is demonstrating immediate recall. If she initiates a series of actions, she is using sequential memory. If the game follows certain "rules" or movements, such as in fingerplays, procedural memory is involved. Children love repetition, so even if adults are bored with "The Itsy Bitsy Spider," they should be mindful that repetition builds memory skills. The adult should begin at the child's level and follow the child's interest lead. The adult can also use these motivating games to introduce new words, expressions, and movements, and the memory cycle will begin again.

Physical Play

As with face-to-face play, physical play can involve imitation, initiation, turn taking, and repetition. Many types of physical play require visual-spatial memory, as the child moves around the environment. Physical activities such as riding a tricycle also involve procedural memory, games such as Duck-Duck-Goose involve memory for rules, and rough-and-tumble play requires memory for social consequences. Although free play capitalizes on recognition and recall of previous play events, it does not challenge higher level memory skills. It is important for adults working with children with special needs to provide all of these types of physical play experiences to help children develop and use all types of memory skills.

Manipulative Play

Free play with manipulatives enables children to recognize and remember what to do with toys. Depending on the child's level of understanding, manipulative play also may involve complex procedures and reconstructive memory, such as is needed for building a block castle. For younger children, adults want to encourage the development of sequential memory by modeling, suggesting, or questioning next steps. For older children, providing unusual combinations of manipulatives will force children to think about how these materials were used in the past and how they can be combined in new ways. For example, putting out a shoe box, action figures, scraps of material, and Legos promotes recall of previous experience, but also prompts the child to make new associations. Building neural networks requires expansion beyond the familiar for children at any age. The adult's role is to continually provide situations in which this can occur and to stimulate memories that will lead children to the next level of learning. In the previous situation, if the child responds to the play materials by repetitively putting the action figure in and out of the box, the adult might say, "It looks like you are putting the man to bed. He needs a blanket to cover him up." This prompt may allow the child to see the scrap of material in a new way, make an association to his own experience, and then add a new, higher level step to his play sequence. The adult needs to continually read the child's actions and try to anticipate what experiences or associations might be familiar to the child. Using the piece of material as a parachute might be an appropriate suggestion for some children, but it will not trigger any memories for many children.

Dramatic Play

Dramatic play requires the use of all forms of memory and thus should be supported at home, in child care, and in school. Dramatic play requires the child to reconstruct his or her world. As with manipulative play, discussed in the previous paragraph, the props and materials available promote creative thinking, but adult facilitation also is critical. Keeping in mind that building and strengthening neural networks for memory is a goal, the adult may introduce dramatic play for the novice dramatic player with familiar props and daily routines, but these should quickly be modified with new materials and activities. Once comfortable with the idea of reconstructing events, the adult should introduce ever-changing dramatic play situations to build on both familiar and new experiences and information. For example, dramatic play props in preschool typically involve kitchen materials and plastic food. After several days of play with these materials, the play is reliant primarily on recall and repetitive reconstruction of the same events. By introducing new materials, such as a stuffed dog, a dog bed, an empty dog food bag, and a leash, the child who has a pet dog at home will immediately transform his or her play in a new direction. The adult may then introduce new props when the puppy gets "sick" and needs to go to the veterinarian. The child now has an opportunity to learn novel vocabulary and new procedures and to reconstruct unique events (particularly if a field trip or visit to the vet is part of the child's experience).

Reading and Learning Routines

Circle Time

Many of the same skills that are addressed in one-on-one reading can be addressed in circle time, but because each group represents a range of abilities, the task for the teacher or caregiver is more difficult and requires the ability to modify interactions to meet individual child needs. Strategies that may help include:

- Have board books for children to hold and look at along with the teacher.

- Use big books that are easier to see.

- Use real objects or props depicted in the book.

- Modify the text in complex books so they are at the child's level.

- Discuss or ask questions at different levels for individual children; for example, instead of asking, "Does anyone remember the name of the rabbit?" which will be answered quickly by a child who does not need this low-level prompt, the teacher should direct that question to the child who is at that level. The higher level child might be asked, "Why would a rabbit want wings?" This requires memory of characteristics of rabbits, memory of the function of wings, and reconstructive memory for what would happen if the rabbit were transformed.

- Use sign language, gestures, and dramatization to illustrate words and actions and provide multisensory input.

- Use assistive devices to enable children at all levels to participate (e.g., picture charts, voice output devices).

One-on-One Book Reading

Most children love to sit on a lap and look at books or be read to. This is a critical time for building semantic memory, or memory for words, sentence structure, inflection, narrative, and concepts of print. Because reading is a complex procedure, it also is a time for helping children recognize and remember all of the procedures involved in reading. From infancy throughout early childhood, adults should take time to read individually to children each day. At home, time for reading to the child is usually available. In child care and preschool, the number of children present often means that individual reading time is sacrificed to group reading. This should not be the case. Throughout the day, teachers need to capture moments to read to individual children. During free play time, when children are going down for a nap, when they are waking up—whenever possible—one-on-one (or even two) interaction enables the adult to address each of the aspects of semantic and procedural memory associated with language and reading based on the child's individual developmental level. During this time, adults model language; discuss vocabulary, actions, sequence, and characters; point out literacy concepts; ask questions to elicit different types of memory skills; relate books to children's experiences; and encourage children to use their emerging language and literacy skills in a supportive situation.

Math and Science

Much of what we think of as math and science (e.g., counting, manipulating numbers, categorizing objects and materials) is based on early concept development and mental comparison of characteristics such as amount; shape; function; similarities and differences; and space, time, and distance awareness. Memory for these aspects and their relationships can be supported by the adult. All of the previous strategies are useful. What is important is the focus of the adult's interactions with the child. Children's own experiences channel their memories, but adults can help direct both the experiences and the actions and thoughts associated with those experiences. For example, a caregiver is interacting with an infant who is playing with a plastic ball with spinners inside. The adult may emphasize that this is a ball and play with it in a fashion similar to other balls, by rolling it back and forth. This reinforces the child's recognition of the object and recall of its use through previous experiences, and it also expands the notion of "types" of balls. The adult also could shake the ball, spin the ball, or rotate it to make the inner spinners move. This interaction would encourage recall of similar cause-and-effect experiences, which might stimulate the child to experiment with imitating this action. Interaction with the same toy with a young child might involve looking at speed or distance when the ball moves down a ramp at different degrees of incline, comparing the spinners to other things that spin, examining the components, or dramatizing a space ship coming from the moon. The actions, discussion, and questions elicited by both the child and adult will influence the types of memory that are stimulated or strengthened.

XENA

Xena is a 3-year-old with Down syndrome. She has some language, mostly labels for objects and names of family members. She is able to walk and play independently, although much of her play is repetitive. Xena's favorite toys are her doll, which she likes to feed; an empty tissue box that she is fond of filling with small objects; a toy piano that she enjoys banging; and a dictionary book of pictures. In terms of memory skills, Xena is ready to increase her memory for words, including objects and actions; improve her memory for sequences of actions with objects and routines; and, in her dramatic play, reconstruct actions she sees others perform. The following suggestions were made to be incorporated into her daily routines at home and at preschool.

Interaction Strategies

1. *Use the activities that Xena likes and show her how to expand the sequence with a new step that is part of her repertoire. This will enable her to learn and remember*

new ways to play with toys. For example, use Xena's favorite tissue box in a variety of ways that incorporates two- to three-step action sequences. For instance, play a game where you put two items that Xena can name in the box. Have her cover the box with a cloth, close her eyes, and then feel to find the item you ask for. This requires her to use memory for words and tactile recognition, and it involves three steps. After you have guided this game several times, let Xena hide items for you to see if she can remember the steps.

2. *Use Xena's box for a variety of types of play. This will help her break the "habit" of using it for only one thing. For example, pretend it is a bed for a small stuffed animal, turn it over and make it a table for her doll, or combine it with blocks and use it as a big block to construct a wall or tower. Again, model several action steps and repeat the play sequences several times. Then leave the materials out to see if Xena remembers these actions independently. You also can involve her peers so they will continue to model for her.*

3. *Use Xena's baby doll in many routines of the day. When Xena eats, she can feed her baby. When she goes to the toilet, her baby can sit on her tissue box. When Xena gets dressed, her baby can get dressed. When Xena is read to and goes to bed, her baby can be read to and put to bed. The adult can model doing actions with the doll and let Xena participate. Use the opportunity to label body parts and actions. The adult can encourage recall by prompting, "Baby is going to. . . ." Make the materials that are used in the routines available in Xena's play area; for example, wash cloths, blanket, toilet paper, pillow, and so forth. After several days, Xena will probably begin to reconstruct these scenarios during her play.*

4. *Use Xena's toy piano in a variety of ways. Use one finger and model pushing on one key and then one more. Sing words that she knows in time to the sounds; for example, "Xe-na-play" and "Mom-my-play." This type of play pairs three types of input—auditory, visual, and tactile. The rhythm helps Xena remember the words and pair them with the actions. Use Xena's pattern (whatever she plays) and add words to her rhythm. Once she gets the idea of the game, you can modify it so that you add notes, or clap a pattern that she plays, or dance to the rhythm. She also may practice new words she learns this way. Place objects next to the piano and then "play" the words, such as "ba-na-na" or "ba-by." This should be a fun game and not "therapy." Follow Xena's lead in when to start and stop.*

5. *Introduce new toys by using simple, interesting actions that are easy for Xena to imitate. Repeat the play activities several times so that she can remember what to do.*

Environmental Modifications

1. *Xena has low tone resulting from Down syndrome. Although she is able to walk and play independently, she will be able to manipulate toys and materials more easily if she is stable without having to lean on her arms or a table. A cube chair will enable her to sit comfortable at a small table. On the floor, encourage her to sit cross-legged or straight-legged rather than in a W-sit. These are stable positions that are not harmful for her hips.*

2. *Xena likes pictures and recognizes the pictures of many objects. Use of picture sequences for routines could help her remember each step of an activity such as going to the toilet or dressing. Picture sequences also will help her caregivers follow a consistent routine and encourage them to have her remember and do the routines independently.*

KEYS TO INTERVENTION BY DEVELOPMENTAL AGE

The following ideas are directed toward children who are functioning at approximately the following levels. The suggestions are not meant to be all-inclusive, but rather are indicative of potential areas for exploration.

Developmental age	Memory skills	Keys to intervention
Birth to 3 months	Imitates facial movements. Repeats interesting actions.	Engage in face-to-face play. Use exaggerated expression. Let child experience actions that cause something to happen.
3–6 months	Recognizes familiar objects. Imitates sounds and movements.	Present objects to see, feel, move, taste, and smell. Use slow movements so the child can see how to imitate. Exaggerate mouth movements and sounds for imitation.
6–9 months	Activates object. Repeats short sequence to attain a goal. Anticipates what is going to happen.	Present materials that do something (e.g., household objects such as light switch or toys that move, light up, or make noise). Model second action after child's initial action. Hold up object or object cue (e.g., car keys) and wait for the child to anticipate next event.
9–12 months	Finds objects. Remembers simple games. Knows meaning of many words. Remembers how others use tools.	Play Hide-and-Seek games with favorite toys. Ask recognition questions (e.g., "Where's the ball?" "Do you want the ball or the rain stick?").
12–18 months	Remembers strategies and applies to new situations. Recognizes and points to objects and pictures. Has names for people and objects. Imitates words. Recognizes places.	Point out similarities in situations. Ask questions related to objects and pictures. Label objects and point out characteristics. Use new vocabulary and encourage imitation. Note characteristics of sites, events, and so forth.
18–24 months	Remembers and talks about experiences. Remembers action sequences for long periods.	Recall and discuss the sequence of actions in books, activities, routines, and events. Provide materials to be used in combination and materials that require action sequences for all types of play.
24–36 months	Dramatizes events. Recognizes and labels books, signs, symbols. Discusses activities of self and others.	Provide real materials from household and community for dramatic play. Elicit comparisons of people, objects, activities, and events. Point out and discuss environmental print and symbols. Share books and discuss details.
36–48 months	Remembers details of events. Remembers whole songs/fingerplays. Fills in missing words from songs, stories, dramatic play scripts. Remembers landmarks. Counts. Uses complex sentences and descriptors.	Recount sequences after an activity, event, or story. Play word games, make up songs and fingerplays. Extend stories into dramatic play. Use materials for unusual purposes. Model a variety of sentence structures in play and routines. Ask open-ended questions to elicit more complex language.
48–60 months	Remembers events in a story. Dramatizes event sequences. Bases behavior on consequences of previous experiences.	Let the child "read" the book. Point out concepts related to reading and print. Discuss consequences of own and others' actions and relate to the child's experiences.

Developmental age	Memory skills	Keys to intervention
48–60 months (*continued*)	Can determine what is missing from situations. Recognizes and names familiar songs.	Play "sabotage" games in which not everything that is needed is present. Play games with simple rules. Play matching games and games requiring naming, comparing, counting, and sequencing.
60–72 months	Can recite verses; detailed memories for experiences; elaborate play scripts and recreation of stories. Remembers sequences of numbers, words.	Play memory games and model memory strategies such as self-talk, using visual-spatial techniques, and associations. Provide opportunities to recite or sing verses. Extend fun experiences (e.g., a trip to the zoo) by reading related books (e.g., *If I Ran the Zoo*), and providing props (e.g., stuffed animals) to dramatize experiences.

7

Facilitating Cognitive Development

III.   Strategies for Improving Problem Solving

Goal Attainment Scale

1	2	3	4	5	6	7	8	9
Recognizes changes in people, objects, or actions.		Is able to see the relationship between a simple action or event and what caused it to occur.		Is able to make a desired familiar event occur using another person or by him- or herself.		Is able to perform a series of actions toward an unfamiliar goal and use trial and error manipulation to make corrections.		Is able to understand complex causal relationships, mentally organize sequences toward a goal, and make modifications as needed. Can then generalize results to new situations.

Understanding problem solving requires a definition of the word *problem*. For purposes of working with young children, the definition is very broad. A problem involves a situation in which something is puzzling to the child. The quandary can be related to what something (e.g., person, object, situation, event) is, what it does, how it does what it does, why it does what it does, or how something can be changed to achieve a specific outcome. Problems can be related to objects, situations, or social interactions.

Problem solving involves identifying a problem, planning what needs to be done, executing a solution, evaluating the result, and making modifications if necessary (Zelazo & Mueller, 2002). Problem solving integrates both conceptual knowledge and procedural knowledge. The brain organizes information from the vestibular, proprioceptive, vision, hearing, tactile, taste, and olfactory sensory systems into perceptual and conceptual systems for understanding objects, people, events, relationships, and abstractions. Depending on how a problem is perceived and interpreted and on the child's goals, individual processing strategies, and physical ability to implement the strategy, outcomes will vary. The problems the child needs to solve and the strategies used will vary at different developmental levels.

Problem solving is critical for all areas of development. Children need to be able to figure out how to make things happen and understand whether they were successful in the areas of thinking skills, social skills, physical skills, and communication abilities. Skillful problem solving in these areas contributes to the development of successful social relations, acquisition of knowledge, and ability to meet one's needs.

Attention and memory in the cognitive domain and emotional and behavioral regulation in the emotional and social domain are closely related to problem solving (see Chapter 7, Section I. Strategies for Improving Attention; Chapter 7, Section II. Strategies for Improving Memory; Chapter 5, Section III. Strategies for Improving State and Emotional Regulation; Chapter 5, Section IV. Strategies for Improving Behavioral Regulation) and should be viewed as interrelated with this section.

APPROPRIATE PROBLEM SOLVING

Infants are born with the ability to discriminate likenesses and differences, changes in actions, and other subtle characteristics of people, objects, and events. As noted in Section II on memory (page 500), the infant soon learns to remember actions and anticipate what will follow; for example, when the mother bares her breast or shows the baby a bottle, the child knows that feeding will follow. Children also learn early in infancy that their actions can cause something to happen; for instance, when they cry, their mother or father will respond. By the end of the first year, infants are gaining voluntary control of their actions and begin to sequence behaviors to achieve a specific result. The infant may crawl over to a ball and then throw it toward a parent in order to get the parent to throw it back. If the ball rolls the wrong way, the infant may pursue it and try again. By the end of the first year, infants can determine whether an effort on their part was successful. Their persistence and ability to try again is a key to their future accomplishments. During the second year, toddlers learn to try multiple ways to accomplish their goals and get their needs met. They experiment with fine and gross motor problem solving, in addition to tackling cognitive tasks. They also begin to encounter conflict with peers and have to learn strategies for solving social problems as well. Adults play a major role in helping children learn how to handle all of these challenging situations. During the preschool and kindergarten years, children can see relationships among and across objects, people, situations, and events. Their problem solving is very concrete, but they are beginning to generalize rules for when, why, and how various things occur.

Appropriate Problem Solving in Practice

▓▓▓▓ **III. A. What behaviors indicate understanding of causal
reasoning skills or problem solving (executive function)?**

Daily Routines (Home and Classroom)

Infant/toddler: The infant drops his spoon off the highchair and looks to his mother to get it.

Young child: The young child runs to the window to see if the birds have come to eat the bread she put out. When she does not see any birds, she says, "The birds are sleeping."

Play Routines (Home and Classroom)

Infant/toddler: The infant swipes at the busy box in his crib, anticipating that its parts will move.

Young child: The young child drops a marble down a hole and then moves around to watch for it to come out the other side.

Classroom Routines

During circle time, the teacher asks a question and the child raises her hand to answer.

▨▨▨▨ III. B. How does the child identify and plan a solution to a problem?

Daily Routines (Home and Classroom)

Infant/toddler: The toddler sees the milk on the floor, says, "Spill," and looks for a towel.

Young child: At bedtime, the child says to his dad, "I'm hungry. I need to eat something before I go to bed."

Play Routines (Home and Classroom)

Infant/toddler: The infant reaches out to catch a bubble and looks at his hand when the bubble disappears. Then he looks back at the adult and reaches toward her.

Young child: The young child says, "You made it too tall and it fell."

Classroom Routines

Out on the playground, one child starts to cry. The teacher said, "What happened?" Another child responds, "Alex took Mary's trike."

▨▨▨▨ III. C. How well does the child organize, monitor, and evaluate progress toward a goal and make corrections?

Daily Routines (Home and Classroom)

Infant/toddler: The toddler opens the drawer, pulls out a shirt, and puts it on his head. He then shouts to his mother for help.

Young child: The young child tries to put on his jacket but has it upside down, so he takes it off and starts again.

Play Routines (Home and Classroom)

Infant/toddler: The toddler puts the square block in the round hole on the shape sorter. When it does not fit, she tries the square hole.

Young child: The child is building a garage for his cars, and he stacks blocks into a tower in each corner and then lays a long block across the top. When one corner is too short, he removes the long block and studies the situation.

Classroom Routines

In the science center, the child tries to put together the dinosaur puzzle. When the piece does not fit, he examines it, looks at the puzzle, and fits it in the right space.

▨▨▨▨ III. D. How quickly can the child analyze a problem situation and respond?

Daily Routines (Home and Classroom)

Infant/toddler: The toddler sees a toy on a shelf and tries to reach it. When he finds he cannot reach it, he pushes over a chair and climbs up to get it.

Young child: In the preschool classroom, the child goes to get another plate for a child who does not have one.

Play Routines (Home and Classroom)

Infant/toddler: The toddler picks up another cube block and this time immediately places it over the square opening and pushes it in.

Young child: The child looks at his block structure and decides that the long block is falling off the top of his two towers because one tower is too short. He adds another block to the short tower and then replaces the long block across the two block towers. He smiles when it does not fall.

Classroom Routines

In the dramatic play center, one child is pretending to be a doctor. The other child says, "I've got a tummy ache." The "doctor" scribbles on a piece of paper and says, "Here's a 'scription.'"

▆▆▆▆▆ **III. E. How well can the child generalize information from one situation to another?**

Daily Routines (Home and Classroom)

Infant/toddler: The toddler takes his mother's car key to his riding car and tries to find a hole to put it in.

Young child: The page of the magazine she is reading with her mother accidentally tears. The young child says, "I can fix it." She goes to the "junk" drawer and brings back cellophane tape.

Play Routines (Home and Classroom)

Infant/toddler: The toddler sees a new toy with a button and she pushes the button to see what will happen.

Young child: The young child is playing house with his sister. She hands him a pretend cupcake. He says, "Thanks," and pretends to peel off the imaginary cupcake paper.

Classroom Routines

The children are watching the hamster run in his cage. The young child goes to the Tinkertoys on the table and tries to make a wheel.

GENERAL PRINCIPLES FOR SUPPORTING APPROPRIATE PROBLEM SOLVING

Help Identify the Problem

Before problem solving can take place, the child needs to recognize that something is amiss. This means that an action does not go as expected, an unexpected outcome occurs, an obstacle is encountered, or an answer is unknown. Adults help children identify that a problem exists. Parents often use sounds with infants to indicate that a predicament has occurred. They often will say, "Uh-oh!" or "Oops!" or "Hm-m-m." These sounds soon become associated with difficulties encountered, and children also begin to use these sounds to indicate that something is wrong. Parents usually follow these sounds with a gesture or comment that indicates the nature of the trouble. For example, when the child's toy falls off the couch, the parent may say, "Uh-oh. There goes your rattle." As the child acquires language comprehension, such comments indicate what occurred that was problematic.

As the child gets older, the parent begins to assist the child in identifying the problem. The parent may point to the issue at hand, frown, gesture "What?" or say, "What happened?" All of these communications are attempts at helping the child see that there is a dilemma.

Explore and Identify Relationships

Most parents follow up the identification of a problem with a clarification of what the problem is or make an attempt to assist the child in discovering why a problem exists. For instance, if banging on the lever does not make the lid on the toy pop up, the caregiver may say, "Uh-oh. Banging doesn't work." The caregiver may then go on to encourage discovery by saying, "Hm-m-m. Try something else." If the child continues to bang or push, the parent may identify a characteristic and an option to try, such as, "It's like a handle. Pull it."

Make a Plan

For older children, caregivers often help the child think about a course of action; for example, "You hurt Sophie's feelings. What do you think you should do to make her feel better?" At this point, the child may either have her own idea or no idea at all. In the first instance, the child may offer a plan. "Say 'sorry,'" or "I give her the doll." The child also may respond with what she feels is an appropriate response, such as going and giving Sophie a hug. If the child does not respond, either because she does not want to or because she has no idea what to do, the parent usually gives the child a suggestion or options. Typically, the parent just tells the child an appropriate response (although giving options would be more thought provoking).

Try Out the Plan

Regardless of the age of the child, experimentation is the path to learning. Whether it is an infant learning that kicking the mobile results in its movement or a preschool-age child discovering that it takes 12 eggs to fill a carton, children learn by testing their hypotheses. The caregiver or teacher supports problem solving by encouraging investigation and persistence in the child's efforts. For example, the teacher might say, "How many eggs do you think it will take to fill the carton for a dozen eggs?" If the child says, "Ten," the teacher would say, "Why don't you put ten eggs in the carton and see if you are right?"

Revise the Plan

When initial efforts at problem solving do not work, the adult helps the child think about what went wrong and how to revise the plan. For the infant who cannot pull the lever to make the lid pop up, the adult may either model pulling the lever, assist the child to pull it, or change the goal and point to the button that can be pushed or banged to open it. For the preschool-age child who discovers that 10 eggs do not fill the carton, the adult may say, "What do you think now? Do you have a new idea?"

Celebrate Success

Typically, caregivers and teachers reward successful outcomes. Parents clap when the child walks without falling down, cheer when the child puts a letter in the mailbox successfully, and give "high fives" when he gets his pants on accurately. Children love to receive reinforcement and they begin to feel a sense of pride in their accomplishments as they begin to recognize that they actually did solve a problem.

THE PRINCIPLES IN PRACTICE

For young children, life is one challenge after another. Fortunately, they do not typically see this as a negative situation. In fact, the problems and dilemmas encountered throughout the day provide the essence of the joy of discovery. The following are examples of how the adults in children's lives support the development of their problem-solving skills.

Daily Routines (Home and Classroom)

Feeding/Eating

At mealtime, the caregiver offers the child a choice between a spoon and a fork to eat pudding. When the child picks the fork, the caregiver lets her eat several bites and then lets her try the spoon. The caregiver comments on how much more pudding the child gets with the spoon. The adult's role is to help the child experiment and compare results, pointing out why one works better than the other.

Diapering/Toileting

As the child begins to understand the sequence of steps in diapering, the caregiver lets the child help with the steps, such as attaching the sticky strip on the disposable diaper or pulling the pants up and down.

Dressing

When the child attempts to snap, button, or zip, the adult does the first step, positioning the fastener, and then uses language to support his or her problem solving; for instance, "Here, I'll hold it. You pull!"

Play Routines (Home and Classroom)

Face-to-Face Play

Peekaboo is a favorite adult–child game that uses problem solving. The adult disappears under a blanket, then waits for the child to pull the blanket off. Initially, the parent models this effort on the child and on him- or herself.

Physical Play

An older version of Peekaboo involves Hide-and-Seek. Adults typically make the hiding spots very easy (in fact, the adult can usually be seen hiding under the table or behind a chair). As the child begins to understand the hiding sequence, the adult begins to make the hiding places more difficult.

Manipulative Play

In Western cultures, cause-and-effect toys involving problem solving often are the first objects the child handles. Objects that make noise or move when shaken, swiped, or hit involve the child figuring out how to get an event to recur. Sometimes the event happens by accident, as when a rattle is moved and it makes noise. Other times the adult shows the child the event and tries to help the child make it happen again, by using hand-over-hand or physical manipulation of the child.

Sensory Play

Problem solving with messy sensory materials and art materials usually is done to experience what the materials feel like, what they can do, and in the case of art materials, how they can be used to make something. Adults encourage problem solving by allowing exploration or trial and error, by asking guiding questions, and by demonstrating.

Dramatic Play

Dramatic play involves a higher level of problem solving, because the child has to make up the sequence of actions and events and the problems the characters will encounter. The adult offers suggestions for problems such as, "Oh, no! The bus ran out of gas!" When the child has difficulty generating a solution to a problem, the adult can offer hints, asking, for example, "What could we use for a gas station?" When no solution is forthcoming, the adult may demonstrate a solution; for instance, "We could use these blocks and make a gas station and gas pumps."

Reading and Learning Routines

Circle Time

Teachers often help children with social problem solving in group situations. They point out the problem and often give children the solution; for example, "I can't hear when everyone is talking. Maddie, you have your hand raised. What would you like to say?"

One-on-One Book Reading

During book sharing, adults point out the problems presented in the books and involve children in predicting the resolution. For instance, when reading *The Three Bears*, the adult may say, "Look what happened when she sat in the baby bear's chair! What is going to happen when the three bears come home? What do you think she should do?"

Math and Science

Opportunities for problem solving in the home, community, and school related to classification, physics, math, and so forth present themselves every day. Adults support learning by pointing out problems, noting what is happening, and helping children to think about what they are experiencing. In the car, for example, they may play a game such as, "I see something that is brown and has a fluffy tail, is climbing a tree, and eats nuts."

PLANNING INDIVIDUALIZED INTERVENTIONS FOR IMPROVING PROBLEM SOLVING

All of the strategies described previously are useful for a broad range of children, with and without special needs. However, additional strategies are needed for children who do not respond to traditional approaches. Children with cognitive delays, information processing challenges, visual or auditory processing problems, attention-deficit/hyperactivity disorder, and many other disabilities encounter difficulties with problem solving. For some children, the difficulties stem from a lack of conceptual understanding of the situation, others lack persistence to try to solve the problem, and still others are unable to see relationships with regard to cause and effect. Children with motor difficulties may have conceptual understanding but lack the ability to put their ideas into practice. Some children can do problem solving relating to concrete objects they can see and manipulate, but they cannot discern causes and consequences in social situations. Problem solving is a complex process and must be examined with regard to all areas of development.

▪▪▪▪ III. A. What behaviors indicate understanding of causal reasoning skills or problem solving (executive function)?

In order to do problem solving, the child has to see relationships and have a basic understanding that something is not as it should be and that something has happened to cause this to occur. Problems solving also requires that the child understand that something needs to happen for a desired outcome to occur. The first part of problem solving is this basic understanding and anticipation of what should happen in the environment.

Many children with delays or disabilities may not even understand there is a problem to solve. They do not notice the characteristics that have created a discrepancy or transformation, and therefore they cannot anticipate what is going to occur. Children with autism, for example, may focus on one aspect of a situation and ignore others that are relevant. For instance, the child may look at and repeatedly spin the wheels on a toy car and not notice the other aspects of the car. Children with attention issues may be easily distracted by other input and not attend long enough to any one thing to discover all the relevant aspects of a situation. Ability to identify a challenge requires a variety of sensory input. Children who cannot see, hear, feel, or explore objects or situations fully due to disabilities may need assistance to identify the relevant characteristics of a situation. For example, a child with motor disabilities may not be able to move her body to orient to a given situation or may not be able to manipulate an object to discover important aspects. Children who are hypersensitive to various types of sensory input may avoid objects or situations in which they are uncomfortable and therefore miss opportunities to use problem-solving skills.

Attending to and noticing that a change has occurred or something needs to happen is the first step to problem solving. Understanding the actual processes that lead to change is another step. This requires understanding cause-and-effect relationships and connections between actions and outcomes. For instance, in order to understand how three crackers got on her highchair tray, how the toy clown started laughing, or why she is in time out, the child has to understand several different aspects of each situation. She needs to know that outcomes are a result of actions or thoughts; that an agent caused the action; and that agents can be other people, objects, or oneself. Children learn very early in infancy that they can cause people to do things; for instance, when he cries, an adult will come; when he smiles, the adult will smile. They also discover that their actions result in changes in the environment. For instance, they discover that by moving various body parts, they can make objects move or make noise.

Understanding *why* these changes occur is the next level of understanding. This requires making a connection between the outcome and the event that occurred. To return to the previous examples:

The crackers were not here before. Mommy just walked over and put her hand on my tray. Mommy must have put the crackers here.

The toy clown was not laughing before Daddy held it. Daddy must have done something to the clown.

I was playing and I hit my brother. Now I am in time out. I must be in time out because I hit my brother.

Such causal understanding is essential for the next steps of purposeful problem solving to occur. This section provides suggestions for adults to support children in gaining understanding of why things happen.

Attention, memory, and conceptualization are critical for problem solving and should be considered in conjunction with all of the aspects of problem solving (see Chapter 7, Section I. Strategies for Improving Attention; Chapter 7, Section II. Strategies for Improving Memory; and Chapter 7, Section VI. Strategies for Improving Conceptual Knowledge). Although many different strategies may be tried, determining which approaches will work with a given child is easier if the adult can use his or her own problem-solving skills to identify what issues may be negatively influencing the child's ability to identify what is occurring in a given situation.

Interaction Strategies

1. *Bring attention to discrepancies or changes.* The adult needs to help the child notice various sensory characteristics, discrepancies, and relationships. For children with visual impairments, this may be accomplished by using touch or sound to help demonstrate key aspects of situations that relate to problems. The infant who is blind may feel and hear a vibrating toy as it is activated. When it stops, the adult can say, "It stopped! Make it go again!" This will encourage the child to find a way to recreate the actions. For children with lack of focus or reduced cognitive understanding, the adult may need to highlight the problem. For instance, if a toy truck is not fitting under the bridge, the adult may use sound to emphasize the problem. "Crash! The truck hit the bridge!"

2. *Use multisensory input to explain what is going to happen.* There are many ways to demonstrate the aspects of a problem to which the child should attend. Sound and action usually are powerful mechanisms to emphasize key elements. In the previous example of the child who is blind, the adult might place the child's fingers in the ring and physically help the child pull the ring to experience the vibration again. The adult should then wait to see if the child makes the connection and pulls the ring independently.

In the second example in #1, the adult used sound to illustrate the problem ("Crash!") and verbally and physically pointed out that the car hit the bridge. He or she might then have the child feel the truck up against the bridge to emphasize the size difference.

3. *Use instant replay.* Instant replay in sports is used not only to review what happened in a situation but also to see why it happened. The same principle can be used with children. Make sure the child is attending and repeat the action. For instance, if the child was not looking when the parent put crackers on the tray, they will seem to have appeared magically. If the child observes the sequence again, with mother reaching into the box, taking out the crackers, and putting them on the tray, the connections between the events can be formed.

Replaying events or steps of processes is particularly important for children with disabilities who may have more difficulty seeing connections. Children with visual impairments or those who are deaf may suddenly feel bombarded with stimuli they were not expecting because they did not see or hear the event occurring; for instance, a spoonful of food suddenly strikes the child's closed lips, or a person behind the child suddenly picks her up. Without experiencing connections, such events are startling and appear to come out of nowhere. Even for children with normal sight and hearing, cognitive disabilities may inhibit their ability to make simple cause-and-effect associations. The adult needs to consciously help children note changes, see relationships, and experience the consequences. For example, with the infant who is blind, the caregiver may have the child feel the baby food jar and the spoon and then place the baby's hand on her own to feel the movement from the jar to the mouth. The parent of the deaf child might position himself in front of the child so that she is aware of the parent's presence. He might then gesture or sign UP to the child to indicate what was going to happen.

4. *Use slow motion or exaggeration.* In addition to repeating actions so the child has the opportunity to experience the same cause-and-effect sequence several times, repeating the actions in slow motion and with exaggerated behaviors emphasizes the connections. Holding the clown, for instance, so the child can see the wind-up mechanism, then turning it slowly with big gestures, will enable the child to see each step in the sequence. If the adult moves quickly, the child may just perceive *clown-still/clown-moving* and not the total sequence.

5. *Help the child experience the event.* Particularly for children with disabilities, just observing things happen may not be enough to translate into cognitive understanding. The adult can help the child *experience* making things happen. If using the strategies described previously, for example, the adult might model building a tower of blocks and knocking it down several times, quickly and slowly. The child may develop a totally different understanding, however, if the adult assists the child with building a tower and then knocking it over or kicking it over together. *Doing* something takes a thought or action beyond awareness to internalization, a higher level of understanding of why something occurs.

6. *Explain why.* Many things that happen in the child's world do not provide obvious sensory cues to explain why or how things occur. For instance, the child wonders what makes it suddenly light in the room when it has been dark (i.e., the child cannot see the light switch being pushed). The child wonders why Mommy can't play with him when she has the phone to her ear (i.e., the child does not understand there is a person and another phone somewhere else). The child wonders why the toy works sometimes when she pushes the button, but not all the time (i.e., the child does not understand about batteries and how they work). Providing explanations at the child's developmental level helps the child formulate an understanding of elements that are more difficult to experience.

7. *Encourage asking why.* Asking questions about why and how things occur and are related is an essential process. Adults need to model asking questions for children and then finding the answers (e.g., "I wonder what cows eat? Let's find out"). Asking *why* encourages the adults to provide an explanation.

Environmental Strategies

1. *Have multipurpose toys and materials.* Have toys that can be activated or used in many ways—by touch, sound, or movement. This allows children with different interests and learning styles to discover cause-and-effect in a variety of different ways. Toys that only can be used in one way quickly become boring to children who like novelty. There are many toys on the market that can be used in only one way; for example, a button is pushed and a tune is played. Unless the child loves the repetition of that song, the toy quickly will become uninteresting. A roll of toilet paper, on the other hand, can be used in many ways. In doll play, it can wipe a doll's nose or bottom, or it can be a diaper, a bath towel, a blanket, a pillow, a table cloth, a napkin, or a dress for the doll. Such adaptable materials promote thinking and problem solving and keep the child motivated and interested. When combined with other objects, such as scissors, glue, glitter, and crayons, the child can envision new uses for toilet paper. The adult's role is to provide interesting materials and situations to prompt the child to think of new ideas or approaches.

2. *Use concrete materials.* Many causal concepts are difficult to understand. Using concrete examples can clarify what is happening. For example, when children paint and use different colors, the colors blend and make new colors. The reason for the new color seems like magic. However, experimenting with colored cellophane or colored plastic sheets can allow children to take apart the colors and put them back together many times to see how and why the variations change.

III. B. How does the child identify and plan a solution to a problem?

Children with special needs often can determine that a problem exists. They cannot always determine, however, how to solve the problem and follow through on a plan. This may be a result of low frustration tolerance, distractibility, lack of conceptual understanding, or difficulty with organizing their ideas in a meaningful way.

Interaction Strategies

1. *Help the child anticipate.* Adults often use one of two common strategies when problems arise: they either tell children what is going to happen or what is happening, or they show them. These approaches often are effective, but letting children think about and explore a situation on their own enables problem solving to take place. For example, when playing, instead of saying, "Get the cups and tea pot so we can play tea party," if the parent says, "Let's play tea party. What do we need?" the child has an opportunity to anticipate the situation and think about what will be needed.

2. *Encourage trying to find a solution.* One of the most important adult supports is to encourage effort. Finding the solution to a problem deserves commendation, but many children give up before they plan or find a solution and they then feel frustrated and defeated. This may lead to giving up on problem solving in general. For this reason, reinforcing *effort* is as important as, if not more essential than, reinforcing success. Phrases such as, "You can do it!" "Try another way," or "You are working *so hard!*" put emphasis on the child's attempts at problem solving rather than the end result. One does not always succeed, but one can always try. This is an important message for children to embrace.

3. *Use a sequenced approach.* A good chef does not take intact meals out of a box from the store. He or she creates them by following discrete steps, with each course consisting of a separate sequence of actions. Anyone could create a meal with the recipes, explanations of why things need to be done a certain way, and encouragement and guidance when problems arise.

In a similar fashion, children can take on complicated tasks as well. Breaking a big problem down into smaller problems can make the task seem more manageable. Many children become easily overwhelmed or frustrated when the problem is complicated and the first thing they try does not work. A large floor puzzle, for instance, can become several smaller puzzles that are then put together into a larger one. A complex motor sequence can be broken down into simple actions.

4. *Ask guiding questions.* Adults frequently provide too much guidance and support for children with special needs. Whenever possible, the adult should merely be the stimulus to get the child to think and act independently. Parents do not want art work created by the teacher to go home with their child's name on it; likewise, they want developmental outcomes for children to result from their own efforts.

5. *Describe and explain.* Depending on the child's level of language comprehension, the adult can cue the child, describe what is happening, explain what to do, and comment on the outcome. This can take the form of simple one-word descriptions or direc-

tions for developmentally lower functioning children. For example, when trying to figure out how to get into a tunnel, the adult might help the child by cuing, "Knees down. Hands down. Head down. Crawl!" If the child forgets to duck his head, the adult might explain, "Ouch!" (while touching her head) and adding, "Head down," while physically moving the child's head down.

6. *Break down processes.* For more complex problems, repeating or slowing down the process may not be sufficient. For problems that involve more than two to three steps (e.g., building a zoo) or a series of action sequences (e.g., acting out a story), the adult can use the strategies discussed previously for each short segment of the problem. Modeling, labeling, explaining, and encouraging are all potential strategies that can be combined for each series of actions.

7. *Help the child see another point of view.* Particularly in social situations, children react from their own perspective, rather than seeing how another person sees the situation. When a child takes a toy from another child, he views the problem as getting the toy he wants, and the solution is to take it. The adult needs to help the child see that the problem is that *both* children want the toy to play with and there is only one toy. Reframing the problem by saying, "There is only one baby, and you both need a baby to play with" changes the problem.

Environmental Modifications

In addition to interpersonal strategies that may support the child to plan and carry out a variety of actions toward a goal, environmental modifications often are useful. Depending on the findings from TPBA2, the team may want to consider some of the following environmental modifications.

1. *Make it easy.* Present simple problems and work up to more complex strategies. For example, most caregivers understand presenting simple separate-piece puzzles before interlocking puzzles. In the same way, problem solving with daily routines or play routines can begin with one or two steps, adding additional steps as the child comprehends the process.

2. *Make it possible.* Many children with disabilities would be able to do more independent problem solving if assistive technology was available to aid their understanding and efforts. Switches can be attached to almost any cause-and-effect device. Voice-output devices can enable children to share what they understand verbally or request assistance when needed to complete a task.

3. *Use enhanced cues.* Color cues (e.g., red and green switches for *stop* and *go*); tactile or color cues that direct attention (e.g., a Velcro patch where the matching shape goes); or taped directions (e.g., "Now turn the page") are all samples of cues that can direct the child's attention to key elements of a situation.

4. *Structure the environment to aid problem solving.* Use sequencing aids, such as setting out materials in a sequence or using "cue" cards, "recipe" cards, or action sequence pictures.

5. *Gradually increase challenging materials.* In many classrooms, the materials, books, toys, and activities change very little over the course of the year. The "kitchen" area remains the same, with few additional materials; books remain the same, only more worn; puzzles and blocks remain the same; and, consequently, the children's' activities are repetitive. The adult's role is to facilitate learning not only through interactions but also through increasing the challenge of materials and activities.

6. *Model different ways to solve a problem.* When children do not have an idea for how to solve a problem, they may become frustrated or angry. On the other hand, they also

may give up, abandon the situation, or let someone else solve the problem. Adults may help children who are not persistent or who give up by modeling for them. The adult may model the next step of a frustrating problem or may model a sequence of steps, depending on the child's memory and ability level.

7. *Have multiples of the same objects.* Children learn through observation and imitation. Having two of the same item allows the child to watch and explore without having to share or take turns with an adult or another child. This encourages uninterrupted exploration.

8. *Provide developmentally appropriate materials and situations.* Children become frustrated when they encounter problems that are above their developmental level. Unless toys are adaptable to various levels (as described in #1), it is important to provide toys and materials that are challenging enough to encourage problem solving, but not *too* challenging so that they discourage effort. Slightly novel and slightly difficult is the desired combination to encourage interest and investigation.

9. *Provide many opportunities for repetition of experience.* Particularly when engaging with objects, children need an opportunity to explore all of the characteristics of a situation so they can identify what will contribute to solving potential problems. The more experiences they have, the more they will be able to categorize and classify those experiences in different ways. Seeing, feeling, smelling, and manipulating objects gives children information that can help them figure out how objects can be used. For instance, how does a child learn that the plastic food in the play area is not meant to be eaten? He discovers that the plastic banana tastes different from a real one, is hard and cannot come apart, and does not smell like a banana. Over time, experience with other fake foods helps the child recognize on sight, or by touch, that the plastic food is just for play. He no longer needs to test each one to see if it is real.

10. *Use picture cues.* A picture of a child sitting and raising her hand to ask a question, followed by a picture of the teacher pointing to that child and smiling, can provide a clue that the reason the teacher is smiling and paying attention to the child is because the child is raising her hand. In a toddler classroom, the teacher has a row of pictures of all of the children with their names under the pictures. When pictures are missing, the spaces are a cue for how many children are absent, and the names underneath the spaces provide clues for who is absent (see Chapter 7, Section II. Strategies for Improving Memory). In the toddler and preschool rooms, pictures of the activities that take place in a specific part of the room provide cues that help the children function independently.

11. *Create environmental problems related to the child's needs.* When the child is expecting objects to be in the environment, such as a chair, a favorite stuffed animal, or a cup, and it is not where it is expected to be, the child needs to find a way to solve the problem. Creating simple problems such as these gives the child an opportunity to practice problem solving with adult support and encouragement.

██████ III. C. How well is the child able to organize, monitor, and evaluate progress toward a goal and make corrections?

Often the child's first efforts toward a goal are not successful. When this occurs, the child must determine what went wrong and modify or change his or her approach. Many times, the child merely repeats the same behavior to see if the outcome changes, much like the adult who keeps pressing the elevator button when the elevator is slow. After several repetitions with no desired result, the child may give up or change the approach. Evaluating why a given approach did not work requires analytical ability. The child needs to see why an approach did not work. Then the child needs to think of another plan.

Children with disabilities often have difficulty thinking of an alternative strategy. Adults can play an important role in helping children to become adaptive thinkers. Creativity requires fluency, being able to think quickly; flexibility, being able to shift thought patterns; and originality, being able to think of unique approaches. Problem solving requires all of these in varying amounts. The first time a child tries anything new, that experience is unique to that particular child. Changing a pattern requires flexible thinking, and often quick thought is required before it is "too late" for a solution. Helping children to develop these skills is important for problem solving.

Interaction Strategies

1. *Focus the child's attention on the problem.* When challenged, many children's responses are emotional. Frustration may cause the child to give up or shift focus of attention. Instead of addressing the child's emotions, use positive affect to redirect the child back to the problematic situation and encourage reexamination. If adult assistance is needed, make sure the child is focused on *what* the issue is and *how* the problem is being addressed, rather than just the resolution.

2. *Encourage trying to find multiple solutions.* There is typically more than one way to solve a problem. Helping children understand that experimentation is a good way to approach a problem is helpful. The message is that if one does not succeed, it is always worth trying again or trying another way. The adult's role is to reinforce experimentation and discovery and not always expect the child to do things in a prescribed way. Particularly for children with disabilities, the means to an end may be unique.

3. *Talk through the analysis.* Help the child find the key aspects on which to focus attention. Point out with gestures or label what can be changed; for example, "Your house needs a roof. We need something big enough to go across the top. It needs to be stiff so it doesn't fall in. Look around and see what you can find."

4. *Prompt experimentation.* Ask questions beginning with "How else . . . ?" Promote flexible thinking by saying, for example, "Let's think of another way to . . . "; "What could we use for a roof? Do you think this string could be a roof?"; "It is long enough, but it is too . . . What else could you use?"

5. *Demonstrate options.* Showing various approaches that may work equally well encourages flexibility. The adult may say, for example, "Let's each find a different way to get the ball to a friend. I'm going to try to throw it through my legs," or "That's a good way to draw a flower. Let's see what happens if you use a brush *and* a pencil."

6. *Encourage originality.* Help children look at situations from new perspectives. For example, draw a table after looking at it from underneath the table. Play with blocks on the floor, on a table, or on a soft mat. This will help children see different approaches to a situation.

Environmental Modifications

In addition to interpersonal strategies that may support the child in analyzing and modifying strategies, environmental modifications often are useful. Depending on the findings from TPBA2, the team may want to consider some of the following environmental modifications.

1. *Modify the environment to require changes in approach.* Use sabotage to make children think. If there are no chairs at the table, what should be done? If the lid on the jar is on too tight, what can be tried? If the baby cannot reach the toys, what options can be added (e.g., a string, a ramp).

2. *Allow alternatives.* Some children who are significantly physically involved can still problem solve mentally. They need a way to express what they are thinking and a means to fulfill actions they themselves cannot perform. A variety of computer programs and symbol or picture systems are available to enable children to express their thoughts. Actions may then be carried out by caregivers or peers so that these children can see their thoughts actualized.

3. *Have novel materials available.* A variety of unusual things that typically are not found together will encourage creative combinations of toys and materials. In manipulative play with blocks, dramatic play, literacy, and art, for example, the inclusion of unique objects or materials can inspire thinking about toys, materials, or situations in novel ways. A Slinky can become a monster's tail in dramatic play, a tunnel in block play, an object to draw or trace, or a tool to make patterns when dipped in paint. Placing objects together that ordinarily are not seen together can trigger imagination, especially when the adult provides a clue or suggestion to prompt the child to see a relationship. For example, what will the children do in the block area with Popsicle sticks, cotton balls, or ribbons? When children see interesting materials, they typically want to use them in some way. In combination with the interpersonal supports described previously, environmental "staging" can encourage problem solving in new ways.

III. D. How quickly can the child analyze a problem situation and respond?

Interaction Strategies

1. *Give the child an opportunity to think and act.* Before the adult provides information or an explanation, the child should have a chance to determine what is going to happen or what the problem is; for example, "Here comes Kitty. I wonder what she is going to do" or, after the wind-up toy stops, "Uh-oh! What happened?" Do not give the answer or solution too quickly. If the child is verbal, give him or her the chance to anticipate or explain. If the child is nonverbal, give him or her time to make a physical response; for example, trying to wind up the toy again.

2. *Help children move from concrete visual, auditory, and tactile input to thinking about situations without seeing them.* After the child has done an activity numerous times successfully, the adult can ask questions about what happened and why, what would happen if . . . , and so forth.

Environmental Modifications

1. *Highlight what is happening.* For example, use a magnifying glass to watch the internal gear mechanisms of a toy, or use a flashlight to focus on what is happening as flour and water mix together. Once children understand a concept, they will be able to think about relationships differently.

2. *Give the child the same problems multiple times.* Speed and fluency can increase when the child has multiple opportunities to solve the same problem. Children love to repeat things they can do successfully. Therefore, when the child learns to operate a new toy, climb up on the couch, or construct with blocks, it is important for him or her to be able to practice repeatedly with these same objects.

III. E. How well can the child generalize information from one situation to another?

In order to generalize, or see how a solution to one problem can be applied to another problem, children need many of the experiences described previously. Generalization requires seeing how situations are alike. Several factors contribute to learning to generalize problem solving: exposure to many different experiences, adults pointing out our similarities and differences in situations, and opportunities to discover the results of one's thoughts and actions.

Interaction Strategies

1. *Create similar problems.* Although adults want children to always be successful, they learn to solve problems by encountering challenges. Adults can make situations challenging for children and then support the generalization across problems. For instance, if the child has difficulty getting her jacket on one day, and the parent provides verbal steps and suggestions to help the child succeed, the parent can present a different jacket or sweater the next day and see how much the child remembers, adding only the prompts that are needed.

2. *Point out the similarities across problems.* When problems or situations are similar, adults need to point out and discuss how they are similar and how the solution to one problem is useful in another problem. In the previous situation with the jacket, the adult can remind the child of how this situation is "like yesterday when you put on your jacket."

3. *Point out outcomes.* Discuss how actions result in similar or different outcomes. Often, children do not relate what happens to another child to what happens to themselves. Preschool teachers often point out how one child's actions resulted in a positive outcome in the hope of getting other children to generalize the actions; for example, "Jeremy is sitting nicely, so I'll let him help me first."

Environmental Modifications

In addition to interpersonal strategies that may support the child in generalizing strategies, environmental modifications often are useful. Depending on the findings from TPBA2, the team may want to consider some of the following environmental modifications.

1. *Provide similar experiences with different materials in close proximity of space and time.* When the infant is exploring cause-and-effect toys, for instance, provide similar but slightly different activities for the child (e.g., different toys that can be swiped or have buttons that can be pushed). For toddlers, dolls, stuffed animals, and action figures can be fed, put to sleep, and so forth. Preschool-age children can problem solve on higher level tasks, such as how gravity makes different objects go down a ramp, what makes things float, and so forth.

2. *Provide opportunities for repetition of thoughts and actions.* Some children have difficulty generalizing actions or behaviors across people. They use social problem-solving behaviors with one person but not with others. It is important for parents and caregivers to be consistent in their expectations for problem solving so that children learn to use their skills in a variety of situations and with different people.

ROUTINES FOR THE CHILD WHO NEEDS SUPPORT WITH PROBLEM SOLVING

Daily Routines (Home and Classroom)

Feeding/Eating

For infants and toddlers, generalizing how to use a fork and spoon can be done with different types of utensils. Using different shapes and sizes of utensils helps children learn how to adjust their hands, fingers, mouth, lips, and teeth. For children with motor difficulties, experimenting with utensils that have varying sizes of handles, shapes, and orientation is important; problem solving to find one appropriate set of utensils is more important than generalization for this child. Experimentation with different types of foods also is important for children. If the child likes a certain type of vegetable, such as carrots, the caregiver can combine this with something else the child likes, such as rice or noodles. Then, small amounts of new vegetables can be introduced in addition to the preferred vegetable. As the child adapts to the new taste, the amount of new vegetable can be increased.

Diapering/Toileting

Problem solving during diapering can be done while the child plays with objects during the diapering process. Activating a mobile and playing with manipulatives are options. Once children start toilet training, they become more actively involved in the problem-solving process. Problem solving can relate to any part of the process, including undressing and redressing, getting on and maintaining balance on the toilet, turning on faucets and using soap, drying hands, and hanging the towel. This also is an opportunity for adults to address safety issues. Adults can help children experiment with water pressure and water temperature, the cause-and-effect of flushing, amounts of toilet tissue, different ways to dress and handle fasteners, and so forth. Each step presents opportunities for adults to help children think about problems, plans to solve problems, alternative solutions, and the effectiveness of their efforts.

Dressing

Toileting addresses the lower garments. Dressing the whole body or adding layers of outer garments presents additional dilemmas for children. Children often have difficulty with pullover clothing. They have difficulty managing putting the right body parts in the arm and head holes. The adult can help by pointing out the parts of the clothing and helping the child analyze which body part goes in each segment, planning the sequence for putting it on, monitoring as the child tries to dress, helping the child determine what may be wrong if an arm ends up in the neck hole, encouraging trying again, and rewarding the effort, whether or not the child is independently successful. In the case of children who have difficulty with sequencing, the adult may need to have the child involved in the final steps first (e.g., pulling the shirt down) and then as he or she succeeds at that, add steps in the reverse order. Another tactic for adults to try is to have the child wear the same type of garment each day (e.g., pullover, zipper pants) for several days in a row. This gives the child an opportunity to practice and generalize these skills in a compressed time frame.

Going Out

Each excursion into the community offers opportunities for problem solving. Whether at the grocery store, the bank, or the mall, children can encounter experiences requiring problem solving. Particularly for children with special needs, who may not ask *why* and *how*, adults need to be particularly alert to situations that can involve children in looking, planning, analyzing, experimenting, and altering their perceptions of efforts. For example, determining how to get into the grocery cart, figuring out how to use the money machine, and talking about how to get on the escalator can be activities the adult does unconsciously *for* the child, or they can become activities that involve the child in active learning and problem solving.

Play Routines (Home and Classroom)

Face-to-Face Play

Particularly with infants, face-to-face play provides opportunities for children to figure out how to get adults to do things. Whether making faces, making noises, or playing turn-taking games, the adult needs to give the child an opportunity to try to initiate and get the adult to participate. The child's efforts may involve using vocalizations or movements. After the child figures out how to get the adult to respond, the adult can wait and make the child "work" harder to get the game to continue.

Physical Play

As with physical play, wait time and letting the child figure out how to elicit social involvement of others is important (except in the case of children who do not initiate interaction). Physical play provides many opportunities for motor problem solving as well as social problem solving. Figuring out how to do action sequences is part of the early childhood experience. Adults can help children anticipate what they need to do, what will happen when they move, and what they need to change if their actions did not work. Physical games that involve turn taking, such as Duck-Duck-Goose and Musical Chairs, are games that allow children to learn from observing each other and being prompted by adults, "Faster, faster! There's a spot!" Such games also allow children to practice moving more quickly so that movements can become more fluid and unconscious. Adults also can change physical games to require modification of movements. Children could, for instance, play Duck-Duck-Goose while crawling or play Musical Chairs while jumping. These modifications help children think more flexibly by seeing alternative approaches.

Sensory Play

Sensory play provides opportunities for children to see what various materials can do. Children need opportunities to find out the characteristics and potential of substances (e.g., tactile materials such as sand, water, paper, cereal, or glue). They also need opportunities with musical instruments and other sound-making objects. Carrying, pushing, and pulling objects teaches children how to problem solve with weight and how to use tools to help them. Almost every found object or material can be used to make something. Adults can help children explore the qualities of materials to discover how they can be used. Let children choose what they want to do (or provide alternatives), then help them think of different ways to reach their goals.

Dramatic Play

All forms of problem solving are needed for dramatic play. Particularly for children with disabilities, who often cannot coordinate social roles and object play (either or both), adult support is needed. Adults can model; ask questions about what needs to happen; suggest alternatives; encourage new ideas; introduce props to stimulate actions; and help children combine thoughts, actions, and language. For children with special needs, involvement of an adult in the dramatization as a play partner is critical. The adult needs to follow the child's lead and be there to identify when a problem arises that the child does not recognize or know how to solve.

Reading and Learning Routines

Circle Time

Problem solving in a group can be individualized by the teacher directing appropriate problem-solving questions to each child. This can range from simple questions relating to what will happen next to complex questions related to the motivations of the characters. Knowing what the child understands is an important first step.

One-on-One Book Reading

Problem solving in reading can range from figuring out how to turn the page to figuring out what words are on the page and what they mean. One-on-one reading time is a perfect venue for problem solving around the content of the book—concepts and what they mean, characters and how they feel and what they intend to do, what will happen next and why, and what else could have happened. Problem solving also is involved in learning about how sounds and letters combine to make words, words combine to make sentences, and sentences combine to make a narrative. The adult's role is to see what problem the child is encountering in all of these aspects and then provide the prompt or assist to help the child work out the problem independently. In the physical sense, this can mean providing aids for turning pages, such as space between pages with "page separators," or showing the child how to follow the line of print with a finger. Assistive technology also is available on computers to aid in highlighting letters and sounds, tracking words, and so forth. Cognitive problem solving often needs support. Abstract concepts may not be able to be solved by looking at pictures or just going by the words on the page. Thinking about the actual characters and events may require adult questioning and suggestions.

Science and Math

Helping children problem solve with science and math concepts involves formulations of relationships, classification and categorization, seeing one-to-one relationships, and sequencing ideas toward a desired goal. Children with disabilities may need assistance with any or all of these steps. Using concrete examples, modeling experimentation and comparison, and helping the child anticipate the next step are all important processes.

▮▮▮▮   *HASSAN*

Three-and-a-half-year-old Hassan is from Somalia and has only been in the United States for a few months. His parents are attending college, and Hassan is in the local child care center during the day. Although his parents speak English, they speak Somali with Hassan. The teacher at the child care center is concerned because Hassan does not play with toys or with the other children. He likes motor play and loves outdoor time, when he becomes more animated. She wants to know whether language differences are the reason for his apparent delays or whether other developmental concerns are present.

TPBA2 was conducted to determine how Hassan is developing. His developmental history revealed no prenatal or postnatal problems. Hassan had been raised in an extended family environment, surrounded by relatives and friends. Discussion with Hassan's parents revealed that in his home in Somalia, toys were uncommon. Children played outdoors in nature, with the "water, the rocks, the dirt and sticks." They made up games, which mostly involved throwing and jumping, or pretending to do what they saw their relatives do. They felt that language was an issue, and perhaps they should start to talk to him in both languages.

Play observations revealed that Hassan was studying his environment, was intrigued by cause-and-effect toys, and was unsure about dramatic play. When he played with his father, they played ball and rough-and-tumble games. With his mother, he looked at a book. With a peer, Hassan primarily observed what the other child was doing. With the play facilitator, he was able to take a turn and imitate her sequences and problem solving when she encouraged him to try. Language and a cautious temperament appeared to be contributing to his lack of play and interaction, more than cognitive or motor limitations.

The following recommendations were suggested to increase Hassan's problem-solving skills while at the same time helping him to learn a new language. It is important to note that although learning how to solve problems was the concern and focus, this area could not be addressed in isolation. Emotional and social as well as language development need to be considered simultaneously.

Interaction Strategies

1. *Sit next to Hassan and slowly demonstrate problem-solving sequences. Point out what he should attend to and use language focused on important actions. Allow him to watch and then imitate each step of the action sequence.*

2. *Reward Hassan's efforts with smiles and Somalian gestures of approval.*

3. *When the children are dramatizing a sequence, take pictures and post them in order of the actions. This will act as a cue for Hassan. A peer partner also can model for him.*

4. *Speak in short sentences, emphasizing the key words needed. Make a list of key Somali terms for prepositions, key nouns and terms related to routines, and common verbs, so that you can use these to reinforce the language term when Hassan is confused.*

Environmental Modifications

1. *Use visual cues for Hassan to support him in learning the schedule of the day or routine sequences. Many of the daily routines are new for him.*

2. *Arrange for Hassan to have a peer buddy for activities requiring sequenced thought, so Hassan can watch one child, instead of many.*

3. *Hassan learns quickly, so start with developmentally simple puzzles, cause-and-effect toys, and so forth. This way, Hassan can learn the basic approach and not be overwhelmed by the complexity of toys and materials with which he is unfamiliar. Use puzzles of things that Hassan knows. Increase the complexity as he learns simple relationships. Use activities that do not require complex language instructions but that can be figured out with visual-spatial or motor investigation.*

4. *Use a Somali story,* The Fox and the Crocodile, *for the theme and have a dramatic play area related to this traditional Somali tale (McParland, Mohammed, & Hewis, 1992), with costumes and props representing the story. This will give Hassan familiar activities and an opportunity to be a leader.*

5. *Use* A Journey Through Somalia *(Buxton, 1997), a dual-language alphabet book about everyday life in Somalia. This book and others could be integrated into the literacy center to help the other children learn about Hassan's country of birth.*

6. *Because Hassan knows outdoor games, he and his father can teach the other children in his class some of these games. This will break down some of the social barriers and give Hassan an opportunity to show what he does well.*

7. *Hassan's mother volunteered to come and teach the children how to make flat bread and a Somali dish as part of their science and math center.*

REFERENCES

Buxton, C. (1997). *A journey through Somalia.* London: Tower Hamlets.

McParland, E., Mohammed, O., & Hewis, B. (Ill.). (1992). *The fox and the crocodile.* London: Learning Design.

Zelazo, P.D., & Mueller, U. (2002). Executive functions in typical and atypical development. In U. Goswami (Ed.), *Handbook of childhood cognitive development* (pp. 445–469). Oxford, England: Blackwell.

KEYS TO INTERVENTION BY DEVELOPMENTAL AGE

The following ideas are directed toward children who are functioning at approximately the following levels. The suggestions are not meant to be all-inclusive, but rather are indicative of potential areas for exploration.

Developmental age	Characteristics of problem solving	Keys to intervention
Birth to 3 months	Tracks objects and faces.	Play face-to-face games and let the infant watch changes in facial expression and movement of objects.
3–6 months	Moves own hand and fingers. Notes actions of legs and feet. Notes disappearance and reappearance of objects and people. Imitates sounds and simple actions. Discovers through mouthing of objects.	Place moving objects within swiping and kicking distance. Play Hide-and-Seek games with people and objects. Play sound and movement imitation games.
6–9 months	Explores and manipulates toys with eyes, hands, and fingers. Moves to get desired goal. Combines actions toward a goal. Tries new approaches. Knows adults solve problems.	Provide toys that produce noises or actions when moved. Place desired objects so movement is needed. Use toys and materials that have interesting features and moving parts. Demonstrate novel movements, sounds, and strategies.
9–12 months	Uses hands together or separately. Can put things in and dump them out. Uses body in new ways to achieve a goal. Uses tools as a means to an end. Generalizes problem-solving approaches.	Provide toys and materials that require use of two hands. Provide large objects for the child to push or place things on or in. Demonstrate how tools can help. Give similar toys and materials for generalization.
12–18 months	Experiments with orientation of objects, distance, and height. Uses deferred imitation of adults in emerging role play. Makes a plan to achieve a goal. Combines objects in new ways.	Play action game involving throwing objects into containers. Have the child involved in household routines and imitating adult actions. Talk about what you are doing while solving a problem. Demonstrate alternative approaches.
18–24 months	Experiments with balancing, moving, and shifting objects for a purpose. Can follow verbal instructions to solve a problem. Uses objects functionally to solve problems.	Place objects in unexpected places and encourage experimentation. Use words to explain where objects are and what is happening. Involve the child in daily problem solving with tools (e.g., household utensils).
24–36 months	Mentally plans how to solve problems without trial and error. Likes taking things apart in various ways. Understands position of words in problem solving. Likes to figure out how mechanisms work. Asks questions with *what, where, why, when, who.* Uses visual-spatial problem solving on puzzles and construction.	Ask *wh-* questions to prompt thinking. Provide materials to take apart. Involve the child in helping to figure out how things turn on, move, change, activate, and so forth. Have the child help decide what things go together and how in daily activities. Have missing parts to prompt questioning. Have or make simple picture puzzles.
36–48 months	Shows ability to organize by what goes together and what does not. Can use materials creatively.	Involve the child in organizing and making decisions about the arrangement of the environment.

(continued on next page)

Developmental age	Characteristics of problem solving	Keys to intervention
36–48 months (*continued*)	Asks about and answers *why* and *how* questions. Categorizes by size, shape, color, and function. Does complex visual-spatial problem solving with interlocking puzzles.	Provide unusual combinations of materials for exploration and creation. Ask *why* and *how* and give explanations. Involve the child in seeing relationships and building categories for concepts.
48–60 months	Can create complex patterns with blocks; creates stories in dramatic play. Invents new uses for objects. Can describe how to do something and why. Can use "rules" and understanding, rather than visual perception, to understand a problem.	Provide everyday objects for dramatic play and construction. Ask the child to explain what she is doing, what is her goal, and why she is doing it this way. Help the child understand the "rules" for why things occur as they do. Relate explanations to the child's own life experiences.
60–72 months	Can use numerical reasoning. Can make a plan, implement and monitor progress, change the approach when needed, and evaluate the result.	Provide opportunities to look at amount (e.g., quantity, size, money) in meaningful contexts. Provide opportunities for projects involving planning, implementing, modifying, and evaluating over time.

7

Facilitating Cognitive Development

IV. Strategies for Improving Social Cognition

Goal Attainment Scale

1	2	3	4	5	6	7	8	9
Does not attend to and/or attach meaning to others' facial expressions, gestures, or body language.		Is able to read and respond to others' facial expressions, gestures, body language, and movements.		Responds to emotions expressed by others by acting to sustain positive emotions and reduce negative emotions.		Anticipates and responds to others' needs, desires, and thinking based on own needs, desires, and logic, which may not match those of others.		Understands and responds to motivation, desires, and thoughts of others, even if they are different from own.

Social cognition is the child's understanding of the social world and the psychological thinking behind how and why people act the way they do under various circumstances (see TPBA2, Chapter 7). Social cognition is concerned with how the child *reasons* about what people want, what they intend, and what motivates them. It involves inferring the thinking behind the social actions of others and the related consequences.

Understanding the thoughts, beliefs, and intentions of other people develops along with cognitive skills such as imitation; awareness of cause and effect; seeing relationships and developing classification systems; and comprehending concepts related to *wanting, feeling, thinking, knowing,* and *believing.* Social cognition is essential for the development of pretend play, joint planning and negotiation, and higher level thinking, including making moral judgments. It also is necessary for understanding the motivations and actions of characters in books, on television, and in movies. Social cognition appears to require the ability to attend to and imitate others and to form mental representations of people's actions (or to put oneself in another's place) before, during, and after an event. Without understanding, children act only to meet their own needs and respond to only the concrete observations of what causes events to occur. They do not grasp the social nuances others provide and cannot use their own experiences to interpret what others may be thinking and feeling. Thus, children with diminished social cognition skills have difficulty understanding how to respond to others' thoughts and feelings.

APPROPRIATE SOCIAL COGNITION

Social cognition develops early in infancy. Infants have an innate interest in the human face and the emotions adults express verbally and facially. They also are fascinated by the actions of adults and the results these actions produce. By 9–12 months, children are demonstrating awareness of the emotional meaning of facial expressions, the intentions behind gestures, and the meaning associated with vocal intonations, and they are anticipating the results of adults' movements. These early foundations help children develop higher level social understanding. As described in the section on problem solving (see Chapter 7, Section III), the ability to imitate lies at the heart of early problem-solving skills. Increasingly sophisticated motor, language, and cognitive abilities enable children to imitate more complex behaviors. Children watch, mentally map, incorporate the other person's behaviors, and then plan how to execute the behaviors, a combination of social and physical problem solving. This ability to recreate others' behaviors contributes to children's learning how the other person thinks and feels during those behaviors. An additional skill, being able to generalize thoughts and feelings from person to person and situation to situation, also is necessary. Children typically develop social cognition in their daily activities with their caregivers.

Appropriate Social Cognition in Practice

▓▓▓▓ **IV. A. What foundational skills related to social cognition does the child demonstrate?**

Daily Routines (Home and Classroom)

- *Infant/toddler:* During diapering, Mother smiles and says, "Look, James!" looking toward the window, and James looks at the window to see what is there.

- *Young child:* The young child is playing on the floor next to his father when his father says, "Look," and points to the television, adding, "That man is fighting an alligator." The child looks up at the television and says, "He looks scared! Would you be scared, Dad?"

Play Routines (Home and Classroom)

- *Infant/toddler:* While playing, one infant falls and starts to cry. The second infant crawls over and watches her, then starts to cry too.

- *Young child:* Freddie stacks up a high tower of blocks, gets up, goes to his teacher, and points to his tower of blocks. The teacher says, "Wow! Look what you made."

Classroom Routines

At the literacy center, Max watches Sara draw an *S* for her name. Max tries to draw an *S* too.

▓▓▓▓ **IV. B. How well does the child infer the thinking and actions of others?**

Daily Routines (Home and Classroom)

- *Infant/toddler:* Marla sees her mother putting her coat on and starts to cry.

- *Young child:* Ali is shopping for a birthday present for his mother. He tells his father, "I think she would like something pretty and sparkly."

Play Routines (Home and Classroom)

- *Infant/toddler:* Dad is chasing 2-year-old Jaime. Jaime is running, stopping, looking back at Dad, laughing, and then running again.

- *Young child:* When Alexander sees his friend twirling, laughing, and falling down, he says, "Wait. I want to be silly too."

Classroom Routines

During circle time, Lilly watches the teacher, who is sitting silently with a book on her lap. Lilly watches the teacher's worried face as she waits for the noisy group to quiet down. Lilly says, "I'm ready to listen, Miss J."

GENERAL PRINCIPLES FOR SUPPORTING APPROPRIATE SOCIAL COGNITION

Social cognition involves problem solving about social situations. Many of the same strategies that were pointed out in the problem-solving section are relevant here as well. The "topic" is just more internal.

Demonstrate Actions and Reactions

The way children learn to anticipate others' actions is to see actions and reactions many times. They see that when the handle is turned, the jack-in-the-box pops up. When children act in specific ways, adults respond in certain ways. Consistency on the part of adults is important. The child will learn that when he picks up his toys, he always gets a hug, a smile, or a "high five."

Use Facial Expressions and Body Language to Show Feelings

Children learn what people are feeling by interpreting their facial expressions. They learn what those facial expressions mean by the actions or words that follow them. In the previous example, the child learns that a picking up toys is associated with a specific reaction, and that reaction is one that feels good. His parent's smile generates a smile from him. He learns that smiles are associated with good feelings. The same is true of other feelings. Children come to understand feelings when they see them on others and feel them themselves and make the association.

Explain What You Are Feeling and Why

Labeling feelings is important. Children understand how to classify various emotions when adults help them by giving a feeling a label. Parents often say things such as, "It makes me mad when you do that!"; "If you don't stop, I'm going to get angry"; and "It makes Mommy happy when you go potty by yourself!" Once children start acquiring labels for feelings, they will begin to ask questions about new labels when they hear them; for instance, "Daddy, what does 'frustrated' mean?" It is important to explain to children *why* the adult is feeling the way he or she is; for example, saying, "I'm very sad right now. That dish that broke was a very special present."

Explain What You Are Doing and Why

Caregivers also support children's development of social cognition by talking about what they are thinking and doing. This helps children understand what a person might be thinking and why specific actions follow. For instance, when the parent says, "We are out of milk. I'm going to have to go to the store," the child has clues to what is happening when Mom goes to get her purse. The phone rings, and Dad says, "That was your grandma. She's coming over to take you to the park." The child starts to learn that when the phone rings, someone is talking somewhere else (although it takes many calls to know it's not always Grandma). If Dad is smiling, he or she knows this is a good thing.

Talk about Actions and Consequences

Caregivers help children see the relationship between their actions and the consequences that result; for example, "Dante, I know you are crying because Lamar hit you. He hit you because he was mad. Do you remember why he was mad? Yes. You took his toy. It makes people mad when you take their toys. And it makes people sad when they get hit. It is not okay to make people mad or sad. Let's think about what could make you both feel happy."

Talk about Feelings and Reasons for Feelings

Children express many emotions in infancy, even though they do not have labels for them. They learn the words for what they are feeling as they see them demonstrated on others and hear the labels used, as described previously. They also need to have their own feelings labeled for them. Parents will use expressions such as, "I know you hate getting your diaper changed, but I'll be very quick"; "I got you ice cream. You love ice cream!" or "You look mad because Sammy took your toy."

THE PRINCIPLES IN PRACTICE

Most adults have no idea what social cognition means or how to promote it. They just naturally use interactions that help children gain a better understanding of thoughts and feelings. The following are typically used strategies that support the development of social cognition.

Daily Routines (Home and Classroom)

Feeding/Eating

During snack time, the caregiver feeds Jackson pears. Jackson makes noises and leans forward for more. The caregiver smiles and says, "You like pears! You want more!" She responds to his emotion with a label and an action. He is learning that his sounds and actions will elicit a response. Soon he will anticipate what his caregiver will do when he opens his mouth and leans forward.

Diapering/Toileting

Dad is changing Cory's diaper. He makes a face and says, "Yuck!" Cory laughs. Dad says, "You think stinky diapers are funny?" Cory says, "Yucky!" and laughs. Dad is modeling an emotional response, commenting on Cory's emotional response, and making the connection between the emotion and the cause.

Dressing

Gabrielle walks into the kitchen wearing her bathing suit. Her mother sees her, laughs, and says, "You dressed yourself! I am so proud of you! But look outside." She is pointing to the snow outside. Her facial expression assumes a worried look. "It looks cold out. Let's find something warm to put over your suit." Gabrielle's mother has demonstrated two different emotions and explained the reason for each.

Play Routines (Home and Classroom)

Face-to-Face Play

Damian is playing with his mother. He is sticking his fingers in his mouth and she is "munching" on them with her lips. He giggles and sticks his fingers in her eye. "Ouch, Damian, that hurt!" Damian looks like he is about to cry. "You can put your fingers in my mouth, not in my eyes." She guides his fingers back to her mouth, smiling again. Damian's smile returns.

Physical Play

During a roughhousing game of tag, Jordan jumps up and down, then runs and jumps on the couch. She stops, looks at her dad, then starts to jump up and down. His expression changes from a smile to a frown. Jordan jumps off the couch and starts to run again. Jordan read her dad's facial expression and determined that he was not happy about her jumping on the couch. No words were necessary.

Manipulative Play

During dramatic play, Linessa invites her mother to a party. When her mother sits down at the table, Linessa pretends to pour tea into her mother's cup, saying, "This is tea. You don't like coffee." Linessa's mother says, "Do you think I should have sugar in it?" Linessa replies, "Yes, you should have sugar. Here is your sugar." Linessa anticipates what she thinks her mother would like to drink rather than pouring her something she herself would like, or something she has seen other adults drink. Her mother encourages her to think about what else she might like.

Sensory Play

During art play in the classroom, Randy gets out the watercolors. He looks at his teacher and asks, "What do you think I should make?" His teacher says, "I think you should think about what you like best in the world and paint that." Randy is recognizing that his teacher has thoughts but she encourages him to think about his own preferences. Thinking about thinking is an important social cognition skill.

Reading and Learning Routines

Circle Time

The teacher is reading *The Three Bears.* She asks, "How do you think the bears are going to feel when they come home and find their house is a mess?" The teacher is asking the children to put themselves in the bears' place and think about what they will see and feel.

One-on-One Book Reading

The caregiver is reading to Chris. She says, "There goes the Mommy duck. And look, all the baby ducks are following her. Where do you think she wants to take them?" Chris likes to go to the park with his mother, so he projects his desires onto the ducks. The teacher replies, "Maybe. I know you like to go to the park, don't you? What else do you think the ducks might like to do?" The teacher tries to help Chris think of another idea related to ducks.

Science and Math

Rachel and Marco are playing in the rocks on the playground. The teacher begins a game with the rocks. She says, "I'm going to pretend these rocks are potatoes. How many do you think I want to cook?"

PLANNING INDIVIDUALIZED
INTERVENTIONS FOR IMPROVING SOCIAL COGNITION

Some children do not understand that adults' expressions, actions, and behaviors communicate what they are thinking and feeling. As a result of many different neurological, developmental, and environmental factors, children with special needs may show delays or impairments in this area. Children with autism spectrum disorders, for example, have a notable lack of understanding of the emotions and intentions of others, which negatively influences their social interactions. Children with emotional problems or cognitive deficits also may demonstrate delayed or impaired social cognition skills. Children also can be influenced negatively by environmental factors such as lack of opportunities to see and experience different emotions, lack of role models, or lack of responsive caregivers.

■■■■■ **IV. A. What foundational skills related to social cognition does the child demonstrate?**

Basic foundations for social cognition include understanding that adults are communicating what they want, what they are feeling, and what they are going to do through nonverbal means such as gestures, facial expression, and actions. As mentioned previously, most children develop these basic abilities by 12 months of age. Strategies that are described previously are helpful for all children, but children with disabilities may need additional strategies to support this aspect of development.

Interaction Strategies

1. *Make sure the child is attending to the gesture or action.* Often, adults use cues such as, "Look at me." This often is ineffective because the child takes these words as a negative cue rather than a positive one. It is more effective to use a cue that indicates that something is worth looking at. Positioning the gesture or action in front of the child's face, moving the gesturing finger in an enticing manner, or putting your face in close frontal proximity to the child may help get the child to look toward the object of interest.

2. *Exaggerate the facial expression, gesture, or action.* Exaggeration or extremes attract attention. Part of getting children to understand what people are thinking or doing is getting them to look at what is happening. As suggested in the preceding paragraph, gestures or actions may help, but often children with disabilities such as autism do not automatically attend to actions of others. For this reason, making the action or object of attention unavoidable is important. Add sounds, sudden movements, or intense gestures.

3. *Use words with facial expressions, sounds, gestures, and actions.* A multisensory approach is effective for some children. Combine noises, such as shaking a bell, tapping the object, snapping the fingers, or making a funny noise near the object to which you want the child to attend. Then attach the word for the object or action you want the child to know. For instance, snap fingers, say, "Ruff-ruff," then point to the dog. When the child is looking at the dog, say, "Doggie. Doggie says, 'Ruff-ruff.'"

4. *Demonstrate the relationship between the gesture and the result.* The reason children do not look when the adult points or gestures is that they do not understand there is a reason to do so. The adult needs to help the child see the reason to look. Begin with the

child's favorite toys or materials as an object of attention. Have the object very close to the child so that the connection between pointing and the object is immediately seen. For example, present the child's favorite toy in front of his face, and point to the object, while naming it. Repeat the presentation of the gesture or pointing several times until the child automatically makes the association between the gesture and something to which he wants to attend. Then substitute something else of high interest as a consequence of looking at where you are pointing. Continue this until the child is beginning to look automatically, then substitute other items as objects of interest and distance them farther away. Include the high-interest objects intermittently so the child does not lose interest in looking at the gesture.

5. *Reward the outcome of looking, acting, or understanding with something meaningful to the child.* Once the child's attention is directed toward the desired object or action, the adult needs to ensure that something of interest to the child occurs. Children will make the connection between the gesture or pointing if the adult makes sure that the gesture is clear and is associated with a real object or something of interest. For example, if the adult continually makes the sign for PLAY and then gives the child her favorite object, the child will soon associate that sign with that object. The adult can then begin to generalize the sign PLAY by presenting another toy, signing PLAY, and acting on the object.

6. *Position the adult's face in a direct line with the child's face.* It is important for the child to see the adult's face as an object that is important to look at. Caregivers want to be able to capture the child's direct attention so he or she attends to direction, listens to comments, and carries on conversations. It is therefore important that the child begins to understand that other people cause things to happen and other people help the child to understand the world.

Environmental Modifications

In addition to interpersonal strategies that may support the child developing the basic foundations of social cognition, environmental modifications often are useful. Depending on the findings from TPBA2, the team may want to consider some of the following environmental modifications.

1. *Use enhanced visual, auditory, or tactile referents.* A bright color amidst muted or dark colors, flashing lights, interesting sounds, shiny surfaces among dull surfaces, or moving objects or parts all attract attention. The adult then needs to *do* something to help the child see a connection between the object and the adult's actions or words. The adult might, for instance, begin a game of pushing a button to make something happen. When the child becomes interested, the adult needs to maintain a role as an instigator, either by holding the object of interest away from the child so that he needs to cue the adult with a sound or gesture to make something happen, or by taking turns with the child in engaging the object. This actually requires a combination of interpersonal and environmental approaches, because the environment needs to be enticing but the adult also needs to require the child to engage the object in some way to keep the interesting effect going.

2. *Position referents so they are accessed easily.* The adult needs to talk to the child or present interesting objects or events from a close proximity to the child, so the child can see, smell, touch, or hear the event within a second or two. Calling the child to come to the kitchen for dinner is too far removed and requires the child to visualize the adult, the situation in the kitchen, and the consequences if she comes when called. It would be more effective to either bring the child into the kitchen to point out and talk about dinner or to bring a piece of food into the living room to show the child what is

in the kitchen. The adult needs to keep in mind that the child cannot always understand words alone.

3. *Use multisensory input.* Letting children see, touch, hear, and experience a situation in multiple ways gives them a much better understanding of a situation than does any one sensory input in isolation. For instance, if the adult holds up a toy, some children may look. If the adult holds up the toy, lets the child feel the toy, then makes a sound to go with the toy (e.g., a motor noise with a toy car) as the adult and the child push the toy in unison, the child is more likely to repeat the actions and understand the relationship of the noise to the object and movement of the object. Objects such as an orange can be seen, smelled, touched for texture, peeled together for action, and experienced for the changing texture and smell, and then eaten for taste. The total experience, if taken in sequence, with adult comment, demonstration, and encouragement of experimentation can result in increased understanding on the part of the child of what humans do to cause events to occur.

4. *Use pointing.* If the child is looking at your finger instead of the object to which you are pointing, move to the object and point again. Place your finger on the object and name it. Repeat this type of action numerous times, both with the same object and different objects. You want the child to begin to understand that he should look toward the object named. The more interesting the object, the more motivated the child will be to look, once he associates the label or the pointing with the interesting object; for instance, "See, your clown is dancing."

5. *Pair pointing with sound.* Point to an object and then have another person turn on or make a sound from the target object. For example, first Mom points and labels, "See doggie." Then Dad either activates the toy or barks to attract the child's attention. With enough repetitions, the child will look when someone points, anticipating that something interesting will happen in the direction of the point. It is important to always label the target of the point, because labels for objects result from this association.

IV. B. How well does the child infer the thinking and actions of others?

Understanding the thinking and actions of others comes as a result of having a mental image of what people are going to do, based on what you would do in the same situation and associating others' intentions and motivations with one's own. At first, children think that everyone acts as they do and for the same reasons they do. It is only as children come to see that others respond differently and hear them explain or demonstrate why they acted as they did that children start to understand that people have their own separate thoughts and motivations. For instance, most young children, when watching their parent open a birthday present, anticipate that something they would like will be in the box. When Dad opens the box and a shirt is in the box, they are surprised and unimpressed. When they see Dad has a happy expression on his face and gives their mother a kiss and a hug, children begin to formulate initial ideas about the differences in people's likes and dislikes. It takes many, many such experiences for children to begin to categorize how different categories of people (e.g., dads and moms, young people and old people, boys and girls) behave differently, how their preferences vary, and how people's actions differ based on their intentions and desires.

Interaction Strategies

1. *Tell the child what you are doing and why.* Often, adults assume that the child knows that "when I have keys in my hand, I am going out in the car." Some children do make this connection; others do not. To some children, the adult is just standing there talking and holding an object in his or her hand, and the disappearance of the

adult comes as a complete surprise. It is better to help the child form a connection between objects and actions; for instance, "Mommy is putting her coat on. Mommy is going to the store in the car (showing the child the keys), and I will be back soon. Molly will stay with you (pointing to Molly, who is standing next to her) while I am gone. Molly is going to play with you (Molly shows the child a toy the child likes and approaches the child to play)." Some children, especially children with autism or developmental delays, may not know, or care, that the parent is leaving. It is still important for the adult to make clear to the child what is happening and why. This will help the child develop the connection between objects, actions, and consequences.

2. *Demonstrate actions and shorten the time frame for results.* Let children see actions and consequences in a short time frame before a longer time frame. For instance, if the child has difficulty with separation, short versions of separation can let the child understand the leaving–coming-back sequence. The parent can say, "I'm going to the bathroom." The parent then leaves the room and comes back in just a few seconds, announcing, "I'm back." These leaving–coming-back episodes can be lengthened so the child understands the sequence.

3. *Tell the child what you think he or she is feeling and why.* Children use many ways to express emotions—facial expressions, body language, vocalizations, or verbalizations. They will not have words for their feelings until they understand the association between what they are feeling and a label provided by an adult. The adult helps the child acquire these labels by pointing out what the child is doing and how the adult is interpreting the behavior; for example, "I hear you screaming. I know you are mad," or "I see that pouting lip (imitating the child). I know you are sad."

4. *Tell the child how you are feeling and why.* Many children see the expressions on adults' faces or see their "body language" (e.g., turning away, leaning forward, picking the child up), but they do not understand what the expressions or movements mean. The adult needs to pair actions with short explanations such as, "You hit me. I'm sad"; "Yeah! Do that again!" or "Mommy loves you. I'm going to kiss you." Keep sentences short for optimal comprehension. Match words with actions.

5. *Explain what others appear to be feeling and why.* Helping children to observe and understand others' feelings is very important. Again, helping the child to attach meaning to expressions and actions can assist the child to develop empathy and appropriate social responses. When children are young, the adult can act as interpreter of behaviors. As children begin to acquire language, the adult should begin to ask the child to interpret the behavior of others; for example, "Why do you think she is hiding her face?" or "Can you think of something to do to make her feel better?"

Environmental Modifications

In addition to interpersonal strategies to support the child's understanding of the thinking and actions of others, environmental modifications often are useful. Depending on the findings from TPBA2, the team may want to consider some of the following environmental modifications.

1. *Exaggerate actions and emotions.* Children who have difficulty reading others' cues and emotions have difficulty understanding the thinking of others. Adults can emphasize what they are doing, what they are feeling, and the consequences of actions through exaggerated facial expressions, body movements, and explanation. The adult's role is to make sure the child experiences what is happening, what caused it to happen, and the consequence of what happened.

2. *Use verbal explanations.* Let children know what will happen next; for instance, "I am going to make you lunch." When lunch follows soon after, the child learns to anticipate what will happen based on repetition of routines, words, and actions.

3. *Use patterned action–response toys.* Toys that have sounds help children make associations and anticipate what will happen. For instance, a wind-up toy may make a noise as it is wound and then an action or song follows. This type of sequence teaches the child to anticipate that something interesting will happen when the adult winds up a toy. This generalizes to other areas as the child sees that varying actions result in interesting outcomes. Children begin to anticipate that others' actions have consequences.

4. *Point out feelings and actions depicted in pictures.* Whether on billboards, on food boxes, or in books, adults can point out expressions and behaviors depicted in pictures and talk about the emotions represented. They also can point out the reason for the actions or what the person will probably do next. This will help them think about and anticipate likely action sequences.

5. *Use bibliotherapy.* Stories (with pictures) that illustrate what happens as a consequence of actions can help older children make a connection between others' actions and their own.

ROUTINES FOR THE CHILD WHO NEEDS SUPPORT TO IMPROVE SOCIAL COGNITION

Expressing emotions, both physically and verbally, and talking to the child about what is happening and why is crucial to the development of thinking, language, and emotional understanding. This can and should happen throughout the day. Each routine and activity presents another opportunity to talk about the child's feelings, actions, and reactions and others' feelings, actions, and reactions.

Daily Routines (Home and Classroom)

Feeding/Eating

Use facial expressions to help children relate their own feelings about food or eating. When a food is not preferred, make a negative face when the child does, so the child can see the expression of dislike. When the child likes a food, make a smiling expression and sounds of pleasure to demonstrate the child's feelings. This will help the child understand what these expressions mean when seen rather than personally experienced.

Diapering/Toileting

Elimination of bodily fluids is a cause-and-effect action. The child wets and then feels water running down a leg. The child defecates and then feels an unpleasant sensation when sitting down. These actions, combined with adult explanations of how using a "potty" can make the child feel better, help the child learn to understand why adults use the bathroom. Adults model, discuss, and explain why for children. This is important in toilet training, because the reason for using a toilet rather than the diaper is not immediately evident.

Dressing

Parents need to model and explain both the dressing process and why various clothing pieces are needed. When it is hot, for example, the parent uses facial expressions and words to say she needs to take off a jacket because she is hot. When it is difficult to get a shirt over the child's head, the adult makes noises to indicate effort, surprise when the head pops through, and then a cheer for success. All of these expressions demonstrate actions and reactions associated with emotions.

Going Out

Leaving the house for any purpose is usually associated with either positive or negative feelings. Children anticipate either something fun or an unpleasant change from the routine. Caregivers can help children to anticipate what is good about what happens next as opposed to what is bad about it. For instance, instead of saying, "You will only need to be in your car seat for a few minutes," the parent can help the child understand why they are going out and also anticipate something positive such as, "We don't have any Cheerios left. You get to ride in the grocery cart and help me find Cheerios!"

Play Routines (Home and Classroom)

Face-to-Face Play

Face-to-face play is a great way to let children see and respond to others' facial expressions and actions. Adults can use various strategies to highlight feelings and consequences of actions. For example, the adult can imitate the child's facial expressions or actions or exaggerate responses to the child's actions. The adult can demonstrate what happens as a consequence of the child's actions, both emotionally and physically. For example, when singing a song and doing a fingerplay such as "Five Little Monkeys," the adult has an opportunity to model happiness (jumping), sadness (bumping one's head), and disapproval (no jumping!). In addition, because this is a repetitive game, the child soon begins to anticipate the actions and facial expressions of the adult, and soon initiates them independently. The words highlight the reason for the emotions expressed.

Physical Play

Physical play, unlike the games described previously, involves real emotions rather than imitated emotions. When the child is tickled, she laughs because it feels good or is funny. When she cries, it is because she is overwhelmed or hurt. Experiencing emotions first hand is important for understanding how others feel. In this type of interaction, turn taking is important so that the child learns that what is done to her and makes her feel good or bad also can be done to others to make them feel good or bad. Being the "agent" that causes others to express positive or negative emotions is a powerful experience, and children can learn quickly the results of their actions on others.

Manipulative Play

Manipulative play, particularly with puzzles, cause-and-effect toys, building blocks, and so forth, often is done in isolation or in parallel play. For manipulative play to be instructive for the purposes of social cognition, it requires the participation of others. In isolated play with manipulatives, children can demonstrate their understanding of what others think and feel, but they can only learn new understanding through social interaction. For this reason, it is important for adults, siblings, and peers to use manipulatives together. Play partners then demonstrate emotional reactions to each other's actions, encourage change in behavior, or demonstrate consequences of actions. Inclusion of "action figures" or toy people or animals into the play increases the opportunities to act out situations or events that might occasion different reactions or emotional responses. For instance, in building a farm, the adult or peer might have the animals be hungry, tired, afraid, bullying, brave, protective, friendly, caring, and so forth. Each situation presents new opportunities for exploration of new actions, reactions, and emotional responses. The adult's job is to continually introduce novel, creative situations for exploration.

Sensory Play

Sensory play is another type of play that is typically done in isolation or in parallel play. The adult can turn this into an activity that increases social understanding by making it into a social game. Begin by imitating what the child is doing; for instance, emptying and filling a cup. Then demonstrate an emotion of excitement when the child does the action. Make sure the child sees, hears, or feels your response. After several repetitions, see if the child appears to anticipate and even wait for your response. Insert other actions, such as sticking your hand under the sand when the child is pouring and make another emotional response, "Oh, no! You poured it on my hand!" Wait to see if the child repeats the action. Sensory play provides opportunities for the child to see various emotional responses—happiness, surprise, disgust, and so forth. The adult's role is to help the child see the connection between actions and emotions.

Dramatic Play

Acting out roles is one of the best ways for children to get to safely "try on" different emotions and responses to emotions in others. Young children act out the roles and emotions they see on their family members and others in dramatic play. They then get opportunities to experience how others respond to those actions and emotions. Adults can use dramatic play as a means for encouraging children to learn about emotions. Role play events that occur cause emotions, and then demonstrate appropriate reactions. Role play favorite stories that contain actions and consequences or emotions and reactions. Use language, gestures, and facial expressions to help the child understand what is happening and why.

Reading and Learning Routines

Circle Time

In a large-group reading activity, the teacher needs to be able to individualize the questions each child is asked, depending on his or her ability to understand people's thoughts and feelings. For example, one child in the group may be able to say that a character is "mad," but not be able to say why. Another child may be able to explain why the character is mad and also predict what will happen as a result. In addition, the teacher can help the children learn by explaining what characters are thinking and feeling and comparing those feelings to what they may have experienced. For instance, if a character in the book is lost, the teacher may ask, "Have any of you ever been lost?" "How did you feel?" "What did you do?" The teacher also should make sure that children know that expressing emotions is good, but it is important to express feelings appropriately, so that one does not hurt oneself or other people. Books can help show children acceptable ways of behaving and expressing emotions. Teachers also should be cognizant of different cultural values relating to when and how emotions can be expressed.

One-on-One Book Reading

As with dramatic play, in which a sequence of events is played out, books also tell stories with actions and their consequent results and emotions. Books present opportunities for adults to talk to children about what is happening to the various characters, how and why they feel the way they do, and how they act in response to their own and others' feelings. They also enable parents to relate the actions and feelings of the characters in the books to their own experiences and feelings. The adult should ensure that whenever characters in books express emotions, he or she takes the time to talk about what the characters are feeling and why. Also discuss what characters are doing and help children think about why they are acting the way they are. Ask them questions about why characters would be acting in certain ways, and have children anticipate what the characters are going to do next. All of these strategies help children get "into" another's mind.

Science and Math

Psychology, or understanding the human mind, is a science in itself. As children learn to classify and categorize experiences, they also learn to understand how different types of emotions relate to specific types of experiences. They learn to understand how sequences of behavior lead to various emotional outcomes. The teacher's role in this discovery is to help children see likenesses and differences in experience, to examine the consequences of behavior, and to think about how others' thoughts and feelings are expressed in similar or different ways. For instance, the teacher can help children think about why some people might like going to the beach and other people might not. They can point out others' behaviors and ask the child what they think the person is doing and why, and what the person may be feeling. For example, on a field trip to a pumpkin patch, the children watch people bent over, picking pumpkins. The teacher asks the children, "Why are the people picking pumpkins?" "What do you think they are thinking about?" "How do you think they feel?" "Have you ever felt excited about doing something?" These types of questions help children to group and classify different types of behaviors and emotions.

▓▓▓▓▓   ELIJAH

Elijah is a 3-year-old identified as having autism. He avoids eye contact, except for when he wants something. Elijah does not show awareness of others' actions and feelings and ignores the peers in his preschool class. He enjoys playing by himself and repeating actions that create visually interesting effects, such as watching the wheels on his toy car with his head lying on the table. In order to make him more aware of others' actions, thoughts, and feelings, his parents and teachers developed a plan to help him become more attentive to people and more aware of emotions.

Interaction Strategies

1. *When interacting with Elijah, use a singing intonation to attract his attention. Use exaggerated facial expressions.*

2. *Indicate that you are happy to see him when he comes near you: "Elijah, I'm happy to see you!" Hug him when he looks at you.*

3. *Engage in turn-taking games with sensory materials that Elijah likes. For example, use tub foam on a table top. Imitate what Elijah does. Make funny noises to attract his attention so he will see that you are imitating him. Wait, watch, and imitate him again. Once he is looking at what you are doing, change your actions slightly and add a word such as "Yucky!" See if you can encourage him to imitate you.*

4. *When playing or engaging in a routine, place the object in which Elijah is interested close to your face, by your mouth and eyes. Label the object and comment on what you are going to do with the object. Then demonstrate.*

5. *Label the emotions that Elijah is expressing. Say why you think he is feeling that way.*

6. *Talk about your own emotions and show him your face. Tell him why you are feeling the emotion in simple terms. "Mommy is upset because the glass broke." When you are upset, hug him and then show him you feel better. Tell him, "Hugs make me feel happy." This will help him see the relationship between actions and feelings.*

Environmental Modifications

1. *When interacting with Elijah, get on his level in front of him. This will make it easier for him to look at you.*

2. *Read books with pictures of children's emotions. Better yet, make a book of pictures of emotions with pictures of Elijah and other family members making expressions of different emotions. Read the book together and talk about what is happening and why.*

3. *Play with cause-and-effect toys in a turn-taking pattern, and hold off on your turn until Elijah looks at you and makes an indication that he wants you to do something.*

KEYS TO INTERVENTION BY DEVELOPMENTAL AGE

The following ideas are directed toward children who are functioning at approximately the following levels. The suggestions are not meant to be all-inclusive, but rather are indicative of potential areas for exploration.

Developmental age	Social cognition characteristics	Keys to intervention
Birth to 3 months	Enjoys studying people's faces. Responds to emotion in others' voices.	Show exaggerated facial expressions when looking at the child. Match the facial expression with the vocal expression.
3–6 months	Repeats things that make him or her feel good. Responds distinctively to different people. Vocalizes to human voices.	Expose the child to people of different gender, age, and physical characteristics. Interaction with a variety of people will also enable children to experience different voices, expressions, and gestures.
6–9 months	Has social smile in response to human face or a smile on another's face. Enjoys watching own and others' actions. Laughs at social and physical play with adults. Reacts to others' emotional expression.	Engage in a variety of social games (e.g., Peekaboo, songs, fingerplays, tickling and imitation games). Demonstrate appropriate emotions with each.
9–12 months	Watches others to see how they accomplish their goals. Reacts to subtle emotions expressed by adults. Pays attention to peers' actions and feelings. Knows others can make him or her feel better.	Point out what others are doing and feeling. Talk about and demonstrate facial expressions. Point out what siblings or other children are doing.
12–18 months	Looks for other person's emotional reaction before acting. Knows one can share emotions or change another's emotions. Knows movement of others means actions toward a goal. Knows what an adult wants and acts to meet the need.	When the child heads for something that is off-limits, make a loud noise to get his or her attention, make a frowning face, and shake the finger *no*. Tell the child what your intentions are when acting. Talk about your needs and what the child needs to do. Provide wait time and give gestures to support what you want.
18–24 months	Knows when someone is pretending. Knows others have different emotions, likes and dislikes; uses vocabulary relating to feelings. Shows concern for another's distress. Anticipates consequences of behavior.	Engage in pretend play and act out situations requiring different emotions. Talk about what each family member or classmate likes and does not like. Ask, "What is going to happen?"

Developmental age	Social cognition characteristics	Keys to intervention
24–36 months	Uses words *pretend, think,* and *know*. Knows people's feelings vary across situations; reads others' feelings and actions in dramatic play; shows empathy; shows signs of guilt. Realizes he or she can cause distress in others. Ascribes thoughts and feelings to dolls and action figures.	Use vocabulary about thinking and feeling. Ask about others' thoughts and emotions. Give children an opportunity to dramatize stories relating to emotions. When someone is hurt, involve the child in kissing and caring. Discuss how the child's behavior affects others. Talk about how dolls and stuffed animals would "feel" in specific situations in dramatic play.
36–48 months	Can describe own feelings; aware of others' thoughts, feelings, and perceptions. Can differentiate own point of view from another's. Understands *if . . . then* behavior and consequences.	Talk about feelings: the child's, yours, and others'. Ask how others are feeling when emotions are expressed. Ask "What will happen if . . ." questions. Ask "What do you think . . . wants?"
48–60 months	Can explain to another what will happen if he or she does something; asks questions to determine how another person thinks or feels. Can discuss another's imagination, knowledge. Makes inferences about another's motives; understands that beliefs and desires determine actions. Can pull tricks on others, knowing they will believe one thing, then do another.	Have children talk together and hypothesize what is going to happen in various situations. Ask questions so children will compare thoughts and feelings. Talk about why people are doing what they are doing. Predict what is going to happen next. Talk about different cultures and beliefs. Play games in which children predict what happens and then something else occurs. Discuss what happened and why. Talk about jokes and tricks.
60–72 months	Can think about multiple characters; their actions, beliefs, and behaviors; and how one influences another.	Involve children in dramatizing stories with emotional themes, then talk about the actions and feelings of the characters. Role play responding in different ways when the child's actions result in making another angry or hurting another's feelings.

7

Facilitating Cognitive Development

V. Strategies for Improving Complexity of Play

Goal Attainment Scale

1	2	3	4	5	6	7	8	9
Enjoys people and investigating the environment with all the senses.		Enjoys sensory exploration, body movement, and exploring objects repetitively.		Enjoys putting things together, experimenting to make things happen, and recreating familiar actions and routines.		Combines various kinds of play to create actual and imagined structures, scenarios, and outcomes.		Demonstrates both logical and creative thinking in all forms of play (i.e., sensory, physical, functional, construction, dramatic, and games with rules). Creates own games with own rules.

The subcategory of Complexity of Play within the cognitive domain examines how children incorporate people, objects, space, actions, and language into their play. Complexity implies both the type of play in which the child engages and how elaborate the actions are within the play. Categories of play include face-to-face play, sensorimotor play, functional/relational play, construction, dramatic play, games with rules, and rough-and-tumble play. Although these forms of play tend to be hierarchical and build on each other, all kinds of play remain important to the child throughout childhood (and even adulthood). Behavioral sequences within play also are indicators of the complexity of the child's thinking.

Play is a significant learning tool for children. Each form of play has a period in childhood when it predominates and promotes various aspects of cognitive, motor, language and communication, and social development. Children learn to problem solve and think for themselves in their play, but they also learn to negotiate social interactions. They learn how to use inner language to talk themselves through problems, but they also learn how to use language in social play. Children learn how to move and control their bodies, but they also learn how to persist when play requires focus and limited movement. Play provides a safe venue for experimentation and discovery for all areas of development. The adults in children's lives play a crucial role in assisting children to transition into higher levels of play and use more complicated thought processes.

APPROPRIATE COMPLEXITY OF PLAY

Depending on the developmental level of the child, complexity will look different. For infants, increased sensory exploration and manipulation of objects will lead to using hands together to combine toys in various ways. For toddlers, increased social, language, and motor skills lead to understanding how to use objects functionally and how to imitate higher level behaviors. Preschool-age children show increased social understanding, more controlled movements, expansion of language concepts, and ability to solve higher level problems. These enable children to demonstrate elaborate physical play, complicated constructions, sophisticated dramatic play, and games requiring social and cognitive strategies.

APPROPRIATE COMPLEXITY OF PLAY IN PRACTICE

▦▦▦ **V. A. What behaviors demonstrate the level and complexity of the child's play?**

Daily Routines (Home and Classroom)

- *Infant/toddler:* Marshall is playing with his mother's measuring cups while she is cooking. He repeatedly puts one cup inside of another.

- *Young child:* While his mother is cooking dinner, Avery gets out a pot and spoon and pretends to cook. "I'm making us spaghetti. What are you making?"

Play Routines (Home and Classroom)

- *Infant/toddler:* Courtney plays with her busy box, twirling the spinner, pushing the noise maker, and pulling the lever to make the face pop up.

- *Young child:* Anderson lines up five chairs and then sits in the first one, holding a paper plate as a steering wheel. "Who wants a ride on my bus? It costs one dollar."

Classroom Routines

The toddler is playing with playdough, rolling it out with a rolling pin and then poking holes in it with a dowel.

▦▦▦ **V. B. What approach typifies the complexity of the child's actions within the listed categories of play? (See Section V. A.)**

Daily Routines (Home and Classroom)

- *Infant/toddler:* Kiley holds a rattle during diapering. She shakes it, mouths it, and then waves it around. She accidentally hits the mobile with the rattle and the mobile moves. She waves the rattle again.

- *Young child:* Maya is in the tub with her twin sister. She dips a cup into the water and says, "I'm the Mommy. I am going to wash you. Now, don't cry." She then pours water on her sister's leg. Later, the cup becomes a turtle floating in the water, and still later, a drum.

Play Routines (Home and Classroom)

- *Infant/toddler:* Shera opens the door on the toy barn and places the cow inside and says, "Night, night, cow."

- *Young child:* Julio is dramatizing a story about a monster. He makes a tail from a scarf and a costume from a shawl and a belt. He then tells his friend to be a sheep and he will come eat the sheep.

Classroom Routines

The young child is building a house out of blocks. His friend Jake "drives" a toy car by and says, "Hey, Ahmjed, you building a garage?" Ahmjed says, "Sure" and starts to lay out blocks for a garage.

V. C. What level of cognition is demonstrated in the child's sense of humor?

Daily Routines (Home and Classroom)

- *Infant/toddler:* Bridget laughs when her father blows on her tummy. She laughs, pushes him away, and then pulls up her shirt for him to do it again.

- *Young child:* Before bed, the young child gets on the bed and jumps, and then drops to his bottom and laughs. He repeats this action over and over.

Play Routines (Home and Classroom)

- *Infant/toddler:* The infant pulls the blanket over her head and waits for her dad to pull it off. When he does, she squeals and laughs. She then tries to put it over her dad's head.

- *Young child:* Logan whispers in his friend's ear, "You are a poopy face!" He laughs. Then they both rock back and forth with laughter.

Classroom Routines

The teacher is reading a book about a princess getting potty trained. She shows the group a picture of the princess with the potty on her head. "Oh, no! Look what she did." The kids howl with laughter.

GENERAL PRINCIPLES FOR SUPPORTING APPROPRIATE COMPLEXITY OF PLAY

Caregivers typically engage in many behaviors to encourage more complex thinking and actions in play. Often this happens without conscious effort. The following strategies frequently are used to help children expand their ideas in play. These strategies can be used with children at all levels.

Provide Opportunities for Many Different Kinds of Play

Children need to engage in many types of play. Face-to-face play, sensorimotor/exploratory play, functional/relational play, construction, dramatic play, sociodramatic play, games with rules, and rough-and-tumble play each encourage different aspects of development. Sensorimotor or exploratory play can involve any of the senses—sight, hearing, smell, taste, touch, movement, or pressure. Cultures, and even individual families, may vary in terms of their acceptance or tolerance for different forms of play.

For example, some cultures or families have traditions of not allowing children to play on the floor, others do not appreciate messy play, and still others have limited toys for economic reasons. The amount of play materials available, the degree of support for play, and the level of parent involvement in play will vary from family to family. Whether outdoors with sand, rocks, and sticks, or indoors with pots, wooden spoons, and other household items, children find ways to play. Regardless of the culture or family preferences, however, most parents find ways to help their children experience numerous types of play. A full range of experiences is essential for optimal learning. As described previously, parents, teachers, and other caregivers present many play options throughout the day.

Bump Up the Play Level

Another strategy used by adults is encouraging the child to move into a higher level of play. Usually this is done through making a suggestion or demonstrating for the child. For example, the mother can transform the child's nesting activity (functional/relational play) into pretending to pour, stir, and drink (dramatic play) by modeling the actions in order to encourage a higher category of play.

Add Materials

When adults observe the child repeating actions or only playing with limited materials, a common strategy is to add new materials. This does not mean buying new toys all the time (although some parents do that). Often just adding a new item encourages the child to use the old materials in a new way. For example, the parent adds a diaper to the doll play to use as a burp cloth. This instantly expands the child's routine play of feeding the baby into a more complex sequence of events relating to feeding. The addition of new items into play encourages the child to think about how the material can be incorporated.

Add Language

Play with children provides unlimited opportunities for using language. Parents add sounds, rhythms, and words to play. For infants, play with the sounds that make up words is important for development. For example, when the baby produces jargon, the mother sings a song with words and the baby joins in the play. Adults also provide vocabulary to explain what is happening in play. They describe, question, and make suggestions that increase children's understanding, make them think, and help them consider alternatives.

Add Actions

Children love to repeat actions. Repetition is their way of practicing a skill. In order to learn new skills; however, it is important for children to discover new play patterns. Often these new approaches are discovered as the child explores the item or situation, but adults play an important role as well. Adults model alternative approaches or uses of materials for children. By demonstrating a new approach, children can pick up new strategies. Instead of rolling a ball, for example, adults may bounce it, throw it up in the air, or toss it in a bucket. Adding actions helps children learn new strategies as well as how to combine actions into a new sequence.

Add Ideas

The strategies described previously all build on what the child is already thinking and doing. Another way adults help children build their play skills is to present novel ideas that they might not have considered. For example, the parent might suggest making a birthday card for grandma, then give the child paper, glue, glitter, feathers, markers, and so forth to combine in his or her own way. If not structured by the adult, this becomes a playful act of creation for the child. Adults and peers can introduce new ideas into many forms of play. They might add an idea in construction play (as the peer did when he suggested the block building could be a garage for his car). They might add an event in dramatic play, such as saying their car ran out of gas. By adding ideas, the adult helps to increase the complexity of children's play.

THE PRINCIPLES IN PRACTICE

Most caregivers and teachers automatically use strategies to prompt higher levels of play throughout the day. The following are examples of strategies adults use throughout the day to encourage more complex play.

Daily Routines (Home and Classroom)

Feeding/Eating

During lunch, Jodi finishes eating the yogurt out of the carton. Her mother then gives her the lid and Jodi tries to put it on. Her mother then takes the crumbs and leftovers from the highchair tray and puts them in the empty cup. Jodi does the same. Her mother then puts the lid on the yogurt cup and shakes it. Jodi shakes it too, and they both laugh.

Diapering/Toileting

Christian is sitting on the toilet. His mother gives him two action figures to play with while he is trying to go to the bathroom. She says, "These are big guys. They already went to the bathroom. They said they want to play with you when you are finished."

Dressing

When dressing Montana, Dad takes Montana's underwear and says, "I need a hat," and puts them on his head. He then puts Montana's socks on his hands and calls them "mittens." Montana laughs, pulls the underwear off his dad's head and puts them on his own. He takes a sock and tries to put it on his hand.

Going Out

While riding in the car, Margo jargons and makes noises. Mother slowly sings a song and Margo makes more vocalizations, with occasional attempts to imitate her mother's words. What was originally sensory play for the child—making sounds—has become functional play. The mother has built on the child's natural vocal play and encouraged adding rhythm and words.

Play Routines (Home and Classroom)

Face-to-Face Play

Mom has her infant, Drushan, on her lap facing her. She starts to sing, "Row, Row, Row Your Boat" while moving Drushan back and forth. When her mother leans forward, Drushan falls back, then pulls forward, anticipating the game. Mother waits for Drushan to signal the next step before continuing.

Physical Play

Father and son are roughhousing on the floor. Dad says, "I'm going to kiss your nose." He lunges and Jordan turns his head. Dad kisses Jordan's ear and says, "I got your nose!" "Did not! That was my ear!" Jordan laughs. The original play was primarily humor built on sensory play; however, the father added higher level verbal humor to the play.

Manipulative Play

Natasha is pretending to feed the doll. The caregiver hands the child a cloth diaper and says, "Is she ready to burp? Here is a cloth for your shoulder, in case she spits up." Natasha puts the cloth on her shoulder and then pats the baby's back. In this situation, the caregiver added a prop and a suggestion to expand the child's play from simple dramatic play with one step of a routine to a series of actions comprising a longer sequence of feeding the baby.

Sensory Play

Teryn is making patterns on paper with fingerpaint. The teacher gives her a variety of items to use on the paint—a wavy ravioli cutter, a cookie cutter, and other tools. Teryn begins to experiment with the tools to make designs and pictures on the paint.

Reading and Learning Routines

Circle Time

During circle time, the teacher put up a sequence of pictures from the book the class had been reading. She then asked who wanted to act out the part of the story depicted in the pictures and have the class guess what was happening.

One-on-One Book Reading

While reading the book to Shoshana, her mother pointed to the cow in the book and made funny mooing sounds. Shoshana imitated her. Her mother then made a deep "moo" for the daddy cow, another sound for the momma cow, and a high-sounding "moo" for the baby cow. Shoshana loved it and wanted to go back to those pages in the book. Such play with language helped Shoshana explore tones, the meaning of sounds, and playful expression of meaning.

Science and Math

In the dramatic play area, Marva is taking the toys in and out of the doctor's bag. The teacher says, "Are you the doctor? I'm sick. Can you listen to my heart?" The child nods, opens the doctor's kit, and takes out the stethoscope. What began as simple exploration by the child was modified into sociodramatic play when the teacher inserted herself into the situation by playing the role of a sick person.

PLANNING INDIVIDUALIZED INTERVENTIONS FOR IMPROVING COMPLEXITY OF PLAY

▄▄▄▄ V. A. What behaviors demonstrate the level and complexity of the child's play?

Many children with developmental delays or specific disabilities demonstrate a lower level of play than would be expected for their chronological age. Many children with disabilities primarily engage in either sensorimotor play or functional/relational play. In sensorimotor play, they enjoy exploring and investigating the sensory characteristics of objects. In functional/relational play, they like to use realistic objects, such as a phone, or combine objects in simple ways, such as banging them together or putting objects in and out of a container. Children may be "stuck" at this level for varying reasons.

Some children choose the play that is at their cognitive level. Children with intellectual disabilities, for example, may continue to play at the sensorimotor or functional/relational level because that is their level of understanding. They will investigate toys, mouth them, move the parts, and put things in and out or together. Other children choose to play at a lower level because that type of play meets a specific need. For example, children with autism may select play opportunities that provide a certain type of stimulation, such as watching things that spin or lining things up in straight lines. They may become fixated on a specific type of sensory input, such as watching their finger flick, and ignore other types of input.

Children with visual impairments may select play that provides input such as movement or pressure and/or gives them interesting tactile and auditory experiences. Because they cannot see, they may miss details in the environment, spatial dimensions, and a concept of what the whole environment contains. In addition, they may miss the nonverbal communication of others. Higher level construction or dramatic play involving events children cannot see or experience in order to understand, such as going in a rocket to space, may be imitated but not fully understood. Making sure children with visual impairments understand these abstract concepts requires creativity on the part of adults. Children with visual impairments also may have difficulty comprehending how events occurred. For example, they may feel that the baby doll is wet, but they do not understand the sequence of events (i.e., giving the baby a bath) that led to this condition. Social play also is affected, because children who are blind cannot see what others are doing.

Children who are hard of hearing or have language impairments also may show delays in play. Although they can see and imitate others, they may have delays in understanding abstract concepts that cannot be seen, such as *hungry*. Their play primarily may reflect actions they can see others perform.

Children with attention deficits also may play at a lower level because their focus shifts before they can engage in more advanced play. As a result, their play may look fragmented and unorganized. Play with peers may be especially difficult because children with attention deficits typically are more focused on objects and movement than on interacting with others.

Regardless of the reason for the delay, children can be supported in moving to a higher level of play. The following are suggestions for helping children with special needs progress to higher categories of play.

Interaction Strategies

1. *Engage the child at his or her level through imitation, and then model a higher level play.* For example, if the child is at a sensory level, mouthing, waving, and banging an object, the adult can position herself directly in front of the child, then imitate the child. Once the child is attending, the adult can position two objects in front of her face (because the infant will most likely be looking at the adult's face) and bang the objects together to make an interesting sound. If the child does not imitate after several turns, the adult can help the child with hand-over-hand banging. Sometimes the child needs to "feel" the action to help him perform it. As children begin to combine objects and use objects functionally (functional/relational play), the adult can begin to model combining toys in more complex ways, such as stacking, lining up, and creating interesting

effects (e.g., rolling a ball down a ramp, pushing a button on a pop-up toy). As children begin to understand how to combine objects and sequence actions, they are ready to imitate actions in daily life. This is the beginning of dramatic play. Adults can prompt this by being a play partner and introducing real objects from the child's daily life into play. When real-life sequences are dramatized spontaneously, the child is ready to use dolls, action figures, and replicas of real objects in his or her play. The adult also can help the child integrate peers into dramatic play in separate roles. This involves observing and anticipating the actions of all of the children and providing a narrative to explain what each child is doing. This adult narration and "brokering" within the play helps children move into sociodramatic play.

2. *Stay primarily at the child's level, occasionally adding higher level actions.* Adults need to understand that children may make gradual advances into the next level of play. Just because the child imitates the adult in pretending to drink from a cup does not mean that pretend play suddenly should become the primary focus. Children need to explore and observe the options for play at multiple levels.

3. *Introduce peers who are playing at one level higher than the child.* Peers can be great teachers! Children are typically interested in watching other children. The peer can become the model for the child to imitate. The adult can help bring the child's attention to what the peer is doing and encourage imitation. "Look, Rebecca! Andrew is driving his car through the car wash. Psh-sh-sh! Your car looks dirty too."

4. *Use language that explains what is happening.* Providing an explanation or narration about the activity helps the child understand the play. In the previous example, the child with cognitive delays might observe the peer driving his car under the toy structure, but he does not understand that the structure represents a car wash. The adult's explanation of the peer's actions, added sound effects of water spraying, and suggestion that the child's car was dirty helped prompt her to both imitate the peer and understand what he was doing.

5. *Provide cues.* Verbal and visual cues, such as described previously, most commonly are provided by adults. Some children, however, need additional cues. Children with visual impairments or children requiring additional sensory input to comprehend situations will benefit from a more detailed examination of all of the elements of a situation. Again, using the previous example, the child may need to feel the car, the moving wheels, and the car wash structure. The addition of the sounds of water from an actual car wash on tape, or actual water flowing over the car wash (or on the sidewalk!), will help the child understand the intent of the play and motivate her to want to participate.

6. *If signing the label for toys or materials, sign it next to the object being labeled.* The proximity of the sign to the object helps the child make the association. Signing or providing clarifying gestures also can help children who are not deaf or hard of hearing, because the sign often is another visual representation of the words being said.

7. *Introduce materials or props that will stimulate ideas and connections.* Provide toys that have multiple parts, with pieces that fit inside, together, or on top of each other, to encourage relational play. Moving dramatic play materials into the block area or sensory area can promote dramatic play. For example, adding action figures to the sand and water table may spur dramatic play on a beach. Even animal puzzle pieces can become dramatic play figures in the block area.

8. *Reenact favorite stories.* After reading a favorite story, let the child play his or her favorite character. Find props and act out the story together. This not only prompts the child to participate in sociodramatic play, but also builds narrative skills for emerging literacy.

Environmental Modifications

In addition to interpersonal strategies that may support the child moving to higher levels of play, environmental modifications often are useful. Depending on the findings from TPBA2, the team may want to consider some of the following environmental modifications.

1. *Highlight the play.* Children with visual impairments (with some sight) may benefit from bold colors or high contrast between the play object of focus and the background. Putting a table cloth that is a sharp contrast to the toys (black or light) on the play table or floor, using a light box, or using a lamp to light an area may help some children. Reducing the number of toys in an area also can help the child focus on the objects at hand. Rotating toys and materials so the child encounters novel experiences is helpful.

2. *Consider clarity and size of materials.* Small objects may be hard for some children to see, manipulate, or relate to their larger real-life counterparts. For example, small Lego figures often are crude representations of actual people or animals. Children may have a harder time understanding that these can be used in play to represent people or animals. More lifelike rubber animals and people may enable the child to use them in dramatic play actions. Pictures, puzzles, or toys that are too "busy" also may inhibit children's understanding of the features of the objects and, thus, the meaning or use of the materials.

3. *Consider location of materials.* Children need to easily be able to see, touch, hear, and experience play materials and objects in their environment. Their play level will be negatively affected if the toy shelves are too high for them to reach, the chairs too high for their feet to touch the floor, the books too far away for them to see, or the important sounds too soft for them to hear. For children who cannot move to access toys independently, make sure objects are placed so the children can reach them. Placing two toys in proximity will encourage the child to combine the toys in some way.

4. *Familiarize the child with where materials can be found.* Just as children rely on routine to be able to guide their day, they rely on predictability of the environment to guide their play. Higher level play requires combining different toys and materials in creative ways. It is important for children to know where these materials can be found in order to help them organize their play. If the child goes to find objects that are needed for dramatic play, for instance, and they are not where they are expected to be, the child may give up on the play, get upset, or require adult assistance. Having an organized, predictable environment can minimize these undesired outcomes.

▬▬▬ V. B. What approach typifies the complexity of the child's actions within the listed categories of play?

Children learn by observing, manipulating, experimenting and combining objects to make play sequences and recreate events they have seen or imagine. As they move into sociodramatic play, they learn how to incorporate others into their play sequences. Children with special needs may have problems with any or all of these skills. They may choose a limited variety of toys and materials, perform a restricted number of actions on objects, combine few action sequences, and repeat the same actions or sequences across all types of activities. For example, a child with developmental disabilities may select the same toy repeatedly, such as a toy car, rather than investigating novel objects. He or she may then repeat familiar actions, such as pushing or throwing, rather than trying new actions and discovering new consequences. Because of the limited number of actions the child performs, the number of play sequences the child creates also is restricted. Lack of expanded actions confines the child to a lower developmental category of play, and results in less complex, less organized play. Consequently, the child may rely on adults or peers to introduce other toys or actions, suggest a play sequence, or structure social interactions. The following are suggestions for increasing the complexity of a child's play.

Interaction Strategies

1. *Watch for the difference between practice and perseveration.* Practice play is important for children. When toys, materials, or actions are new, repetitive play enables the child to practice a new skill. When repetition appears to be all that the child can do or wants to do, then it becomes perseverative. The adult needs to give the child another option for play by modeling another action or giving the child something that can be combined with the toy to encourage another action. For example, if the child is repeatedly pushing cars around and does nothing else, the adult can model doing something different with the cars. For example, the adult might put tape on the floor for a "road" or add a ramp made out of magazines for the car to go down. A dump truck could be added and the back filled with blocks. Note that the adult is adding variations to what motivates the child. If the toy or action becomes an obsession, it may be necessary to introduce a replacement that also will be motivating.

2. *Introduce combinatorial play.* Toys and materials can be combined in many ways. As in the previous example, the addition of tape or blocks may be enough to motivate the child to try new actions. Sometimes introducing unique actions or materials will capture the child's interest and encourage imitation of novel actions; for instance, driving the car into a shoe box "garage," pretending to feed the doll a real apple instead of a plastic apple, or hiding the preferred ball and other items in an empty tissue box and playing Hide-and-Seek.

3. *Demonstrate novel actions with toys.* Wind-up toys or toys that provide a lot of stimulation can frequently draw the child's attention and encourage experimentation to get the effects to recur. Notice what effects (e.g., auditory, visual, tactile, movement) the child prefers and provide toys that produce that effect but require different causal actions. For instance, if the child likes things that make noise, find objects that make noise but require different actions to produce the noise (e.g., a radio with a knob, the TV control with a button, a wind-up toy with a small key, a jack-in-the-box with a crank). This will help the child learn to investigate the possibilities of different toys.

4. *Add one more step to the actions the child performs.* Whatever the child does, whether one action or a three- or four-step action, the adult can always model one additional action to the child's sequence. Modeling a new action gives the child a new idea to add to his or her repertoire. For example, if the child is repetitively feeding the baby and then putting it to bed, the adult can add a step. "Uh-oh! The baby is wet. She needs her diaper changed." If this step is added several times during the play with adult suggestion, the child is more likely to add the step spontaneously at a later time without adult support.

5. *Discuss the characteristics of toys.* Frequently, a child with special needs focuses on only one characteristic or function of an object. Adults can help children learn to analyze materials to determine characteristics that relate to certain functions. The adult can point out features and relate them to something the child already knows; for instance, "Look, Brianna. It has a button just like your tape recorder." See if the child makes the association and pushes it. If more prompting is needed, the adult might say, "I wonder what will happen if you push it." If the child does not respond, the adult can

then model pushing the button so the child can observe the relationship between the action and what happens after.

6. *Ask questions to encourage investigation.* Asking questions can help a child consider another action or step in a play sequence; for instance, "What else can we put in the hole?" "Can you find another way?" or "Now that the baby is full, what does she want to do?" Such questions can help children think beyond what they are currently seeing or thinking.

7. *Do not forget vocal play.* Regardless of the child's developmental level, playing with sounds and rhythms, songs, and dance can motivate the child to try creative forms of play.

8. *Play with movement also can involve higher levels of play.* Movement can be part of dramatic play as well. A rocking horse, stairs, a fishing pole, and other toys and materials that encourage movement can become part of the props for creating a narrative. The horse (hobby horse) may be ridden to a mountain for a hike (up the stairs) or to a lake where there is fishing (to use the fishing pole). Almost any materials can be made into representations of another object for creating a story.

Environmental Modifications

In addition to interpersonal strategies that may help children increase the complexity of their play, environmental modifications often are useful. Depending on the findings from TPBA2, the team may want to consider some of the following environmental modifications.

1. *Determine the "right" number of toys or materials.* Having options is important so that the child is motivated—but not so many options that the child is overwhelmed by the variety of choices.

2. *Have duplicates of toys.* Duplicate toys reduce conflict between children. Duplicates also enable the child to observe another person playing with the toy and have a model for actions.

3. *Provide adaptations for toys and materials.* Adaptations can make toys easier for children to manipulate. Options include large knobs on puzzle pieces or turning devices, grips on crayons or markers, easily activated switches on mechanical devices, tactile pieces glued onto the toys to enable children to identify key aspects, aromas added to playdough for an added attraction, and high-contrast colors or lights to make toys easier to see.

4. *Provide adaptations to the environment.* Adaptations can make play easier for children with special needs. For instance, adaptive seating for children who have difficulty sitting without support can allow the child to have more control of his or her arms, hands, and fingers for play. Additions to toys (e.g., Velcro on blocks) can provide support for children who have difficulty controlling movements. Stabilizing materials, such as taping down the paper so the child can draw without worrying about the paper moving, is a simple adaptation.

5. *Select toys and materials that capitalize on the child's strengths.* For example, a toy that makes noise as a consequence of hitting a switch does not benefit a deaf child, but a toy that has flashing lights might. Children who are tactually defensive might not want to play with stuffed animals or fingerpaints. This does not mean that the child is never exposed to these materials; rather, the adult can introduce toys the child avoids or resists gradually, if this is important for the child's development.

▰▰▰▰ V. C. What level of cognition is demonstrated in the child's sense of humor?

What children find humorous can reveal a great deal about their cognitive understanding, particularly for children who cannot express cognitive skills through movement or language. What people find funny is cumulative. As adults, we can still laugh at sensory experiences such as tickling, but we also laugh at sophisticated jokes that require comprehension of language and incongruities in life experience and world events. Therefore, as children develop conceptual understanding, evidence of increasing appreciation of humor should be apparent. For children, sense of humor often is most evident in their play. Facilitation of the development of the child's sense of humor is important primarily for social reasons. Joint laughter can bring children together in a way that is qualitatively different from other types of social interaction. The following strategies highlight ways to provide opportunities for sense of humor to develop.

Interaction Strategies

1. *Explain why a situation is funny.* The child may not see or comprehend the incongruities that make a situation humorous. For example, when reading a book about a porcupine, the parent can point out the picture of the porcupine holding an umbrella. The porcupine's quills are all poking through the umbrella. The child might not understand why this is funny without the parent's explanation.

2. *Create funny situations.* Adults love to make children laugh with sensory experiences, especially when they are infants and toddlers. They tickle, toss, and tumble with them. This playful interaction should continue as the child gets older but also should expand into higher level types of humor. The parent can use objects in unusual ways (e.g., trying to put the child's shoes on the adult's feet) and begin to use words in more than one way. Almost any word that has multiple meanings can be used in a humorous way. For instance, the parent and child are coloring and the child says, "Do you want an orange?" The parent replies, "Oh, yes, I love to eat oranges!" The child laughs and says, "No, Mommy! Not that kind of orange, this kind of orange!" (holding up the orange crayon). This helps the child increase conceptual understanding and, at the same time, develop a sense of humor.

3. *Point out funny things to the child.* Bring humorous situations to the child's attention. Throughout the day, small events are humorous. Look for opportunities to point these out to the child; for example, the ant that carries a crumb 10 times its size, the spilled milk that looks like a bird, the noise the water makes when it goes down the drain, and so forth.

4. *Use humor to defuse a difficult situation.* Humor can distract and redirect feelings. For example, when the child is trying to put on her shoes and is crying because she is frustrated, the parent might say, "No wonder you can't get them on. Those are MY shoes!" and then struggle to put one on.

5. *Share books, songs, and poems.* Use exaggerated affect and intonation when reading or singing funny material. This emphasizes the funny parts for the child. When the adult laughs, it often triggers laughter in the child. The adult may need to explain what was funny, however.

6. *Point out what is* not *funny.* Humor can be hurtful to others. Adults need to help children understand when saying certain things (e.g., "You are fat like Santa!") is not funny, and why some situations may look funny but are not funny in real life (e.g., the elephant that sits on a dog in a cartoon).

Environmental Modifications

1. *Have funny books available.* Read books that demonstrate humorous use of language (e.g., *Moo, Baa, La-la-la!; Food Fight!; Knuffle Bunny: A Cautionary Tale*), funny situations (e.g., *Don't Let the Pigeon Drive the Bus; Olivia*), and funny poems (e.g., *Where the Sidewalk Ends*). Use the previous strategies as the book is read.

2. *Provide toys that do surprising things.* Humor is about surprise, so toys, games, and materials that have unexpected actions or consequences provide opportunities for laughter (e.g., shoot bubbles into the air, have frogs that leap, have parts to make silly characters).

ROUTINES FOR THE CHILD WHO NEEDS SUPPORT TO INCREASE THE COMPLEXITY OF PLAY

Daily Routines (Home and Classroom)

Feeding/Eating

Although mealtime is not typically a time to play, there are aspects of play that can be encouraged during mealtime. Observation of others, turn-taking, imitation, and vocal play can be integrated easily into meals. In addition, what occurs during meals often is later reenacted in dramatic play, so eating actually encourages dramatic play. Adults and children alike can be models for younger children, modeling actions (e.g., pouring milk), making sounds (e.g., "yum, yum!"), and talking during the meal. Adults also can demonstrate using tools (e.g., knife and fork together), emphasize a sequence of actions (e.g., scooping the food, placing it in the mouth, chewing, and swallowing), and imitate what others are doing (e.g., "Daddy blew on his hot chicken. I'm going to blow on my chicken, too"). Mealtimes also provide opportunities for laughing at funny language or situations.

Diapering/Toileting

Although diapering and toileting are typically not playful situations, making them so is actually beneficial for both the child and the parent. During diapering, the child can hold and play with objects, engage in face-to-face play, and use his or her feet in playful interactions. This can be a time for vocal play and singing. For children learning to use the toilet, dramatic play can be highly motivating. Children can engage in dramatic play, putting their dolls through the toileting sequence and then going through the sequence themselves (or vice versa).

Dressing

Dressing can easily become a play activity, either with dolls, as noted previously, or in a game with a caregiver. Dressing can involve songs (e.g., "This is the way we put on our shirt, put on our shirt, put on our shirt"), guessing games (e.g., "I've got something with two legs that is blue"), or turn-taking actions (e.g., "Let's put the shirt on your baby, then put your shirt on").

Going Out

Walking or driving to destinations can involve singing, dramatic play, or turn-taking games. If walking, motor games can be played that include going "fast" and "slow" or hopping, jumping, and skipping. The child can pretend to be taking the dolls to the store or the park. In the car, singing and doing fingerplays can entertain, or I See games can be played; for example, "I see a stop sign! Who else sees a stop sign?" "What do you see?" For older children, clues can be used, such as "I see something that is big, has a trunk, and has green leaves."

Play Routines (Home and Classroom)

Face-to-Face Play

Face-to-face play is the first type of play in which children engage, but face-to-face play is fun for children throughout the early years. Infants begin with facial imitation and move to imitation of gestures in games such as Peekaboo. By preschool, children love to join adults in songs and fingerplays. Fingerplays are a great way to help children engage in more complex verbal and gestural play. Fingerplays require sequencing of both thoughts and actions. After the child can imitate simple gestures easily, fingerplays can be introduced. The adult should talk or sing slowly, making the corresponding gestures simultaneously. Let the child imitate the words and/or the gestures before moving to the next step of the sequence. As the child begins to anticipate the words and gestures, the adult can increase the tempo. Let the child choose which songs and fingerplays she wants to do, and let her lead the actions as much as she can. This will support the development of memory for sequences.

Physical Play

Physical play often involves sequencing of actions (e.g., getting on a tricycle, positioning feet and hands, and coordinating reciprocal movement of the feet). Adults can increase the complexity of physical play by introducing props or steps that require additional thinking and action. For example, as children learn to crawl, introduce objects they can crawl through, over, under, and around, increasing their ability to plan motor movements. Placing a desired toy in a place that requires new movements is a simple motivator. Toddlers have the ability to climb and move their bodies with increasing balance and skill. They can begin to imitate songs that require whole-body movements, such as "I'm a Little Teapot." For most children, the words will stimulate memory for the actions, although the reverse also is possible. Preschool-age children are much more coordinated and are beginning to engage in actions that require differentiated use of body parts, such as riding a tricycle. Play that involves obstacle courses and games that involve motor sequences, such as the Hokey-Pokey, enable children to practice sequences of movements. Adult demonstration can prompt participation initially but should be replaced by peer modeling.

Manipulative Play

Manipulations of small objects and play with toys that require the use of fingers is difficult for some children with disabilities. Use of larger materials may help them be successful. For instance, if the child has difficulty with small Legos, large Duplo blocks may be easier to manipulate. Children also may resort to simple combinations, such as putting toys inside something and then taking them out again. In order to increase the level of manipulative play, children need to think of different actions and try new approaches to play. Introducing new objects that have similar properties may help children gain a new perspective. For example, if the child has difficulty with the buttons on the doll's shirt, a game of putting pennies through a lid with a slot may help the child understand the sequence. The adult can then point out the similarity as the child is dressing the doll: "Remember how you put the pennies in the slot? Put the button in the slot. Now pull it through!"

For children with fine motor concerns, adaptations of materials may be helpful. Adding a handle to preferred toys may help. A material such as Theraplast can be molded to form a shape that the child can hold.

Children with visual impairments may need reduced clutter in the play area to be able to see the small items. Attention to the color and background also is important for these children. Use of magnification devices also may be helpful.

Increasing the number of actions in a play sequences and the variety of actions the child uses may require an adult or peer model, a verbal suggestion, or a physical prompt.

Sensory Play

Sensory play typically is exploratory in nature. Play in the sandbox or in the tub often is characterized by "dump" and "fill." The addition of water to the sand can move the child into construction play, making sand castles or walls. Snow can be used to make snowmen or snow forts. Adding kitchen objects to the tub, such as a sieve, a measuring cup, or turkey basters, can encourage experimentation. Materials such as bath foam and bath crayons help children create art on the sides of the tub, and action figures and plastic bowls can become pirates and boats to promote dramatic play in the water. Adding a plastic baby doll, a sponge, baby shampoo, and other bath items can encourage play and also help the child practice the action sequence for bathing.

Dramatic Play

Dramatic play begins with acting out familiar routines. As pointed out previously, adding dolls to the daily routines encourages children to reenact these sequences in play. To move children into a higher level of dramatic play, adults can encourage dramatization of stories in books or movies. Provide props related to the story to prompt memory for actions. Dramatization of stories takes children beyond role play of simple action sequences into the dramatization of event sequences and retelling of narratives.

Children with developmental delays may need adult or peer play partners to model or remind them of the next actions in the sequence. Children with disabilities that affect gross and fine motor skills may need environmental adaptations to enable them to participate in dramatic play. Space for a wheelchair or use of a walker or "stander" may be needed. Props may need to be placed at lower levels for easier access. For children who have difficulty holding toys, Velcro also can be glued to toys and a Velcro strap made that goes around the child's palm.

Use of real or realistic props is important for children with cognitive delays or vision problems. The adult needs to ensure that the child with vision impairments understands what each object in the dramatic play is and how it is used before beginning dramatic play. Adults need to familiarize children with where props are located and narrate what is happening for children who have vision impairments and cannot see what peers are doing or where props are located. Positioning props in the order in which they will be needed can assist children who are engaging in a dramatic play scenario for the first time.

For children who are deaf or hard of hearing, the adult needs to teach peers how to position themselves in front of the child so they can see their mouths, gestures, and/or signs. Pictures of the sequences of actions in the story or the event being enacted also can be posted so the child can see what happens next.

Reading and Learning Routines

Circle Time

When reading to a group of children, the adult should incorporate the children in the process as much as possible. Make sure that all children can see, hear, and understand what is being read. This may mean using big books, using real objects to explain concepts, using signs and gestures, acting out the story, or letting the children tell the story in their own way. Circle time should be a fun, interactive time.

One-on-One Book Reading

Reading should be a fun experience for children. Learning will occur, but it should not be the only emphasis when a book is being shared with a child. Let the child's interest guide the reading. Depending on the child's developmental level, the adult can assist him or her in learning the sequences of actions; predicting what will happen next; and filling in words, phrases, or sentences from the book. The adult also can point to words as they are read. This demonstrates for the child the sequence of how books are read and the association between the spoken word and the written word, and, as the story becomes familiar, enables the child to begin to recognize words from the story. As children begin to recognize letters, they can be prompted to associate letters and letter-sounds.

Science and Math

Science and math involve discovery of relationships. As children play, adults can help children make comparisons, point out similarities and differences, relate ideas, and understand causal relationships. For example, as the child is putting together a puzzle of farm animals, the adult may comment, "Ducks and chickens both have two wings and two legs. They are both birds. You found the cow. How many legs does the cow have?" Such a discussion can continue as long as the child is interested.

▰▰▰ *RAEL*

Rael is a 2-year-old whose family—including his father Marco, his mother Ana, and his brothers Juan and Carlito—has just moved to the United States from Spain. His two older brothers have been identified as having fragile X syndrome. After genetic testing, Rael also was determined to have fragile X. Rael's parents are anxious to have early intervention for Rael. They indicated that they are concerned about his short attention span and repetitive play. They would like for him to be able to play both independently and with his brothers. Rael's favorite toys are cars and trucks, but his play with these items is limited to making car noises and pushing the cars across the floor. He occasionally goes to other toys, but his attention is fleeting. He plays in the same area as his brothers, but does not observe or engage with them.

During the first visit to the home, Kim, the early interventionist, wants to watch Rael's play skills and help the family develop a plan for intervention. She first sits with Rael and his parents on the floor. Rael has a truck and is pushing it back and forth without releasing it. Kim suggests that Rael's father sit behind him and his mother sit a few feet away in front of him. She indicates that she would like to help Rael make his favorite play into a social activity. She asks Marco to help Rael push and release the car toward Ana. She also suggests they show excitement and approval when he releases and when Ana catches the car. Ana then pushes the car back to Rael and they cheer again. After several back-and-forth turns, Kim suggests that Marco not help Rael and see if he can take a turn by himself. Ana waits expectantly for the car with her hands reaching out. Rael pushes it to her. Marco and Ana look at each other, then at Rael, and smile and cheer. After several more turns, Ana gets 5-year-old Juan to sit in front of her. The game begins again, with the brothers pushing the car back and forth. Kim explains that this game will benefit the social development of both of the boys, and that they may need some support in this game until they find pleasure in the activity without the encouragement of their parents. Kim then builds a tunnel of couch pillows for the car to go through and demonstrates for the boys how to aim the car at the tunnel. She introduces a ball into the game as well.

Kim indicates that she would like to see Rael expand his play interests and his actions with toys. She suggests they begin by trying to combine other toys and materials with the cars and trucks. She asks about other materials or objects that Rael likes. Marco says he loves water and his bath; Ana adds that Rael loves to splash. The interventionist suggests that maybe they can figure out a way to combine what Rael likes to expand his play repertoire. They agree to let Rael take a bath so that they can try out some new ideas. Rael is thrilled with the prospect of a bath, and Marco leads Rael to the bathroom to start filling the tub. Kim asks Ana to bring a plastic bowl or container from the kitchen, and other kitchen utensils that can go in the tub. Kim brings some plastic cars and people with her to the bathroom. Rael has his clothes off and is in the tub within a minute. He splashes and laughs. Marco says, "He loves to splash! We need ten towels to clean up!" Kim says, "Let's see if we can get him interested in playing with the toys in the water." She takes his favorite truck and places it in a bowl so that it is floating in the water. Rael stops splashing and looks at the truck. He picks up the truck and tries to "drive" it on the water. It floats for a few seconds, then sinks. He watches it. Kim pulls it out of the water, dumps the water out and puts it back in the bowl. Rael repeats the sequence again. Kim narrates what is happening. "Look, Rael. The bowl floats! The truck is sinking! Here it is! Dump the water out!" She explains to Marco and Ana that Rael is now using the truck for a different purpose and is experimenting with cause and effect. They smile, get down next to Rael, and start playing with the toys and kitchen utensils. The following plan evolved from the follow-up discussion with Rael's parents:

Interaction Strategies

1. Use exaggerated actions and emotions in play to entice Rael to watch and want to participate.

2. After several turns of what Rael likes to do, introduce another action, sound, word, toy, or material to the play.

3. Involve Juan in play with Rael; tell Juan what to do and why, so he can repeat the play when you are not present. This will benefit both boys.

4. Rael likes what is familiar to him, but he needs to learn new ways to play too. He responds to structure, so when introducing new routines, toys, or actions, have Rael sit between your legs and guide him through the actions until he understands the sequence. You will need to make the new activity interesting by making it into a game with noises and big movements.

5. Don't be afraid to be silly. Rael likes to laugh and make noises, so make play fun for everyone!

Environmental Modifications

1. Position family members close to Rael so he is aware of their presence.

2. *Use toys and materials that Rael likes in order to expand his play sequences. Add interesting or surprising materials to attract his interest.*

3. *Use bath time as a fun time to play games and introduce new words and play sequences. Try using one or two toys at a time and changing them so each bath time is a little different and new play sequences can be introduced.*

4. *Have play dates with other children, if possible, so the brothers have other role models and playmates.*

5. *Use real objects from the various rooms in the house in play. You can then model using these items in pretend play routines with the boys.*

REFERENCES

Boynton, S. (1995). *Moo, baa, la-la-la!* New York: Little Simon.
Falconer, I. (2000). *Olivia.* New York: Atheneum Books.
Shields, C.D. (2002). *Food fight!* Brooklyn, NY: Handprint Books
Silverstein, S. (1974, 2004). *Where the sidewalk ends.* New York: HarperCollins.
Willems, M. (2004). *Knuffle bunny: A cautionary tale.* New York: Hyperion Books.
Willems, M. (2003). *Don't let the pigeon drive the bus.* New York: Hyperion Books.

KEYS TO INTERVENTION BY DEVELOPMENTAL AGE

The following ideas are directed toward children who are functioning at approximately the following levels. The suggestions are not meant to be all-inclusive, but rather are indicative of potential areas for exploration.

Developmental age	Play interests	Keys to intervention
Birth to 3 months	Likes watching people; moving arms and legs; exploring with the senses, especially the mouth.	Engages in face-to-face play; physical play. Play with objects that can be mouthed. Model exaggerated mouth and arm movements.
3–6 months	Likes sensory play, beginning cause and effect with hands and feet. Enjoys sounds (e.g., rattles); physical play; vocal play; moving to get desired objects.	Demonstrate cause-and-effect actions. Arrange environment so child's actions cause interesting effects. Engage in mouth games (e.g., making bubbles) and tickling.
6–9 months	Enjoys social games (e.g., Peekaboo) Combines objects; uses objects for different purposes.	Demonstrate banging objects together. Use toys that require different actions (e.g., poking, pushing, pulling, turning) to get something to happen (e.g., busy box). Consider characteristics of objects.
9–12 months	Likes making things "go." Beginning dramatic play (e.g., pretend drinking, eating); enjoys social games (e.g., "So Big"). Likes chase games; likes combining objects (e.g., putting things "in").	Introduce toys that can be pushed or pulled, toys with strings and handles. Use plastic dishes and cups to pretend to drink and eat, and practice taking turns. Cue the child to social games by beginning with the first word or action. Provide different sizes of containers with varying openings for children to put things into. Demonstrate different ways to combine objects (e.g., on top, inside, together, under). Use adaptive equipment when needed (e.g., switch toys).
12–18 months	Imitates others; likes doll play; activates toys to "do" something (e.g., move, light up, make sound). Enjoys water and messy play.	Introduce dolls into a variety of routine situations (e.g., bathing, dressing, feeding, going for a walk) and let the child plan how to include the doll.

Developmental age	Play interests	Keys to intervention
12–18 months (*continued*)	Parallel play with peers; plays functionally with realistic toys (e.g., phone); stacks objects on top of each other.	Include toys and materials in bath time; have play dates. Demonstrate stacking and nesting to encourage experimentation with size, shape, and balance.
18–24 months	Uses objects symbolically in play (e.g., pretends to pour); combines objects in dramatic play (e.g., fills dump truck). Combines 3 steps in play (e.g., feeds doll; puts to bed; says, "Night, night").	Engage in pretend play around everyday situations and special events. Use real objects in dramatic play. Model one more action when the child stops or starts to repeat. Use adaptive devices as needed.
24–36 months	Engages in simple construction with blocks; make-believe play; more than 4 steps in dramatic play. Dramatizes scenes from books, movies; finds some words funny. Dramatizes feelings; substitutes unrealistic object in dramatic play (e.g., stick for a banana).	Use a variety of types of materials for building (e.g., blocks, milk cartons, sticks, sand). After seeing a movie or reading a favorite book, introduce props for reenacting, starting with what the child remembers. Play songs and do fingerplays. Do a variety of playground motor activities requiring multiple steps.
36–48 months	Constructs enclosures; likes miniatures in dramatic play; likes puzzles; prefers play with peers. Likes developing a theme in play (e.g., being a hero) and dramatizes events from own life. Enjoys music, singing, and dancing.	Construct miniature scenarios and include action figures and story dialogue. Encourage peer play by having each child contribute to the ideas for the play. Incorporate music and dance into play with costumes and instruments. Integrate dramatic play into gross motor activities outdoors. Begin indoor and outdoor turn-taking games where imitation is possible.
48–60 months	Creates elaborate stories in dramatic play; likes rhyming and silly words. Likes chase games; makes up own rules in turn-taking games (e.g., card or board games). Negotiates roles in sociodramatic play; creates own costumes.	Provide simple turn-taking games both indoors and outdoors. Make up rhyming songs and dances Provide unusual props and materials to encourage creation of social play with miniatures and dramatic play with costumes.
60–72 months	Likes making up complex stories and performing them. Enjoys card and board games. Beginning games with rules (e.g., sports).	Encourage children to create their own plays, dialogue, props, and costumes (each involves sequences of planning and creating). Play a variety of games that involve strategy.

7

Facilitating Cognitive Development

VI. Strategies for Improving Conceptual Knowledge

Goal Attainment Scale

1	2	3	4	5	6	7	8	9
Recognizes familiar sounds, smells, tastes, people, actions, and objects.		Notices salient properties, sees similarities and differences, and has simple labels for some animals, people, objects, actions, and events.		Recognizes, discusses, or uses concrete similarities and differences to categorize or group animals, people, objects, actions, and events into constructs, such as type, location, use, relationship, and/or causality.		Recognizes, describes, and organizes thoughts and actions by both concrete and abstract concepts and categories. Is forming a classification system into which new concepts and rules are structured and related.		Describes, compares, differentiates, and understands both featural and dynamic (e.g., who, where, when, why, and how) aspects of concepts. Has an understanding of logical relations among mathematical, physical, biological, psychological, and literacy concepts, and can share ideas through symbolic representations.

Conceptual knowledge is the understanding children develop as a result of making connections between and among "pieces" of information by combining them into categories. Categorization allows young children to compartmentalize sensory information into manageable units of things that are alike. Categorizing information makes retrieving information easier and provides a means for comparing and organizing new information.

Children grow in their appreciation of how the world works by being able to differentiate characteristics of objects, people, and events. Several steps are involved in concept development: 1) recognizing the salient properties of objects, actions, or events; 2) noting similarities and differences; and 3) beginning to develop categories of concepts by identifying their common properties and grouping these into inclusive constructs. Thus, attention, memory, and problem solving are necessary for conceptualization (see TPBA2, Chapter 7, Subcategories: Attention, Memory, and Problem Solving; and Chapter 8 in this volume).

Conceptual and categorical knowledge is thus the means of organizing input to the brain so that it can be used. The development of concepts related to physical knowledge and the cognitive processes involved in mentally manipulating these concepts leads to classification systems and higher level thinking related to psychology, biology, mathematics, and physics.

The development of categorical knowledge provides an important organizational framework for the sensory information the child processes. Classifying information into categories enables an individual to manage an infinite amount of detail. It enables organized storage of information in the memory, making retrieval more efficient. Categorization of information also enables new stimuli to be quickly analyzed and assimilated into existing conceptual categories. The assignment of words to these categories then helps children communicate their ideas. Which categories are most relevant depends partially on what the child experiences.

For example, children first learn to figure out what kind of animal they are seeing by analyzing its characteristics, the number of feet, whether or not it has wings, the shape of the body, the type of body covering, how it moves, and so forth. In addition, as the child encounters different animals in real life, in books, and on various media, he or she begins to think about animals in different categories. These categories will be influenced by logic and experience. A child who lives in the country may classify animals primarily by whether they are "wild" or "farm." A child who lives in the city may originally think of animals as "farm," "zoo," or "pets." A child who lives in a village where animals primarily are used for food may classify animals by whether or not they can be eaten or if they are dangerous. For this child, the ability to categorize animals may be a matter of life and death, so the classification system may become much more detailed and defined than that of children from the country or the city. Although there are undoubtedly some universal categories in terms of how the elements of the environment are classified, development, culture, and experience also contribute to the level and degree of sophistication of each individual's conceptual system.

APPROPRIATE CONCEPTUAL KNOWLEDGE

Infants begin categorizing sensory input even before they are born. They feel movement, hear sounds, and are aroused and comforted by different types of input. After birth, they begin immediately to notice people and to recognize familiar people, sounds, smells, and tastes. Children start to take in the dynamic, or changing, aspects of their environment as well as familiar features. Increasing attention and memory skills help them start to differentiate people, objects, actions, and events. By the end of the first year, children recognize toys that operate in different ways and those that require the assistance of an adult, and they can recognize different animals, people, actions, and events.

APPROPRIATE CONCEPTUAL KNOWLEDGE IN PRACTICE

▟▟▟▟ **VI. A. What similarities and differences can the child recognize?**

Daily Routines (Home and Classroom)

- *Infant/toddler:* The infant recognizes a bottle, even a novel one, and shows readiness to suck. The toddler recognizes Grandma's house and gets excited.

- *Young child:* The young child recognizes that she is not at the park and gets upset.

Play Routines (Home and Classroom)

- *Infant/toddler:* The infant sees his favorite rattle next to another object and picks up the rattle and puts it in his mouth. The toddler gets her doll, finds a toy bottle, and feeds her baby.

- *Young child:* The young child looks through the toys, searching for the action figure to go with the motorcycle.

Classroom Routines

During circle time, when the teacher asks, "Has anyone here ever been afraid like the girl in the story?" Jeremiah answers, "I was afraid when I got lost."

▬▬▬ VI. B. What evidence is seen of the child's conceptual and/or categorical knowledge?

Daily Routines (Home and Classroom)

- *Infant/toddler:* The infant sees a new toy, picks it up, and mouths it. The toddler sees a robin and says, "Chicken."

- *Young child:* The young child takes the fruit loops cereal and organizes the pieces into piles according to color.

Play Routines (Home and Classroom)

- *Infant/toddler:* The infant crawls over to the coffee table, pulls up to stand, laughs, and starts throwing every object on the table on to the floor. The toddler sits on the floor with the puzzle and puts the shapes in the right spaces.

- *Young child:* The young child sorts through the toy box, pulling out all of the dinosaurs.

Classroom Routines

At the science center, Meghan is placing things that float in the water in one pile and things that sink in another.

▬▬▬ VI. C. What behaviors demonstrate that the child integrates concepts into a classification system?

Daily Routines (Home and Classroom)

- *Infant/toddler:* The infant cries when unfamiliar adults approach. The toddler searches among the family's shoes for her own.

- *Young child:* The young child takes the lettuce off his plate and says," I don't like vegetables."

Play Routines (Home and Classroom)

- *Infant/toddler:* The infant waves then bangs each toy she picks up. The toddler lines up each baby doll, then covers each with a blanket.

- *Young child:* The young child dresses her doll systematically, from underwear to outer wear and from top to bottom.

Classroom Routines

In the dramatic play area, Miguel is playing doctor. He puts his "instruments" in a bag, lines up his lotions and bandages, and makes a sign that says *X R A*, which he tapes over the cot.

VI. D. What understanding of measurement concepts in math and science does the child demonstrate?

Daily Routines (Home and Classroom)

- *Infant/toddler:* The infant hears a dog barking and crawls to the window. The toddler sees her brother get two cookies and cries because she only has one.

- *Young child:* The young child helps set the table and gets enough napkins for the five family members.

Play Routines (Home and Classroom)

- *Infant/toddler:* The infant takes one block in each hand and bangs them together. The toddler says, "I want three crackers."

- *Young child:* The young child is playing a board game and counting three spaces with his game piece.

Classroom Routines

In dramatic play, "Dr." Miguel tells Ariel to stand on the scale. He looks at the scale and says, "You weigh 4 - 0." He puts the thermometer in Ariel's mouth. "You have a temperature of 200 degrees." He puts the stethoscope to Ariel's chest. "You are very sick. I counted 11 bumps."

GENERAL PRINCIPLES FOR SUPPORTING APPROPRIATE CONCEPTUAL KNOWLEDGE

Many of the interactions adults have with children throughout the day encourage children to differentiate among and classify experiences. The following are strategies that often are unconsciously implemented by adults in their interactions with children.

Point Out Similarities and Differences

Adults often help children analyze their experiences. They may make comparisons to other people, objects, or events, indicating similarities and differences. For example, in the preschool class the teacher frequently has children line up by a certain characteristic. She says, "All the children who have brown hair can line up. All the children who are wearing pants can line up. Now, all the children who have curly hair can line up." This activity encourages the children to look at themselves and at others to determine characteristics. They can then see how they are alike, but also how they are different. This type of analysis is fundamental to conceptual understanding.

Group Like Items

As children develop, adults help them understand groupings by location, type of objects, and uses. Most adults organize where things are located in the home by where they are used. Dishes and silverware go in the kitchen. Towels and toilet paper are in the bathroom. Adults also typically group things that are alike together. Plates are stacked together in one place, glasses lined up in another. Sheets and blankets are on the beds in bedrooms. Adults also group things by function. Things we eat go in the refrigerator or a cupboard. The coats we wear outside go in the closet. Such organization helps children see relationships. They learn to organize their own toys and materials in the same way. All the trucks and cars go on one shelf. The books go on another shelf. In homes where no organization is evident or chaos reigns, children may have more difficulty forming logical patterns of relationships.

Demonstrate Relationships

Seeing similarities and differences is only one aspect of understanding concepts. Children not only learn to compare, but also to identify relationships. Understanding relationships between and among concepts leads to a higher level of thinking. For example, Annie will first learn the concrete concepts of family, such as "Mommy," "Daddy," and "Jack." Later she will learn that Mommy is a specific person in the group called "mothers" and Jack is a specific person in a group called "brothers." Still later, Annie will understand that Mommy has a mother and that she is Annie's grandmother, and all are part of Annie's "family." Her classification system develops as Annie sees the relationships and begins to make sense of them in relation to what she already knows.

Label Categories

Adults also support children in their concept development by providing labels for different categories of experience. Language itself is a means of organizing experience. Each word in a given language is associated with a concept. Nouns or labels for objects or people are learned first, actions later, and more abstract concepts such as numbers are learned still later. As labels for individual items are learned, categories into which these items fit also acquire a label. For example, a banana is an object, it is also classified as a fruit, and it is also part of a larger category called food. Children learn these relationships by hearing adults and other children use these terms. The adult may say, "Are you hungry? Do you want some food to eat? How about some fruit? Oh, here is a banana!" Without really thinking about it, the adult has just helped the child to learn several concepts and how the word *banana* fits into a classification system.

Classify Experiences

Adults help children to classify experiences. For example, the parent may say, "We need to get dressed up for church" or "Let's take off your good clothes so that you can play outside." These comments help children begin to classify experiences and the parameters around experiences. This is particularly important for learning the "rules" of a culture. Children also come to understand abstract concepts such as feelings through observation of cause and effect and adult narration of experience. The adult may say, "Sophie is crying because you hit her and it hurt" or "I love your drawing! I will put it up on the refrigerator!" Judgments about the value of an object, person, or experience also come from listening to others' evaluations and emotional responses. Prejudice, for example, is acquired as much through incorporating others' appraisal as it is through determining one's own.

THE PRINCIPLES IN PRACTICE

As noted previously, adults play an important role in helping their children organize and understand concepts. The following are examples of how the preceding strategies are used throughout the day.

Daily Routines (Home and Classroom)

Feeding/Eating

While feeding the infant, the caregiver says, "Let's eat the peas first. They will make you strong. Then you can have the peaches for dessert." The caregiver is differentiating between the foods, their purpose, and the order of eating them.

Diapering/Toileting

During toilet training, the toddler sits on the potty and mother reads from a book about how all animals and people poop: "Oh, look what you did. You made a big poop, just like all the animals!" By reading the book about what the child is doing, the parent helps the child understand the toileting process as an action that is common to others. This is one small step toward understanding broader biological concepts.

Dressing

Dad tells the young child it is cold outside and he needs to dress warmly. The child goes to his room and gets out socks, pants, and a sweatshirt. "Is this warm?" he asks. "Do I need mittens?" The child is developing a classification system for clothing and its functions. Dad is guiding this process by pointing out relationships between the weather and clothing.

Play Routines (Home and Classroom)

Face-to-Face Play

The class has sung "If You're Happy and You Know It, Clap Your Hands" many times. The teacher now lets the children take turns making up new verses to show how they are "happy." Whitney says, "Run around." Baylor says, "Jump up and down." Christopher says, "Turn a somersault."

Physical Play

The children are playing Simon Says out on the playground. The teacher varies directions, such as "walk fast," "skip slowly," "crawl slowly," "jump fast," and so forth. Some children move as directed; others watch to see what their friends do. Here, the teacher is helping children to develop movement concepts as well as to categorize *how* they are moving.

Manipulative Play

Ingrid and Brennan are creating a veterinary clinic with the stuffed animals their classmates have brought in to the classroom. They have dogs in one area, "zoo animals" in another, and "farm animals" and "forest animals" in two other areas. The teacher suggests that the animals may need different kinds of beds and food. She gives them animal books to look at, in order to decide what they might need in their pretend play.

Sensory Play

It is spring and the class is creating a mural for their wall. The teacher asks each child to talk about what he or she saw on a class walk and what the class should put in their mural. They mention clouds, rain, flowers, grass, butterflies, and dandelions. The teacher writes each of their ideas on a piece of paper. She then asks about each item's characteristics and what they could use to represent each on their mural. The children say the clouds are white and could be represented by toilet paper, writing paper, cotton, or white cloth. Jessie says, "Clouds are soft. We need something soft."

Reading and Learning Routines

Circle Time

The teacher reads *Three Billy Goats Gruff* to the children. They discuss the similarities and differences among goats, sheep, and cows. They talk about whether all animals eat grass. They compare sizes of children and discuss what it means to be brave, a bully, or a big brother. They also talk about what to say to someone who is mean.

One-on-One Book Reading

Sara's mother is reading her a story about a lost animal that is looking for its mommy. She asks Sara, "What do you think his mommy would look like? How do you know that the cow is not his mommy?"

Science and Math

In the science center, the children are studying what lives in the ocean. They are looking at books with pictures of different kinds of fish. They have made tape marks in the hall to measure the size of a guppy, a goldfish, a catfish, a dolphin, a shark, and a whale.

PLANNING INDIVIDUALIZED INTERVENTIONS FOR IMPROVING CONCEPTUAL KNOWLEDGE

Children with special needs often have delayed conceptual development as a result of deficits in attention, memory, understanding, organization, or experience. Unlike typically developing children, who piece together their experiences into levels of conceptualization and categorization without special supports, children with disabilities may need guidance to create a hierarchy of understanding of the world in which they live. The following ideas are applicable to all children but may be particularly beneficial for children with limited conceptual understanding.

VI. A. What similarities and differences can the child recognize?

Young children attend to both *featural* characteristics (e.g., contours, face, texture, color) and *dynamic* characteristics (e.g., how and why something moves). Dynamic aspects give the child clues about agency (who is doing something), intentionality (why someone is doing something), or goal-directedness (what is going to happen as a result) (Gelman & Opfer, 2002). Children who have difficulty recognizing such characteristics will have problems with language development, social development, and elements of cognitive development, such as problem solving. It is therefore important to look at whether or not the child is able to differentiate features and identify dynamic aspects and similarities and differences across objects, people, and events in order to know where and how to focus intervention.

Problems can arise if children cannot discern characteristics, record information, process (i.e., compare and contrast) characteristics, retain (remember) characteristics, or communicate their understanding. Each of these presents different issues for adults addressing these concerns.

Children with attentional concerns may have difficulty focusing on, or maintaining focus on, objects or events long enough to register similarities and differences between featural or dynamic characteristics. Difficulty with this first step in conceptualization negatively affects other aspects of concept development as well, which may result in the child appearing to have deficits in processing and problem solving (see TPBA2, Chapter 7, Subcategory: Attention, p. 316).

Children with autism or other similar disorders may fixate on specific characteristic of situations and ignore others, thus missing the larger picture of what an object "is" or can "do" and how it relates to other objects or situations. On the other hand, they may be able to understand specific events or activities in great detail. For instance, they may come to understand the physical properties and dynamic balance of things that spin to an exceptional degree. Other children develop unusual talents and may exhibit an extraordinary ability to differentiate and process one type of experience. For example, a few children are able to hear, differentiate, remember, and relate minute sound variations in order to play incredibly complex music by ear. This ability, however, may not translate to other areas of conceptualization.

Children with vision impairments or children who are deaf or hard of hearing have a different type of input issue. Most children take in information about specific situations using all senses. This is not the case for children with sensory impairments. Children who cannot see rely on their other senses, particularly hearing and touch, to learn about their world. Depending on what they hear or touch, their understanding may be limited. It is like the old story of the blind men investigating an elephant. Depending on the part of the elephant they touched—the ear, leg, truck, or tail—their impression of the elephant was very different! Children who are deaf or hard of hearing have a similar, but different, issue. They can see the world but cannot hear the nuances of sounds or explanations of relationships for concepts that cannot be seen. Children with sensory deficits involving tactile, vestibular, or proprioceptive input also may have a distorted or limited understanding of aspects of their environment. They may either avoid specific types of input or seek out certain types of input to the exclusion or minimization of others. In either case, a distorted understanding of objects, people, or events may result, thus limiting conceptual understanding.

Children with mental retardation or cognitive delays may demonstrate adequate attention but may not be able to retain or process information about their experiences. They have difficulty generalizing or relating information from one situation to another. They require numerous repetitions for the concept or pattern to be remembered and applied to similar situations or activities. For these children, activities need to be concrete and meaningful so that previous knowledge is related more easily.

Children with motor disabilities such as cerebral palsy, even if they do not have deficits in other areas, may have difficulty accessing various objects or participating in activities in such a way as to gain sufficient sensory information to be able to adequately categorize what they have experienced. For example, if the child can only swipe at toys rather than hold and explore them with both hands, he or she may not discover all of the characteristics of the object. Restricted sensory access can limit understanding.

Interaction Strategies

1. *Help the child note characteristics of people, objects, and events.* Although adults typically do label and point out characteristics for young children, it is important to consider each child and which characteristics may be overlooked, avoided, or misinterpreted. The adult should consider all aspects of a situation and think about what needs to be emphasized for an individual child. Help the child look, touch, listen, move, and

experience each important aspect of the environment. Label and describe features and actions.

2. *Provide opportunities for generalization (similarities).* Generalization requires that some aspects of a situation be similar; for instance, both toys have switches you can push, you can talk on all types of telephones, round things usually roll, and so forth. Adults can point out similarities of situations and give children an opportunity to recognize these characteristics and generalize the actions. Ask questions to promote generalization; for instance, "Look, Miranda, this phone looks kind of like your toy phone at home. What should we do with it?"

3. *Emphasize differences.* In the same way that adults point out similarities, they need to point out differences. Children who are nonverbal will try to act on objects in familiar ways. When these ways do not work, the adults can help children learn a new strategy. For example, if Miranda picked up an old-fashioned rotary dial phone, she might have recognized it as a phone and tried to push the numbers in the dial. The adults can use this opportunity to help her to see differences and to problem solve. "You're right, Miranda, this is a phone. It is a little different from yours. Nothing happens when you push the numbers. What else should we try?" (Miranda pushes the numbers again.) Her dad demonstrates turning the dial. Miranda pushes again. Her father takes her finger and helps her pull down on the dial. Miranda smiles as the dial rotates back into place. She tries to pull down the dial on her own.

4. *Allow for sensory comparison.* Even children who cannot hear explanations or see differences can make comparisons. Present high-contrast items together to the child, so the child clearly experiences the difference; for example, a furry blanket and a silky blanket. Then label or sign the object, "blanket," and the characteristic you want the child to learn, "furry blanket" and "smooth blanket." When swinging the child, the adult can demonstrate going fast and slow, while signing or labeling the action. The adult can then say or sign, "Do you want to go fast?" and watch for the child's nonverbal reaction. If the child shakes his or her head or makes a negative face, the adult can ask, "Do you want to go slow?" watch for cues, and react by swinging the child slowly.

As the child acquires the contrasting concepts, more subtle comparisons can be added. Knowing extremes of a concept helps variations to be considered in relation to these extremes.

Environmental Modifications

In addition to interpersonal strategies that may support the child being able to determine similarities and differences, environmental modifications often are useful. Depending on the findings from TPBA2, the team may want to consider some of the following environmental modifications.

1. *Organize the environment to highlight similarities.* Children without disabilities can figure out similarities on their own. Children with special needs may need some environmental "engineering." In other words, adults can arrange the environment so that similarities are identified and labeled more easily. Placing blocks in one place, books in another, and dolls in yet another helps the child see similarities and organize mental categories. In preschool settings, further delineation of categories (e.g., by size or shape) often are used.

2. *Play with toys with similar mechanisms at the same time.* Having a variety of toys that have similar aspects, such as startup mechanisms, presented at the same time can help children see both similarities and differences and learn how to adapt for each. For example, a toy with a button, one with a wind-up key, and one with a switch can all help

children understand similarities (they all do something) and differences (you need to change the action to make it work). Presenting these at the same time allows the child to make immediate comparisons, rather than having to try to remember from previous experiences. The same can be done with other materials. For example, let children experiment with pencils, markers, crayons, and paint all at one play time.

3. *Provide concrete sensory experiences.* Many children with disabilities need more extensive sensory experiences with materials to fully comprehend the concepts being presented. In order to fully comprehend what an egg is, you need to know that it comes from a chicken, that it contains a yoke and a white part, and that it can either become a live chicken or food to eat. This knowledge is learned most effectively when children have an opportunity to experience all aspects of an egg, from the biological concept of seeing the egg in the nest, to seeing the baby chick peck its way out and grow bigger. For the food concept, children feel and smell an egg, they need to crack it, smell and feel its inner parts, and cook and eat an egg in different ways—boiled, fried, poached, and scrambled, or as part of a recipe for cookies. Such experiential learning gives children a more complete concept of the object and its functions. Thoughtful planning can enable children to experience many concepts in this way. (See example of Lia at the end of the chapter.)

▰▰▰▰ VI. B. What evidence is seen of the child's conceptual or categorical knowledge?

Some children remember concepts but cannot retrieve the right words to express what they know. This is a problem with processing information (see Chapter 6, Section I. Strategies for Improving Language Comprehension, p. 343). For other children, even recognizing concepts is difficult. It is as if every experience is a new one. This is a problem with retaining information (see Chapter 7, Section II, Strategies for Improving Memory, p. 499). Because these issues are discussed in other chapters, just a few suggestions will be offered here.

Interaction Strategies

1. *Provide wait time.* Some children just need more time to think of concepts. Provide several seconds before repeating a request or providing a cue.

2. *Provide a sound cue.* Cue the child with the first sound of a word. This may be enough of a cue to help trigger the word for the concept.

3. *Give a choice.* Giving the child a choice between two concepts narrows down the total number of options available. For example, the adult asks a question such as, "What is this animal called?" The adult waits, and when the child does not respond, asks, "Is it a cow or a sheep?"

4. *Give clues.* Often, providing clues or ideas about the concept can help the child think of a concept. Clues can be seeing part of a picture, hearing related words, or feeling or experiencing an aspect of the concept. For example, some children's books show a part of an object such as a flower to help the child conceptualize the whole flower. Children can hear a line of a song and remember the whole song. Children also can recognize objects or parts of objects by touch, so letting a child feel or touch aspects of an object may trigger recognition. In the same way, reexperiencing an event also may spark the memory for concepts. For example, tramping over a bridge may stimulate the retelling of the story of *Three Billy Goats Gruff.*

5. *Pair objects with pictures, symbols, actions, or gestures.* Combinations of various types of sensory input help children integrate various aspects of a concept. Multiple types of

input also give the child more than one type of clue as to what is going on. For example, when the parent takes the child's clothes off, then wraps the child in a towel and heads for the bathroom, the child knows what event is about to take place even if no words have been spoken.

6. *Name and explain.* Children have to hear concepts labeled and explained, preferably as they are experienced in a concrete way. If a concept cannot be experienced, such as riding in a boat, then explanation has to include varying levels of understanding: looking at pictures of boats in the water, playing with toy boats in a tub or pool, pretending to drive a boat when moving in the car, or making sounds or hearing sounds of an engine.

7. *Use concepts frequently across multiple situations.* To really integrate concepts so that they are easily recognized or recalled, they need to be experienced repeatedly in a variety of different ways. If the child sees pictures of cows in only one book, he or she may not recognize a different picture of a cow in a different book or a real cow as the same animal as in the picture.

8. *Accept alternatives to words as communication.* Recognition of something is easier than recalling or generating the label. Therefore, allow children who have difficulty producing language to use recognition strategies. For example, they may be able to use eye-pointing to make a choice or indicate what they want. They may be able to point to a picture when given picture options. Even movement toward a person or object can indicate understanding. For example, if the adult says, "Do you want Daddy or Mommy to take you?" and the child leans toward Daddy, this is an indication of comprehension.

Environmental Modifications

In addition to interpersonal strategies that may help the child recognize or recall concepts, environmental modifications often are useful. Depending on the findings from TPBA2, the team may want to consider some of the following environmental modifications.

1. *Use concrete objects.* Children learn first from actual experiences and real objects. A real rabbit implies the concept of rabbit better than a stuffed rabbit. In fact, if the stuffed animal is called "rabbit," the child may come to think of many stuffed animals as rabbits, or only his or her stuffed rabbit as the concept "rabbit." Real objects also can be used as cues to symbolize upcoming events (e.g., a spoon symbolizes "time to eat"). Children who have cognitive delays or are deaf or hard of hearing may benefit from this approach in addition to use of signs and gestures.

2. *Use technology to reinforce concepts.* Assistive technology can help children generate concepts. Picture or symbol systems can present concepts that children can recognize and point to. Switch mechanisms that activate voice responses also can help children with motor disabilities.

3. *Use multisensory approaches.* Providing means for children to obtain a variety of sensory input enables them to combine and make sense of many different forms of information. A child who plays with wooden toys, helps her dad cut wood, plays with sawdust, tries building with wood scraps, and is shown all of the things that can be made with wood will have a much deeper understanding of the concept of wood than the child who sees wood in only one context.

4. *Allow exploration from different perspectives.* If a table only is seen from the top, one's perception of a table is of a flat, two-dimensional surface. Children who have lim-

ited ability to move and are always carried often have limited understanding of a concept because of limited opportunities to explore. Therefore, it is important to allow children to explore objects in many different ways and from many different positions.

5. *Highlight important aspects of concepts.* Any concept has various characteristics. The adult can ensure that the key aspects of objects, people, situations, or events are pointed out or emphasized. This may mean raising the sound level, using color or lighting to highlight characteristics, demonstrating movement or outcomes, or verbally describing characteristics.

VI. C. What behaviors demonstrate that the child integrates concepts into a classification system?

Simple labels for people, objects, events, and other types of concepts is the first level of a hierarchy of conceptual understanding. Children first conceptualize objects as a whole (e.g., "this is a table"). Once an object in a class has been assigned a label, that label applies to other members of the class (e.g., "this big one is also a table"); and different objects (e.g., chairs, tables) have individual labels, and different objects cannot be assigned the same name. As children assign labels to the entities in their environment, they then can begin to pay more attention to the characteristics of each of these entities to form larger conceptual categories (see TPBA2, Chapter 7, Subcategory VI: Conceptual Knowledge).

As the child develops and has more experiences, each of these labels can be included in a more complex network of relationships. Different kinds of furniture are found in various rooms or places. For example, beds are found in the bedroom and highchairs are found in the kitchen. One kind of bench is found in a church and another kind of bench is found in the park. As noted previously, the child starts to differentiate both features and dynamic aspects of his or her environment. Children form mental systems for categorizing objects and events: What is it? What are its characteristics? How is it similar to or different from other things I know? What does it do? Why does it do what it does? How do other people perceive it?

Such mental discovery helps the child move concepts into a classification system or a hierarchy; for example, 1) this is my chair; 2) these things you sit on are chairs; 3) different kinds of chairs have different names; 4) all of the types of chairs are called "furniture;" 5) other objects, like tables and beds, also are considered "furniture"; and so forth. This leads to more complex integration of concepts, such as potential materials, functions, or variations.

In addition to expanding the understanding of the relationship of terms, children simultaneously expand the *way* they communicate their ideas. As they begin to understand abstract representations, such as pictures, they expand the way they communicate their understanding. They begin to share concepts through drawings, gestures, pantomime, and dramatization. Abstract *representation* of concepts extends language into such symbolic forms, as well as sign language, fingerspelling, and the written word.

Physical understanding of the world provides the foundation for the development of systems of knowledge related to at least four areas: *physics* (understanding of how things work), *mathematics* (understanding of measurement of quantity), *biology* (understanding of life processes), and *psychology* (understanding of mental processes). This book does not attempt to address all of these areas, but the basic principles for intervention to increase understanding of how concepts fit into a system apply to all areas.

Interaction Strategies

1. *Build vocabulary.* Children need a broad range of vocabulary as a foundation for classification. Take every opportunity to label and explain objects and events. See previous sections as well as the communication domain (see TPBA2, Chapter 5).

2. *Group items or materials so relationships are obvious.* If relationships can be seen or experienced, they are internalized more easily. For example, instead of having all the same size toy dishes and utensils, vary the sizes. That way, the child can learn the concept of sizes (e.g., little, big, biggest) by comparing through sight and touch. The adult can question and guide as the child places the cup, plate, and silverware together. A higher level prompt could then be to ask the child where the adult, the child, and the doll should sit to eat. This requires the child to think about both features (size) and dynamic aspects (why) of placement.

3. *Demonstrate or point out categories based on features.* Children with special needs may learn the labels for many different things in their environment but have difficulty organizing those "things" into larger categories. For example, they may know the names for many foods they eat without knowing the concepts of "fruit," "vegetables," or "meat." Adults can help by pointing out and grouping things that belong to various categories and talking about why they are all alike and what the concept is called. For example, when shopping at the grocery store, adults should identify each area of the store (e.g., the bakery, meat section, produce area) and discuss the characteristics of each (e.g., meat comes from animals such as cows). Classifying things beyond the basic label often requires adult support for children to be able to fit concepts into categories.

4. *Demonstrate or point out categories based on dynamic aspects.* Just as "things" can be grouped into larger categories based on recognizable features, dynamic aspects also can be grouped into larger categories. Dynamic aspects, as noted previously, include understanding what is causing something to occur (e.g., a person, mechanism, biological cause), why it is occurring (e.g., to meet a need, effect of one object on another), and what will happen as a result (e.g., feelings, actions). These concepts are more difficult to comprehend and use and require adults to demonstrate, explain, and allow children to experience in concrete ways. For example, for an infant, putting a toy on a blanket and then pulling the blanket toward the child will show the child how the blanket can be a tool. Repeated with other toys and different supports, such as a newspaper, the infant begins to see the connection between the toy and the support. For young children, watching water move a water wheel in the tub and pushing water to make "waves" to move a toy boat, along with adult explanation, can help the child understand that water has "force" to move things. This is harder for a child to grasp than the concepts of "water," "boats" or "wheels," all of which can be seen rather than inferred.

5. *Do not underestimate the child's ability to form higher level understanding.* Often, adults who interact with children with special needs make assumptions about the limits of the child's abilities. This is a mistake. Make every effort to build conceptual understanding at more than a simple level of object identification. Explain, demonstrate, illustrate, compare, describe, relate, and help the child gain a greater degree of understanding.

Environmental Modifications

In addition to interpersonal strategies that may support the child organizing concepts into a system, environmental modifications often are useful. Depending on the findings from TPBA2, the team may want to consider some of the following environmental modifications.

1. *Group by category.* As indicated in item 2 in the previous section, how the adult arranges the environment is important. Teachers often arrange the room by activity area, such as dramatic play, sensory play, and book areas. This is a form of categorization. Grouping like items together and then grouping them into another category is an-

other form of categorization. How the adult groups items will influence how the category is perceived. For example, placing all of the different types of blocks together in a block area is one form of categorization. It tells the child that regardless of materials (e.g., wood, plastic, cardboard, foam), size (e.g., tiny, small, medium, large), or type (e.g., magnetic, Velcro, bristle, stacking, interlocking) they are all "blocks." Another way of grouping would be to have all of the blocks combined with other construction items, such as Tinkertoys, Lincoln Logs, and K'NEX, called "construction materials." Still another way of grouping would be to place small toys together (e.g., small blocks, puzzles, wind-up toys) into an area called "manipulatives." The adult needs to consider the developmental level of the child and his or her ability to group by like characteristics.

2. *Use visual cues to help the child categorize.* Teachers can support organizing concepts through environmental cues. For instance, marking books and their corresponding containers with a stamp or sticker indicating a category can help children learn the classification. For example, books marked with a stamp of a farm animal should be put in the corresponding book box labeled "farm animals"; this will help children learn that the book about sheep goes in the "farm animals" box and so does the book about horses. The teacher needs to support this by explaining the category and not just making the task one of matching stickers.

3. *Use visual cues to show dynamic results.* Just as picture directions on a box can help explain what needs to happen, picture sequences for children can help demonstrate relationships and outcomes. A picture of one child handing another a toy, followed by a picture of the child with the toy smiling, conveys how sharing makes one feel good. Such picture cues convey cause and effect and are helpful for children who have difficulty comprehending lengthy verbal explanations.

4. *Use tactile and other sensory cues for classification.* For many children, input from multiple senses helps in classification. For instance, feeling the difference between feathers and fur helps children classify animals, hearing the difference between drums and horns helps them classify sounds, and hiking for a mile helps the child classify distances. The adult not only can provide the experiences, but also can help children think about how to fit the experience into a pattern of other experiences by comparing and contrasting different elements.

VI. D. What understanding of measurement concepts in math and science does the child demonstrate?

A child understands the world in logical sequences. The process of learning scientific concepts is influenced through experience, and with adult support shifts from understanding at a concrete level to understanding through mental representation. Mental representations of science and math concepts move from thinking about local clusters, to linear relations, to configural relations. For example, the child understands the concept of space first in relation to his own body, then his body and an external but nearby referent, and later he can think about objects in space in relation to each other (see TPBA2, Chapter 7).

Learning to sequence is fundamental to logical relations. The child first develops an ability to sequence actions and moves to sequencing ideas. Concurrently, the child learns to compare and order, or seriate, a series of aspects and place them in order from one end of a continuum to another, beginning with two and increasing to an ever-larger number of elements. In order to do this, the child must be able to see the relationship between any element in the series and the one that precedes it and the one that follows it, and also to understand the equivalence of units. Across physical, mathematical, biological, and psychological concepts, the child works to relate and organize concepts in a way that allows systematic comparisons to be made using "units" of thought against this type of mental reference line.

As discussed in the previous sections, children make similarity matches before they make comparisons of other features such as equivalency. Children are drawn to the similarities of items, and first recognize equivalence when objects they are examining are identical entities or are from the same category. Children first notice similarity in amounts, then they develop the ability to think about differences in amounts and discrete number. The concepts of "more/less" and "one/many," which can be determined *perceptually*, are acquired first.

Figurative understanding comes as children begin to use number words, first as if *onetwothreefour* is one word; then with the numbers differentiated in a rote manner; then with one-to-one correspondence, as children understand that one number word is associated with each item counted. At first, children may point to each item counted, although not necessarily with the right number. They also may skip some items or count some objects more than once. As children come to understand the relationship of the numbers to each other, *cardination,* or the understanding that the last number counted represents the total set of items, develops. Children conceptualize numbers in terms of amounts, and understand that five is one more than four and one less than six. They understand the use of numbers for determining quantity and for measurement of amount. They begin using their fingers for simple addition in preschool.

Children with cognitive impairments may be at a lower level of understanding of math and science concepts. Intervention needs to begin with understanding what procedures and concepts each child does understand. Children with sensory impairments need to compensate by using other types of sensory input to help them develop representational abilities. Children with attentional impairments need assistance to focus and attend to the relevant aspects of number for their developmental level. Children with language impairments need concrete approaches to help them make sense of number words and to use them appropriately.

Interaction Strategies

1. *Present opportunities to see equivalence.* (See the previous section on perceiving similarities and differences.) It is important for children to experience things that are the same using all of their senses to help them notice discrepancies. This includes similarities in appearance of objects, but also all types of math and science concepts; for instance, seeing blocks of the same size and shape next to each other, hearing sounds at different distances from the child, or having two objects that weigh the same in each hand.

2. *Demonstrate comparing amounts (for various types of quantity).* Once children can group like objects, they are determining a perceptual equivalence. They then can begin to make comparisons of different math and science concepts. For example, when one ball is placed close to the child and the other far away, the child learns through movement of his body to determine the difference in spatial distance between them. Dropping items off a highchair or dropping them down a flight of stairs teaches the child about height and time (before it hits bottom). Sitting in a child-sized chair and then sitting in Daddy's overstuffed chair teaches the child about size, height, and shape differences. Playing with different sizes and shapes of blocks teaches children about balance, distance, height, length, shape, weight, and space. Having obvious differences is important, because children can discriminate wide discrepancies before subtle differences. The adult's role is to present the opportunities to experience these concepts perceptually first. Conceptual understanding will grow with experience and social mediation by adults and other children.

3. *Point out the features or aspects that are different.* The adult can provide labels to clarify what the child is seeing, hearing, feeling, smelling, or tasting. Children may be able to discriminate a difference between items independently, but they need adults to label what they are experiencing. Adults can use words that describe the difference or discrepancy. Using comparison words such as "smaller/larger," "bigger/biggest," "sour/sweet," "rough/smooth," and so forth, can help children develop a vocabulary to describe what they know.

4. *Demonstrate the procedure of counting or measuring.* When naming a number, count to show what that means. For example, "You are 3 years old, 1, 2, 3" (counting on fingers). Learning the words for numbers precedes understanding what the words mean; thus, rote counting is to be encouraged but supported with explanation.

5. *Practice using number words and quantity words.* Number and size words are part of everyday life and should be used whenever possible. Over time, the child will piece together the meaning of all of the various uses; for instance, "Nana lives at 2541 Cook Street"; "Let's call Grandpa. You push the numbers . . . 3-0-3 . . . "; "You can pick out two cookies"; "We are going to the 3rd floor. Push the number 3." Quantity words also are important to use: "You have more than I do"; "The snow is all gone"; "Your glass is empty!"

6. *Support use of one-to-one correspondence.* Show children how to count using one-to-one correspondence. Point to each item as it is tagged with a number. Demonstrate how one item corresponds to another; for example, "This baby has two feet. We need two shoes"; "Let's put out one plate for each of us: one for Daddy, one for Mommy, one for Molly, and one for Teddy." Help the child see the relationship between amounts: "Daddy is very hungry. We'll give him a big piece. I am not very hungry. I'll have a little piece. How hungry are you?"

7. *Help the child understand cardinality.* Children do not always understand that the last number stated when the last item is tagged represents the total amount of items counted. Adults often assume that this understanding is present. To help children understand this concept, the adult can ask, "So, how many do we have all together?" (gesturing to show the whole amount). "You counted five, so we have a total of five blocks." Using words like "total" and "all together" are concepts that also will be helpful as math vocabulary is acquired. Understanding of cardinality is necessary in order to be able to perform mental operations on different forms of quantity, without having to use concrete one-to-one counting or measuring. Children often need help to conceptualize a number as all of its parts considered together.

8. *Help the child develop the concept of a mental number line.* In order to understand the relationship of amounts to one another, the child needs to be able to understand that each number stated represents an actual amount and that that amount is one more than the previous number and one less than the number after. This comes as the child develops the concept of cardinality, discussed previously. Once the child understands the meaning of a number in terms of amount, the adult can help children see how adding or taking away one unit changes the total amount. The adult can assist the development of this mental number line by challenging the child to think about what comes before and what comes after in terms of both number and amount. Play games in which the adult counts forward and backward and the child fills in the next number. Sing songs with fingerplays that involve counting and adding or subtracting numbers, such as, "Ten little monkeys jumping on the bed, one fell off and bumped his head."

9. *Provide opportunities to add and take away amounts.* Children learn to manipulate amounts by experimenting and having opportunities to compare amounts as situations change. They need opportunities to play with and investigate space, discontinuous quantity (i.e., separate items), continuous quantity (e.g., water), distance, and time. Challenging children by having them compare amounts, measure using different approaches, and explain what they have found is important. Involving children in measuring amounts for recipes, or seeing how deep the snow or the water in the tub is, for example, helps them to learn about distance. Looking at the thermometer and talking about the temperature helps them see the relationship between higher numbers and amount of heat. Watching the moon get fuller each night provides an opportunity to discuss size and time. Walking around the block provides a means for counting blocks and quantifying space. Everyday activities also can enable children to add or subtract numbers; for example, "Usually we set four plates for dinner, but Mommy is not here tonight. How many plates should we put out?"

Environmental Modifications

In addition to interpersonal strategies that may support the child, environmental modifications often are useful. Depending on the findings from TPBA2, the team may want to consider some of the following environmental modifications.

1. *Modify the environment to help focus attention.* Arrange items or group items so that various concepts are enhanced. For example, rather than having all of the blocks out in a pile, lining up a long line of blocks and a short line of blocks next to each other allows the child to see a pattern. The adult can then relate to these rows in different ways, depending on the level of understanding of the child, by talking about greater or lesser amounts, number, length, distance, space, projected height, and other concepts. Think about the arrangement of materials before presenting them to the child. Even food on a snack plate presents opportunities for talking about one-to-one correspondence, adding and subtracting, and so forth.

2. *Make math and science meaningful.* All of the events that occur during the day have some connection to math and science. Take advantage of the natural environment encountered each day to point out space, distance, number, amount, temperature, time, and so forth. Worksheets allow practice but are not meaningful to the child. Thinking about concepts related to real events encourages thinking and problem solving.

3. *Provide means for exploration with multiple senses.* Use of all of the senses results in distributing neurological input to different areas of the brain. The more ways the brain comes to understand a phenomenon, the more opportunity the child has to make sense of the different types of input. However, for some children, too many types of input at one time can lead to overload and shutting down. It is important for the adults to observe what type and amount of sensory input is most useful for each individual child. This may mean modifying the environment so that input is provided through different channels at different times. For example, seeing, touching, hearing, and moving the balls down a spiral ramp toy may be overwhelming to some children. So much information is being processed at one time that the number of balls, the effect of the ramp, and the distance down from different holes—all of this is missed by the child. For this child, eliminating some of the input, for instance, sound, and just looking at one ball at a time may be necessary. The adult's comments and questions also can direct attention to specific aspects.

ROUTINES FOR THE CHILD WHO NEEDS
SUPPORT TO INCREASE CONCEPTUAL KNOWLEDGE

Daily Routines (Home and Classroom)

Feeding/Eating

Label the foods eaten, depending on the child's level, by basic name or by category of food. Compare and describe colors, textures, and tastes. Arrange or present the food, so you can count items (e.g., number of beans, number of things on the plate). Use number words (e.g., "Can you eat two beans?"), size words (e.g., "I'm going to take a *tiny* bite"), amount words (e.g., "Is your plate empty?"), and so forth. Use both commenting to model vocabulary and questioning to elicit concepts. Give choices to demonstrate (e.g., "Do you want a *long* bean or a *short* bean?" [while holding up two sizes]).

Diapering/Toileting

Diapering offers many opportunities for identifying and counting body parts and describing and comparing different textures and smells. There also are many untapped opportunities for science exploration in the bathroom; for example, counting squares of toilet tissue; talking about sizes, shapes, and amount of poop; talking about the height of the toilet, potty chair, or sink; and talking about time.

Dressing

Dressing often is an opportunity for identifying body parts and counting to two—arms in the sleeves, legs in the pants, sock, shoes. However, dressing also can be a time for talking about directionality (e.g., up, down, out, in, top, bottom); number and size (e.g., of clothing); comparison of sizes (e.g., big, bigger); physiological changes (e.g., growing up); measuring (e.g., length, height), and so forth. Adults also can talk about the functions of various clothing pieces and differences of clothing across people. The adult can ask, "Do animals wear clothing? Why not?"

Going Out

When out on errands, the adult has many opportunities to point out and label objects, people, animals, actions, places, and events. These can be compared and categorized in games such as I Spy. Going out is a perfect opportunity for talking about space and distance, time, and location. Terms such as "near/far," "soon," "in 10 minutes," or "5 miles" can help children begin to understand such concepts. Count various items seen, and use order words; for example, "First, we are going to get gas; second, we will go to the store; and third, we'll stop at Nana's house." Reviewing the sequence at the end of the trip also helps the child create a mental sequence. During shopping, the adult also can encourage labeling, comparing, classifying (e.g., fruit versus vegetables), and use of counting and math skills: "Let's see how many bananas are in this bunch. You count them." After counting, ask, "So how many bananas are in the bunch?"

Play Routines (Home and Classroom)

Face-to-Face Play

Playing face-to-face games with infants allows adults to help children experience different perspectives and distances. Babies love to be lifted in the air, look at the world upside down, experience movement, touch faces and fabric, and taste the adult's chin—and everything else they can get to their mouth. Toddlers and young children love counting fingerplays, tickling games, and roughhousing. Adults can label body parts, actions, and quantity words and insert questions to encourage thinking; for example, "Do you want more tickles, or less?" "Count to ten and then I'll get you."

Physical Play

Physical play often involves running and chasing, playing ball, riding bikes, jumping, swinging, and climbing. These activities offer opportunities to talk about these actions, places where the actions are occurring, and events involving the actions. For children at the appropriate level, the adult also can talk about distance (e.g., "You can ride to the corner, that's not too far"); number (e.g., "See if you can jump 15 times"); space (e.g., "Let's see how high you can throw it"); speed (e.g., fast or slow); or time ("In 5 minutes it is time to come inside"). The adult can support children depending on developmental level, by assisting them in counting or helping them see relationships; for example, "I pushed you 12 times on the swing. How many times should I push you now? Is 15 more or less than 12? Let's see how many more."

Manipulative Play

Manipulative play with toys and miniature figures and scenarios (e.g., house, farm, zoo) allows the adult to help the child learn labels for objects, people, animals, parts, actions, locations, and functions as well as understanding of causality. Manipulative play with construction toys (including art materials) provides great opportunities for experimentation with quantity, spatial understanding, balance, symmetry, distance, and weight. Although many children will gain understanding of these concepts through discovery, many will need adult guidance to see relationships. Adults can help children plan and think about what is happening as they are constructing. They can ask questions to promote thinking, such as, "How many blocks do you think we will need to make the road to the garage? Let's see if you are right." They can help children to analyze situations. "You're putting the triangle on top of the square. It has a point on top. Do you think you can put another block on top of the triangle? Why not? That's right. It's not flat." Adults also can explain why something occurred: "You cut a big triangle for your tree. It is too big for your card. We need a piece of paper bigger than your tree."

Sensory Play

Sensory play enables experimentation and comparison of many different concepts. Children can label and describe the objects within the sensory play, compare characteristics such as color and texture, describe actions they are doing with the material, and discuss the functions of utensils with which they are playing. The adult not only can provide the materials and help the child find the vocabulary to label concepts, but also can comment or guide the investigation as needed. For example, in a sand and water table, children investigate amounts and results of combining two materials: "Let's add the ¼ cup of water and see what happens." They can shape and build with wet sand and discover properties of weight and height. The adult can prompt or model, "My sand is not sticking together. I'm going to add another ¼ cup of water. Now I can shape it! How is yours? Do you need more water or more sand? Let's see how high we can build before it falls over. Oops! What happened? Was it too tall or too skinny? Let's make it fatter and see how high we can go." Such exploration can be done with all kinds of materials and all types of sensory exploration. The adult just needs to think about the potential properties of the material and relate those to desired science and math concepts.

Dramatic Play

Dramatic play with very young children involves reenacting daily routines. Within this type of play, the adult can reinforce the application of concepts that apply to the child's life. Concepts related to labeling objects (e.g., baby), actions (e.g., eating), and events (e.g., going to bed) are incorporated naturally. As the child gets older, adults incorporate concepts related to function (e.g., "We need something that pours"), comparison (e.g., "This dress is too small"), and classification (e.g., "I would like meat for dinner"). As the child begins to understand discrete amounts, the adult can encourage use of props that will stimulate use of science and math concepts. For example, in kitchen play, having measuring cups and spoons and varying sizes and weights of materials (e.g., cans of real food and empty food boxes) is important. Expanding dramatic play beyond house play also is important so that children can investigate a wide variety of dramatic play scenarios. For example, props for a beauty shop, police station, shoe store, archaeologist, veterinarian, and construction worker give children a wide range of alternatives for counting, measuring, weighing, determining space, and so forth. Again, the adult can observe and comment as needed to prompt thinking and using concepts related to math and science.

Reading and Learning Routines

Circle Time

Individualizing questions or comments is important during circle time. Although many comments will be directed to the group, the adult can direct specific questions to individual children that are geared to their level of understanding. Particularly in preschool this is important, because the range of understanding may be greater. Making adapted versions of books for children with special needs also may enable the child who needs modified input to look at a different version of the book; one with fewer pictures, added texture, picture symbols, or other adaptations. The adult talking to or reading to the children can alter the level of comment and questions, as described in the previous section.

One-on-One Book Reading

Books for very young children encourage learning labels for people, animals, actions, and events. The adult plays an important role, both providing and eliciting appropriate terms. The adult also comments and asks questions to encourage thinking about causality (e.g., what happened and why), description (e.g., color, texture, size), comparison (e.g., nice versus mean), and classification (e.g., Spot, dog, animal, mammal). Every book presents opportunities for counting, whether counting objects on a page, opening to the "first" page, or counting pages in the book. Although not always prompted by the text of the book, adults also can find ways to incorporate math and science concepts. For example, on a page with pictures of different animals, the adult might ask, "Which do you think is heavier, the mouse or the squirrel?" "Which is taller, the dog or the cat?" "Which animal do you think eats the most food?" "Why?" Discussion about sequential order also can be included; for instance, "What did Olivia do first? What did she do second? What happened last?"

Science and Math

The understanding of math and science begins at birth, so children of all ages should have opportunities to investigate the physical, biological, and mathematical properties of their environment. For infants, this involves discovering how things work in their immediate vicinity; for toddlers, discovery expands to the space in which they move; and for young children, the world expands even further to whatever they can manage to get away with! For all children, the world beyond their home and school is dependent on adult introduction. Even without field trips to parks and museums, however, children can learn much about the way the world works. Children of all ages need experiences first to learn *what* things are and what purposes they serve, then *how* things happen, and then *why* things occur the way they do. Comprehending *why* is the step that leads to true conceptual understanding. Children of all developmental levels can be guided through these steps if they are allowed to 1) investigate the properties of objects or situations, 2) determine actions which can be performed or sensations experienced, 3) relate experience to resulting consequences, and 4) understand the reasons for specific outcomes. Investigation should enable children to experience both static and dynamic properties of objects and situations encompassing the physical, biological, and mathematical world.

LIA

Lia is a 3-year-old Asian child who has cortical blindness. Her parents have been teaching Lia to use her hands to search around her for what she wants. They have used Lia's own body parts to help her identify the parts on her doll and understand that it is a small "person" like her. The doll, Mai, is now Lia's favorite toy. Mai takes a bath with her, and Lia washes Mai's hair, sponges her off, and dries her. At mealtime, Lia feeds Mai after she eats. Mai is put to bed before Lia. Her parents have taught Lia to use her fingers to identify the key parts of objects and then to "teach" Mai about the objects. For example, when Lia puts on her pants, her mother helps identify the waist of the pants by laying out the pants so that the two legs are pointing away from Lia. Lia can then sit down and put her legs in the pants and pull them up. Lia then teaches Mia how to put on her pants. In this way, Lia is practicing new skills and verbalizing her strategies while she teaches her doll.

Another strategy that Lia's parents are using with her is providing a variety of sensory experiences to help her learn about a concept and to learn strategies for investigating other concepts. For example, Lia is learning about carrots. She helps to plant the seeds, feels the ground each day to see if anything has changed, waters the ground, and finally pulls the carrots as they grow. Then she examines, feels, and tastes the carrot from the garden. She helps to wash it and cut off the greens and the tip. They experiment with cutting the carrot in various ways—sliced, julienned, peeled, and curled. They taste and examine the carrots raw, boiled, steamed, and cooked in soups and other dishes.

Lia is learning about all of the foods she eats in this way, by being involved as much as possible in examining and preparing the foods she eats. Lia is learning to identify the foods by smell and by touch. In this way, she knows what is for dinner and if and how it has been cooked.

Lia also is learning about how ingredients are combined. She helps her mother make a carrot cake with carrots from her garden, flour, sugar, and eggs. Each of the ingredients is felt and tasted before being measured in special cups and spoons that enable Lia to feel the number of the amount in braille. Lia's mother tells her how much of each ingredient is needed and then tells Lia to find the right cup. She helps Lia measure and feel the bowl before dumping in the ingredients and stirring them up. Lia's mother also tells her about baking the cake in a hot oven. They open the oven door and feel the heat coming out. Lia's mother helps her feel the temperature and turn the knob. She also feels the timer and they set the timer to go off in 1 hour. Lia then helps to put the soap in the sink to wash the dishes. She then puts the silverware back in the correct compartments in the kitchen drawer.

These events, although wonderful for a child who has a vision impairment, are just as valuable for a sighted child. Children need to experience as much from every situation as they can. We rely too much on having children watch and/or listen to adults explain. How can you explain the taste of cinnamon or the feel of an egg yolk? All children will learn more through experiencing events with all of their senses and by taking part in each step of the discovery.

The following are suggestions that were incorporated into Lia's intervention plan.

Interaction Strategies

1. *Lia cannot see when someone or something is approaching, so you need to warn her. Let her know when you are going to present something or touch her, so as not to startle her. For example, say, "Lia, I am going to pour shampoo on your head so we can wash it. Here it comes." Describe what she will experience: "It will feel cold and wet."*

2. *Before experiencing an object or event, prepare Lia for what to expect. For example, "Lia, here is a yummy fruit called papaya. Try a taste." Tell her to what the object or event is similar and of what it consists: "It is sweet and a little like the peaches you like, only softer." As you explore an object, label the characteristics Lia is experiencing: "See, it is wet and slippery when you touch it." After exploring an object, talk about what the experience was like: "Did you like papaya? What did you like? What other fruit is it like?"*

3. *Lia can benefit from multisensory experiences to learn about a concept. She needs to explore all of an object's properties across many situations. For example, when teaching Lia the label for a new food, let her touch, smell, and taste it, both when it is raw and cooked. When teaching her a concept such as "chair," show her many chairs of different sizes and shapes and softness, so she learns to generalize the concept across variations.*

Environmental Modifications

1. *Provide materials adapted for children with visual impairments. Many of these are provided free of charge through various organizations. These include materials with braille, tactile and braille books, and other materials that enable blind children to play and function more independently. For resources, go to the web site for the American Foundation for the Blind (http://www.afb.org).*

2. *Arrange materials so that Lia can find them with a tactile search. Start with only one or two items and work up to identification of a desired item from among many.*

3. *Use toys and materials that provide tactile or auditory feedback when Lia has done something correctly. For example, use toys that make a sound when activated or toys that allow her to use texture to guide how they are combined (e.g., puzzle pieces with textures added).*

REFERENCES

Gelman, S., & Opfer, J. (2002). Development of the animate-inanimate distinction. In U. Goswami (Eds.), *Blackwell handbook of childhood cognitive development* (pp. 161–166). Malden, MA: Blackwell Publishers Ltd.

KEYS TO INTERVENTION BY DEVELOPMENTAL AGE

The following ideas are directed toward children who are functioning at approximately the following levels. The suggestions are not meant to be all-inclusive, but rather are indicative of potential areas for exploration.

Developmental age	Conceptual interests	Keys to intervention
Birth to 3 months	Observes differences in patterns, contrasts, tastes, sizes, animate/inanimate objects, voices, people.	Present contrasting stimuli, so the child can look from one to the other, or hear contrasting sounds, or touch contrasting textures to stimulate interest in comparison.
3–6 months	Recognizes sounds, objects, familiar/unfamiliar people. Likes to look at things upside down; explore body parts; and make things happen.	Engage in face-to-face play and experiment with looking at the world from different perspectives. Move in different planes (e.g., forward/back; up/down; side to side; around). Count fingers and toes (for rhythm of the language and differentiation of parts).
6–9 months	Compares objects. Knows near and far. Looks at objects named. Displays fear of heights.	Place objects in different locations around the child to encourage movement and exploration of distances. Drop objects from varying heights and into different sizes of containers. Roll balls down the stairs, across the room, and under chairs to encourage discovery of distance and angles, force, and space.
9–12 months	Knows adults can make things happen. Knows body parts. Puts things in/out, on/off; associates properties of objects; knows same gender; uses first labels for objects.	Present toys or objects that can be activated with a simple switch or button, or toys with wheels. Share picture books of different categories of items, such as people, animals, toys, and foods.
12–18 months	Attends to physical characteristics of objects. Combines related objects. Uses objects by function; matches circle shape. Puts like objects together. Understands number 1, concept of "more."	Experiment with combining different blocks, putting objects in different shaped holes, lifting objects of different weights, climbing on different obstacles, putting things together, moving at different speeds. Play with water. Practice counting items, and point to objects as they are counted. Use "amount" words, such as *all gone, one more,* and so forth.

18–24 months	Understands and uses
	    agents (e.g., *mama*)
	    actions (e.g., *run*)
	    objects (e.g., *cup*)
	    recurrence (e.g., *more*)
	    cessation (e.g., *stop*)
	    disappearance (e.g., *all gone*)
	Makes collections of things that are alike in some way (e.g., puts toys with wheels together).
	Knows location (e.g., "there"); nests objects (relates sizes); matches circle, square, triangle; one-to-one correspondence with two objects; points to and names body parts.
	Distinguishes living and nonliving things; has knowledge of basic-level categories such as plants, animals, and people.
	Understands "more"; compares and matches form, size, color.
		Begin experimenting to help develop concepts.
		Explore
		    What happens to objects in water?
		    What makes things "go"?
		    How can things go together?
		    How do things change as they grow?
		    How are plants alike? Animals? People?
		Point out comparisons and describe objects, actions, and events.

24–36 months	Rote counts to three; counts two objects, knows "one more."	Count objects whenever possible with one-to-one correspondence.

(continued on next page)

Developmental age	Conceptual interests	Keys to intervention
24–36 months (*continued*)	Recognizes and points to functions of objects; recognizes size differences (e.g., pointing to little, big); names at least one color. Understands most common descriptors; understands gender; gives both first and last name; can do simple form puzzles; asks *what, where, why, when, who* questions. Makes spatial designs with blocks; knows directional words (e.g., *up, down, out, in, over, under*). Understands numbers 2 and 3 with one-to-one correspondence; understands concepts of "all" and "none."	Try using objects in different ways (e.g., a stick, a spoon, or a fork for a shovel). Try to figure out why something happened. Experiment with changing events (e.g., run cars down a short or long ramp, steep or slight incline). Experiment with making new things out of old (e.g., mixing colors, making things out of blocks or socks). Talk about characteristics and what changed.
36–48 months	Counts to 3 meaningfully. Knows several shapes, colors, sizes, and textures. Knows variety of spatial relationships. Knows what objects go together functionally and how they are used; understands functions of body parts. Matches wide range of colors. Can name examples of objects, animals, and so forth, in a class (e.g., fruit). Asks questions about bodily functions.	Use counting to solve problems of what is needed. Make "collections" of like things and like amounts. Study what happens to things in nature. Create imaginary animals, plants, people, and transportation. Use props in dramatic play to stimulate exploration and use of categories, and counting and measuring. Use routines to talk about time. Talk about money when making purchases and let the child use money to pay for items.
48–60 months	Uses terms *longer, shorter*; recognizes *day* and *night* and relates to experience. Counts to 4 with one-to-one correspondence. Can do simple analogies (e.g., the stove is hot, the refrigerator is cold). Uses hypothetical reasoning (e.g., "what would happen if . . . ?"); talks about past, present, and future time. Understands "same number as"; correctly rote counts to 20. Recognizes commonly used coins (e.g., nickel, dime, penny). Can explain the similarities and differences between objects, people; compares weight (e.g., light, heavy). Points to and names wide range of colors; uses relational words (e.g., *forward, then, when, first, next, backward, behind, in front of*). Can identify the class when members of the class are named (e.g., apple, banana, and pear are fruit).	Use one-to-one correspondence and counting to measure lengths, heights, and weights with different units (e.g., length of string, shoes, sticks, rocks). Look for equivalence before differences. Compare the physical, mathematical, and biological properties of entities. Document findings in drawings, charts, and dictations. Compare amounts by comparing the number of units in a set, and talk about cardinality. Use concrete means to compare amounts that differ by one or two (up to five) items. Associate written number symbols with spoken numbers. Measure time by movement of the clock to major numbers associated with daily routines. Practice games where items of a category are remembered (e.g., things people drive). Watch the life processes of animals and plants.

8

Strategies for Supporting Emerging Literacy

with Forrest Hancock

Goal Attainment Scale

1	2	3	4	5	6	7	8	9
Listens to sounds, recognizes familiar voices, and likes rhythms.		Likes to explore books, look at pictures, listen to the rhythms of someone reading, and make marks on paper.		Listens to a simple story, turns pages, labels pictures, repeats adult's words from a book and imitates intonation. Tries to represent objects or people on paper.		Listens to longer stories, pretends to read, talks about pictures, can retell a story, and makes letter-like forms on paper or writing surface.		Understands stories, uses book-reading behaviors, has phonemic awareness, and has letter and some word recognition in meaningful contexts. Also draws, writes letters, or uses writing-like marks. Uses invented spelling. Composes written products such as lists, notes, and stories.

Note: In TPBA2 and TPBI2, literacy is discussed as a subcategory within the cognitive development domain but also is highlighted in a separate chapter to stress the importance of literacy for success in school. For consistency among volumes, the questions under the literacy subcategory in TPBI2 Chapter 8 are numbered as VII. A., VII. B., and so forth. In TPBA2, see Chapter 7 (starting on page 371) for the Conceptual Development Observation Guidelines, Observation Notes, and Observation Summary Forms for cognitive development, which include literacy as a subcategory. A separate Age Table for conceptual development (Math/Science and Emerging Literacy) can be found on page 391 of TPBA2.

Emerging literacy is the gradual growth of language skills that eventually leads to independent reading and writing. Learning in the area of emerging literacy begins at birth (or, as some believe, prenatally) and continues to develop through supportive interactions with others. A large part of the emergence of literacy evolves from experiences with books: discovering how to use them; listening to them; learning from the meaning they convey; focusing on the words and sounds they contain; learning the letters of the alphabet, their associated sounds, and how they can be manipulated to form different words; and developing an awareness of how words and sentences can be used to convey thoughts and ideas to readers. Emerging literacy is important because it is the foundation for competence in literacy, which is the key to learning and success in school and throughout life.

APPROPRIATE EMERGING LITERACY

Because emerging literacy develops from birth until the child is an independent reader and writer, its characteristics vary over time. Researchers have found that prelinguistic behaviors such as gestures, vocalizations, listening and understanding words, and use of objects during play are correlated significantly with later competence in language. These early prelinguistic behaviors lay the foundation for the development of vocabulary, phonological awareness, understanding the alphabetic principle, and print knowledge, which are strong predictors of literacy competence.

Developmental indicators of emerging literacy are easily observed in the child's behavior. Early-developing behaviors that support the emergence of literacy include the child's ability to listen and respond to people, environmental sounds, rhythms and rhymes, and stories being read. Another feature of emerging literacy can be seen when the child notices and understands print in the environment, such as logos and signs for stores and restaurants, road signs, entrance and exit indicators, restroom labels, and so forth. Many indicators of emerging literacy can be observed by the child's use of books, which includes a broad range of behaviors such as manipulating and exploring books, looking at them, and turning pages; labeling pictures and knowing which are the words and which are the pictures; knowing that one can read the words, pretending to read, and then later actually reading the words; and understanding stories and being able to retell them. Writing develops concomitantly with reading and includes skills such as making marks, scribbling, drawing, making letterlike forms, writing alphabetic letters and combining them to form words, using invented spelling, and composing written products (e.g., notes, cards, lists, stories) that are dictated or written independently.

Literacy emerges as infants, toddlers, and preschool-age children interact linguistically with others during naturally occurring daily routines, caregiving, and play and during supportive learning activities such as dialogic reading. Mastery of literacy is evident when children are able to read and write independently; they can decode and understand print as well as encode print and generate novel linguistic texts, use written language to communicate with others, and engage in purposeful reading and writing. The following are examples of typical emerging literacy behaviors and ways adults can support their development during everyday activities. The role of the adult is to be responsive to the child, to set up or use features of the environment to support literacy development, and to provide instruction when appropriate.

Appropriate Emerging Literacy in Practice

■■■■ **VII. A. What listening skills does the child demonstrate?**

Daily Routines (Home and Classroom)

- *Infant/toddler:* The infant crawls away rapidly when his mother says, "Time for a dry diaper." While on a walk outside, the toddler looks up at the sky, points up, and says, "ah-pain" when she hears an airplane overhead. Her father says, "Yes, that's an airplane."

- *Young child:* The young child selects a book for his teacher to read when she says, "Ryan, today you get to choose a book for storytime."

Play Routines (Home and Classroom)

- *Infant/toddler:* The infant smiles broadly and looks expectantly at the piece of cloth hiding her father's face when he says, "Peekaboo." When the toddler claps his hands, his mother says, "Pat-a-cake, pat-a-cake." They engage in singing and clapping together as they play the Pat-a-cake routine.

- *Young child:* During outdoor playtime, the young child stops playing and runs to line up to go inside when her teacher rings the bell.

Classroom Routines

During circle time, the children listen as a visiting third grader reads a storybook.

VII. B. How does the child use books?

Daily Routines (Home and Classroom)

- *Infant/toddler:* The infant is sitting on her mother's lap in the pediatrician's waiting room. When her mother gets a cloth book out of the diaper bag, the infant reaches for it, waves it in the air, and then chews on the corner. After his sister gets home from school, the toddler brings her the family photograph album. As they look at it together, the toddler insists on holding the book and turning the pages. When he points to a photograph, his sister names the people in it.

- *Young child:* During center time the young child pretends to be the teacher in the dramatic play area as she reads a book to a group of dolls that she has placed in a semicircle in front of her.

Play Routines (Home and Classroom)

- *Infant/toddler:* When the infant opens and closes the book his mother is holding, she pairs the words "open" and "close" with each action. The toddler places his favorite book in his stroller and pushes it from room to room in his house. When his mother says, "Do you want me to read to you?" he hands her the book.

- *Young child:* After the young child looks at pictures of rocket ships in a book, she says, "I want to be an astronaut when I grow up." The teacher says, "Tell me what you will do when you are an astronaut."

Classroom Routines

In the book center, the children lie on beanbag cushions and rugs while they look at picture books during center time.

VII. C. What does the child comprehend when looking at or sharing a book?

Daily Routines (Home and Classroom)

- *Infant/toddler:* The infant pats the book as her father reads it to her at bedtime. She looks from her father to the book repeatedly during the book sharing. While reading his favorite storybook with his older brother, the toddler points to the picture of the red bird when his brother says, "Red bird, red bird, looking at me."

- *Young child:* The young child asks her child care provider to read a book with her in the book area during center time. As they read, the adult asks, "I wonder what will happen next?" The child says, "The puppy will find his mommy."

Play Routines (Home and Classroom)

- *Infant/toddler:* The infant offers a nursery rhyme book to an adult, then retrieves it. The adult states, "You have a book." The toddler sways side to side as her mother reads *Humpty Dumpty, Jack and Jill,* and *Hickory Dickory Dock.* When she stops reading, the toddler says, "More," to which the mother replies, "You want to read more poems."

- *Young child:* The young child laughs when her teacher reads *Froggy Gets Dressed.*

Classroom Routines

After the teacher reads *Caps for Sale,* he asks, "I wonder what the monkeys will do with all those caps?"

■■■■■ VII. D. What does the child recall of words, phrases, storylines, and content from familiar stories?

Daily Routines (Home and Classroom)

- *Infant/toddler:* The infant imitates his mother's facial expressions as she sings, "Twinkle, Twinkle, Little Star" at bedtime. As the toddler eats goldfish crackers during snack, he makes them "swim" and calls one cracker, "Nemo," which is the main character in his favorite storybook, *Can You Find Nemo?*

- *Young child:* When the teacher pauses as he reads *Drummer Hoff,* the young child fills in the appropriate word(s), phrase, or repeated line.

Play Routines (Home and Classroom)

- *Infant/toddler:* The infant anticipates the actions that accompany *Pat the Bunny.* She leans forward to smell the flowers when that page is shown. When his father says, "Buzz, buzz, busy bees," the toddler runs to get his storybook with that repeated line in it and hands it to his father to read.

- *Young child:* The young child says, "I think I can. I think I can" as he pushes a toy train over a pillow.

Classroom Routines

As the teacher reads *The Very Hungry Caterpillar,* she pauses and waits for the children to say the repeated line. She stops periodically during the reading and asks, "What will the caterpillar eat next?" After she has read the storybook, the teacher asks the children to recall what the caterpillar ate and if they can think of other things he might eat.

■■■■■ VII. E. What emerging literacy skills are evident in the child's attempts to read?

Daily Routines (Home and Classroom)

- *Infant/toddler:* At naptime, the infant looks at the pictures of his mother, father, sister, and brother that are hanging on the wall near his crib. His mother notices and says, "Where's Sissy?" When he looks at the picture of his sister, his mother says, "Yes, there's Sissy!" During bath time, the toddler plays with sponge letters floating in the water. When he holds up the letter *m* to show his mother, she smiles and says, "That's an *m*. You have an *m*!"

- *Young child:* While riding in the car, the young child points to a sign for McDonald's and says, "I want a Happy Meal."

Play Routines (Home and Classroom)

- *Infant/toddler:* The infant vocalizes mewing cat sounds as she turns the pages of her favorite picture book about cats and kittens. The toddler lifts the flap on each page of the interactive book *Where Is Baby's Belly Button?* and points to the body part on her own body.

- *Young child:* The young child gets her favorite storybook and reads it to her dolls.

Classroom Routines

During circle time, the children read and then sing a song that their teacher has written on a chart using words and pictures.

▧▧▧▧ VII. F. What does the child understand about writing?

Daily Routines (Home and Classroom)

- *Infant/toddler:* The infant grabs the pen from his mother's hand as she is writing and pushes it on the paper, noticing the marks he makes. While at the park, the toddler pushes her wagon in the sand and notices the tracks left by the wheels. Her father then uses a stick to make more marks in the sand. The toddler takes the stick from her father and imitates him by making marks in the sand as well.

- *Young child:* The young child makes three horizontal lines of cursive-like scribble on the notepad where his mother writes her shopping list. He asks her to put it on the refrigerator where shopping lists are routinely placed.

Play Routines (Home and Classroom)

- *Infant/toddler:* The older infant watches as marks appear on paper while her father draws a picture of a flower. She leans forward to smell it when he is finished. The toddler makes marks on a piece of paper and hands it to her mother and says, "Read it."

- *Young child:* The young child shows his drawing of a dinosaur to his teacher and asks how to write "T-Rex." The teacher says, "You know the first letter because it's just like the first letter in your name, Todd." Then she models writing the remaining letters (pairing each with its phonemic sound as she writes) and gives it to Todd to copy.

Classroom Routines

With support and guidance from their teacher the children generate a morning message that describes what they will do in school that day. They dictate the message to the teacher who writes it for all to see. When it is finished, they read it all together.

▧▧▧▧ VII. G. What characterizes the child's writing?

Daily Routines (Home and Classroom)

- *Infant/toddler:* The infant swirls her hands in the pureed peaches that have spilled onto the tray of her highchair. She explores moving the peaches with her hands and observing the result. While observing his mother sign a birthday card, the toddler gets a crayon and makes marks on a piece of paper. When his mother says, "Read it to me," the toddler says, "Happy berday, Nana."

- *Young child:* The young child writes a thank-you note to his aunt for the dinosaur book she sent him by drawing a picture of a dinosaur and writing her name and his name beside it.

Play Routines (Home and Classroom)

- *Infant/toddler:* The infant holds a crayon and starts to put it in his mouth. His mother says, "No, we write with crayons." Then she moves his hand so the crayon makes a mark on a piece of paper and says, "Look what you did!" The toddler scribbles with a pencil on a large piece of paper.

- *Young child:* In the dramatic play area at her preschool, Ava writes her name on a piece of paper and tapes it to a necklace saying, "This is my necklace for the party."

Classroom Routines

The children have created a restaurant in the dramatic play area. One child hands out menus to the others and writes their orders on a notepad.

GENERAL PRINCIPLES FOR SUPPORTING EMERGING LITERACY

Because literacy is a language skill, the strategies adults use to support the development of emerging literacy are similar to those used to support language development. As children mature and their interests expand to the use of written language, adult support focuses on helping children understand, read, and generate symbolic language such as pictures, logos, letters, words, and stories. The following are examples of ways in which adults can support emerging literacy development.

Recognize and Comment on the Child's Listening Skills

When the parent or caregiver notices that the child is attending to sounds or voices, the adult can name the source of that sound. For example, if the mother observes her infant turning her head toward her father's voice, the mother can identify the source of the voice by saying, "Daddy. That's Daddy!" As the child matures, she begins to attend to sounds outside the immediate environment such as a telephone ringing, doorbell chiming, dog barking, siren blaring, or airplane engine whining. By the adult labeling the sound source, the child learns to understand the meaning of the sound. Once the child has a repertoire of known sounds and voices, the adult can ask her to anticipate, recognize, label, and search for the source of the sound. These accomplishments build the foundation for listening skills that will be needed later for more sophisticated tasks such as following directions, engaging in conversations, intentionally attending to speech sounds, and listening to stories.

Talk to and with Children

During the prelinguistic period of language development, it is important for adults to be vigilant for and responsive to the infant's initiations. By interpreting the infant's gestures and vocalizations as conversational turns, the adult attaches meaning to them, which prepares both members of the dyad for interactive turn taking. Conversational turn taking lays the foundation for the development of pragmatics and is evident in early language games such as Peekaboo and Pat-a-cake. These early language games become more sophisticated when the child is ready to engage in songs, fingerplays, chants, poems, and rhymes. The focus on words and sounds in these games supports children in learning the components of phonological awareness. Other linguistic advantages of conversations with children include growth in vocabulary, use of abstract language, syntax/grammar usage, and word knowledge, all of which are components of emerging literacy.

Capitalize on Opportunities and Experiences to Build Vocabulary

A rich vocabulary in early childhood is positively and significantly correlated with reading ability in grade school. Adults can support vocabulary growth for infants and toddlers by naming objects they show interest in, describing actions they engage in or observe, and purposefully planning experiences that will stimulate learning the meaning of new words. Vocabulary words should be taught by pairing them with real objects, people, and events in functional, naturally occurring daily routines before they are presented symbolically in photographs, pictures, drawings, or written words.

Provide a Print-Rich Environment of Reading and Writing Materials That Are Easily Accessible

By providing literacy materials and modeling their use, adults can support children's interest in exploring and using these materials themselves. The environment should contain reading and writing materials that are appropriate for the child's developmental level, easily accessible, and interesting to him or her.

In the home, a print-rich environment may contain developmentally appropriate books; toy catalogs; and various types of writing paper in different locations, such as paper for notes beside the telephone, paper for list making, paper for drawing, cards, envelopes, and so forth. The drawing and writing materials should reflect the types of writing that occur in the home so that the child can imitate or role play his or her observations and experiences.

In the preschool classroom, there should be a variety of labels for materials and locations where they are displayed. These labels can display a sample of the real object or a representation of the object (e.g., miniature object, salient part of an object, photograph, drawing, picture from the container it came in) paired with the written name of the object. Labels provide a rich opportunity for literacy growth by illustrating the match between the real object, its visual representation, and the written form of its name.

The print-rich preschool classroom contains many choices of literacy materials that are easily accessible and representative of the children's interests and cultural heritages. There should be opportunities for children to explore using a variety of media and tools for expressing themselves (e.g., crayons, paint, clay, pencils, markers, different types of paper). These materials can be made available throughout the classroom, such as blueprint paper in the block area; recipe cards, menus, a telephone book, address book, and list making paper in the dramatic play area; books and materials to create books in the book or art area; songs in the music area; and so forth. In this way, children can develop an understanding of literacy and creatively generate their own literacy products.

Talk About Print

By experiencing print-rich environments at home and at school, children have the foundation for extending their knowledge about print to the greater environment in their neighborhoods and communities. They may notice signs, logos, and numerals that they can read or that more competent readers can interpret for them. Adults can point out environmental print and talk about its meaning with children. In this way, children learn that literacy is more than reading storybooks; it surrounds us everywhere we go.

Read with Children

Parents and teachers can support the development of comprehension and decoding skills by focusing on both as they read to children. Comprehension of what is read is as important as understanding the components of what is written (i.e., the letters, their sounds, and how they can be manipulated). By using the principles of dialogic reading such as talking with the child about the story, asking and answering questions, and stimulating the child to think about the story, the adult engages the child as an active participant in the reading activity and expands the child's ability to understand what is read. When adults point out and label isolated letters or words, they help the child learn about the sounds of the letters (phonemes) and how they can be blended to make words or arranged to make different words to say, read, and write.

Reading with children should be an enjoyable, comfortable, engaging experience. The reader's voice should reflect enthusiasm and an accurate portrayal of the author's intent. Books that children select and that reflect topics of interest to them will entice them to participate in the book reading. Often, young children select the same books over and over. Through repeated readings of a storybook, children can make predictions, join in the reading, and eventually begin to read the story independently. Some storybooks have these features built in, such as repeated lines and predictable stories, which facilitate the child being an active partner in the reading activity.

Encourage Children to Create Their Own Stories

Enjoyment of storybook reading and hearing stories that others tell can encourage children to create their own stories. A child can orally tell her story to another, dictate the story so it can be written and read again later, or write it herself. Carrying her creativity a step further, the story can then be acted out by the author or others who want to join in the active retelling. By creating their own stories, children are empowered to be writers and authors.

THE PRINCIPLES IN PRACTICE

The strategies outlined previously can be used by parents, caregivers, and teachers throughout the daily routines to support the child's development of emerging literacy skills. The following are examples of some ways adults can integrate these strategies naturally into daily activities.

Daily Routines (Home and Classroom)

Feeding/Eating

For infants and toddlers, caregivers can enhance vocabulary development during mealtime by naming the foods and commenting on what the child is eating (e.g., "You are eating bananas, yum!"). Caregivers can offer choices of food. For example, while showing the child each food container or the actual food, the caregiver can say, "Do you want sweet potatoes or green beans?" being sure to match each food name with the appropriate food item.

For older children, parents may point to the labels on food containers as they read them or ask the child to predict what is in the container based on the label. Some restaurants have picture menus that children can use to make choices and order their food. Adults can model reading restaurant and grocery store logos or signs, and when children read labels, logos, or signs, adults should recognize and value their accomplishment as an indication of literacy.

Diapering/Toileting

For infants and toddlers, parents can talk about the diapering or toileting routine as it occurs, thus building vocabulary and sequencing skills. The adult can point to and name a package or container that holds an item used during the diapering routine. For example, they could hold up the wipes, point to the container, and say, "Wipes help clean," or they might point to the picture on the label and name it "wipes." Diapering or toileting time can be used as an opportunity for learning songs or rhymes; for example, singing "The Wheels on the Bus" can become part of the toileting routine as the child sits on the potty.

In preschool, the teacher will help the children learn to read labels and signs associated with toileting and hygiene such as "boys," "girls," "restroom," "hot," "cold," and so forth. Picture communication symbols or photographs placed near the sink can be used to help children learn the proper hand washing routine.

Dressing

Parents of infants and toddlers can use dressing time as an opportunity to enhance vocabulary by naming body parts as they help the child get dressed (or undressed), naming the items of clothing, and commenting on what the child is doing (e.g., "Shirt on, pants are next"). Toddlers and older children can be given choices of what to wear. For example, while holding two tops, the mother may say, "Do you want to wear the red shirt or the blue shirt?" or simply "Red shirt; blue shirt. You choose." Whichever one the child indicates by eye-pointing, reaching, touching, naming, and so forth, becomes the selected one to wear. Through interactions such as these, the child learns the names of body parts, clothing, and colors; the use of prepositions; as well as choice making.

For young children, dressing can be used to further support vocabulary growth by naming more sophisticated body parts (e.g., shoulder, elbow, ankle, waist), increasing the use of adjectives (e.g., color words such as beige, maroon, navy blue; long- or short-sleeved shirt; pullover or button-up shirt), and using more complex prepositions (e.g., in front of, in back of, behind, between, underneath). Often, t-shirts have words printed on them that parents or teachers can comment on and either read to the child or ask the child what it says (e.g., Power Rangers, princess, child's name, name of school).

Play Routines (Home and Classroom)

Face-to-Face Play

Face-to-face games provide an opportunity for adults and infants to read and react to each other's gestures, vocalizations, and facial expressions; all of which are important for language development and correlate strongly to the development of literacy skills. During face-to-face games with toddlers and young children, adults can support the development of vocabulary, listening skills, and the use of objects in play, which also are strongly correlated with later literacy skills. When young children become interested in playing board games, more opportunities arise to support emerging literacy skills, such as understanding the symbols on the board, learning that often such games have rules that are written and included with the game, and learning how to find out what to do when it is your turn (e.g., reading the number on the dice, reading a card that is drawn, reading what it says in the space on the game board).

Physical Play

Outdoor physical play offers opportunities for children to use muscle movements that will support the development of handwriting skills. Young children can be offered large pieces of chalk for drawing on sidewalks or on large expanses of paper, such as butcher paper, attached to a fence. They can use paintbrushes dipped in water to "paint" a fence. During physical play, children can engage in games that require listening skills and following oral directions, such as Duck, Duck, Goose or Simon Says.

Manipulative Play

Play with small "manipulative" toys such as cars and trucks, blocks, doll house objects, and so forth, often involves the use of small muscles that will be needed for the fine motor skills used in handwriting. Also, group play with toys can evolve into creating scenarios with roles for each player. For example, young children might build a structure with blocks, pretend that it catches on fire, and then drive the fire trucks to put the fire out and rescue the people inside the structure. Manipulating magnetic letters on a metal surface is a way for children to explore the shapes of the letters of the alphabet; find letters that have meaning for them, such as the first letter in their name; and experiment with stringing letters together to make words and changing them to make new words.

Sensory Play

Play with messy materials such as shaving cream, mud, fingerpaint, and playdough supports children in developing fine motor skills that will be needed later for handwriting. Also, sensory play provides opportunities for experimenting with drawing and early writing. Preschool-age children can explore and experiment as they creatively make marks, draw, and write, choosing from a variety of available materials.

Dramatic Play

During dramatic play, children engage in language and communication skills at the upper limits of their current developmental level (i.e., the zone of proximal development). The play allows them to be creative and unrestricted in their language use. Storytelling skills can develop during this type of play as the players develop the theme of the play and act it out. Other emerging literacy skills that can be incorporated into dramatic play include listening (e.g., to the other players), using books (e.g., telephone book), and writing (e.g., phone message). The teacher can place menus from favorite community restaurants in the dramatic play area. If the children choose to play "restaurant," it may result in reading (e.g., the menu), listening (e.g., to the food orders), and writing (e.g., the orders).

Reading and Learning Routines

Circle Time

During circle time, the preschool teacher can read engaging storybooks and encourage children to retell and/or dramatize familiar stories or stories they have created. Circle time also is a good time for children to sing, chant, and perform fingerplays, which include rhymes and rhythmic language that support the development of phonological awareness.

One-on-One Book Reading

One-on-one book reading should be a fun and engaging experience for both participants (i.e., reader and listener). Reading lift-the-flap and touch-and-feel books with infants and toddlers encourages them to participate in the reading activity. During individualized book reading, the adult or older child can read a book of special interest to the child; for example a favorite storybook; a book on a topic of interest to the child; or a type of book that the child enjoys, such as a flap book, repeated-line book, or a book with rhyming words. Either of the reading partners can read or they can take turns reading to each other. Providing a cozy, comfortable environment for one-on-one book reading conveys an invitation to read and interact. One-on-one reading provides opportunities for the more skilled reader (the adult or an older child) to support the listener's emerging literacy skills such as vocabulary, print awareness and book conventions, phonological awareness, phonemic awareness, alphabet knowledge, and reading comprehension. The reader can use strategies including asking questions, labeling pictures or their features, retelling the story, and helping the child relate the contents in the book to real people and personal experiences.

Science and Math

Science and math activities provide opportunities for multisensory learning and investigations. The use of real objects and functional activities are key components for learning to occur. For example, cooking activities can span science, math, language, and emerging literacy. During cooking activities, children can be actively engaged in listening, following written and/or oral directions, sequencing, measuring, counting, predicting, observing, changing the physical properties of a substance, calculating and manipulating quantity, and so forth. Children can recall what they did and what happened following math and science activities. They can describe their recollections to generate experience stories which can be written by the children or dictated for an adult to write. The stories can be illustrated in ways chosen by the children.

PLANNING INDIVIDUALIZED
INTERVENTIONS FOR IMPROVING EMERGING LITERACY

Because emerging literacy is language based, children who have language delays or disabilities will likely experience difficulties in developing the skills for this area of development. In addition, because emerging literacy relies strongly on visual and auditory processing, children who have impairments in these sensory areas may need specific, individualized intervention strategies in order to acquire emerging literacy skills. Specialists who are trained and certified in specific areas of disability should be consulted and involved in the planning and intervention for children with speech-language, visual, and auditory impairments. Specialists in the area of assistive technology also are knowledgeable about a wide range of devices and intervention strategies for supporting literacy development of children with disabilities. They are important team members to consult as well. The following suggestions can be used for all children but may be especially beneficial for children with disabilities.

▧▧▧▧ VII. A. What listening skills does the child demonstrate?

Children may have difficulty listening to books for a variety of reasons such as a language delay or disability or a hearing impairment that interferes with ability to understand spoken language. Also, children with an autism spectrum disorder, cognitive delay or dysfunction, or attention-deficit/hyperactivity disorder (ADHD) may require extra time and/or specific interventions in order to focus on and process auditory information.

Children with severe visual impairment need concrete, realistic experiences and references in order to understand verbal information. They may be candidates for learning braille. Children with low vision may have no difficulties in listening to books, but they may need specific lighting, enlarged pictures or text, or magnification in order to see the book, pictures, or words as books are being read.

Children with severe hearing impairments may need specific and individualized amplification devices and strategies in order to receive and comprehend auditory information. Some children with hearing loss have had a cochlear implant and need specifically planned interventions in order to benefit efficiently from their implant. Certified teachers of children who are hearing impaired know a wide range of teaching strategies and how to acquire, maintain, and use assistive technology devices for these children. These teachers can offer suggestions and advice for children with mild to moderate hearing loss as well. Children with physical impairments such as those caused by cerebral palsy, spina bifida, or traumatic brain injury may need specialized intervention and assistive technology devices in order to use, develop, and reveal their listening skills.

Interaction Strategies

1. *Use story props.* Story props are objects that help illustrate and demonstrate the content of a story. For example, story props for "Goldilocks and the Three Bears" might include three sizes of chairs, bowls, beds, and bears. Using props while reading a storybook may help children focus on the story. Props enhance attention and understanding of the content of the story. Children can manipulate the props during or after the storybook reading in order to tell or retell the story. Props may help children who have ADD or autism attend to the story by giving them something to hold as they are listening, which could be used as a reminder to focus on listening. Props for children with sensory impairments can support understanding as they see, feel, and manipulate the objects.

2. *Encourage active participation.* When children actively participate in storybook reading, their listening and attention increase. For example, children can perform actions that are in the story, turn the page or tell the reader when to turn the page, supply the next word, and so forth.

3. *Use stories with repeated lines.* Stories with repeated lines encourage children to actively participate in the storybook reading by saying the repeated line all together on cue with or without the reader joining in. Children can independently read familiar books with repeated lines, so they need to be easily accessible within the environment.

4. *Predictable stories.* Predictable storybooks can increase listening through the active participation of the listeners, the expectation that a prediction will be made, and the eagerness and curiosity to find out if a prediction is correct.

Environmental Modifications

In addition to interpersonal strategies that may support the child in listening during book reading, environmental modifications often are useful. Depending on the findings from TPBA2, the team may want to consider some of the following environmental modifications.

1. *Monitor the noise level.* The noise level in the area where a storybook is being read may affect the ability of some children to listen and understand the content. The reader needs to be aware of the needs of the listeners in this regard.

2. *Simplify the language and/or the story.* Children who have problems listening to stories read orally may need to have short stories with simple language read to them so

they can experience success in listening. The stories can gradually grow in length or complexity as the children are ready. Another strategy would be for children to dictate a story and listen as the teacher reads it back.

3. *Offer choices.* When reading a storybook to children who have problems listening, it may be helpful to offer choices of stories that are interesting to them. For example, the adult can hold two books and provide an opportunity for the children (or a child) to select one. Because children enjoy hearing well-loved stories read repeatedly, a favorite book frequently can be offered as one of the choices.

4. *Consult the team of specialists.* The transdisciplinary team of specialists who are trained to teach children with disabilities such as autism, visual or auditory impairment, language delay or disability, mental retardation, or physical impairment can offer advice for individualized environmental modifications to help children listen to stories.

▨▨▨▨▨ VII. B. How does the child use books?

Some children may have problems accessing books, handling or holding books, or turning the pages of a book. Each child will present with unique strengths and needs for the team to address. The following suggestions provide support for children who are experiencing difficulties using books.

Interaction Strategies

1. *Provide adult support.* The adult can hold and support the book while the child turns the pages.

2. *Offer choices.* For children with motor problems, the adult or another child can offer choices of books and hand the child the one he or she chooses as indicated by eye-pointing, gesture, vocalization, or verbalization. Begin the choice making by showing only two familiar books. When the child is proficient in making choices, the number and variety of books can be increased appropriate to the child's developmental level.

3. *Observe and respond to what the child needs.* When sitting beside a child with a disability who is handling a book, the sensitive adult will react to cues from the child about how and when to offer support. If the adult is still wondering how to support the child, the transdisciplinary team (e.g., speech-language pathologist [SLP], occupational therapist, physical therapist, teacher of children with visual or auditory impairment) can be consulted.

4. *Support the child with a visual impairment.* A child who has a visual impairment may need specific instruction or guidance in ways to handle and use books. Books may need to be modified in order to support the child with a visual impairment in exploring them (e.g., add tactile features so the child can identify the book, pair real objects with the book topic, enlarge the pictures and print). Real objects may need to be paired with objects in the storybook so the child can experience them by touch, manipulation, or smell as he learns new vocabulary or recognizes familiar objects.

5. *Support the child with a physical impairment.* A child with physical limitations may need physical support from an adult or a device in order to turn pages, or access, hold, and explore books. The child may benefit from having the book placed at an angle so she can access it visually. It is important to provide the appropriate support for her posture so she is stabilized while sitting and can focus her energy on handling books.

6. *Support the child with an autism spectrum disorder.* A child who has autism may play with books by lining them up or placing them in specific places in the environment,

and he may become upset when the arrangement is disturbed by another. Adults can support a child with behaviors such as these by recognizing his interest in books and asking if he wants to choose one to look at together. Just sitting beside a child with autism and silently looking at a book about something of interest to him may help by providing a role model for reading. Often, the child with autism has very specific interests such as trains, machines, objects, or shapes. He may find books containing pictures of a favorite interest enticing to look at and read. Watch for signals that the child is ready to engage in the reading activity. A social story about how to read a book may help a child with autism understand how and why books are read. Children with autism often enjoy predictable books, stories with repeated lines, and books with rhymes and rhythm. They frequently like having books read repeatedly, enjoying the predictability and familiarity of the words, pictures, and story.

Environmental Modifications

In addition to interpersonal strategies that may support the child using books appropriately, environmental modifications often are useful. Depending on the findings from TPBA2, the team may want to consider some of the following environmental modifications.

1. *Use adapted books.* Adapt books for ease in page turning by separating the pages with spacers made from foam, Velcro, clips, and so forth. Board books have thick pages that may be easier for a child to turn, but some children may still need spacers between the pages. Young children and children with physical impairments may be able to carry books with handles more easily than conventional books.

2. *Adapt the space for book reading.* Place the book on a nonsliding surface (e.g., Dycem, nonslip shelf paper) so it is stabilized for the child who has difficulty turning pages. Provide a support to hold the book at an angle according to the child's visual and physical needs.

3. *Adapt the book for children with visual impairments.* If the child has a severe visual impairment, the book can be adapted with tactile information or tactile symbols to help her choose the one she wants, explore it, and understand the contents of the book.

▨▨▨▨ VII. C. What does the child comprehend when looking at or sharing a book?

Children who struggle to understand a story may have auditory processing problems or insufficient vocabulary or experiences to relate to the content in the storybook. These children may need individualized support strategies to enhance their comprehension.

Interaction Strategies

1. *Use real objects.* Use real objects to enhance children's interest and understanding of the book. The children can use the real objects to reenact the story later in the day.

2. *Use props.* Use props that go with the storyline to help children understand and engage in the storybook reading.

3. *Ask questions and talk about the story with the child.* Help the child relate the story to his own experiences or provide experiences to support his understanding of shared storybooks. Questions can be planned to help the child think about the story, recall details, and share feelings.

4. *Support understanding and learning vocabulary.* If the child's limited vocabulary is hindering his understanding the content of shared storybooks, select books that contain

words the child knows in order to allow him to focus his cognitive energy on story meaning instead of learning new words. However, it also is important to build the vocabulary of children who have limited lexicons. Create experiences and seek opportunities during the daily routines for building the vocabulary of children who have insufficient word knowledge to understand storybooks. Vocabulary grows from real experiences in which the child is an active participant.

Environmental Modifications

In addition to interpersonal strategies that may support the child understanding a shared book, environmental modifications often are useful. Depending on the findings from TPBA2, the team may want to consider some of the following environmental modifications.

1. *Monitor the environmental noise level.* Attend to the noise level in the environment to enhance listening and thus understanding of a shared book.

2. *Support the child with a visual impairment.* For a child with a visual impairment, the following environmental features are important: color, contrast, time, space, and illumination. Consult with the teacher for children with visual impairment about this child's individual needs and ways in which the environment can be modified.

3. *Support the child with a hearing impairment.* A child with a hearing impairment may need specific environmental accommodations in order to engage in book sharing. Consult with the teacher for children with hearing impairment in order to modify the environment for this child's specific needs.

4. *Support the child with ADHD or autism.* A child with ADHD or autism may have difficulty focusing attention during a shared book experience. The adult may need to discover specific book features that support the child in attending to and understanding stories. Also, the area where the shared reading occurs needs to accommodate the child's needs for noise level and degree of stimulation. Parent input and observations during TPBA can provide insights and suggestions for this area of concern.

VII. D. What does the child recall of words, phrases, storylines, and content from familiar stories?

Verbal recall is difficult for children who have language disorders, cognitive impairments, and neurological dysfunctions. Adults can provide structure to support children's success in this skill. The following are some examples of ways to scaffold for children who have problems recalling information from stories.

Interaction Strategies

1. *Use books with repeated lines.* Read books with repeated lines and encourage the children to join in when it is time for the repeated line.

2. *Use repeated readings of favorite books.* Engage in repeated readings of favorite, well-liked books. Focus on a storybook for an extended amount of time so that children become familiar with the characters, plot, and storyline. The perceptive and observant teacher will be aware of the children's level of enjoyment as they experience a storybook and thus can gauge how long to continue to focus on the story.

3. *Act out stories.* Support children in acting out a familiar story. Their participation and active involvement in reproducing the story will support recall.

4. *Read stories with rhythm and rhymes.* Read stories and poems with rhythm and rhymes (e.g., *Drummer Hoff; Brown Bear, Brown Bear, What Do You See?; "A" Was Once an Apple Pie;* Dr. Seuss books). The song-like, steady beat can aid in recall of the story.

5. *Read stories with alliteration.* Read stories that contain alliteration (e.g., *Dr. Seuss's ABC, All About Arthur [An Absolutely Absurd Ape], Animalia, Zoophabets*). Encourage children to engage in language play as they contribute to or extend the story by making up words that start with the same phoneme.

6. *Use songs and chants.* Singing or chanting a story or selected lines in the story are helpful strategies for supporting recall.

7. *Use props with storybooks.* Use props along with reading a story to enhance understanding and recall. Allow the children to play with the props during center time. Encourage them to use the props to retell the story for another class or a child who was absent.

8. *Ask questions.* Stop reading during a favorite, frequently read storybook and say, "I wonder what happens next?" Write the children's predictions and refer to them after the next part of the story is read. Plan to ask questions that will be cognitively challenging for the children, such as "What would you do if you were in this story?" "What's a different way for this story to end?" or "What do you like (or dislike) about this story?"

9. *Use advanced notice and problem solving.* Tell the children what part of the story they will be recalling before the story is read. If children know that they will be asked to recall specific parts of the story, they may be focused on this as they listen and then be ready to respond. Ask them to think of ways to help remember the word(s), phrase, line, or idea from the story (e.g., "What can we do to help us remember what the hungry caterpillar ate?"). Implement one or more of the children's ideas after the story is read.

Environmental Modifications

In addition to interpersonal strategies that may support the child recalling words, phrases, lines, and content from books, environmental modifications often are useful. Depending on the findings from TPBA2, the team may want to consider some of the following environmental modifications.

1. *Provide visual representations of the story or parts of the story.* The reader can visually represent a story with pictures that are displayed as the story is being read. Or the reader can display a chart that visually represents the story, repeated line, words, or phrases to be recalled, so children can reference this as they recall. Use pictures from the story to support the children in recalling the sequence of events. The visual mode is a strong avenue for supporting learning and recall.

2. *Use props in the environment.* Large, interactive, story-related props in the environment that children can play in or on can serve as avenues for supporting recall of the story. For example, if a large box becomes the three bears' house, the children can add more props, decide who plays which role, and reenact the story. Their active involvement in planning and performing the story retelling will support recall.

3. *Act out stories.* Children can use puppets or put on dress-up clothes to reenact stories. The reenactment will encourage the children to recall what the characters said, their actions, and/or the plot of the story.

VII. E. What characterizes the child's attempts to read?

Children with disabilities often need to be guided and supported in a structured way in order to learn the components that lead to independent reading and writing. Some of the following suggestions may appear didactic compared with learning through play and discovery; however, this should not preclude using a playful, engaging approach while teaching the components of emerging literacy.

Interaction Strategies

1. *Sing the "ABC Song."* Sing the "ABC Song" with children to help them learn the names of the letters of the alphabet. While singing, link the song to visual representations of the alphabet letters.

2. *Use three-dimensional letters.* Provide a variety of types of three-dimensional letters (e.g., magnetic, foam, plastic, felt) and a space to place them so children can explore their shapes and manipulate them into a variety of arrangements.

3. *Learn letters of the alphabet.* Because children typically focus on the first letter in their first name as they begin learning about the alphabet, provide opportunities for them to notice that alphabet letter in words and in the environment.

4. *Learn sounds of the alphabet letters.* Use songs and chants to help children experience making and listening to the sounds of the letters of the alphabet. Provide opportunities for children to manipulate alphabet letters and comment on the sound associated with each letter. For example, stamps of the letters of the alphabet and ink pads can be made available for children to produce letters on paper. As they stamp an alphabet letter, the adult can say the phoneme that goes with that letter.

5. *Use a multisensory approach to teaching sounds of the letters.* Use a multisensory approach to teach the sounds of the letters of the alphabet; for example, combine tactile, visual, auditory, and kinesthetic behaviors so the child is simultaneously touching the letter; seeing the letter; saying the letter's sound or phoneme; and physically forming the letter either by tracing it or producing it independently.

6. *Use a multisensory approach to decoding written words.* Use multisensory approaches to decode words; for example, saying the sounds of the letters while tracing them. In this way the child is using visual, auditory, tactile, and kinesthetic senses simultaneously.

7. *Show blending and segmenting of phonemes.* Using three-dimensional alphabet letters, visually show how letter sounds (phonemes) can be blended to make words and how sounds and their respective letters can be changed to make new words. Pair each word with a visual representation such as a picture, photograph, or line drawing to add the component of meaning and comprehension of the word created by the blending of the phonemes.

8. *Dictate sentences and stories.* Support children in generating sentences and stories about topics of interest. Write their dictated sentences or stories, and read the dictation with the children. Adding pictures will help support reading the sentences or stories later.

9. *Support the child with hyperlexia.* Some children are compelled to read print in their environment. Often, such children have memorized books yet do not understand the content of the books. Children with hyperlexia typically have problems understanding what they read and often have delayed language skills. An improvement in language frequently leads to improvement in reading comprehension for these chil-

dren. Adults can use the unique ability of the child with hyperlexia by pausing as they read a familiar book and allowing the child to interject the succeeding word(s) or phrase. The SLP on the transdisciplinary team can contribute ideas and expertise for supporting the child's language development.

10. *Support the child with a hearing impairment.* Reading may be difficult for children who learn American Sign Language (ASL) because the syntax of ASL and that of English is different. Also, children with mild-to-moderate hearing loss often have difficulty with phonemic awareness skills because of distortions or inability in hearing the speech sounds and associating them with the letters of the alphabet. For children who have hearing impairments, consult with the teacher for children with auditory impairments and/or the SLP to find ways to support these children in developing and using emerging literacy skills in attempts to read.

Environmental Modifications

In addition to interpersonal strategies that may support the child using emerging literacy skills in attempts to read, environmental modifications often are useful. Depending on the findings from TPBA2, the team may want to consider some of the following environmental modifications.

1. *Support the child with a visual impairment.* In order to use their emerging literacy skills efficiently, children with visual impairment may need specific, individualized modifications depending on their vision. Some will need to use braille, tactile symbols, enlarged print, glasses, or magnification. Some may need a specific amount or angle of lighting in order to see pictures and/or print in a book.

2. *Noise level.* The amount of noise in the environment can affect a child's ability to focus on reading. When the adult notices that a child is unable to concentrate she can use the opportunity to engage the child in problem solving. For example, the adult may say, "It's too loud to read our story, what should we do?"

3. *Recorded stories at a listening center.* Provide equipment and recordings of familiar and favorite storybooks for children to listen to independently. The storybook should be available for the child to follow as he or she listens to the recording. Story props may be made available as well.

VII. F. What does the child understand about writing?

Knowing about writing—why we write and how we write—can be a difficult task for children who have cognitive, communication, physical, visual, or auditory impairments. The transdisciplinary team can work together to develop individualized strategies for children who experience problems in understanding writing and actually engaging in writing.

Interaction Strategies

1. *Use three-dimensional letters.* Using three-dimensional alphabet letters visually shows how letters can be blended to make words and how letters can be changed to make new words. Children can manipulate the concrete letters to form arrangements that may or may not be words that can be read.

2. *Experience stories.* Following a common experience (e.g., field trip, special visitor, class party), the adult can support the children in developing a written account of the experience. Through discussion and agreement, the story is developed and then dictated to the scribe, who writes it on a large piece of paper for all to see. After the story is written, it is read by the children and/or the scribe. The children can decide ways to illustrate their story using photographs, drawings, or objects.

3. *Use dictation.* Support children in generating sentences and stories about topics of interest to them, write their dictated sentences/stories, and read the dictation together. Provide materials for children who are interested in illustrating the sentence or story.

Environmental Modifications

In addition to interpersonal strategies that may support the child in understanding the writing process, environmental modifications often are useful. Depending on the findings from TPBA2, the team may want to consider some of the following environmental modifications.

1. *Use labels in the environment.* Environments in which objects and spaces are labeled convey a sense of organization. They help children (and visiting adults such as substitute teachers, observers, parent helpers, and so forth) know where things belong. When a new item is added to the classroom environment, the adult can encourage the children to develop a label for the item and a label for where it will be stored. This activity helps children not only learn about the writing process, but also learn about why we write.

2. *Leave notes on the refrigerator for the child to see.* The refrigerator often is the communication center for families. Notes that the child can read using pictures, symbols, and/or words can be placed at eye level where he or she can see them easily. Paper can be made available for the child to leave notes as well.

3. *Label the areas where toys are stored.* Generate labels for toys using pictures, drawings, photographs, objects, or parts of objects, along with words naming the toy. The label should be placed in the location where the toy is stored and an identical label should be affixed to the container that holds the toy. Reading the labels is supported by pairing the toy with the visual representation of the toy and the written word on the label. The child can contribute ideas for where to store the toy and how to draw or make the label. The child may actually make the label which would encourage and support development of written language.

VII. G. What characterizes the child's writing?

Some children may struggle with the physical process of handwriting, others may find it difficult to express their intended message in written form, and still others may have problems organizing and then recalling their thoughts before recording them in writing. When children experience problems with writing, they may become intimidated, fearful, or hesitant about engaging in the writing process. The insightful, sensitive adult will use a combination of the child's interests and fun, motivational strategies to entice the child to overcome his or her inhibitions and attempt to write. For example, if a child is fearful of making written marks on paper, he could form letters with pipecleaners, make letters in sand or shaving foam, use letter stamps to write messages, use a pen that contains disappearing ink, or engage in air writing (use large arm movements in the air to form letters).

Children who struggle to organize and then recall what they intend to write can benefit from learning metalinguistic methods for structuring and organizing their thoughts and ideas. For example, they would think about what they want to write, how they will organize their thoughts, and how they will put their thoughts on paper so they are planning their own writing process. Often, these children need to learn specific strategies or develop their own strategies for self-organization.

Adaptations that support the unique needs of children with communication, physical, visual, or auditory impairments should be discussed and developed by each child's transdisciplinary team. Assistive devices and methods may include specialized or adapted writing utensils and/or specialized paper, proper seating and positioning, proper lighting, voice-activated technology, use of dictation, teaching a child who uses American Sign Language (ASL) how to write using English syntax, and so forth.

Interaction Strategies

1. *Encourage purposeful, functional writing.* Support children in engaging in purposeful writing, such as sending cards to friends who are sick, writing a thank-you note, sending a birthday card, leaving a message, making a list, and so forth.

2. *Use the child's interests.* Discover the child's interests and use them to create engaging opportunities for the child to write (e.g., make a label for a new toy and decide where to store it in the classroom, make a list of friends to invite to a birthday party, write a note or send a drawing to a friend who moved away).

3. *Provide unique writing tools.* Provide unique writing tools for the child; for example, Magna Doodle, Etch A Sketch, paint and paintbrushes, chalk, markers, Magic Slate. Try fingerpainting in shaving cream or using sticks to write in dirt or sand outside. Write or draw with chalk on the sidewalk.

4. *Individualize support to ensure success.* Support the child at the level at which she can be successful, such as drawing, making marks, or scribbling if she has problems writing (e.g., make tally marks, use marks to measure the height of children in the class, draw what she wants to communicate).

5. *Sing songs to help learn spelling.* Sing songs that support learning about spelling (e.g., "BINGO"; the *Sing and Read Storybook* [Scholastic, Inc.] songs for spelling color words such as red, blue, and yellow). Make up songs to familiar tunes for spelling words.

6. *Use strategies for learning how to spell words.* Teach the child strategies for finding out how to spell words independently; for example, sound it out phonetically, ask a friend, find the word in the environment and copy it, use a "pictionary" (i.e., a picture dictionary with pictures and words), or ask an adult to write it on an index card and keep the card in a specific place in case it is needed again later.

7. *Use dictation.* Support children in dictating a story to an adult or older child, allowing the child to write or draw any of the words in the story that he is interested in contributing. After the story is written, read it out loud with the child, stopping at appropriate intervals for him to read a word independently.

Environmental Modifications

In addition to interpersonal strategies that may support the child in learning to write, environmental modifications often are useful. Depending on the findings from TPBA2, the team may want to consider some of the following environmental modifications.

1. *Provide a variety of writing materials.* Provide writing materials in classroom centers, especially types of materials the child observes being used at home, at school, and in the community so he can imitate or role play how adults use the materials.

2. *Support the child with fine motor problems.* Children with fine motor problems may need to have a pencil grip, large writing tools, or individually adapted writing tools. Provide fun and engaging ways for the child to develop fine motor skills, such as a variety of materials to create art work (e.g., painting at an easel, playdough, small objects to glue and tape on paper). Use sabotage to elicit fine motor use. For example, screw the cap tightly on the paint tube, ask the child to squeeze paint from the

paint tube into a jar for the painting easel, or make opening the door a part of the door-holder classroom job.

3. *Adapt the writing space.* The physical plane of the writing space (e.g., horizontal, vertical, angled) may be adapted to support the child's ability to write. Note which is the dominant hand and if the writing space complements the child's use of that hand.

4. *Adapt the paper on which the child writes.* Paper with tactile features such as raised lines helps some children know where to write on the paper. Some children may need paper with large spaces between the lines, thus giving them sufficient space to write and the visual support of the lines to help organize where to place their writing on the paper.

5. *Support the child with a physical impairment.* The child with a physical impairment may need a variety of modifications, including adapted writing utensils, specialized seating and positioning, appropriately angled writing surface, or unique ways to write such as dictating to a scribe.

6. *Support the child with a visual impairment.* A child who has a visual impairment may need environmental support that can be provided by specialized lighting, location of the writing activity in the work space, magnification, paper with tactile features (e.g., raised lines), or technology such as a braille writer.

ROUTINES FOR THE CHILD WHO NEEDS
SUPPORT TO DEVELOP LITERACY SKILLS

Daily Routines (Home and Classroom)

Feeding/Eating

The adult holds two jars of baby food with the labels facing the child and says, "Pears" (as she moves the open jar closer to the child to allow her to smell the contents) and "Bananas" (as she then moves this jar closer to the child, allowing her to smell it). Then, holding both jars side by side, the adult uses facial expression and says, "You choose." Later, this strategy can evolve to using photographs or picture communication symbols of food and drink choices with words written beneath them to support the children in making choices for breakfast, lunch, dinner, and/or snack. For example, the parent, caregiver, or teacher may present a drawing of apple slices with the word *apple* written underneath and a drawing of orange slices with the word "orange" written underneath and tell the child he can choose apple or orange slices as she points to the respective picture and pairs each spoken word with the picture and written word. It is important to provide enough wait time for the child to process the choices mentally and respond using eye-pointing, gestures, or verbalization.

Diapering/Toileting

Photographs of the child or picture communication symbols of the diapering or toileting routine can be placed near the changing or toileting area. The adult can direct the child's attention to these visual representations as the routine progresses from step to step. The adult can match language with each step, thus working on vocabulary, comprehension, and sequencing skills. For older children, teachers may use photographs, picture symbols, or line drawings along with words for each picture to illustrate, for example, the hand-washing sequence. These pictures can be posted in the area of the environment where children wash their hands after toileting.

Dressing

The routine of dressing holds rich opportunities for language and communication, choice making, use of visual representations of the sequential steps, and use of fine motor and self-help skills. The adult can enhance the child's vocabulary by naming items of clothing, physical actions, and body parts and by using counting words (e.g., one sock, two socks), and adjectives (e.g., red shirt, blue shirt). The adult can offer choices of articles of clothing (e.g., while holding up the two choices, verbalize, "Do you want to wear Batman or Superman underpants today?"). The steps of the dressing routine can be represented visually through photographs of the child getting dressed or through picture communication symbols arranged left to right and in sequential order. The adult can refer to the visual representations to ask, "What's next?" "What's first?" or "What's last?" As the child dresses himself, the adult can use language to comment on his actions (e.g., "Reece put on his socks"). Also, the adult can give the child a choice of receiving help in dressing or doing it himself. When the child needs help dressing at preschool (e.g., putting on his coat, shoes, paint smock), the adult can wait, observe, and step in when she sees that the child needs help by asking, "What do you need?" This is an opportunity for the child to use language to describe his needs or desire for help.

Going Out

Before leaving to go on an errand with the child, the parent can use picture communication symbols to represent the sequence of events for the errand. After showing and explaining the pictures, arranging and displaying them left to right in sequential order, the parent places the arranged sequence of pictures where the child can see them during the errand. As each portion of the sequence is accomplished, that picture is removed, thus showing what is left. This strategy helps teach sequence, time, prediction, task accomplishment, and literacy as the symbolic pictures are read and interpreted. For recall, the parent and the child can replace the pictures in sequential order when they get home after the errand is accomplished. For a child with a visual impairment (depending on the child's functional vision ability), the parent can offer tactile symbols, give the child a tangible representation of the purpose or destination of the errand, explain when and how they will go on the errand, and explain how long it will take. The child with autism also may benefit from holding a tangible object associated with the errand as well as use of the picture communication symbols to illustrate the errand, the destination, and the passage of time as each picture is removed as the errand is gradually accomplished.

Play Routines (Home and Classroom)

Face-to-Face Play

Face-to-face play is a time when adults can focus on supporting children's listening skills and enhancing their vocabulary. Often, children enjoy playing with telephones and imitating how others talk on them. Because talking is the purpose of the telephone, it serves as a functional toy for stimulating conversations, asking and responding to questions, and encouraging children to initiate during conversational turn taking. Using real phones (e.g., discarded/outdated cell or landline phones) can be motivating for children. Two phones are needed for face-to-face play, with each play partner having one. For most children, when the adult follows the child's lead in the role play or in choosing conversational topics, the child's play will be richer and last longer than if the adult takes the lead.

Physical Play

During outside play, the teacher places "traffic" signs in the area where children ride tricycles. The signs indicate *Stop, Go, Wait,* and *Look.* Provide materials for children to make and display their own signs. Ask the children what other props (toys) they need (e.g., whistles, flags, a box for a gas station). Engage children who want to join the play and cannot ride tricycles by providing wagons or scooters with wheels that the children can sit on and propel themselves or be pushed by another child or adult. The adult can model reading and responding to the traffic signs as she engages in the play along with the children.

Manipulative Play

Using sponge alphabet letters floating in water, children can explore the letters, find letters they recognize, and name the ones they know. Often, children learn the letters in their own names (especially the first letter of their first name) before other letters. The adult can make sure that the letters of the children's names are floating in the water. As an extension of this play, the adult can provide paper on which the children can stamp the wet letters, thus making imprints. The adult can support this type of play by being available to name and help find letters as the children request or show interest. The adult also can say the sound (i.e., phoneme) of each letter the child selects if the child is developmentally ready for this information.

Sensory Play

The adult can build on the alphabet sponge play described in the previous paragraph by providing materials for the children to paint with the sponges. The adult can support the play and learning in the area of emerging literacy by commenting on the letters the child uses in her painting. Notice and comment if the child uses a letter from her name or a friend's name in her painting, if she makes a word or an approximation of a word, or if she uses one letter repeatedly in her picture.

Dramatic Play

A large box often will stimulate creativity during dramatic play. Play themes emerge along with rich opportunities for language. The box can be placed inside or outside, and the play theme will most likely vary per setting and current area of interest. When children use an object to represent something else (e.g., a box becomes a house or a car), they are using symbolic skills, which is what literacy is all about.

Reading and Learning Routines

Circle Time

The teacher can use circle time as an opportunity to engage children in developing a morning message about the day ahead that they can dictate to the teacher, read together, and reflect on at the end of the day. The words can be accompanied by child- or adult-generated drawings which will support the children in reading the message.

One-on-One Book Reading

One-on-one reading provides an opportunity for the child to make choices, broaden his vocabulary, and enjoy individual attention from an adult or older child. The adult can easily individualize the interaction to accommodate the child's unique needs and interests. The child can choose the book that is read and participate in the storybook reading process (e.g., turning pages, pointing to pictures, labeling pictures, supplying a word when the reader pauses). The adult can help the child extend his understanding of the story by relating it to experiences, creating an experience that is similar to the story and engaging the child in conversations about the story.

Science and Math

Most children enjoy the process of combining ingredients to make something. For example, the children can be guided to make playdough. This activity holds many opportunities for supporting emerging literacy skills, such as listening to the directions; learning the names of the ingredients; labeling the actions needed to make the playdough; reading the recipe, along with visual representations that accompany the ingredients and directions; following the sequence of steps; measuring and counting as ingrediants are added; recalling the steps and/or ingredients; and manipulating the product, which builds fine motor skills needed for handwriting. Choices can be included easily in the activity, such as what color to make the playdough, whether and what scent or flavor to add, what to do with the playdough once it is made, and so forth. The adult can add cookie cutters of alphabet letters to extend the learning experience. The activity can be recorded using a digital camera, and then the adult can support the children in writing an experience story that they can illustrate with the digital photographs.

NAOMI

Naomi is a 4-year-old child who has cerebral palsy. She uses a wheelchair and has limited movement in her arms and hands. Although she is faced with profound physical challenges, Naomi loves to interact with people. Her face lights up with a big smile and happy-sounding vocalizations when people talk to her. Her parents stated, "Naomi is an intelligent little girl trapped in a body that won't allow her to do the things she really wants to." They realize that as their daughter learns how to read, they will need to help her develop the skills she needs in order to be literate.

Naomi enjoys being read to. She looks at pictures in books and can eye-point to show which book she would like read to her. Her parents are wondering what else they can do to help her learn how to read. Because Naomi is nonspeaking and nonambulatory, she has limited ways to communicate and interact with others. She becomes an observer in many situations, especially because most people do not understand how to interact with her.

The following are suggestions that were incorporated into Naomi's intervention plan for emerging literacy.

Interaction Strategies

1. *Provide opportunities for Naomi to eye-point to indicate choices by using real objects, photographs, and picture communication symbols to represent the choices visually. Label each choice symbol with its associated written name.*

2. *Use a voice-output communication aid (VOCA) programmed with a young girl's voice to allow Naomi to engage in scripted communicative exchanges, join in with other children saying the repeated line during storybook reading, and participate in daily routines in the classroom.*

3. *Support Naomi's vocabulary development during naturally occurring daily routines, during book reading, and during planned experiences at home, school, and in the community.*

4. *Provide an assistive technology communication device that Naomi can use to initiate and engage in naturally occurring conversations with others. The complexity of the device (i.e., high-tech versus low-tech) should be selected to match Naomi's cognitive, language-communication, and motoric ability levels. The device should provide ease of use in the settings where she lives, learns, and plays.*

5. *Read and/or comment on the labels, logos, and environmental signs that Naomi sees throughout her day, so she will learn to read them herself.*

6. *Read her favorite storybook(s) repeatedly when she chooses to hear it.*

7. *Find ways in which Naomi can be an active participant during storybook reading (e.g., holding the book, turning the pages or indicating when to turn the pages, eye-pointing to pictures or text, using her communication device to say repeated lines, make predictions, and respond to questions about the story).*

8. *As other children in the class are beginning to focus on and learn the letters in their first names and as Naomi indicates interest in learning about her own name, provide the appropriate three-dimensional letters for her to manipulate, explore, and/or examine visually.*

9. *Provide alphabet letters on Naomi's communication device to support exploration of their use for writing, spelling, and communicating with others.*

Environmental Modifications

1. *Make sure Naomi is positioned correctly to support use of her communication devices and to give her stability during storybook reading time and other activities of the daily routine. Also, make sure the primary device is accessible for Naomi to use throughout the daily routines.*

2. *Ensure that Naomi has visual access for storybook reading and for using her communication devices.*

3. *Ensure that the lighting in the environment is appropriate for Naomi's needs.*

4. *Ensure that the noise level in the environment is appropriate for Naomi's needs.*

5. *Adapt storybooks so Naomi can handle and explore them as independently as possible.*

6. *Support Naomi in engaging in art and writing, science, and math activities by using adapted equipment, adapted tools, and supportive strategies such as hand-over-hand as appropriate and needed.*

7. *Support Naomi in engaging in daily routines as independently as possible.*

REFERENCES

Base, G. (1997). *Animalia.* New York: Harry N. Abrams.

Carle, E. (1969). *The very hungry caterpillar.* New York: Scholastic.

Carle, E. (1974). *All about Arthur (an absolutely absurd ape).* Danbury, CT: Franklin Watts.

Carle, E., & Martin, B., Jr. (1996). *Brown bear, brown bear, what do you see?* New York: Henry Holt & Co.

Dr. Seuss. (1963). *Dr. Seuss's ABC.* New York: Random House.

Emberley, B., & Emberley, E. (1967). *Drummer Hoff* (2nd ed.). New York: Simon & Schuster Children's Publishing.

Katz, K. (2000). *Where is baby's belly button?* New York: Little Simon.

Kunhardt, D. (2001). *Pat the bunny* (reissue edition). New York: Golden Books.

Lear, E., & Macdonald, S. (2005). *"A" was once an apple pie.* New York: Orchard Books/Scholastic.

Logan, J. (1992). *Froggy gets dressed.* New York: Puffin Books.

RH Disney. (2005). *Can you find Nemo?* New York: Random House.

Slobodkina, E. (1987). *Caps for sale: A tale of a peddler, some monkeys and their monkey business* (reissue edition). New York: HarperTrophy.

Tallon, R. (1979). *Zoophabets.* New York: Scholastic.

KEYS TO INTERVENTION BY DEVELOPMENTAL AGE

The following ideas are provided for children who are functioning at approximately the levels indicated. The suggestions are not meant to be all-inclusive, but rather are indicative of potential areas for exploration.

Developmental age	Emerging literacy skills	Key to intervention
Birth to 3 months	Looks at contrasting patterns, touches pictures, orients toward a variety of sounds. Can locate the direction of sound's origin.	Seek appropriate locations to display objects and simple, high contrast pictures. Black and white appear to be effective contrasting colors for very young infants. Comment on human, animal, and environmental sounds (e.g., "That's kitty. Kitty says, 'Meow, meow, meow'"). While sitting in a comfortable place and holding the infant, engage in reading aloud so the baby begins to associate it with a pleasant experience.
3–6 months	Looks intently at pictures for several seconds. Listens to adult while attending to pictures. Recognizes familiar objects and people; starts to make vocal sounds such as "coo" and a variety of open vowel sounds; engages in vocal play.	Label pictures using short, simple words, phrases, or sentences. Notice and comment when the baby shows recognition of a familiar person or object (e.g., "That's Sissy" or simply, "Sissy!"). Respond to the infant's vocalizations (e.g., coos) as if they are parts of a conversation. Provide a pause to allow the infant an opportunity to initiate. Allow for turn taking between the infant and the conversational partner. Look at photograph albums, turning pages and labeling the familiar people in the pictures. Provide a cozy, warm environment for looking at short picture books that have simple language and clear, simple, noncluttered pictures cloth and vinyl books, touch-and-feel books, and board books. Seek opportunities to attend to the same event, action, object, person, animal, and so forth, as the infant, thus building joint attention skills.
6–9 months	Responds to own name and some familiar words. Begins to babble (e.g., *mama, dada, yaya*). Reaches for and grasps books. Brings book to mouth to chew or suck. Explores and manipulates books (e.g., opens, closes). Helps turn pages. Offers book to adult to read. Holds book in both hands.	Respond sensitively to the infant's initiations for linguistic interactions involving language and communication. Respond to infant's babble as if it carries meaning and is the infant's conversational turn. Provide a variety of developmentally appropriate books for the infant to manipulate and explore. Provide a warm, cozy environment for looking at or reading books with the infant. Expand the variety of types of books to include interactive flap books; easily manipulated photograph albums; and books with textures, such as touch-and-feel books. Accept the book offered by the infant or offer a choice of two books and focus on the one the infant offers/selects by looking at it with the infant.

Developmental age	Emerging literacy skills	Key to intervention
6–9 months (continued)		Include books with simple pictures, simple language, and rhymes that can be read using vocal prosody (i.e., melody and rhythm) and body movement to match the beat of the rhythm of the words. Seek opportunities to develop joint referencing by attending to the same event, object, person, and so forth, as the infant and commenting or labeling it (e.g., "It's Mommy! Mommy's home!").
9–12 months	Pulls books off shelf. Plays Peekaboo with books. Vocalizes while pointing to pictures. Pats pictures. Prefers pictures of faces. Laughs or smiles at a familiar picture. Smiles when an adult makes an interesting sound or reads in an interesting way. Sits on adult's lap for extended periods of time to look at books. Gestures to request repeated reading of a book. Turns pages independently but not one at a time. Begins to label objects. Moves to rhythms. Scribbles.	Continue to engage in reading with the child, allowing her to choose books to read, turn pages, and interact with the book and the reader. Engage in play with books following the child's initiations; label pictures the child points to or looks at. Share books with pictures of babies, animals, and familiar objects. Enthusiastically read books that have rhythm and rhyme in order to provide full enjoyment of the experience. Physically move/sway to the cadence of the rhythm while holding or sitting near the child. Continue following or leading the child's attention to objects, people, and events outside the close proximity of the dyad, thus building joint referencing skills (e.g., "That's a big truck! A big, noisy truck!"). Provide materials that encourage the child to explore making marks (e.g., paper, markers, large crayons). Sit beside the child and engage in similar exploration as the child, so the child leads the art or writing activity. Comment on the actions and products of both participants, thus indicating interest and attention and capitalizing on an opportunity to build vocabulary.
12–18 months	Turns an inverted book right-side up or tilts head. Holds book open with help. Turns pages in clumps when looking at books. Shows a preference for a favorite page of a book by searching for it or holding the book open to that page repeatedly. Carries books around while walking. Selects books on the basis of content. Gives book to adult to read. Sustains interest for at least 2–5 minutes looking at named pictures. Makes animal sounds when looking at pictures of animals in book. Shows familiarity with the text on seeing illustration (says some of words in text). Names objects pictured. Points correctly to a familiar object when asked, "Where's the . . . ?" Relates an object or an action in a book to the real world. Uses "book babble" (jargon that sounds like reading).	Continue reading picture books and storybooks to the child; provide a variety of choices of books (e.g., interactive, lift-the-flap, touch-and-feel, photograph/picture, board books) and books to carry around). Allow the infant to turn the pages of the book being looked at and/or read. Include books and experiences that will build vocabulary as well as books with pictures to which the child can point and name or make associated sounds (e.g., books about clothing, food, animals, daily routines). Ask the child to point to familiar objects in the book (e.g., "Where's the doggy?"). If the child responds incorrectly, avoid saying "No"; simply say, "There's doggy" while pointing to the appropriate picture. If the child responds correctly, respond by saying "Yes" or "Yes, that's doggy" or "Doggy! There's doggy!" The experience should be fun and engaging; it should not feel like a test. Pause during storybook reading to allow the child to contribute a familiar word or name of something pictured.

(continued on next page)

Developmental age	Emerging literacy skills	Key to intervention
12–18 months (*continued*)		Acknowledge "book babble" as reading. Provide materials (e.g., paper, writing utensils, art materials) for the child to explore ways to make marks, use his hands, and make creative products. Sensitively respond to the infant's initiations for linguistic interactions involving language and communication, gradually building on language using expansions and rephrasing.
18–24 months	Takes books off shelf and replaces them. Carries books around the house. May use book as transitional object. Sits for several minutes looking at a book. May accidentally or unintentionally tear pages. Points to a picture and asks, "What's that?" or indicates that a label is requested. Distinguishes print from nonprint. Recognizes some printed words. Notices print rather than just pictures. May point to labels under pictures when pictures are named. Uses "book babble" while reading. Recites parts of well-known stories, rhymes, songs. Performs an action shown or mentioned in a book. Shows empathy for characters or situations depicted in books. Makes associations across books. Enjoys a variety of interactive books. Explores making marks with pencil or crayon. Scribbles evolve into more controlled vertical and horizontal lines.	Continue to provide and read a variety of storybooks and opportunities for the child to contribute to the storybook reading process (e.g., choosing which book to read, holding the book, turning pages, providing sounds or words when the reader pauses). Repeated readings of favorite storybooks support the child in participating in the reading activity as well as spontaneously reciting sounds, words, or lines from well-known stories. When appropriate, associate the pictures or story with familiar experiences or daily routines. Provide labels for objects, people, and events and provide experiences to build vocabulary. This is a time of tremendous growth in vocabulary, so the child will be requesting and listening for names of things in the environment. Watch for opportunities to supply child-requested labels and names of objects. Continue to make a variety of writing and art materials available for the child to explore and experiment using.
24–36 months	Searches for favorite pictures in books. Can usually indicate which is picture or writing, understands what print is. Coordinates words that are read with pictures. Listens to longer stories. Talks about characters and events in books in ways that show understanding of the story. Relates stories to own experiences. Fills in a word or phrase in the text when the reader pauses. Says the next word or phrase before the reader does, or reads along with the reader when a predictable/familiar book is read. Protests when adult misreads a word in a familiar story; typically offers correct word. Moves finger or hand across a line of familiar print and verbalizes or paraphrases text. Reads to dolls, stuffed animals, or self. Reads some environmental print (e.g., familiar signs). Copies vertical line and horizontal line. Makes marks on paper randomly with little muscle control. May engage in early scribble writing and makes organized marks.	Read longer stories as well as the much-loved favorites. Pause during reading of familiar books for the child to supply the next word(s) or phrase. Ask "I wonder what's next?" or "What's next?" during reading of familiar books to provide opportunities for the child to learn to predict and recall. Slow the pace of the reading if the child indicates she wants to read along. Adult moves his or her finger under the print during shared storybook reading and encourages the child to do the same. Encourage the child to move her finger along the print during storybook reading if she is interested in doing so. Help the child relate the story to her own experiences (e.g., "We saw a truck like that at the park yesterday!"). Make writing materials available that are similar to those used by others in the environment (e.g., pencils, pens, markers, paper, cards, envelopes). Provide a variety of art materials for child to explore manipulating and to use to make creations.

Developmental age	Emerging literacy skills	Key to intervention
36–48 months	Knows that alphabet letters can be individually named. Can identify 10 or more alphabet letters (especially those in own name). Begins to attend to the beginning sounds in familiar words. Begins to make letter–sound matches. Differentiates between letters and numbers. Begins to identify rhymes and rhyming sounds in familiar words. Generates rhymes to simple words. Attends to alliteration. Can identify simple high-frequency written words. Begins to break words into syllables. Recognizes own name in print. Recognizes print in the local environment. Knows that it is the print that is read in stories. Can retell sequence of a simple story. Connects information and events in stories to real-life experiences. Questions and comments demonstrate understanding of literal meaning of story. Begins to predict what will happen next in an unfamiliar story. Reads drawings as if there were writing on them. Begins to realize that written symbols convey meaning and starts to produce own symbols. May intend that his or her scribbling is writing. Scribbling goes from left to right in lines across the page with repeated patterns and increased muscle control. Knows that different forms of text are used for different purposes. Attempts to write messages. Displays reading and writing attempts to others. Draws simple pictures. Draws person with head and 1–4 features. Makes visual representations (e.g., scenes, familiar items, animals, designs) that are recognizable but not precise. Draws lines and shapes (e.g., circle, square, diagonal line, cross). Dictates words, phrases, and sentences for others to write.	Read alphabet books, supply letter names and sounds as the child requests, and encourage the child to name letters he knows. Point out and name the letters and their corresponding sounds in the child's first name. In the preschool environment, use the child's name paired with a symbol he chooses to label his space or assignment (e.g., cubby, where to sit at circle time, his classroom job). Read engaging counting books and encourage the child to join in the rhythmic reading and counting routines. Use rhythm during counting routines, and pair one counting word to one object by pointing and moving from left to right as often as possible. Thus, the child is learning one-to-one correspondence for counting and reinforcing the left-to-right movement needed for reading and writing. Extend rhyming activities by supporting the child in creating her own rhymes and dictating them to be written and then read later. Read books that contain alliteration, and encourage the child to join in the reading of frequently read books. Encourage the child to predict what happens next in familiar and unfamiliar stories. Continue to seek ways to help the child build a broader vocabulary. Use expansions of child utterances and cloze procedures (i.e., fill-in-the-blank) during storybook reading to support language development. Add literacy materials to the classroom learning centers, such as a phone book, notepad, dry-erase board, menus from familiar community restaurants and restaurant-type order forms, and recipes in the dramatic play area. Visit the library in the preschool setting or the community. Help the child select a book to check out. Look at or read the book with the child. Provide writing materials for a variety of writing purposes (e.g., writing utensils, cards, lists, labels, signs, messages, stories). Provide art materials for creative expression and exploration.
48–60 months	Recognizes and names all upper- and lower-case letters. Knows many, but not all, letter–sound correspondences. Demonstrates understanding that spoken words consist of sequences of phonemes. Able to listen to and then blend phonemes into words. When hearing a word, can generate a rhyming word. Reads frequently occurring words and environmental print. Knows the parts of a book and their functions. Tracks print when listening to a familiar story or when reading own writing.	Provide opportunities for the child to decode new words using his phonetic skills as well as logical thinking skills (e.g., "Since I'm reading about elephants in the jungle, that word that starts with a 'j' is probably 'jungle'"). Seek opportunities to talk about the sounds that the letters of the alphabet make as familiar words are read (e.g., the child's first and last name). Use big books with a group of children so all can see the print and illustrations. Run her hand under the words as you read them and pause periodically at words the child knows how to read.

(continued on next page)

Developmental age	Emerging literacy skills	Key to intervention
48–60 months (*continued*)	Can name some book titles and authors. Able to recognize several types or genres of text. Can answer questions about stories read aloud. Makes predictions based on illustrations or portions of text. Begins to write alphabet letters or close approximations in combination with scribble; gradually, letterlike forms and actual letters replace scribbles in writing. Copies a few words from the environment. May use a group of known letters (often consonants) to form a word. Writes own first and last name. Writes names of some friends and classmates. Puts spaces between written words. Independently writes capital and lower-case letters of the alphabet. Writes messages left to right and top to bottom of page. Begins to use punctuation in writing. Frequently reverses letters when writing. Uses both invented and conventional spellings. Begins to build a repertoire of conventionally spelled words. Dictates messages and stories. Writes labels and captions for illustrations. Draws a person with head and 8 or more features.	Engage children in making their own big book about a common interest or experience. With adults' support, they can develop, write/dictate, and illustrate the story. The children who write the big book can sign the first page as authors and/or illustrators, thus not only using writing skills, but also learning what authors and illustrators do. The same process can be used to create poems or stories with rhyming words. A child can volunteer to read the story to other children. During this developmental period, children usually become interested in board games. Use games such as Candy Land, Memory, or BINGO (with letters of the alphabet in the boxes instead of numbers) to build literacy skills. I Spy is a good game to play for listening skills. Continue to focus on vocabulary expansion; teach alternate words for known words (e.g., "Yes, that's a dog. It's a kind of dog called a *cocker spaniel.*"). Continue to read to children as an avenue for enjoyment, vocabulary growth, and learning new information or concepts. Engage children in discussions about stories as they are being read to them (i.e., implement dialogic reading strategies). Continue to visit the library in the preschool setting or the community. Help the child select a book to check out. Look at and/or read the book with her if she requests. Continue to provide a variety of art materials for children to use to generate creative representations/expressions.
60–72 months	Language repertoire expands. Identifies first and final sounds in spoken words. Generates rhyming words and distinguishes rhyming from nonrhyming words. Blends and segments syllables in spoken words. Blends and segments phonemes in one-syllable spoken words. Uses letter-sound correspondences to read. Uses picture cues to support reading and comprehension. Recognizes common, irregularly spelled words by sight. Has a reading vocabulary of 300–500 words. Reads and understands simple written directions. Monitors own reading and self-corrects when the word does not fit cues or context. Reconstructs/retells stories. Understands information in parts of a book (e.g., cover, title, table of contents). Can predict and justify prediction of next occurrence in a story. Identifies story problem and plot. Describes information gained from a text. Reads and comprehends developmentally appropriate fiction and nonfiction. Prints name and simple words. Writes or copies letters or numbers. Uses basic capitalization and punctuation in writing.	Because children this age are expanding their ability to decode written words independently, provide storybooks they can read to other children without adult support. Continue to read to children and challenge their growth in reading by engaging in dialogue or conversations about stories by asking questions and discussing features such as plot, characters, outcome, the problem and its resolution, how or if the story relates to their own experiences, and so forth. Ask children to make predictions about what will happen next in a story. Encourage children to search for and read books for information. For example, if a child is interested in hamsters, the adult can guide him in ways to find books about hamsters and how to learn more about hamsters from books. Continue to visit the library in the school setting or the community. Help the child select a book to check out. Look at and/or read the book with him if he requests. Use experiences and expository books to give continued support for the child's vocabulary development. Encourage children to write and illustrate their own stories, which they can read or act out for others.

Developmental age	Emerging literacy skills	Key to intervention
60–72 months *(continued)*	Uses invented spellings by spelling words phonetically.	Although children in this age range often will use invented spelling, they also are interested in ways to find out correct spellings. The adult can guide the child in learning strategies for discovering the spelling of words.
	Spells 3- and 4-letter words with short vowel sounds correctly.	
	Shows awareness of need to use conventional spellings.	
	Uses resources to find correct spelling.	
	Selects own literacy activities such as reading a book, looking up information, writing a note to a friend.	
	Dictates messages and stories.	
	Creates own written texts for others to read.	
	Makes up and tells stories of real or imaginative content containing plot and structure.	
	Produces various types of compositions showing understanding of combined use of text and illustrations.	

Index

Page numbers followed by *f* indicate figures; those followed by *t* indicate tables.